# DINKY TOYS & MODELLED MINIATURES

1931–1979

*Mike and Sue Richardson*

With a Preface by Cecil Gibson,
Chapter 3, 'The Ships' by H. N. Twells,
and Chapter 4, 'Aeroplanes' and
Appendix 3, 'Dinky Toys Numbering
System' by Alan Dimmock.
This edition includes the
Dinky Toy Compendium
by Patrick Trench

FRANK HORNBY
1863–1936

## New Cavendish Books

**LONDON**

To our eleven-year-old son, Gary, who sometimes wishes toy cars had never been invented; and to all wives and sweethearts who mirror his sentiments.

'There is no subject so old that something new cannot to be said about it.'

Dostoyevsky, *A Dairy of a Writer*

**First edition published in Great Britain by New Cavendish Books - 1981.**

**Revised and reprinted - 1986.**
**Second revision 1989, reprinted 1989.**
**Reprinted 1992**
**Reprinted 1993 (seventh printing)**
**Reprinted 1995.**
(Revise from mono to colour on pages 174, 218 and 231).
**Specification: 312 pages, over 700 illustrations including 404 in full colour.**
**Plus 72 page Compendium.**

The publishers thank Airfix Limited and Meccano Limited for the use of the names 'Modelled Miniatures' and 'Dinky Toys' and for the reproduction of their house material.

The Hornby Companion Series.

Design – John B. Cooper
Text production and supervision – Narisa Chakra
Editorial direction – Allen Levy

Phototypset by Wyvern Typesetting Ltd., Bristol.

Printed and bound in Hong Kong.

New Cavendish Books, 3 Denbigh Road, London W11 2SJ

ISBN 0 904568 33 4

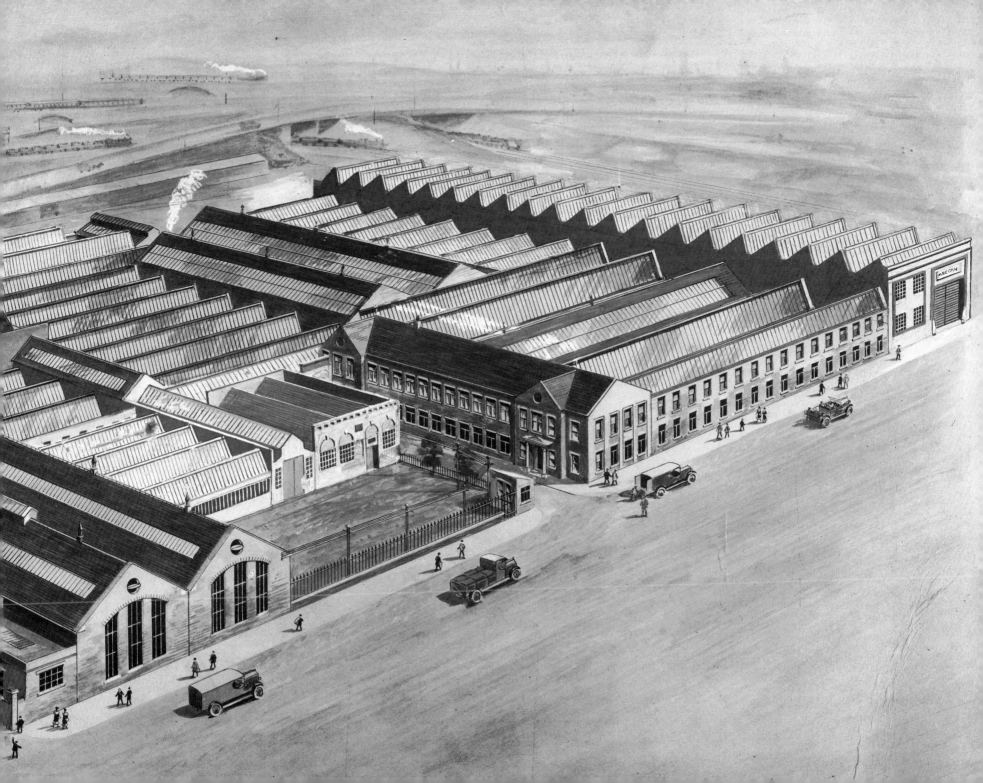

# Preface

by Cecil Gibson

It is a great pleasure to write a few words of introduction to this splendid book, if only to repay the debts of a long friendship dating from the early days of collecting, when the author's own Modelled Miniature was lying in his pram (Mint Boxed, as it were) or, and I am not sure, even before he was in the catalogue.

Model car collecting is a young hobby, and only 20 years ago in this country there was very little organisation, no clubs, swapmeets, specialist magazines or books on the subject. Magazine articles, few in number, were concerned with slot-racing or scratch-building and I was agreeably surprised in 1964 when *Model Cars* accepted five articles on pre-war Dinky Toys written in 'an attempt to straighten out the numbering system', The articles later expanded into a book, still available folks, (to my delight) and now into its fifth printing.

It has been obvious for some time that serious collectors needed something up-to-date, incorporating the complete Dinky range (now, alas, proved to be finite) utilising valuable archive material from the Factory as well as a great deal of research work by hundreds of collectors over the years, and this is the book you now hold in your hand. It is a magnificent production, and I am particularly pleased to find so many colour pictures of the early car issues as well as aircraft and ships. The amount of work involved in producing this sort of book is staggering, but the result, as you can see, is well worth while. I said in my own book that I did not pretend to have written a Dinky Bible, simply a Concordance . . . It seems to me that Mike and Sue, Nelson Twells and Alan Dimmock have now written that Bible.

# Contents

Several years ago, we and a group of collecting-friends talked of updating the then only publication on Dinky Toys and we came to the conclusion that it was a task well beyond the capabilities of one individual. Writing this book has confirmed this and we are indebted to the work of many, many individuals. H. N. Twells and Alan Dimmock have both contributed much more than the sections which are written under their names and our indebtedness to Cecil Gibson and Ed Symons extends far beyond what is apparent from reading their existing publications. We have read, analysed and digested every scrap written in magazines such as *Modellers' World* and all the others and would like to thank all contributors for their efforts. Without the archive material from Meccano Ltd. our task would have been more difficult and the book much less complete. We would also like to acknowledge the assistance of Johnston Brothers (Engineering) Ltd., The Ford Motor Company, The B.B.C. and the M.S.M.C. Library.

Arthur Close and The Ashley Collection lent us the bulk of the pre-war and post-war models respectively that were so expertly photographed by Nick Nicholson of Hawkley Studio Associates Ltd., and we also borrowed models from and were supplied with information and/or archive material by Graham Bridges, Ian Cook, Julian Loffet, Doug McHard and John Mainprise. Many others also helped directly in a multitude of ways: Anthony Armstrong, Vic Bailey, John Barker, Leslie Hurle Bath, Carlo Beux, Colin Bull, Peter Cox, Robin Dove, Alan F. Ellis, Ed Force, Ron Ford, Michael Foster, Olav Glasius, Guy Harrison, Chris Jelley, Allen Levy, H. R. Lines, John Marr, Reg Miles, Fritz Mønstead, Geoffrey Moorhouse, Len Nash, Piero Pagliano, Neil Pankhurst, John Phillips, Arthur J. Roberts, Jean-Michel Roulet, Tony Sawell, Glynn Sharp, Alan Turner and also all those with whom we have ever discussed the subject and who have ever sold us a Dinky Toy for our collection.

When we were asked to compile this book we were initially extremely flattered and then we realised the mammoth task that our acceptance of the request had created. Every Dinky Toy issued from Binns Road, including 'Modelled Miniatures' (the early name for Dinky Toys), from 1931 to 1979 when the factory was effectively closed had to be included, though it was decided to exclude 'Dinky Builder' as this is a constructional system much more like Meccano than a Dinky Toy. Tinplate pressings were also used for a very much later series of large vehicles marketed under the name 'Mogul' and though these are automotive they likewise bear no relationship to Dinky Toys and have therefore been excluded. Related products such as French Dinky Toys sold in the U.K. and English Dinkies sold abroad also had to be found a place, as had many other items related in one way or another to the toys. The models have been placed in their historical context both as far as world events are concerned and also within the evolution of Meccano Ltd.

There are well over 1000 Dinky Toys without considering major casting or colour variations and without adding in the number of boxed sets that were produced and this mass of material has been organised broadly into four sections: Pre-war and post-war re-issues of road and rail vehicles; Ships; Aeroplanes; and Post-war vehicles. However, this subdivision still leaves a mass of unwieldy information and further subdivisions have been made into types of vehicle. Before the War, conveniently, Meccano produced sets of similar vehicles and gave them set numbers with the individual items being distinguished by a letter suffix, and most of the Pre-war section and part of the Post-war is subdivided on the basis of the Dinky Toy numbering. However, all is not so neat that it will fit this system. Thus, for instance, Trains and allied items, Motor bikes and related product, etc. are treated separately. In the post-war period, although number blocks were allocated by Meccano to particular types of vehicle, the overlap became greater and therefore section heads no longer refer to the Dinky number, but the toys are still grouped in types of vehicle. Sometimes it is a little difficult to categorise a particular item and such cases are cross-referenced to where they can actually be found. The main subdivisions are Cars, Commercials, Overseas Issues etc., but these may be further subdivided as in the Aeroplane section into date blocks. In some cases, not only are there fairly clear divisions in time but also these coincide with distinct differences in the appearance of the toy. The cars have been allocated sections depending on the country of origin of the real vehicle because many collectors collect say only British Cars or only American Cars. The Commercial vehicles have been separated into the type of model, for example, 'with advertising' (as that is one collecting theme) or the type of work for which the vehicle was originally designed, i.e. all the farm and garden products are grouped together. The categories which have been selected and which were required to make the material coherent may not suit everyone's collecting interests, so there is extensive cross-referencing to provide easy access to models in different sections.

Each section has its own numerical table. The introduction date has been taken as the first year in which the model appeared in a retail or trade catalogue, or in advertising literature (whichever is earlier). The deletion date is the last year it so appeared. This diverges from many other lists of deletion dates, where the date given is that of the first year the model did *not* appear in retail catalogues, but we prefer to work on material that shows an item existed rather than that which indicated the contrary. We did not have access to *every* trade catalogue, which in some cases would show that an item was still being sold from factory stock despite its non-appearance in the retail catalogue (most of which in any event do not claim to be complete lists of all available product). The year rather than the month of introduction and deletion is normally given because *Meccano Magazine* and other sources of printed information are frequently not accurate to a month or two, especially as the years pass by, and accuracy to a year is normally close enough for most purposes. If, however, the month of introduction is significant, the text will be more specific than the time given in the table. It must also be borne in mind that the period in which a toy appeared in a catalogue does not always coincide with the time that it was available in the shops, for at certain times, the distribution was patchy. Scotland may have received models later than say the Liverpool area. In other cases an item may have been deleted but remained available in the shops for a considerable time after the official deletion. Where models disappeared from the catalogue to reappear later, this is not shown in the tables, though if the deletion was significant it is mentioned in the text.

Many of the technical 'variation' details are included as general comments in the introduction to each section but where changes apply to more than one section, for example, wheels, they are covered in the Historical Survey. Because of the lack of availability of the models to the general readers, virtually all known variations in castings and colours of pre-war vehicles are given in the text, but in the post-war period only major variations are mentioned in the text and listed colours are to be found in the tables (to include every little detail would cause the story of the toys to disappear in a mass of peripheral facts). While this approach enables the collector to participate in the 'glory of the chase' for the less usual colours, care must be taken to ensure the item is not a repaint, for there are many about. The collector should try to establish that it is the sort of colour/two-toning/decalling etc. that was in use at the time by careful scrutiny of the photographs and colours listed for its age-mates. Because a colour or casting does not appear in the book, it does not mean that the model has a greater rarity value. We have made every attempt to include those examples which are uncommon and thus have an added value, although we are sure that more will inevitably be found and become desirable.

Virtually all Liverpool-made Dinky Toys are visibly marked underneath with at least 'Dinky Toys Made in England by Meccano Ltd.' The few known exceptions to this general rule are dealt with in the text. Certain importations from Meccano, France, relevant to the scope of this book display similar information i.e. 'Dinky Toys, Meccano made in France' (or sometimes 'Fab en France'). Therefore it is usually easy to tell if a model is a Dinky or not, though if the model is broken it may not be so obvious. The model should then be compared with the photographs and illustrations to further authenticate it. An un-numbered Dinky with no model name on it may be pre-war, but on an 'actuarial basis' it is much more likely to be post-war. A simple check is to look at the wheels: pre-war smooth; post-war with a concentric ridge. Once this is established, a scan of the section devoted to that type of vehicle and the accompanying photographs should make identification relatively easy.

Meccano Ltd. hold very few records that date back beyond the last few years and correspondence about anything in this book should not be addressed to them. Whilst some of the models are still current at the time of writing, all the catalogues and other material reproduced have been superseded. Please write to us if you wish but replies are only guaranteed if a stamped addressed enveloped is enclosed. Finally, we don't sell Dinky Toys, we only collect them.

Mike and Sue Richardson, August 1981.

# CHAPTER 1
# A Historical Survey

Frank Hornby was a man in the great English Tradition of entrepreneur and inventor mixed with a Scottish trait of emphasis on sound educational values and improvement of the mind. He was a true turn-of-the-century Briton who invented Meccano and began manufacturing it in commercial quantities in 1901, eventually building a factory to accommodate its production in Liverpool, the famous 'Binns Road', which was to remain centre of operations until 1979. The *Meccano Magazine* was published to encourage the use and purchase of Meccano Sets and his restless mind was always looking for new products to manufacture. Thus 'Hornby Trains', being made of tinplate were a logical development of Meccano and were announced in 1920. The scope of both ranges was constantly increased with more and more items peripheral to the basic requirements of the toys being released, i.e. an excavator bucket to suit both Meccano and stations for the 'O' gauge trains. It was inevitable that eventually it would be decided to produce figures of people likely to be found around railway stations and in 1931, a set of Station Staff and a lineside effect, the Hall's Distemper advert, were released under the label 'Modelled Miniatures' as a subsidiary part of 'Hornby Accessories', and as such were in 'O' gauge (approximately 7m to 1ft), a scale more commonly referred to by model car collectors as '1/43rd'. Following the practice with their other products, the items were available in sets or individually, a sales pattern which was maintained until wartime.

The story of pre-war products can be traced through the *Meccano Magazine* which was used to publicise their wares and much of the following material has been extracted from this source, but care must always be taken when reading this publication as it does not tell the full story, nor is everything that was printed an exact representation of the facts. The first mention in *M.M.* cannot always be taken as the release date and therefore, in most cases we refer to

'Spring', 'Autumn' etc. of a particular year, nor can the photographs always be trusted, for many of them are heavily retouched or have drawings superimposed on them. There is also a smattering of typographical errors as one would expect from a monthly produced to a deadline. Artwork tended to be used and re-used, as did models appearing in adverts and text, so that quite significant casting changes were often not made apparent.

The first vehicles released as 'Modelled Miniatures' were trains, small and push-along, aimed at the child who was not yet old enough for clockwork

'O' gauge that had to be wound up and located on rails. From their issue in 1932, variations on these little sets remained in the catalogue until wartime. A year later, the first set of road vehicles was issued and it is at this point that the average model vehicle collector really becomes interested, for it is this group of two cars, a van, a lorry, a tractor and a tank that are regarded as the first Dinky Toys even though the name had not yet been invented. They were simple castings, brightly coloured and running on metal wheels, and must have been most appealing to a small boy of the time, for as the early 1934 Trade

## MECCANO MINIATURES

Our die-cast miniatures are enjoying a remarkable popularity among the younger children. The large number of repeat orders we are receiving indicate that dealers' stocks are rapidly being sold. Novel additions to the range are being made this year as described below. Each component of the various sets of Meccano Miniatures is available packed in boxes of six for separate sale. It is important that the price of each item displayed should be clearly marked. A special card price list showing the full range and giving prices of the complete sets, and also of the components, is now being prepared. Applications for copies of this card will be dealt with as soon as supplies are ready.

Meccano Miniatures No. 6 - Shepherd Set
Retail Price, Complete, 1/2
Each separate item is also supplied boxed in half dozens.
No. 6a Shepherd, 3d. No. 6b Dog, 3d.
No. 20 Sheep, 2d. each

Meccano Miniatures No. 29 Motor Bus
Retail Price 6d. each
Boxed in half dozens, assorted colours

Meccano Miniatures No. 24 - Motor Cars (with Rubber Tyres) Retail Price (set of 8 models) 6/6d
Each separate item is also supplied boxed in half dozens
No. 24a Ambulance 9d No. 24b Limousine 9d
No. 24c Town Sedan 1/- No. 24d Vogue Saloon 9d
No. 24e Super Streamline Saloon 9d
No. 24f Sportsman's Coupe (2 seater) 9d
No. 24g Sports Tourer (4 seater) 1/-
No. 24h Sports Tourer (2 seater) 1/-

Meccano Miniatures No. 18 - Goods Train Set
Retail Price, Complete, 1/9
Each separate item is also supplied boxed in half dozens.
No. 21a Locomotive 9d. No. 21b Wagons 4d. each

Meccano Miniatures No. 19 - Mixed Goods Train Set
Retail Price, Complete, 1/11d.
Each separate item is also supplied boxed in half dozens.
No. 21a Locomotive 9d No. 21b Wagon 4d
No. 21d Petrol Tank Wagon 6d No. 21c Lumber Wagon 5d

Meccano Miniatures No. 20 - Passenger Train Set
Retail Price, Complete, 2/6
Each separate item is also supplied boxed in half dozens.
No. 21a Locomotive 9d. No. 20a Coaches 7d. each
No. 20b Guard's Van 7d each.

Meccano Miniatures No. 23 - Racing Car
Retail Price 6d each
Boxed only in half dozens, assorted colours

Meccano Miniatures No. 26 Rail Autocar.
Retail Price 6d each
Boxed only in half dozens, assorted colours.

Meccano Miniatures No. 25
Commercial Motor Vehicles (with Rubber Tyres)
Retail Price (set of 6 models) 4/6d
Each separate item is also supplied boxed in half dozens
No. 24a Wagon 9d No. 25b Covered Van 9d
No. 25c Flat Truck 9d No.25d Petrol Tank Wagon 9d
No. 25e Tipping Wagon 9d
No. 25f Market Gardeners Van 9d

Meccano Miniatures No. 27 - Tram Car
Retail Price 6d each
Boxed only in half dozens, assorted colours

*February 1932 Trade Catalogue. Note, 29 Motor Bus is a drawing and it was never issued in this form with protruding cab and rear entrance. It was the 'centre entrance' bus that actually came out on the number 29.*

# MECCANO

## Dinky Toys

### Meccano Dinky Toys No. 1
### STATION STAFF

| | | |
|---|---|---|
| No. 1a | Station Master ... ... ... | each 3d. |
| No. 1b | Guard ... ... ... ... | ,, 3d. |
| No. 1c | Ticket Collector ... ... | ,, 3d. |
| No. 1d | Driver ... ... ... ... | ,, 3d. |
| No. 1e | Porter with bags ... ... | ,, 3d. |
| No. 1f | Porter ... ... ... ... | ,, 3d. |
| | Price of complete set 1/6 | |

Boys, Meccano Dinky Toys are the most realistic and the most attractive models in miniature ever produced. They are made of the best material obtainable, and are all finished in beautiful colours.

Many of these toys are ideal for giving the finishing touch to your model railways. You must have railwaymen to deal with your trains, and passengers to travel in them ; car attendants to look after the railway and its equipment. You want farmyard animals for lineside fields, and you should have at least one of the famous " Hall's Distemper " advertisements alongside your line !

Then there are the miniature train sets, rail autocar and various other types of motor vehicle. You can have hours of fun running these on the table or on the floor, arranging road and rail transport services from one point to another.

These splendid toys may all be purchased separately at the prices shown, or they may be obtained in complete sets. Ask your dealer to show you the complete range of Meccano Dinky Toys.

### Meccano Dinky Toys No. 3
### PASSENGERS

| | | |
|---|---|---|
| No. 3a | Woman and Child ... | each 3d. |
| No. 3b | Business Man ... ... | ,, 3d. |
| No. 3c | Male Hiker ... ... | ,, 3d. |
| No. 3d | Female Hiker ... ... | ,, 3d. |
| No. 3e | Newsboy ... ... | ,, 3d. |
| No. 3f | Woman ... ... | ,, 3d. |
| | Price of complete set 1/6 | |

### Meccano Dinky Toys No. 4
### ENGINEERING STAFF

| | | |
|---|---|---|
| No. 4a | Electrician ... ... | each 3d. |
| No. 4b | Fitters ... ... ... | ,, 3d. |
| No. 4c | Storekeeper ... ... | ,, 3d. |
| No. 4d | Greaser ... ... ... | ,, 3d. |
| No. 4e | Engine Room Attendant | ,, 3d. |
| | Price of complete set 1/6 | |

### Meccano Dinky Toys No. 5
### TRAIN AND HOTEL STAFF

| | | |
|---|---|---|
| No. 5a | Pullman Car Conductor | each 3d. |
| No. 5b | Pullman Car Waiters | ,, 3d. |
| No. 5c | Hotel Porters ... | ,, 3d. |
| | Price of complete set 1/3 | |

PRODUCT of MECCANO LIMITED LIVERPOOL

PRODUCT of MECCANO LIMITED LIVERPOOL

### Railway Accessories No. 3
### PLATFORM MACHINES, Etc.
Price of complete set 1/6
Railway Accessories No. 4
This set contains all the items that are included in Railway Accessories Nos. 1, 2 and 3
Price of complete set 3/9

### Meccano Dinky Toys No. 13
### HALL'S
### DISTEMPER ADVERTISEMENT
This miniature of a well-known line-side advertisement is intended to be placed in the fields adjoining the railway track. Price 9d.

### Railway Accessories No. 1
### MINIATURE LUGGAGE AND TRUCK
Price of complete set 1/6

### Meccano Dinky Toys No. 18
### GOODS TRAIN SET

| | | |
|---|---|---|
| No. 21a | Tank Locomotive ... | each 9d. |
| No. 21b | Wagons ... ... ... | ,, 4d. |
| | Price of complete set 1/9 | |

### Railway Accessories No. 2
### MILK CANS AND TRUCK
Price of complete set 1/6

### Meccano Dinky Toys No. 19
### MIXED GOODS TRAIN SET

| | | |
|---|---|---|
| No. 21a | Tank Locomotive ... | each 9d. |
| No. 21b | Wagon ... ... ... | ,, 4d. |
| No. 21d | Petrol Tank Wagon ... | ,, 6d. |
| No. 21e | Lumber Wagon ... ... | ,, 5d. |
| | Price of complete set 1/11 | |

### Meccano Dinky Toys No. 20
### PASSENGER TRAIN SET

| | | |
|---|---|---|
| No. 21a | Tank Locomotive ... | each 9d. |
| No. 20a | Coaches ... ... ... | ,, 7d. |
| No. 20b | Guard's Van ... ... | ,, 7d. |
| | Price of complete set 2/6 | |

### Meccano Dinky Toys No. 23
### RACING CAR
Assorted Colours. Fitted with rubber tyres.
Price 6d. each

### Meccano Dinky Toys No. 26
### RAIL AUTOCAR
Assorted Colours ...    Price 6d. each

### Meccano Dinky Toys No. 2
### FARMYARD ANIMALS
| | |
|---|---|
| No. 2a Horse, each 3½d. | No. 2c Pig, each 2d. |
| No. 2b Cow ,, 3½d. | No. 2d Sheep ,, 2d. |
| Price of complete set 1/6 | |

### Meccano Dinky Toys No. 24
### MOTOR CARS
Fitted with rubber tyres and silver plated radiators.

| | | |
|---|---|---|
| No. 24a | Ambulance ... ... | each 9d. |
| No. 24b | Limousine ... ... | ,, 9d. |
| No. 24c | Town Sedan ... ... | ,, 1/- |
| No. 24d | Vogue Saloon ... ... | ,, 9d. |
| No. 24e | Super Streamline Saloon | ,, 9d. |
| No. 24f | Sportsman's Coupé ... | ,, 9d. |
| No. 24g | Sports Tourer (4 seater) | ,, 1/- |
| No. 24h | Sports Tourer (2 seater) | ,, 1/- |
| | Price of complete set 6/6 | |

### Meccano Dinky Toys No. 22
### MOTOR VEHICLES

| | | |
|---|---|---|
| No. 22a Sports Car each 6d. | No. 22d Delivery Van each 8d. | |
| No. 22b Sports Coupé ,, 6d. | No. 22e Tractor ,, 9d. | |
| No. 22c Motor Truck ,, 8d. | No. 22f Tank ,, 1/- | |
| Price of complete set 4/- | | |

### Meccano Dinky Toys No. 28/1
### DELIVERY VANS

| | |
|---|---|
| Manchester Guardian Van | each 9d. |
| Palethorpes Sausage Van | ,, 9d. |
| Hornby Trains Van ... ... | ,, 9d. |
| Pickfords Removals Van ... | ,, 9d. |
| Oxo Van... ... ... ... | ,, 9d. |
| Ensign Cameras Van ... ... | ,, 9d. |
| Price of complete set 4/6 | |

### Meccano Dinky Toys No. 6
### SHEPHERD SET

| | | |
|---|---|---|
| No. 6a | Shepherd ... ... ... | each 3d. |
| No. 6b | Dog ... ... ... ... | ,, 3d. |
| No. 2d | Sheep ... ... ... | ,, 2d. |
| | Price of complete set 1/2 | |

### Meccano Dinky Toys No. 25
### COMMERCIAL MOTOR VEHICLES
Fitted with rubber tyres and silver plated radiators.

| | | |
|---|---|---|
| No. 25a | Wagon ... ... ... | each 9d. |
| No. 25b | Covered Van ... ... | ,, 9d. |
| No. 25c | Flat Truck ... ... | ,, 9d. |
| No. 25d | Petrol Tank Wagon ... | ,, 9d. |
| No. 25e | Tipping Wagon ... ... | ,, 9d. |
| No. 25f | Market Gardener's Van | ,, 9d. |
| | Price of complete set 4/6 | |

**MANUFACTURED BY MECCANO LTD., LIVERPOOL 13**

Catalogue says 'Our die-cast miniatures are enjoying a remarkable popularity among the younger children.' That this was not just advertising propaganda is indicated by the plethora of new models released in 1934. As the range became established in its own right and not just as a part of 'Hornby Accessories', it became clear that 'Modelled Miniatures' left much to be desired as a name, for it is not 'snappy' or memorable. Neither can it be said to roll of the tongue. Early in 1934 'Meccano Miniatures' was tried but that had little more to recommend it, so it was changed again and by happy design 'Dinky Toys' were christened.

The Concise Oxford Dictionary tells us that 'dinky' is a colloquial adjective of Scottish origin meaning 'pretty, neat, of engaging appearance' and as such is a name perfectly fitted to the product. To enable this new name to acquire the reputation of the other products and to establish the name of the manufacturer, the designation given was 'Meccano Dinky Toys', and it remains so on the day of writing (Spring 1981) although soon 'Dinky Toys' was printed in larger bolder type, so that while 'Meccano' was still there, it was in effect dropped from the title. Dinky Toys publicity always used the two words together, never 'Dinky' on its own, though the child customer did so shorten it as Meccano realised, for in the *Meccano Magazine* of January 1941 referring to a letter from a reader the following line appears: '"Dinkies" as boys often call them'. The plural spelling of the word thus gained authenticity not merely from usage, but also had the acceptance of the manufacturers. The new name was revealed to the public in the April 1934 *Meccano Magazine*.

Not content with only producing road vehicles, ships and planes were also released so that by November 1934, the advertising was claiming '150 Varieties' of Dinky Toys. With the increase in size of the range, *Meccano Magazine* began to give Dinky Toys the same sort of coverage that had previously been afforded to Meccano and Hornby Trains, though the articles were not so frequent. Maybe the product was selling so well that it did not need the additional coverage, but more likely the lack of frequency was occasioned by running out of new things to say. However, they began in a big way with two pages devoted to the subject in the December 1934 issue.

THE MECCANO MAGAZINE

# Collecting Meccano Dinky Toys

## A New and Fascinating Hobby

THERE is a peculiar fascination about miniature reproductions of familiar things. We pay little attention to the normal full-sized objects to be seen every day in our streets and elsewhere, but a miniature reproduction of one of them immediately attracts our notice, and most of us feel a desire to possess it!

Some years ago a set of platform accessories—luggage and truck, milk cans and truck, seats, and automatic machines—was introduced with the object of making Hornby Station platforms more realistic. This proved immediately popular, but Hornby Railway owners were not satisfied. They demanded miniature railwaymen and passengers to give "life" to the platforms, and in response to this demand two further sets of figures were produced, one consisting of station staff and the other of typical passengers. Miniature train sets followed, each made up of a locomotive and two or three coaches or goods vehicles.

The requirements of railway enthusiasts were thus fairly well provided for, but nothing had been done for those whose interests lay in other directions. We were repeatedly asked for other miniatures, mainly of motor cars, aeroplanes and ships; and finally it was decided to introduce a comprehensive series of models under the general title of Dinky Toys. This series met with an enthusiastic welcome, and it has been rapidly extended until it now includes well over one hundred items, with many others in active preparation.

The Dinky Toys form the most attractive set of miniatures in existence. They are well designed and beautifully finished in colour, and they include the utmost amount of detail possible in such tiny reproductions. All of them form delightful ornaments for table or mantelpiece, especially if arranged in sets. In addition many of them can be used with striking effect in Hornby Railway layouts, to which they add a remarkable touch of realism. This is specially the case with layouts incorporating some of the Countryside Sections. Horses, cattle and sheep can be placed in the fields, and pedestrians and motor vehicles of various types distributed at suitable points along the roads. The effects that can be produced in this manner are quite extraordinary, and the general scheme can be varied almost indefinitely.

With a few exceptions all the Dinky Toys are arranged in sets, but every item can be purchased separately. One of these sets, or even a single model, forms an ideal Christmas present.

The train sets, of which there are four, have already been mentioned, Set No. 17 consists of a locomotive and tender, coach and guard's van, and Set No. 20 of a tank locomotive, two coaches and guard's van. For those who prefer goods trains there are Sets No. 18, consisting of a tank locomotive and three open wagons, and No. 19, comprising a tank locomotive, an open wagon, a petrol tank wagon and a lumber wagon. By purchasing additional coaches or wagons these trains can be increased to quite impressive proportions, and as all the items are to the same scale the trains can be rearranged and made up in any way desired.

Motor car enthusiasts are particularly well catered for. Set No. 24

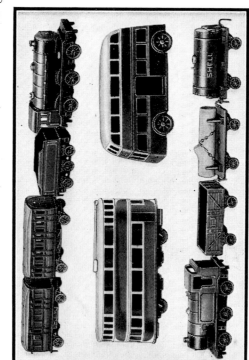

This illustration shows two of the Meccano Dinky Toy Train Sets, the Tramcar and the Motor Bus. The Racing Car, which is available in a variety of sporty colour schemes, is shown below.

alone includes seven different types of up-to-date private cars, ranging from a sports two-seater to a handsome limousine, together with a splendid model of a typical ambulance. All these vehicles are fitted with rubber tyres and silver-plated radiators. Then there is Set No. 25, which provides an equally attractive collection of commercial vehicles. There are six of these, an open wagon, a flat truck, a covered van, a petrol tank wagon, a market gardener's van, and a tipping wagon that actually tips!

Another interesting model is the Racing Car (No. 23). This is a realistic little model of a typical modern speed car. It is fitted with rubber tyres and is obtainable in a variety of attractive colours. Even more striking is the "Airflow" Saloon (No. 32). This is an exceptionally handsome model, which demonstrates excellently the principles of streamlining. It is fitted with rubber tyres, silver-plated radiator and bumpers, and is obtainable in various colours. Still another very attractive vehicle is the "Holland Coachcraft" van (No. 31). This is a model of one of the most modernistic commercial vehicles now on the road.

Turning now to aeroplanes, we find six splendid models in Set No. 60. The largest of these is a realistic reproduction of an Imperial Airways liner, which gives a good idea of the massive proportions and handsome appearance of these machines. Smaller but equally attractive are the models of a D.H. "Leopard Moth," a Percival "Gull," a low wing monoplane, and a General of a Cierva "Autogiro." This tiny model, with its revolving vanes, has proved exceptionally popular, which shows clearly not only the high quality of the model, but also the widespread interest that is now being taken in this type of aeroplane.

One of the outstanding events of 1934 was the launch of the giant Cunard White Star Liner "Queen Mary," on 26th September. This ship has attracted more attention than any other vessel built for many years, and therefore it is fitting that a special model should be included in the Dinky Toys series. This model (No. 52) is designed to a scale of 150 ft. to 1 in., and is nearly 7 in. in length. It contains a surprising amount of intricate detail work, particularly in the boat deck and the superstructure generally. It is finished in correct colours and shows how the real "Queen Mary" will appear when she is completed and ready for her maiden voyage in the early part of 1936. Then, everyone hopes, she will recover for Great Britain the much coveted "Blue Riband" of the Atlantic.

Set No. 51 includes six liners of world-wide fame. There is Norddeutscher Lloyd "Europa," and the Italian liner "Rex," which at present holds the Atlantic record with a crossing between Gibralter and New York made in four days 13 hours. Coming now to British ships, there is the C.P.R. "Empress of Britain," the P. & O. "Strathaird," the Furness Withy "Queen of Bermuda," and the Cunard White Star "Britannic."

All these ships are what are known as "waterline" models; that is to say, they represent the vessel as she appears in the water when loaded down to her normal level. It is impossible to convey in words any adequate impression of the daintiness of these models. They include every detail for which room could be found, and they are beautifully finished in correct colours.

All boys are interested in warships, and Set No. **50** provides a set of ships of the British Navy ranging from battle-ships to submarines. Heading the Set are the mighty battle cruiser "Hood" and the battleship "Nelson." Then there are three typical cruisers, "Effingham," "York" and "Delhi," and two destroyers of the "Broke" and "Amazon" classes respectively. Smallest of all are models of submarines of the "X" and "K" classes. All these warships are painted in battleship grey, with a dull matt finish that gives a strikingly realistic appearance. Keen boys will appreciate the fact that the gun turrets on the cruisers and battleships, although so small, will actually swivel!

The Dinky Toy ships are just the thing for giving the finishing touches to models of harbours and docks. Large models of this nature are very popular just now with Meccano Clubs, and they look astonishingly realistic with one or two Dinky Toy liners at the quayside. The effect is enhanced by a small fleet of warships lying at anchor in the "roadstead."

From this necessarily brief survey it will be evident that the Meccano Dinky Toys provide all the material for a fascinating collecting hobby. The range of subjects is so great as to provide ample variety, and as many of the models can be obtained in several different colours, there is scope for an extensive collection of outstanding interest. The Dinky Toys that are now in preparation will be announced in the pages of the "M.M." immediately they are available, and collectors should keep a sharp look-out for details.

In next month's "M.M." we hope to include an article describing in detail how Meccano Dinky Toys can be put to use in the fascinating hobby of table-top photography. This hobby consists of arranging on a table miniature scenes, composed of tiny models and scrap material of all kinds. These scenes are then photographed, and the results appear as though they were quaint reproductions of real scenes. A great deal of the fun in this kind of photography lies in making use of the simplest of household articles to produce realistic effects, and in next month's article we shall describe some of the unlimited possibilities in this direction.

One difficulty in the past has been that the household material available has usually been seriously deficient in models small enough to be used for the purpose. This problem is now solved by the appearance of the Dinky Toys. The motor cars and wagons lend themselves perfectly to the production of necessary road scenes; the trains provide the necessary railway material, and the ships make it possible to produce harbour or coastal scenes in great detail. The aeroplanes, too, can be made to play an important part, and in the article special reference will be made to their employment.

No doubt keen and enthusiastic readers will discover other interesting uses for the Dinky Toys, and we should be glad to receive descriptions and if possible photographs of any such schemes.

A beautiful miniature of the world's largest ship the Cunard White Star "Queen Mary" is included in the Dinky Toy Series, and a full size reproduction of the model is shown here. Dinky Toy motor vehicles and an Imperial Airways Liner are illustrated at the top of this page.

By this time, metal hubs with white tyres had begun to be substituted for the metal wheels, and thereafter the range continued to expand with more versions of cars, trucks, ships and planes being produced. New products such as motor bikes, garages, petrol pumps were also made, but it wasn't until 1936 that completely new ideas were again introduced with the release of the 'Dolly Varden' doll's house and furniture aimed at a new market, little girls. It was this year that Dinky Toys began to feature in the monthly competitions in *Meccano Magazine*.

A most attractive advert from the same year shows a Dinky Toys layout with pavements, garages and so on, and serves as an illustration of the care with which such publicity must be regarded, for not only is the picture heavily retouched, but the car (bottom right) resembling an Armstrong with a boot was never actually made.

1937 saw the introduction of what developed into a very fine range of military vehicles. They were all approximately in the same scale, but were of a smaller scale than the bulk of the other wheeled vehicles. This variation in scale was nothing new, as the Ships and Aeroplanes also had their own peculiar scales. (Motor vehicles very approximately: 1/43. Military vehicles about: 1/60. Planes: 1/200. Ships: 1/1800.) Selected items manufactured at the French Meccano factory at Bobigny outside Paris were imported in 1937 and incorporated into the advertising and sales brochures. They are all distinguished by a 'z' suffix on the catalogue number and represent only a very small proportion of the products of the French Meccano factory. The total production was now so large that the catalogue numbering system began to break down. Since the product marketing strategy was based on the sale of vehicles in sets with each item also available separately, the set as a whole was given a number, say 28, and each individual vehicle, in case a series of vans, was allocated the same number and an individual letter, eg. 28a, 28b . . . Letters such as 'i' that could be easily confused with figures were generally omitted. So many versions of the 28 vans were made that there were not enough letters in the alphabet and the last set had to be given a new number (280). Despite these early warning signs of a system collapse, it wasn't until 1954 that the whole

# Competitions for All Readers
## A Novel "Dinky Toys Layout" Competition

This month we announce the third of the special summer competitions. These contests are of such a nature that entries may be prepared either indoors or out in the open. There is no model-building to do and all that a competitor requires to enable him to prepare his entry are a copy of this issue of the "*M.M.*," a pencil, and a sheet of paper.

The illustration on this page shows a complex Dinky Toys road and traffic layout, which is fully equipped with various Road Signs, Traffic Signals, Motor Vehicles, and other appropriate items from the Dinky Toys Series. In designing the layout and arranging the traffic several ridiculous mistakes have purposely been made. For example, some of the Road Signs are in the wrong places and Traffic Signals are facing the wrong directions. If the illustration is carefully studied a large number of other errors will become apparent, and readers are invited to test their powers of observation by trying to find as many of these as possible. Many of the mistakes are obvious and will be seen at a glance, but some of them will only be revealed by a very careful examination of the illustration.

Numerous errors have been made in the arrangement of this Dinky Toys traffic layout and prizes are offered to readers who can find the greatest number. Full details of the contest are given on this page.

The competition is open to readers of all ages, living in any part of the world, and all entries will be grouped into one section and judged together.

The following instructions should be noted. On one side of a sheet of paper competitors should make a list of all the mistakes they can "spot," and explain exactly where each occurs in the layout. They must then write their name and address on the other side of the sheet, and enclose it in an envelope addressed to "Dinky Toys Layout Competition," Meccano Ltd., Binns Road, Liverpool 13.

The following prizes will be awarded to the competitors who discover the greatest number of errors, in order of merit. First, Meccano Products value £2/2/-; Second, Products value £1/1/-; Third, Products value 10/6. Prizewinners will be notified by letter, and the result will be announced in due course in the Magazine.

In the event of a tie for any of the prizes the judges will take into consideration the neatness of the entries concerned.

All entries must be posted in time to reach Liverpool on or before the 31st October, 1936. Any received after that date will be disqualified.

referencing scheme was revamped and the suffix letters deleted entirely.

Meanwhile, the *Meccano Magazine* publicity machine ground on with the educational (sic) value of Dinky Toys being promoted in an article entitled 'L.M.S. Motor Drivers Go To School. Dinky Toys Vehicles For Road Instruction.' which tells us that on 'a table arranged as a model highway . . . To illustrate the rules of safe driving . . . "traffic" consisting of Meccano Dinky Toys road vehicles is run . . .'

and that by this means the time taken on the drivers' training course is much reduced. Customer involvement in the product was also encouraged in a Monthly Competition in October of that year: 'write on a postcard 10 suggestions for new items not already covered in the Dinky Toy Series.' Unfortunately, the results were not published but the volume of replies no doubt gave the New Products Committee ample food for thought.

1938 saw further consolidation of the range which was gradually edging towards containing 300 varieties of toy. There were no major innovations, probably because the new product effort was being directed towards an entirely new range, Hornby Dublo Trains. When this system was released, the *Meccano Magazine* copywriters scrabbled around the Dinky range to find vehicles that would be vaguely consistent with the scale. Because of the wide variation in scales, they came up with some that were fairly good and some that would just about do, 29c Double Deck Bus, 35 series Small Cars, 25 series Commercial Vehicles etc. But, of course, the event that had the most effect on Meccano products, was the outbreak of war in September 1939. The inevitability of fighting occasioned a flurry of activity, including such hasty measures as announcing new product considerably earlier in the development stages than was usual. The 38 series of Sports Cars were first featured in June, utilising poor drawings, almost as if to reassure the manufacturers themselves that there would not be the total breakdown of civilisation that was to be feared. In September a batch of models was withdrawn from sale only to be reintroduced in March of the following year. Prices had gone up, and down, since the introduction of the range, but on September 15 an across-the-board price rise was imposed reflecting the scarcity of materials occasioned by the build up in armament production. By now all vehicles were fitted with black tyres.

When the cataclysm did not happen and minds became adjusted to the situation, the marketing skills of the organisation reasserted themselves and new product ideas springing from the times were brought out; the Petrol Tanker was liveried in the grey and white of the common petrol 'Pool' and camouflage was introduced on the aeroplanes, beginning with the Spitfire, and for a time the advertising heavily featured the military vehicles and planes. Also in 1940, completely new items were released, for example, three of the 38 Sports Cars. However, supplies were limited and though the January 1941 price list shows that most items were available, they were not to be found in the smaller shops nor in great quantities in the larger ones. It would appear that the policy was to make the stocks

stretch as far round the country as possible and last as long as possible, so that when production resumed neither the retailer nor the customer would forget about the brand. A certain diminution in demand was occasioned by the imposition of Purchase Tax in October 1940 which effectively increased retail prices by about 20%, and this tended to help the strategy of stock stretching. After January 1941, as uncertainty increased once again, prices became sub-

ject to change without notice, no new liveries were introduced and supplies became scarcer and scarcer until officially stopped by government orders; the first in January 1942 forbidding manufacture of metal toys and the second in September 1943 stopping further distribution of any still left in warehouses.

While the 'Battle of Britain' was in progress and the R.A.F. stocks of fighter planes were being daily

*Meccano Magazine February 1936.*

xiv       THE MECCANO MAGAZINE

TOYS OF QUALITY MADE BY MECCANO LTD.

The above illustration shows in a striking manner the realistic effects that may be obtained with Dinky Toys. The components used are listed below, **excepting** the pavements and hoardings which are quite easily made of cardboard or plywood.

| Item | | Dinky Toys No. | | | Price each | Item | | Dinky Toys No. | | | Price each |
|---|---|---|---|---|---|---|---|---|---|---|---|
| Pillar Letter Box. G.P.O. | ... | No. 12a | ... | ,, | 3d. | Sportsman's Coupé | ... ... | No. 24f | ... | ,, | 9d. |
| Pillar Letter Box. Air Mail | ... | No. 12b | ... | ,, | 3d. | Sports Tourer (four seater) | ... | No. 24g | ... | ,, | 9d. |
| Robot Traffic Signals. Two-way (4) | ,, | No. 47c | ... | ,, | 3d. | Vogue Saloon | ... | No. 24d | ... | ,, | 9d. |
| Belisha Beacons (6) | ... ... | ,, | No. 47d | ... | ,, | 1d. | Vauxhall Car | ... | No. 30d | ... | ,, | 9d. |
| Road Signs "Roundabout" (2) | ,, | No. 47r | ... | ,, | 1½d. | Petrol Tank Wagon "Texaco" | ,, | No. 25d | ... | ,, | 9d. |
| Road Sign "No Entry" | ... ... | ,, | No. 47q | ... | ,, | 1½d. | Wagon | ... | No. 25a | ... | ,, | 9d. |
| Petrol Station | ... | No. 48 | ... | ,, | 1/6 | Daimler Car | ... | No. 30c | ... | ,, | 9d. |
| "Theo" Petrol Pump | ... | ,, | No. 49c | ... | ,, | 4d. | Atco Lawn Mowers Van | ,, | No. 28n | ... | ,, | 6d. |
| "Shell" Petrol Pump | ... | ,, | No. 49d | ... | ,, | 4d. | Newsboy | ... | No. 31 | ... | ,, | 3d. |
| Oil Bin (Pratts) | ... | ,, | No. 49e | ... | ,, | 3d. | Woman and Child | ... | No. 3a | ... | ,, | 3d. |
| Garages (2) | ... | No. 45 | ... | ,, | 1/6 | Storekeeper | ... | No. 4c | ... | ,, | 3d. |
| Market Gardener's Van | ,, | No. 25f | ... | ,, | 9d. | Business Men (7) | ... | No. 3b | ... | ,, | 3d. |
| Covered Van | ... | No. 25b | ... | ,, | 9d. | Women (3) | ... | No. 3f | ... | ,, | 3d. |
| Mechanical Horse | ... | ,, | No. 33a | ... | ,, | 6d. | Electricians (2) | ... | No. 4a | ... | ,, | 3d. |
| R.A.C. Motor Cycle Patrol | ,, | No. 43b | ... | ,, | 9d. | Male Hiker | ... | No. 3c | ... | ,, | 3d. |
| A.A. Motor Cycle Patrol | ,, | No. 44b | ... | ,, | 9d. | Dogs (2) | ... | No. 6b | ... | ,, | 2d. |
| Breakdown Car | ... | No. 30e | ... | ,, | 9d. | Fitter | ... | No. 4b | ... | ,, | 3d. |
| Palethorpes Sausage Van | ,, | No. 28f | ... | ,, | 6d. | Greaser | ... | No. 4d | ... | ,, | 3d. |
| "Manchester Guardian" Van | ,, | No. 28c | ... | ,, | 6d. | Guard | ... | No. 1b | ... | ,, | 3d. |
| "Kodak" Cameras Van | ... | ,, | No. 28g | ... | ,, | 6d. | | | | | | |

denuded, Meccano Directors came up with the idea of selling their Spitfire model in aid of a fund to purchase a 'Meccano Spitfire' for presentation to the R.A.F. The appeal was launched in the October 1940 *Meccano Magazine*. 'To help to carry out this scheme our Directors have arranged for the production of a special miniature "Spitfire" in the form of a pendant. This pendant is available beautifully enamelled in bright green with red propeller, or in bright red with green propeller; and is fitted with a split ring so that it can be worn on the lapel of a coat or costume. The pendant will be sold at 2/6, and every penny of this, without deduction of any kind, will go to a fund to purchase a "Spitfire". This miniature forms a most

delightful souvenir, and will be specially attractive to all ladies. Make sure that your mother, sisters and all your lady friends have one.' The success of the appeal can be gauged from Lord Beaverbrook's message in the next month's magazine. (£2000 equals 16 000 2/6.)

During the War, the factory was turned over to war work as diecastings are an essential part of engines and other types of machinery. Judging by what was not re-issued after the war, many of the toy dies were 'lost' during this period, perhaps having been melted down because of the steel shortage or perhaps having been damaged beyond repair. By early 1945, it was obvious that it was only a matter of time

# DINKY TOYS

### BOYS! START THIS FASCINATING COLLECTING HOBBY TO-DAY!

Dinky Toys collecting is one of the most fascinating of all hobbies. These wonderful miniatures are unique in their realistic accuracy, rich colouring and perfection of finish.

The Dinky Toys Series is always up to date. Nowadays everybody is interested in the mechanised units of the British Army, and among the most popular Dinky Toys models are the two Royal Tank Corps Sets. These have been followed recently by a Mobile Anti-Aircraft Unit and an 18-Pounder Quick-Firing Field Gun Unit, which promise to enjoy even greater popularity.

Many of the Dinky Toys are splendid for adding realism to Hornby and Hornby-Dublo railway layouts; others, such as the Traffic Signals, Road Signs and Motor Vehicles, are ideal for making up fascinating road scenes.

Hours of fun can be had in playing with these miniatures. Exciting race games can be devised for the Sports Cars, and thrilling gliding races can be held with the Aeroplanes.

All Dinky Toys can be bought separately, and many also in complete sets.

**Owing to difficulties that have arisen in recent months, we regret that it has been found necessary to suspend the manufacture of certain Dinky Toys. These items will be reinstated as soon as conditions permit.**

*1939 Catalogue.*

# Lord Beaverbrook Thanks Meccano Boys!

On the Editorial page we print in full the message received from Lord Beaverbrook, Minister of Aircraft Production, in acknowledgment of the cheque for £2,000 sent to him as a first instalment towards the purchase of a "Meccano Spitfire."

## HAVE **YOU** DONE YOUR SHARE?

Have you told your father and mother, and all your relatives and friends, about the Fund, and persuaded each of them to buy a Spitfire Pendant?

Every Meccano boy is full of enthusiasm for the splendid work of our Fighter Command—the magnificent pilots who have fought and beaten, and continue to beat, the most powerful bombers the Germans can put into the air. Here is a glorious opportunity to express this enthusiasm, and to show these pilots that their heroic exploits are watched with ever-growing excitement and admiration in every British home.

*Up to the time of going to press the*
*Fund has reached £3,250*

*Every Pendant sold is another step towards your own Meccano Spitfire*

*Fig. 1. Reprint of p. 323 of* Meccano Magazine *August 1947.*

# Dinky SUPERTOYS
## A Fine New Series of Models

THIS month we announce the arrival of the first of our new products—the Dinky SUPERTOYS. These fine models have been given this name because they are die-cast miniatures similar in general style to our famous Dinky Toys, but much larger.

Take for instance the Foden Wagon shown on the right. The overall measurements of the actual wagon are 29 ft. 7½ in. long and 7 ft. 10 in. high; the corresponding measurements of the SUPERTOY model are 7½ in. and 1¹⁰⁄₁₆ in. The same dimensions of the Guy Lorry are 20 ft. 1½ in. and 7 ft. ¾ in.; those of the SUPERTOY are 5¼ in. and 1½ in.

These big SUPERTOYS are very striking in appearance. Their size alone is impressive, and the great amount of accurate detail that has

**Dinky Supertoys No. 501 Foden Diesel 8-wheel Wagon.**

**Dinky Supertoys No. 502 Foden Flat Truck.**

**Dinky Supertoys No. 511 Guy 4-ton Lorry.**

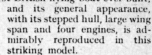

**Dinky Supertoys No. 512 Guy Flat Truck.**

been included in them makes them wonderfully realistic. The Foden Wagon and the Guy Lorry illustrate these features well. They have the same distinctive appearance as their prototypes, to which the roomy cab in a forward position contributes greatly. The front is faithfully reproduced, with the chromium-plated radiator grille

flanked by the two headlights. On the near side of the chassis, tucked under the body, is a miniature of the tank, and there is even the spare wheel, bolted in its correct place under the body at the rear. The bodywork is equally realistic. Two types are available, one with head, side and tail boards, the other a flat truck.

Equally attractive is the fine model of the famous Short "Shetland" Flying Boat illustrated at the foot of this page. This will be welcomed by all who are interested in aircraft. The "Shetland" is the largest British flying boat ever built, and its general appearance, with its stepped hull, large wing span and four engines, is admirably reproduced in this striking model.

**Dinky Supertoys No. 701 "Shetland" Flying Boat.**

before hostilities would cease and life would be able to return gradually to 'normal'. As war work tailed off, time was found to start thinking about Dinky Toys again. Indeed, some of the drawings show alterations dated May 1945, some time before V.E. Day. *Meccano Magazine* started predicting that the toys would soon be back and there were approximately fifty different models on sale for Christmas 1945. It is possible that some of these were pre-war stocks that had been 'frozen' by government order in September 1943 and therefore had all the features of pre-war manufacture. Production was, however, quickly getting under way again and there were sufficient stocks to enable a reasonable size catalogue to be produced for export markets, which, on government insistence, took priority over the home market, in order to start paying off the massive war debt that had been incurred. (See: Display and Marketing—Catalogues for the 11/45 Canadian Catalogue.)

The April 1946 *Meccano Magazine* carried a quarter page advert heralding '. . . the first of the new Dinky Toys for which you have waited so long.', a 38c LAGONDA which had been designed in 1939 and the completely new 153a JEEP. This set the trend of introducing new models via *Meccano Magazine* for at this time there were no regular catalogues and some means had had to be found to keep purchasers on their toes waiting for new releases. At the time, Meccano virtually had the diecast toy field to itself, for many of the small pre-war manufacturers had not survived the war and the new ones had not yet got into production. Usually, the magazine announcements coincided with the release of models to the retailers but frequently enough to be significant they did not. Thus 40a RILEY was in the shops in May 1947 and not in the magazine until June. This lack of coincidence did not signify anything new as it was also a feature of pre-war advertising. Other new models followed. August 1946 saw the issue of the first new plane 70a AVRO YORK and November another 38 series, 38f JAGUAR, and another aeroplane, 70e GLOSTER METEOR. By December, the size of the adverts had increased to a full page and during this period there was some considerable emphasis on their ability to fit with Dublo Railways, although judicious selection had to be employed to give such an impression.

*Fig. 2. Reprint of pp. 24–5 of Meccano Magazine January 1954.*

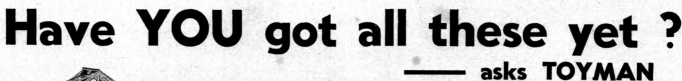

# Have YOU got all these yet ?
## —— asks TOYMAN

**No. 752
Goods Yard
Crane**
Base 4 in. square
Length of Jib 7 in.

Here displayed all together for you are the new Dinky Toys of 1953, except for the International Road Signs. Have you got them all yet? Whether you buy Dinky Toys to play with individually, or to use together on Dinky Toys layouts or in games of various kinds, or just to display in a cabinet for sheer pleasure in their appearance, you cannot do without any of these additions of the past year.

There is no need for me to describe them in detail, as all of them have been illustrated in issues of the Magazine during 1953. Five of them are brilliant miniatures of racing cars, in the racing colours of various countries. The rest provide plenty of variety and all are splendid for use on many different kinds of layouts, including those that I have constructed myself and have described and shown to you in pictures in recent months. Many of you have enjoyed as much real fun with them as I have, and I hope to hear more of your layouts, and of the many ways in which you make use of your Dinky Toys.

There is no new Dinky Toy this month, and I suppose that you all noticed that no new one was announced in the Christmas issue either. The reason for this is very simple. The demand for the Dinky Toys that are already in production is still so enormous that it has been quite impossible as yet to squeeze any new ones in! But I promise you that during 1954 there will be many splendid newcomers that will add still further to the pleasure that these world-famous miniatures give to all of you. So look out for them.

**No. 581
Horse Box**
Length 6¾ in.

**Leyland Cement Wagon
No. 533**
Length 5¼ in.

**No. 30w
Electric Articulated Lorry**
Length 5¼ in.

**No. 27n
Field-Marshall Tractor**
Length 3 in.

**No. 673
Scout Car**
Length 2⅝ in.

**No. 582
Pullmore Car Transporter**
Length with ramp raised 9⅝ in.

**No. 40j
Austin Somerset Saloon**
Length 3½ in.

**No. 27ak
Massey-Harris Tractor
and Hay Rake**
Length 6 in.

**No. 23k
Talbot-Lago Racing Car**
Length 4 in.

**No. 23j
H.W.M. Racing Car**
Length 3¾ in.

**No. 23n
Maserati Racing Car**
Length 3½ in.

**No. 23h
Ferrari Racing Car**
Length 4 in.

**No. 23g
Cooper-Bristol Racing Car**
Length 3½ in.

1947 saw the re-introduction of more pre-war models including 52c QUEEN MARY and the issue of some new ones, featuring amongst them 'Supertoys' in the form of Guys, Fodens and the Shetland Flying Boat. But the following year production declined to approximately one a month, mainly commercials (especially in the Farm and Garden categories) and 'working' models, for instance the Fork Lift Truck and Bulldozer. The hopes for a quick return to the status quo were not to be fulfilled and in 1949, production of all the aeroplanes had to be suspended. This was the first example, post-war, of the need to take such steps and it was to happen again but not on such a wide scale, so that occasionally an item would disappear from the catalogues for a short time only to reappear later. Most of the models that were issued were small items; amongst them the sack truck and wheelbarrow, whose '. . . inclusion in Dinky Toy layouts of various types will add realism.' (so said Meccano Magazine) and also would not use much metal. Despite the cut-backs a prestige item was produced on the Guy chassis, the Slumberland Van. 1950 did not see much of an improvement with introductions running at about one a month, and the following year was no better with models coming out in small batches but with no increase in the total number.

However, the post-war boom was gathering momentum and 1952 was a much more productive period with more pre-war items being re-released such as the Railway Accessories and the re-introduction of the planes from 1949. Amongst the new items were the first of the Gift Sets signalling an increase in consumer spending power. It was not only Meccano that was affected by the improvement and competitors such as Lesney and several small toy firms (which latterly were not to have great success) in the diecast toy field were beginning to appear. Interestingly, it is around this period that Airfix, who were later to produce plastic kits which fought for the weekly pocket money and eventually took over Meccano Ltd., was also finding benefits from the general improvement in trading conditions. The metal shortage occasioned by the Korean War was still somewhat acute and Meccano began looking at alternative materials, although in the event their use was not required because of an easing of their supply

problems. To boost sales, the tail end of the year saw the beginning of a new series of articles in Meccano Magazine describing in glowing detail the merits of the new Dinky Toys, a series which was to last for many years. In 1953, releases, including re-issues, were at the rate of up to three a month and 'To meet the increasing demand for Dinky Toys we have built a new Works where we have installed the most up-to-date plant resulting in improved methods of production which have enabled us to reduce prices.' This was Speke, a trading estate on the outskirts of Liverpool. Speke only did the diecasting, all other processes being retained at Binns Road. The release of a 'New Dinky Toys Booklet in Colour' was also announced in October though this was not in fact the first colour catalogue to be produced. (See: Display and Marketing—Catalogues.) Dinky Toy articles in Meccano Magazine acquired the title 'Dinky News' and were written by 'The Toyman', a pseudonym used by a selection of magazine staff writers.

Introductions continued apace into 1954 with the production of the first of the new group of army vehicles, but one of the most significant developments, at least as far as the collector is concerned, was renumbering. The suffix letter system was finally deemed to be no longer manageable, and a new numbering system based on blocks of numbers allocated to types of vehicles was gradually introduced in 1953 when, for instance, the drawing of the Austin Devon had the new number 152 added to it. (Original sales number—40d.) Obviously, it was impossible to change the whole lot overnight and it was not until November 1954 that the instruction was released to alter the numbers of the racing cars which had been 23 to the block starting 230. Both numbers appeared for a time on the boxes and in the catalogues but after the implementation of the instruction drawn up in January 1955 to change the markings on the remainder, all reference to the earlier number was deleted. New releases were slotted into the new system as they appeared. For full details of the numbering system, see Appendix.

No new Supertoys were introduced at this time and the 'Marking on Dinky Toys' list (see Appendix) shows some models being upgraded to Supertoy category and others being demoted from it, indicating that ideas about the continued use of the name

were in a state of flux. There is, after all, nothing to distinguish Supertoys from the rest of their product except size and hence cost. However, the sales potential of the title was recognised and, despite the fact that they hadn't been anywhere, there was a promise that 'Dinky Supertoys will return' in the 1955 Meccano Magazine. There was said to be a 'wonderfully brilliant finish that will be given to them and to Dinky Toys also—by the use of a new range of enamels.' Seventeen of the largest toys were to be re-classified as Supertoys in an attempt to make the child believe they were not just more expensive than the others but were actually better. This was partially true because some always were, for example, the Guy Vans. This marketing vein was continued for some years with the 1958 catalogue proclaiming that 'Dinky Supertoys are the "big brothers" of Dinky Toys, being produced in the same superlative quality to a larger scale.'

In 1956 another competitor arrived on the scene, Corgi Toys, diecasts with features that Dinky Toys didn't possess such as windows and even, on some, friction motors. Dinky's 'answer' was to produce just what they had before but in two-tone! But to encourage consumer loyalty, 1957 saw the founding of the Dinky Toy Club (See: Display and Marketing). In this 'never had it so good' era there was an acceleration in demand and Corgi did not appear to be much of a challenge despite its manufacturer, Mettoy, having a long history in the toy field. December of this year saw the announcement of an 'entirely new series', Dublo Dinkies, which were not as popular as was hoped, for by this time 'Matchbox' had got themselves well established in the market for small scale diecasts. About this time the 20mph roundel on the rear of the trucks was discontinued.

It was 1958 before Dinky replied to the challenge offered by Corgi and the other European manufacturers, notably Tekno from Denmark and Solido from France, by fitting special features to their models. Not only did they start off behind but when they did introduce new ideas they tended not to do them quite as well as the other, so they began to lose their pre-eminence amongst toy manufacturers. April saw the release of 176 AUSTIN A 105 with windows and, apart from 183 FIAT 600 and 160 AUSTIN A 30 which appeared in the following two months, all cars produced from this time were so equipped. The first of the new style spun metal wheels which looked much more realistic were fitted to 192 DE SOTO FIREFLITE in December and gradually became standard. An indication of increased prosperity can be gained from the introduction of a new batch of Gift Sets. 150 ROLLS ROYCE SILVER WRAITH came out in February 1959 with four-wheel suspension of primitive design, a piece of spring steel which allowed the axle to move up and down in slots in the tin base. In April, windows were extended to Dublo (Royal Mail Van) and in May to the commercials (B.B.C. T.V. vehicles). At this time, Meccano were co-operating with Triumph over the production of a model of the new Triumph Herald so that the release of the toy coincided with the launch of the actual vehicle. This relationship between the manufacturers was to prosper to the extent that a later *Meccano Magazine* could report that 'It has been said— jokingly, of course,— that Dinky Toys are a subsidiary of Standard-Triumph Ltd. . . .' Similar co-operation was practised over the years with Ford and other vehicle producers. French Dinkies were imported and distributed by Meccano and there was a promise of some French Dinkies being made in the U.K. The Renault R16 die was shipped to the U.K., cast here and fitted with an English Dinky baseplate and given an English Dinky number but the project ran into technical difficulties because many of the dies were not compatible with the casting machines. The KENEBRAKE STANDARD ATLAS (295) was the unlikely first recipient of interior detail, seats and

steering wheel, amongst the closed vehicles (May 1960). In August, the refinement of 'Directional Control' or as it was more commonly known 'Fingertip Steering', in which the whole axis pivoted instead of the wheels moving independently, appeared on 195 JAGUAR 3.4. Many accessories, for example petrol pump stations were introduced about this time (See: Street Furniture).

Pausing for breath in 1961 from the introduction of so many new gimmicks, twenty or so new models were put into the shops and the change-over from plain to treaded tyres was begun on the cars, although Supertoys, tractors and military vehicles had sported them for some time. August 1962 is remarkable for 276 AIRPORT FIRE TENDER with flashing lights; October for 113 M.G. B with opening doors; and November for 198 ROLLS ROYCE PHANTOM V with opening windows and 'polychromatic', i.e. metallic finish and 142 JAGUAR MARK 10 with opening boot. According to the advertising, this was 'another 1st' but if you can make one thing open, you can make another. Prestomatic steering was somewhat of an improvement on the earlier type though the whole of the axle still swung. By now Meccano were rather scratching around for 'new' developments and 1963 is significant for engine detail, tipping seat backs, a safety belt that unclipped and many other minor items. Perhaps the only one of significance to the collector was the fitting of 196 HOLDEN SPECIAL SEDAN and many subsequent models with jewelled headlamps.

Of far greater import to the company than any

increase in sales that these refinements may have produced, was the trading loss that Meccano Ltd. sustained in 1963, partly caused by the effort in 1959 of re-tooling to change the Hornby Dublo Train system over from three rail to two to keep up with the competition, partly by the purchase of the plastic building construction system, Bayko, in the year that Lego was launched, partly by the disruption of their U.S. distribution system, and partly by the increasing penetration of their traditional markets by Corgi and Lesney in the U.K. and Solido and Tekno in Europe. Moreover a new extension had been built to the Binns Road factory enabling Speke to be closed. The time was therefore ripe for a take-over, and Lines Bros. of Triang fame, manufacturers of a rival range of diecasts, Spot-On, and many other toys and child-related products were to be the bidders. The Binns Road factory was found to be rather the worse for wear but Lines Bros. were impressed by the tool room and the quality of the tool-makers employed there and this discovery played no small part in the decision to gradually abandon the Spot-On range in favour of the Dinky.

There was pressure on the Meccano management to break into the character merchandise field and after a half-hearted attempt with 'Dinky Beats'

and the FATHER CHRISTMAS MODEL T, they got down to business in 1967 with the release of Lady Penelope's FAB 1 and THUNDERBIRD 2. The mid-sixties also saw the introduction of the cost-saving stickers to replace the waterslide and spirit-based transfers as well as the sprayed or stamped-on decalling that had been in use. The production of a few models in Hong Kong in 1966 was an attempt to reduce costs sufficiently in order that the models would sell again into America but this hope was not fulfilled. The search for new product led in 1968 to the production of 1/35 scale military vehicles that had originally been designed by Lines Bros. for the American market but which had not gone ahead and the beginning of a new range of large aeroplanes. Now commercial vehicles had acquired some of the refinements of the cars and 917 MERCEDES-BENZ TRUCK and TRAILER was fitted with opening doors and character merchandise and military vehicles were 'action packed' with shells and rockets, etc.

In June 1969, once again behind their competitors, Speedwheels were fitted to some of the cars and they were to become standard on virtually everything. Six years after the take-over of Meccano by Lines Bros., the name of the firm was changed to Meccano-Triang Ltd., a bad omen, for in 1971 after a general recession in the toy trade, their heavy bank loans were called in and the whole of the Lines Group went into liquidation. The group was split up into bits and pieces and Binns Road and the other 'Meccano' assets were transferred to a new company, Maoford Ltd., which was subsequently renamed Meccano (1971) Ltd. Secretary of State approval was needed for the name to be changed back to Meccano Ltd. and the company sold by the Lines Receiver to Airfix Industries. New product lines were desperately needed as more and more toys came on the market designed specifically for boys, i.e. Action Man. Reflecting Airfix's expertise in the modelling of military vehicles in plastic kits, Dinky produced many in diecast fully finished. Kits did appear in the following year, as might be expected, as did other new lines, 1/25 scale cars, and some new ships, the first for many years. None of these sold as well as was hoped and nothing else was found to enliven the range. Even Mogul, large pressed steel vehicles which do not fall within the scope of this book because they were not put out under the Dinky label, did not supply enough competition for the already established Tonka toys and fell somewhat flat.

The 1977 catalogue shows an indication of desperately needed new thinking. 1/35 scale cars were illustrated with a lot of thought behind the design to make the casting lighter and finer and with the judicious use of plastic to make their production and assembly easier and cheaper, examples being the 122 VOLVO 265, DL ESTATE, 123 PRINCESS 2200 HL, and 244 PLYMOUTH POLICE CAR. An attempt to capture the younger end of the market was made with the Convoy range using a standard cab/chassis unit with a variety of bodies, another cost saving exercise. However, despite the happy accident of 1977 being the year of the Queen's Silver Jubilee and therefore something of a bonanza for the toy manufacturers as they rushed to produce souvenirs, the promise of the catalogue was not fulfilled. The next and last catalogue (No. 14) contains the TR 7 (a masterpiece of design with the bumpers and interior being moulded in one and secured between the two castings of the body and chassis), 180 ROVER 3500 which was made in Hong Kong in an attempt to cut costs and even the most up-to-the-minute vehicle possible, the Space Shuttle. But by now the hand of doom was resting on Binns Road and even the Shuttle project was hit by the delay in the launch of the real thing so that the model had to be shelved. Many sets were put together in an attempt to improve sales but several of the proposed new items never reached the casting stage. Even a scheme for shipping dies to America (the old Brinks Truck die) did not prosper and the Binns Road factory was effectively closed on November 30 1979. The closure did not save the parent company, which was in difficulties particularly in America and Airfix was later to call in a receiver.

Though Dinky Toys continued to be produced elsewhere after the closure of the factory, this book stops at that point. It is a celebration of the wonderful toys that were produced under the Dinky name over a period of approximately forty-five years. We hope that it is not also an epitaph.

### How Dinky Toys Are Made

Once a decision had been taken to produce a particular model, a wood mock-up was made, sometimes the same size as the finished product and sometimes larger with fine detail perhaps worked in

*Fig. 4. The 24 series castings modified to produce the prototypes of the 36 series.*

*Fig. 5. The wooden mock-up of the M.G. Record Car.*

*Fig. 6. The production model (on plinth) with the wood and brass mock-up.*

*Fig. 7. Suggestions for colour schemes at production stage.*

*Other mock-ups.*

brass. Alternatively, if there was sufficient similarity to an existing model that would be modified, for instance the 24 series into the 36 series. The pictures show 24 series with brass radiators in the form of those of the 36s and the modification to produce the Rover having had side pillars added and an insert in the base.

The prototypes were presented for approval and once this was received, drawings to enable the dies, moulds, decals and any other required parts were produced. After scrutiny, the go-ahead to make the tools would be given and in due course the first raw castings came off the machines, After a trial assembly of these parts, the required corrections were made, for example after increasing the axle diameter

from .062in to .078in on all vehicles in August 1945, it was found that the alteration of the drawings of the 38 series had not been done correctly and the castings sat too high when mounted on the wheels, so the drawings and then the dies were again modified to produce the right effect.

The first batch of castings were painted a variety of colours to enable the New Product Committee and Sales Director to choose the finish that was thought to be the most saleable. This was also done throughout the life of a vehicle if it was thought that a colour change was in order or if there was a requirement from an outside source, e.g. a company wishing to use a current Dinky Toy as a promotional vehicle in a finish different from that which was in normal production. The photographs show examples of hand-painted camouflage on military models which was probably done for a large London store.

The detailed procedure followed in making a toy once all the pre-planning and tooling was completed is described in the following hand-out prepared at Binns Road. Despite dating from the late fifties or early sixties, the techniques changed so little over the years that it can be taken as a good representation of how things were.

## Producing Dinky Toys

'Dinky Toys are true engineering products made with special equipment installed in the Works of Meccano Limited at Binns Road, Liverpool 13. The best way of illustrating exactly how models are made is by taking a fairly simple example, such as a lorry, and then following its production from start to finish. Generally, one of these is in two main parts, the cab and chassis on the one hand and the body on the other, with, of course, the wheels, axles, the base of the cab and the interior fittings in addition. Both the cab and chassis and the body are die-cast which means that they are made by forcing molten Mazak, almost pure zinc, into a mould or die that gives the metal the required shape when it cools and solidifies. The die is made by a skilled toolmaker working with the greatest accuracy. It is in two main sections, which are mounted in an automatic die-casting machine for the actual casting. One section is bolted to the machine itself, and the other to a moving part, called a platen, that can be moved horizontally to close the two half dies, while molten metal is forced into the space between them, and to separate them when this has been done.

'The metal solidifies almost immediately on entering this space. When cooled the resulting castings are trimmed to remove any unwanted metal, the last traces being removed by rotating them in large six-sided barrels, made of steel and lined with rubber, in which there are small graded stones and soapy water. From these the castings emerge bright and shining, with perfectly smooth faces. Then they undergo a chemical treatment known as Bonderising, which gives protection against corrosion, and also etches the surfaces slightly, so that the enamel that is applied later will adhere firmly.

'Enamelling is a fascinating process. Every Dinky Toy casting receives a first coating of its basic colour, usually in automatic machines in which several compressed air spray guns, set at different angles, cover it completely as it is rotated at high speed, to make sure that every part is covered with the enamel. From the automatic sprayers, the castings pass directly to a large conveyor oven through which they move slowly while they are heated to a temperature of about 200 deg. F. This not only dries the enamel, but hardens it and gives it the wearing

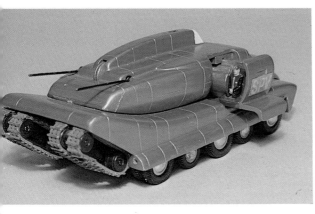

*Fig. 8. Other wooden mock-ups.*

qualities that distinguish Dinky Toys.

'The flashes, radiators, lamps and other parts that require a second coating are then sprayed. This is done with hand spray guns after placing the castings behind ingeniously designed masks that cover all the parts that are not to receive the second colour. This process too is followed by oven treatment in order to dry and harden the new coating. The conveyor table along which mask spraying of this kind is carried out is a fascinating place. At each station there is a miniature spraying booth in which the work is done, with an exhaust tube leading upwards to carry away fumes and unused spray.

'After enamelling and baking the castings are then ready for assembly by fitting the various parts together. Preparations for this begin with the die-casting itself, for in many instances, including cars and lorries, the main casting is made with projecting pins or spigots that fit into holes in the base. On the assembly line the two are brought together, with the spigots projecting through the correct holes, and by means of a special spinning tool the ends of the

spigots are spread out to fix the two parts firmly together. Before this happens, however, all the various fittings, such as windows, seats, steering wheel, etc., are added.

'Each Dinky Toy requires its own special assembly methods, but all cars and lorries want wheels and axles. The wheels themselves are either die-cast or turned, depending on the model for which they are intended, and they are then sprayed the necessary colour. Tyres are placed on them and they are fitted on the axles, where they are retained by rivet-shaped heads formed on the ends of the axles by pressure applied by a specially shaped tool.

'At the end of the assembly line on which these processes are carried out, the Dinky Toys are complete except for final inspection. Indeed, they are inspected at all stages of production, so that only perfect products reach the end of the assembly line, where they are packed in the familiar boxes in which they appear in the shops of Dinky Toys dealers, ready for their enthusiastic admirers.'

## Materials

Originally, a lead casting alloy was used. Later, a heavy, relatively soft material, butthen mazak (a zinc alloy) was introduced. Mazac had many advantages for Meccano, being a more satisfactory material than lead, but causes many problems for the collector if it is not pure for then 'fatigue' can occur and gradually the toy will fall to bits. We reprint the following extract from *Modellers' World*.

## Fatigue

'Mazak is an alloy containing 3–4% aluminium, 1–2% copper, 92–6% zinc and a trace of magnesium. Besides these elements there are minute amounts of other metals present as impurities. As little as 0.008% of lead and 0.006% of cadmium can give severe "intergranular corrosion" problems, known to model collectors as "fatigue". When viewed through a microscope all cast metals have a granular appearance. The impurities gradually move towards and locate themselves at the grain boundaries. This gives the alloy a non-uniform chemical composition, and when moisture is present at the metal surface (in a damp warehouse, for example) the grain boundaries are attacked. The attack is due to the difference in chemical composition between the grain boundaries and the grains themselves, causing a complex electro-chemical reaction resulting in corrosion. This corrosion product is formed between the grains, pushing them apart and causing the metal to distort, crack and grow. Eventually the model disintegrates.

'Once mazak has been contaminated with lead or cadmium nothing can be done to stop the corrosion completely. However, it can be slowed down by keeping the models in a dry atmosphere. Normal room temperature fluctuations probably do not affect the rate of deterioration of the models to any great degree, and if a relatively old model has not yet shown signs of cracking then it was most likely made out of "clean" alloy, and will not suffer from fatigue. This explains why many models suffer from fatigue in the wheels only, while the body is perfect. It is quite noticeable that the more difficult the casting was to make, the fewer seem to suffer from this problem. Compare the number of fatigued Double Deck Bus chassis there are in relation to the number

*Fig. 10. A very fatigued lorry.*

of fatigued bases. This is probably because the height of the body casting required very clean metal to get the correct flow through all the small passages in the die (the window pillars) whereas the much flatter base casting could be made with inferior quality metal. This lower quality would be the result of re-melting sprues and flash, with probably the addition of bits and pieces swept up off the casting shop floor and lead was in use at Binns Road throughout the whole period which has produced fatigued castings.'

The shortage of raw materials in the early 1950s led to a search for alternatives, but there is no evidence that any of these except aluminium was actually used. Cast iron was suggested for the Dumper Bucket and lead for the Speed of the Wind. Aluminium was proposed, but probably not used, on the Goods Yard Crane. However, the Horse Box doors, the Car Carrier body and rear ramp were made from aluminium as was the Avro Vulcan (See: Aeroplanes). Plastic was listed in 1951 as an alternative to mazak for the ridged wheels used on most of the smaller Dinkies at the time, but it is doubtful if it was ever used. The Bulldozer and Ruston Bucyrus Excavator were produced both in metal and plastic.

To begin with spirit-based transfers were applied and then waterslide ones, but at the same time decalling was also applied with rubber stamps and later sometimes sprayed on through masks. However, in the mid-sixties there was a change to self-adhesive stickers.

Interestingly, until the change to plastic, the small figures were always made from a lead alloy.

## Notes on Dinky Toys
## by Norman Craig

EDITOR'S NOTE. Norman Craig spent forty years with the Meccano Company, retiring in 1964 as Sales Director. This article is, therefore, to say the least, authoritative. It originally took the form of a personal letter to the author of *A History of British Dinky Toys* and is reprinted here by permission.

### Numbering

'The problem of changing numbers and the occasional apparently inconsistent use of numbers stems from a variety of causes. Firstly, when starting a new venture one can never see just how it will develop; the project may be affected by a large number of factors which cannot be foreseen, e.g. changes in the adult world of which toys may be a reflection in miniature; changes in public taste; trade acceptance; changes in manufacturing technical possibilities, etc.

'When Modelled Miniatures/Dinky Toys were first conceived in the 1930s, world economics were in a sorry plight and the purchasing power of the public was limited. As a natural extension to the Hornby railway accessories it was thought that some *sets* of figures, animals, etc. would add both to the interest of the toy railway user and to the profit of the manufacturer. As you know, these were followed, very naturally, by *sets* of miniature trains. (The larger 'O' gauge trains were sold in sets.) The next step of thought; try a small *set* of toy vehicles. Thus the sets were numbered. When later it was discovered there was a demand for individual pieces it seemed logical to identify these pieces by the set number and a distinguishing letter of the alphabet.

'This persisted until a change of internal accounting to what was then a modern four digit system (Power-Samas) made it necessary to change, and this was followed by a further change to the computer system needing five digits.

'The seemingly haphazard numbering of models to which you refer on page 54 [this and all page numbers refer to *The History of British Dinky Toys*, Ed.] was probably caused by the system whereby the number of the model was allocated to it as soon as the first decision was made to produce it. This number then followed it through the drawing office, tool room, etc. for the gestation period from "conception to delivery"—sometimes during this period a further decision had been made which would appear to make a nonsense of things. This seeming nonsense is made to appear much worse by the variation in the gestation period of different models. I have no doubt that the decisions to make the Dinky 197 Morris Traveller and the 198 Rolls Royce were taken in that order; the decision to offer the Mini Traveller in an alternative finish as an Austin would be taken later but before either the 197 or the 198 had appeared on the market. It is, of course, possible that Austin only announced the prototype 'Countryman' after the number 198 had been allocated to the Rolls.

'As you say, certain numbers only appear in connection with special finishes for overseas markets including a fair number of U.S. military finishes. The old delivery van 28 in the "Bentall" livery (pp. 57 and 86–7) was a special finish never offered to the public through the retail trade, and was used by Bentall's, the well-known Kingston-on-Thames store for a special publicity campaign.

25t (p. 57) was used for 25c and 25g packed together, as a set. The "Z" suffix was, as you say, used on French products, mainly pre-war. As I recollect, these were all imported, the only one I can remember being cast in Liverpool from borrowed French tools was the Renault Dauphine (what fun we had with the London taxi-drivers' Union over the "Mini-cab"!).

'Re-issues with a change of number and finish, e.g. racing cars, were made from time to time when an item might still appeal as a toy but would have been the subject of criticism on the grounds of age, inaccuracy, etc. as a model.'

### Finishes or Liveries

'As usual, a variety of reasons caused a variety of decisions; some from a general principle held at that particular time, some from "ad hoc" reasons which had no general application.

'In the paragraph previously on *Numbering* the point of re-issue of certain racing cars was mentioned, and we have also touched on the importance of the set idea assumed and held (although with changing emphasis as we shall see). Even though items such as the 1953 racers were issued separately, the idea of a set was considered as well. It was for this reason that the Ferrari was produced in Argentinian colouring, with the justification that Fangio, then the World Champion driver, was an Argentinian, even although the car he actually drove was in Italian colours (pp. 47–8). The same thought made us use Swiss colours for the Maserati by this means producing a variety of colours in the set instead of a predominance of all-red cars.

'The use of advertisers' names on the trucks, etc. had three advantages (1) the road scene had more variety, colour and authenticity (2) the boy might be persuaded to buy more than one version (3) the cost of the transfers and of fixing them would be paid for

by a prior arrangement with the advertiser concerned (this last arrangement had worked with the Hornby "O" gauge "private owner" wagons). This scheme did have one or two disadvantages, for instance when the article had a different name or an unhappy one in certain overseas markets. 'Swiss Rolls' are 'Tootsie Rolls' in the U.S.A. and 'Ovaltine' is known as 'Ovomaltine' in a number of overseas countries. Again, an advertiser might withdraw from the scheme at an awkward moment due to a change in policy or an over-spent advertising budget.

'The "Top Rank" co-operation (p. 57) on the 434 crash truck was made after the colour work had been done for the Magazine (and, I think, the box labels) but before production of the toy had started.

'The one colour of the Volvo, No. 184 (p. 54) was a late decision made for costing reasons in order to get a "round" price particularly in the Swedish market. The changes in the American Police Car No. 258 (p. 54) were probably caused by tool trouble or possibly because the "De Soto" mark was dropped by Chrysler about this time.'

## Boxing

'This had its secondary effect on finishes. Individual boxing of Dinky Toys did not start until the late 1940s and prior to that models were in sets or in boxes, usually of six or rarely in four or in threes. There is a good picture of the end of such a box with a Daimler ambulance on page 45. The contents of such boxes might contain a mixture of colours, e.g. 29c double-decker bus. Occasionally, the factory was left with the problem of a surplus of boxes or transfers, or of part-finished toys, and the economic run-down of any such inequalities sometimes caused curious re-issues, or other anomalies.'

## Scale

'Probably nothing has caused as much argument, both inside the organisation, and outside. So a universal scale would please the purist, but might bankrupt the individual manufacturer. If, for example, the double-decker bus had been produced in anything like the same scale as private cars it would have been priced out of the market, and not become one of the biggest-selling toys, both at home and overseas of all time. And a strict adherence to scale could also mean that certain features easily seen in the prototype would not be apparent in the toy, e.g. the slope of the radiator in a Riley or an Armstrong Siddeley should be exaggerated to be seen. In the same way the play value of any individual toy would be lost if it had been produced in its "proper" scale, e.g. the 60Y Refuelling Tender compared to the 60 series aircraft.'

[Editorial Interpolation: the above remarks show very clearly the difference in outlook between the manufacturer and the 'purist' collector.]

## General

'As you know (p. 12), the very early Modelled Miniatures and Dinky Toys were of a relatively soft metal and made on the "fill and spill" method with all its usual weaknesses and crudities. The credit for the first use of pressure die-casting using the zinc-based metal alloy (Zamak in U.S. and France but more usually called "Mazak", in the U.K.) in toys I think must go to Dowst in the States for the first of their better Tootsietoys with rubber tyres. The developments and improvements which have followed over the years since Meccano imported their first "Madison Kipp" machine have been fantastic. It seems curious that the Americans, who had this ball at their feet, never seemed to make either the commercial or technical developments in the toy field that the British and subsequently the French and Danes made. Germany and Japan also never made the progress that might have been expected. Outside the Meccano organisation, probably the best "developers" have been Fairbairn at Mettoy (Corgi) and Smith and Odell at Lesney (Matchbox).

'Tootsietoy never recognised the importance of making a toy a true model, and associating it with a prototype name. They probably found the American automobile manufacturers as unresponsive and suspicious as we did when it came to getting authentic drawings, and as for advance information— phew!'

## Minor Points

'"Bowser", "Wayne" and "Theo" were makes of pumps not motor spirit (p. 24). "Pratts" was the early name for what later became Esso spirit and oil.

'"Supertoy" or "Dinky Toy". The segregation of models caused confusion and heartburnings from time to time—should size, price, function, etc. be the qualification to the "higher" tag? If you put them in a different number group, do you catalogue and illustrate them on a page away from their natural but smaller "club members" e.g. military vehicles? Some difficulties also arose in overseas markets in registering the trade mark of "Supertoy" or "Dinky Supertoy" '

# CHAPTER 2
# Pre-war Issues

The 22 series set is probably the most famous group of Dinky Toys ever made, and it is the only group of road vehicles issued under the 'Modelled Miniatures' label. It was by no means the earliest issue in Modelled Miniatures, nor was it the last, despite the fact that 22 was the highest number allocated to any of that Series. Their run as Modelled Miniatures didn't last very long, because in February 1934 they were referred to as 'Meccano Miniatures' and by April 1934, the name 'Dinky Toys' had come into being. Though the six vehicles were not advertised in *Meccano Magazine* until December 1933, all were available by October 1933, as the six items are separately referred to in 'How to Add "Life" to Layouts' in that month's magazine: 'Yet another set of Modelled Miniatures is now available, No. 22 . . .' Maybe they were available even earlier, as in *Meccano Magazine* for September 1933, there is a photograph taken at the Advertising and Marketing Exhibition at Olympia of a model of Fleet Street designed by G. McConnell Wood and exhibited by the *London Evening Standard*, with a large fleet of 22d VANS carrying the newspapers to their destinations. The date of this exhibition was July 17–22, 1933, so this vehicle at least must have been in production then, though it is quite possible that it was not at that time on general sale. It is likely that the vans were lettered 'London Evening Standard', though it is not possible to distinguish this from the rather poor reproduction in *Meccano Magazine* and unfortunately, the original is no longer in the *London Evening Standard* Archives, so the existence of potentially the first diecast U.K. promotional vehicle must remain for the time being a matter of speculation. But wouldn't it be exciting if one did turn up! An even earlier picture reference exists in the April 1933 issue of *Meccano Magazine* in which the four road vehicles from the 22 series are used as lineside effects. It is not possible, however, to tell whether these are finished castings or mock-ups. All the models were made of an alloy with a very high lead content so that they do not suffer from the fatigue problems of later production. Though most were only available for two years, the tractor and tank were not deleted until the war years.

**Modelled Miniatures—22 series**

22a SPORTS CAR is a fairly complicated one piece casting, incorporating body, wings and seat, with another single casting for the toe-board, dashboard, windscreen surround and four-spoke steering wheel. This part has a peg on the concealed part of the toe-board which is an interference fit in a slot in the main casting. The screen part is extremely fragile and bendable as one would expect from such a thin piece of lead, and is frequently broken off in examples still extant. The body was painted red with cream wings and interior, cream with red wings and interior, or yellow with green wings and interior. Normally the radiator grille was painted to match the wings, but occasionally the overpainting was omitted so that it is the same colour as the main body. The grille had a shiny tinplate surround held on by a tab at the base and a small pin in the position of the radiator cap. The wheels and tyres are represented by a solid metal disc covered with a thin metallic colour wash of green, purple, blue, yellow etc. Despite production of the Sports Car continuing into the year after the introduction of the name 'Dinky Toys', all are marked 'Hornby Series' up underneath the bonnet.

22b SPORTS COUPÉ is constructed on similar lines but without the addition of a second casting, for there is no interior detail and the hood is cast in with the body. There is a separate tinplate radiator surround affixed as before and this one carries an additional decorative bar down the centre of the grille. The same type of wheel was used and all are marked 'Hornby Series'. The body colour is yellow with green wings and hood or red with cream wings and hood.

22c MOTOR TRUCK was made up of two large castings, one cab and chassis, the other the sided truck bed, the former normally painted blue and the latter red. A tinplate surround was fitted to the grille and the wheels were colour-washed metal like the cars. The inside of the cab roof bears the name 'Hornby Series' but the back casting carries no identification marks at all.

22d DELIVERY VAN utilises the same cab and chassis casting as the Motor Truck with an additional slot in the roof to accept the tinplate clip holding the van back on. The back is plain, there being no refinements like opening doors or transfers, and it carries no identifying marks. The grille surround is the same as that used on the lorry and the wheels are the 'standard' for the series. The cab is usually orange and back blue. In August 1934, when the 28 series vans were allocated individual numbers the one carrying the 'Meccano' decal was given the number 22d, so it is quite likely that from this time until the set was deleted, the vehicle carried transfers.

22e FARM TRACTOR looks a much more complicated piece of work but it still consists only of two main castings plus wheels. The grille/engine cover/seat unit slots at the front into the engine/ mudguard casting and is held at the rear by the back axle. The wheels are specific to this vehicle and are all metal. The tractor was the longest in production of all the 22 series vehicles, and late production was fitted with diecast front wheels which are prone to fatigue. The early ones are marked 'Hornby Series' but with the passage of time, this was changed to 'Dinky Toys'. There was, coincidentally, a slight casting change as a rear towing hook was added to the rear of the upper casting. The wheels are normally red though yellow is also found. The body can be green, yellow or, unusually, blue with the contrasting engine/wing unit in yellow, blue or, unusually, white.

22f ARMY TANK has two castings, one very large casting for the main body and side skirts and a smaller one for the turret which actually rotates. A

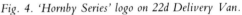

*Fig. 4. 'Hornby Series' logo on 22d Delivery Van.*

This fine model of Fleet Street, with Ludgate Hill and St. Paul's Cathedral, designed by Mr. G. McConnell Wood, was exhibited by the London "Evening Standard" at the recent Advertising and Marketing Exhibition at Olympia, London. A specially interesting feature of the model is the large fleet of Hornby miniature Delivery Vans, Modelled Miniatures No. 22, which contributed greatly to the realistic effect of the scene. Our illustration is reproduced by courtesy of the "Evening Standard."

*Fig. 2. Meccano Magazine September 1933.*

Complete Pullman trains form the most important expresses in the Hornby Series. This realistic photograph shows an all-Pullman express approaching a level crossing, while road traffic is held up for the train to pass.

*Fig. 1. Meccano Magazine April 1933.*

*Fig. 3. Boxed set of no. 22 Modelled Miniatures.*

*Fig. 5. Modelled Miniatures no. 2, Farmyard Animals.*

## SHEPHERD SET

Dinky Toys No. 6. Price of complete set 1/-

| | | |
|---|---|---|
| No. 6a Shepherd | ... ... ... ... ... ... | each **3d.** |
| No. 6b Dog | ... ... ... ... ... ... | ,, **2d.** |
| No. 2d Sheep (4) | ... ... ... ... ... ... | ,, **2d.** |

great deal of attention was paid to modelling louvres and rivet heads on both pieces. Four large and six small wheels carry the tracks which were initially made of red rubber and then of green. The red tracks look particularly attractive as they contrast well with the body colour. The first colour combination used was green for the body with an orange turret but later the vehicle was painted all-over drab grey. The Tank was also in production for a fairly long time and its marking of 'Hornby Series' was altered to 'Dinky Toys' part way through its production run.

### Modelled Miniatures—Miscellaneous
'(For details see page 37.)'

13 HALL'S DISTEMPER ADVERTISE-MENT was amongst the first group of Modelled Miniatures issued in late 1931/ early 1932 and as the catalogues said, 'This miniature of a well-known lineside advertisement is intended to be placed in the fields adjoining the railway track.' In keeping with the larger than life originals, these two men are much bigger than any of the other Modelled Miniature

people, being 6cm from base to hand holding the cardboard advertising board. The figures are not solid metal, but as can be seen from the neat hole in the centre of their caps, a form of slush moulding was used so that the main body of the casting is hollow. This enables there to be a fair saving in metal and weight and though unusual for Meccano, it was a process commonly used by toy soldier manufacturers. Both the figures are the same and have nice detail painting round the edges of their collars. The colour of the paint in their pots and on the brush bristles varies; red, blue, green and any combination of colours may be found in one box. They were packed in sets of two men and one hoarding originally as a 'Hornby Series' issue which pre-dated their designation as 'Dinky Toys'. In the absence of the box, it is extremely difficult to date this set as the differences that are found are not deliberate design changes, but can be put down to mould wear. Just as most of these types of advertisement disappeared during the war and were not re-erected, so this set lasted until the war and was not re-issued.

## MODELLED MINIATURES

| No. | Name | From | To | Notes |
|---|---|---|---|---|
| 002 | | | | Renumbering of 2 |
| 006 | | | | Renumbering of 6 |
| 1 | Station Staff | | | See: Trains |
| 2 | Farmyard Animals | 1932 | 1955 | Renumbered 002 |
| 2a | Horses (Two in set) | 1932 | 1955 | |
| 2b | Cows (Two in set) | 1932 | 1955 | |
| 2c | Pig | 1932 | 1955 | |
| 2d | Sheep | 1932 | 1955 | See: Shepherd Set |
| 3 | Passengers | | | See: Trains |
| 4 | Engineering Staff | | | See: Trains |
| 5 | Train and Hotel Staff | | | See: Trains |
| 6 | Shepherd Set | 1934 | 1955 | Renumbered 006 |
| 6a | Shepherd | 1934 | 1955 | |
| 6b | Dog | 1934 | 1955 | |
| 13 | Hall's Distemper Advertisement | 1931 | 1941 | |
| 22 | Modelled Miniatures – Vehicles | 1933 | 1935 | |
| 22a | Sports Car | 1933 | 1935 | |
| 22b | Sports Coupé | 1933 | 1935 | |
| 22c | Motor Truck | 1933 | 1935 | |
| 22d | Delivery Van | 1933 | 1935 | See: Other Pre-war Vehicles |
| 22e | Farm Tractor | 1933 | 1941 | |
| 22f | Army Tank | 1933 | 1939 | |
| 22g | Streamlined Tourer | | | See: Other Pre-war Vehicles |
| 22h | Streamlined Saloon | | | See: Other Pre-war Vehicles |
| 22s | Search Light Lorry (small) | | | See: Military Pre-war |

**Trains and Modelled Miniatures**

*MECCANO MAGAZINE*: MARCH 1933: Page 229

## MINIATURE TRAIN SET

'An interesting addition made some time ago to the Hornby Series was Set No. 21 of Modelled Miniatures. This consists of a small train set made up of a tank locomotive and four goods vehicles of different types. The idea of its introduction was to provide the very junior Hornby Railway enthusiasts with a locomotive and train more suitable for management by them than the smallest existing trains running on rails and propelled by clockwork. Even a "push along" train has a tremendous fascination, and its activities are not limited by the extent of the system of rails. Unlike most trains sets of small proportions, this Hornby Train is well designed and complete in detail, and the enamel finish is pleasing, the components of the set being die cast in hard metal.

'First there is the Locomotive. This runs on six wheels, and in its general design is typical of the average tank locomotive built in actual practice for ordinary goods and shunting work. It has side tanks and looks very modern with the large boiler fitted. The smoke-box is of correct design and in the course of assembly the boiler is let into it so that the correct appearance of a raised smoke-box is the result. The construction is interesting in that the main frames, footplating and smoke-box form one complete unit, while the boiler, tanks, cab and bunker form another, the wheels of course being mounted in the main frames as in actual practice. The details are very complete, even to minute rivet heads on the smoke-box and main frames. Brake blocks and their hangers are represented also, and steps and guard irons add to the completeness of the underframe. The boiler has a squat dome and tiny safety valves of the Ross "pop" pattern, and even the boiler bands and handrails are not forgotten. The boiler, tanks, cab and bunker are painted a cheerful red, and the frames and smoke-box are picked out in a darker colour.

'Each of the four wagons has a similar type of base or underframe; consisting practically of a flat truck mounted on four wheels. The Open Wagon is formed by the attachment of miniature wagon body to this underframe. Typical features of up-to-date practice are incorporated in the details shown on the wagon body. The sides and ends are duly "planked" and the corners protected by raised corner plates complete with bolt heads. The side and end strapping—the latter of T-section—is also shown, and the hinge straps of the side doors; and even the pins and small chains for securing the latter may be seen. For detail within fine limits these wagons would be hard to beat.

'The Crane Truck is simple, but none the less effective. The crane base, turntable and jib form a single casting secured to the standard underframe. The design on the whole follows that of the ordinary Gauge O Crane Truck of the Hornby Series. A miniature crank handle, hook and length of thread "cable" make it possible for the crane to work. The crane position can be rotated on the base if required.

'The "Shell" Petrol Wagon is a fine piece of work, the large capacity tank with its fittings forming a complete casting. The tank appears to rest on three supports, and raised straps secure it to the two outer ones. The special frames for retaining it in position lengthways are also provided, and the manhole and valve on the top of the tank and the raised rivets complete the details. The word "Shell" is in raised letters on the tank sides and shows up well.

'The Lumber wagon is made up of the standard underframe to which a pair of bolsters complete with stanchions have been added, so that it is of a simple nature. The load provided is a very realistic piece of modelling, however, and has the appearance of a length of tree trunk mounted on the bolsters. A representation of crossed chains securing it appears on the trunk. It is finished in a natural brown colour, while the red bolsters and stanchions of the wagon have a smart appearance.

'Hook and loop couplings enable the complete train to be assembled, and as these are of strong wire let into the various bases during the process of casting they are not likely to come loose easily or break off, which is a common fault with miniature rolling stock of this kind. The engine has no coupling at the front end, but there is a small hole behind the buffer beam intended to take a string if necessary. This may be made use of when it is required to run the engine backward with its load. The hooks on the wagons will drop into the hole easily and the train thus may be worked in either direction'.

The above article from *Meccano Magazine*, March 1933, pretty well says it all about the first diecast train set which was issued early in 1932 not long after the introduction of 'Modelled Miniatures' themselves. However, a few comments can be added. The bulk of the Modelled Miniatures are train related as one would expect from a company one of whose major projects was tinplate trains, and which was experimenting with diecasting techniques of which they had had little previous experience. Thus it is no surprise that their first diecast vehicles should be trains and rolling stock. Why they should have given this set such a high number is a mystery as many of the lower numbers were not used until some time later.

Modelled Miniature 21 HORNBY TRAIN SET was in production for less than two years, possibly because of the difficulty of casting the crane, for it is this item alone that does not figure in any of the other goods sets issued. The casting material used was lead and each vehicle was composed of two major castings running on diecast wheels. 21a LOCOMOTIVE is red with the frames and smokebox dark blue; 21b WAGON has a blue base and soft green sides; 21c CRANE is similar with blue base and green crane; 21d 'SHELL' PETROL WAGON has a red tank and blue base, and as the above text says the letters of 'Shell' are raised and are not picked out in a separate colour; 21e LUMBER WAGON has a red base and some have green stanchions while the tree trunk is finished in deep yellow, which is hardly the 'natural brown' claimed in the text.

Not until early 1934 were the other two goods train sets issued, and in both cases no new castings were utilised but were those from the 21 set.

19 MIXED GOODS TRAIN is identical to 21 with the omission of the Crane Truck. By this time the engine colours had become more prototypical, and a maroon close in tone to LMS maroon and a green close to the GWR green were used for the body casting. (Neither of these railway companies survive today.) The frame and smokebox casting is black with the buffer beam picked out in red. A further realistic touch is provided by the painting of the cab roof black. Authenticity was not however extended to the rolling stock, as this set is usually found in the toybox colours of green, red, blue and yellow as in 21, though shades may vary. The box of the set photographed shows that it is the latest issue reading 'Dinky Toys' whereas the others show the intermediate title between this and 'Modelled Miniatures' i.e. 'Meccano Dinky Toys'. A further technical box detail of more academic interest is that where a maroon or green dot appears on the end by the label it refers to the colour of the engine contained in the box. Contents: 21a TANK LOCOMOTIVE, 21b

WAGON, 21d PETROL TANK WAGON, 21e LUMBER WAGON.

**18 TANK GOODS TRAIN SET** utilises only the engine in green or maroon and the wagon, also in green or maroon with black bases and wheels, which makes it look a lot less toy-like than the previous sets. Contains 21a LOCOMOTIVE and 3×21b WAGON. A few items of rolling stock are found cast in mazak, though lead is the usual material.

**20 TANK PASSENGER TRAIN** used the tank engine of the previously mentioned sets but had two new items, the COACH and the GUARD'S VAN. There were two 20a COACHES, nicely detailed castings for which lead was used, but more are found with mazak bodies than lead. However, the bases are still lead and utilise the construction principles of the truck bases: wire hooks and loops cast into the chassis and cast wheels. Again the engine is green or maroon and the coaches are brown or maroon with cream roofs. The chassis is red or green. 20b GUARD'S VAN completes the set and has the same characteristics as the coaches.

**17 PASSENGER TRAIN SET** has got a new LOCOMOTIVE numbered 17a and a TENDER numbered 17b. The loco uses the chassis of the TANK LOCOMOTIVE and the painting details are also the same, but the tender is, unusually for this range, a single casting. It uses six of the standard cast wheels and is the same colour as the engine. The other two parts of the set are 20a COACH and 20b GUARD'S VAN, and all the details are the same as above. (see Set 20.)

All the four sets, 17, 18, 19, 20 were still in production at the outbreak of war.

This section ends with an intriguing note culled from a 1932 Trade Circular 'MINIATURE TUNNEL! This Tunnel will be supplied to dealers at the special price of 3/6d per dozen nett. We have not fixed a retail price for it, and it will not appear in any of our price lists, but it may be sold to interested customers at a price that allows a margin of profit. It is primarily intended for use with Modelled Miniatures Train Set No. 21, with which it should be associated in window and counter displays.' No number, no retail price, no material, no size is mentioned. What were Meccano up to?

Set **16 STREAMLINED TRAIN SET** was designed in the year that the first streamlined crack express from L N E R took to the rails, and became available some seven months later in mid-1936. Such a revolutionary shape needed completely new drawings from the previous diecast trains that had been produced, and it was sold as a complete unit for the individual items, Locomotive, Centre Coach and Rear Coach were not given separate numbers. Each of the three castings was a single piece with representations of wheels incorporated into the casting. The wheels on which it could be propelled are hidden inside and are the type used generally on the rest of the vehicles; smooth hubs and white rubber tyres. L N E R and the number 2590 are cast in on the tender and cab sides. The front coach has a shallow curve on the leading edge and a deep concave curve at the rear which allows the convex curve of the rear coach to nestle inside it. Thus it was not possible to incorporate additional coaches to produce a long train. The overall finish was silver as befitted its first title 'Silver Jubilee', the real train being so named because King George V's Silver Jubilee had occurred in 1935. Some had the prototypical grey paint on the smokebox door, side panels, running gear, and cab and tender roof, but orange, red and light blue were also used. The colour was also supplied to the lower panel of the coach sides. After a short time the designation 'Silver Jubilee' was dropped and it was renamed 'Streamlined Train Set'. It was still in production at the outbreak of war, and while hostilities were still in progress, thought was being given to re-issue because the factory drawings show a modification dated October 1943, which planned to fill in the previously cut out windows with a sunk panel. No doubt these were giving flash problems as the die wore, and rather than re-make the tool, an expensive operation, this small alteration was preferred. Remember that metal onto the finished product is equivalent to metal off the die, an operation of little difficulty. Post-war issues therefore have filled in windows and a new paint scheme with black rubber tyres. The loco was now deep blue with black detail and L N E R picked out in gold while the coaches are teak with cream roofs and windows. In 1953, further die modifications were made to enable a tinplate base to be fitted, and the line below the windows on the carriages was extended full length through the doors. One assumes that at this time, or possibly a little later, L N E R was removed from the tender sides to allow room for the transfer of the British Railways Lion motif. The use of this logo coincided with another paint change in 1956 to the British Railways colours of green on the loco (with black detail), and maroon lower and cream upper and roof on the coaches. The very latest issues, around about 1958, had white treaded tyres as were being used on some of the American cars. In May 1954, it had been renumbered to no. 798, and had reverted to the name actually used on the original drawings: 'EXPRESS PASSENGER TRAIN'.

**16z STREAMLINED DIESEL ARTICULATED TRAIN**—see French Dinky Products sold on the U.K. market.

**26** was initally known as the RAIL AUTOCAR but later as the G W R RAIL CAR, and it is by this second designation that it is more commonly known. Produced in early 1934, it is a single piece diecasting for which lead was used initially and then mazak. The lower half is virtually any of the bright colours in use on Dinky Toys at the time; red, green, yellow, brown, etc., with the windows and roof painted cream. If you want the prototypical one, find the brown and cream as these are the G W R colours. The internal 'wheels' are actually red or green plastic rollers of two or three different designs. (Plastic rollers are used on the tram and the ships amongst other items). It was not re-issued after the war.

**26z DIESEL RAIL CAR**—see French Dinky Products sold on the U.K. market.

**15 RAILWAY SIGNALS** were issued in the spring of 1937 and were in production for three years or so. The bases and poles (all one casting) are diecast and marked 'Meccano Dinky Toys' on the base. Unfortunately they are extremely prone to fatigue, so that one may be left with a pile of little bits and some nicely printed tinplate signal arms. The colours

Fig. 7. Modelled Miniatures no. 21, Hornby Train Set.

Fig. 8. Modelled Miniatures no. 19, Mixed Goods Train.

Fig. 11. Modelled Miniatures no. 17, Passenger Train.

Fig. 9. Modelled Miniatures no. 18, Tank Goods Train.

Fig. 10. Modelled Miniatures no. 20, Tank Passenger Train.

Fig. 12. Modelled Miniatures no. 16, 'Silver Jubilee' Train Set.

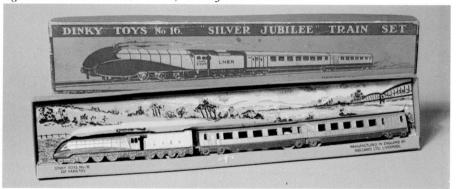

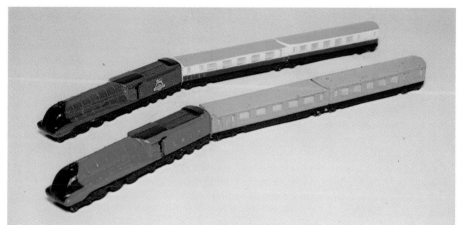

Fig. 13. Post-war liveries of Dinky Toys no. 16, Express Passenger Train.

can be identified from the original drawings for the tinprinting of these arms. Most unusually, Meccano gave the same number to two different items, and they did it twice! 15a SINGLE ARM SIGNAL 'Home' can be seen at the right hand end of the box while 15a 'Distant' is to be found at the left hand end. Similarly, centre right is 15c JUNCTION SIGNAL 'Home' and centre left is 15c 'Distant'. The other two are the same, 15b DOUBLE ARM SIGNAL. One 'Home' and one 'Distant'.

At the same time as the first diecast trains were released, a selection of little figures came on to the market. These fall into two categories: the first, suitable for adding realism to the railway station, consisted of railway staff and passengers; the second, enhancing the Hornby Countryside Sections, were of farm animals. There are two different castings on the railway accessories, the first being bigger than the second (averaging respectively 4cm and 3.5cm) and there are also changes in the stance; for instance, the little girl is on her mother's right in the larger figure but on her left in the other and so on. Some of the figures were also available post-war, and these can be identified by the simpler painting which is typified by the use of fewer colours of harsher hue and less careful brushwork. The larger figures were Modelled Miniatures and the smaller Dinky, although illustrations of the larger were still in use after the smaller ones had been introduced as can be seen from the 1938–9 *Hornby Book of Trains*.

1 STATION STAFF were the first set of people released, but more significant than that, they were also first in the Modelled Miniature series. Both large and small versions were issued; the former are re-illustrated in the reproduction from the *Hornby Book of Trains* and the latter in the photograph. Each item was available separately or you could buy the whole set. The figures are unmarked. From left to right in the photograph we have 1d DRIVER, 1a STATION MASTER, 1e PORTER WITH BAGS, 1f PORTER, 1b GUARD, 1c TICKET COLLECTOR. They all wear dark blue uniforms with gold or silver buttons except for the driver, who is in a lighter blue. They were all in production up to the war, but the post-war re-issue set did not contain the PORTER. It was renumbered 001.

4 ENGINEERING STAFF followed over a year later in mid-1932 and used the same castings, but a neat bit of attention to the colour schemes makes them look quite different. Now they are painted fawn or blue and some are in white shirtsleeves. From left to right in the box they are as follows: 4b FITTER in blue (casting as PORTER), 4a ELECTRICIAN in blue (as PORTER WITH BAGS), 4c STOREKEEPER in brown (as STATIONMASTER), 4e ENGINE ROOM ATTENDANT in slightly darker blue (as TICKET COLLECTOR), 4d GREASER in brown (as ENGINE DRIVER), 4b FITTER in brown (as PORTER). They were issued in both sizes and were available up till the war. They were re-issued post-war, but the set contained only five items as the ELECTRICIAN was no longer included. The figures were no longer available individually, and the set was eventually renumbered 004.

5 TRAIN AND HOTEL STAFF were issued at the same time as set 4 and were produced over the same timespan. Again some of the castings of the first set were utilised. Large and small sizes were both produced. From left to right: 5b PULLMAN CAR WAITER with blue trousers and white jacket (as Porter), 5c HOTEL PORTER with brown trousers and red jacket (as Porter with Bags), 5a PULLMAN CAR CONDUCTOR again in blue and white (as Ticket Collector), another 5c with blue trousers and green jacket, another 5b. The set was re-issued post-war but the figures were no longer available individually, and it was renumbered 005.

3 PASSENGERS joined the scene in early 1932 and were made in large and small sizes. This time the casting differences between the two are much more noticeable, particularly on the Woman and Child and the Newsboy. All were new castings and not paint variations on the first set. They remained in production until 1955, but after the war the figures were not available individually. Renumbered 003. 5a WOMAN AND CHILD. In the earlier set the Child is on the Woman's right and dressed in a red jacket and yellow trousers, whereas in the later set not only has the Child changed sides but is now wearing green, and the Lady's coat is more 'modern' in style.

3b BUSINESS MAN wears a blue suit. 3c MALE HIKER is in brown while 3d FEMALE HIKER has a blue skirt and white top. 3e NEWSBOY is in blue and in the first set is running, while in the second set he is standing still. 3f WOMAN has a white skirt and red jacket.

Post-war, two sets of metal figures were issued as Dinky Toys in '00' scale, using pre-war castings which had been given 'D' prefixes showing they were then regarded as part of the Hornby Dublo Train series. 1001, renumbered 051 was a set of 6 STATION STAFF and 1003 renumbered 053 was a set of 6 PASSENGERS. After their deletion three sets of plastic Dublo scale figures were introduced, the first two consisting of twelve items each. 050 RAILWAY STAFF had a contents change part way through its life, as a Shunter with pole was substituted for a Policeman with hands behind his back. 052 PASSENGERS had eleven figures and a seat and 054 STATION PERSONNEL consisted of four people with platform 'hardware' such as Refreshment Trolleys etc. Though given Dinky Numbers most collectors regard them as properly belonging to the story of Hornby Dublo and not Dinky, and full details can be found in the Companion Book in this series *Hornby Dublo Trains* by Michael Foster pp. 261–6.

Dressed in a navy blue frock coat is an isolated figure which was issued post-war and even then must have appeared as a bit of an anachronism 13a COOK'S MAN (renumbered 013). He was a representative of the travel firm Thomas Cook and acted as a courier to the wealthy at railway stations etc.

After many years of having steered clear of non-motorised diecast trains it was decided to re-introduce one. The wisdom of this can be judged by noting the length of its run in the catalogues—2 years!

784 DINKY GOODS TRAIN SET consisted of a stubby tank loco painted blue and lettered 'G E R' (Great Eastern Railway—a company that disappeared in the 1920s), and two different trucks, the yellow having lower sides than the red. Though no track was required it could be used on OO/HO track.

Fig. 14. No. 26, Rail Autocar, later G W R Rail Car.

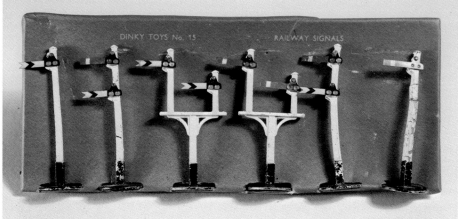

Fig. 15. No. 15, Railway Signals.

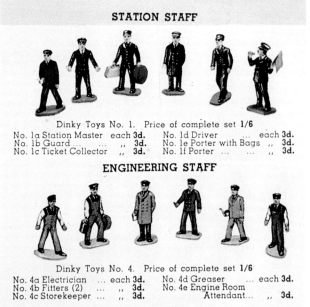

**STATION STAFF**

Dinky Toys No. 1. Price of complete set **1/6**

| | | |
|---|---|---|
| No. 1a Station Master | each **3d.** | No. 1d Driver ... each **3d.** |
| No. 1b Guard ... | ,, **3d.** | No. 1e Porter with Bags ,, **3d.** |
| No. 1c Ticket Collector | ,, **3d.** | No. 1f Porter ... ,, **3d.** |

**ENGINEERING STAFF**

Dinky Toys No. 4. Price of complete set **1/6**

| | | |
|---|---|---|
| No. 4a Electrician | ... each **3d.** | No. 4d Greaser ... each **3d.** |
| No. 4b Fitters (2) | ,, **3d.** | No. 4e Engine Room |
| No. 4c Storekeeper | ,, **3d.** | Attendant... ,, **3d.** |

**PASSENGERS**

Dinky Toys No. 3. Price of complete set **1/6**

| | | |
|---|---|---|
| No. 3a Woman & Child | each **3d.** | No. 3d Female Hiker each **3d.** |
| No. 3b Business Man | ,, **3d.** | No. 3e Newsboy ... ,, **3d.** |
| No. 3c Male Hiker ... | ,, **3d.** | No. 3f Woman ... ,, **3** |

**TRAIN AND HOTEL STAFF**

Dinky Toys No. 5. Price of complete set **1/3**

| | |
|---|---|
| No. 5a Pullman Car Conductor | ... each **3d.** |
| No. 5b Pullman Car Waiters (2) | ,, **3d.** |
| No. 5c Hotel Porters (2) | ,, **3d.** |

Fig. 19. Figures, Sets 1, 3, 4, 5 and 6.

*Fig. 18. No. 1, Station Staff and No. 4 Engineering Staff.*

*Fig. 20. No. 3, Passengers.*

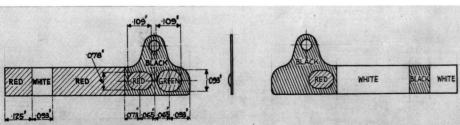

*Fig. 16. Tinprint Layout—Dinky Toy Signal Arm—'Home'.*

*Fig. 17. Tinprint Layout—Dinky Toy Signal Arm—'Distant'.*

*Fig. 21. 784, Goods Train Set.*

**784** Dinky Goods Train Set
(non motorised) (*no track required*)
May be used on OO/HO track

115 mm    92 mm    92 mm

784

"COOKS AGENT" – JOB No. 10987

# TRAINS AND MODELLED MINIATURES

| Cat. No. | Model | Intro. date | Deletion date | Comments |
|---|---|---|---|---|
| 001 | | | | Renumbering of 1 |
| 003 | | | | Renumbering of 3 |
| 004 | | | | Renumbering of 4 |
| 005 | | | | Renumbering of 5 |
| 013 | | | | Renumbering of 13a |
| 051 | | | | Renumbering of 1001 |
| 052 | Passengers | 1961 | 1969 | |
| 053 | | | | Renumbering of 1003 |
| 054 | Station Personnel | 1962 | 1971 | |
| 1 | Station Staff | 1931 | 1955 | Two distinct sets of castings pre-war. 1a omitted from post-war set. Renumbered 001. |
| 1a | Station Master | 1931 | 1941 | Post-war only as part of set. |
| 1b | Guard | 1931 | 1941 | Post-war only as part of set. |
| 1c | Ticket Collector | 1931 | 1941 | Post-war only as part of set. |
| 1d | Driver | 1931 | 1941 | Post-war only as part of set. |
| 1e | Porter with bags | 1931 | 1941 | Post-war only as part of set. |
| 1f | Porter | 1931 | 1941 | |
| 3 | Passengers | 1932 | 1955 | Two distinct sets of castings pre-war. Renumbered 003. |
| 3a | Woman and Child | 1932 | 1941 | Post-war only as part of set. |
| 3b | Businessman | 1932 | 1941 | Post-war only as part of set. |
| 3c | Male Hiker | 1932 | 1941 | Post-war only as part of set. |
| 3d | Female Hiker | 1932 | 1941 | Post-war only as part of set. |
| 3e | Newsboy | 1932 | 1941 | Post-war only as part of set. |
| 3f | Woman | 1932 | 1941 | Post-war only as part of set. |
| 4 | Engineering Staff | 1932 | 1955 | Two distinct sets of castings pre-war. 4c omitted from post-war set. Renumbered 004. |
| 4a | Electrician | 1932 | 1941 | |
| 4b | Fitters (two in set) | 1932 | 1941 | Post-war only as part of set. |
| 4c | Storekeeper | 1932 | 1941 | Post-war only as part of set. |
| 4d | Greaser | 1932 | 1941 | Post-war only as part of set. |
| 4e | Engine Room Attendant | 1932 | 1941 | Post-war only as part of set. |
| 5 | Train and Hotel Staff | 1932 | 1955 | Two distinct sets of castings pre-war. Renumbered 005. |
| 5a | Pullman Car Conductor | 1932 | 1941 | Post-war only as part of set. |
| 5b | Pullman Car Waiters (two in set) | 1932 | 1941 | Post-war only as part of set. |
| 5c | Hotel Porters (two in set) | 1932 | 1941 | Post-war only as part of set. |
| 13a | Cook's Man | 1952 | 1956 | Renumbered 013. |
| 15 | Railway Signals | 1937 | 1941 | |
| 15a | Single Arm Signal | 1937 | 1941 | One 'Home' and one 'Distant' |
| 15b | Double Arm Signal, home and distant | 1937 | 1941 | |
| 15c | Junction Signal | 1937 | 1941 | One 'Home' and one 'Distant' |
| 16 | Streamlined Train Set | 1937 | 1959 | Also known as 'Silver Jubilee'. Re-issued post-war. Renumbered 798. |
| 16z | Streamlined Diesel Articulated Train | | | See: French production |
| 17 | Passenger Train Set | 1934 | 1939/40 | |
| 17a | Locomotive | 1934 | 1939/40 | |
| 17b | Tender | 1934 | 1939/40 | |
| 18 | Tank Goods Train Set | 1934 | 1941 | Made up of 21a & 3×21b |
| 19 | Mixed Tank Goods Train Set | 1934 | 1941 | Made up of 21a, b, d, e |
| 20 | Tank Passenger Train Set | 1934 | 1939/40 | Also contained 21a |
| 20a | Coach | 1934 | 1939/40 | |
| 20b | Guard's Van | 1934 | 1939/40 | |
| 21 | Hornby Train Set | 1932 | 1934 | |
| 21a | Tank Locomotive | 1932 | 1941 | |
| 21b | Wagon | 1932 | 1941 | |
| 21c | Crane | 1932 | 1941 | |
| 21d | Petrol Tank Wagon | 1932 | 1941 | |
| 21e | Lumber Wagon | 1932 | 1941 | |
| 26 | Rail Autocar/G W R Railcar | 1934 | 1940 | |
| 26z | Diesel Rail Car | | | See: French Production |
| 784 | Dinky Goods Train Set | 1972 | 1974 | |
| 798 | Express Passenger Train | | | Renumbering of 16 |
| 1001 | Station Staff | 1952 | 1959 | Renumbered 051 |
| 1003 | Passengers | 1952 | 1959 | Renumbered 053 |

## Modelled Miniatures—Miscellaneous

2 FARMYARD ANIMALS was released in early 1932 and the beasts are very good models of the various breeds. Some are marked 'Hornby Series' on their stomachs, and they were issued in one size only. The set consisted of 2a HORSES, two, one brown, one white, 2b COWS, two, one black and white, one brown, 2c PIG, pink and 2d SHEEP, white with black ears, nose and legs. It was re-issued post-war, renumbered 002 and deleted in the mid-fifties.

6 SHEPHERD SET followed early the next year, its introduction coinciding with the change from 'Modelled Miniatures' to 'Meccano Dinky Toys' and it remained in the catalogue until the outbreak of war. 6a SHEPHERD was dressed in brown and carried a lamb under his arm. To start with, he wore a dark brown hat and leggings with black boots and the lamb was picked out in cream. However, later the painting was much simplified and he was all brown with green hat and collar to match the green of the base. 6b DOG is a black and white collie and the four SHEEP are numbered 2d and are the same casting as that in the previous set, except that 'Hornby Series' does not appear on their stomachs. Though the *Hornby Book of Trains* and *Meccano Magazine* adverts show three white sheep and one black, the set was normally issued with four white sheep. It was re-issued post-war, renumbered 006 and deleted in the mid-fifties.

## 23 Series Racing Cars—Pre-War

The popularisation of the sport of motor racing took place in the 1930s with large crowds attending Brooklands and other race tracks and Meccano latched onto this new enthusiasm by producing their first racing car in 1934. Thereafter, up to the outbreak of war, they produced some of the better known racing cars of the times and even dabbled in the record car field. Though they only made seven basic shapes in all, production runs of some of them were very high with all of them being re-issued post-war. The seven shapes can be conveniently divided into three types, the first consisting of 23a and b, the second of 23c, d and e, and the third of 23m, p and s.

The first two types have single piece bodies without baseplates and are fitted with large white (later large black) smooth tyres. Both are marked 'Made in England' up inside the bodywork which enables one to distinguish them from the very similar items that were 'Fab. en France'.

23 RACING CAR was issued in April 1934 on 23 without a letter suffix, but a month before the release of 23b when it had been decided to develop a series of racing cars the number was changed to 23a RACING CAR. It was based on the two M.G. Record/racing cars driven in 1933 and 1934 by Capt. George Eyston, although it was never given this designation by Meccano, and was issued on two main castings and a plethora of colour schemes. The

*Fig. 22a. 23a Racing Car, showing the change to the exhaust system.*

*Fig. 23. The prototype of the first type of 23a Racing Car, Capt. Eyston's 'Magic Midget'.*

first casting, based on the 4-cylinder 'Magic Midget' EX-127 is of lead and therefore heavier than the others, and has an open cockpit without a driver and four stub exhausts in two groups of two protruding from the nearside bonnet. Early examples have the type of wheel hub with the small central circular boss. By December 1934, the casting had been changed to incorporate a driver's head, and a 6-branch exhaust system (including a silencer and fishtail) had been added to the nearside of the car to represent the later 6-cylinder M.G. Magnette (M.G. designation EX-135) also driven by Capt. Eyston who had the real car painted in the 'Humbug' pattern of brown and cream stripes. (This car was subsequently sold to Major Gardner who had it rebodied and its features in this guise as Dinky no. 23p. See this chapter, Fig. 27.) There is a raised circular ridge

*Fig. 23a. The prototype of the second type of 23a Racing Car, Capt. Eyston's 'EX-135, M.G. Magnette', showing the 'Humbug' paint job.*

Fig. 26. 23m 'Thunderbolt' Speed Car.    Fig. 27. 23p M.G. Record Car.

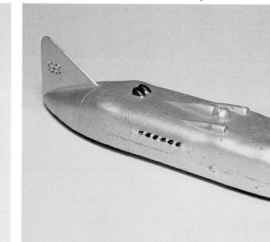

Fig. 22. Painting variations on 23a Racing car.

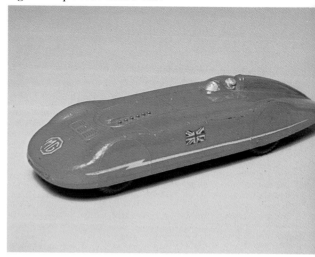

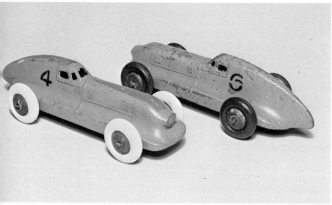

Fig. 24. 23b, Hotchkiss.

on either side of the body in which to locate the racing number. The positioning of 'Meccano Dinky Toys' and 'Made in England' cast in the interior has also changed. In fact, this is not just a die modification but a completely new one. Further small modifications were made as time went on. The locating ring for the number was removed and then, presumably as the die wore, the rearwards vertical part of the windscreen was filled in. The change from the first to the second die can be dated fairly accurately to December 1934, because in that month, *Meccano Magazine* published the article 'Collecting Meccano Dinky Toys' (see vol. 7) and it contains a photograph of 23a with a driver's head obviously drawn in, though the advertisers in *Meccano Magazine* continued to use the original illustration until 1936, and some catalogues until the outbreak of war. All are painted two-tone, and there are three different versions. They do not seem to have been used consecutively, because both early and late second type castings are found with the same design on them. The commonest has the subsidiary colour running from the high point of the bonnet, widening out to encompass the cockpit area and then continuing along the top section of the tail fin. The radiator (and stub exhausts if the scheme is on the first casting) are also painted the same colour. The second type has the overpainting running from the lower edge of the

nose up to a point in front of the cockpit and also along the whole of the tail fin. And the third and prettiest example consists of the 'Humbug' pattern of alternate colour stripes running the length of the body shell. Numbers, for instance '3', '4', '11', etc., were frequently applied, and the coloured stencilled roundel allowed the main body colour to show through to create the number so that a blue body would have a blue number, a red body a red number, and so on. Frequently, the roundel colour was that of the subsidiary colour flash, but a third colour was also used, e.g. red body, cream flash, silver roundel, etc. Many colour combinations are found, such as (main colour first) cream/green, cream/red, red/cream, blue/white, blue/silver, orange/green, brown/cream, and so on. The model was re-issued post-war.

23b HOTCHKISS RACING CAR was released in mid 1935, and is a much less complicated little beast than 23a. The same construction method of a single piece body casting on wheels with no base was used. There were no significant casting changes during its entire life. Despite it being a model of a French manufactured car, it was designed at Binns Road. All were painted two-tone with the main body colour showing through as the racing number, which was usually '5'. These were applied high up on either side of the enclosed cockpit behind the windows, though early examples did not have them. The roundel could be the same colour as the flash, which runs along the top of the body right from the nose to the tail. The usual colours are blue/white, green/yellow and red/silver. The model was re-issued post-war.

23 RACING CARS set was first advertised in *Meccano Magazine* in late 1936 though the three vehicles that comprised the set were actually issued some six months earlier. They were 'Fitted with drivers and detachable rubber *racing* tyres' (Authors' italics) and so they were. The tyres are larger than any others used pre-war, are black and have a herringbone pattern tread round the outside edges. The chassis were tinplate with the sump, differential etc. pressed in and were individual to each car. They were held in by the one-piece body casting which was deformed at critical points after the bases were fitted. Racing circles and numbers were applied in the same manner to this group as they were to 23a and b, namely with a stencil which allowed the body colour to show through for the number. The circles were either yellow or white and were usually applied to the Mercedes-Benz and Auto-Union but not normally to the 'Speed of the Wind'. The drivers were white, and goggles, steering wheel, windscreen, radiator, exhaust, air intakes etc. were touched in with silver. 23c and d were sold in France but they were not manufactured there. 23c MERCEDES-BENZ RACING CAR is a model of the Merc W 25 and the driver is integral with the body casting. It can be found in red, shades of blue, and yellow. The decals are positioned on either side of the tail in front of the scuttle.

23d AUTO-UNION RACING CAR is really a model of a Record Car, and came in red, blue, green or silver. The driver is a separate piece and slots up into the body casting.

23e 'SPEED OF THE WIND' RACING CAR is also a model of a Record Car, this time one of Capt. Eyston's. The driver is part of the body casting and is crudely modelled so that he looks more like a deep sea diver than a racing driver. Colours: blue, yellow and green. With very small changes, these

## 23 SERIES RACING CARS—PRE-WAR

| Cat. No. | Model | Intro. date | Deletion date | Comments |
|---|---|---|---|---|
| 23 | Racing Car | 1934 | 1935 | Renumbered 23a |
| 23 | Racing Cars | 1936 | 1941 | |
| 23a | | 1935 | | Renumbering of 23. Re-issued post-war. |
| 23b | Hotchkiss Racing Car | 1935 | | Re-issued post-war. |
| 23c | Mercedes-Benz Racing Car | 1936 | | Re-issued post-war. |
| 23d | Auto-Union Racing Car | 1936 | | Re-issued post-war. |
| 23e | 'Speed of the Wind' Racing Car | 1936 | | Re-issued post-war. |
| 23m | 'Thunderbolt' Speed Car | 1938 | 1941 | |
| 23p | Gardner's M.G. Record Car | 1939 | | Re-issued post-war. |
| 23s | Streamlined Racing Car | 1939 | | Re-issued post-war. |

*Fig. 25. 23c Mercedes-Benz, 23d Auto Union and 23e 'Speed of the Wind' racing cars.*

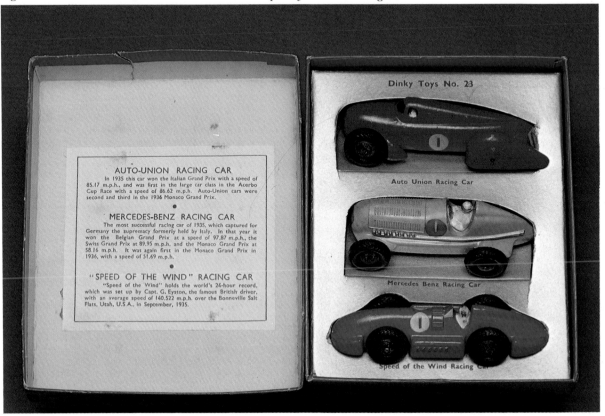

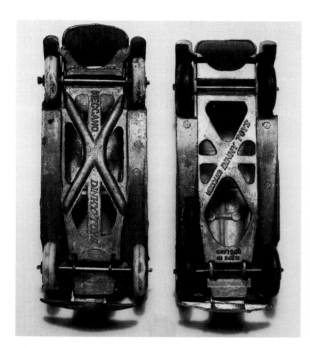

*Fig. 29. First and Second type chassis for the 24 Series.*

*Fig. 30. First type grille—diamond type.*

*Fig. 31. Second type grille—Bentley style (no badge).*

*Fig. 32. Third type grille—Bentley type (with badge).*

were all re-issued post-war.

The third group consists of three models, but only two castings, as 23m 'THUNDERBOLT' SPEED CAR and 23s STREAMLINED RACING CAR are the same thing with different paint finishes. They were one piece castings with tinplate bases rivetted on. It was a big car, as can be seen from the small size of the driver's head. 23m is 'A fine model of the car in which Capt. G. E. T. Eyston set up a world land speed record of 312mph at Bonneville, Utah, U.S.A. in 1937' and Meccano had it in production by April 1938 before interest in the achievement had evaporated. (The original drawing is dated 30. 11. 37.) This version is always silver with black exhausts and air intakes, and the Union Jack transferred on either side of the tail. 'Ready during February' of 1939 was 23s STREAMLINED RACING CAR 'Similar in type to the "Thunderbolt" Speed Car.', and distinguishable by its 'Assorted colours' e.g. light green with dark green air intakes and exhausts, light blue with dark blue detailing, etc. It did not have the Union Jack on the tail. 23s was re-issued post-war but 23m was not.

If 23p GARDNER'S M.G. RECORD CAR had actually appeared in September 1939 as advertised in *Meccano Magazine*, it would have been something of a record for Dinky because the car only made the two sets of records at the end of May and beginning of June of that year, which would have meant a bare three months from record breaking run to the toy in the shops. It didn't actually appear till December, but even this later date reflects a pretty creditable turn of production speed. It is 'A scale model of the car in which Major A. T. G. Gardner set up new world speed records for cars up to 1,100cc on the Bitterfeld-Dessau Autobahn, Germany, in May, 1939. His speed for the flying kilometre was 203.7mph, and for the flying mile, 203.2mph. After having the engine rebored, Major Gardner set up new records for cars up to 1,500cc over the flying kilometre, mile and five kilometres, with speed of 204.2mph, 203.8mph and 200.6mph respectively.' It is a very good model of the car indeed, being finished in dark green with the 'MG' logo on the nose and the Union Jack on the sides. The white lightning flash found on the side of some of the cars was on the car

when it took the records. Re-issued post-war.

For post-war re-issues and new issues in the 23 series: See Post-war—Racing Cars.

### 24 Series—Motor Cars

The first advertisement for 'Dinky Toys', in 1934, contained details of the 24 set of Motor Cars—the fact that the first in the list was an ambulance seems not to have worried the factory at all! Even though we would now regard it as a commercial vehicle, it is relevant to deal with it along with the rest of the series because it shares the significant features of the other 24s. As a group, the eight vehicles represent the major types of body styles that were on the roads at the time, and that they were meant only to be models of generic vehicles can be seen from their nomenclature, since apart from 24d Vogue Saloon they were not given the names of particular makes of car. This was in keeping with what other toy manufacturers were doing at the time in England, for the earliest Minic cars were similarly designated 'Town Coupé', 'Four Seat Tourer', etc.

*Fig. 33. 24a Ambulance.*

*Fig. 34. 24b Limousine.*

*Fig. 35. 24c Town Sedan, with and without spare wheel.*

*Fig. 36. 24d Vogue Saloon.*

*Fig. 37. 24e Super Streamlined Saloon.*

*Fig. 38. 24f Sportsman's Coupé, with and without spare wheel.*

*Fig. 28. The 24 Set of Motor Cars.*

At the time, the real car manufacturers were advertising the advantages of the different body styles they made, if anything, more heavily than their own name, and it was not really until later on in the thirties that each marque developed its own easily recognisable identity.

There are many detail variations in the 24 series vehicles over the six or so years that they were in production, and because of the scarcity of examples it is very difficult to arrive at a clear order amongst them. Many didactic statements have appeared in writings over the years based on the examples that each author has had in his possession plus a good bit of guesswork. Therefore, although the authors of this work believe that the following comments are correct, it must always be borne in mind that a model could turn up that does not seem to fit within the designated categories. There are features common to all of the 24 series vehicles (apart from wheels and tyres) and these are the chassis and the grilles. The chassis is commonly known as the 'criss-cross' chassis, but as can be seen from the photograph, there are two distinct versions, the first and earlier having 'Meccano Dinky Toys' on a bar running centrally up the chassis and the second and later having the legend running diagonally across the chassis. It is probable that the first type was not in use for very long as it is found less frequently than the later one, but the reason for the change from one to the other is not obvious from looking at them, and the drawings which would give some explanation are no longer extant. Both of these chassis were made in two versions, with and without a spare wheel slot in the nearside running board. By the late thirties, the use of the chassis with spare wheel slot was suspended so that all the latest issue items did not have a spare wheel. There were two basic types of grille, one with a diamond in the centre of the bumper and one 'Bentley' type. The diamond-type is similar to those used on French Dinkies before the war and is found with both types of chassis. Though it is less common than the Bentley-type and seems to occur more frequently on the earlier chassis, one cannot say that it is the earlier because the Bentley-type is also found on both chassis. It seems that they were both in use at the same time. To make the confusion even worse, there are two versions of the Bentley grille. The

*Fig. 39. 24g Sports Tourer (Four-Seater).*

*Fig. 40. 24h Sports Tourer (Two-Seater).*

## 24 SERIES—MOTOR CARS

| Cat. No. | Model | Intro. date | Deletion date | Comments |
|---|---|---|---|---|
| 24 | Motor Cars | 1934 | 1940 | |
| 24a | Ambulance | 1934 | 1941 | Same body used on 30f |
| 24b | Limousine | 1934 | 1940 | |
| 24c | Town Sedan | 1934 | 1941 | |
| 24d | Vogue Saloon | 1934 | 1940 | |
| 24e | Super Streamlined Saloon | 1934 | 1940 | |
| 24f | Sportsman's Coupé | 1934 | 1940 | |
| 24g | Sports Tourer (4-Seater) | 1934 | 1941 | |
| 24h | Sports Tourer (2-Seater) | 1934 | 1941 | |
| 24kz | Peugeot Car | | | See: French Dinky Products |

earlier is a simpler casting with no badge on the radiator cowling and no over-riders on the bumpers. The later carries both these features. This is the grille that is found on the 36 series Bentley and it is fairly safe to assume that it was only fitted to the 24 series cars after the introduction of the 36 series in mid-1938. It may have been a deliberate decision to use both types of the Bentley grilles on the 24 series or it may have been a long-running mix-up on the production line. The spare wheel on the running board or tail of the open cars was still in use in 1938 as examples of these exist with the grille carrying the badge and over-riders. To sum up there are two overlapping sequences; as follows:

First type chassis with slot for spare and without slot—in use at the same time
*followed by:—*
Second type chassis with slot for spare and without slot—in use at the same time
*followed by:—*
Second type chassis without slot, and Grille with diamond probably used concurrently with grille without badge or over-riders
*followed by:—*
Grille without badge or over-riders
*followed by:—*
Grille without badge or over-riders used concurrently with grille with both features.
The only possible permutation of the above two

sequences that does not seem to occur, is the use on the same vehicle of the first type chassis and the Bentley grille with badge and over-riders.

The wheels and tyres require a special note, for although most are found with the standard smooth hubs and white tyres of the pre-war issues, some very early examples are found with wheel hubs similar to those used on Tootsietoys from America, i.e. smooth with a small central circular boss (see photograph of 24d Vogue Saloon). Some early vehicles also have tyres in red, green or blue rubber instead of the usual white. The wheel hubs are usually black, but the blue is also common and other colours such as green can be found as well as chrome plated ones. Despite their dull appearance now all the grilles were 'silver' plated. Nearly all the vehicles were two-tone with the chassis in the darker shade, black, blue, green, brown, red and some even grey, cream or maroon etc. The bodies were maroon, yellow, green, blue, red, fawn, grey, cream and even pink. Of some of the colours, more than one shade was used. Theoretically, except for the ambulance, any colour or any pair of colours could turn up on any of the vehicles, so the colours will not in general be mentioned when the individual models are detailed.

All the items in the set 24 MOTOR CARS appeared at the same time in 1934 and all were available into the war, though some went out of production slightly earlier than others. 24a AMBU-

LANCE was issued with a light grey body and a dark grey chassis, and then with a cream body and grey or brown chassis, followed by the cream body, this time on a red chassis. It is often thought that it was also available in grey with a red chassis, but according to *Meccano Magazine* advertising and catalogue references, this colour scheme was used for the 30f AMBULANCE. The early issues of the 30f AMBU-LANCE (pre-1938) are indistinguishable from the 24a AMBULANCE in body and chassis, because the 30 series chassis will not fit the ambulance body. After the introduction of the 30 series, they can only be told apart by their colour. After 1938, this problem does not arise, as then the 30f was fitted with the 36 series slotted chassis. That is not to say that one could not find a grey and red ambulance in a boxed set of 24 series that is still as it was issued from the factory, because the end-of-production line packers would hardly care about the colour, as long as they

had the right casting to complete the work quota. The reason for being firm about the allocation of colours is merely that the intention of Meccano was that the 30 series ones should be grey and red, and the 24 series the other colour combinations. It is not found with a spare wheel. 24b LIMOUSINE is not found with a spare wheel and has two body castings, the earlier having the three parallel bonnet louvres vertically above each other, and the later having them diagonally above each other. The body is similar to that used on the 36a ARMSTRONG SID-DELEY. 24c TOWN SEDAN is found with and without spare wheel in the wing. The screen, dash and steering wheel are a separate diecasting, giving the model a very 'Tootsietoy-ish' appearance. The body style was not available on any other series. 24d VOGUE SALOON is the only model that was given a 'real' name. It came with and without a spare wheel in the wing. The body is similar to that used

on the 36d HUMBER VOGUE SALOON. 24e SUPER STREAMLINED SALOON did not have a spare wheel in the wing. The body is similar to that used for the 36d ROVER. 24f SPORTSMAN'S COUPÉ came with or without the spare wheel in the wing, and its body is similar to that used for the 36b BENTLEY. 24g SPORTS TOURER (FOUR-SEATER) was available with or without a spare wheel on the rear (the hub is part of the body casting). On earlier issues, the tinplate screen is 'open', i.e., consists only of the screen frame, whereas on later ones it is 'solid', i.e., the glass is represented by an indentation on a solid piece of tin. There are two castings for the steering wheel/dashboard insert, one of which has the spokes positioned 45° and the other 22.5° to the horizontal. The body, very slightly modified, was used for 36f BRITISH SALMSON 4-seater. 24th SPORTS TOURER (TWO-SEATER) uses a very similar casting, again with or without a spare wheel on the tail. The same screens and dash/steering wheel units were fitted. This body with very little change appears on 36e BRITISH SALMSON 2-seater.

## 25 Series—Commercials

A series of commercial vehicles was issued in the Spring of 1934, and their announcement in *Meccano Magazine* coincided with the first use in that magazine of the name 'Dinky Toys'. This was a carefully prepared venture as all six vehicles shared a standard chassis, five had the same cab, and the lorry beds all had the same number of 'planks'. The chassis, which was usually painted black, was in use for the whole of the pre-war period and has three large triangular holes. Differences between one chassis and another are found quite commonly, but these are no help in dating the model for there appears to have been more than one chassis die. Also, die wear caused differences to develop over the years even when the same die was in use, and so many of the castings have been distorted by fatigue to a greater or lesser extent, that detailed study of chassis produces little information of any accuracy. The chassis is truly common to the range as they all have the fixing for the tipping mechanism of the Tipping Wagon, and although the towing hook was redundant on the petrol tanker, no different casting was used, the hook being nipped off

*Fig. 48. The Pool Petrol Tanker.*

(with shears) after casting. If the chassis is no help in dating a model, the radiator grille is a little better. They all began life with plated tinplate radiators which clipped in through a slot in the top of the bonnet and were folded up underneath at the bottom. Two very similar pressings were used, one which fitted the five open-backed vehicles and one slightly wider for the tanker. Very soon after their introduction and certainly by late 1935, the switch over from tinplate to the plated diecast type with integral headlamps was begun. It is unlikely that they were all changed at the same time, for a major bonnet modification was required and it is likely that this was done vehicle by vehicle. The Dinky Display Board which can be dated to mid to late 1935 shows the Wagon and the Covered Van (which is the same thing with a tin tilt) having the diecast grille. Unfortunately, the Market Gardeners Wagon in the same photo is shown from the rear, but it is probable from pictures in *Meccano Magazine* showing it still with a tinplate radiator in 1936, that it was one of the latest to be changed. (It is not wise to put too much reliance on these pictures as there is no way of knowing when they were actually photographed or whether the latest models were used in them anyway, as Dinky Toys are frequently merely adjuncts to a train layout.)

The advertising consistently mentioned 'Silver-plated radiators' and both the tinplate and diecast types were plated with a variety of metals to give them a silver finish. The tinplate ones have in many cases kept their appearance unless they have become damp and turned rusty, but the diecast ones almost without exception have dulled down to a grey-black. The very latest production had little stickers (transfers) on the offside rear of some vehicles comprising a white 20 in a black circle, because at this time such heavy vehicles were restricted to a maximum speed of 20 miles per hour!

25 COMMERCIAL MOTOR VEHICLES consisted of six vehicles, but the six that could be bought together in a boxed set changed somewhere between mid-1936 and 1939. Initially it was constructed from the first six vehicles that were released at the same time in early 1934: 25a WAGON, 25b COVERED VAN, 25c FLAT TRUCK, 25d PET-

ROL TANK WAGON, 25e TIPPING WAGON, 25f MARKET GARDENER'S VAN. After the issue of more vehicles on the number 25, the WAGON and FLAT TRUCK were omitted and their places taken by: 25g TRAILER and 25h FIRE ENGINE. (For details of this model see the section on Fire Engines.) In the following recital of the colours most commonly found, no attempt is made to segregate those on tinplate radiator and those on diecast radiator vehicles, partly because in many cases this would lead to a boring repetition of colours, but partly because virtually any colour that was in use in the factory at the time seems to have found its way onto one vehicle or another. In nearly all cases the chassis were black though other colours can be found. 25a WAGON and 25b COVERED VAN share the same diecasting and bearing in mind the penchant of small boys for swapping bits around, it is now very difficult to tell whether an example existing now started from the factory in one form or the other. The cab and back can be found in maroon, green, grey and blue most commonly with 'runners up' in brown and orange. This last colour looks particularly attractive when found with a green chassis. Tin tilts are found in cream, grey or green. Some of the tin tilts carried advertising. 'Meccano En-

gineering for Boys' and 'Hornby Trains' are found on a cream tilt; 'Carter Paterson Express Carriers London' on a green one with the Carter Paterson red stripe across the top, and 'Carter Paterson Special Service to the Seaside' on a cream one. These legends should appear on green vehicles, green being the house colour of Carter Paterson. Extreme care should be taken to examine these decalled tilts thoroughly before accepting them as authentic because there were so many plain tilts produced that small boys could apply their own decals too, and recently some excellent reproduction ones have been made. Every so often, a new 'rare' one is reported. None of these have been included as we have not been able to authenticate them personally. 25c FLAT TRUCK comes most often in royal blue, which looks particularly good if the wheels are the same colour, but sometimes in green, etc. The range of colours found seems to be less on this vehicle than on some of the others. 25e TIPPING WAGON has a three piece casting instead of the usual two piece, so three colours can be found on any one vehicle. Again, the chassis is usually black and the cab a different and darker colour than the tipping bed. Maroon cab, yellow back is the usual combination but brown/light blue, brown/brown, fawn/fawn, grey/grey,

etc. are also found. 25f MARKET GARDENER'S WAGON or VAN is typically yellow or green with a black chassis, but the yellow one with a green chassis is perhaps the most attractive. In the middle of 1935, some considerable time after the rest of the items were issued, 25g TRAILER appeared being advertised as 'For use with Dinky Toy Commercial Vehicles No. 25'. It was usually green or dark blue. A tinplate towbar affixed to the swivelling front axle mounting enabled it to be towed by any of the aforementioned vehicles. 25d PETROL TANK WAGON had a completely different style of cab from the others, being wider and altogether more detailed. On the very earliest tinplate radiator examples, the little windows behind the cab doors were open but very quickly these became flashed over and most are found with them filled in. It was issued in red or green, with or without 'Petrol' in black or white on the sides. The word seems to have been applied with a rubber stamp and is very susceptible to wear from children's fingers which, in play, grip the model just where the legend was applied. Quite when the Petrol Company transfer versions were issued is not known but it was certainly not long after the vehicles were released as examples have been found on the earlier tin radiator type. The following decal/colour schemes have been found:

| Petrol Company | Transfer Colour | Vehicle Colour |
| --- | --- | --- |
| SHELL-BP | gold | red |
| ESSO | gold | green |
| REDLINE-GLICO | gold on red band | blue |
| POWER | gold | green |
| TEXACO | white | red |
| MOBILOIL | blue on white band | orange |
| CASTROL | red and black | green |
| POOL | white stamp | grey |

This last one is the best documented as it was announced as 'new' in the January 1940 issue of *Meccano Magazine*. Though the body was always grey, the chassis was painted either black or white. Any of the decal varieties, including 'Pool' can be found in the boxed set. (For post-war re-issues and new releases in the 25 series: See Post-war—Commercials.)

*Fig. 41. The 25 Series Commercial Motor Vehicles, second type.*
*The green tanker at top right is a post war version included to fill the space left by the 'lost' pre war version.*

Fig. 42. 25b, Covered Wagon, 'Hornby Trains'.

Fig. 45. The yellow and green 25f Market Gardener's
Wagon.

Fig. 46 & 47. The 25d Petrol Tank Wagons with
advertising.

## 28 Series Vans

The 28 series of vans were the first group of vans with advertising that were produced and in one form or another they continued from 1934 until the war-time years. On this number, 28, three distinct castings were released and each casting was common to the decals in use at the time. Meccano's numbering did not distinguish between castings so there could be three different castings on the same number, but each was deleted before the next one was introduced.

The first casting, which was first advertised in April 1934, utilised the tool of the van in the 22 series, 22d. It was in use for a very short length of time, for trade catalogues show illustrations of the new shape as early as June 1935, though retail advertising in *Meccano Magazine* did not reflect this until August of that year. Some of the early casting have 'Hornby' underneath in the manner of the early 22 series but most of them are marked 'Meccano Dinky Toys'. To begin with the individual transfers were not allocated letter suffixes but these were added by August 1934. 13 different transfers were issued, the vans being grouped in two sets of six with one short-term substitution in one set. The sets were allocated the numbers 28/1 and 28/2 but the individual items did not have /1 or /2 as part of their designation. The second set contained the 'Meccano Engineering for Boys' van which began life as 22d, presumably because the van in the 22 set had by this time acquired these decals (though it started off plain), but when it was dropped from the 22 set in about April 1935, it was renumbered 28n. The decals were usually the same on both sides of the van, but two, the 'Oxo' and 'Ensign', sported different ones either side. The ENSIGN VAN (28e) was replaced for a very short time, round about September 1934, by 'Firestone Tyres' which was white with gold lettering but the substitution only seems to have lasted about a month. Bad handwriting in the advertising office probably led to an error in the numbering of 28e ENSIGN for it appears occasionally as '28l'; however, this number had already been allocated to the CRAWFORD'S BISCUITS VAN.

Pictures of the second casting first appeared in trade information in June 1935 but *Meccano Magazine* didn't let the readers into the know until August. This re-design of the vehicles is quite dramatic, the

### 28 SERIES VANS

| 28/1 | Delivery Vans | April 1934 | June 1935 | Contained 28a,b,c,d,e,f. |
|---|---|---|---|---|
| 28/2 | Delivery Vans | May 1934 | June 1935 | Contained 28g,h,k,l,m,n. |
| 28a | Hornby Trains Van | 1934 | 1935 | |
| 28b | Pickfords Removals Van | 1934 | 1935 | |
| 28c | Manchester Guardian Van | 1934 | 1935 | |
| 28d | Oxo Van | 1934 | 1935 | |
| 28e | Ensign Cameras | 1934 | 1935 | Briefly substituted by 28e★ |
| 28e★ | Firestone Tyres Van | 1934 | 1934 | |
| 28f | Palethorpe's Sausages Van | 1934 | 1935 | |
| 28g | Kodak Cameras' Van | 1934 | 1935 | |
| 28h | Sharp's Van | 1934 | 1935 | |
| 28k | Marsh and Baxter's Van | 1934 | 1935 | |
| 28l | Crawford's Biscuits Van | 1934 | 1935 | |
| 28m | Wakefield's Oil Van | 1934 | 1935 | |
| 28n | Meccano Van | 1934 | 1935 | Numbered 22d until April 1935 |

small curvaceous van with a Ford-type radiator looking much more modern than the square castings of the lead type. The new version was used for most of the pre-war period, for it was not replaced until 1940, or possibly very late 1939. None of the advertising literature shows the third type and there was no fuss made of the change, possibly because the two castings are alike in size and were thought of as merely a sensible update taking advantage of the earlier die or dies wearing out. Though superficially similar, there are in fact many differences between the two. The earlier with the Ford-type grille (vertical grille bars) has five bonnet louvres, the door is straight-edged and much wider at bottom than top, the square rear windows are closed and there is no front bumper nor rear numberplate. The later Bedford-type (squared grille bar pattern) has three bonnet louvres, made by the leading edge of the tool, not just a modification. Unfortunately, the quality of the metal used was very poor indeed and the vast major-

ity of the vans suffer to a greater or lesser extent from fatigue—a great sadness to see such pretty things crumble before one's eyes. The wheel hubs are usually black, though coloured examples such as blue are found. Most were on white tyres. Being a single casting there was not much scope for two-tone colour schemes and with one exception, the whole casting is painted a single colour with beautifully printed decals in several colours, gold being the predominant one.

The first two sets using the new castings came out at the same time and used transfers from the first, lead set with the exception of 'Ensign Cameras'. For some reason two of the vehicles swapped sets, 'Oxo' going to the second and 'Meccano' to the first. Because of the aforementioned confusion over the letter suffix of 'Crawfords' it was renumbered 28p. 28k is always referred to as 'Marsh and Baxter's Sausage Van' but the decals omit 'Baxter's'. In each of these two sets numbered 28/1 and 28/2, there are six ve-

Fig. 52. Reverse side of 28e and 28d.

Fig. 55. 28 3rd (Bedford) type Vans.

Fig. 51. 28/1 Boxed Set of Delivery Vans.

*Fig. 53. (3 pictures) 28/2 set of Delivery Vans.*

*Fig. 54. A selection of 28 2nd type and 280 Vans.*

hicles, but over the years substitutions were made so that in all, seventeen different vans were produced. Two, 'Meccano' and 'Sharps' were produced so briefly that they were never illustrated in catalogues which instead showed 'Atcol' and 'Dunlop' from the start. Over the years, 'Pickfords' was replaced by 'Seccotine', 'Hornby Trains' by 'Golden Shred' (if one believes *Meccano Magazine* advertising the sequence goes: 'Hornby Trains', 'Golden Shred', 'Hornby Trains', 'Golden Shred') and 'Palethorpes' by 'Virol'.

In 1936, another group of six were released and numbered 28/3. This time there were only six different ones.

A year later, another set came out, and because by this time all the suitable suffix letters had been used up, they were numbered 280. In all, nine different advertisements appeared on the sides. 'Ah! Bisto' became 'Bisto', 'Lyons' became 'Hartleys' and 'Ekco' became 'Yorkshire Evening Post'.

In addition some promotional vans were released; 'Bentalls' and 'Bonneterie' were made for shops, one in London and the other in Amsterdam. There was also apparently one made for the newspaper, the *Liverpool Echo*, although we haven't seen this one.

## 28 SERIES VANS

| | | | | 2nd casting | 3rd casting | body colour | decal colour |
|---|---|---|---|---|---|---|---|
| 28/1 | Delivery Vans | 1935 | 1941 | Contains 28a,b,c,e,f,n | | | |
| 28/2 | Delivery Vans | 1935 | 1941 | Contains 28,d,g,h,k,m,p | | | |
| 28/3 | Delivery Vans | 1936 | 1941 | Contains 28r,s,t,w,x,y | | | |
| 280 | Delivery Vans | 1937 | 1940 | Contains 280a,b,c,d,e,f | | | |
| 28a | Hornby Trains Van | 1935 | 1936 | 2nd casting | | yellow | gold |
| 28a | Golden Shred Van | 1936 | 1941 | 2nd casting | 3rd casting | cream | red & blue |
| 28b | Pickfords' Removal Van | 1935 | 1935 | 2nd casting | | dark blue | gold |
| 28b | Seccotine Van | 1935 | 1941 | 2nd casting | 3rd casting | light blue | gold |
| 28c | Manchester Guardian | 1935 | 1941 | 2nd casting | 3rd casting | red | gold |
| 28d | Oxo Van | 1935 | 1941 | 2nd casting | 3rd casting | dark blue | gold |
| 28e | Firestone Tyres Van | 1935 | 1941 | 2nd casting | 3rd casting | white or blue | red |
| 28f | Palethorpe's Sausages Van | 1935 | 1938 | 2nd casting | | grey | colours |
| 28f | Virol | 1938 | 1941 | 2nd casting | 3rd casting | yellow | black etc. |
| 28g | Kodak Cameras' Van | 1935 | 1941 | 2nd casting | 3rd casting | yellow | red |
| 28h | Sharp's Van | 1935 | 1935 | 2nd casting | | red | gold |
| 28h | Dunlop Tyres Van | 1935 | 1941 | 2nd casting | 3rd casting | red | gold |
| 28k | Marsh and Baxter's Sausages Van | 1935 | 1941 | 2nd casting | 3rd casting | dark green | gold |
| 28m | Wakefield's Castrol Oil Van | 1935 | 1941 | 2nd casting | 3rd casting | green | red |
| 28n | Meccano Van | 1935 | 1935 | 2nd casting | | yellow | red & gold |
| 28n | Atco Mowers Van | 1935 | 1941 | 2nd casting | 3rd casting | green | gold |
| 28p | Crawford's Biscuit Van | 1935 | 1941 | 2nd casting | 3rd casting | red | gold |
| 28r | Swan's Van | 1936 | 1941 | 2nd casting | 3rd casting | black | silver |
| 28s | Fry's Van | 1936 | 1941 | 2nd casting | 3rd casting | dark brown | gold |
| 28t | Ovaltine Van | 1936 | 1941 | 2nd casting | 3rd casting | red | gold |
| 28w | Osram Van | 1936 | 1941 | 2nd casting | 3rd casting | yellow | gold |
| 28x | Hovis Van | 1936 | 1941 | 2nd casting | 3rd casting | white | gold |
| 28y | Exide and Drydex Van | 1936 | 1941 | 2nd casting | 3rd casting | red | gold |
| 280a | Vyella Van | 1937 | 1940 | 2nd casting | 3rd casting | pale blue | white |
| 280b | Lyon's Van | 1937 | 1939 | 2nd casting | | blue | red & white |
| 280b | Hartley's Van | 1939 | 1940 | 2nd casting | 3rd casting | cream | red & green |
| 280c | Shredded Wheat | 1937 | 1940 | 2nd casting | 3rd casting | cream | red & black |
| 280d | Bisto Van (Ah! Bisto) | 1937 | | 2nd casting | | yellow | colours |
| 280d | Bisto Van | | 1940 | 2nd casting | 3rd casting | yellow | colours |
| 280e | Ekco Van | 1937 | 1939 | 2nd casting | | green | gold |
| 280e | Yorkshire Evening Post Van | 1939 | 1940 | 2nd casting | 3rd casting | cream | gold |
| 280f | Mackintosh's Van | 1937 | 1940 | 2nd casting | 3rd casting | red | gold |
| | Bentall's Van | | | 2nd casting | | green & yellow | green |
| | Maison de Bonneterie Van | | | 2nd casting | | red | gold |
| | Liverpool Echo Van | | | | | | |

## 30 Series—Motor Vehicles

The group of seven vehicles given '30' numbers are a strange mixture and the set lacks the coherence of other pre-war groups. It consists of the first American car issued by Meccano, three U.K. cars which were given the names of actual vehicles and which do have the significant recognition factor of those vehicles incorporated in the model, an ambulance, a breakdown truck and eventually, a caravan. Moreover, the individual items were not issued together and one was even renumbered! Even the construction methods were not the same—three are one piece castings and four are two piece. On the two piece vehicles there are two chassis, one vehicle using chassis from other series and three having their own. Very confusing! It is the chassis used on the Rolls, Daimler and Vauxhall that is thought of as the 30 series chassis and it can be distinguished from the others having the wings integral with the base by the existence of two different size triangular holes with their apexes pointing towards a small central circular hole.

*Fig. 56. The 30 Series Motor Vehicles, showing the 3 versions of 30d Vauxhall, the earliest being on the right.*

30 MOTOR VEHICLES always consisted of six items, four cars, a breakdown lorry and for the first eighteen months of its issue, an ambulance. For the rest of the pre-war period, the ambulance was replaced by a caravan. 30a CHRYSLER 'AIR-FLOW' SALOON was issued in late 1934 as number 32 with no letter suffix. It is not obvious why it was renumbered 30a but this designation was used from June 1935 onwards. The bodies, some of which have been found made out of lead, are one piece castings with a separate radiator/front bumper unit and a separate rear bumper, this being the only pre-war vehicle that carried one. It is a good model of this futuristic vehicle, though it has a more delicate appearance than the original. The variety of colours found is wide, shades of blue and green abound, and it is also in turquoise, maroon, cream and red. Though the wheel hubs are usually black or chromed, colours such as blue and red were also used leading to some very attractive combinations. The hubs were fitted with large tyres. It was released in France with white tyres carrying the 'Dunlop' name.

30b ROLLS ROYCE CAR has body and chassis secured together with the axles which fit through lugs in the body, and is fitted with a fair representation of a Rolls radiator grille which has lights and bumper attached to it. The chassis is as described above. Usually it is painted black but other colours are found, and the body may be blue, red, cream, grey or fawn and some of the colours are in more than one shade. The tyres are the smaller of the two sizes. The Rolls was issued in the late summer of 1935 along with most of the other 30 series. 30c DAIMLER CAR shares chassis and wheels with 30b and is similarly distinguished by its Daimler radiator/light/bumper unit. Again, the chassis is usually black and the body colours may be in shades of blue, green, fawn, cream, yellow, turquoise. A spectacular sight is one that has a pink body and a maroon chassis! Not quite the thing for a Daimler, surely. 30d VAUXHALL CAR utilises the tyres of the previous two and the body casting has the distinctive Vauxhall bonnet flutes. The chassis is similar to the one used for 30b and c, but initially it had a slot in the nearside to accommodate the spare wheel that was pinned into the side of the body. Later, the spare wheel was deleted and so was the chassis slot. Two different grilles were used, the first had raised lines in a chequered pattern and is commonly called the 'criss-cross radiator'; the second was the more conventional shield shape. Both grilles are found on vehicles with spare wheel and without spare wheel. Normally the chassis is black and the body can be blue, green, grey, yellow or brown in a variety of shades. 30e BREAKDOWN CAR is actually a lorry. It utilises the one piece casting of the 22c LORRY with a cast insert for the back incorporating the searchlight and crane. This is rather an oddity in the set as it is wildly out of scale with the other items. It ran on small tyres and early examples had the front and rear wings painted black. The whole of the rest was one colour, red, yellow, grey, brown, green, blue, etc. It is found with black, chromed or coloured wheel hubs. The hook is merely a piece of bent wire. 30f AMBULANCE was only part of the set for a short time, although it remained in production until 1941. The body is identical to that used for the 24a AMBULANCE and for the first few years of its life it utilised the 24 series chassis. In 1938, when the 36 series was released, the chassis was changed to the slotted one. It was not possible to use the chassis

## 30 SERIES—MOTOR VEHICLES

| Cat. No. | Model | Intro. date | Deletion date | Comments |
|---|---|---|---|---|
| 30 | Motor Vehicles | 1935 | 1937 | Containing 30f Ambulance |
| 30 | Motor Vehicles | 1937 | 1941 | Containing 30g Caravan |
| 30a | Chrysler 'Airflow' Saloon | 1935 | | Previously numbered 32 Re-issued post-war |
| 30b | Rolls Royce Car | 1935 | | Re-issued post-war |
| 30c | Daimler | 1935 | | Re-issued post-war |
| 30d | Vauxhall Car | 1935 | | Re-issued post-war |
| 30e | Breakdown Car | 1935 | | Re-issued post-war |
| 30f | Ambulance (grey with red cross) | 1935 | | Re-issued post-war |
| 30g | Caravan Trailer | 1936 | 1941 | |
| 32 | Chrysler 'Airflow' Saloon | 1934 | | Renumbered 30a |

from the Rolls, Daimler and Vauxhall because the Ambulance body simply wouldn't fit on it. The only way to distinguish between a 24a and a 30f is the colour. The latter has a grey body and a red cross. Two radiators were used, both 'Bentley' types; earlier, the plain one without the badge or overriders,

and then after the introduction of the 36 series, the type with the winged 'B' above the radiator bars. It runs on the large tyres. When the Ambulance was dropped from the set, it was replaced by 30g CARAVAN TRAILER which was another one piece casting and it is the only one of the group that was not

*Fig. 57. 30a Chrysler 'Airflow' saloon.*

*Fig. 59. The post-war 30e.*

re-issued post-war. With small tyres and a wire towing hook it was issued 'For use with the Saloon Cars in Dinky Toys Nos. 24 and 30' in 1936 and joined the boxed set in 1937. Some of the latest issue have the roof light windows filled in, no doubt caused by wear on the die, and at some point the name 'Meccano' was added to the wording 'Dinky Toys Made in England' cast inside the roof. The wheels could be black or some other colour, and the bodies were always two tone with the lighter shade above the waistline: cream/blue, grey/red, two-tone green, fawn and chocolate and various other combinations.

## 30 Series—Post-war

All the 30 series except the Caravan were re-issued for varying lengths of time after the war, with very small body changes in two cases. The chassis of the Rolls, Daimler and Vauxhall were initially the same as before with two triangular holes in the base, but later these were filled in giving a much more solid structure. The grilles were unchanged. The ridged hubs carried black tyres, and sometimes a treaded tyre more normally associated with the military vehicles was used. The chassis were always black and the range of body colours drastically reduced.

30a CHRYSLER 'AIRFLOW' SALOON has no casting changes and still did not have a chassis. It was only available for a short time and was finished in green, cream, blue or red. 30b ROLLS ROYCE CAR is found in shades of blue and fawn. 30c Daimler can be fawn, green and cream. These two were both available for about four years. 30d VAUXHALL is scarcer being in for only two years, and came in brown, green and yellow. 30e BREAKDOWN TRUCK has a slight casting change in that the rear cab window is now filled in. It is single tone red, green or grey. 30f AMBULANCE is fitted with the post-war 36 series chassis and the first issues are found with the windows open as before, but later all the rear windows (those behind the cross) were filled in. The bodies were grey or cream with red crosses. The radiator carried the Bently badge.

### 30 SERIES—POST-WAR

| Cat. No. | Model | Intro. date | Comments |
|---|---|---|---|
| 30a | Chrysler 'Airflow' Saloon | 1948 | Re-issue |
| 30b | Rolls Royce | 1950 | Re-issue |
| 30c | Daimler | 1950 | Re-issue |
| 30d | Vauxhall | 1948 | Re-issue |
| 30e | Breakdown Truck | 1948 | Re-issue |
| 30f | Ambulance | 1948 | Re-issue |

Fig. 58. The 2 chassis for 30b, c and d, the earlier one on the left

# Road-Rail Services for Hornby Railways

## By "Tommy Dodd"

THE various miniature motor vehicles of the Meccano Dinky Toys Series have made possible the splendid fun of operating road services in conjunction with the trains running on Hornby railways. This month I am dealing with a recent introduction that is of special interest; that is the Mechanical Horses and Trailer Vans included in No. 33R of the Series of Meccano Dinky Toys. These realistic little vehicles are finished in the colours of the four British railway groups, and therefore which-ever real group is followed as the prototype of the miniature railway, the appropriate road vehicles can be used.

Just as the real ones do, the Meccano Dinky Toy Mechanical Horses and Trailers form together an articu-lated unit, the front end of the Trailer being supported on, and coupled to, the tail of the power unit. This articula-tion renders the whole unit extreme-ly flexible, and cap-able of manoeuvring readily within close restrictions of space.

The whole idea in introducing into real practice the so-called "mechani-cal horse" was to produce a motor unit occupying no more space than the four-legged horse used for railway cartage work almost exclusively until recent years. And of course the mechanical horse on wheels had to be as easily persuaded this way or that as the real horse on legs. This was not an easy thing to attempt, as anyone will realise who has seen a carter getting his horse to back a van in a confined space between various obstructions. However, the problem was solved by the three-wheeled units, that have become such familiar sights during the past few years.

Naturally the Meccano Dinky Toy reproductions—No. **33R**—are very similar to the originals, both in details of construction and finish. The horse unit is a three-wheeler as in actual practice, and is fitted as usual with rubber tyres. The bonnet of the vehicle has the radiator repre-sented in relief on the front, and there is also the regis-tration number plate and a spotlight. At the sides of the bonnet are represented the usual louvred openings. Behind the cab the frame narrows, and on it between the rear wheels is mounted what we may term a coupling block. This has a slot pierced in it in the centre, into which the tongue of the tow-bar of the Trailer fits. The coupling block widens towards the rear, and its surface gradually slopes down rearwards. The reason for this construction

will soon become apparent.

A feature of the real units is that special coupling gear is fitted, so that when the "horse" is backed on to the trailer the two become automatically coupled together. Similarly this operation can be reproduced with minia-ture ones if the Trailer Van is restrained from moving backwards, as it would be, for instance, when standing against a Goods Platform. The swivelling coupling and unit and dummy supporting wheels at the front of the van must be set straight, then if the Horse unit is backed up carefully, square with the Van, the coupling tongue on the latter will ride up the slot of the coupling block on the Horse and will settle in the slot. It is restrained from wandering by the raised edges of the coupling block, which guide it safely into the slot. Very young "drivers" of these vehicles may need a little practice before they are able to do this correctly each time, but the older boys will have no difficulty at all. The ability to couple Horse and Van in this manner adds greatly to the fun of operating them.

The Trailer Vans are attractive vehicles. All have the swivelling coup-ling and supporting

A busy scene at the Goods Platform on a jointly-operated Hornby railway. Mechanical Horses and Trailer Vans in L.M.S.R. and G.W.R. colours are shown backed up to the platform.

unit at the front end, and the rear runs on the usual rubber-tyred wheels. Large opening doors are represented at the rear. The floor level at this end is conveniently low for loading and unloading purposes.

The L.M.S.R. units are finished in the familiar Midland red of that company, except that the upper part of the van body and the cab roof of the Horse are finished in black. The initials "L.M.S." decorate each component of the unit, and the words "Express Parcels Traffic" stand out boldly on the upper surface of the Van sides. Similar decoration schemes are used for the L.N.E.R. and S.R. units, with the L.N.E.R. dark blue and the familiar Southern green taking the place of the red of the L.M.S.R. vehicles. An interesting variation also is that the full title "Southern Railway" appears on the Trailer Vans of that company, and not merely the initials.

The G.W.R. units are finished in an extremely attrac-tive manner. The standard brown and cream used for the company's coaching stock and road motors is employed, brown being used for the Horse and Van lower bodywork. The upper parts of the Horse cab and the Van body are cream. Each component of the unit carries the new G.W.R. monogram, and below this on the Van sides appear the words "Express Cartage Services."

## 33 Series—Mechanical Horses and Trailers

The three-wheeled Mechanical Horse used to be quite a popular form of tractor unit, especially for use in areas where space was limited and a fair amount of manoeuvring was required to be done. It was a particular favourite with the railway companies, though also used by other enterprises.

33 MECHANICAL HORSE AND FIVE ASSORTED TRAILERS was released in mid-1935, and all the individual items remained in production until the war with two of them being re-issued post-war. However, by 1939 the set had changed to MECHANICAL HORSE AND FOUR ASSORTED TRAILERS, though the same number was used. The trailer that was no longer part of the set was 33d BOX VAN which was sold separately. 33a MECHANICAL HORSE is a single casting with a slot between the rear wheels to accept the hook of the trailers. This hook is part of a tinplate pressing which is common to all the trailers, and also carries the dummy wheels which support the trailer when it is detached from the tractor unit. The colour of the tractor unit, green, blue, yellow, etc. is also found on the various different trailers. 33b is the FLAT TRUCK and 33c the OPEN WAGON. Apart from the heights of the ends and sides, the only difference between them is that the flat Truck has two lugs cast in on the bed which, when it is used as part of 33f PETROL TANK WAGON, serve to retain the tinplate tank in place. This was either red with 'Esso' decals or dark green with 'Wakefield Castrol' transfers, though both colours have been seen without any transfers at all. The wagon is usually the contrasting colour to the tank, i.e. red tank with green wagon and green tank with red wagon. 33c OPEN WAGON is used for the base of 33e

Fig. 60. The 33 Set of Mechanical Horse and 5 assorted trailers, with the alternative liveries of the box van shown.

*Fig. 62. The 4 liveries of the Mechanical Horse and Trailer Van.*

DUST WAGON. The tinplate top has an opening hatch and is most commonly found in turquoise blue on a yellow or cream trailer, but it must be borne in mind that the tinplate insert was readily removable and would fit any 33c TRAILER, so that it is hardly possible with the lack of contemporary documentation to say what was or was not a colour combination issued by the factors. 33d BOX VAN was at first available as part of the Set, but later it was omitted and was only available on its own. The base is diecast with a neat tinplate pressing for the roof and sides. It came plain in a variety of colours though frequently green, or green with 'Meccano Engineering For Boys', or blue with 'Hornby Trains British and Guaranteed' transfers.

33w MECHANICAL HORSE AND OPEN WAGON issued after the war was a combination of 33a and 33c. It was no longer possible to buy the two items separately, which is the reason for the allocation of a different number. There are no casting differences, though the date of issue can be ascertained from the wheels. The commonest colour is that of the latest issue, a bright blue Horse and cream Trailer, though brown, yellow and olive green are also found. Despite the colour, the latter is *not* an American Army issue! Renumbered 415.

33r RAILWAY MECHANICAL HORSE AND TRAILER VAN came in four different versions. They were available as one unit for which the above number was used, or separately, 33Ra RAILWAY MECHANICAL HORSE and 33Rd TRAILER VAN, but the four were not issued together as a set. The four available liveries were LMS, LNER, GWR, and SR, and they were accurately painted in the correct railway company colours. As so often happens with railway items, the SR vehicle is less common than the others, and the one in the photograph has had its wheels and tyres overpainted, probably by its original owner, and its cream roof has been painted black. Available from late 1935 to 1940, and utilising the castings of 33a and 33d.

*Fig. 61. The post-war 33w/415, Mechanical Horse and Open Wagon.*

## 33 SERIES—MECHANICAL HORSE AND TRAILERS

| | | | | |
|---|---|---|---|---|
| 33 | Mechanical Horse and Five Assorted Trailers | 1935 | 1937 | Available until introduction of next item |
| 33 | Mechanical Horse and Four Assorted Trailers | 1937 | 1940 | |
| 33a | Mechanical Horse | 1935 | 1940 | Issued post-war as part of 33w |
| 33b | Flat Truck | 1935 | 1940 | |
| 33c | Open Wagon | 1935 | 1940 | Issued post-war as part of 33w |
| 33d | Box Van | 1935 | 1940 | Available without decals or with 'Hornby' or with 'Meccano' |
| 33e | Dust Wagon | 1935 | 1940 | May have been issued post-war |
| 33f | Petrol Tank | 1935 | 1940 | Available without decals or with 'Esso' or with 'Castrol' |
| 33r | Railway Mechanical Horse and Trailer Van | 1935 | 1940 | Available in LMS, LNER, GWR, SR liveries |
| 33Ra | Railway Mechanical Horse | 1935 | 1940 | Liveries as 33r |
| 33Rd | Trailer Van | 1935 | 1940 | Liveries as 33r |
| 33w | Mechanical Horse and Open Wagon | 1947 | 1957 | Re-issue of 33a & 33c |
| 415 | | | | Renumbering of 33w |

## 35 Small Cars

These small, virtually 'OO' scale cars are quite good representations of real vehicles. The set is the smallest dimensionally and certainly numerically amongst the smallest issued, consisting as it does of only three vehicles. Quite why this group was issued in this scale is not clear, because their issue is some two years before that of Hornby Dublo Trains, and there was very little else compatible issued except perhaps 29c DOUBLE DECKER MOTOR BUS. The set was introduced in April 1936 using one piece castings and the same sort of all-rubber wheel/tyre as the Motor Bikes, but of smaller diameter.

35 SMALL CARS consisted of 35a SALOON CAR which is often given the misnomer, 'Austin 7 Saloon' by today's collectors, though Dinky did not themselves fall into this trap. Undoubtedly the rear end is Austin 7, but the front wings and radiator grille show it to be a Triumph Super 7. The colours are single-tone grey, turquoise and shades of blue or duo-tone grey or blue, with the darker shade on the spare wheel cover on the rear. It was re-issued post-

### 35 SMALL CARS

| Cat.<br>No. | Model | Intro.<br>date | Deletion<br>date | Comments |
|---|---|---|---|---|
| 35 | Small Cars | 1936 | 1941 | Consists of 35a,b,c, only |
| 35a | Saloon Car | 1936 | 1948 | |
| 35az | Fiat Two-seater Saloon | | | See: French Dinky Products |
| 35b | Racer | 1936 | 1957 | Renumbered 200 |
| 35c | 'M.G.' Sports Car | 1936 | 1948 | |
| 35d | Austin 7 Car | 1938 | 1948 | |
| 200 | Midget Racer | | | Renumbering of 35b |

war in single-tones only and can be found in grey and blue. 35b RACER is a model of the M.G. R type and was initially released with an open cockpit and painted red, and then with an integral driver and painted silver with a red grille, though the colours do overlap and there are some red ones with drivers and some silver ones without. It was re-issued post-war with driver in red and silver. After renumbering to 200 it was known as a MIDGET RACER. 35c 'M.G.' SPORTS CAR is based on the M.G. Midget or P type and came in maroon, dark blue, red or green with silver on the radiator, screens, steering wheel and spare wheel. On its post-war release the colour range was reduced to red and green, and only the radiator was silvered.

35d AUSTIN 7 CAR was modelled on the Austin 7 Opal 2-seat tourer and as the catalogues say: 'This model is the same as No. 152c (included in the Royal Tank Corps Light Tank Set) except that it is finished in a range of different colours.' It is not quite the same as there is no hole in the seat for a driver but this is the only difference, both having an otherwise identical casting and a wire windscreen surround. The cars are normally single-tone blue, yellow, grey or green, but some are also two-tone with a different colour on the spare wheel at the rear, for example, yellow with orange spare. The steering wheel is silver, as is the grille. It was released in 1938, later than the others but concurrent with the military version. Re-issued post-war without the wire screen, it is found in fewer colours: fawn, blue and yellow and there is no two-toning or silver on the steering wheel.

*Fig. 64. The 35 Series Small Cars, showing the duo-tone paint schemes on 35a and 35d.*

*Fig. 67. The pre-war 36 Series Motor Cars.*

from the time of introduction of the 36 series in mid-1938 until manufacture ceased during the war. If the whole vehicle is available, a 36 is easily distinguishable from a 24 by the presence of the drivers and passengers which are an essential part of the model, for they were advertised as 'Motor Cars (With Drivers, Passengers, Footmen)'. It is possible that very late on some were issued without people, but these would be *very* late items when the exigencies of war precluded the manufacture of any more parts but when the factory still had a stock of bodies and chassis suitable for assembly.

Two different materials were used for the people. The saloon cars had small lithographed tinplate ones in the front seats and the open cars had diecast drivers. The tinplate people were made in pairs with the inside arm touching, and consist of two separate pieces of tin, one for the front and one for the back. The driver and passenger are respectively a man in a blue suit without a hat and a lady in a cream dress with a blue hat. The driver and footman are both in navy blue livery with red collars and cuffs, wearing blue chauffeurs' hats. The detail of the lithography is quite fine and it is a pity they are not more easily seen through the windows. The diecast driver looks more female than male and has her hands on the steering wheel at ten and four. A peg on her bottom fits into a hole in the driving seat to secure her behind the wheel.

The chassis, which is common to all six cars, carries slots to take the tabs of the tinplate people and is more realistic than that on the 24s, having sidelights on top of the wings and dummy transmission underneath. The cutaway at the rear accommodates a caravan towing hook if so required. The grilles are more accurate being distinctly 'Rover', 'Salmson', etc. and were all 'silver' plated. The Bentley grille has the winged 'B' cast in on the cowling, and was also used instead of the plain grille on the 24 series cars and ambulance. The body was usually painted a different colour from the chassis, though sometimes it was just a different shade of the same colour, i.e. light grey body, dark grey chassis, light green body, dark green chassis, etc. Apart from these a whole gamut of other colours are found—red, maroon, black, blue, fawn, brown, yellow and all of these in various shades.

## 36 Series—Motor Cars

The 36 series of cars has very similar body styles to six of the 24 series cars, and indeed if you found just the body shell in the bottom of a box you could have difficulty allocating it to the correct group. However, each body does have certain differences such as a changed angle on the bonnet louvres, a grille fitted within the bodywork, etc., so that in the unlikely event of just the body turning up a careful comparison of it and the pictures of the two series will enable it to be identified. Despite the similarity, the original 24 dies were not modified to produce the 36s because both ranges were in production together

Fig. 65. Driver and Footman in 36c Humber Vogue Saloon.

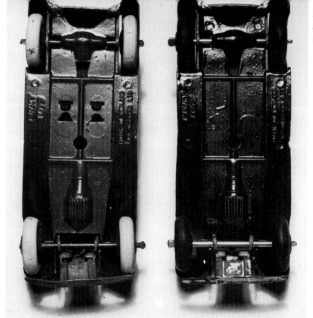

Fig. 68. 36a Armstrong Siddeley (Limousine) pre-war.

Fig. 69. 36b Bentley (2-seater sports coupé) pre-war.

Fig. 70. 36c Humber (Vogue saloon) pre-war.

Fig. 71. 36d Rover (Streamlined saloon) pre-war.

Fig. 72. 36e British Salmson (Two-Seater sports) pre-war.

Fig. 73. 36f British Salmson (Four-Seater sports) pre-war.

Fig. 74. 36g Taxi with driver.

36 MOTOR CARS (WITH DRIVERS, PASSENGERS, FOOTMEN) were first put on the market in mid-1937, were still available in 1941 and were re-issued post-war. 36a ARMSTRONG SIDDELEY (LIMOUSINE) WITH DRIVER AND FOOTMAN is similar to the 24 series Limousine but with detail changes on the bonnet louvres and door handles. The bonnet has been extended to enclose the realistic Armstrong grille. 36b BENTLEY (TWO-SEATER SPORTS COUPÉ) WITH DRIVER AND PASSENGER bears many similarities to the Sportsman's Coupé but carries the Bentley grille with badge and over-riders. 36c HUMBER (VOGUE SALOON) WITH DRIVER AND FOOTMAN has a longer bonnet than the 24 series Vogue to accommodate the flush-fitting Humber grille. 36d ROVER (STREAMLINED SALOON) WITH DRIVER AND PASSENGER is like the 24 Super Streamlined Saloon but has an additional side door pillar and a very recognisable Rover grille. 36e BRITISH SALMSON (TWO-SEATER SPORTS) WITH DRIVER is little different from the 24 Two-seater Sports but is easily distinguishable by the hole in the seat for the driver and the Salmson grille. The driver is painted in a variety of colour schemes. She may have a green, brown, or even red coat; grey, black, brown or red gloves and scarf; brown, black or silver hair . . . The tinplate screen is more usually 'solid' than 'open'. 36f BRITISH SALMSON (FOUR-SEATER SPORTS) WITH DRIVER has the same significant features as 36e and bears a similar relationship to the 24 Four-seater Sports. It does not, however, have a spare wheel on the tail.

36g TAXI WITH DRIVER is frequently thought of as being part of the set. It was never available in a box with the others but always on its own. The driver and steering wheel are part of the chassis casting and the grille is part of the body casting, so that the whole vehicle is constructed of two main pieces only held together by the axles. The same item was re-issued post-war and the earlier can be distinguished not only by the smooth wheel hubs but by the existence of the open back window. The roof, wings and interior are always black but the body comes in shades of green, blue, maroon, yellow, red, grey and fawn, i.e. the colours that are found on the 36 cars. The 'Taxi' sign on the roof and the Hackney Carriage licence plate on the rear are in black and silver.

## 36 SERIES—PRE-WAR

| Cat. No. | Model | Intro. date | Deletion | Comments |
|---|---|---|---|---|
| 36 | Motor Cars (with Drivers, Passengers, Footmen) | 1937 | 1941 | |
| 36a | Armstrong Siddeley (Limousine) with driver and footman | 1937 | 1941 | Re-issued post-war without people |
| 36b | Bentley (Two-seater Sports Coupé) with driver and passenger | 1937 | 1941 | Re-issued post-war without people |
| 36c | Humber (Vogue Saloon) with driver and fooman | 1937 | 1941 | Re-issued post-war without people |
| 36d | Rover (Streamlined Saloon) with driver and passenger | 1937 | 1941 | Re-issued post-war without people |
| 36e | British Salmson (Two-seater Sports) with driver | 1937 | 1941 | Re-issued post-war without people |
| 36f | British Salmson (Four-seater Sports) with driver | 1937 | 1941 | Re-issued post-war without people |
| 36g | Taxi with driver | 1937 | 1941 | Re-issued post-war |

## 36 SERIES—POST-WAR

| Cat. No. | Model | Intro. date | Deletion | |
|---|---|---|---|---|
| 36a | Armstrong Siddeley | 1946 | 1950 | Re-issue |
| 36b | Bentley | 1946 | 1950 | Re-issue |
| 36c | Humber Vogue | 1946 | 1950 | Re-issue |
| 36d | Rover | 1946 | 1950 | Re-issue |
| 36e | British Salmson 2-Seater | 1946 | 1950 | Re-issue |
| 36f | British Salmson 4-Seater | 1946 | 1950 | Re-issue |
| 36g | Taxi | 1946 | 1950 | Re-issue |

Fig. 75. Post-war re-issues of the 36 Series Motor cars, showing the harder post-war colours.

**36 Series—Post-war**

All the 36 vehicles were re-issued post-war with certain minor changes. The chassis are the same except that the slots for the driver and passenger are filled in. (Some pre-war chassis with slots are found on very early post-war items.) The grilles are unchanged. The bodies are identical except for the deletion of the spare wheel from the tail of the Two-Seat Tourer and the filling in of the rear window of the Taxi, after its brief appearance with a rear window. The colours are common to the group but they are not as bright as those on the pre-war issues, and the range is more restricted. The chassis are always black and the body colours comparatively harsh—green, red, brown, grey, blue in various shades. There are, of course, no people.

## 38 Series—Open Sports Cars

In June 1939, *Meccano Magazine* announced a set of Open Sports Cars, numbered 38a to f. However, unlike the usual practice, these models were not available in the shops at the time or very soon afterwards. In fact, the times were unusual, because by June it was fairly obvious that war was not very far away and there was a rush to get things done before the holocaust. In common with the 39 series, which were in a more advanced stage of planning, the magazine illustrations are artists' impressions of the cars and not very good ones at that. It was widely believed that the outbreak of war would lead to a total breakdown in communications, though not in the manufacturing base, and Meccano no doubt felt that they had better advertise their wares while it was still possible to do so. There was no holocaust and Britain entered a period of 'Phoney War' in which the hostilities hardly impinged on the man in the street at all. The urgency to get things done diminished greatly, and at the same time the manufacturing capability still remained, so that it was still possible to pursue the development stages of a product, albeit at reduced speed. Therefore, three of the 38 series were actually produced and made available in June 1940, these being 38a FRAZER-NASH B.M.W., 38b SUNBEAM-TALBOT and 38d ALVIS. 38c LAGONDA and 38f JAGUAR were

| Cat. No. | Model | Intro. date | Deletion | Comments |
|---|---|---|---|---|
| 38a | Frazer-Nash B.M.W. Sports Car | 1940 | 1954/5 | Export No. 100 |
| 38b | Sunbeam-Talbot Sports Car | 1940 | 1954/5 | Export No. 101 |
| 38c | Lagonda Sports Coupé | 1946 | 1954/5 | Export No. 102 |
| 38d | Alvis Sports Tourer | 1940 | 1954/5 | Export No. 103 |
| 38e | Triumph Dolomite Sports Coupé | | | Not issued |
| 38e | Armstrong-Siddeley Coupé | 1946 | 1954/5 | Export No. 104 |
| 38f | Jaguar Sports Car | 1946 | 1954/5 | Export No. 105 |

not released until after the war, and 38e TRIUMPH 'DOLOMITE' was never issued but replaced post-war by 38e ARMSTRONG-SIDDELEY.

Over the years, the columns of modelling journals have been full of speculation as to what happened to the Dolomite and of reports that 'a friend of a friend' saw/bought one many years ago from a toyshop in Liverpool, etc. However, there is no factual evidence at all that would indicate that the model was ever produced nor indeed, to go one stage further back, that the die was ever made. Let us look at the documentary evidence that does exist. First, the *Meccano Magazine* announcement of the series in June 1939; it is clear from the release publicity in the same magazine a year later, that the models were only at the planning stage and in all probability, though the drawings had been done, the tools had not been made. Second, the Dolomite drawing itself, though still on file until at least December 30, 1946, the date of the last amendment, offers no evidence that a die had been made from the drawing. The alterations to the drawing are general to the range, i.e. the increase of axle slots from .070 to .088 was necessitated by the post-war use of a thicker gauge wire, and not only the 38 series drawings but every drawing in the factory would have been altered to accommodate this change whether the model was in production or not. The Issue 6 alteration applied to all the 38 series as it was occasioned by the use of thicker gauge celluloid for the screens. In other words, none of the amendments were caused by the unsatisfactory working of the die, and therefore none of them are any help in deciding whether one was ever produced or not. Even if a die was ever made, and now it will certainly not turn up because all the old dies have been scrapped, there will be no

proof that it ever existed until a casting is found or the toolroom or production records of the time are located. However, these have most probably been destroyed too. The probability is, on the evidence known to exist, that either the die was never made, or if it was that it was lost or damaged during the war.

As was the trend at the time, the models were all one piece castings (some with separate headlamps), with tinplate baseplates. The bases are riveted on and serve to hold the axles in place. A slot also locates the celluloid screen which slots through the body. All the bases are marked with the name of the vehicle. Pre-war, they were coated with a clear lacquer, post-war with black paint. Early issues had a thin band of silver painted round the edge of the screen to represent the frame. The steering wheel had the space between the spokes either filled in or open. The wheels were generally black and each vehicle had the seats and/or tonneau cover painted a different (matt) colour from the body. Though the six items disappeared from U.K. catalogues in about 1950, they were certainly available for four more years as they figure in export catalogues until 1954–5, and during this period batches were also released onto the U.K. market.

**38a FRAZER-NASH B.M.W. SPORTS CAR** is 'A realistic scale model of a famous car that has won many successes in motor sports', said *Meccano Magazine*—certainly realistic and very pretty, though not an accurate scale model. It was finished in various shades of blue or grey with seats in fawn and grey, though blue and red were also used. A most attractive piece is the one seen in light grey with red seats and red wheels.

*Fig. 76. The 38 series Sports Cars. Back row 38c, 38d, centre 38e, 38b, front 38f and 38a.*

38b SUNBEAM-TALBOT SPORTS CAR, 'A scale model of one of the finest equipped sports cars on the road' has separate headlamps and is found in a wide range of colours, blue, grey, red, brown, green, yellow and maroon with tonneau cover matt grey, fawn, blue, green or maroon. The red one with red wheels and a maroon tonneau is particularly delightful. 38c LAGONDA SPORTS COUPÉ was promoted as '. . . a fine model of one of the outstanding cars that will soon be familiar on our roads.' and also has separate headlamps. Usually found in maroon, grey or green, the seats are blue, green, grey, black or maroon. 38d ALVIS SPORTS TOURER is 'A scale model of a popular luxury car of the sports type' and is finished in green, maroon or blue with the seats and folded hood in grey, red, brown, blue, green or black. 38e ARMSTRONG-SIDDELEY COUPÉ is 'A handsome model that reproduces splendidly the fine lines and modern style of an attractive post-war car.' *Meccano Magazine* rather overdid the praise, as this is a rather unprepossessing vehicle and the least attractive of the 38s. Cream, grey, green or red body with grey, green, maroon, or blue seats. 38f JAGUAR SPORTS CAR was called an S.S. JAGUAR pre-war and was billed as '. . . a model that will make a special appeal to all sports car enthusiasts.' Fitted with separate headlamps, it came in blue, grey, red and brown with seats and tonneau in blue, grey, maroon and black.

*Fig. 78. The post-war re-issues of the 39 Series Saloon Cars.*

*Left rear 39c, right front 39a, centre 39c, 39f, 39d and 39b.*

*Fig. 77. The 39 Series Saloon Cars, pre-war boxed set.*

## 39 Series—U.S.A. Saloon Cars

The group of vehicles numbered 39 constitute a new concept in Dinky Toys. They had one piece diecast bodies with flowing lines and were accurate representations of specific vehicles with tinplate baseplates inscribed with the vehicle names. Though it was not the first time that Dinky had issued such accurate models, these are the first in the scale that came to be used for most of the toy cars for many years to come, and also the first to use this form of construction. These vehicles, which could be recognised for what they were from any angle and not just from the front and rear (when the radiator grille

63

| Cat. No. | Model | Intro. date | Deletion date | Comments |
|---|---|---|---|---|
| 39 | Saloon Cars -or- U.S.A. Saloon Cars | 1939 | 1941 | |
| 39a | Packard 'Super 8' Tourer | 1939 | | Re-issued post-war |
| 39b | Oldsmobile Sedan | 1939 | | Re-issued post-war |
| 39c | Lincoln 'Zephyr' Coupé | 1939 | | Re-issued post-war |
| 39d | Buick 'Viceroy' Sallon | 1939 | | Re-issued post-war |
| 39e | Chrysler 'Royal' Sedan | 1939 | | Re-issued post-war |
| 39f | Studebaker 'State Commander' Coupé | 1939 | | Re-issued post-war |

| Cat. No. | Model | Intro. date | Comments |
|---|---|---|---|
| 39a | Packard 'Super 8' Tourer | 1950 | Also 'Made in France' |
| 39b | Oldsmobile Sedan | 1950 | -1952. Issued in special colours in the U.S.A. |
| 39c | Lincoln 'Zephyr' Coupé | 1950 | -1952. Issued in special colours in the U.S.A. |
| 39d | Buick 'Viceroy' Saloon | 1950 | |
| 39e | Chrysler 'Royal' Sedan | 1950 | -1952. Issued in special colours in the U.S.A. |
| 39f | Studebaker 'State Commander' Coupé | | Also 'Made in France' |

could be identified or the name read) reflected a developing trend echoing the real world, i.e. away from a saloon body, a tourer body, and so on, that could fit any chassis and be powered by any engine, to the design of a whole car as an integral unit that could be a Ford, a Vauxhall, etc. In other words, marques with their own distinctive identity had developed, and by 1939 were sufficiently recognisable for Meccano to follow suit.

The one piece body signalled a great development in diecasting expertise, as the tools to produce such an item were much more complicated to make and operate than those for a two or three piece model. More pieces are required to produce a more intricate shape; the larger the casting, the wider the die has to open to allow ejection of the casting, and so on. The baseplates were individual to each vehicle, made of tinplate, and secured to the vehicle by the axles which slipped through lugs cast in with the body. The complexity of the casting was therefore compensated for by ease of assembly. The base was black on the inside and lacquered on the outside to produce a yellow silver finish. (The economies that were required in production, especially during the war, are exemplified by the existence of one or two of this series that have tinplate bases produced from scrap tin—in one case, pieces that had been lithographed originally as Hornby Dublo teak coaches!) Incidentally, each base has a cut-out or hole that will take the hook of the caravan if required. Despite the popularity in America of whitewall tyres, the wheels and tyres of the 39 series were always black. If you are interested in the details of how this series was created from wooden mock-ups, turn to the chapter on how Dinky Toys were made, Chapter 1.

39 SALOON CARS were all models of American vehicles and are the first group of 'foreign' cars produced at Binns Road, though the 30 series Airflow predates them. They were later designated in catalogues as U.S.A. SALOON CARS, which is a much more informative title, and were available as a set from the early Autumn of 1939 until 1941. 39a PACKARD 'SUPER' 8 TOURER is one of the two in the group with separate headlamps, and the commonest colours are green, grey, black and royal blue, though other colours are found, and it looks particularly distinctive in yellow. 39b OLDSMOBILE SEDAN has a more restricted colour range, normally found in black or green. 39c LINCOLN 'ZEPHYR' COUPÉ comes in grey and green but also yellow. 39d BUICK 'VICEROY' SALOON also has separate headlamps and is found in maroon, green and blue. 39e CHRYSLER 'ROYAL' SEDAN is usually blue, green or grey. 39f STUDEBAKER 'STATE COMMANDER' COUPÉ comes in grey, green or yellow.

The November 1939 catalogue contains the following lyrical description of the vehicles:

'The six models in this fine set are accurate scale miniatures of outstanding modern cars, each beautifully enamelled in attractive colours.

'The Packard "Super 8" Touring Sedan is a typical example of a modern American luxury car. It has an eight-cylinder 32.5hp engine, and a four-door body capable of seating five passengers.

'Another big roomy car is the Oldsmobile "Six" Sedan, which is a five-seater powered by a six-cylinder engine rated at 28.4hp

'One of the most distinctive American cars is the Lincoln "Zephyr" Coupé, which seats three passengers. It has a body of very advanced streamlined design and a V-type, 12-cylinder engine of 36.3hp

'The Buick "Viceroy" Saloon also has a very distinctive appearance, due to the beautifully streamlined design of the front wings and the bonnet. Its engine has eight cylinders in line and is rated at 30.6hp. The gear lever is mounted on the steering column.

'A good example of a seven-seater car of the sedan type is the Chrysler "Royal". A safety all-steel body with a seamless top is fitted, and the six-cylinder engine is rated at 27.34hp

'The attractively streamlined Studebaker "State Commander" Coupé is powered by a six-cylinder engine of 26.35hp. The gear-box is fitted with remote control from a lever on the steering column. The body is of one-piece seamless steel construction.'

## 39 Series—Post-war

Very soon after the factory got back to making toys after the war, the 39 series was re-issued with no changes to the body casting or to the tinplate pressing of the base. It is only by the use of ridged wheel hubs and the colour of the base that one can distinguish the later issues from the earlier. The base is now black on the outside (and grey on the inner surface). The body colours in which they were available also show some differences—yellow is not found post-war, but generally the variety of shades has increased.

39a PACKARD 'SUPER 8' TOURER was issued in various shades of brown, blue and green including a most attractive olive green. 39b OLDSMOBILE SEDAN came in greys, blues, greens, brown and fawn. 39c LINCOLN 'ZEPHYR' COUPÉ comes in grey, brown and cream and, unusually for this series, in red. 39d BUICK 'VICEROY' SALOON is normally painted in dark shades of fawn, maroon, grey, blue, etc. but occasionally in a bright colour such as green. 39e CHRYSLER 'ROYAL' SEDAN is found in a variety of colours and it is on this vehicle that one is most likely to find coloured wheel hubs, e.g. light blue with light blue wheels, cream with light green wheels etc. It was also issued on other shades of blue, grey and many different shades of green. 39f STUDEBAKER 'STATE COMMANDER' COUPÉ was available in dark shades of blue, grey, green, fawn with an occasional light shade as well. Note: The above colours are those *commonly* found, and any of the cars could be found painted in any of the darkish shades in use in the factory at the time, and even in some quite unexpected and untypical ones.

Briefly, after the war, it appears that the Studebaker and Packard were manufactured in France, for they are found with baseplates in French and some of these are fitted with French Dinky all-metal wheels.

Though deleted from U.K. catalogues in 1950, three of them were still being made until 1952 and painted in special colours for the American market, namely the Oldsmobile, Lincoln and Chrysler. (See: American Issues).

## Pre-war General—Street Furniture

Over a period of three years various POST OFFICE items were issued which eventually ended up being sold as a set. It is one of the scarcer sets because it was only available as such for a couple of years. The first two items are two Pillar Boxes: 12a PILLAR BOX GPO (General Post Office) is painted red with white 'time of collection' panels. The 'Post Office' transfer on the oval surmounting the pillar box is yellow with red printing, and an arrow points in the direction of the nearest Post Office. The crown and 'GR' (George Rex i.e. King George) are merely raised on the casting and not separately coloured. Some were issued without the oval, no doubt because this part began to cast unsatisfactorily as the die wore. As real pillar boxes of both types were used, this alteration would have caused no problems. Luckily for the collector, the Pillar boxes are marked 'Meccano Dinky Toys' down the centre of the back, thus enabling the Dinky to be distinguished easily from amongst the plethora of Pillar Boxes emanating on to the toy market at about the same time. Issued mid-1935. 12b PILLAR BOX AIR MAIL was released at the same time and used the same casting. This time it was painted blue with 'time of collection' panels and 'AIRMAIL' in white. It was not until nearly a year later that 12c TELEPHONE BOX was produced, painted cream with silver windows, and detailing picked out in red. Later it was also produced in red with silver windows and the detailing was now in black, for the Post Office changed its colour schemes to standardise on red, and Dinky followed suit. The same casting was also used post-war, but the black painting round the windows was omitted so it is easy to tell the difference. There has been some discussion that different castings were used. However, it appears that differences in size can be put down to fatigue growth even on items where cracks are not visible to the naked eye. In 1938, two figures were added: 12d TELEGRAPH MESSENGER is in mid-blue with a light brown pouch at his waist for holding the telegrams. 12e POSTMAN was at first dressed in dark blue with red bands on his cuffs and carried a dark brown bag. Subsequently, the blue and brown were both lighter and the detail red painting was eliminated. Both were re-issued post-war, on 011 and 012

respectively. 34b ROYAL MAIL VAN was the only vehicle issued in the set and it also came out in 1938. Unusually, for pre-war, this meant that a set consisted of items with different numbers. Painted Post Office red with black roof, bonnet and wings, and with the raised lettering of 'Royal Mail' picked out in black and the crown and 'GR' in gold, it is a superb model of that type of van body style so common in the mid-thirties. The oval windows at the rear are open. It was re-issued in precisely this form immediately after the war, and the van in the photograph is one of these. Subsequently, the back windows were filled in and later the roof was no longer painted black. This, added to the brighter red that was used, makes the item lose a lot of its period charm. The whole set was available until the war.

Another group of street furniture was issued in 1935; traffic lights, Belisha Beacons and road signs. Despite them all being on the same number, 47, only the road signs were issued as a set. 47a were FOUR FACE TRAFFIC LIGHTS, or 'Robot Traffic Signals', 47b were THREE FACE TRAFFIC LIGHTS and 47c were TWO FACE TRAFFIC LIGHTS. These were of two types, for the two rows of lights were either back to back or at right angles to each other—another of the few examples of more than one item being issued on the same catalogue number. Though the painting was, of course, similar for all of the traffic lights, the three and two face versions can be found with either the green or the red 'showing' in any particular direction, so that there are two painting schemes on each of these three types. Only the Four Face was re-issued post-war, the only distinguishing feature at first being that the underneath of the bases are white on first issue and black on re-release. However later, the yellow beacon on the top was deleted, being replaced with a simple white pointed finial. This 4-face Traffic Signal was renumbered 773. At first, the Belisha Beacons were advertised as being sold in pairs, but normally they could be purchased separately. Numbered 47d, they were first available in mid-1935. These beacons were named after the Home Secretary at the time of their introduction, Sir Hore Belisha. They were also available after the war with black instead of white under the base, and renumbered 777.

The set that was issued on the number 47 was

made up of 12 ROAD SIGNS, which look somewhat antiquated to the eye used to the current International Road Signs. 47e 30 MILE LIMIT was, and is, the normal speed limit in towns. 47f DE-RESTRICTION meant exactly what it said, as at that time there was not the upper limit of 70. 47g SCHOOL carries the 'Torch of Learning' emblem. 47h STEEP HILL. 47k BEND. 47m LEFT-HAND CORNER. 47n RIGHT-HAND CORNER. 47p ROAD JUNCTION. 47q NO ENTRY. 47r MAJOR ROAD AHEAD. 48s CROSSING, NO GATES signifies a Level Crossing where railway line crosses road, and the warning symbol is that of a little steam engine puffing smoke. 47t ROUND-ABOUT. Re-issued post-war with black instead of white underneath the bases. The missing letters 'i', 'l', 'o' are not items that it was decided not to introduce, but letters that might too easily be confused with others, and were not used for that reason. Available numbered 770 on the export market after being deleted from U.K. catalogue. Post-war: only available as a set.

To use the items from the previous ones issued on the number 47, you might have wanted 46 PAVEMENT SECTIONS, made from grey cardboard with the lines between the paving slabs printed a darker grey. The pieces are a standard width but vary in length, and the box contained 4 sections 30cm in length, 6 sections of 15cm and 4 of 7.5cm, plus four 90° corner pieces. The pieces were not given individual letters as it was not possible to purchase them separately. They were issued from 1937–40 and then again from 1948–50, when the colour was stone grey as opposed to the darker elephant grey previously employed.

*Fig. 79. The pre-war G.P.O. items.*

*Fig. 80. Box of 12 Pillar Boxes, Airmail.*

*Fig. 80a. The three main versions of 34b Royal Mail Van.*

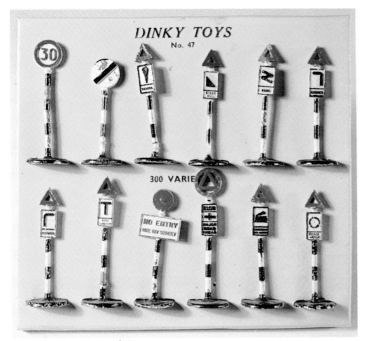

Fig. 82. No. 47, Road Signs.

| Cat. No. | Model | Intro. date | Deletion | Comments |
|---|---|---|---|---|
| 011 | | | | Renumbering of 12d |
| 012 | | | | Renumbering of 12e |
| 12 | Postal Set | 1938 | 1941 | |
| 12a | Pillar Box G.P.O. | 1935 | 1941 | |
| 12b | Pillar Box Air Mail | 1935 | 1941 | |
| 12c | Telephone Box | 1936 | 1962 | Renumbered 750 |
| 12d | Telegraph Messenger | 1938 | 1959/60 | Renumbered 011 |
| 12e | Postman | 1938 | 1959/60 | Renumbered 012 |
| 34b | Royal Mail Van | 1938 | 1952 | |
| 46 | Pavement Sections | 1937 | 1950 | |
| 47 | Road Signs | 1935 | 1954/5 | See 47e—t below. Renumbered 770. |
| 47a | Traffic Signal 4-face | 1935 | 1963 | Renumbered 773 |
| 47b | Traffic Signal 3-face | 1935 | 1941 | |
| 47c | Traffic Signal 2-face Right angle or back-to-back | 1935 | 1941 | |
| 47d | Belisha Safety Beacon | 1935 | 1963 | Renumbered 777 |
| 47e | '30 Mile Limit' Sign | 1935 | 1941 | Available until 1954/5 as part of set 47/770 |
| 47f | 'Derestriction' Sign | 1935 | 1941 | Available until 1954/5 as part of set 47/770 |
| 47g | 'School' Sign | 1935 | 1941 | Available until 1954/5 as part of set 47/770 |
| 47h | 'Steep Hill' Sign | 1935 | 1941 | Available until 1954/5 as part of set 47/770 |
| 47k | 'Bend' Sign | 1935 | 1941 | Available until 1954/5 as part of set 47/770 |
| 47m | Left-hand 'Corner' Sign | 1935 | 1941 | Available until 1954/5 as part of set 47/770 |
| 47n | Right-hand 'Corner' Sign | 1935 | 1941 | Available until 1954/5 as part of set 47/770 |
| 47p | 'Road Junction' Sign | 1935 | 1941 | Available until 1954/5 as part of set 47/770 |
| 47q | 'No Entry' Sign | 1935 | 1941 | Available until 1954/5 as part of set 47/770 |
| 47r | 'Major Road Ahead' Sign | 1935 | 1941 | Available until 1954/5 as part of set 47/770 |
| 47s | 'Crossing. No Gates' Sign | 1935 | 1941 | Available until 1954/5 as part of set 47/770 |
| 47t | 'Round-About' Sign | 1935 | 1941 | Available until 1954/5 as part of set 47/770 |
| 750 | | | | Renumbering of 12c |
| 770 | | | | Renumbering of 47 |
| 773 | | | | Renumbering of 47a |
| 777 | | | | Renumbering of 47d |

Fig. 81. Traffic Lights and Belisha Beacons.

## Pre-war General—Garages etc.

Unlike some of the other toy manufacturers, Meccano were not particularly interested in providing garages in which to park toy cars, or petrol stations at which to refuel them. This paucity of buildings is a little surprising when one considers the stations, engine sheds and so on that were produced as accessories for O Gauge trains. Perhaps the explanation is that the ones they did make didn't sell very well. However, one garage of the private, next-to-house type was made, and one petrol station which could be enhanced by a separate set of diecast petrol pumps.

45 GARAGE is designed to take two cars (yes, there were a few two car families in those days) and was introduced late in 1935. The detail of the tiled roof, window glazing, creepers growing up the walls, tulips in the surrounding flower beds and so on is lithographed onto the tinplate in soft washed out colours. The bright green base is 12.7×9cm. It is marked 'Manfd. by Meccano Ltd. Liverpool' on the apex of the rear wall.

48 PETROL STATION carries the designation 'Filling and Service Station' on its header board. The lithography is quite garish compared with the subdued tones of the garage, though the overall appearance is considerably modified by the different colour combinations used for base and roof. As well as the bright green of the example shown, blue and dark green were also used for the bases and yellow and brown for the roofs. However, the centre section printed with the windows, mechanic advancing through the open door, oil bins and so on remains the same. 'Made in England by Meccano Ltd.' appears on the right hand end underneath a 'Pratt's' advertising roundel. Introduced in mid-1935, it was in production until the war and not re-issued.

49 PETROL PUMPS were of a suitable scale to use with the Petrol Station no. 48. Mainly diecast, they are very accurate models of various types of pump in use in the 1930s. Of course, to today's eyes, they look antiquated indeed. The names, 'Wayne', 'Bowser' and 'Theo' are not brands of petrol but the makes of the pumps. All the items were re-issued post-war with little change beyond the replacement of the white rubber hoses with yellow plastic ones. Starting with the smallest one, 49b WAYNE PET-ROL PUMP is pale blue and about 4cm high. 49a BOWSER PETROL PUMP is green and about 4.5cm tall. 49d SHELL PETROL PUMP is red with a wire pump handle and stands at about 5.5cm. The tallest, 49c THEO PETROL PUMP is 6cm approximately and was blue pre-war and brown post-war. 49e OIL BIN is a necessary accompaniment to petrol pumps, and has a diecast main body with a hinging top of tinplate which raises to reveal three oil pumps picked out in red against the grey interior. It is always yellow and before the war carried the legend 'Pratts Motor Oil'. Post-war, this printing was deleted. They were renumbered 780 for the export market.

## Motor Bikes and Related Items

One of the commonest forms of transport for the private individual, especially in the 1930s was the motor bike. However, the variety of types was not reflected in Dinky production, for not only did they not make many, but all the ones that were issued were variations of the same basic casting. The full detail of the casting is easiest to see on the solo bikes and although they were not the first to be released, they will be dealt with first. The three items on no. 37 were not issued as a set, though they could be bought in boxes of six of the same thing. They were all made available at the same time—in the late autumn of 1937. The castings are one piece and approximately 4.5cm long, with a non-prototypical bar incorporated beneath the front of the engine to enable the machine to be stood upright. It is virtually impossible to say which make is being modelled, especially since many of the large heavy-duty bikes of the time looked very much the same anyway. On the solo there is no room for any maker's mark. The wheels are all solid rubber, white at first but changing to black in 1939. (They are larger than the type used on the 35 series 'Small Cars'.) Those that were re-issued later had black wheels changing to grey plastic at the very end of the production run. All pre-war bikes had silver engine and exhaust detail, whereas post-war did not; thus one can date a black wheeled one with accuracy.

37a MOTOR CYCLIST—CIVILIAN rode a black bike with silver handlebars and was dressed in blue, green or black with brown boots. His leather, close-fitting, biking cap similar in shape to a flying helmet could be brown or white. Post-war he was dressed in drab grey with a brown helmet. The helmet itself now has a little more of a peak than before, but this is a scarcely noticeable difference as the heads on all of the civilian drivers seem a little misshapen. Renumbered for export after 1954.

37b MOTOR CYCLIST—POLICE is virtually the same except for his hat, which is the flat topped type worn by police drivers then and now. The chinstrap holding it secure against the breeze is painted on the face. The post-war re-issue is much more crudely painted so that the blue of the cap merges into the blue of the uniform. Also renumbered for export.

37c ROYAL CORPS OF SIGNALS DESPATCH RIDER uses the same casting as the Police Motor Cyclist and is dressed in khaki. The bike is painted green with no silvering on the handlebars. On his upper right arm he wears the blue and white armband of the Signals Corps. Not re-issued after the war.

The Motor Cycle Combination appeared in several guises, all using the same casting which is itself very similar to that of the solo. There is an extra hole at the front of the engine casting to take the axle-like support for the front of the sidecar, and the rear axle hole has an additional piece on the side to provide extra support for the longer rear axle. No stand is needed as the unit supports itself on its three wheels. Since the combination was issued before the solo it is likely that it was designed first and that the solo is a modification of the with-sidecar casting, not the other way round. The wheels are the same, being white rubber to start with and then black immediately before the war, black again after the war, and then plastic for items that remained in the catalogues long enough. The sidecar castings are marked in the usual way up inside the casting so that there are no identification problems.

42 POLICE HUT, MOTOR CYCLE PATROL AND POLICEMEN was the lowest numbered set to make use of the combination, and it was issued in the summer of 1936. 42b MOTOR CYCLE PATROL has the same colour scheme and painting details as the solo on the bike itself, with a green sidecar with a blue tonneau cover. The post-war re-issue can be identified by the lack of detailed painting on the heads of the policemen. It was available for export after being deleted from the U.K. catalogues. 42a POLICE HUT or as it was more commonly designated POLICE BOX was diecast and painted regulation dark blue with silver detail and red round the finial. It was re-issued post-war and survived renumbering when it became 751. The only change was the use of a slightly harsher blue paint. The set was completed with two policemen both unmarked and about 4cm tall. 42c POINT DUTY POLICEMAN (IN WHITE COAT) and 42d POINT DUTY POLICEMAN in blue uniform with white gauntlets. Neither of these reappeared post-war.

43 R.A.C. HUT, MOTOR CYCLE PATROL AND GUIDES came out in late 1935 and again consisted of four items. 43b R.A.C. MOTOR CYCLE PATROL utilises the same bike but has a sidecar adapted for carrying car repair tools, not a passenger. The colour matched the blue of the driver's uniform and was a lighter shade than used by the police. The early issues had quite detailed painting showing the driver's white shirt and red sash, whereas later and post-war these niceties were omitted. The post-war run was very short. 43a R.A.C. BOX was of lithographed tinplate in blue and white, and is an accurate representation of those in use at the time and from where you could telephone for help in case of a breakdown. 43c R.A.C. GUIDE DIRECTING TRAFFIC and 43d R.A.C. GUIDE AT THE SALUTE are unmarked and are clothed in blue with red sashes, though later the painting was simplified, and stand 3.6cm tall. Only 43b was re-issued.

## MOTOR BIKES AND OTHER RELATED ITEMS

| Cat. No. | Model | Intro. date | Deletion | Comments |
|---|---|---|---|---|
| 14z | Three-Wheeled Delivery Van | | | See French Dinky Products |
| 37a | Motor Cyclist—Civilian | 1937 | 1954/5 | Export No.041 |
| 37b | Motor Cyclist—Police | 1937 | 1954/5 | Export No. 042 |
| 37c | Royal Corps of Signals Despatch Rider | 1937 | 1941 | |
| 42 | Police Hut, Motor Cycle Patrol and Policemen Set | 1936 | 1941 | |
| 42a | Police Box | 1936 | 1960 | Renumbered 751 |
| 42b | Motor Cycle Patrol | 1936 | 1954/5 | Export No. 043 |
| 42c | Point Duty Policeman (in white coat) | 1936 | 1941 | |
| 42d | Point Duty Policeman | 1936 | 1941 | |
| 43 | R.A.C. Box, Motor Cycle Patrol and Guides | 1935 | 1941 | |
| 43a | R.A.C. Box | 1935 | 1941 | |
| 43b | R.A.C. Motor Cycle Patrol | 1935 | 1948/49 | |
| 43c | R.A.C. Guide Directing Traffic | 1935 | 1941 | |
| 43d | R.A.C. Guide at the Salute | 1935 | 1941 | |
| 44 | A.A. Box, Motor Cycle Patrol and Guides | 1935 | 1941 | |
| 44a | A.A. Box | 1935 | 1941 | |
| 44b | A.A. Motor Cycle Patrol | 1935 | 1963 | Renumbered 270. Export No. 045 |
| 44c | A.A. Guide Directing Traffic | 1935 | 1941 | |
| 44d | A.A. Guide Saluting | 1935 | 1941 | |
| 270 | | | | Renumbering of 44b |
| 271 | T.S. Motor Cycle Patrol | | | Belgian market only |
| 272 | A.N.W.B. Motor Cycle Patrol | | | Dutch market only |
| 751 | | | | Renumbering of 42a |

(R.A.C. = Royal Automobile Club)

44 A.A. BOX, MOTOR CYCLE PATROL AND GUIDES was released at the same time as the R.A.C. set in 1935. 44b A.A. MOTOR CYCLE PATROL had the standard bike but a sidecar of the more angular A.A. pattern, finished in bright yellow. To begin with the driver sported a blue collar and sash, and the petrol tank was painted yellow. However, before the introduction of black tyres these expensive touches were deleted. The A.A. badge transferred on the sidecar was .5cm across but, probably on post-war re-issue, this was increased to .7cm. The brown of the driver's uniform changed to a lighter shade of fawn some time after the increase in badge size, and the very latest issue had grey plastic wheels. For U.K. sales it was renumbered 270 and for export 045. 44a A.A. BOX was of complex tinplate construction with tinplate signs on the roof directing the traveller to Liverpool, Glasgow and London, giving it a putative location somewhere near the outskirts of Manchester enabling the traveller to find the Meccano factory more easily!

From the drawing dated April 30 1935 can be seen the complexity of making this piece, especially when one considers that the walls were lithographed in three colours and only two were the same. Not surprisingly it was not re-issued post-war. Neither were 44c GUIDE DIRECTING TRAFFIC nor 44d GUIDE AT THE SALUTE, which used the same castings as the R.A.C. guides, but dressed them in brown with blue collars and sashes on the early issues.

Two further versions of the A.A.-type Motor Cycle Patrol were released post-war for overseas markets. The casting and colouring cannot be distinguished and the only difference lies in the decal applied. (A.A. = Automobile Association)

271 T.S. MOTOR CYCLE PATROL was produced for the Belgian market, (T.S. = Touring Secours)

272 A.N.W.B. MOTOR CYCLE PATROL was made for Holland A.N.W.B.

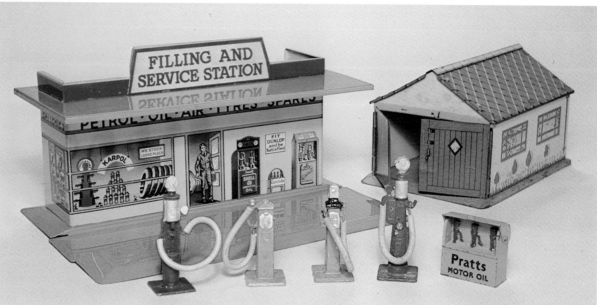

Fig. 84. No. 45, Garage, No. 48, Petrol Station and No. 49 Petrol Pumps.

Fig. 86. No. 37b, Motor Cyclist Police and 37c, Royal Corps of Signals Despatch Rider.

Fig. 86a. 37c Royal Corps of Signals Despatch Rider, showing the armband.

Fig. 92. 271 T.S. Motor Cycle Patrol and 272 A.N.W.B. Motor Cycle Patrol.

Fig. 91. Stages in the changes which occurred in the course of production, the first version is on the left, the final post-war version on the right.

Fig. 92a. Meccano drawings for the transfers for nos. 271 and 272. Of the 2 diagrams for the Belgian issue (271) only the 'T.S.' version was produced.

Fig. 85. Box of 37a, Motor Cyclist—Civilian.

Fig. 87. No. 42, Police Hut, Motor Cycle Patrol and
Policemen.

Fig. 88. No. 43, R.A.C. Hut, Motor Cycle Patrol and
Guides.

Fig. 89. No. 44, A.A. Box, Motor Cycle Patrol and
Guides.

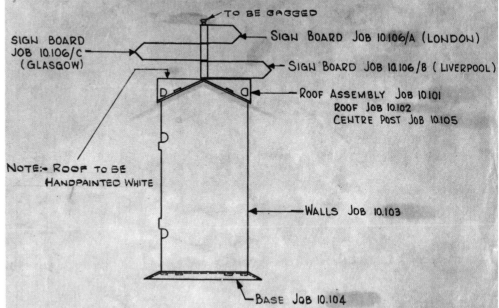

Fig. 90. Works Drawing of Miniature A.A. Hut.
Complete, first drawn in April 1935.

# The most attractive miniature house and furniture ever produced

## "DOLLY VARDEN" DOLL'S HOUSE

READY IN MID-JULY

The Couch Hammock, Tennis Net, Garden Seats, Dinky Toys Garage, Motor Cars and Figures, and the Hornby Trees and Hedging featured in the illustration below are not included with the Doll's House and Garden.

### DIMENSIONS
The following are the overall dimensions of the "Dolly Varden" Doll's House when built up ready for play.

Length ... ... 1 ft. 6¾ in.
Depth ... ... 10¼ in.
Height ... ... 1 ft. 6¾ in.

The open container on which the house stands measures 3 ft. 3½ in. by 2 ft. 5½ in.

When the house is dismantled and packed in container, the overall dimensions of the complete parcel are ¾ in. x 1 ft. 7½ in. x 2 ft. 5½ in.

The "Dolly Varden" Doll's House illustrated below has been specially designed for use with Dinky Toys Doll's House Furniture.

The house is collapsible and the exterior is designed to represent a half-timbered dwelling, while the interior decorations ... ich are printed in nine colours, are in an attractive mod ... tyle.

... orced leather board is the material of which the house is co ... cted, and when set up it is as strong as a wood structure. The ... iner, which also is made of reinforced leather board, opens out to show a lovely garden with Tennis Lawn, Carriage Drive, and Rockery, providing an exquisite setting for play with Dinky Toys and Hornby Trees, Hedging, etc.

The Doll's House will be ready in mid-July.     Price 9/6

## DINKY TOYS
### DOLL'S HOUSE
# FURNITURE

The extension of the range of Dinky Toys to include true-to-scale modern Furniture will be welcomed by all who know the charm of these perfect miniatures. Much care and thought have been given to the design, finish and presentation of every article of this Furniture series. There is a tone and individuality of style about them which cannot fail to appeal. Among the most attractive features are the opening doors and drawers. This furniture is far superior to anything of its kind that has ever before been produced for the delight and pleasure of young people. The Dinky Toys Furniture is now ready. See it at your dealer's.

**DINING-ROOM FURNITURE. Dinky Toys No. 101**
Price of complete set 2/3

| | | | |
|---|---|---|---|
| No. 101a. | Table | ... | 5d. each |
| No. 101b. | Sideboard (Opening doors) | ... | 9d. „ |
| No. 101c. | Carver Chairs | ... | 3d. „ |
| No. 101d. | Chairs | ... | 2d. „ |

Supplied in walnut finish only.

**BEDROOM FURNITURE. Dinky Toys No. 102**
Price of complete set 2/11

| | | | |
|---|---|---|---|
| 102a. | Bed | ... | 6d. each |
| 102b. | Wardrobe (Opening door) | ... | 9d. „ |
| 102c. | Dressing Table (Opening drawers) | ... | 10d. „ |
| 102d. | Dressing Chest (Opening drawers) | ... | 6d. „ |
| 102e. | Dressing Table Stool | ... | 2d. „ |
| 102f. | Chair | ... | 2d. „ |

Supplied in two colour schemes—mauve and gold; light green and dark green.

**KITCHEN FURNITURE**
Dinky Toys No. 103
Price of complete set 2/6

| | | | |
|---|---|---|---|
| No. 103a. | Refrigerator (Opening door) | ... | 8d. each |
| No. 103b. | Kitchen Cabinet (Opening doors and drawer) | | 10d. „ |
| No. 103c. | Electric Cooker (Opening door) | | 6d. „ |
| No. 103d. | Table | ... | 4d. „ |
| No. 103e. | Chair | ... | 2d. „ |

Supplied in two colour schemes—light blue and white; light green and cream.

**BATHROOM FURNITURE. Dinky Toys No. 104**
Price of complete set 2/-

| | | | |
|---|---|---|---|
| No. 104a. | Bath | ... | 6d. each |
| No. 104b. | Bath Mat | ... | 1d. „ |
| No. 104c. | Pedestal Hand Basin | ... | 6d. „ |
| No. 104d. | Stool | ... | 2d. „ |
| No. 104e. | Linen Basket (Opening lid) | ... | 4d. „ |
| No. 104f. | Toilet (Lifting lid) | ... | 4d. „ |

Supplied in two colour schemes—pink and white; light green and white.

**MECCANO LIMITED
BINNS ROAD, LIVERPOOL 13**

*Fig. 97. The announcement of 'Dolly Varden' items in the July 1936 Meccano Magazine.*

## Dolly Varden

In producing the 'Dolly Varden' Doll's House and Dinky Toy Doll's House Furniture, Meccano broke into completely new territory: toys for girls. This was a very uncharacteristic move and one not often repeated. The doll's house was collapsible and made out of re-inforced leather board, a material not used for any other item in the Dinky toy range, and was most probably 'made out', as it would not have been worth setting up tooling just for this. The furniture was diecast and tinplate and therefore produced in the same sort of way as the rest of the toys. Unfortunately, the metal used was heavily contaminated and it is rare to find a piece that does not suffer severely from fatigue.

The introductory advert in the July 1936 *Meccano Magazine* claims that it is 'The most attractive miniature house and furniture ever produced'. Lines Bros., who had been in the doll's house business for some time, would no doubt have taken exception to this statement and doll's house collectors today probably would also, but the furniture has captured the essence of Thirties' design and is therefore exceedingly collectable for those interested in the era. There is nice attention to detail, for you can see yourself in the tinplate mirrors, the fridge has a sheet of printed tinplate food just inside the opening door, and the backing board to which the individual items are strung can be used as a carpet for that particular room, being printed with tiles or carpet borders where appropriate.

Dolly Varden Doll's House
101 Dining Room
102 Bedroom
103 Kitchen
104 Bathroom
Not re-introduced after the war

**FOOTNOTE:**
Dolly Varden is a character in 'Barnaby Rudge' by Charles Dickens, whose name had been used in preceding years for marketing attractive female clothing, for she has 'the face of a pretty, laughing girl, dimpled, and fresh, and healthful—the very impersonation of good humour and blooming beauty'.

## Other Pre-war Vehicles

Whilst most of the pre-war vehicles and accessories were produced in sets there are a few items that weren't, and although some can be dealt with in other sections, e.g. 22g SEARCHLIGHT LORRY with Military Vehicles, there are a small handful that do not really 'fit' anywhere. It is this rather strange mixture that is dealt with in this section.

22c MOTOR TRUCK was issued in 1935 as a replacement for the lead 22c MOTOR TRUCK that figures in the 22 MODELLED MINIATURES. (Note: Dinky never issued two different vehicles on the same number at the same time. All items were out of production before the number was re-allocated.) To distinguish the two numbered 22c, this one is often referred to as the 'little Bedford' but this is nomenclature given by collectors and not by Meccano. From this description it can be gathered that it is of a fairly small scale, being only 8.5cm long. The casting is one piece and before the war sported an open rear window in the cab. It came in red, green and blue. Post-war, the rear window was filled in and it was painted brown, green or red. It was used as the basis of the 22g SEARCHLIGHT LORRY.

22g STREAMLINED TOURER and 22h STREAMLINED SALOON have identical front ends with sweeping grilles of the 'Airflow' type. They were issued subsequent to the 32/30a Chrysler 'Airflow' Saloon, and not only have grilles integral with the casting but are of a smaller scale altogether. Both have one piece body castings but the Tourer has a separate windscreen/dash/steering wheel casting which is an interference fit in interior channels in the body. They were both available in red, blue and cream though black has been seen on the Tourer. The wheels could be a contrasting colour to the body. A real oddity is the Streamlined Saloon fitted with a plain tinplate baseplate, French Dinky turned metal wheels and treaded tyres, indicating post-war production. The ones seen are painted bronze and are very pretty indeed. A mint example turned up in the late Sixties and when the authors queried its authenticity of the French Dinky Factory at Bobigny, they received a very cagey reply which, while not admitting they made it nor how many were made, did not deny it either! We have wondered ever since just what they were up to.

25s SIX-WHEELED WAGON is a one piece casting (with small diecast insert for the dash/steering wheel unit) and is merely the 151b THREE-TON TRANSPORT WAGON in civilian guise. It was issued in early 1938 and billed in advertising as 'An interesting model of a modern three-ton wagon. In assorted colours.' One can quibble with its modernity and with the assortment of colours, for it is usually found in brick red, a reddish brown. It does not have the tinplate insert in the back that comes with 151b to provide seating accommodation and the pictures in the catalogue show it without tin tilt, but some examples are found with this accessory painted grey. Post-war, the colours included reddish brown, green and blue and it was normally fitted with the grey tilt. (Note: The tilt for this vehicle and 25b COVERED WAGON are not interchangeable as the bed of 25b is noticeably longer.)

34a ROYAL AIR MAIL SERVICE CAR was issued in late 1935. Although it is on the same digits as the 34b ROYAL MAIL VAN it was not packaged with it. (34b was part of 12 Postal Set.) Nor was it ever sold with 12b AIR MAIL PILLAR BOX. It is a very attractive and accurate casting and provides a very accurate representation of the real vehicle which was only used for about a year in 1934–35 for promotional purposes by the Post Office. Its special body was made by Duple Bodies and Motors Ltd. and fitted to a Morris Commercial Chassis. Both real vehicle and model were finished in a most attractive blue and carried a finely drawn decal 'ROYAL AIR MAIL SERVICE' in silver and the crown and post horn in gold.

60y REFUELLING TENDER is a pretty model of the Aircraft Refuelling Tender made by Thomson Bros. and a common sight on airfields at the time. The number fits in with those allocated to the aeroplanes but the scale does not, for the planes are about 200th scale while this model is about 72nd. The original was a very large vehicle indeed and was basically a fuel tank on wheels powered by a small Ford sidevalve engine at the rear. A derelict example was recently still in existence, lying at the side of a shed at Brooklands and being used by the children as a climbing frame! The *Meccano Magazine* and current

| Cat. No. | Model | Intro. date | Deletion |
|---|---|---|---|
| 22c | Motor Truck | 1935 | 1950 |
| 22g | Streamlined Tourer | 1935 | 1941 |
| 22h | Streamlined Saloon | 1935 | 1941 |
| 25s | Six-Wheeled Wagon | 1938 | 1948 |
| 34a | Royal Air Mail Service Car | 1935 | 1941 |
| 60y | Refuelling Tender | 1938 | 1941 |

catalogues specifically say that it is a 'Thompson' but the decalling on the sides reads 'SHELL AVIATION SERVICE' in yellow on either side, colouring which shows up well against the red of the main body. (The wings are black and the driver and cockpit brown.) A tinplate base was fitted to a single piece casting and is retained by the rear axle and front wheel mounting. The base is marked 'Dinky Toys' but the casting is not, so care should be taken, if the base is missing, that this vehicle is not mixed up with the 'Skybird' version which is slightly smaller and just as scarce, the scarcity being occasioned by it not being introduced until early 1938 and not being reintroduced after the war. The front wheel is the type used on the 35 series and the rear are like those used on the motor bikes.

There are very few pre-war buses and fire appliances and these are detailed with the post-war releases in a later section. Post-war re-issues of 23 series racing cars and 25 series commercials are also dealt with in a later post-war section.

*Fig. 98. No. 22c, Motor Truck.*

Fig. 93. No. 101, Dining Room.

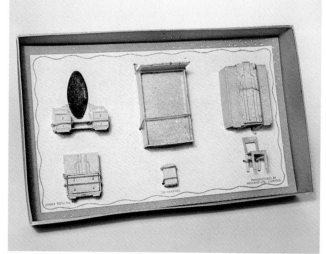

Fig. 94. No. 102, Bedroom.

Fig. 95. No. 103, Kitchen.

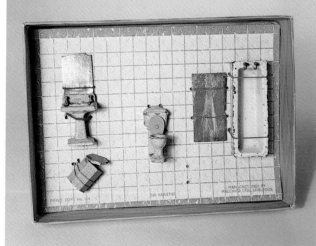

Fig. 96. No. 104, Bathroom.

*Fig. 99. No. 22h, Streamlined Saloon and 22g Streamlined Tourer.*

*Fig. 100. No. 25s, Six-Wheeled Wagon, post-war on the left, pre-war on the right (Note: the driver was not supplied with the wagon).*

*Fig. 101. No. 34a, Royal Air Mail Service Car.*

*Fig. 102. No. 60y, Refuelling Tender.*

## Military—Pre-war

The early years of Dinky Toys were the years of appeasement when the thought of another war was so terrible that the politicians, the press and therefore the public pushed war thoughts and preparations to the backs of their minds. The British toy manufacturers did likewise and neglected the toy army vehicle almost completely, except, of course, Britains whose main production always had been military, soldiers at first, then vehicles, etc. Although the very first set of Dinky vehicles incorporated a tank, it was not until Autumn 1937, a mere two years before the official declaration of war, that the first of what are thought of as 'Military Dinkies', the Medium Tank, was put on the market. *Meccano Magazine* reflected this attitude as well and there are very few general educational articles that mention anything even slightly militaristic. The first acknowledgement of the true situation came in December 1937 with the publication of one of their 'publicity' articles where the relevance of Dinky Toys to real life is explained. Details are given of the history of tanks, the one upon which the toy is modelled being detailed and the attributes of the toy expanded upon. By now, pacifism had changed to chauvinism and the attitude of the article can be thought to be too pro-British, an understandable fault for the time but one that distorts historical reality, as there is no mention at all of the importance for tank development of the Renault. And we weren't fighting the French, were we?

The pre-war production life of all the military Dinkies was very short as the Meccano factory was turned over to war work and the use of valuable metal for toys and other non-essential items was stopped. The records no longer exist which said when the last batch of this or that went down the production line or was shipped from the factory, and best that can be said is that it was sometime during 1940 or 1941. Where products were still being manufactured they were being made in greatly reduced quantities so that what the lad hadn't got for Christmas 1939 was most likely to stay unacquired.

Despite their very old fashioned looks, the tanks, guns, etc. are very good models as can be seen from the *Meccano Magazine* reproduction. The vehicles on which they were modelled were still of World War I design. Dinky did not, in fact, start producing a

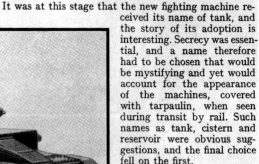

# The Royal Tank Corps
## Unique Models in the Dinky Toy Series

THE mechanisation of armies is a process now in progress in all countries, and in the main it is taking two courses. On the one hand cavalry regiments are being transformed into mechanical units, making use of armoured lorries and trucks instead of horses; on the other hand the armoured fighting machines known as tanks are being rapidly developed and increased in number.

The tank made its first appearance as a practical fighting machine during the Great War. This had only been in progress a few months when it was realised that the machine-gun had given the defensive a great advantage, for a few resolute men armed with machine-guns could hold up what formerly would have been overwhelming forces of infantry. This lesson was learned in many bitter struggles, and the idea of providing infantry with protection was then taken up and steadily worked out in the face of many difficulties.

The tank may be regarded as the land equivalent of the armoured ship. A land battleship has been the dream of many inventors. In the 15th century a German military enthusiast produced a four-wheeled van equipped with guns, which was drawn by horses into a position where it could do most damage. Others tried similar schemes, but their machines had the defects that they were not self-propelling, and could only travel on roads, for they were not fitted for rough and broken ground. The development of the petrol engine overcame the first of these difficulties, for this made the machine self-contained; the second was met by the use of caterpillar or creeper track.

It is impossible to name any one man as the inventor of the tank, but the first suggestion for its employment seems to have come from Colonel Swinton, who as early as October 1914 had seen the necessity for some sort of armoured machine that could force its way through

Army tanks of the Medium type crossing Magdalen Bridge, Oxford. A splendid Dinky Toys representation of this tank is shown on the opposite page.

barbed wire, climb across trenches, and crush machine guns. In that month he submitted to the War Office a design for armoured machine gun tractors mounted on creeper tracks.

This was the beginning of the story. The idea was not received with great enthusiasm, and it was not until the following year that experiments were begun. In the meantime similar suggestions had been made independently at the Admiralty, and a committee under the direction of Mr. Tennyson d'Eyncourt, Director of Naval Construction, had been formed to consider them. When this became known a combined effort was made, which resulted in the production of a machine designed by Mr. Tritton and Lt. Wilson. This was capable of climbing a vertical wall 5 ft. high and of crossing a ditch 8 ft. wide, and its success in trials early in 1916 led to orders for the construction of a large number and the training of men to handle them.

It was at this stage that the new fighting machine received its name of tank, and the story of its adoption is interesting. Secrecy was essential, and a name therefore had to be chosen that would be mystifying and yet would account for the appearance of the machines, covered with tarpaulin, when seen during transit by rail. Such names as tank, cistern and reservoir were obvious suggestions, and the final choice fell on the first.

The appearance of the new weapon in actual warfare was an instant success, although comparatively few were used. This was in an attack in September 1916, when the battle of the Somme had almost come to a standstill. Only 60 tanks were available, but their effect was amazing. The first news of the success of this powerful new weapon reached the public in a dramatic message, sent back by an observer in a low-flying aeroplane, from which the attack was being observed. This read: "A tank

The Dinky Toys Light Tank, No. 152a. It is fitted with a wireless mast, and is correctly armed and protected.

*Fig. 103. An article from Meccano Magazine December 1937.*

is walking up the High Street at Flers, with the British Army cheering behind."

The Germans were amazed and terrified as the monster approached them slowly but irresistibly, and it seemed as if means of overcoming their resistance without the appalling losses of previous offensives had been discovered. There were still many who had no faith in the tank, however, and on one occasion orders for the construction of large numbers actually were cancelled. Fortunately higher authorities intervened.

The improved tanks devised after the first successes showed their efficiency in the great offensive at Cambrai in 1917. The Germans responded to the challenge of the tanks by constructing similar machines, and tank met tank for the first time near Villers-Bretonneux in April 1918. After an artillery duel a British tank knocked out the first German tank encountered by three hits with 6-pounder shells, and two others that came up in support backed away. The earliest German tanks were only lightly protected on the roof, and their thick side armour covered their creeper tracks, making them clumsy. They could not cross large shell holes or trenches more than 8 ft. wide. In number and effectiveness the German tanks never reached the standard of the British machines.

The full value of the tanks was not realised until 1918, when they had been made still more efficient and were used in greater numbers. They helped to stem the great German offensive in March of that year; and in the battle of 8th August at Amiens, the first of the great hammer blows that ended the War, 400 tanks played a great part in the resounding success achieved. The Germans were demoralised when tanks were employed in force. If the war had continued they would have been called upon to face even larger numbers, for orders had been given for the production of 6,000 larger tanks, which were designed for all-round fire and did not suffer from the high internal temperature that was a great defect of the earlier models.

The tanks of the present day are far superior in every respect to those used in the Great War. The equipment of the Royal Tank Corps consists of two types, the Medium Tank "Mark" II and the Light Tank "Mark" VI. The former is a 12-ton vehicle with a 90 h.p. engine of the air-cooled aero type. It has a speed of 22 m.p.h. and carries a crew of five.

The Dinky Toys Medium Tank No. 151a, which is illustrated on this page, is a splendid miniature of this type. Its turret swivels completely round, and in front of it is a miniature two-pounder quick-firing gun, with a machine gun beside it, while the driver's look-out manhole is below and to the right. A further machine gun is placed on each side of the tank. On top of the turret is a vertical tube representing the one that in the real tank houses a Morse signalling lamp. To the rear is a look-out manhole, known familiarly in the Corps as "The Bishop's Hat," and behind this is the radio mast. Every detail is shown, even the headlights being covered by metal protecting boxes, exactly as in the prototype.

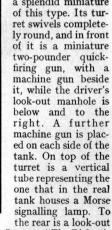

Some of the Medium Tanks of the Royal Tank Corps are equipped with a mortar instead of a two-pounder. The purpose of this is to enable it to fire smoke-shells in order to create a smoke-screen behind which an advance can be made. A tank equipped in this manner is known as a "close support" tank.

The light tank is much faster than the medium one. It weighs 4½ tons, and its lorry engine of 25 h.p. gives it a speed of 40 m.p.h. There are three men in its crew. In the Dinky Toys Series it is represented by the Light Tank No. 152a, shown in the lower illustration on the opposite page. Its turret swivels round in the same manner as its original. In front of it are two machine guns, and on top are two look-out manholes and a radio mast. There is a tubular projection along the right-hand side to represent the exhaust pipe and silencer. Both Dinky Toys Tanks are scale models, one sixteenth full size, and are fitted with creeper tracks that move independently in a fascinating manner as they are pushed along.

The Tanks, Medium and Light, are included in the Dinky Toys Royal Tank Corps Sets Nos. 151 and 152 respectively. Next month we shall describe the other components of these Sets.

Army dispatch riders waiting while a light tank crosses a road during manœuvres on Salisbury Plain.

The Dinky Toys Medium Tank, No. 151a, is correct in detail, even to the protected boxes for headlights.

range of 'modern' fighting vehicles until the 1950s. Compared with other land vehicles that Dinky were making at the time, the castings incorporated a great amount of detail; not only were there rivet heads by the score, but radio aerials were fitted and a new concept, moving parts, was incorporated, for the turrets rotated as did the searchlight, and the gun elevated. All the items were available separately or (except for 22s) in sets, packed in lovely blue boxes with details of the real vehicles printed on the top and representations of green trees printed on the inside. Helpfully, the models contained in the box are printed on it, so should you find a base without a lid you will know to which set it belongs. These boxes are worth money in their own right even if there are no models inside. The vehicles were painted either gloss or matt green and some that began gloss now look matt, as bad overall fatigue can stretch the paint and cause it to become matt. Some of the items were produced in camouflage but were never advertised as such in Dinky Catalogues or *Meccano Magazines*. It was however advertised as 'Mechanised Army Camouflaged' in a wartime Hamleys catalogue. Children also camouflaged some, so turn to the Plane section for the characteristics of factory finish camouflage.

In describing the vehicles, the order runs back to front beginning with the last set, which was first advertised the month after war broke out in October 1939 and is the biggest of the lot. It is also one of the scarcest Dinky Sets.

**156 MECHANISED ARMY SET.** Consists of Sets: 151 without the driver; 152 without the driver; 161; and 162. Introduced at 12/6 it was the most expensive set you could buy, and the price had risen to 18/6 by the introduction of Purchase Tax in 1940, and to 25/– with tax in 1941. (For details see below)

**151 ROYAL TANK CORPS MEDIUM TANK SET.** Four units plus a driver were included in this set. 151a MEDIUM TANK was issued both with and without the white triangular squadron marking and ran on chain tracks of intricate configuration. The chain is peculiar to Dinky Toys and is not one of the types available for use with the Meccano Sets. It is normally bright unpainted metal.

The body is diecast with a tinplate chassis. More tinplate is used on 151b, the TRANSPORT WAGON the military version of 25s which not only has this material for the chassis but also for the tilt and the back insert, which incorporated a floor and bench seats along either side. There are holes in the seats to take the pegs on the bottoms of the passengers which had to be purchased separately. A spare wheel was fitted on the offside just behind the driv-er's door. 151c was the COOKER TRAILER which was equipped with a bent wire stand underneath that could be folded down so that it was freestanding. A nice little touch was incorporated inside, a small seat with a hole in it for the cook. (No separate cook was issued but a seated Private would do nicely!) This was one complete casting without base. The all cast 151d WATER TANK TRAILER completed the mobile parts of the set, but it also included 150d the

ROYAL TANK CORPS DRIVER dressed in dark blue with a dark blue beret.

152 ROYAL TANK CORPS LIGHT TANK SET had three vehicles and a driver. 152a the LIGHT TANK was all diecast except for the same chain tracks that were used on the Medium Tank. It also came with or without squadron markings. Supplies of chain must have run out at some time, because

Fig. 104. Mechanised Army Set.

Fig. 108. 162 18-Pounder Quick Firing Field Unit, showing the boxed set and, in the foreground, the tractor unit with rubber wheels.

Fig. 105. 151 Royal Tank Corps Medium Tank Set.

Fig. 109. 150 Royal Tank Corps Personnel.

Fig. 106. 152 Royal Tank Corps Light Tank Set.

Fig. 107. 161 Mobile Anti-Aircraft Unit.

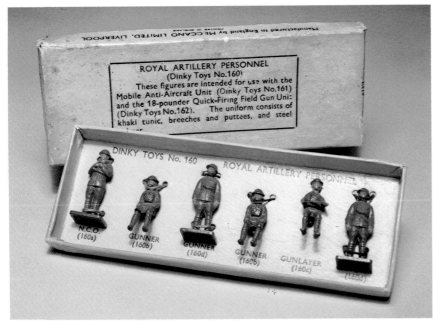

Fig. 110. 160 Royal Artillery Personnel.

Fig. 111. 22s Searchlight Lorry.

some examples have been found with the black rubber wheels normally used for the 35 series instead of the cast spiked wheels and chain track. Another using a tinplate base was 152b the RECONNAISSANCE CAR, a most attractive vehicle which is normally found with black tyres but sometimes has white. (Military vehicles were normally fitted with black tyres.) This is an exceedingly good model of a Morris Commercial. The AUSTIN 7 CAR, no. 152c is an open tourer with a wire windscreen surround. The casting is the same as the civilian 35d and was issued at the same time. It has, of course, 35 series black rubber tyres. There's a hole in the seat to take the 150d TANK CORPS DRIVER which is the last item in the set. More Austin 7 Tourers are found in camouflage than any of the rest of the military items, but they are still extremely difficult to find possibly because this casting is very susceptible to fatigue. There have been suggestions that there were a variety of moulds used for this vehicle because of the differing measurements that are found from one casting to another. However, it is our opinion that these differences have been caused by expansion of the castings due to metal fatigue.

**161 MOBILE ANTI-AIRCRAFT UNIT.** This is a small set consisting of only two items. 161a, the LORRY WITH SEARCHLIGHT uses the basic casting of 151b but instead of the tilt it has a new tinplate floor with two 'seats' (i.e. holes) behind the cab, and a diecast swivelling searchlight is fitted in a slightly modified floor casting. This tows the A.A. GUN ON TRAILER which is mainly diecast but has tinplate flaps (part of the gun platform) which fold up for towing and down for firing and a tinplate range-finder. Seven seated gunners can be accommodated but no figures were included in the set.

**162 18-POUNDER QUICK-FIRING FIELD UNIT.** The No. 162a LIGHT DRAGON tractor unit was used to tow an ammunition trailer and gun. Again it is diecast with chain tracks and the facility for fitting personnel into peg holes. (No figures supplied.) Some were fitted with 35 series rubber wheels and later ones, which could be pre-war and also post-war, have a circular protruberance underneath the base similar to the fitting required for a search-

| Cat. No. | | Intro. date | Deletion | Comments |
|---|---|---|---|---|
| 22s | Searchlight Lorry (small) | 1939 | 1941 | See: 22c Lorry |
| 37c | Royal Corps of Signals Despatch Rider | 1938 | 1941 | See: Motor Bikes |
| 150 | Royal Tank Corps Personnel | 1937 | 1941 | |
| 150a | Royal Tank Corps Officer | 1937 | 1941 | |
| 150b | Royal Tank Corps Private | 1937 | 1941 | Seated. Also available in boxes of 12 |
| 150c | Royal Tank Corps Private | 1937 | 1941 | Standing. Also available in boxes of 12 |
| 150d | Royal Tank Corps Driver | 1937 | 1941 | Also available in boxes of 12 |
| 150e | Royal Tank Corps N.C.O. | 1937 | 1941 | Also available in boxes of 12 |
| 151 | Royal Tank Corps Medium Tank Set | 1937 | 1941 | |
| 151a | Medium Tank | 1937 | 1941 | Re-issued post-war |
| 151b | Transport Wagon | 1937 | 1941 | See: 25s. Re-issued post-war |
| 151c | Cooker Trailer | 1937 | 1941 | Available post-war |
| 151d | Water Tank Trailer | 1937 | 1941 | Available post-war |
| 152 | Royal Tank Corps Light Tank Set | 1937 | 1941 | |
| 152a | Light Tank | 1937 | 1941 | Re-issued post-war |
| 152b | Reconnaissance Car | 1937 | 1941 | Re-issued post-war |
| 152c | Austin 7 Car | 1937 | 1941 | |
| 156 | Mechanised Army Set | 1939 | 1941 | |
| 160 | Royal Artillery Personnel | 1939 | 1941 | |
| 160a | Royal Artillery N.C.O. | 1939 | 1941 | |
| 160b | Royal Artillery Gunner | 1939 | 1941 | Seated |
| 160c | Royal Artillery Gunlayer | 1939 | 1941 | |
| 160d | Royal Artillery Gunner | 1939 | 1941 | Standing |
| 161 | Mobile Anti-Aircraft Unit | 1939 | 1941 | |
| 161a | Lorry with Searchlight | 1939 | 1941 | |
| 161b | A.A. Gun on Trailer | 1939 | 1940 | Re-issued post-war |
| 162 | 18-Pounder Quick Firing Field Unit | 1939 | 1941 | |
| 162a | Light Dragon Motor Tractor | 1939 | 1941 | Re-issued post-war |
| 162b | Trailer | 1939 | 1941 | For ammunition Re-issued post-war |
| 162c | 18-Pounder Gun | 1939 | 1941 | Re-issued post-war |

light (as 161a). Some castings have no holes for figures. 162b TRAILER is a covered ammunition trailer, all diecast and 162c is an 18-POUNDER QUICK-FIRING FIELD GUN mainly diecast but with a tinplate shield.

Two more sets containing figures only were also issued. 150 ROYAL TANK CORPS PERSONNEL contained: 1×150a OFFICER, dressed in khaki and standing with binoculars in his hands; 2×150b PRIVATE sitting down with arms crossed; 2×150c PRIVATE standing at ease; and 1×150e N.C.O.

walking forward. All the lower ranks are dressed in blue, and all have the Tank Corps Beret on their heads which is also blue. Not contained in the set but part of the same series is 150d DRIVER who is similar to the seated private but has his arms out to grasp the steering wheel. All seated personnel have pegs on their bottoms.

160 ROYAL ARTILLERY PERSONNEL are all dressed in khaki and wear tin helmets, also khaki. The set consists of: 1×160a N.C.O. standing with

*Fig. 112. 153a Jeep.*

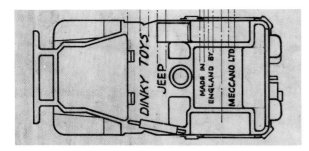

his hands in front of him; 2×160b GUNNER sitting down with his hands on his knees; 1×160c GUN-LAYER sitting down with his hands out so he could be used as a driver, but officially he isn't; 2×160d GUNNER standing with his hands at his sides. Pegs as 150 personnel.

It is very easy to confuse Dinky and Skybirds military personnel as they are about the same size and neither are marked with the manufacturer's name. The Skybirds people are on the whole more carefully modelled and painted and have a more delicate look to them.

Not contained in any of the sets and a bit of an oddity is 22s SEARCHLIGHT LORRY. It is to a much smaller scale than the rest of the military items and is the 22c LORRY with a diecast searchlight in the back. The searchlight is too big as it is the searchlight used on 161a.

**Military—Post-war Re-issues and 153a**

In 1946, as production of Dinky Toys resumed, some of the pre-war items were re-issued. It appears that there were stocks of castings available in the factory because some models exhibiting both pre-

## MILITARY POST-WAR

| Cat. No. | Model | Deletion | Comments |
|---|---|---|---|
| 151a | Medium Tank | 1953/4 | Re-issue |
| 151b | Transport Wagon | 1953/4 | Re-issue. Export No. 620 |
| 152a | Light Tank | 1954/5 | Re-issue. Export No. 650 |
| 152b | Reconnaissance Car | 1953/4 | Re-issue. Export No. 671 |
| 153a | Jeep | 1954/5 | Same casting as 25j. Export No. 672 |
| 161b | A.A. Gun on Trailer | 1954/5 | Re-issue. Export No. 690 |
| 162 | Field Gun Unit | 1954/5 | Re-issue. Export No. 691 |

and post-war characteristics are to be found. If a model has any post-war trait at all, such as wheels with hub ridges, it must be regarded as of post-war issue, though a major part of it may have been made much earlier. Two items most probably fall into this category, for while examples are found with post-war wheels and collectors with long memories can remember buying them in the late forties, they did not appear in any Meccano literature that has so far come to light as being officially re-issued. These are 151c COOKER TRAILER and 151d WATER TANK TRAILER. Some were available for export after deletion from the U.K. catalogues. (see U.S. issues)

However, the first post-war batch of military subjects, with one exception, the Jeep, were re-issues with the expected change to ridged wheels and one or two other minor differences. The most obvious change was in the colour: gloss green was not used at all, the colours being matt green or less commonly matt brown. A tyre with a light tread was also commonly used.

151a MEDIUM TANK. Whilst until recently this was regarded as not having been available post-war, information has recently come to light showing that it was. An example with black underbase and no squadron markings was found in Canada. It also appears in U.K. and Canadian literature and in a U.S. dealer's price list between the years of 1946 and 1949.

151b TRANSPORT WAGON came with or without the tinplate floor insert that enabled passengers to be seated in the back.

152a LIGHT TANK appeared with black chain tracks and the white squadron markings were standard.

152b RECONNAISSANCE CAR looks particularly attractive in brown, as does 161b A.A. GUN ON TRAILER

162 FIELD GUN UNIT was only available as a set and consisted of: LIGHT DRAGON MOTOR TRACTOR usually with black chain tracks, but there are examples with black 35 series rubber wheels, and a round protruberance on the base. It is a matter of conjecture whether these are pre- or post-war. Instead of these being sent to the retailer in boxes of six as was standard practice at this time, there were three, each towing the Ammo Trailer and 18-Pounder Gun, though it was not necessary to buy the three pieces together. They are often referred to, because of this, as the 'Light Dragon Set', but Dinky didn't issue them in this way under a separate number, though many a lad must have bought the three together. AMMUNITION TRAILER and 18-POUNDER GUN complete the re-issues. The group was renumbered 691 for the export market.

153a JEEP with the white U.S. star on the bonnet is the first post-war designed military vehicle, and it shared a casting with 25j the civilian Jeep. Mainly diecast, it has a tinplate windscreen panel and is always matt green. The one photographed is a bit of an oddity, for it has pre-war wheels and steering wheel, i.e. smooth hubs and the space between the spokes filled in. However, it can't be pre-war because the vehicle itself wasn't designed until war-time.

# CHAPTER 3

# The Ships

The introduction of the Dinky Toy range which followed the success of the Hornby Modelled Miniatures is well covered elsewhere in this book and since Meccano Ltd. were reported as receiving suggestions from the public in the early months of 1934 for new models to add to the range, it would indeed have been surprising if no requests for models of ships had been amongst a large mail-bag of suggestions.

As it was the Company devoted a great deal of attention and finance to new models and by December 1934 there were seventeen different waterline models available, out of a total of more than 150 Dinky toys in all. As the Company commented in the *Meccano Magazine*, 'they represent the vessel as she appears in the water when loaded down to her normal level'. The ships were to a scale of 150ft to 1 inch, of necessity a much smaller scale than the range of motor vehicles and other models intended for the 'O' gauge railway scene. The Company also commented in its advertising literature, 'It is impossible to convey in words any adequate impression of the daintiness of these models. They include every detail for which room could be found, and they are beautifully finished in correct colours.' Nearly half-a-century later, no one can argue with those comments, indeed, the wealth of detail in even the smallest models is superb and in some instances surpasses so-called detailed models produced today.

The 'Flag-ship' of the Dinky range was no less than a model of the new Cunarder 'Queen Mary', the star launch of 1934 and one which attracted a great deal of publicity, not only in this country, but also abroad.

As is sometimes the case, the name of a new vessel remains a closely guarded secret until the actual launching ceremony, but until this time the growing hulk of the new vessel is known by its yard number. The 'Queen Mary' was Liner No. 534 and

the earliest issues of the Dinky Toy model carried the full title 'Cunard White Star Liner 534'. The launch took place on September 26, 1934, and very soon afterwards the lettering beneath the model was changed to 'Cunard White Star Liner "534" "Queen Mary"', so this became the second issue of this model for a short period. By late 1934 or early 1935 the model die had changed yet again, with the removal of '534', and the lettering remained unchanged until the 'Queen Mary' model was withdrawn in 1949.

The other six Liner models were to the same scale as the 'Queen Mary' but somewhat smaller by varying degrees. All were well detailed. Two were foreign vessels, the 'Europa' and 'Rex,' and the remaining four British, and set alongside one another were an attractive sight. Apart from minor painting variations these models were unchanged until they were withdrawn as part of the general wartime cutback, and destined never to return after the war.

Numbering commenced at 51b with the boxed set numbered 51, and one is left wondering whether Meccano intended the number 51a to be used on another vessel. In addition to the individual models, the boxed set made an attractive presentation pack.

Further Liner models were planned, but only the French Lines 'Le Normandie', which was introduced into the United Kingdom in 1935 with the number 52c materialised, and this was made in the Meccano factory in Paris.

The announcement was made in the 1939 catalogue that the 'Cunard White Star Liner "Queen Elizabeth"' was to be added as number 52e, but despite very intensive research not one single model has come to light. Many collectors have been approached in the course of these enquiries, many swapmeets visited, and in some cases collectors who were sure they had the model, were disappointed when they found nothing more than a 'Queen Mary'. Just as with the 38e TRIUMPH DOLO-

MITE SALOON, it is a pity because there can be no doubt that had the model appeared it would have been just as delightful as the other ships.

The Dinky Toy series also included ten ships of the British Navy, issued individually and as a boxed set containing fourteen models. No. 50b BATTLESHIP 'HMS NELSON' was also available as 'HMS Rodney', a separate casting, but never listed as such in catalogue or magazine. In addition two types of Destroyer were listed, the 'Broke' class, and 'Amazon' class, and there were three of each of these in the No. 50 boxed set. The Destroyers and two types of submarines were flat-bottomed castings and carried no lettering.

When the Naval ships were introduced six carried names beneath the model and were advertised with these names. At some time later the names of the vessels were removed from the castings and other minor changes made. The Meccano archives have failed to throw any light on when this change was made, in fact there is virtually nothing in the official records on the ship range. In the opinion of the writer, this change most probably took place around the outbreak of war in 1939. The full-size

naval counterparts were then prime military targets and a black-out of all official information was imposed. The only feasible alternative is that the un-named models could have been produced during the later war years and as some of the Naval ships had been war casualties the models were issued anonymously. There are boxed sets which have un-named models and this lends weight to the possibility that the change took place around 1939–40, using the cardboard box with labels carrying a printing code of October, 1934. It is true also that the names of the ships were used in catalogues and the magazine issued in the early war years.

The Naval boxed set was also exported to France before the war and sold as a 'Battleship set—Flotte de guerre' and the printing on the box was in French.

The ship models were all long and slim and the earlier models are often to be found in varying stages of metal fatigue, and this condition can be seen in some of the models included in this chapter. The later models, and mainly the un-named castings, appear to be of a more stable metal mixture and on the under-sides quite bright, almost resembling aluminium. Many of the ships illustrated have been in

my collection for many years and there has been no further deterioration in their condition during this period. They have been kept in a constant dry temperature and free from vibration.

We have already questioned reference 51a and it can be nothing more than conjecture what was intended for number 52d . . .

More detailed descriptions are shown alongside each model illustrated, but at this point I would like to thank Keith Winter for the loan of his Set 51, Ken Mansfield of the Hamilton House Toy Museum in Ashbourne for his boxed 534, and my parents and relatives, who many years ago first introduced me to Dinky Toys, and provided a fascination for a lifetime.

50 Boxed set of SHIPS OF THE BRITISH NAVY mid-1934 to 1942. A large blue box containing fourteen models of warships set to capture the interest of boys of all ages. Most were one piece castings, but the larger models had gun turrets which swivelled. Wire masts were cast into the model rather than being added later. The set contained three of each type of Destroyer and two of the large Battleships, and single examples of the other ships in the range. As the following photographs of individual models show there were two castings of each of the named vessels but the actual date when the change took place is not known. As with the Famous Liners set 51, the names of the Naval vessels were also printed on the base of the box below the model which was held in place with cord.

50a BATTLE CRUISER 'HMS HOOD'. The flag-ship of the Dinky Naval ships and the largest model with four gun turrets, two fore and two aft of the main superstructure. Amidships there were three torpedo tubes on either side, very delicately cast and on the early casting the name was on the underside. An impressive miniature of what was said at the time to be the largest and most powerful warship in the world.

50b BATTLESHIPS 'NELSON' CLASS 'HMS NELSON' and 'HMS RODNEY'. Although both models were listed as 50b there were two separate castings, with a third casting when the names were omitted. The three gun turrets were on the forward deck. The under-sides of the three castings are shown and the uppermost one is the last. On the

*Fig. S2. 50a Battle Cruiser 'HMS Hood'. Length approx. 5¾".*

earliest castings the rivets for the turrets are recessed, whereas only the centre one is so treated on the un-named casting. The two named castings are definitely different—the 'Nelson' has a pronounced stud which is visible in the photograph, in the stern section, and there are other small variations.

50c CRUISER 'HMS EFFINGHAM'. Rather smaller than the 50a and 50b but again much detailed with very small single-gun turrets as part of the casting detail. Once the name had been removed from the under-side, an indentation was made beneath the forecastle, no doubt in an effort to economise on the amount of metal used.

50d CRUISER 'HMS VICTORY'. Another Cruiser, slightly smaller than the 'Effingham' with all detail cast as one. An interesting model with covered deck space. The un-named casting has been recessed more deeply beneath the forecastle but unfortunately this detail cannot be seen in the photographs.

50e CRUISER 'HMS DELHI'. The smallest of three Cruisers and the simplest casting. The second casting also has a metal-saving recess in place of the ship's name.

50f DESTROYERS 'BROKE' CLASS. A simple small casting, three of which comprised the class, and no identification lettering, not even the Dinky Toy name.

*Fig. S3. 50b Battleships 'HMS Nelson' and 'HMS Rodney'. Length approx. $4\frac{11}{16}''$.*

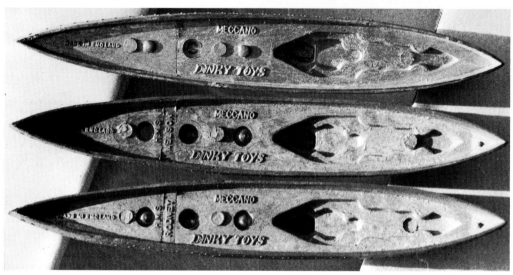

*Fig. S4. 50c Cruiser 'HMS Effingham'. Length approx. 4".*

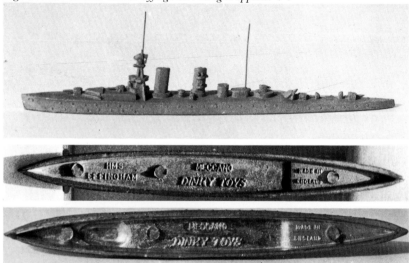

*Fig. S5. 50d Cruiser 'HMS York'. Length approx. $3\frac{7}{8}''$.*

84

Fig. S7. 50f Destroyers 'Broke' Class. Length approx. 2¼".

Fig. S8. 50h Destroyers 'Amazon' Class. Length approx. 2¹⁄₁₆".

Fig. S6. 50e Cruiser 'HMS Delhi'. Length approx. 3³⁄₁₆".

Fig. S9. Left: 50g Submarine 'K' Class. Length approx. 2¼". Centre & right: 50k Submarine 'X' Class. Length approx. 2⁷⁄₁₆".

Fig. S10. 53az Battleship 'Dunkerque'. Imported from France.

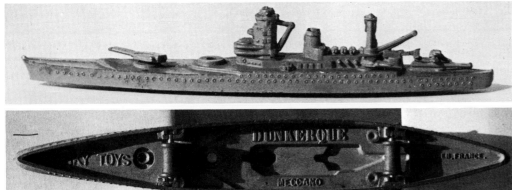

**BATTLESHIP "DUNKERQUE"**

Dinky Toys No. **53az**

Scale model of the French 26,500 ton Battleship "Dunkerque," which has an overall length of 702 ft. 9 in., and a main armament of eight 13 in. guns. (Made in the Meccano Factory in Paris) ... ... Price **9d.** each

**50h DESTROYERS 'AMAZON' CLASS.** Another small casting, hardly different to 50f but approximately 7mm shorter in length.

**50g SUBMARINE 'K' CLASS (L)**
**50k SUBMARINE 'X' CLASS (C & R).** Very simple flat-bottomed castings giving a good impression of the prototypes. The left and centre models shown are pre-war issues with wire masts: the remaining example has metal cast around the wire mast. It is perhaps not surprising that some confusion arose in the advertising of the two submarine models. In the 1934 Catalogue, 50g was listed as 'X' Class, 50k as 'K' Class. This was changed by December 1934 in a M.M. illustration and all subsequent listings. However, in the July 1936 printing of the 1937 Catalogue the numbering of the silhouette

illustrations for these two models was transposed. What prompted this change is not known—perhaps nothing more than a printer's error.

**53az BATTLESHIP 'DUNKERQUE'.** This scale model was imported from the Paris factory of Meccano some months after first release in France. This model in my collection certainly has one turret and the two small masts missing and these are all discernible. Although the models sold in France and the catalogue illustrations used in the United Kingdom have a trail of smoke back from the funnel, the model sold in this country did not have the smoke trail. This had been removed and the top of the funnel painted black, but not entirely so that part is light grey as the entire model. There is certainly

some dainty detail on this model, the only Naval vessel produced by the Company in France. The under-side carried bold lettering, and special retaining lugs were provided to hold the axles for the rollers, which on my model are a green plastic-type material. In France this model was sold boxed, with or without rollers, but only one version was listed in this country. The price remained constant at 9d.

**51 boxed sets of six FAMOUS LINERS.** The six liners were models of the flag ships of their respective shipping companies and serve as an historic reminder of the great pre-war shipping years of passenger travel on the high seas. All were one piece castings with the wire masts bedded into the metal and a great amount of detail was on each model. As

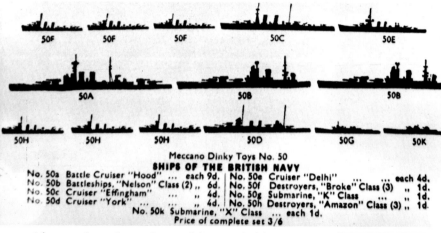

*Fig. S11. Meccano Magazine December 1934.*

**Meccano Dinky Toys No. 50**
**SHIPS OF THE BRITISH NAVY**

| | | | |
|---|---|---|---|
| No. 50a Battle Cruiser "Hood" ... each 9d. | No. 50e Cruiser "Delhi" ... ... each 4d. | | |
| No. 50b Battleships, "Nelson" Class (2) „ 6d. | No. 50f Destroyers, "Broke" Class (3) „ 1d. | | |
| No. 50c Cruiser "Effingham" ... ... „ 4d. | No. 50g Submarine, "K" Class ... „ 1d. | | |
| No. 50d Cruiser "York" ... ... „ 4d. | No. 50h Destroyers, "Amazon" Class (3) „ 1d. | | |

No. 50k Submarine, "X" Class ... each 1d.
Price of complete set 3/6

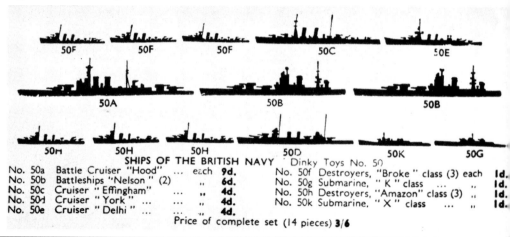

*Fig. S12. 1937 Catalogue.*

**SHIPS OF THE BRITISH NAVY** Dinky Toys No. 50

| | | |
|---|---|---|
| No. 50a Battle Cruiser "Hood" ... each 9d. | No. 50f Destroyers, "Broke" class (3) each 1d. | |
| No. 50b Battleships "Nelson" (2) „ 6d. | No. 50g Submarine, "K" class ... „ 1d. | |
| No. 50c Cruiser "Effingham" ... „ 4d. | No. 50h Destroyers, "Amazon" class (3) „ 1d. | |
| No. 50d Cruiser "York" ... ... „ 4d. | No. 50k Submarine, "X" class ... „ 1d. | |
| No. 50e Cruiser "Delhi" ... ... „ 4d. | | |

Price of complete set (14 pieces) 3/6

with most boxed sets the models were held in with Meccano cord to make a fine presentation set. The base of the box was covered with a grained light-blue paper, to resemble the water, upon which the names of the various ships was printed, and the front side of the bottom half dropped down for easy viewing of the models. The price of this set on introduction was 3/6, 2d cheaper than the cost of six individual models, and this was unchanged until early 1939 when the price was reduced to 2/11. The individual prices were then set at 6d each. However, by the Autumn 1939 the boxed set reverted to a price of 3/6 and the single ships were then 7d each. The front label of the box was printed in blue, whilst the end label was red printing on yellow background, and carried an October, 1934 printing code. The following individual models are also shown 'under-side', and it is interesting to note that the lettering is not standardised, nor are the names consistently placed. In addition 51b and 51d have lettering with the stern on the left as it is read, the remaining four reading from the bows on the left.

**51b NORDDEUTSCHER LLOYD 'EURO-PA'.** The largest model in the six Liners, a former 'Blue Riband' holder of the Atlantic, and originally priced at 9d. Later 6d and then 7d. A black hull with white decks and superstructure, and light brown funnels, on either side of which were air vents finished in red. There were detail differences in paint finish from time to time, and generally those models

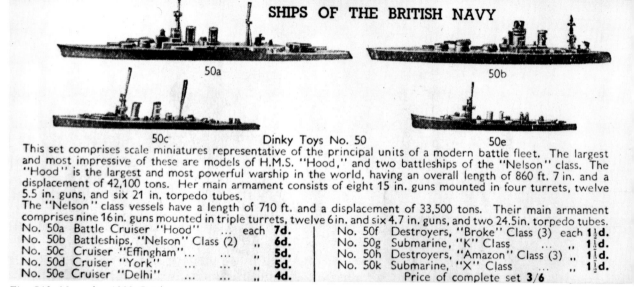

**SHIPS OF THE BRITISH NAVY**

Dinky Toys No. 50

This set comprises scale miniatures representative of the principal units of a modern battle fleet. The largest and most impressive of these are models of H.M.S. "Hood," and two battleships of the "Nelson" class. The "Hood" is the largest and most powerful warship in the world, having an overall length of 860 ft. 7 in. and a displacement of 42,100 tons. Her main armament consists of eight 15 in. guns mounted in four turrets, twelve 5.5 in. guns, and six 21 in. torpedo tubes.
The "Nelson" class vessels have a length of 710 ft. and a displacement of 33,500 tons. Their main armament comprises nine 16 in. guns mounted in triple turrets, twelve 6 in. and six 4.7 in. guns, and two 24.5 in. torpedo tubes.

| | | |
|---|---|---|
| No. 50a Battle Cruiser "Hood" ... each 7d. | No. 50f Destroyers, "Broke" Class (3) each 1½d. | |
| No. 50b Battleships, "Nelson" Class (2) „ 6d. | No. 50g Submarine, "K" Class ... „ 1½d. | |
| No. 50c Cruiser "Effingham" ... ... „ 5d. | No. 50h Destroyers, "Amazon" Class (3) „ 1½d. | |
| No. 50d Cruiser "York" ... ... „ 5d. | No. 50k Submarine, "X" Class ... „ 1½d. | |
| No. 50e Cruiser "Delhi" ... ... „ 4d. | Price of complete set 3/6 | |

*Fig. S13. November 1939 Catalogue.*

included in the boxed sets were given a little more attention. Other vents were also picked out in red on some models, as were the sides of the life-boats on the upper deck, 12 on either side. The two on the rear-lower deck were often left plain white. On some models the tops of the funnels were blacked.

**51c ITALIA LINE 'REX'.** Yet another 'Blue Riband' liner, and the one which eventually surrendered supremacy to the 'Queen Mary'. Again a

finish of black hull and white decks, but the Italia Line's colours were carried on the funnels—top half of each funnel was red, lower half white with a green line around just below the red top, and a red disc below the green line on the funnel sides. Air vents were also picked out in red. Also originally 9d, later 6d and 7d.

**51d CPR 'EMPRESS OF BRITAIN'.** The Canadian Pacific Railway Company had a substantial interest in shipping and this was their latest addition. The model was all white with light-stone funnels and light brown masts and hatch-covers. The model was included in the set had plain white lifeboats; on the individually sold one in my collection these are dark brown. Originally priced at 8d, and adjusted later to 6d, then 7d.

**51e PENINSULAR AND ORIENTAL STEAM NAVIGATION COMPANY 'STRATHAIRD'.** This model is unfortunately affected by fatigue, the front bows showing signs of splitting apart. However, this was a smaller ship than the previous three, which was also finished in white, with funnels in light stone and forecastle and masts in light brown. Issued at 6d and remained unchanged until Autumn 1939 when it was increased

to 7d. The under-side of this model had rather more stepped levels following the contours of the decks.

**51f FURNESS WITHY 'QUEEN OF BERMUDA'.** The smallest of the six models and the one to carry the most attractive livery and a great amount of detail for a model so small: 3⅞in or 99mm in length. The hull was light grey, white deck superstructure and lifeboats picked out in brown. The funnels were red with black top-quarter and black

*Fig. S15. 51b Norddeutscher Lloyd 'Europa'. Length approx. 6½".*

*Fig. S16. 51c Italia Line 'Rex'. Length approx. 6".*

*Fig. S17. 51d C.P.R. 'Empress of Britain'. Length approx. 5⅛".*

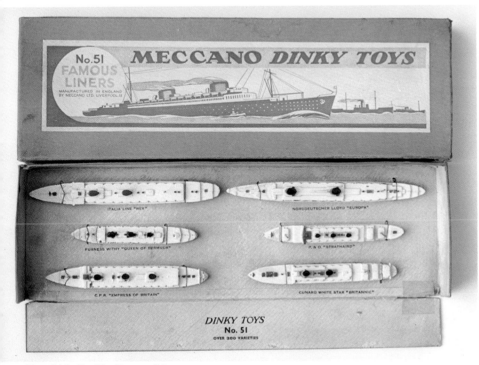

*Fig. S14. Set 51. Famous Liners.*

*Fig. S18. 51e Peninsular and Oriental Steam Navigation Company 'Strathaird'. Length approx. 4½".*

band, and the masts and front only of the forecastle were light brown. Hatch covers were grey. On the under-side the two outer round pieces of metal provide a depth into which the masts are set.

**51g CUNARD WHITE STAR 'BRITANNIC'.** The Britannic, the second of the Cunard Liners to be included in the Dinky Toys range, but not nearly so impressive a model as the 'Queen Mary'. Again finished in black and white with light brown top deck and funnels, the top third of which were black. This was the only model with lettering in the bow and stern sections.

**52 CUNARD WHITE STAR LINER 'NO. 534'.** The first boxed issue of this model which appeared in mid-1934, before the actual naming ceremony took place at the launch on September 26, 1934. The box label was a colourful artist's impression of the liner showing its massive proportions against smaller tugs and a dockside crane. The model was a two-part casting, the upper part being the top deck, with funnels and air vents, etc. and forecastle, and rear staged decks. This fitted into the main casting of the hull, which had all deck levels and a row of

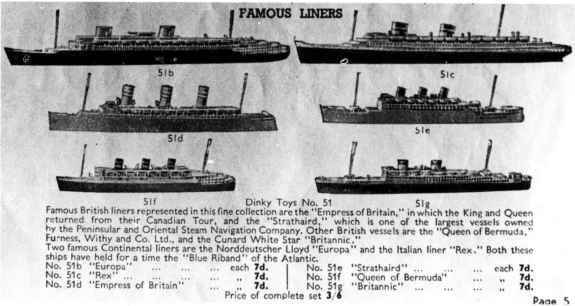

*Fig. S27 & 28. Showing two styles of illustration, one photographs, the second silhouettes—both from pre-war catalogues.*

**FAMOUS LINERS**

Famous British liners represented in this fine collection are the "Empress of Britain," in which the King and Queen returned from their Canadian Tour, and the "Strathaird," which is one of the largest vessels owned by the Peninsular and Oriental Steam Navigation Company. Other British vessels are the "Queen of Bermuda," Furness, Withy and Co. Ltd., and the Cunard White Star "Britannic."
Two famous Continental liners are the Norddeutscher Lloyd "Europa" and the Italian liner "Rex." Both these ships have held for a time the "Blue Riband" of the Atlantic.

| | | | | | |
|---|---|---|---|---|---|
| No. 51b "Europa" | ... | each **7d.** | No. 51e "Strathaird" | ... | each **7d.** |
| No. 51c "Rex" | ... | " **7d.** | No. 51f "Queen of Bermuda" | ... | " **7d.** |
| No. 51d "Empress of Britain" | ... | " **7d.** | No. 51g "Britannic" | ... | " **7d.** |

Price of complete set **3/6**

Page 5

*Fig. S19. 51f Furness Withy 'Queen of Bermuda'. Length approx. 4".*

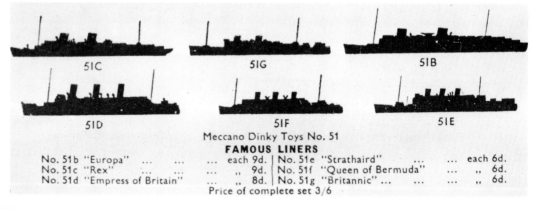

Meccano Dinky Toys No. 51
**FAMOUS LINERS**

| | | | | | |
|---|---|---|---|---|---|
| No. 51b "Europa" | ... | each 9d. | No. 51e "Strathaird" | ... | each 6d. |
| No. 51c "Rex" | ... | " 9d. | No. 51f "Queen of Bermuda" | ... | " 6d. |
| No. 51d "Empress of Britain" | ... | " 8d. | No. 51g "Britannic" | ... | " 6d. |

Price of complete set 3/6

*Fig. S20. 51g Cunard-White Star 'Britannic'. Length approx. 4¾".*

88

fifteen lifeboats on either side. The masts were a continuous piece of wire suitably bent which fitted between the two castings. The model was correctly finished in black and white, with red and black funnels, and orange or light brown masts.

52 CUNARD WHITE STAR LINER 'QUEEN MARY'. The later boxed issue has the same colourful label but the printing style has changed and the full title of the vessel is used. There are two styles of label used on the ends of the boxed issues. Neither the ends nor the fronts of the boxes carried a printing date. The under-sides of the cast-

ings showing the three variations in the title of the 'QUEEN MARY' model in order of appearance. The top casting is the earliest and space has been left beneath the '534' for a later name. The middle one is the rarest version and was produced for only a short period before the '534' was removed from the mould, even then not entirely as can be seen in the third casting—the outer inverted commas remaining. The third and final casting has the tinplate attachment carrying the small plastic—or similar material—roller wheels. These rollers were either red or gold coloured.

52c LE TRANSATLANTIC 'LA NORMANDIE' 1/6. This model was imported from the Meccano (France) Ltd. factory in Paris and was available in the United Kingdom from May or June 1935, although the History of French Dinky Toys by Jean-Michel Roulet gives the introduction as 1937. Almost identical in length to the 'Queen Mary', 'La Normandie' had larger and therefore more prominent funnels, and the model was again a two-part casting with the wire for the masts between the two parts. It was sold in a French produced box which carried the vessel's principle statistics on the card-

*Fig. S22. Later style 'Queen Mary' box.*

*Fig. S26. 'Queen Elizabeth' advertised but never issued.*

### CUNARD WHITE STAR LINER "QUEEN MARY"

Dinky Toys No. 52a
Fitted with rollers and in presentation box ...     ...     Price **1/-** each
Dinky Toys No. **52m**
Without rollers and not packed in presentation box     Price **9d.** each

*Fig. S24. '534' and 'Queen Mary' castings.*

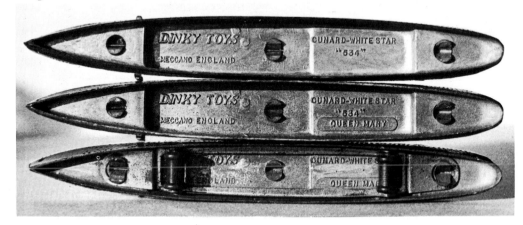

### "NORMANDIE"

Dinky Toys No. **52c**
A scale model of the French Line's giant steamship. (Made in the Meccano Factory in Paris) ...     ...     ...     ...     ...     ...     Price **1/6** each

### CUNARD WHITE STAR LINER "QUEEN ELIZABETH"

Dinky Toys No. **52e**
The Cunard White Star Liner " Queen Elizabeth," at present building at the Clydebank yard of John Brown and Co., Ltd., was launched on 27th September, 1938, by H.M. the Queen. The vessel will be completed and ready for service sometime in 1940, and her length of 1,031 ft. and 85,000 tons gross weight will make her easily the world's largest liner.
Price **1/-** each

*Fig. S23.*
*Two styles of box end labels.*

*Fig. S21. 52 Cunard-White Star Liner 'No. 534'. Length approx. 6⅞".*

*Fig. S25. 52c Le Transatlantic 'La Normandie'. Box 8" × 2⅜" × 1".*

Catalogue variations in the listing of CUNARD WHITE STAR LINER QUEEN MARY

*1934/5 Catalogue*

| | | | | |
|---|---|---|---|---|
| 52 | '534' | 1/– | mid-1934 to Autumn-1934 | 1st Issue |
| 52 | '534' 'Queen Mary' | 1/– | Autmn 1934 – | 2nd Issue |

*December 1934 Meccano Magazine*

| | | | | |
|---|---|---|---|---|
| 52 | 'Queen Mary' | 1/– | December 1934 – | 3rd Issue |
| 52a | 'Queen Mary' with rollers | 1/– | December 1934 – | 3rd Issue |

*August 1935 Catalogue*

| | | | | |
|---|---|---|---|---|
| 52a | 'Queen Mary' with rollers | 1/– | | 3rd Issue |
| 52b | 'Queen Mary' (without rollers) | | Formerly listed as No. 52. | 3rd Issue |

*July 1936 Catalogue*

| | | | | |
|---|---|---|---|---|
| 52a | 'Queen Mary' with rollers and in presentation box | 1/– | | 3rd Issue |
| 52m | 'Queen Mary' without rollers nor boxed | 9d | Formerly listed as No. 52b | 3rd Issue |

(Price of this model now reduced to 9d)

*June 1939 Catalogue*

As July 1936 listing

*November 1939 Catalogue*

| | | | |
|---|---|---|---|
| 52m | 'Queen Mary' | 1/– | 3rd Issue |

The 52a listing is not included, but this need not necessarily indicate that the model had been discontinued.

The following description appeared beneath the model in this catalogue:

'The Cunard White Star Liner "Queen Mary" holds the "Blue Riband" of the Atlantic with a record set up in September 1938. She crossed from Bishop Rock, Scilly Isles, to the Ambrose Light, off the entrance to New York Harbour, in 3 days 21 hrs 48 min., at an average speed of 31.6 knots. On the return trip eastward she achieved a record average speed of 31.69 knots.

The "Queen Mary" has a length of 1,081 ft. and provides accommodation for 2,000 passengers. Her crew numbers 1,200.'

*October 1947 Meccano Magazine*

| | | | |
|---|---|---|---|
| 52a | 'Queen Mary' with rollers | 3/6 including purchase tax | 3rd Issue |
| | | Available mid-1947 to late 1949 | |

board inner fitting, and it is perhaps an indication for the date of introduction that the inner fitting states '150 varieties'. A simple livery of black hull, white again for the upper decks and red and black funnels. At the rear of the ship is a small blue patch, picked out to represent the swimming pool. The price of 1/6 remained unchanged.

*The larger liners as advertised in the 1939–40 Catalogue.* The two listings for the 'Queen Mary' and the 'Normandie' need no further comment, but the 'QUEEN ELIZABETH' was advertised for the first and only time in this catalogue. Had it been produced it would have been slightly longer than the 'Queen Mary', but greater in depth and with taller masts. We must, regretfully, console ourselves with the thoughts of what might have been, unless of course, someone is able to produce an example.

During the mid-1970s six ships were produced which have nothing in common with pre-war issues except that they too are waterline models—running on Speedwheels! Mostly, they are metal-hulled with plastic accessories but 674 COASTGUARD AMPHIBIOUS MISSILE LAUNCH is not only all plastic but less prototypical and more futuristic than the others. All were equipped with very inefficient missile systems. Prototypes of some of these have survived. (See: 'How Dinky Toys Are Made.')

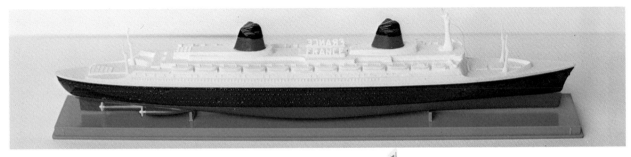

Fig. S29. The French post-war Liner 'France'—This model was sold in a presentation packing with the model on supports. The base of the hull was removable to give a waterline model with small rollers for children to push along. The model was produced to a scale of 1/1200 at the request of the owners, Compagnie Generale Transatlantique. Whilst this model was never officially listed as available in the U.K., it is believed that small quantities found their way onto the shelves of various London Souvenir Shops. Length 10⅜".

672 OSA Missile Boat 206 mm

671 MK1 Corvette 260 mm

675 Motor Patrol Boat 170mm

678 Air Sea Rescue Launch with pilot and dinghy 170 mm

All run on concealed wheels – will not float

674 Coastguard Amphibious Missile Launch 155mm

673 Submarine Chaser 197mm

new

Fig. S30. Illustrations from 1976 & 1977 Catalogues.

## SHIPS PRE-WAR

| Cat. No. | Dinky Name | Intro. date | Last catalogue reference |
|---|---|---|---|
| 50 | Ships of the British navy | mid 1934 | 1942 |
| 50a | Battle Cruiser 'Hood' | mid 1934 | 1942 |
| 50b | Battleships 'Nelson' (2) (or: Rodney) | mid 1934 | 1942 |
| 50c | Cruiser 'Effingham' | mid 1934 | 1942 |
| 50d | Cruiser 'York' | mid 1934 | 1942 |
| 50e | Cruiser 'Delhi' | mid 1934 | 1942 |
| 50f | Destroyers 'Broke' class (3) | mid 1934 | 1942 |
| 50g | Submarine 'K' class | mid 1934 | 1942 |
| 50h | Destroyers 'Amazon' class (3) | mid 1934 | 1942 |
| 50x | Submarine 'X' class | mid 1934 | 1942 |
| 51 | Famous liners | mid 1934 | 1940 |
| 51b | 'Europa' | mid 1934 | 1940 |
| 51c | 'Rex' | mid 1934 | 1940 |
| 51d | 'Empress of Britain' | mid 1934 | 1940 |
| 51e | 'Strathaird' | mid 1934 | 1940 |
| 51f | 'Queen of Bermuda' | mid 1934 | 1940 |
| 51g | 'Britannic' | mid 1934 | 1940 |
| 52 | '534'/'Queen Mary' | | see separate table |
| 52a | '534'/'Queen Mary' | | see separate table |
| 52b | '534'/'Queen Mary' | | see separate table |
| 52c | French Liner 'Normandie' | May 1935 | Autumn 1939 |
| 52m | 'Queen Mary' | | see separate table |
| 53az | Battleship 'Dunkerque' | 1938 | 1939 |

## SHIPS—POST-WAR

| Cat. No. | Model | Intro. date | Last catalogue reference |
|---|---|---|---|
| 671 | Mk 1 Corvette | 1975 | 1977 |
| 672 | OSA 2 Missile Boat | 1976 | 1977 |
| 673 | Submarine Chaser | 1977 | 1978 |
| 674 | Coastguard Amphibious Missile Launch | 1976 | 1978 |
| 675 | Motor Patrol Boat | 1973 | 1977 |
| 678 | Air Sea Rescue Launch | 1974 | 1977 |

# CHAPTER 4
# The Aeroplanes

The name 'Dinky Toys' has long been associated with toy cars, and it is true that the vast majority of Dinky items have been road vehicles. But aircraft form probably the second largest subject group and, apart from the Second World War years and a brief period from 1949 to 1952, there were always some included in the range. Most of the models made before 1965 were approximately 1/200 scale (though they did vary between 1/150 and 1/220) and the resulting small size (2″ to 5″ wingspan) undoubtedly contributes to their charm. Although a modern youngster (reared on finely-detailed plastic aircraft kits) might find much fault in them, the miniatures were generally accurate in outline, the proportions looked right and they were compatible with one another. Following developments in the model car range, the aircraft introduced since 1965 were generally made to larger scales (5″ to 8″ wingspan) in order to include interior detail or, later working features— such gadgets needed to attract the toy buyer in a more sophisticated age.

Generally, the models are described in their order of introduction, though later versions of individual items are detailed with their earlier counterparts where appropriate, etc. and they are divided into four broad production periods: 1934 to 1941 plus post-war re-issues, 1945 to 1949, 1952 to 1965, 1965 to 1980—the 'Big Planes' range.

The 1930s were still very much pioneer years of aviation, with the opening up of commercial air routes and creation of new long-distance records, bringing the aeroplane to the public's attention in much the same way as achievements like those of the NASA Space Shuttle do today.

Meccano Ltd. appear to have monitored closely the latest developments, and the introduction of Dinky aeroplanes was often preceded by notes on the real aircraft in the *Meccano Magazine* 'Air News' features and other articles. The choice of subjects mainly centred on new machines which were distinctive in appearance and thought likely to be successful, and those types which had achieved recognition through the breaking of a speed or distance record—they were topical and models of them could be expected to sell well. Some of the chosen types are rather obscure today, but we are looking at the range from hindsight. In some instances, the aircraft never achieved what was expected of them—all part of the pioneer era! However, a sizeable number remain well-known and the pre-war period can be regarded as halcyon days for Dinky planes—by 1940 some 45 varieties were listed, not counting seven boxed sets and some French imports. The range has never been as wide since.

The identification and dating of old models can be important to the enthusiast. Whilst the main characteristics of each model are set out in individual descriptions which follow, some general preliminary notes may be helpful. Initially (like most early Dinky Toys) the models carried no name details— only the 'Meccano Dinky Toys Made in England' inscriptions. These models are best identified by looking at photos in this book, and then finding the appropriate references in the text. Some models always carried names, e.g. the 60h SINGAPORE FLYING BOAT introduced in 1936, but it was not until around 1938 that inclusion of the type name became standard. Where present, the type name itself can be useful in dating some models. After 1938, nearly all of the pre-war aircraft models had proper aircraft names inscribed, e.g. 62m AIRSPEED ENVOY. Where the type was re-issued post-war, in most cases, the name inscription was changed to a vague description, e.g. 62m LIGHT TRANSPORT. Another factor is the absence or presence of a 'Gliding Game' hole in the casting. The 'Gliding Game' was featured on a special leaflet enclosed with most of the aeroplanes from 1937 to early 1940.

The idea was for the Dinky aeroplane to 'glide' down a piece of string fixed at an angle. In some instances, a special wire clip was supplied to slip over the model; in others a small square hole was provided in the centre of the wings or fuselage for the insertion of a split pin, the string passing through the loop of the pin. It is the small hole that provides the clue to dating, since of the models affected, only those made between 1937 and early 1940 have the hole. The March 1938 *Meccano Magazine* reported another use for the 'Gliding' hole and split pin. A Manchester boy devised a scheme for miniature bombing operations by fitting an air-gun slug under the fuselage of his Dinky Whitley Bomber, the 'bomb' being released by pressing down the 'Gliding' split pin. It was suggested that a suitable target be made out of wood and Meccano parts, with numbered sections for points scoring.

Various types of pins were used to retain propellers in place, and these can also be a guide to dating early models. Three basic types exist. The earliest was much like an ordinary household pin (i.e., thin and with a very small head). Around 1939, this type was gradually replaced by a larger one with a thicker stem and a hemispherical head, and some castings were thickened on the inside to provide a better fixing for the pin. In 1940 a further type was introduced, which had a flat disc head. This was used concurrently with the second type and both were also used after the war.

When registration letters were first applied to some of the earlier models they were generally smaller and 'rounder' in outline than those applied from 1938 onwards, which were larger and 'squarish' in shape. Unless otherwise stated, these were in black. In all cases where landing wheels were fitted, these were in a light gold-buff colour, somewhat prone to corrosion (this type of landing wheel actually lasted until the mid-1960s).

## 1934 to 1941—60 Series

60 AEROPLANES SET. This first set of Dinky planes made its appearance in the June 1934 *Meccano Magazine* advertisement page. It comprised six items Nos. 60a to 60f (as detailed below) packed in a blue box with colourful label on the lid. The set lasted until the end of production due to the War—in 1940 it was issued with the models in camouflage finish (see No. 66 of 1940). The models were also supplied to dealers in boxes of six of one type, for separate sale.

60a IMPERIAL AIRWAYS LINER. This was based on the Armstrong-Whitworth Atalanta, a four-engined monoplane in use on Empire air routes. The model consisted of a cast fuselage/tail unit, with a tinplate wing secured by tabs slotted through the fuselage and bent over. Cast radial engine units were fixed to the undersurface of the wing and small, two-bladed propellers (in bright uncoloured tinplate) were fitted. A simplified undercarriage was included, with two wheels fitted onto a single axle. The fuselage casting featured 'open' side windows and cockpit—later airliner models represented these details more basically with raised surface indications only. Until 1936, 60a was finished in bright, two-colour schemes without registration letters; in yellow with blue wingtips and tailplane; gold and blue with a 'sunray' effect of radiating bands of colour on the wings; and red and cream with a similar 'sunray' finish. After 1936, a single-colour finish was adopted of gold or silver, with the registration letters G-ABTI. In 1939, the designation 'Imperial Airways Liner' was added under the starboard wing. A camouflaged version was announced in 1940 under the name 'Heavy Bomber' 66a.

60b DH 'LEOPARD MOTH'. Three experimental Leopard Moths took part in the 1933 King's Cup air race and one of them, piloted by the designer Geoffrey de Havilland, crossed the winning line first. The machine was a single-engined high-wing monoplane. The Dinky version's construction was similar to that of the 60a Airliner. Until 1936, the toy was painted in two-colour schemes without registration letters; green and yellow, or dark blue and orange, the second colour being applied to the wingtips and tailplane. Later models were in a single colour; green, silver or gold, with the registration G-ACPT. Around 1939, the inscription 'DH Leopard Moth' was stamped under the starboard wing, and the side window openings in the casting were left solid from late 1939 or 1940. The camouflaged version was issued in 1940 under the name 'DIVE BOMBER FIGHTER' 66b.

60c PERCIVAL 'GULL' (from 1936 also available as 60k). This was a high performance three-seat cabin monoplane famous for several record flights in the 1930s. One was flown to Australia in 1933. The Dinky version went through several variations and was the only original 60 set model to be re-issued (albeit in a slightly different form) after the war. Construction of this toy was similar to that of 60a and 60b, but with a propeller larger than that fitted to the Leopard Moth. Earlier, it was finished in two-tone schemes; overall white with blue wingtips and tail area, or buff and red, without registration letters. In May 1936, Amy Mollison created a new record in this aeroplane, covering the distance of 6700 miles to Capetown in a little more than three days. Meccano Ltd. quickly arranged for a souvenir version of their Dinky Gull to be put into production, finished in the colours of Amy's aircraft—light blue fuselage and fin, silver wings and tailplane, with registration letters G-ADZO in blue. Packed in individual boxes carrying a suitable inscription, this version was separately identified as 60k. It was probably the inclusion of registration letters on this model that

# GLIDING — A NEW GAME WITH DINKY TOYS AEROPLANES!

A fascinating game known as "Gliding" has been devised for owners of Dinky Toys Aeroplanes. The idea is clearly shown in the diagram. Line A is passed through the eye of a special fitting now supplied with Dinky Toys aeroplanes (except the Autogiro). By means of line B, which is tied to its tail, the aeroplane is hauled to the top of line A. Line B is then released, and down glides the aeroplane in the most thrilling and realistic manner.

Gliding is the greatest fun imaginable, and it can be played either outdoors or indoors. Try it as a change from kite-flying. The only materials required are a reel of thread, two small screw-eyes and a peg to be driven into the ground or a weight of some kind.

### How to begin the Fun

To play the game in the garden, fix the two screw-eyes, one half an inch below the other, into a fence or tree at a height of, say 9 ft., or into the top of a ground floor window frame. Tie one end of a length of thread to the peg, pass the thread through the eye of the aeroplane fitting so that the tail of the machine points away from the peg, and tie the other end to the upper screw-eye. This is line A. Now tie one end of a second length of thread to the tail of the aeroplane, and pass the other end through the lower screw-eye, leaving enough thread to reach the ground with a few feet over. This is line B. For indoors insert the screw-eyes into a door post or picture rail, and replace the peg by a weight such as a flat-iron.

Line A should be slack enough to allow the aeroplane to land a yard or so before reaching the peg or weight. A piece of cardboard or linoleum makes a smooth runway for landing. The speed of the glide is controlled by the steepness and tightness of line A, and the length of the loose portion of line B.

### Races and Landing Tests

The greatest fun is obtained when two or three boys play together, each one fixing up his own glide, so that races and landing tests can be arranged. The heavier aeroplanes can be handicapped against the lighter ones by slackening the glide line slightly. Many other excitements are possible, such as formation flying with the aeroplane tail lines connected together so that the machines maintain formation during their glide.

Some of the Dinky Toys Aeroplanes, such as the "Singapore" Flying Boat (shown gliding in the illustration) are provided with a split pin, which is passed through a hole in the upper plane and held in place by opening out its legs slightly. The other Dinky Toys aeroplanes (except the Autogiro) are supplied with a spring clip that is attached as shown in the small drawing in the circle

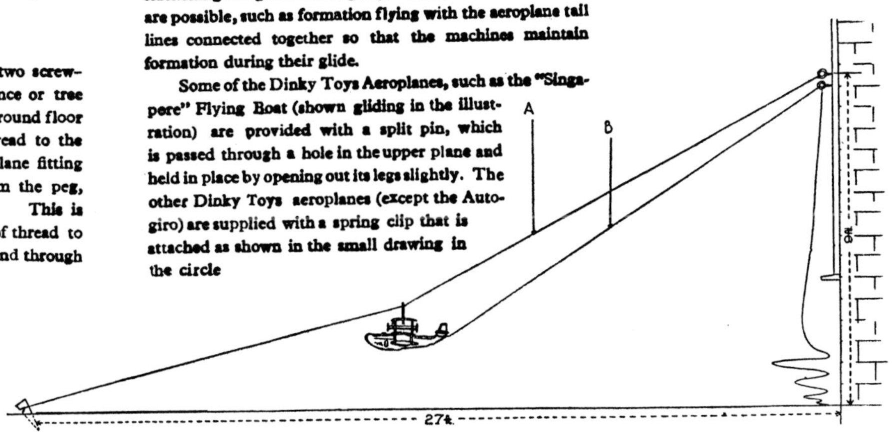

A
B

27t.

MECCANO LIMITED — LIVERPOOL 13 — ENGLAND

4/1137/400                                                    Printed in England

*Fig. A1. Gliding Game Instructions.*

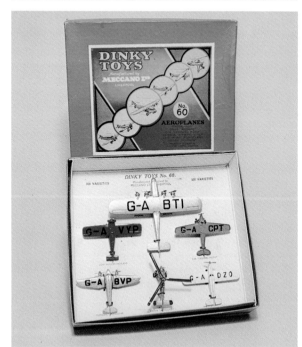

inspired Meccano to extend the feature to other aeroplanes in the range, the improvement in realism being obvious. Subsequently, the ordinary 60c model also had the registration G-ADZO applied to it, but in black and on a single-colour finish; white, red, yellow or light blue. Later 60k souvenir models represented the plane as flown by H. L. Brook in another record South African flight. These are similar to the Amy Mollison version but have the registration letters G-ADZO in black rather than blue. Models dating from late 1939 or early 1940 have the side windows left solid rather than cast open, and the name 'Percival Gull' was added to the underside of the starboard wing sometime during this period. The pre-war models all had 'Meccano Made in England' cast under the tailplane. The Gull was re-issued in late 1945 as 60k LIGHT TOURER, with the inscription under the tailplane altered to 'Made in England Meccano Ltd.', in single-colour finishes without registration letters. Some of these post-war versions were obviously made with pre-war stocks of wings—examples with 'Percival Gull' over-stamped with 'Light Tourer' can be found, making the inscription seem to read 'Percival Tourer'. Later models have just 'Light Tourer' inscribed under the starboard wing, and are in dark green, light green, red or silver. Post-war versions have been seen with either small or large two-blade propellers, both types in red. The version in camouflage was available for a short time from 1940 as a 'TWO SEATER FIGHTER' 66c.

60d LOW WING MONOPLANE was based on the Vickers Jockey, a design dating from 1930 which did not enter production. However, the toy resembled several single-radial-engined types of the period. It featured an open cockpit, and the construction was the same as the other 60 set models. The first issues were finished in the usual two-tone schemes without registration letters; red with cream wingtips, fin and tailplane; orange and cream, gold and blue. These had the cockpit cast as an open 'hole'. Subsequently, the casting was altered to include a representation of a pilot's head finished in a single colour (red, orange or silver) with registration G-AVYP on the wings. A large two-blade un-coloured propeller was fitted to all versions. The 1940 camouflaged model was called a 'TORPEDO DIVE BOMBER' 66d.

60e GENERAL 'MONOSPAR'. The Dinky model is a fairly good representation of the Mono-spar ST/25, a light twin-engined five-seat cabin monoplane developed from the ST/10, which won the 1934 King's Cup air race. The name 'Monospar' related to a (then) new type of wing construction involving the use of a single spar for strength. This was the first Dinky plane to be completely diecast, the distinctive shape of the wings probably precluding the use of tinplate. The fuselage/tail unit was press-fitted into four slots in the cast wing piece. A pair of undercarriage legs was cast under each wing, each pair having its own short axle to hold the wheel in place, a far neater arrangement than the single long axle method used on the 60a–60d models and a method later to be adopted as standard. Only the front cockpit panes were cast open on this model, the side windows being represented by raised lines in the casting. Small two-blade uncoloured propellers were fitted. First versions were in two-colour finishes without registration letters, in gold with red wingtips, fin and tailplane, or a silver and blue finish. In 1936–7 a single-colour scheme of silver or gold was adopted with registration letters G-ABVP. Later the name 'General Monospar' was added to the wing casting under the starboard side. The camouflaged version which came out in 1940 was listed as a 'MEDIUM BOMBER' 66e.

60f CIERVA 'AUTOGIRO'. Invented by Juan de la Cierva, the Autogiro was really the forerunner of the modern helicopter, although its main rotor was unpowered. The Editorial of the January 1934 *Meccano Magazine* referred to a new form of Cierva Autogiro without lateral stabilising wings, heralding this as 'an outstanding event in aviation'. The Dinky model appears to be based on this type. It is a real 'period piece', nicely modelled and quite scarce today. A one-piece casting without any inscriptions at all, measuring about 50mm in length, it was fitted with a one-axle, two-wheel undercarriage, a large three-blade tinplate main rotor, and a small two-blade propeller. Like 60d, it was produced in two versions; in the first type, the cockpit area consists of a round hole just aft of the rotor support struts, later models include a representation of the pilot's head and this area of the casting is solid. The model never

Fig. A4. 60a Imperial Airways Liner.

Fig. A5. 60b DH 'Leopard Moth'.

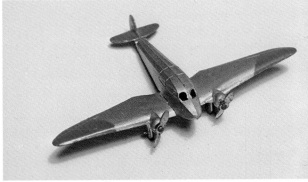

Fig. A6. 60c Percival 'Gull'.

DINKY TOYS No. 60k

Scale Model Souvenir

of actual

Percival "Gull" Aeroplane

flown by Mrs. Amy Mollison

on her record flight to

Capetown and back.

Fig. A8. 60d Low Wing Monoplane.

Fig. A9. 60e 'General' Monospar.

Fig. A7. 60k Amy Mollison's Percival 'Gull'.

Fig. A10. 60f Cierva 'Autogiro'.

carried registration letters, but was always finished in an all-over colour with a second colour applied to the main rotor, the tail fins, and as a band round the engine cowling. The only known scheme is gold with blue trim. A similar model was produced by Meccano (France) and this was imported into the U.K. as part of a set of French aircraft (No. 60z). Models in colour schemes other than blue and gold are possibly from this set, and are all of the first type without pilot's head. A military version listed as 'ARMY CO-OPERATION AUTOGIRO' 66f was issued in 1940.

After a twelve-month hiatus, the next aircraft item appeared—60g DH. 'COMET' AERO-PLANE. In 1933 Sir Macpherson Robertson put up the prize money for the Centenary of Victoria air race from England to Melbourne. All existing air-craft with the necessary performance were Amer-ican, and the Comet was born of the de Havilland company's determination to counter this threat and to build a winning machine. Three were ordered almost at once, by Jim and Amy Mollison, Bernard Rubin and A. O. Edwards (the managing director of Grosvenor House Hotel, London). It was a small, low-wing monoplane of all wood construction hav-ing a very thin section wing. The model, released in the spring of 1935, was a one-piece casting originally finished in two-tone colours without registration letters—red with gold ailerons, elevators and fin, and vice-versa, or silver and blue. Small two-bladed uncoloured tinplate propellers were fitted and the landing wheels were properly enclosed in stream-lined fairings. Later, probably in 1936, a single over-all finish was applied—red, silver or gold with regis-tration letters G-ACSR, that being the registration of the machine owned by Bernard Rubin. About 1938 the name inscription 'D H Comet' was added under the starboard wing. The model was re-issued after the War, as 60g LIGHT RACER, with that name moulded under the starboard wing and 'Dinky Toys' under the port wing (instead of beneath the fuselage as on the original model). This version car-ried the spurious registration G-RACE on the wings, and was finished in overall yellow, red or silver with red three-blade propellers.

60h 'SINGAPORE' FLYING BOAT was a four-engined, long-range reconnaissance flying boat

used by the R.A.F. It had four gun positions, one in the nose, two amidships and one in the extreme tail. Introduced in 1936, the model was the largest aircraft subject so far attempted and today it has a good vintage look about it, being both a biplane and a flying boat. The hull was a diecasting, incorporating the tailplane and fins, and the wings were tinplate pressings interconnected by cast engine and strut units, diecast floats being fixed under the lower wing. Large two-blade propellers (originally un-coloured) were fitted. During its production life the model went through several variations (and was also available in civilian garb numbered 60m). The first version had fully-modelled bows, was not fitted with a roller, and had no 'Gliding Game' hole. Later in 1936 a small roller, made in a plastic material but later occasionally wood, was included within the hull casting. From 1937 to 1940 there was a 'Gliding' hole in the centre of the upper wing. In 1940 the hull casting was modified under the bows so that less metal was used. It was usually coloured silver, although in 1940 it became available in light grey for a while. Large roundels were carried on the upper wings. Initially, these were just blue circles with a red dot in the middle, the silver base colour showing through to represent the white part of the markings. From 1939 proper red, white and blue roundels in transfer form were applied. Also about this time, the propellers were painted silver instead of being left uncoloured. 'Singapore Flying Boat' was inscribed under the lower starboard wing of all versions. 60m FOUR-ENGINED FLYING BOAT. Someone at Meccano must have been so pleased with the appearance of the Dinky Singapore that they were inspired to have 'two bites at the cherry' by making the same model available in an alternative finish under a different catalogue number. There was actually no real civilian version of the Singapore III. However, this did not stop Meccano producing the Singapore III in bright colours with fictitious regis-tration letters, though they did have the grace to change the catalogue description to 'Four Engined Flying Boat', and that name appears under the lower starboard wing. The structural variations are basic-ally the same as the 60h, though 60m does not appear to have been produced in the first version. The finish was an overall single bright colour—red, light green,

dark blue and silver, with registrations G-EUTG, G-EVCU, G-EXGF or G-EYCE across the top wings. The propellers were usually painted silver on the red models and red on models in other colours.

60n FAIREY 'BATTLE' BOMBER (60s in camouflage). The 'Battle' was the latest thing in military aircraft when it made its appearance in 1936. It was a two-seat medium-range day bomber and saw action in the Second World War, though by then it was outclassed by more modern types. The Dinky was introduced during the first half of 1937 and consisted of a one-piece casting fitted with a red three-blade propeller. The original models included undercarriage legs with each wheel having its own axle. In 1938 the name 'Fairey Battle Bomber' was added under the starboard wing, and in 1940 the model was issued without undercarriage—cheaper to manufacture and producing a more realistic 'flying' model. Originally finished in silver (with cockpit canopy picked out in greyish blue), a change to light grey was made in 1940. Roundels were applied to the upper wing surfaces; blue circles with red dots of paint on early models, and proper red, white and blue transfers from about 1939. An alternative version in camouflage finish was made available from 1938. Originally listed as 60s 'MEDIUM BOMBER', it was advertised as 'similar to Fairey Battle Bomber (No. 60n) but with new Air Ministry Shadow Shading'. The 'shadow shading' consisted of the now well-known green and brown camouflage pattern in a semi-matt finish applied to the upper surfaces of the wing, fuselage and tail areas. The undersurfaces were in black and the cock-pit canopy was finished in silver. Originally, only one roundel was applied to one wing—this was not an error but followed actual practice—but later the usual roundels were applied to both wings. Initially these were red, white and blue with a yellow outer ring, but in 1940 a change to the red and blue type was made. For a time the models were available in boxed pairs, in 'mirror finish', one model having the camouflage pattern arranged exactly the opposite to the other one. The structural variations were the same as for the 60n 'standard' version. The model was listed as 60s 'FAIREY BATTLE BOMBER (CAMOUFLAGED)' from 1940, and this coincided with a change to a darker shade of green in the finish.

*Fig. A11. 60g DH 'Comet'.*

*Fig. A13. 60m Four-Engined Flying Boat.*

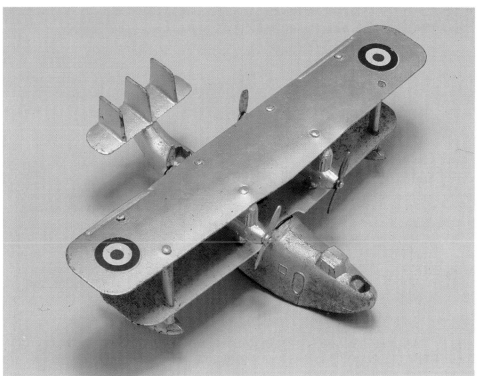

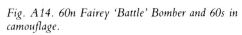

*Fig. A14. 60n Fairey 'Battle' Bomber and 60s in camouflage.*

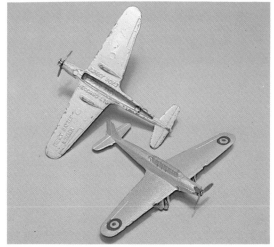

*Fig. A12A. 60h hull modification on bows.*

*Fig. A12. 60h 'Singapore' Flying Boat.*

**60p GLOSTER 'GLADIATOR' BIPLANE.** Introduced in 1936, the Gladiator was the last biplane fighter to serve with the R.A.F. Although obsolete by the time war broke out, it is probably best remembered by the exploits of 'Faith, Hope and Charity'—the three aircraft used in the defence of Malta. The model, introduced in 1937, measured only 38mm in length, but was neatly modelled. One casting formed the fuselage, undercarriage legs, lower wing and tail areas; the separately-cast upper wing was fixed via a central spigot through a hole in the fuselage and spaced with tiny metal pressings to represent the struts near the wingtips. Landing wheels on a single axle were fitted, the smallest to appear on a Dinky aeroplane. The two-blade propeller was finished in red, with the model itself originally in silver with R.A.F. roundels consisting of blue circles with red dots of paint on the upper wings. The next development was the addition of the 'Gloster Gladiator' name under the lower wings, and around the same time (1939) the roundels in red, white and blue were applied by transfers. In 1940 the model was issued in light grey for a short time. Unfortunately, it was not re-issued after the War and it is now a scarce item much prized by collectors.

**60r EMPIRE FLYING BOAT.** The Short 'Empire' was a large all-metal four-engined flying boat, 29 of which were originally ordered by Imperial Airways for use on Empire air routes. In the Editorial of the April 1937 *Meccano Magazine*, under the heading 'World Airways Development', it was stated that '. . . we are on the threshold of . . . important developments, for Atlantic air services are now in sight. The great flying boats that will undertake flights between Great Britain and America are now beginning their long-range experimental work . . .' The first Dinky Empire Flying Boat, the 'Caledonia', was announced in the September 1937 *M.M.* Advertisement. This was the name of one of the machines that had been making the experimental flights. It was stated that models of five others would also be made available shortly. Something of a prestige item at the time, the 'Caledonia' was initially packed in special individual blue boxes with the name on the card inset. The models were cast in two main sections, the hull and tail area forming one piece and the wings (with the four engines) the other,

cast floats being fixed under each wing. A plastic roller was fitted within the hull and it had small red three-blade propellers. From its introduction until 1940, there was a 'Gliding' hole in the centre of the wing casting. In 1940 the hull casting was modified at the bows like the Singapore, the 'Gliding' hole was deleted, and some models were fitted with wooden rollers. After the War, the roller was made of brass. The finish was always silver with registration letters on the wings, and a neatly lettered name applied each side of the nose. The original six names were eventually extended to a range of twelve; though in fact there are fifteen variations, since when one of the real machines had the misfortune to crash, the equivalent Dinky name was withdrawn and another substituted. The full list of names and registrations produced is as follows:

| | |
|---|---|
| CALEDONIA | G-ADHM |
| CANOPUS | G-ADHL |
| CORSAIR | G-ADVB |
| CHALLENGER | G-ADVD |
| CENTURION | G-ADVE |
| CAMBRIA | G-ADUV |
| CALPURNIA | G-AETW |
| CAPELLA | G-ADUY |
| CERES | G-AETX |
| CLIO | G-AETY |
| CALYPSO | G-AEUA |
| CAMILLA | G-AEUB |
| CORINNA | G-AEUC |
| CHEVIOT | G-AEUG |
| CORDELIA | G-AEUD |

Before the war, all the models were supplied in individual boxes, and by the time the different names were available, they were a standardised type slightly smaller than that used originally. The name of the particular aircraft enclosed was printed on a gummed slip stuck on one end of the box lid. The post-war models are more usually found with the 'Cambria' name and registration G-ADUV. The scarcest names seem to be 'Calypso', 'Corinna', 'Ceres' and 'Clio', and assembling a full set is very difficult today. **60x ATLANTIC FLYING BOAT** was a 'fictional' model—really the same as the 60r Empire, but finished in a range of colours with different names and registrations, all non-authentic. Construction was identical to the Empire model,

except that the under-wing inscription was 'Atlantic Flying Boat', but the writer has never seen a version with the 'hollowed out bows' hull casting of 1940. 60x is exceptionally scarce, and the only examples seen have had the fuselage and tail areas finished in light blue, 'Dauntless' each side of the nose, and the spurious registration G-AZBP on the cream-coloured wings. However, the toy was advertised as being available in assorted colours, names and registrations, so other finishes are possible—indeed, one unconfirmed report indicates that the name 'Dreadnought' was used. Introduced late in 1937, 60x was not re-issued after the war.

**60v ARMSTRONG WHITWORTH WHITLEY BOMBER** (62t in camouflage). The 'Whitley' heavy bomber entered production for the Air Ministry in 1936, and it was the first British bomber to bomb Germany, in March 1940. The model first appeared in *Meccano Magazine* advertisements late in 1937. It was a one-piece casting, with pairs of undercarriage legs (each with short axle and wheel) under each engine, small three-blade red propellers, and a 'Gliding' hole in the centre of the fuselage, finished in silver, with roundel transfers on each wing. In January 1939, the same model was released in an alternative camouflage finish as 62t. This was the same green and brown colouring as applied to 60s, with black undersurface and red, white and blue roundels with a yellow outer ring on the wings. In 1940 this was changed to the darker green shade with red and blue roundels. Both versions were packed in individual boxes which had details of the real aircraft printed on the lid.

**60t 'DOUGLAS DC3' AIR LINER.** The American DC3 is probably the most famous transport plane ever made. It was a successful follow-up to the DC2, and the model was probably planned at the same time as arrangements were being made for the real aircraft to be produced under licence in Europe by the Fokker company in Amsterdam. Released early in 1938, the Dinky was another one-piece casting, perhaps spoilt by the hollow fuselage with straight sides. It was fitted with the same type of undercarriage as 60e, 60v, etc. and also had, uniquely for this scale, a tiny tail wheel. Finished in silver, with three-blade red propellers, the model carried the Dutch registration PH-ALI on the wings and included the 'Gliding' hole in the centre of the fuselage. This was a rather basic toy with no window markings on the fuselage sides, though it was described as a 'scale model' on the lid of the individual box in which it came. Strangely enough, although real DC3s (Dakotas) were widely used in the post-war years, the model version did not re-appear after the War, and it is therefore scarce.

60w FLYING BOAT 'CLIPPER III'. The United States was also very much involved in trying to conquer the Atlantic in 1937. The 'Clipper III' was a Sikorsky design used by Pan-American Airways in their trans-Atlantic experimental flights. The Dinky was introduced early in 1938 and consisted of two main castings; the fuselage with tailplane and fins, and a separate wing piece fixed to the pylon included in the fuselage. Floats were fixed under each wing area, and it had the standard plastic roller. Each engine had a small red three-blade propeller. It was finished in silver, and carried the letters 'USA' on the port wing with the registration NC 16736 on the starboard. A 'Gliding' hole was included, and the inscription 'Pan American Airways Clipper III' was cast under the starboard wing. The model was packed in individual boxes bearing notes on the real aircraft. It was re-issued after the War as just 'Flying Boat' with the under-wing inscription altered to show that. The roller was of brass or plastic. The finish was much simplified, to all-over silver, dark green or light blue, with no registration or nationality markings.

## 1934 to 1941—62 Series

62k AIRSPEED 'ENVOY' KING'S AEROPLANE. The Airspeed Company had already been successful with their twin-engined Envoy light commercial aircraft when the firm was commissioned to supply a specially-fitted and finished version for the use of King George VI. The King's Flight version was painted in the colours of the Brigade of Guards. The model was issued early in 1938. A one-piece casting with red two-blade propellers, it was fitted with undercarriage legs each with axle and wheel, and was finished in the colours of the actual machine—silver wings with the registration G-AEXX in blue, with red and blue fuselage and tail fin, and the window areas picked out in silver. The inscription 'The King's Aeroplane' was under the starboard wing. Packed in individual boxes. 62m

AIRSPEED 'ENVOY' is the ordinary civilian version of 62k. Introduced at the same time, it was finished in a single all-over colour, red, silver, blue or green with black registration letters G-ACVI, G-ACVJ, G-ADCB, G-ADAZ or G-AENA. The inscription under the starboard wing was 'Airspeed Envoy'. After the War, the model was re-issued as No. 62m LIGHT TRANSPORT, with that name under the starboard wing. The fictitious registration G-ATMH was applied and colours are red, silver or blue.

62n JUNKERS Ju 90 AIR LINER was a new four-engined German aircraft, which in June 1938 had set up new altitude records for landplanes carrying useful loads of 5 and 10 tons respectively. The wingspan was nearly 115 feet, with an almost straight trailing edge and a leading edge swept sharply back to the blunt wingtips. The aeroplane was adopted by Deutsche Lufthansa which was operating routes to parts of Europe and also one to South America at the time. The April 1939 *Meccano Magazine* featured the Ju 90 on the front cover and included a special article, which no doubt assisted sales of the Dinky Toy version which had already been pictured in the December 1938 *M.M.* advertisement page. A large one-piece casting, the model was finished in silver with three-blade red propellers, and had windows and doors represented in greyish-green by transfers applied on each side of the fuselage. Authentic German registrations were applied to the wings: D-AALU, D-AIVI, D-AURE and D-ADLH. The now-standard undercarriage legs, each with axle and wheel were included, and a 'Gliding' hole was present in the casting. 62y GIANT HIGH-SPEED MONOPLANE shared the same casting as 62n, but was finished in a range of colours with a fictitious registration. Announced in February 1939, a note in the *Meccano Magazine* declared 'some of the Dinky Toys civil aircraft are available in various colours, and these models appeal particularly to enthusiasts who like to build up fleets of particular types, all the aircraft finished in a certain colour being regarded as representing the fleet of a certain air transport company'. This sales gimmick was possibly aimed at younger children, the brighter colours of models 60m, 60x, 62x and 62y perhaps appealing to them more than the semi-authentic silver finish of the equivalent models 60h, 60r, 62p and 62n. The

'Giant High Speed Monoplane' carried that name under the starboard wing and was finished in an over-all base colour (without window transfers) with the ailerons and elevators picked out in a second colour. The registration was D-AZBK. Known colours are: blue with brown trim, light blue with dark blue, light green with dark green. Six schemes were stated to be available, so other colours may yet be found. 67a JUNKERS Ju 89 HEAVY BOMBER (German Service Colours). The Ju 89 was a military development of the Ju 90 airliner, using the same basic casting, although the real aircraft differed somewhat and the resulting model was not really authentic. Finished in black with light blue undersurfaces, it carried German markings in white on the wings with swastikas on the tail fins. The name 'Heavy Bomber Junkers Ju 89' was cast under the starboard wing. Packed in individual boxes, it had a short life and was not re-issued after the war. It seems to have been particularly prone to 'fatigue', this factor no doubt contributing to its rarity today. 62y was re-issued after the war, with the spurious British registration G-ATBK, in all-over silver, light green with dark green trim, grey with green trim, medium green with dark green trim.

62p 'ENSIGN' AIR LINER. Imperial Airways had also placed orders with Armstrong Whitworth for a number of large landplanes, and *Meccano Magazine* in September 1938 featured both a 'cut-away' diagram and a photograph of the first of these, named 'Ensign', which had achieved a new record for four-engined aircraft of 70 minutes for the London-Paris route, during its acceptance trials. The Dinky was first pictured in the December 1938 *M.M.* advert, initially being produced with the name 'Ensign' each side of the nose and with the registration G-ADSR, on an overall silver finish, with three-blade red propellers. It was cast in two pieces, the fuselage and tail area forming one casting and the wings another, which was fixed into the top of the fuselage. Undercarriage legs were incorporated in the wing casting, each pair having its own axle and wheel. In January 1939 the model was made available with five more names, and the full range of markings on offer became:

| | | | |
|---|---|---|---|
| ENSIGN | G-ADSR | ECHO | G-ADTB |
| ELSINORE | G-ADST | ETTRICK | G-ADSX |
| EXPLORER | G-ADSV | ELYSIAN | G-ADSZ |

Fig. A15. 60p Gloster 'Gladiator' Biplane.

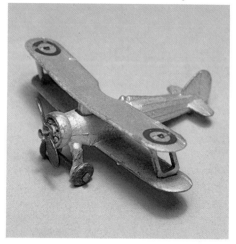

Fig. A16. 60r Empire
Flying Boat.

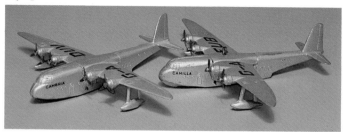

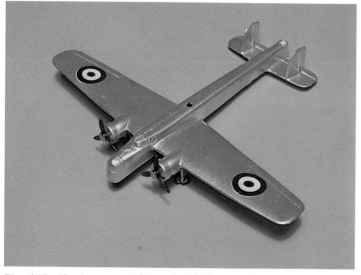

Fig. A18. 60v Armstrong Whitworth 'Whitley' Bomber and
62t in camouflage.

Fig. A17. 60x Atlantic Flying Boat.

Fig. A19. 60t Douglas DC3 Air Liner.

Fig. A20. 60w Flying Boat 'Clipper III'.

Fig. A21. 62k Airspeed 'Envoy' King's Aeroplane.

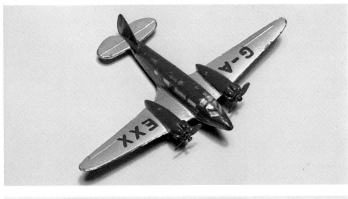

DINKY TOYS No. 67a

JUNKERS Ju 89 HEAVY BOMBER

The Junkers Ju 89 is one of the largest long-range heavy
bombers used by the German Air Force. It has been
developed from the Junkers Ju 90 4-engined 40-seater air
liner, and can carry about 8,000 lb. of bombs. It has a
gun turret in the nose of the fuselage and another in the
stern, and each contains a movable cannon. There are
also machine gun positions in the top and bottom of the
fuselage. The four engines develop a total of some
4,000 h.p., and give the bomber a top speed of about
260 m.p.h. With full load the machine has a range of
approximately 1,500 miles.

The Ju 89 is a low wing monoplane. The wings taper
very sharply at the leading edges, and the slightly tapered
trailing edges are fitted with the familiar Junkers "double
wing" flaps.

Fig. A22. 62m Airspeed 'Envoy'.

Fig. A24. 67a Junkers JU 89 Heavy Bomber.

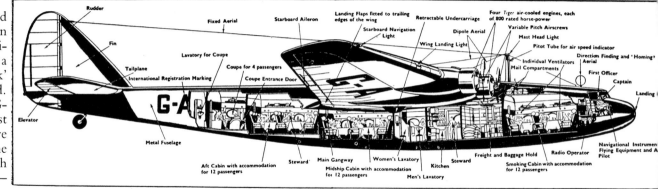

The internal arrangements of an Imperial Airways "Ensign" class air liner for service on the company's European air routes. There is accommodation for 40 passengers crew of five. "Ensigns" operating on the Empire air routes will carry 27 passengers and 1¾ tons of freight and mail. Illustration by courtesy of Imperial Airways Ltd.

'Ensign Class Air Liner' was cast under the starboard wing. Until 1940, the 'Gliding' hole was included in the fuselage. All the models were packed in individual boxes with the relevant name printed on a gummed label on the side of the lid. 'Echo', 'Ettrick' and 'Elysian' seem to be the most difficult to find. 62p was re-issued after the War as ARMSTRONG-WHITWORTH AIR LINER, with that title cast under the starboard wing. Two types of finish were applied, either all-over silver, or in two-tone schemes similar to those used for 62x, but both carried the pre-war 62p names and registrations—usually 'Explorer' G-ADSV on blue with silver trim, grey with green, green with silver, and all-over silver. The 'Ensign' tools were also used to produce a brightly-coloured non-authentic version for younger children. 62x BRITISH 40 SEATER AIR LINER was announced with the 62y in February 1939, and carried this name under the starboard wing. Finished in all-over base colour with a second colour applied to the ailerons and elevators and as a flash along the top of the fuselage, it carried the spurious registration G-AZCA, in red with maroon trim, light green and dark green, yellow and maroon, light blue and dark blue. Two other finishes have yet to be discovered! The propellers were generally silver rather than red. There was a camouflaged version in 1940—No. 68a.

62r DE HAVILLAND 'ALBATROSS' MAIL LINER and 62w IMPERIAL AIRWAYS 'FRO-BISHER' CLASS LINER. The de Havilland 'Albatross' was originally produced to meet a requirement for a mail plane capable of crossing the Atlantic. It was a beautifully streamlined four-engined machine designed by A. E. Hagg, the designer of the Comet racing aircraft. Imperial Airways ordered a fleet of Albatrosses in 1938, and the models were introduced in January 1939. They were made from two castings in a novel manner, one piece forming the wings and lower half of the fuselage, the other the upper half with the tailplane and fins. Undercarriage legs and wheels were fitted as standard. 62r represented the Air Ministry mail plane, finished in silver with registration G-AEVV on the wings, and including the name 'D H Albatross' under the port wing. 62w used the same castings, but had the name 'Frobisher Class Air Liner' cast under the port wing; like 62r, it

was finished all-over in silver but had different registrations, and also carried the names of the aircraft each side of the nose. The first to be released was 'Frobisher' itself; later, two other names were also made available, as follows:

FROBISHER G-AFDI
FALCON G-AFDJ
FORTUNA G-AFDK

62r and 62w each had its own individual box carrying details of the respective versions of the real aircraft, and in the case of the 62w models, a gummed label on the lid showed the name of the particular aircraft inside. The tools were used to produce a similar model from 1945 to 1949, called 62r FOUR-ENGINED LINER, with that title under the port wing. Initially this was produced without registration letters in a two-tone colour scheme, the bulk of the model in one colour, with a second colour for the ailerons and elevators, in grey, light blue and silver, all with red trim. Later, a single colour (grey, fawn, light blue or silver) was applied with the spurious registration G-ATPV. Although shown pre-war with two-blade propellers, all versions—pre- or post-war—have been seen only with three-blade (red) propellers. A camouflaged version, 68b, was issued in 1940.

63 MAYO COMPOSITE AIRCRAFT. The Mayo Composite Aircraft, invented by Major R. H. Mayo, was built by Short Bros. to the order of the Air Ministry for experimental flights by Imperial Airways. The purpose of the experiments was to solve the problem of getting a heavily-laden aircraft

into the air, and involved the use of a larger machine as an in-flight 'launching platform'. The *Meccano Magazine* for June 1938 included a detailed descriptive article on the novel Composite aircraft—the flying boat 'Maia' and the seaplane 'Mercury'. The 'Maia' was similar to an Empire Flying Boat, but with a strut formation in the centre of the wings to support the 'Mercury', which was a smaller four-engined aircraft with large floats. Announced in January 1939 *M.M.* advertisement, the model consisted of 63a FLYING BOAT 'MAIA', a modified version of the 60r EMPIRE, with the addition of a metal pressing to simulate the support struts; and, completely new, 63b SEAPLANE 'MERCURY', consisting of a basic one-piece casting to which separate cast floats were fixed under each wing, with a spring clip fitted beneath the fuselage for the model to be fastened onto the back of 'Maia'. The whole assembly came in a presentation box with details of the real Composite on the lid, but the two components could also be purchased separately. 63a was finished in silver with the registration G-ADHK on the wings and the name 'Maia' each side of the nose. First versions had the fully-modelled bows; in 1940, this changed to the 'hollowed out' type in the same manner as 60r. Plastic rollers gave way to wooden ones also in 1940. 63b 'Mercury' was also finished in silver, with the registration G-ADHJ on the wings. Small two-blade red propellers were fitted. The under-wing casting inscription was 'Mercury Seaplane', and the name 'Mercury' was transferred each side of the nose. This model was withdrawn during the war years, but re-appeared in a modified version in 1945 as 63b SEAPLANE. This version did not have the spring clip fitted, bore the fictional registration G-AVKW, and was inscribed simply 'Seaplane' under the starboard wing. It was also minus the name transfers. In this guise, the model was withdrawn in 1949, but was re-issued in 1952 (with black 'flat disc' type propeller pins), re-numbered as 700 in 1954, and finally deleted in 1957—some eighteen years after its original introduction!

62s HAWKER 'HURRICANE' SINGLE SEATER FIGHTER (62h in camouflage). Little needs to be said here about the Hurricane and its use in the Second World War, though its fame is somewhat eclipsed by the Spitfire. The model was introduced in February 1939 when the real aircraft was already in service with the R.A.F. It was a neat little casting, originally fitted with single undercarriage legs with a return to the one-axle method holding both tiny wheels in place. Available as 62s in silver (advertised as 'aluminium finish') with red, white and blue roundels on the wings; or in 'shadow shading' camouflage green and brown with red, white, blue and yellow roundels and all-black undersurface, as 62h, it was fitted with a two-blade red propeller. In 1940, the model was re-issued without undercarriage, perhaps to ease the cost of manufacture and to provide a more realistic 'flying' model, and the 62h version appeared in the darker green and brown camouflage with red/blue roundels and with the undersurface half black and half white. The 1940 casting was re-issued in silver finish with red/blue roundels on the wings plus red, white and blue

roundels (some with yellow outer ring also) on the fuselage sides. This post-war 62s was fitted with a three-blade red propeller.

62g BOEING 'FLYING FORTRESS'. Another famous aircraft of the Second World War, the Flying Fortress was an all-metal long-range four-engined bomber, with five gun positions. The model was of the early B–17B version and was announced in the summer of 1939. A two-piece casting, one piece forming the wings and lower fuselage areas, the other for the upper part of the fuselage, tailplane and fin, it had single undercarriage legs under each wing with wheels fitted to the outer sides, red three-blade propellers, and an overall silver finish with USAAC markings on the wings and fin. 'Boeing Flying Fortress' was cast under the starboard wing. At first, it came packed in individual boxes which included a small leaflet giving a diagram of the real aircraft. Later, this diagram was to appear on the box lid itself. It was re-issued in 1945 in identical finish, plus in some cases a greyish-blue tinted cockpit and nose, with the under-wing inscription altered to its new title of LONG RANGE BOMBER.

The first few months of the war did not greatly affect production of Dinky Toys. Although some items had been suspended in September 1939, they were made available again in March 1940, according to the Meccano Magazine. New models had continued to appear. Meccano Ltd. took an optimistic outlook, since special articles on the now-extensive range of Dinky aircraft appeared in the February and March 1940 issues of the M.M., which compared the Dinky models with their real-life counterparts.

62a VICKERS-SUPERMARINE SPITFIRE FIGHTER (62e in camouflage). The famous Spitfire was already giving a good account of itself when the Dinky model was announced in the April 1940 Meccano Magazine. A tiny, one-piece casting without undercarriage, it was originally based on a Mark I and was available in two finishes: 62a in silver, with red, white and blue roundels on the wings, or as 62e in camouflage green and brown with half black and half white undersurface, originally with red, white and blue roundels with a yellow outer ring, later changing to the red and blue type with a darker green in the camouflage finish. In the original M.M. advertisement, 62a was stated to be in 'service grey', but a note at the back of the Magazine refers to the usual 'aluminium finish' (silver). Certainly, the writer has never seen one in grey, although the Singapore, Fairey Battle and Gladiator were available in that colour in 1940. The Mark I Spitfire was not re-issued after the War, but a modified version—based on a much later Mark—was produced in 1945 with the same number, 62a. Finished in silver, with red/blue roundels on the wings and (usually) red, white, blue and yellow ones each side of the fuselage, the cockpit area was a different shape from that of the 1940 casting, and the nose extended a further 2mm from the leading wing edge.

62b BRISTOL 'BLENHEIM' BOMBER (62d in camouflage). The Blenheim was a twin-engined medium bomber, the toy being based on the Mark IV. Introduced in May 1940, it was another one-piece casting without undercarriage, also available in the two finishes of silver (62b) or camouflage (62d).

*Fig. A33. 62a First casting.   Fig. A34. 62a Second casting.*

Fig. A25. 62p 'Ensign' Air Liner and 62x British 40-seater Air Liner.

Fig. A30. 63 Mayo Composite Aircraft.

Fig. A27. 62r De Haviland 'Albatross' Mail Liner.

Fig. A28. 62r Four-Engined Liner, post-war.

Fig. A29. 62w 'Frobisher' Class Air Liner.

Fig. 31. 62b Bristol 'Blenheim' Bomber and 62s Hawker 'Hurricane' Single-seater Fighter.

Fig. A31a. 62h: Hawker 'Hurricane' (Camouflaged).

Fig. A31b. 62d Bristol 'Blenheim' Bomber (Camouflaged).

Fig. A35. 62a Vickers-Supermarine 'Spitfire' Fighter and 62e (Camouflaged).

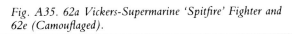

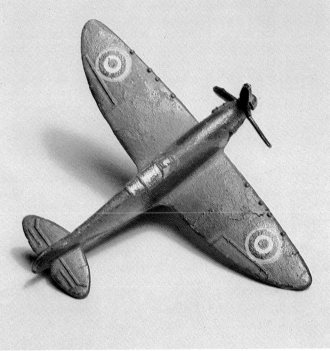

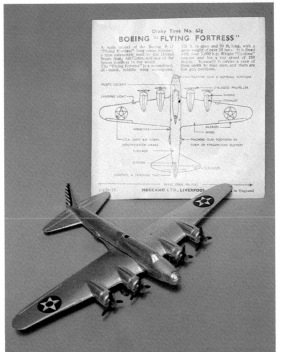

Fig. A32. 62g Boeing 'Flying Fortress'.

The camouflaged was the usual green and brown with red, white, blue and yellow roundels on the wings and also red, white and blue roundels each side of the fuselage. The undersurfaces were half black and half white. The inscription under the starboard wing on these 1940 models was 'Dinky Blenheim Bomber'. 62b in silver was re-issued after the War, listed as MEDIUM BOMBER, with 'Dinky Toys Medium Bomber' under the wing. This had red, white and blue roundels on the wings and red, white, blue and yellow roundels each side of the fuselage.

### 1934 to 1941—Mixed Sets

61 R.A.F. AEROPLANES SET was made available in 1937, about the same time as the Nos. 60n FAIREY BATTLE and 60p GLOSTER GLADIATOR were introduced. It consisted of 60h SINGAPORE FLYING BOAT, flanked by two each of 60n and 60p models, in a blue box with lid (but no coloured label). There being no Trades Description Act then in force, the statement printed on the inside of the box 'Each aeroplane in this set is an exact scale model' probably went unchallenged! To be fair, at the time the toys were better than anything else available in terms of realism for their size.

64 PRESENTATION AEROPLANE SET. Announced in May 1939, this set consisted of six of the smaller models which had already been available separately, packed in a blue box with a leaflet describing the aircraft represented. The set was comprised of one each of 60g DH COMET, 62h HURRICANE (camouflaged) 62k The KING'S AEROPLANE, 62m AIRSPEED ENVOY (commercial version), 62s HURRICANE (silver finish) and 63b SEAPLANE 'MERCURY'. However, according to a 1940 Canadian catalogue, one of the Hurricanes was later replaced in the set by a Spitfire, though it is not clear whether this was the silver or camouflaged version.

65 PRESENTATION AEROPLANE SET. Also introduced in May 1939, this set comprised eight of the largest Dinky aircraft, all of which had previously been available as separate items. Packed in a large blue box with coloured label illustrating six of the models, the blue liner card had the names and numbers luxuriously printed in silver. The contents were 60r EMPIRE FLYING BOAT, 60t DOUGLAS D.C.3, 60v WHITLEY BOMBER, 60w CLIP-

PER III FLYING BOAT, 62n JUNKERS Ju 90, 62p ENSIGN CLASS AIRLINER, 62r D. H. ALBATROSS MAIL LINER, and 62w FROBISHER CLASS AIRLINER.

66 CAMOUFLAGED AEROPLANE SET was announced in the July 1940 Meccano Magazine; it is now exceptionally hard to find. It was basically the old No. 60 set of six models, but all (except the Autogiro) finished in the darker shade of green and brown camouflage with black undersurfaces and red and blue roundels on the wings. The models were also available separately and were listed as types of military aircraft, even though the resemblance was slight in most instances! The propellers were of the same type as on the civilian counterparts in the No. 60 set, but were painted silver or red. 66a HEAVY BOMBER was the 60a IMPERIAL AIRWAYS LINER (Atlanta), without the name inscription. 66b DIVE-BOMBER FIGHTER was the 60b LEOPARD MOTH, in final version with 'solid' side windows but without the name under the wing. 66c TWO SEATER FIGHTER was the PERCIVAL GULL 60c, also in the version with 'solid' side windows but without a name inscription. 66d TORPEDO DIVE-BOMBER was the LOW-WING MONOPLANE 60d in its second type casting with pilot's head, without name inscription. 66e MEDIUM BOMBER was the 60e GENERAL MONOSPAR and this did have the 'General Monospar' name cast under the starboard wing. 66f ARMY CO-OPERATION AUTOGIRO was the same as the second type of 60f AUTOGIRO with pilot's head, but finished in silver-grey with red, white and blue roundels on the fuselage sides. The rotor was silver and the propeller red.

68 AIRCRAFT IN SERVICE CAMOUFLAGE. This prestige set was also announced in July 1940. It was comprised of 13 aircraft, but only two types were actually new and even these merely colour changes. The contents were: 2 of 60s FAIREY BATTLE, 2 of 62d BRISTOL BLENHEIM, 3 of 62e SPITFIRE, 3 of 62h HURRICANE, one 62t WHITLEY and also a 68a 'ENSIGN' CLASS AIRLINER and a 68b 'FROBISHER' CLASS AIRLINER. The camouflaged military aircraft were all as before. The Ensign and Frobisher were identical to 62p and 62w, apart from their finish in camouflage green and brown with black undersurfaces, red and

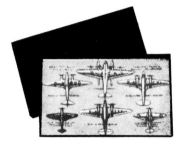

Dinky Toys No. 64

*Fig. A37. 64 Presentation Aeroplane Set.*

blue roundels on the wings and red, white and blue roundels on each side of their fuselages (without 'Gliding Game' holes). 68b FROBISHER has been seen in both light and dark camouflage colours; 68a ENSIGN only in the dark green and brown finish. 68a and 68b were also available as separate items, according to the Meccano Trade Bulletin No. 403 of August 1940 and contemporary price lists.

### 1934 to 1941—French

All the French models in the 60z and 61z sets included undercarriages and wheels in a similar fashion to the British 60 set models, though the wheels enclosed in the streamlined fairings of the Arc-en-Ciel were of the type fitted to Dinky Toy railway rolling stock, somewhat larger than usual. The models all carried the inscriptions 'Dinky Toys Fab en France Meccano' but did not include the type name (apart from the second type of DEWOITINE D338, No. 61az).

60z AEROPLANES was a French set of six aircraft made by Meccano (France) Ltd. and imported into the U.K. from late 1937 or early 1938. It was the French equivalent (numbered 60) of the Liverpool No. 60 set. It became No. 60z to distinguish it from this, and came in a similar blue box with coloured label. It consisted of models of typical French aircraft of the period, as described below. Only one item from the set was also made available for separate sale in the U.K., the No. 60az ARC-EN-CIEL which was a two-piece casting of a large triple-engined aircraft, very streamlined in shape for the period, finished in gold with red, blue or green wingtips and fuselage top. Large two-blade propellers, on plated finish, were fitted. The cockpit window areas were cast 'open'. Potez 58 was a small high-wing monoplane, similar in construction to the Leopard Moth. It had a tinplate wing attached to a cast fuselage/tail unit and a large two-blade plated propeller. Colour schemes are yellow-orange with grey trim, or yellow with white trim. (The same model with a separate colour scheme was also available in set No. 61z). Hanriot Type 180T was an unusual type known as a sesquiplane, really a high-wing attached to a cast fuselage and was fitted with a two-blade plated propeller. The lower wing was in the form of cast projections from the fuselage sides and really formed the top of the undercarriage legs. Finishes: green, with white or red trim (leading edges of wings and tips of tailplane). The model was also included in set No. 61z as a Hanriot 180M. Dewoitine Type 500 is a low-wing monoplane fighter, and had a tinplate wing slotted through the cast fuselage sides and an open cockpit (with 'hole' in the casting). It was fitted with a two-blade plated propeller, and is in white with parts of the wing and tailplane tips in red. The same model in overall silver with military roundels was included in the 61z set. Breguet Corsair is an attractive little model of a single-engined low-wing monoplane with a dual cockpit, and had a tinplate wing with pressed-in rib lines, slotted through a die-cast fuselage/tail unit which incorporated two triangular shaped holes to represent the cockpit areas. A plated two-blade propeller was fitted and the only known colour is red with a green pattern on the wings and tailplane. The Autogiro is basically the same as the first type of British No. 60f model, i.e. without a pilot's head included in the casting. The colours are distinctive—silver fuselage with red tail fins and a cream rotor, or silver with green rotor, tail fins and engine cowling band. Some rotors have the undersurface of the blades in black.

61z AEROPLANES (FRENCH SET) was imported into the U.K. about the same time as 60z. Some of the models were identical to those in the 60z set, apart from colour finish, and others were earlier castings modified to represent different aircraft. Six models were included, but again, only one was also available separately, 61az DEWOITINE D338, which was originally merely an altered version of the Arc-en-Ciel casting, fitted with radial engines and three-blade propellers. However, this was later replaced by a completely new one-piece casting which was a more accurate replica of the real airliner in use

by Air France. It is thought that it was this version that was on sale separately in the U.K. in overall silver finish with registration F-ADBF on the wings, and two-blade red propellers. Potez 56, a small twin-engined aircraft, made use of the Hanriot fuselage casting fitted with a tinplate wing secured under the fuselage above the lower stub wings and undercarriage legs. Cast engine units seem to have been 'welded' onto the tinplate wing and each has a small two-blade red propeller. Blue with silver engines and fuselage top. Farman F360 was produced from the same components as the Breguet Corsair model, though the wingtips and tailplane were clipped off at right angles and the finish was basically silver with a yellow or blue flash in silver with (in some cases) French Air Force roundels on the wings. Dewoitine de Chasse 500d is the same as the Dewoitine 500 in the 60z set, but finished overall in silver with French Air Force roundels on each wing. Potez 58 Sanitaire is the same as the Potez 58 in the 60z set, but finished in either white or silver with red cross markings on the wings.

64az AMIOT 370. Announced in the July 1939 *M.M.*; this was an imported model, made by Meccano (France) Ltd. The Amiot 370 was a twin-engined military reconnaissance aircraft which had been developed from the Amiot 340 long-range bomber. In the U.K., it was available only in silver finish, with French roundels on the wings. It was a one-piece casting, with undercarriage, and red three-blade propellers (somewhat larger than the Liverpool ones of the period). The model could have had only a short life in the U.K., importation probably ceasing later in 1939 due to war conditions. It was not included in August 1940 price lists. 64bz BLOCH 220 was another French-made import, announced at the same time as the Amiot 370. The Bloch 220 was a twin-engined 16-seat airliner capable of a top speed of 220mph, in regular use by Air France. The Dinky was a solid, one-piece casting with undercarriage, finished in silver with the registration F-AOHJ on the wings; it had small three-blade red propellers fitted.

No further Dinky aeroplanes were to appear before the 1942 Government Order came into force, prohibiting the manufacture of metal toys. However, it is known that Meccano had several more new Dinky aircraft in the planning stage, one of which

was 62f DH FLAMINGO, a twin-engined commercial type, which was pictured in the 1939–1940 general Meccano products catalogue (printing date June 1939). This model was not mentioned in any *Meccano Magazine* of 1939 or 1940, and was apparently not put on the market, even after the war, despite later appearances on the back covers of wartime *M.M.*s, together with a Buick Car, rep-

*Fig. A40. 68 Aircraft in Service Camouflage.*

107

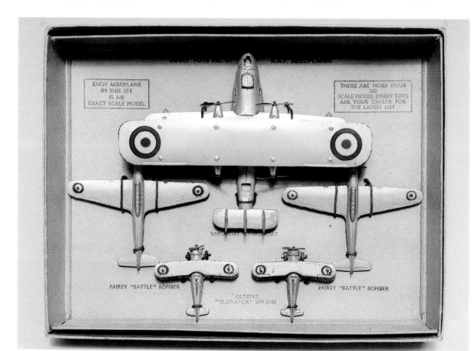

Fig. A36. 61 R.A.F. Aeroplanes Set.

Fig. A38. 65 Presentation Aeroplane Set.

Fig. A39. 66 Camouflaged Aeroplane Set.

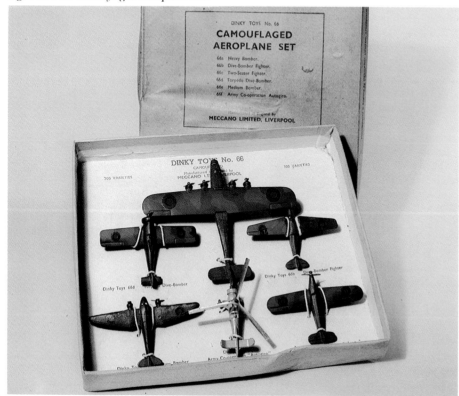

Fig. A41. 68a 'Ensign' Air Liner (Camouflaged) and 68b 'Frobisher' Air Liner (Camouflaged).

Fig. A42. 60z French Aeroplanes Set.

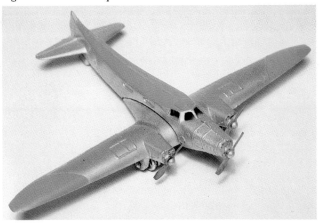

Fig. A43. 60az Monoplane 'Arc-en-Ciel'.

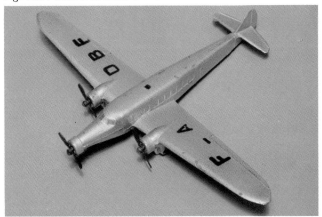

Fig. A45. 61az Dewoitine D338.

Fig. A46. 64az Amiot 370 and 64bz Bloch 220.

Fig. A44. Clockwise from bottom left: Potez 58 (60), Dewoitine 500(60), Breguet Corsair (60), Hanriot 180T (60), Potez 56 (61), Hanriot H180M (61), Farman F360 (61), Dewoitine de Chasse 500D (61), Potez 58 (61).

109

resenting the time when Dinky Toys would be available again. Probably a wooden mock-up was made and used for the catalogue illustration, but preparation of tools did not proceed, production being postponed in favour of the topical Spitfire and Blenheim models. By the time the war was over, other aircraft types were more topical, and it would not have been worthwhile to develop the Flamingo model. Other subjects under consideration in 1940 included a Blackburn Skua, a Heinkel 111, a Messerschmitt Me 110, as well as a Barrage Balloon. None of these appeared in any literature of the time, but old factory records indicate that drawings were prepared. The Messerschmitt Me 110 was eventually released after the War as No. 70d 'TWIN-ENGINED FIGHTER' (see next section), but the other items didn't get off the ground. Dinky aeroplanes were regularly advertised in the *Meccano Magazine* (along with other Dinky Toys of course) until 1942, and there may well have been sufficient stocks in the shops for them to be on sale throughout this period, but after 1943 it was made illegal to sell any metal toys (new or second-hand). It was to be late in 1945 before some of the pre-war models were re-issued and 1946 before any new items appeared.

D.H. " FLAMINGO " LINER

Dinky Toys No. **62f**
Scale model of the latest British transport monoplane. It has a top speed of 245 m.p.h. and can carry 12 to 20 passengers.     Price **6d.** each

*Fig. A47. 62f DH 'Flamingo' Liner (not produced).*

**Aeroplanes 1945 to 1949**

Meccano Ltd. was fairly quick off the mark in getting Dinky Toys into production again after the war. By the end of 1945 some 50 models had been re-issued in time for the first post-war Christmas, albeit in small quantities and with export having preference. These included 12 aircraft, some with new titles and modifications (see Aeroplanes 1934–1941):

## AEROPLANES 1934–41 AND POST-WAR RE-ISSUES

| Cat. No. | Model | Intro. date | Deletion | Comments |
|---|---|---|---|---|
| 60 | Aeroplanes/British Aeroplanes | 1934 | 1941 | Contains: 60a,b,c,d,e,f |
| 60a | Imperial Airways Liner | 1934 | 1941 | See also: 66a Heavy Bomber |
| 60az | Monoplane 'Arc-en-Ciel' | 1937/8 | 1940 | See also: 60z |
| 60b | DH 'Leopard Moth' | 1934 | 1941 | See also: 66b Dive Bomber Fighter |
| 60c | Percival 'Gull' | 1934 | 1941 | See also: 60k and 66c Two Seater Fighter |
| 60d | Low Wing Monoplane | 1934 | 1941 | See also: 66d Torpedo Dive Bomber |
| 60e | General 'Monospar' | 1934 | 1941 | See also: 66e Medium Bomber |
| 60f | Cierva Autogiro | 1934 | 1941 | See also: 66f Army Co-operation Autogiro |
| 60g | DH 'Comet' Aeroplane | 1935 | 1941 | Re-issued post-war |
| 60g | =Light Racer= | 1945 | 1949 | Re-issue |
| 60h | 'Singapore' Flying Boat | 1936 | 1941 | See also: 60m |
| 60k | Percival 'Gull' Monoplane | 1936 | 1941 | See also: 60c. Re-issued post-war |
| 60k | =Light Tourer= | 1945 | 1949 | Re-issue |
| 60m | Four-engined Flying Boat | 1936 | 1941 | See also: 60h |
| 60n | Fairey 'Battle' Bomber | 1937 | 1941 | See also: 60s |
| 60p | Gloster 'Gladiator' Biplane | 1937 | 1941 | |
| 60r | Empire Flying Boat | 1937 | 1949 | See also: 60x |
| 60s | Fairey 'Battle' Bomber/Medium Bomber Camouflaged | 1938 | 1941 | See also: 60n |
| 60t | Douglas DC-3 Air Liner | 1938 | 1941 | |
| 60v | Armstrong Whitworth 'Whitley' Bomber | 1937 | 1941 | See also: 62t |
| 60w | Flying Boat 'Clipper III' | 1938 | 1941 | Re-issued post-war |
| 60w | =Flying Boat= | 1945 | 1949 | Re-issue |
| 60x | Atlantic Flying Boat | 1937 | 1941 | See 60r |
| 60z | French Aeroplanes | 1937/8 | 1940 | Contains: 60az |
| 61 | R.A.F. Aeroplanes | 1937 | 1941 | Contains: 60h, 2 of 60n, 2 of 60p |
| 61az | Dewoitine D338 | 1937/8 | 1940 | |
| 61z | French Aeroplanes | 1937/8 | 1940 | Contains: 61az |
| 62a | Vickers-Supermarine 'Spitfire' Fighter | 1940 | 1941 | See also: 62e |
| 62a | Spitfire | 1945 | 1949 | |
| 62b | Bristol 'Blenheim' Bomber | 1940 | 1941 | See also: 62d. Re-issued post-war |
| 62b | =Medium Bomber= | 1945 | 1949 | Re-issue |
| 62d | Bristol 'Blenheim' Bomber Camouflaged | 1940 | 1941 | See also: 62b |
| 62e | Vickers-Supermarine 'Spitfire' Fighter Camouflaged | 1940 | 1941 | See also: 62a |
| 62f | DH Flamingo | | | Not issued |
| 62g | Boeing 'Flying Fortress' Monoplane | 1939 | 1941 | Re-issued post-war |
| 62g | =Long Range Bomber= | 1945 | 1948 | Re-issue |

**=Flying Boat=, this sign indicates a re-issue.**

| Cat. No. | Model | Intro. date | Deletion | Comments |
|---|---|---|---|---|
| 62h | Hawker 'Hurricane' Single Seater Fighter Camouflaged | 1939 | 1941 | See also: 62s |
| 62k | (Airspeed 'Envoy') King's Aeroplane | 1938 | 1941 | See also: 62m |
| 62m | Airspeed 'Envoy' Monoplane | 1938 | 1941 | See also: 62k. Re-issued post-war |
| 62m | =Light Transport= | 1945? | 1949 | Re-issue |
| 62n | Junkers Ju 90 Air Liner | 1938 | 1941 | See also: 62y |
| 62p | (Armstrong Whitworth) 'Ensign' Air Liner | 1938 | 1941 | Re-issued post-war. See also: 62x, 68a |
| 62p | =Armstrong Whitworth Air Liner= | 1945 | 1949 | Re-issue |
| 62r | De Havilland 'Albatross' Mail Liner | 1939 | 1941 | See 62w, 68b. Re-issued post-war |
| 62r | =Four-Engined Liner= | 1945 | 1949 | Re-issue |
| 62s | Hawker 'Hurricane' Single Seater Fighter. Aluminium Finish | 1939 | 1941 | See 62h. Re-issued post-war |
| 62s | =Hurricane= | 1945 | 1949 | Re-issue |
| 62t | Armstrong-Whitworth 'Whitley' Bomber Camouflaged | 1939 | 1941 | See 60v |
| 62w | Imperial Airways 'Frobisher' Class Liner | 1939 | 1941 | See 62r |
| 62x | British 40-Seater Air Liner | 1939 | 1941 | See 62p |
| 62y | Giant High-Speed Monoplane | 1939 | 1949 | See also 62n |
| 63 | Mayo Composite Aircraft | 1939 | 1941 | Consists of 63a,b |
| 63a | Flying Boat 'Maia' | 1939 | 1941 | |
| 63b | Seaplane 'Mercury' | 1939 | 1941 | Re-issued |
| 63b | =Seaplane= | 1945 | 1954 | Re-issue. Renumbered 700 |
| 64 | Presentation Aeroplane Set | 1939 | 1941 | Contains: 60g, 62h,k,m,s, 63b. See text |
| 64az | Amiot 370 | 1939 | 1940 | |
| 64bz | Bloch 220 | 1939 | 1940 | |
| 65 | Presentation Aeroplane Set | 1939 | 1941 | Contains: 60r,t,v,w, 62n,p,v,w |
| 66 | Camouflaged Aeroplane Set | 1940 | 1941 | Contains: 66a,b,c,d,e |
| 66a | Heavy Bomber | 1940 | 1941 | See also: 60a |
| 66b | Dive-Bomber Fighter | 1940 | 1941 | See also: 60b |
| 66c | Two-Seater Fighter | 1940 | 1941 | See also: 60c |
| 66d | Torpedo Dive-Bomber | 1940 | 1941 | See also: 60d |
| 66e | Medium Bomber | 1940 | 1941 | See also: 60e |
| 66f | Army Co-operation Autogiro | 1940 | 1941 | See also: 60f |
| 67a | Junkers Ju 89 Heavy Bomber | 1940 | 1941 | See also: 62n |
| 68 | Aircraft in Service Camouflage | 1940 | 1941 | Contains: 2 of 60s, 2 of 62d, 3 of 62e, 3 of 62h, 62t, 68a,b |
| 68a | Armstrong Whitworth 'Ensign' Liner in Service Camouflage | 1940 | 1941 | See also: 62p |
| 68b | 'Frobisher' Liner in Service Camouflage | 1940 | 1941 | See also: 62r,w |
| 700 | =Seaplane= | | | Renumbering of 63b |

| | | | |
|---|---|---|---|
| 60g | Light Racer | | (DH Comet) |
| 60k | Light Tourer | | (Percival Gull) |
| 60r | Empire Flying Boat | | |
| 60w | Flying Boat | | (Pan-American Airways Clipper III) |
| 62a | Spitfire | | |
| 62b | Medium Bomber | | (Bristol Blenheim) |
| 62g | Long Range Bomber | | (Boeing Flying Fortress) |
| 62m | Light Transport | | (Airspeed Envoy) |
| 62p | Armstrong Whitworth Air Liner | | (Ensign Class Air Liner) |
| 62r | Four-Engined Liner | | (DH Albatross) |
| 62s | Hurricane | | |
| 63b | Seaplane | | ('Mercury' Seaplane) |

Later, a further model was to be re-issued:

| | | |
|---|---|---|
| 62y | Giant High-Speed Monoplane | |

In the majority of cases, it will be seen that there was a change to a general descriptive name (the original pre-war type names are given in brackets). This change occurred on the lists and on the toys themselves, and it is assumed that this was to make the models appear less dated. Plans for new models were in hand, however, and August 1946 saw the announcement in the *Meccano Magazine* of the first of the post-war 70 series of Dinky aircraft, with five more following during the next twelve months.

*Fig. A48. Meccano Magazine, August 1946.*

These were all similar in style and construction to the pre-war range, except that inclusion of an undercarriage was the exception rather than the rule. The propellers tended to be larger than before. The colour is silver unless otherwise specified, and cockpits usually tinted blue. Renumbering took place circa 1954.

The Dinky range was 'slimmed down' in 1949, with many of the models originating from pre-war days being withdrawn, since a sizeable number of completely new items had been introduced. The withdrawals included all the aircraft—even the recent post-war types—and production concentrated on road vehicles, including the expansion of the Supertoys range; but all the 70 series plus the 63b SEAPLANE were to re-appear in 1952.

70a AVRO 'YORK' AIR LINER. There was a dearth of British-made passenger aircraft at the end of the War, and the York was developed from the Lancaster bomber, using the same wings and en-

*Fig. A51. 70d Twin-Engined Fighter.*

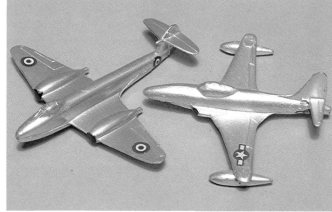

*Fig. A50. 70e Gloster Meteor Twin-Jet Fighter and 70f Shooting Star Jet Fighter.*

*Fig. A49. 70a Avro 'York' Airliner.*

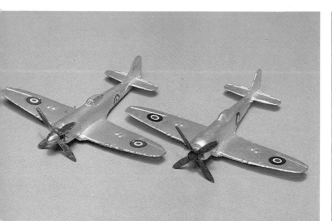

*Fig. A52. 70b Tempest II Fighter.*

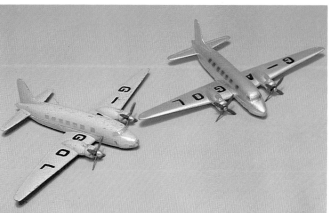

*Fig. A53. 70c Viking Air Liner.*

*Fig. A54. 701 Shetland Flying Boat.*

gines. It provided B.O.A.C. with a serviceable machine until the British aircraft industry could start production of more suitable civil types; later it was much used by charter companies, especially during the Berlin Airlift. The model followed pre-war practice in its two-piece construction, with pairs of undercarriage legs included in the wing casting, but a new feature was a tinplate base rivetted under the hollow fuselage casting. Withdrawn in 1949, it was re-issued in 1952, with the centre tail fin slightly thickened. Renumbered 704.

70e GLOSTER METEOR TWIN-JET FIGHTER was the first operational British jet, developed from the Gloster-Whittle experimental aircraft. When the model was introduced in October 1946, the Meteor was also the holder of the World Absolute Speed Record. A one-piece casting without undercarriage, the model had especially good undersurface detail. The R.A.F. roundels varied in type over the years, but generally fuselage roundels with yellow bands are pre-1949, and the wing roundels of that period are larger than those of later production. Renumbered 732.

70d TWIN-ENGINED FIGHTER was not announced in the *Meccano Magazine*, but it was probably put on the market in 1946. Originally planned in 1940 as a miniature of the Messerschmitt Me 110, Meccano records indicated that in October 1945 it was decided to produce it under the vague title of 'Twin Engined Fighter', presumably out of respect for British and Allied sensitivities in those early post-war days. Why Meccano Ltd. decided to go ahead with it anyway is a bit of a mystery, since it was an unsuccessful type, out of date in 1945. An unusual error occurred on later production, the letter 'N' in Meccano' being reversed in the under-wing inscription. Renumbered 731.

70b TEMPEST II FIGHTER. The Hawker Tempest was in use against the 'Doodlebug' flying bombs in the latter part of the war, and the fast Tempest II radial-engined version entered peacetime service with the R.A.F., though the age of the jet had arrived, making all propeller-driven fighters obsolete. The December 1946–49 production had a special large pointed spinner to retain the propeller, giving a very realistic appearance. This type of retaining pin was used also on the first issues of 70c

AEROPLANES 1945–49

| Cat. No. | Model | Intro. date | Deletion | Comments |
|---|---|---|---|---|
| 70a | Avro York Air Liner | 1946 | 1959 | Renumbered 704 |
| 70b | Tempest II Fighter | 1946 | 1955 | Renumbered 730 |
| 70c | Viking Air Liner | 1947 | 1962 | Renumbered 705 |
| 70d | Twin-Engined Fighter | 1946 | 1955 | Renumbered 731 |
| 70e | Gloster Meteor Twin-Jet Fighter | 1946 | 1962 | Renumbered 732 |
| 70f | Shooting Star Jet Fighter | 1947 | 1962 | Renumbered 733 |
| 70g | Avro Tudor | | | Not issued |
| 700 | =Seaplane= | | | Renumbering of 63b. See also: 1934–41 |
| 701 | Shetland Flying Boat | 1947 | 1949 | |
| 704 | =Avro York Air Liner= | | | Renumbering of 70a |
| 705 | =Viking Airliner= | | | Renumbering of 70c |
| 730 | =Tempest II Fighter= | | | Renumbering of 70b |
| 731 | =Twin-Engined Fighter= | | | Renumbering of 70d |
| 732 | =Gloster Meteor Twin-Jet Fighter= | | | Renumbering of 70e |
| 733 | =Shooting Star Jet Fighter= | | | Renumbering of 70f |

VIKING, and on the SHETLAND 701. At this time, there was also a yellow band on the fuselage roundels. Renumbered 730.

70c VIKING AIR LINER was another civil machine developed from a bomber (the Wellington). It was used by B.E.A. on short-range and feeder routes in the early post-war years, and later by charter firms. The model was produced from two castings, one for the upper half of the fuselage, nose and tailplane/fin areas; the other forming the lower part of the fuselage with the wings and engines. Early models could be grey with silver window details. No cast representations of the windows were made, the squarish 'blobs' of colour perhaps giving a more realistic impression on the sleek fuselage sides. Renumbered 705.

70f SHOOTING STAR JET FIGHTER. An early American jet design, this Lockheed used engines developed from British examples sent over to the States during the war. In 1947 it attained a world-record speed of 623.8mph. Announced in the August 1947 *Meccano Magazine*, initial production had the cockpit tinted blue. 1947–49 production can be distinguished by the under-wing inscription 'MADE IN ENGLAND BY MECCANO LTD',

the later production having the letters re-spaced and the word 'BY' omitted. Renumbered 733.

701 SHETLAND FLYING BOAT. The Short Shetland was a logical development of the Sunderland and C Class Empire Flying Boats, and was produced when many people still considered there was a bright future for such craft. The Shetland was larger than any previous British flying boat, but in the event only two prototypes were built, and the registration of the second was used on the model which was included in the first group of Dinky Supertoys, announced in August 1947. It was a large impressive-looking replica, cast in three main sections—the fuselage or hull, with tailplane and fin; the wings and engines; and a separate planing surface fitted under the hull. Cast floats were fixed under each wing. There were extra-large four-blade propellers, unusually in black rather than red. It was packed singly in utility-looking boxes of buff cardboard, but with striking labels in red and black. It may have been this accent on realism for their new range of Dinky Supertoys that made Meccano decide to omit a roller within the hull casting, though this must have made it awkward to handle as a toy. Withdrawn in 1949, and not re-issued.

## Aeroplanes 1954 to 1965

Although all the '70' models and the 63b SEA-PLANE had gradually been put back into production during 1952, and it was to be another two years before any further activity occurred on the aviation scene. By 1953 the British Aircraft industry was getting back into its stride after the Second World War and the jet engine was making its mark. Meccano were taking stock of developments and plans were being made to introduce some of the latest types. I well remember my own excitement at seeing the full-page announcement in the October 1954 *M.M.* of a new Dinky aircraft, the DH Comet Airliner, and the mention in the 'Dinky News' pages that this was to be the first of a new series of aircraft models. After renumbering and, where applicable, re-allocation to the 'Supertoy' category, the under-wing markings were altered to suit.

702/999 DH COMET JET AIRLINER, carrying the same name as the pre-war de Havilland record-breaker, was the world's first jet airliner to enter commercial service. Unfortunately, faults developed which enforced the grounding of the whole fleet but these were overcome and the re-designed Comet eventually became a very successful aircraft.

The model, resplendent in authentic B.O.A.C. colours, captured the look of the original and was the first Dinky airliner to carry full livery. Originally the model carried the registration G-ALYV but after renumbering it was changed to G-ALYX and about 1964 the silver finish was altered to a metallic grey.

992 AVRO VULCAN DELTA WING BOMBER. The Vulcan was the first of Britain's 'V-Bombers'. The March 1953 *M.M.* carried a picture of the Vulcan on its front cover and a feature on the plane covering its impressive performance at the Farnborough Air Show in 1952. The planning of the model was anything but straightforward resulting in the Dinky Vulcan being an exceptionally rare item today. Perhaps the story is best told by quoting from some correspondence I had with Meccano Ltd. It was discovered '. . . that the Vulcan was originally allotted sales number 703 previously destined for the Herald, but that it was eventually at drawing board stage given the number 707. It was then decided that because of the bulk of the model—it measured 6¼″ span by 6″ long—it would be very heavy to cast in mazak, and since at the time there was a severe shortage of the material following the Korean War (we are talking of 1955) the decision was made to cast

the model in aluminium. A special machine was produced for this purpose but, unfortunately, the dies were not really suitable for the high temperatures involved in aluminium casting, and as a result of attempting to use them for this purpose, they were damaged . . . The change (of number) to 749 was made at the time it was decided to make the model in aluminium, we believe this was done to identify it as a non-mazak casting.' In the event the model was never announced officially in the *Meccano Magazine* and was not sold in the U.K. However, it was listed in Canada and the United States in 1955 and 1956 under the Dinky Supertoys tag with the number 992. Although packed in a Supertoys blue-and-white-striped box with the nuber 992 on the lid, the model itself carried the Dinky Toys logo and the number 749. Further points to emerge from later correspondence were that 'the wing tips were originally very much more pointed and squared off, but because of the thinness of these extremities and their distance from the main bulk of the model they did not 'fill' properly in the mould, which, after one or two shots, was blocked to round off the wingtips.' There were no longer any records relating to Vulcans leaving the factory but it was stated that 'various

Fig. A58. 992 Avro Vulcan Delta Wing Bomber.

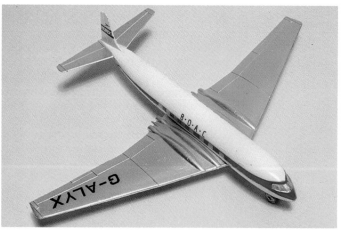

Fig. A55. 702 DH Comet Jet Airliner.

**MECCANO LIMITED, 675 KING STREET WEST, TORONTO**

**MODELS NOT ILLUSTRATED**

| | $ | | | $ | | | $ |
|---|---|---|---|---|---|---|---|
| 011 Telegraph Messenger | 0.15 | 053 Passengers (00) Set of 6 | 0.55 | 751 Police Hut | 0.30 |
| 012 Postman | 0.15 | 200 Midget Racer | 0.20 | 992 Avro Vulcan Delta Wing | |
| 013 Cook's Man | 0.15 | 220 Small Open Racing Car | 0.30 | Bomber | 1.40 |
| 051 Station Staff (00) Set of 6 | 0.55 | 750 Telephone Box | 0.25 | | |

Fig. A57. 1956 Canadian Catalogue.

stories have been heard of upwards of 500 castings being produced before the tools finally became useless and it is the opinion of one who was here at the time that they were all despatched to Canada and that this was the only order ever made . . .'

A bunch of three fighters finished in grey and green camouflage were produced between July 1955 and May 1956. 736 HAWKER HUNTER was probably the best known British jet fighter of the 1950s. 734 SUPERMARINE SWIFT entered service with the R.A.F. in 1954 but was not to prove as successful as the Hunter, handling problems leading to its withdrawal from service in 1955. 735 GLOSTER JAVELIN DELTA WING FIGHTER was an all-weather delta-wing fighter in service with the R.A.F. from 1956 until 1967. Originally the model was equipped with the same type of smooth buff-coloured landing wheel as all earlier models, but in 1965 a change was made to a new treaded type in black.

706 VICKERS VISCOUNT AIRLINER (AIR FRANCE). The Viscount was a very successful British four-engined turbo-prop airliner. Introduced in the early 1950s some are still flying today. The Dinky model was introduced in September 1956 and withdrawn just over a year after introduction, following the issue of the B.E.A. version. 708 VICKERS VISCOUNT 800 AIRLINER (B.E.A.) introduced in September 1957 was exactly the same as the Air France model except, of course, for the colour finish. It was initially produced in silver with red 'British European Airways' markings on each side of the fuselage, the upper part of which was white. The silver part of the finish was later changed to a metallic grey. The wheels changed from the smooth buff

type to the treaded black in 1965. On these later models the B.E.A. lettering on the port wing changed too—it was upright instead of sloping and included full stops after each letter.

Two helicopters were produced during this period. 715 BRISTOL 173 HELICOPTER was a 14-seat twin-engined helicopter with tandem rotor layout, Britain's first attempt at this design. It included stub wings fore and aft to lessen the load on the rotors in forward flight. The prototype first flew in 1952 but the model was not introduced until November 1956. 716 WESTLAND-SIKORSKY S.52 HELICOPTER was one of several American designs produced in England by Westland, although production of this particular type had ceased in 1951 in the U.S.A. It was in use by the British Services under the name of 'Dragonfly' and the model was introduced in February 1957. Both 715 and 716 used

*Fig. A60. 706 Vickers Viscount Airliner (Air France).*

*Fig. A61. 708 Vickers Viscount 800 Airliner (B.E.A.).*

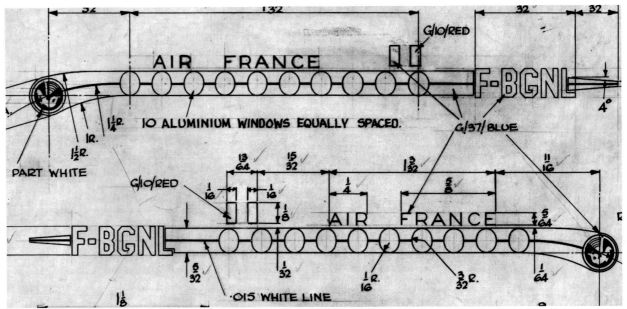

*Fig. A62. Transfer Drawing for Vickers Viscount.*

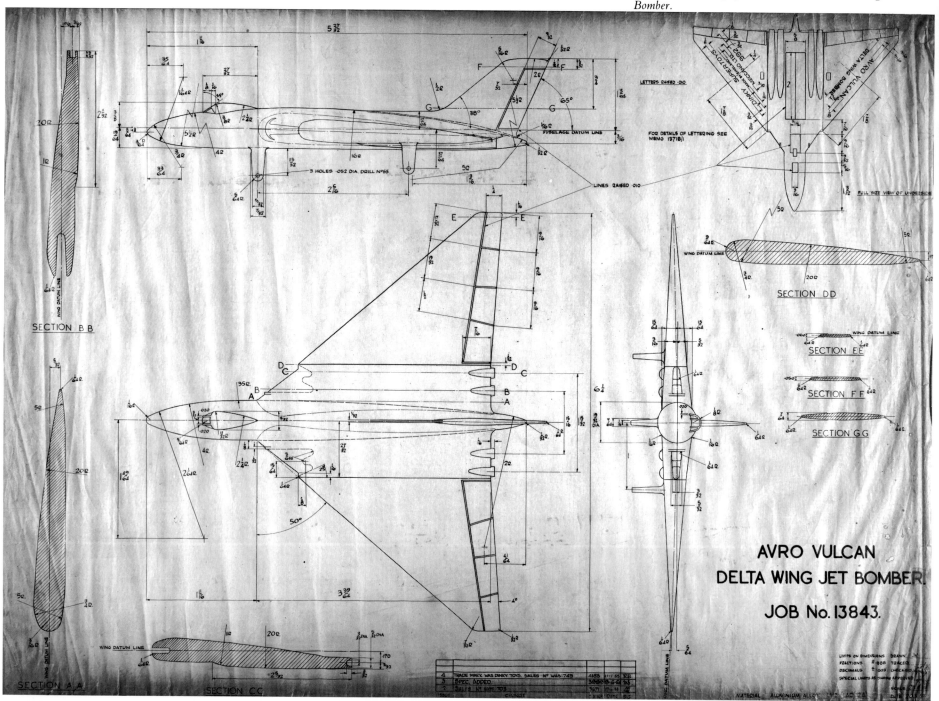

**AVRO VULCAN
DELTA WING JET BOMBER.
JOB No. 13843.**

# Dinky Toy Flies Faster than Sound!

## Shock Waves from the Gloster Javelin Delta Fighter

MANY of you have seen pictures like two of those on these pages, and will recognise them as shadow photographs showing the wave systems produced in the atmosphere by an aircraft in flight. Some of you may have realised that the aeroplane in these pictures is not a real one at all! It is in fact a Dinky Toys Gloster Javelin Delta Wing Fighter, No. 735, and the interesting thing is that it is actually in free flight at the Mach number of 1.4.

The Mach number is the ratio of the speed of the aircraft to that of sound in undisturbed air. As in this instance it is well over one, it is clear that the Gloster Javelin in the pictures has broken through the sound barrier! And it has done it very thoroughly, for its speed was about 1,500 feet per second, while that of sound in air is approximately 1,100 feet per second.

The photographs were taken at the Aeroballistics Range of the Canadian Armament Research and Development Establishment at Valcartier, Quebec, Canada. This range is used for aerodynamic tests of model shell, rockets, guided missiles and aircraft. Recently a test launching was made as a demonstration of the techniques employed, and it was in this test that the Dinky Toys Gloster Javelin was used. During this trial photographs were taken from which the two illustrations referred to have been reproduced, by courtesy of CARDE.

The Dinky Toys Gloster Javelin model was prepared for use in these tests by filing off the landing gear, so that the model represented the flight arrangement of the miniature aircraft. The modified Dinky Toy was then fired from a small bore gun with a bore diameter of 3¼ in., which was actually made by removing the rifling from a 17-pounder anti-tank gun.

While in the gun the model was carried in a "sabot." This is a special device, the outside surface of which fits the gun bore, while the inside surface fits the model. It is used in tests of this kind for two purposes in addition to giving the model aircraft the desired speed. One of these is to provide the necessary base for propelling the model, as the Dinky Toys aeroplane could not fit the gun bore exactly; the other is to protect the Dinky Toy from the hot gases produced on firing the gun. On emerging from the gun the sabot falls away behind and sideways, leaving the model to fly on alone.

The model was photographed while in free flight by means of a "shadowgraph" optical system. This method shows up disturbances in the air caused by the model flying through it, in much the same way as hot air rising from a stove is made visible by the shadows it throws in a beam of sunlight, although in the one case the air disturbances are caused by the physical motion of the model through the air and in the other by differential heating.

The photographs show the model in

flight at about 1,500 ft. per second, as already noted, which is roughly 1.4 times the speed of sound. The air disturbances made visible by the method of photography used are of course the waves created in the

air by the passage of the aircraft through it. When an aeroplane is in flight at speeds less than that of sound, the air in front of it gets advance warning from the pressure waves sent ahead. These waves move with the speed of sound, and form streamlines, moving the air out of the way. When the speed is above that of sound no such warning is given, because the aeroplane gets there first and moves the air forcibly out of the way.

This explains how shock waves are formed, and it is this effect that produces the sonic boom when an aircraft passes through the sound barrier. In our illustrations, with the Dinky Toys aircraft flying steadily at a speed above that of sound, the shock waves can be seen just ahead of the nose of the fuselage in the pictures.

One particularly striking fact of immense interest to all Dinky Toys enthusiasts emerged from this remarkable application of a Dinky Toys aeroplane. This was that from observations all along the range it was concluded by the observers that the Dinky Toys Gloster Javelin Delta Wing Fighter is a good stable aircraft, and that it flew well at its supersonic speed. This is indeed a wonderful testimony to the design of the model itself and to the magnificent finish of the fuselage and wings. The Dinky Toys aircraft in fact flew at its unaccustomed speed above that of sound in much the same efficient way as a real aeroplane expressly designed for supersonic flight.

Dinky Toys Gloster Javelin Delta Wing Fighter, No. 735.

*Fig. A65. 998 Bristol Britannia Airliner.*

*Fig. A66. 737 P.1B Lightning Fighter.*

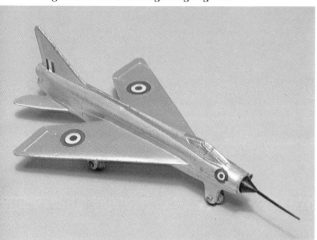

*Fig. A67. 738 DH 110 Sea Vixen Fighter.*

*Fig. A64. 715 Bristol 173 Helicopter and 716 Westland-Sikorsky S.51 Helicopter.*

*Fig. A69. Advertisement from Meccano Magazine, August 1961.*

Fig. A71. 700 Spitfire Mk II Diamond Jubilee of the R.A.F.

Fig. A72. 710 Beechcraft S.35 Bonanza.

Fig. A73. 715 Beechcraft C55 Baron and 712 U.S. Army T-42A.

Fig. A74. 717 Boeing 737.

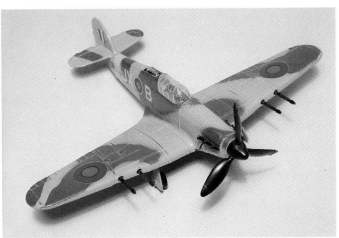

Fig. A75. 718 Hawker Hurricane IIc.

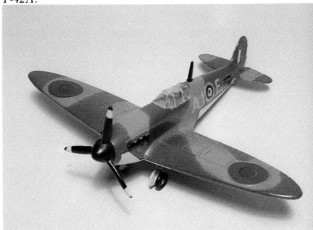

Fig. A76. 719 Spitfire Mk II.

Fig. A77. 721 Junkers JU 87b Stuka.

Fig. A78. 722 Hawker Harrier.

Fig. A79. 723; HS125 and 728; R.A.F. Dominie.

the Autogiro pressing for the main rotor.

998 BRISTOL BRITANNIA AIRLINER. This four-engined turbo-prop earned the nickname of the 'Whispering Giant' in its heyday, due to its quiet operation in spite of its size, a wingspan half the length of a football field. It saw service with several major airlines and is still in use by charter companies today. The Supertoy was introduced in April 1959, some two years after the previous aircraft model. Construction was similar to that of the Comet and Viscount and the red large four-blade propellers were similar to those on the long-obsolete Shetland. The model carried the livery of Canadian Pacific, the bulk of it being in silver but with the upper part of the fuselage and tail fin in white. The three cheat lines and fin flash were originally also in blue, but about 1961 these were changed to red. Around 1964 metallic grey was used on those part of the model formerly silver.

737 P.1B LIGHTNING FIGHTER. The English Electric all-weather supersonic interceptor, first saw service with the R.A.F. in 1960. The Dinky model was announced in September 1959, when the actual machine was entering production and at a time when its performance details were still secret. It was the first Dinky plane to use plastic in one of its parts—the black nose probe. It was originally finished in silver but from 1964 in metallic grey. In 1965 the smooth buff wheels were replaced by black treaded ones. This was the last of the old miniature style of Dinky aircraft to remain in production, being withdrawn in 1969.

738 D.H.110 SEA VIXEN FIGHTER entered Royal Navy service as a carrier-based interceptor fighter in 1959. The Dinky, introduced in 1960, was the only twin-boom type to be modelled.

997 CARAVELLE SE 210 AIRLINER. The Sud Aviation Caravelle first flew in 1955 and entered production in 1958—it was the French equivalent of the Comet. A novel distinctive feature was its rear-mounted jet engines. The Dinky was introduced to the U.K. market in January 1962, but it originated with the French Dinky Supertoy No. 60F available in France since 1959. Produced in Liverpool from the French tools, the model featured a hinged gangway under the rear of the model which could be swung up and down like the real thing. The registration F-

## AEROPLANES 1954–65

| Cat. No. | Model | Intro. date | Deletion | Comments |
|---|---|---|---|---|
| 702 | D.H. Comet Jet Airliner | 1954 | 1965 | B.O.A.C. livery. Renumbered 999 |
| 703 | Handley-Page Herald | | | Not issued |
| 706 | Vickers Viscount Airliner (Air France) | 1956 | 1957 | Air France livery |
| 708 | Vickers Viscount Airliner (B.E.A.) | 1957 | 1965 | B.E.A. livery silver & white. Later metallic grey & white. |
| 715 | Bristol 173 Helicopter | 1956 | 1962 | Light blue. Later turquoise. Red rotor |
| 716 | Westland Sikorsky S51 Helicopter | 1957 | 1962 | Red |
| 734 | Supermarine Swift | 1955 | 1962 | Camouflaged |
| 735 | Gloster Javelin Delta Wing Fighter | 1956 | 1966 | Camouflaged |
| 736 | Hawker Hunter | 1955 | 1963 | Camouflaged |
| 737 | P.1B Lightning Fighter | 1959 | 1968 | Silver. Later metallic grey |
| 738 | D.H. 110 Sea Vixen Fighter | 1960 | 1965 | Grey & white. R.N. |
| 749 | Avro Vulcan Delta Wing Bomber | | | See also 992 and text |
| 992 | Avro Vulcan Delta Wing Bomber | 1955 | 1956 | Silver. See text |
| 997 | Caravelle SE210 Airliner | 1962 | 1965 | Air France livery |
| 998 | Bristol Britannia Airliner | 1959 | 1965 | Canadian Pacific livery. Silver & white, blue lines. Later red lines. Later metallic grey & white |
| 999 | =D.H. Comet Jet Airliner= | | | Renumbering of 702 |

BGNY in blue was carried on the starboard wing. It should be noted that the markings are slightly different from those on the French-made model, the main difference being that the French one had black registration letters spread over both wings. However, the under-wing inscriptions make it quite clear whether British or French manufacture is involved—despite the British version including the French 60F designation as well as the number 997 and later French models having both these numbers but being sold under the number 891! The first had smooth buff wheels but after 1965 the black treaded type. Incidentally, these types were different to the metallic brown ones fitted to the French Dinky Caravelle.

During the 1950s there was apparently one further Dinky aircraft in the offing—703 HANDLEY-PAGE HERALD (as briefly mentioned in connection with the numbering of the Vulcan). However, this was never made. It would have been good to see further types in the range of this period—a Canberra would have made an excellent choice, but Meccano seem to have been wary of producing bombers since their experience with the Vulcan.

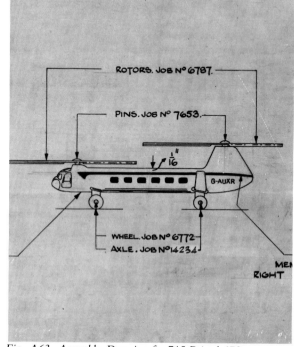

Fig. A63. Assembly Drawing for 715 Bristol 173 Helicopter.

## Aeroplanes 1965 to 1980. The 'Big Planes' Range

In 1965 the Dinky Toy Aeroplane underwent a complete change in concept. At this time, details such as seating and opening doors were being included on many Dinky cars and youngsters expected this standard of realism and play value which the previous type of aeroplane did not provide. It was decided to introduce new models to scales (1/65 to 1/90) large enough to incorporate special features, initially in the form of transparent plastic windows, seating and opening luggage compartments but later more novel features such as retractable undercarriages, cap-firing bombs, battery-operated motorised propellers and even gunfire noise and an ejecting pilot! The choice of new subjects was governed mainly by the sort of action feature that could be built in as much as any other factor.

Two castings to 1/77 scale (almost 'OO' gauge) were made in the mid-1960s. 710 BEECHCRAFT S.35 BONANZA had three major colour changes and many minor ones during its 10 years. The final change to blue, red and white finish was apparently at Beechcraft's request to match one of theirs. 715 BEECHCRAFT C.55 BARON had two main colour schemes with minor variations and in military finish was 712 U.S. ARMY T42A.

In October 1969, Meccano sprang a real surprise, large-scale models in connection with the film 'Battle of Britain'. The models were packed until about 1972 in colourful cartons which included scenes from the film. 719 SPITFIRE MK.II was a good deal bigger than the 1940 62a and had a battery operated spinning propeller. It was replaced by the non-motorised 741. A special version of this in chrome finish was produced to mark the Diamond Jubilee of the Royal Air Force in 1978, packed in a luxurious blue box with transparent cover. The onyx-like display stand bore commemorative script. Numbered 700, it was not available until 1979 and even then not widely. It is certainly a most attractive ornament and something different from the usual type of Dinky Toy. 721 JUNKERS Ju87B STUKA in 1/72 scale had a cap-firing bomb clipped under the fuselage.

717 BOEING 737 in Lufthansa livery was actually nearer in scale to the old 1/200 than to that of its contemporaries. 722 HAWKER HARRIER (1/72 scale) was introduced in 1970 when the real aircraft

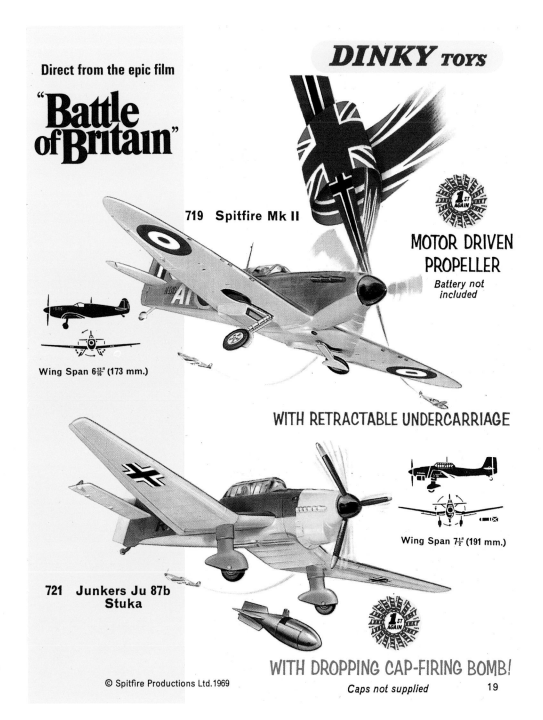

Direct from the epic film

**"Battle of Britain"**

**DINKY TOYS**

719  Spitfire Mk II

**1ST AGAIN**

**MOTOR DRIVEN PROPELLER**

*Battery not included*

Wing Span 6¹³⁄₁₆" (173 mm.)

**WITH RETRACTABLE UNDERCARRIAGE**

Wing Span 7½" (191 mm.)

721   Junkers Ju 87b Stuka

**1ST AGAIN**

**WITH DROPPING CAP-FIRING BOMB!**

© Spitfire Productions Ltd. 1969

*Caps not supplied*     19

*Fig. A70. 'Battle of Britain' Dinky Aircraft.*

was just entering service with the R.A.F. The modern red and blue roundels shown in some late 1970s catalogues were never fitted, red, white and blue being standard. 723 HAWKER SIDDELEY HS125 EXECUTIVE JET was to the rather odd scale of 1/108, and 728 R.A.F. DOMINIE with non-prototypical camouflaging used the same casting. 724 SEA KING HELICOPTER had a winch-operated Apollo capsule but this was not included in the kit version. With sonar device instead of capsule it became 736 BUNDESMARINE SEA KING HELICOPTER and the same casting unmotorised and finished in semi-matt service green figured in 618 A.E.C. ARTIC. TRANSPORTER WITH HELICOPTER. (See: Military post-war.) The PHANTOM casting was used four times: for 725 ROYAL NAVY version, 730 U.S. NAVY, 733 BUNDESLUFTWAFFE for the German and Austrian markets only and 727 U.S. AIR FORCE for the American market. Because of a shortage of finished units before Christmas 1974, wings finished in the Bundesluftwaffe splinter grey and green camouflage were fitted to fuselages in the all-grey gloss finish of the U.S. Navy type! 732 BELL POLICE HELICOPTER is also found in 299 POLICE CRASH SQUAD (See: Police Vehicles) and 303 COMMANDO SQUAD (See: Military post-war) and was scheduled to be given M★A★S★H stickers. (See: Character Merchandise). 734 P47 THUNDERBOLT and 739 A6M5 ZERO-SEN were Second World War fighters in 1/65 scale. For details of the others made between 1965 and 1980 see table. Some were available in kit form (See: Kits).

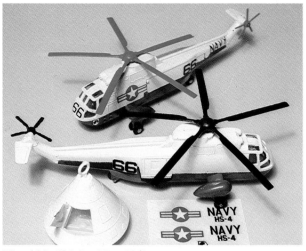

*Fig. A80. 724 Sea King Helicopter.*

*Fig. A82. 726 Messerschmidt Bf 109E.*

*Fig. A81. 725 F-4K Phantom.*

*Fig. A83. 727 U.S. Air Force F-4 Phantom II.*

*Fig. A84. 729 Multi-Role Combat Aircraft.*

Fig. A85. 730 U.S. Navy Phantom.

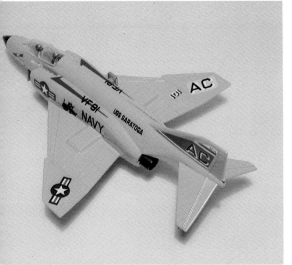

Fig. A89. 734 P47 Thunderbolt.

Fig. A88. 733 F-4K Phantom II Der Bundesluftwaffe.

Fig. A86. 731 S.E.P.E.C.A.T. Jaguar.

Fig. A91 739 A6M5 Zero-Sen.

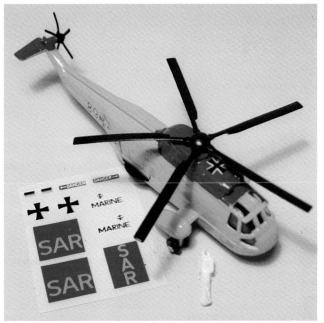

Fig. A90. 736 Bundesmarine Sea King Helicopter.

123

Fig. A92/1. 62e 'Spitfire'.

Fig. A92/2. 62d Bristol 'Blenheim'.

*Fig. A92. Some of the wooden patterns made of the aeroplanes.*

Fig. A92/3. 62g Boeing 'Flying Fortress'.

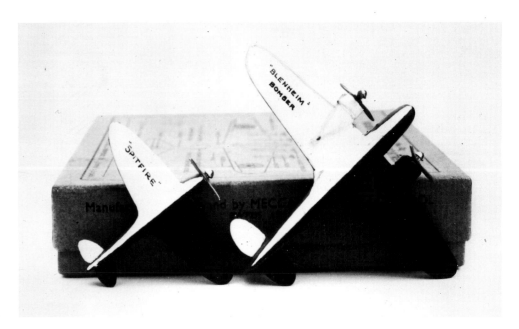

Fig. A92/4. 62k The King's Aeroplane.

Fig. A92/5. The undersides of the 'Spitfire' and 'Blenheim'.

| Cat. No. | Name | Intro. date | Deletion | Colours etc. |
|---|---|---|---|---|
| 700 | Spitfire Mk II Diamond Jubilee of the R.A.F. | 1979 | 1979 | Chromed |
| 710 | Beechcraft S.35 Bonanza | 1965 | 1976 | Red & white. Later bronze & yellow. Later blue, red & white |
| 712 | U.S. Army T-42A | 1972 | 1977 | Military finish: grey-green |
| 715 | Beechcraft C55 Baron | 1968 | 1976 | White: Later red |
| 717 | Boeing 737 | 1970 | 1975 | White engine pods. Later blue |
| 718 | Hawker Hurrican Mk IIc | 1972 | 1975 | Camouflage: grey & dark green |
| 719 | Spitfire Mk II | 1969 | 1978 | Camouflaged. Replaced by 741 |
| 721 | Junkers Ju87B Stuka | 1969 | 1980 | Grey-green. Still in production at factory closure |
| 722 | Hawker Harrier | 1970 | 1980 | Camouflage: metallic light blue & olive green. Still in production at factory closure |
| 723 | Hawker Siddeley HS125 Executive Jet | 1970 | 1975 | Yellow & white. Later metallic blue & white |
| 724 | Sea King Helicopter | 1971 | 1979 | White with metallic blue |
| 725 | F-4k Phantom | 1972 | 1977 | Dark blue and pale blue |
| 726 | Messerschmitt Bf 109E | 1972 | 1976 | Desert camouflage. Later grey-green |
| 727 | U.S. Air Force F-4 Phantom II | 1976 | 1977 | Camouflage: brown & green |
| 728 | R.A.F. Dominie | 1972 | 1975 | Camouflage: metallic blue & olive green |
| 729 | Multi-Role Combat Aircraft | 1974 | 1976 | Camouflage: grey & dark green |
| 730 | U.S. Navy Phantom | 1972 | 1976 | Grey & white |
| 731 | S.E.P.E.C.A.T. Jaguar | 1973 | 1976 | Camouflage: metallic light blue & green |
| 732 | Bell Police Helicopter | 1974 | 1980 | Blue, orange & white. Still in production at factory closure |
| 733 | F-4K Phantom II Der Bundesluftwaffe | 1973 | ? | Camouflage: Grey-green. German & Austrian market only |
| 734 | P47 Thunderbolt | 1975 | 1978 | Metallic silver grey |
| 736 | Bundesmarine Sea King Helicopter | 1973 | 1978 | Grey |
| 739 | A6M5 Zero-Sen | 1975 | 1978 | Metallic green & grey |
| 741 | Spitfire Mk II | 1978 | 1980 | Camouflaged. Still in production at factory closure |

# CHAPTER 5

# Post-war Issues & Production

**To the close of Binns Road**

### 23 Series Racing Cars

All the castings that were still in use at the outbreak of war, i.e., all of them except the first casting of 23/23a, were re-issued post-war, many with detail modifications that are not visible from the outside and some that can't be seen unless the bases are prised off, because they consist of such things as extra casting webs to strengthen the body, spigots to give better location points for bases, and so on. All the drawings that are still extant show these changes to have taken place in 1945, so it is relatively safe to assume that quite a few of the post-war castings are that very little bit different from the pre-war. Most collectors will, however, not be concerned about such minor details as they do not affect the look of the toys.

23a RACING CAR can hardly be distinguished from pre-war issues by anything other than the wheels. They were all two-tone, and the colour split is the same as that of the commonest pre-war one, with the subsidiary colour running from the high point of the bonnet, widening out to encompass the cockpit area, and continuing along the top of the tail fin. The colour range was much restricted—to red and silver and blue and silver. The racing numbers are stencilled as before in black or silver so that the body colour shows through for the number which is almost invariably '4'. It was renumbered 220, by which time it was known as the SMALL OPEN RACING CAR, and stayed in the catalogues until 1956. Being thus available for 22 years (ignoring the enforced wartime hiatus) makes it the longest production run of any Dinky Toy Vehicle. 23b HOTCHKISS RACING CAR came in red or silver, with stencilled circles in red, black or silver carrying the number '5' in the main body colour. This was issued for a couple of years only. 23c MERCEDES-BENZ RACING CAR was known as LARGE OPEN RACING CAR, and the tinplate base had 'Mercedes-Benz' added to the wording. It came in

Fig. 113. 23a, Post-war issue.

Fig. 114. 23b, Post-war issue.

Fig. 115. 23p, Post-war issue.

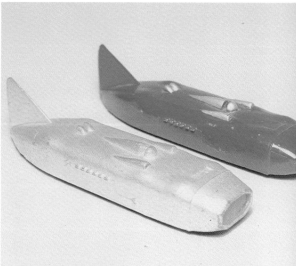

Fig. 116. 23s, Post-war issue.

blue and silver. It was in production until 1950, as was 23d AUTO-UNION RACING CAR, which was available in red, silver, green and blue. The stencilled roundels were red, silver or black with '2' showing through. There are no slots for a driver, and the base is marked with the model name. 23c and d were also made in France, but are clearly marked as such. 23e 'SPEED OF THE WIND' RACING CAR or, as it was later dubbed, RECORD CAR, is a close contender for the 'longest running Dinky' award, as it was available for 21 years. The tinplate base was marked with the name and riveted to the body. It was renumbered 221, and almost always painted silver, though there are some red ones. (For illustration see Chapter 2, Fig. 25.) 23p GARDNER'S RECORD CAR re-appeared only briefly. The base was marked with the name and the 'MG' logo featured on the nose and the flags on the sides, but the Lightning Flash was not applied. The colour was always green. 23s STREAMLINED RACING CAR also had a long run and was available in a

Fig. 117. The post-war new issues.

multiplicity of colourways: blue, green and silver with air intakes, etc. in contrasting blue, green and silver. Sometimes the radiator was coloured to match the air intakes. Renumbered 222, it remained in production until 1957.

As racing resumed after the war, Dinky were preparing a new batch of racing cars with diecast bodies incorporating the drivers and tinplate bases. Most of the group that were issued on the number 23 were in production for about 12 years with no major casting changes, the most significant modification being merely the use of plastic wheels towards the end of their run. There are no paint changes except on 23h FERRARI which has two slightly different nose schemes, the first having a completely yellow one and the second a yellow triangle on the nose. The racing numbers were white or yellow numbers applied directly to the bodies behind the driver. The 23f ALFA ROMEO was an update of a pre-war car and had a 1½ litre supercharged engine, while the 23k TALBOT-LAGO was a 4¼ litre unsupercharged. However, Formula 1 racing was soon superseded by Formula 2 (2 litre unsupercharged) and the other four models are representatives of this capacity. The models were all renumbered in 1954 and those that were subsequently available in bubble packs had yet another number which only appears on the packaging, not the model itself. Bubble packs were introduced in 1962.

**Colours:**
23f ALFA-ROMEO: red, white '8'
23g COOPER-BRISTOL: green, white '6'
23h FERRARI: blue, yellow nose, yellow '5'
23j H.W.M.: green, yellow '7'
23k TALBOT-LAGO: blue, yellow '4'
23n MASERATI: red, white flash, white '9'

Of the six new ones, five (23k being omitted) figured as Gift Set No. 4 RACING CARS. The set was renumbered 249. Later, a new set 249 was released, this time containing six vehicles; the TALBOT-LAGO and the later No. 239/210 VANWALL being included, and 235 H.W.M. omitted. They were tied onto a showcard, entitled : World Famous Racing Cars.

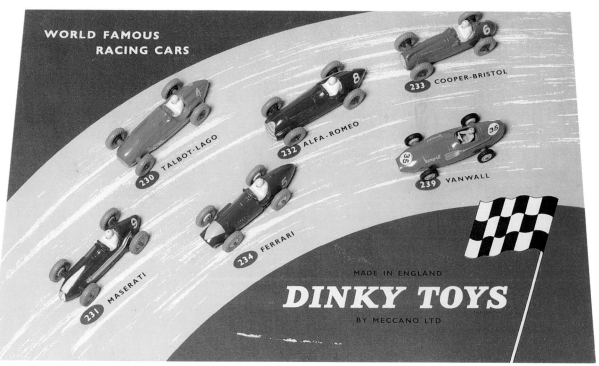

*Fig. 118. 249, World Famous Racing Cars.*

*Fig. 119. An example of the Bubble-pack used for the racing cars.*

| Cat. No. | Model | Intro. date | Deletion | Comments |
|---|---|---|---|---|
| No. 4 | Racing Cars | 1953 | 1958 | Renumbered 249. Contains: 23f Alfa-Romeo, 23g Cooper-Bristol, 23h Ferrari, 23j H.W.M., 23n Maserati |
| 23a | Racing Car | | 1956 | Re-issue. Renumbered 220 |
| 23b | Hotchkiss Racing Car | | 1948 | Re-issue |
| 23c | Large Open Racing Car | | 1950 | Re-issue of Mercedes-Benz |
| 23d | Auto-Union Racing Car | | 1950 | Re-issue |
| 23e | 'Speed of the Wind' Record Car | | 1949 | Re-issue. Renumbered 221 |
| 23f | Alfa-Romeo Racing Car | 1952 | 1964 | Renumbered 232. Bubble pack number 207 |
| 23g | Cooper-Bristol Racing Car | 1953 | 1964 | Renumbered 233. Bubble pack number 208 |
| 23h | Ferrari Racing Car | 1953 | 1964 | Renumbered 234. Bubble pack number 209 |
| 23j | H.W.M. Racing Car | 1953 | 1960 | Renumbered 235 |
| 23k | Talbot-Lago Racing Car | 1953 | 1964 | Renumbered 230. Bubble pack number 205 |
| 23n | Maserati Racing Car | 1953 | 1964 | Renumbered 231. Bubble pack number 206 |
| 23p | Gardner's M.G. Record Car | | 1947 | Re-issue |
| 23s | Streamlined Racing Car | | 1957 | Re-issue. Renumbered 222 |
| 205 | =Talbot-Lago Racing Car= | | | Bubble pack no. of 23k |
| 206 | =Maserati Racing Car= | | | Bubble pack no. of 23n |
| 207 | =Alfa-Romeo Racing Car= | | | Bubble pack no. of 23f |
| 208 | =Cooper-Bristol Racing Car= | | | Bubble pack no. of 23g |
| 209 | =Ferrari Racing Car= | | | Bubble pack no. of 23h |
| 210 | =Vanwell Racing Car= | | | Bubble pack no. 239. See next section |
| 220 | =Racing Car= | | | Renumbering of 23a |
| 221 | ='Speed of the Wind' Record Car= | | | Renumbering of 23e |
| 222 | =Streamlined Racing Car= | | | Renumbering of 23s |
| 230 | =Talbot-Lago Racing Car= | | | Renumbering of 23k |
| 231 | =Maserati Racing Car= | | | Renumbering of 23n |
| 232 | =Alfa-Romeo Racing Car= | | | Renumbering of 23f |
| 233 | =Cooper-Bristol Racing Car= | | | Renumbering of 23g |
| 234 | =Ferrari Racing Car= | | | Renumbering of 23h |
| 235 | =H.W.M. Racing Car= | | | Renumbering of 23j |
| 249 | =Racing Car= | | | Renumbering of Gift Set No. 4 |
| 249 | World Famous Racing Cars | 1962 | 1963 | Contains: 230 (23k) Talbot-Lago, 231 (23n) Maserati, 232 (23f) Alfa-Romeo, 233 (23g) Cooper-Bristol, 234 (23h) Ferrari, 239 Vanwall |

(Later Racing Cars)

| Cat. No. | Model | Intro. date | Deletion | Comments |
|---|---|---|---|---|
| 236 | Connaught Racing Car | 1956 | 1959 | Green |
| 237 | Mercedes-Benz Racing Car | 1957 | 1968 | White |
| 239 | Vanwall Racing Car | 1958 | 1965 | Green. Renumbered 210. See previous section |

## Later Racing Cars

A group of three cars were released, beginning at the end of 1956 whose numbers followed on from the previous batch but mixed in with them was a No. 238 D-TYPE JAGUAR which Dinky called a racing car but which is actually a sports car (see: Sports Cars). The three racing cars are all Formula 1 vehicles which at the time required 2½ litre engines.

In 1963–4, four of the first of the rear-engined Formula 1 cars was released. They were also available in a set, with four plastic people.

For some reason the grip of Formula 1 racing cars on the childish imagination was lost and a mere handful of such cars were made in the 1970s. A large scale, 1/32, was tried for the F.1s and the Super

Fig. 120. 238 D-Type Jaguar, 237 Mercedes and 236 Connaught.

Fig. 121. 239, Vanwall.

| Cat. No. | Model | Intro. date | Deletion | Comments |
|---|---|---|---|---|
| 201 | Racing Car Set | 1965 | 1968 | Consists of: 240, 241, 242, 243 |
| 121 | Goodwood Racing Gift Set | | | See: Sports. Sports Racing Cars |
| 240 | Cooper Racing Car | 1963 | 1969 | Blue, white stripes |
| 241 | Lotus Racing Car | 1963 | 1969 | Green |
| 242 | Ferrari Racing Car | 1963 | 1971 | Red |
| 243 | B.R.M. Racing Car | 1964 | 1971 | Green, yellow engine cowl |

| Cat. No. | Model | Intro. date | Deletion | Comments |
|---|---|---|---|---|
| 222 | Hesketh Racing Car 308E | 1978 | 1980 | Dark blue. Still in production at factory closure |
| 225 | Lotus F.1 | 1970 | 1976 | Metallic red. Later blue |
| 226 | Ferrari 312/B2 | 1972 | 1980 | Red, later gold. Still in production at factory closure |
| 228 | Super Sprinter | 1970 | 1972 | Blue |
| 370 | Dragster Set | 1969 | 1974 | Yellow |

No. 242 See page 53

No. 241 See page 53

**DINKY** TOYS

No. 243 See page 53

No. 240 See page 52

**201 Racing Car Set**

*Fig. 122. 201, Racing Car Set (1966 catalogue).*

*Fig. 124. 225 Lotus and 226 Ferrari.*

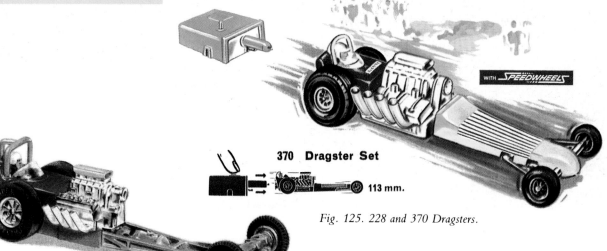

WITH *SPEEDWHEELS*

**370 Dragster Set**

113 mm.

*Fig. 125. 228 and 370 Dragsters.*

Sprinter and Dragster are representative of the new sport of Drag Racing. None of them can be called good models of the originals but they were not intended to be. For example, the Press Release on the Hesketh merely claimed it was 'based on' a modern F.1. Though named 'DRAGSTER SET', no. 370 consisted only of one car plus the impulsion unit which was also available separately. The unit was low in power so there was little danger of chipped skirting boards.

For illustration of number 222, see 1979 Catalogue, Chapter 9.

**228 Super Sprinter**

## Sports Cars—100 Series

The first post-war issues of Sports Cars released in 1955 and over the next few years were allocated numbers in the early 100s. This has lead to them being described by collectors as the '100 series'. We have retained this title because of its common usage but it must be pointed out that it is a little misleading for no. 106 (renumbered 140a) AUSTIN ATLANTIC CONVERTIBLE does not 'fit' with this category (See: British Saloons, Estates, etc.) nor do the numbers from 112 onwards. What we are talking of is a group of five castings of contemporary sports cars that were first released in a competition finish with racing numbers and a white-overalled racing driver and then in a touring finish with a grey-suited gentleman behind the wheel. Thus from 5 castings one gets 10 vehicles each on its own number and each of this ten was released in two finishes, the competition types having two different numbers as well. There were a few competition types released in unusual colours without racing numbers but, provided that the white racing driver is still *in situ* it is possible to distinguish them from a touring car version in an unusual colour. Normally the wheels are painted the same colour as (though not necessarily the same shade) the interior of the cars but later on some of the competition finish items acquired shiny hubs and treaded tyres. The M.G. MIDGET was renumbered 129 and repainted red or white for the American market. It did not have a driver. The AUSTIN-HEALEY 100 features as 128 in internal Meccano memos as a U.S. market issue but there is no firm evidence that it was actually shipped there. The Sports versions figured in a gift set.

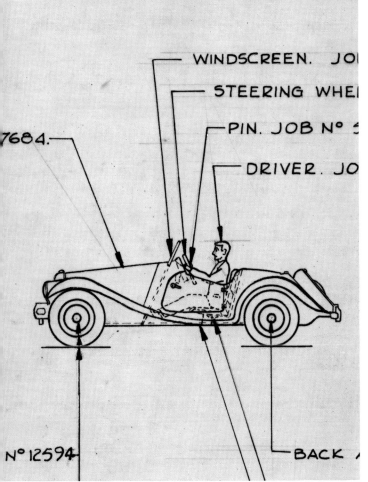

*Fig. 126. M.G. Midget Assembly Drawing.*

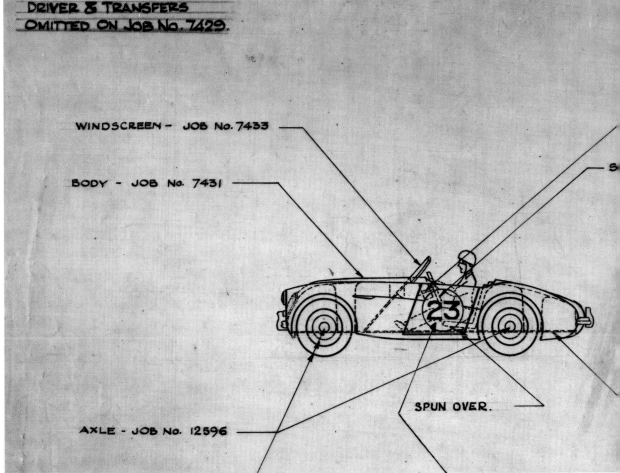

*Fig. 127. Austin-Healey Assembly Drawing.*

*Fig. 128. 149, Sports Car Gift Set (from left to right: nos. 108, 109, 107, 110 and 111).*

## SPORTS CARS—100 SERIES

| Cat. No. | Model | Intro. date | Deletion | Comments (Racing Number in quotes) |
|---|---|---|---|---|
| 101 | Sunbeam Alpine (touring finish) | 1957 | 1960 | Light maroon, tan seats |
| | | | | Turquoise blue, blue seats |
| 102 | M.G. Midget (touring finish) | 1957 | 1960 | Light green, tan seats |
| | | | | Yellow, red seats |
| 103 | Austin-Healey 100 (touring finish) | 1957 | 1960 | Cream, red seats |
| | | | | Red, grey seats |
| 104 | Aston Martin DB3S (touring finish) | 1957 | 1960 | Light blue, blue seats |
| | | | | Salmon pink, red seats |
| 105 | Triumph TR2 Sports (touring finish) | 1957 | 1962 | Yellow, green seats |
| | | | | Grey, red seats |
| 107 | Sunbeam Alpine (competition finish) | 1955 | 1959 | Pink, grey seats. '34' |
| | | | | Light blue, tan seats. '26' |
| 108 | M.G. Midget (competition finish) | 1955 | 1959 | White, maroon seats. '28' |
| | | | | Red, tan seats. '24' |
| 109 | Austin Healey 100 (competition finish) | 1955 | 1959 | Cream, red seats. '23' |
| | | | | Yellow, blue seats. '21' |
| 110 | Aston Martin DB3S (competition finish) | 1956 | 1959 | Grey, blue seats. '20' |
| | | | | Green, red seats. '22' |
| 111 | Triumph TR2 (competition finish) | 1956 | 1959 | Turquoise, red seats. '25' |
| | | | | Pink, blue seats. '29' |
| 129 | M.G. Midget | | | American issue. red or white |
| 149 | Sports Cars Gift Set | 1957 | 1959 | Contains: 107, 108, 109, 110, 111 |

*Fig. 129. The Sports Cars in touring finish.*

### Cars—40 Series

The nine vehicles in the 40 Series can be regarded as the first truly post-war set as they were all planned and produced post-war. Indeed, they are all models of post-war vehicles which are nearly all 'family saloons'. The lead time between the issue of the drawings and the production of the models is approximately one year, much longer than before, and gives an indication of the slow gearing up of production in this immediate post-war phase. The introduction and deletion of the models was spread over several years, from 1947 to 1954 and from 1958 to 1962 respectively. All had a diecast one-piece body (40a and b having separate headlamps) and a tinplate baseplate except the Taxi which has a diecast one. The axles are riveted both ends. Initially they were packed in boxes of six of the same vehicle and they were never available as a boxed set each model being packed singly in its own box. At renumbering they were all, except the Taxi, allocated numbers in the 150s and 160s (approx 1954). In 1956 some of the

Fig. 131. A selection of the many colours which have appeared on the 40 Series cars.

Fig. 133. Left: 40g Morris Oxford, right: 40f Hillman Minx, rear: 40a Riley.

Fig. 134. Left: 40d Austin Devon, right: 40h Austin Taxi, rear: 40j Austin Somerset.

Fig. 136. 40e Standard Vanguard Saloons, showing the casting modification and also the earlier plain box.

Fig. 132. Some more colours, including the later two-tone variations.

Fig. 135. A box of six 40b Triumph 1800 Saloons, showing the later coloured box.

Fig. 137. 40h Austin Taxi showing various single-tone and the two-tone paint finishes. The black one has the latest type of spun metal wheels. The yellow version had either a black or brown chassis and interior.

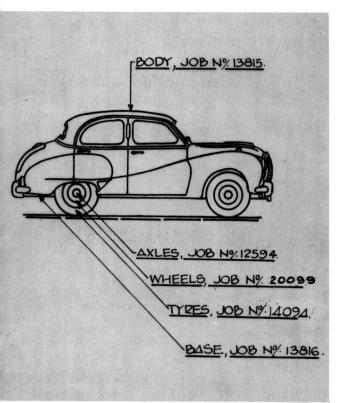

BODY, JOB No. 13815.

AXLES, JOB No. 12594.

WHEELS, JOB No. 20099

TYRES, JOB No. 14094.

BASE, JOB No. 13816.

*Fig. 130. Austin Somerset Saloon Drawing.*

CARS—40 SERIES

| Cat. No. | Model | Intro. date | Deletion | Comments |
|---|---|---|---|---|
| No.3 | Passenger Cars (Gift Set) | 1952 | 1953 | Contains: 27f Estate Car, 30h Daimler Ambulance 40e Standard Vanguard 40g Morris Oxford, 40h Austin Taxi 140b Rover 75 |
| 40a | Riley | 1947 | 1960 | Renumbered 158 |
| 40b | Triumph 1800 | 1948 | 1960 | Renumbered 151 |
| 40d | Austin Devon | 1949 | 1960 | Blue/yellow, green/pink. Renumbered 152 |
| 40e | Standard Vanguard | 1948 | 1960 | See text. Renumbered 153 |
| 40f | Hillman Minx | 1951 | 1958 | Green/cream, pink/blue. Renumbered 154 |
| 40g | Morris Oxford | 1950 | 1960 | Green/cream, white/red. Renumbered 159 |
| 40h | Austin Taxi | 1951 | 1962 | Green/yellow. Renumbered 254 |
| 40j | Austin Somerset | 1954 | 1960 | Black/cream, yellow/red. Renumbered 161 |
| 151 | =Triumph 1800= | | | Renumbering of 40b |
| 152 | =Austin Devon= | | | Renumbering of 40d |
| 153 | =Standard Vanguard= | | | Renumbering of 40e |
| 154 | =Hillman Minx= | | | Renumbering of 40f |
| 158 | =Riley= | | | Renumbering of 40a |
| 159 | =Morris Oxford= | | | Renumbering of 40g |
| 161 | =Austin Somerset= | | | Renumbering of 40j |
| 254 | =Austin Taxi= | | | Renumbering of 40h |

models acquired the newly fashionable two-tone finish and during 1958 the bases were painted glossy black on both sides. Many colours were employed, most of them prototypical. (For colours other than two-tone: see colour photographs.) 40c JOWETT JAVELIN was never issued, though it would have sold as well as the others. The only significant casting changes took place on the 40e STANDARD VANGUARD SALOON, which was initially issued with 'open rear wheels', but these were covered with spats in 1950. The type with a line horizontally across the lower boot was not deliberately conceived as the drawing was not modified to produce the change, so it is sign of die wear or repair.

Three of the 40 Series with three other contemporary vehicles were issued in Set No. 3 PASSENGER CARS.

**Sports Cars, etc.**

The rest of the many sports, sports racing and rally cars don't fall into obvious large groupings so they are all dealt with together in this section which has been subdivided to a certain extent to make the material easier to refer to. Only those with significant variations or of particular interest are dealt with in the text. For details of the rest see tables.

At the same time as the '100 series' were being released three cars especially designed as sports-racers were produced. This was the post-war heyday of Le Mans when the Manufacturers were using the track as a test-bed for their current production and the cars on the Circuit were not very far removed from the ones that the public could buy.

The original plans for 133 CUNNINGHAM show that it was to be issued without numbers.

In the late 1950s and early 1960s, sports cars fully representative of the era were made, a Sprite, an M.G.B., etc. An intriguing early number is to be found amongst the Meccano archive material for the JAGUAR XK 120—139d. This is part of the American series of numbering and possibly indicates that the numbering system was in a considerable state of flux while the vehicle was being designed. It was never released on this number in the U.K., being allocated 157. Almost unbelievably, the XK was released in horrific two-tone colour schemes in its later life. 185 ALFA ROMEO SUPER SPRINT has the significance of being one of the first group with 'finger tip steering', a not very sophisticated system of allowing the front wheels to follow the direction in which one was pushing the car. Four of this selection were included in the Goodwood Racing Gift Set No. 121, which had nine typical racing pit characters

| Cat. No. | Model | Intro. date | Deletion | Comments |
|---|---|---|---|---|
| 133 | Cunningham | 1955 | 1960 | White with blue stripes |
| 163 | Bristol 450 | 1956 | 1960 | Green (See Fig. 151) |
| 238 | D-type Jaguar Racing Car | 1957 | 1964 | Light blue-green (See Fig. 120) |

*Fig. 139. 121 Goodwood Racing Gift Set, top row 113 M.G.B. and 182 Porsche 356A Coupé, bottom row 112 Austin-Healey Sprite and 120 Jaguar E-type.*

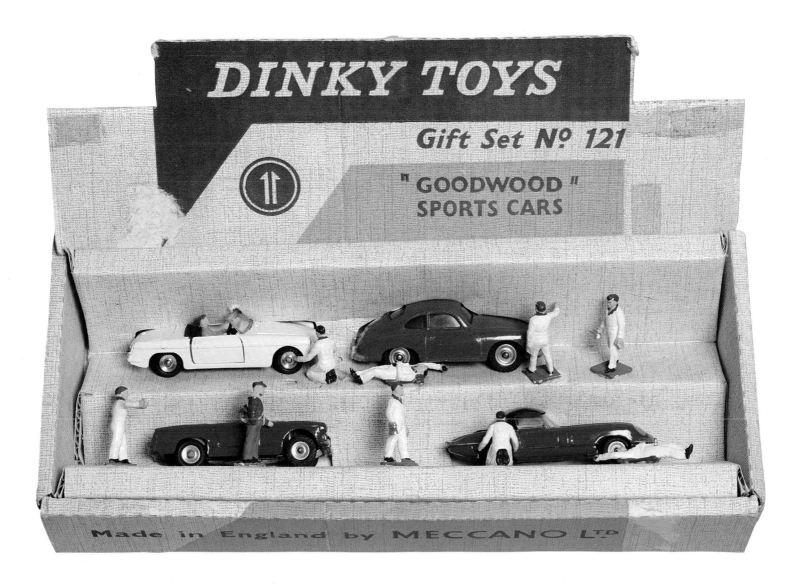

*Fig. 138. 133 Cunningham.*

| Cat. No. | Model | Intro. date | Deletion | Comments |
|---|---|---|---|---|
| 112 | Austin-Healey Sprite Mk II | 1961 | 1965 | Red |
| 113 | M.G.B. | 1962 | 1968 | Cream |
| 114 | Triumph Spitfire | 1963 | 1970 | Silver-grey, gold, red |
| 120 | Jaguar E-type | 1962 | 1967 | Red, black hard top |
| 121 | Goodwood Gift Set | 1963 | 1965 | Contains: 112, A-H Sprite 113 M.G.B., 120 Jaguar E-type, 182 Porsche 356A plus 9 plastic figures |
| 157 | Jaguar XK 120 | 1954 | 1962 | Red, yellow, green, white. Duotone: Pir & turquoise. Grey and yellow |
| 167 | A.C. Aceca | 1958 | 1963 | Red and grey, cream and brown |
| 182 | Porsche 356A Coupé | 1958 | 1965 | Blue, cream |
| 185 | Alfa Romeo 1900 Super Sprint | 1961 | 1963 | Red, yellow |

*Fig. 140. 157 Jaguar XK 120 showing single and two-tone colours.*

**DINKY TOYS**

**114** Triumph Spitfire. 3½″ – 89 mm.

**113** M.G.B. Sports Car. 3⅜″ – 86 mm.

**112** Austin Healey Sprite Mk. II. 3⅛″ – 79 mm.

**120** E Type Jaguar. 3⅝″ – 92 mm.

2

**185** Alfa Romeo 1900 Super Sprint. 4″ – 102 mm.

*Fig. 142. 1963 catalogue (U.K. 11th).*

to create the scene selected from 009 SERVICE STATION PERSONNEL.

Rally cars were not a popular subject with Dinky for they only made five, all of which were existing castings painted and decalled in rally guise, with occasional additions, e.g. a roof-mounted spotlight on 212 CORTINA. The TR 7 is most attractive with its blue and red decalling and 'Leyland' sticker on the rear.

The bulk of 'the rest' were produced in the late 1960s and early 1970s and many were in production for five or six years with very minor casting and decal changes. The majority are fairly unmemorable reflecting the decline in the popularity of the sports car for a variety of reasons including the soaring price of petrol, the imposition of maximum speed limits and the United States safety and emission control regulations. 212 FIAT-ABARTH 2000 did have a casting change, having to begin with a recessed slot in the nose but later a grille was incorporated in the casting. Beware the 1973 catalogue, for in it the illustrations for 187 DE TOMASO-MANGUSTA 5000 and 189 LAMBORGHINI MARZAL have been transposed. There are two versions of the TRIUMPH TR 7 (in addition to the Rally Car), the first of which was available only briefly, painted a metallic blue and in a box slightly

larger than normal. The date on the back of the box, 1975, is the date of the car not the model. Meccano made a great deal of fuss about the introduction of this vehicle in the vain hope it would signal a turn in the fortune of Dinky Toys. 219 LEYLAND JAGUAR XJ 5.3 COUPÉ was made to a larger scale than usual as was the trend in the late 1970s and immediately before the closure of the factory almost the same casting on the same number was released as the 'Big Cat' Jaguar with red, black and white stickers incorporating a grinning Jaguar face on the bonnet and the leaping emblem on the sides. Two Gift Sets were released containing between them five of this group plus 188 JENSEN FF (see: British Saloons and Estates).

| Cat. No. | Model | Intro. date | Deletion | Comments (Rally number in quotes) |
|---|---|---|---|---|
| 205 | Lotus Cortina Rally Car | 1968 | 1972 | White & Red. '7' |
| 207 | Triumph TR7 Rally Car | 1977 | 1980 | White. '8' Still in production at factory closure |
| 212 | Ford Cortina Rally Car | 1965 | 1969 | White. '8' |
| 213 | Ford Capri Rally Car | 1970 | 1974 | Red. '20' |
| 214 | Hillman Imp Rally Car | 1966 | 1968 | Blue. '35' |

**205 Lotus Cortina Rally Car**

*Fig. 143. Page 8 of 1971 Catalogue.*

**213 Ford Capri Rally Car**

*Fig. 141. 182 Porsche 356A and 167 A.C. Aceca.*

*Fig. 144. The Press Release picture of 207 Triumph TR7 Rally Car, December 1977.*

*Fig. 146. 211 Triumph TR7 Sports Car.*

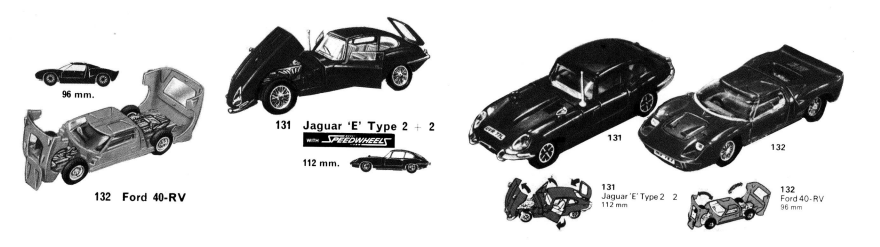

96 mm.

131 **Jaguar 'E' Type 2 + 2**
WITH *SPEEDWHEELS*
112 mm.

132 **Ford 40-RV**

131

132

131 Jaguar 'E' Type 2 2
112 mm

132 Ford 40-RV
96 mm

187

189

187
De Tomaso Mangusta 5000
102 mm

189
Lamborghini Marzal
108 mm

190

200

202

190
Monteverdi 375L
116 mm

6

200
Matra 630
105 mm

202
Fiat Abarth 2000
91 mm

*Fig. 145. Pages 4, 5, 6, 7, 8 and 9 of 1973 Catalogue (no. 9) (Note: captions of 189 Lambourghini Marzal and 187 De Tomaso Mangusta are reversed—an error by Meccano Ltd in the catalogue).*

204

208

210

216

217

204
Ferrari 312P
99 mm

208
VW Porsche 914
89 mm

210
Alfa Romeo Tipo Le Mans
107 mm

7

216
Dino Ferrari
98 mm

217
Alfa Romeo Scarabeo 0S1
90 mm

*Fig. 147.*

⅜″ (111 mm.)

**110   Aston Martin DB 5**

New  **219**

**219**
"Big Cat"
Jaguar
137 mm

SPORTS CARS

| Cat. No. | Model | Intro. date | Deletion | Comments (Racing numbers in quotes) |
|---|---|---|---|---|
| 110 | Aston Martin DB5 | 1965 | 1970 | Metallic red, black or cream interior |
| 131 | Jaguar E-type 2+2 | 1968 | 1974 | Gold. Later mauve & white |
| 132 | Ford 40-RV | 1967 | 1973 | Silver. Later metallic green |
| 153 | Aston Martin DB6 | 1967 | 1971 | Silver-blue. Later Silver-green |
| 187 | De Tomaso Mangusta 5000 | 1968 | 1976 | Red & white. '7' |
| 189 | Lamborghini Marzal | 1969 | 1977 | Green & white. Later blue and white |
| 190 | Monteverdi 375L | 1970 | 1973 | Dark red |
| 200 | Matra 630 | 1971 | 1974 | Blue |
| 202 | Fiat-Abarth 2000 | 1971 | 1974 | Orange & white |
| 204 | Ferrari 312P | 1971 | 1974 | Red. '60' or '24' |
| 208 | VW Porsche 914 | 1971 | 1980 | Yellow. later blue with black bonnet. Still in production at factory closure |
| 210 | Alfa Romeo 33 Tipo Le Mans | 1970 | 1973 | Orange. '36' |
| 211 | Triumph TR7 Sports Car | 1976 | 1980 | Metallic blue. Later red. Still in production at factory closure |
| 215 | Ford GT Racing Car | 1965 | 1973 | White. Later green. '7' |
| 216 | Dino Ferrari | 1967 | 1974 | Red |
| 217 | Alfa Romeo Scarabeo OSI | 1969 | 1974 | Red. Later day-glo orange |
| 218 | Lotus Europa | 1970 | 1974 | Yellow with blue or with black detail |
| 219 | Leyland Jaguar XJ 5.3 Coupe/ | 1977 | 1979 | White. 'Leyland' decals |
| 219 | 'Big Cat' Jaguar | 1979 | 1979 | White 'Cat' decals |
| 220 | Ferrari P5 | 1970 | 1974 | Red |
| 223 | McLaren Can-Am | 1970 | 1977 | White and blue. Later green '5' or '7' |
| 224 | Mercedes-Benz C 111 | 1970 | 1973 | Metallic dark red |
| 245 | Superfast Gift Set | 1969 | 1972 | Contains: 131 Jaguar E-type. 153 Aston Martin DB6. 188 Jensen FF |
| 246 | International GT Gift Set | 1969 | 1972 | Contains: 187 De Tomaso, 215 Ford GT, 216 Dino Ferrari |

See the 1979 Catalogue for illustration of number 219, 1979 issue. Chapter 9.

**218**
**220**
**223**
**224**

**218**
Lotus Europa
96 mm

**220**
Ferrari P5
96 mm

**223**
McLaren M8A Can Am
94 mm

**224**
Mercedes-Benz C111
102 mm

## British Saloons and Estates

Meccano's general early post-war strategy (initiated with the previously described 40 series) was to produce the cars that could be seen on the street and then to keep them in production for approximately the life of the real vehicle, i.e. four years or so. At first there was a preponderance of family saloons but gradually luxury cars were incorporated so that in the early 1960s luxury cars and the top end of the family saloons predominated. This trend continued to the extent that in the 1970s there were fewer and fewer family cars being made and the emphasis shifted to the super-luxury vehicles, most of which fall into the 'sports car' category. This was a deliberate policy, the theory being that children did not want to play with cars that dad and grandad owned but with the models that dad or grandad would like to have owned given sufficient wealth. Albeit with hindsight one wonders about the wisdom of this proposition. Occasionally a car lasted well beyond its expected span. 197 MORRIS MINI TRAVELLER was in the catalogue for nine years but the longevity record (in this group of British Saloons and Estates) goes to the Rolls Royce Phantom which, with a casting change and two numbers, 152 and 124, was shown first in the 1965 catalogue and finally in the one for 1979!

| Cat. No. | Model | Intro. date | Deletion | Comments |
|---|---|---|---|---|
| 106 | =Austin A90 Atlantic= | | | Renumbering of 140a |
| 156 | =Rover 75= | | | Renumbering of 140b |
| 140a | Austin Atlantic Convertible | 1951 | 1958 | Blue, black, pink. Renumbered 106 |
| 140b | Rover 75 Saloon | 1951 | 1958 | Maroon, cream, red, duo-tone blue & cream, dark & light green. Renumbered 156 |

Despite the self-congratulatory sentiments in the catalogues, Dinky were rarely 'first' at introducing new features such as opening doors, etc. Two years after Corgi did so, Dinky released the first cars with windows (1958) on the 176 AUSTIN A105 SALOON. Unsophisticated suspension came in the following year on 150 ROLLS ROYCE SILVER WRAITH. They waited until 1960 to introduce 'Fingertip Steering' and 1969 to phase in 'Speedwheels' represented in this section by 165 CAPRI. None of these innovations were as technically brilliant as those fitted by Tekno (Denmark), Solido (France) or the Japanese Toy Manufacturers and even the first batch of models with opening parts had badly fitting doors, bonnets, etc. Most of the Gift Sets involving vehicles in this section are detailed at the end.

The first two are contemporaneous with the 40 series and were both renumbered. One isn't a saloon but it fits in this group as it can hardly be called a sports car, the Austin Atlantic Convertible. The Rover 75 is in Gift Set 3 PASSENGER CARS. (See 40 series.)

This group dates from the late 1950s and early 1960s and contains the first cars with windows and suspension. There are few casting variations, the most significant being the existence of the Humber Hawk with and without front number plate. The Hillman Minx is the 1957 model, not a re-issue of the 40 series.

The mid-1960s saw an increase in the number of expensive cars in the range, one of them being 195 JAGUAR 3.4 LITRE MARK II which was the first

BODY    JOB Nº 13661
BASE    JOB Nº 13662
AXLE    JOB Nº 12598
WHEEL   JOB Nº 20099
TYRE    JOB Nº 14094.

*Fig. 148. 140B Rover 75 Drawing.*

*Fig. 149. 140b Rover 75 and 140a Austin Atlantic.*

Fig. 150. 176 Austin A105 Saloon, 141 Vauxhall Victor
Estate Car and 150 Rolls Royce Silver Wraith.

| Cat. No. | Model | Intro. date | Deletion | Comments |
|---|---|---|---|---|
| 150 | Rolls Royce Silver Wraith | 1959 | 1962 | Two-tone grey |
| 160 | Austin A30 | 1958 | 1962 | Fawn, blue |
| 162 | Ford Zephyr | 1956 | 1960 | Cream & green, two-tone blue |
| 164 | Vauxhall Cresta | 1957 | 1960 | Maroon & cream, green & grey |
| 165 | Humber Hawk | 1959 | 1963 | Maroon & fawn, green & black, green |
| 166 | Sunbeam Rapier | 1958 | 1963 | Cream & orange, two-tone blue |
| 168 | Singer Gazelle | 1959 | 1963 | Cream & brown, grey & green |
| 175 | Hillman Minx | 1958 | 1961 | Pink & green, grey & blue |
| 176 | Austin A105 Saloon | 1958 | 1963 | Grey & red, cream & blue |
| 189 | Triumph Herald | 1959 | 1963 | Green & white, blue & white |

Fig. 151. 162 Ford Zephyr and 164 Vauxhall Cresta with
163 Bristol 450 at the rear.

Fig. 153. 195 Jaguar 3.4 litre Mark II and 135 Triumph
2000 with 189 Triumph Herald in the foreground.

Fig. 152. Back row: 166 Sunbeam Rapier and 165 Humber
Hawk. Front row: 145 Singer Vogue, 168 Singer Gazelle and 175 Hillman Minx.

Fig. 154. 183 Fiat 600 Saloon and 160 Austin A30.

car with 'Fingertip Steering'. There are two COR-TINAS in the group, 139 being the first type, and 133 the second with modified grille, etc. Both appeared very soon after the full-size cars were re-leased so Meccano presumably had access to draw-ings and photographs before the public announce-ment by Ford. 130 CORSAIR figured with the HEALEY SPORTS BOAT ON TRAILER as 125 FUN A'HOY GIFT SET, and 135 TRIUMPH 2000 in 118 TOW-AWAY GLIDER SET which was slightly larger than the car by itself. The glider was not available separately. 146 DAIMLER 2½ LITRE SALOON was a modification of 195 JAGUAR 3.4 LITRE MARK II where the grille had been altered.

The late 1960s group includes 164 FORD ZODIAC, one of the first with opening doors which, on its release, was one of the 'lows' of Dinky casting. 152 ROLLS ROYCE PHANTOM V LIMOUSINE was in production until 1975 first

*Fig. 156.*

## BRITISH SALOONS AND ESTATES

| Cat. No. | Model | Intro. date | Deletion | Comments |
|---|---|---|---|---|
| 118 | Tow-Away Glider Set | 1965 | 1969 | Contains 135 Triumph 2000 & plastic glider and trailer |
| 125 | Fun A'Hoy Gift Set | 1964 | 1967 | Contains 130 Corsair & 796 Healey Sports Boat on trailer |
| 127 | Rolls Royce Silver Cloud III | 1964 | 1971 | Metallic green, later metallic bronze |
| 130 | Ford Consul Corsair | 1964 | 1968 | Red, light blue |
| 133 | Ford Consul Cortina | 1964 | 1968 | Metallic yellow & white |
| 134 | Triumph Vitesse | 1964 | 1967 | Metallic green, metallic blue |
| 135 | Triumph 2000 | 1963 | 1968 | Blue with white roof, cream with blue roof, etc. |
| 136 | Vauxhall Viva | 1964 | 1972 | White, blue |
| 138 | Hillman Imp | 1963 | 1972 | Metallic green, metallic red |
| 139 | Ford Consul Cortina | 1963 | 1964 | Blue |
| 140 | Morris 1100 | 1963 | 1968 | Blue |
| 141 | Vauxhall Victor Estate Car | 1963 | 1967 | Yellow |
| 142 | Jaguar Mark 10 | 1962 | 1968 | Metallic blue |
| 143 | Ford Capri | 1962 | 1966 | Green & white |
| 145 | Singer Vogue Saloon | 1962 | 1966 | Metallic green |
| 146 | 2½ litre V.8 Daimler | 1963 | 1966 | Metallic green-blue |
| 155 | Ford Anglia | 1961 | 1964 | Blue |
| 194 | Bentley 'S' Series Coupé | 1961 | 1966 | Grey. Red interior |
| 195 | Jaguar 3.4 litre Mark II | 1960 | 1964 | Maroon, cream |
| 198 | Rolls Royce Phantom V | 1962 | 1968 | Silvery-green & cream, two-tone-grey |

142

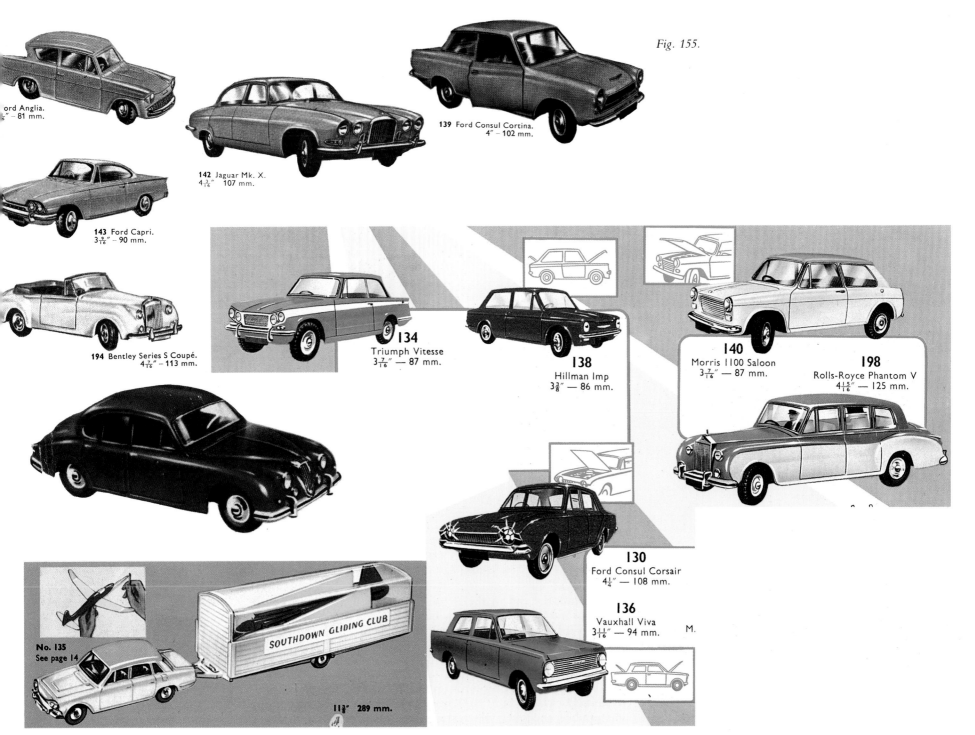

Fig. 155.

ord Anglia.
" — 81 mm.

142 Jaguar Mk. X.
4 3/16" 107 mm.

139 Ford Consul Cortina.
4" – 102 mm.

143 Ford Capri.
3 9/16" – 90 mm.

194 Bentley Series S Coupé.
4 7/16" – 113 mm.

134
Triumph Vitesse
3 7/16" — 87 mm.

138
Hillman Imp
3 3/8" – 86 mm.

140
Morris 1100 Saloon
3 7/16" – 87 mm.

198
Rolls-Royce Phantom V
4 15/16" — 125 mm.

130
Ford Consul Corsair
4 1/4" – 108 mm.

136
Vauxhall Viva
3 11/16" – 94 mm.

No. 135
See page 14

SOUTHDOWN GLIDING CLUB

11 3/8" 289 mm.

M.

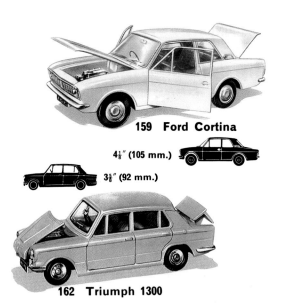

**159 Ford Cortina**

4⅛" (105 mm.)

3⅝" (92 mm.)

**162 Triumph 1300**

**165 Ford Capri** WITH *SPEEDWHEELS*

**168 Ford Escort**

**158 Rolls Royce Silver Shadow**

*Fig. 157.*

| Cat. No. | Model | Intro. date | Deletion | Comments |
|---|---|---|---|---|
| 123 | Princess 2200HL Saloon | 1977 | 1980 | Gold & black. Still in production at factory closure |
| 124 | Rolls Royce Phantom V Limousine | 1977 | 1979 | Metallic blue |
| 151 | Vauxhall Victor 101 | 1965 | 1968 | Yellow. Later metallic red |
| 152 | Rolls Royce Phantom V Limousine | 1965 | 1975 | Dark blue. Later metallic blue |
| 158 | Rolls Royce Silver Shadow | 1967 | 1972 | Metallic red. Later blue |
| 159 | Ford Cortina Mk II | 1967 | 1969 | White |
| 162 | Triumph 1300 | 1966 | 1969 | Blue |
| 164 | Ford Zodiac Mk IV | 1966 | 1971 | Silver. Later bronze |
| 165 | Ford Capri | 1969 | 1975 | Green & metallic purple |
| 168 | Ford Escort | 1968 | 1975 | Blue. Later red |
| 169 | Ford Corsair 2000E | 1967 | 1969 | Silver & black |
| 171 | Austin 1800 | 1965 | 1967 | Blue |
| 180 | Rover 3500 | 1979 | 1980 | White. Still in production at factory closure |
| 188 | Jensen FF | 1968 | 1974 | Yellow |

See the 1979 Catalogue for illustration of numbers 123, 124 and 180. Chapter 9.

| Cat. No. | Model | Intro. date | Deletion | Comments |
|---|---|---|---|---|
| 178 | Mini Clubman | 1975 | 1979 | Bronze |
| 183 | Morris Mini Minor (Automatic) | 1966 | 1974 | Metallic blue & black. Red & black |
| 197 | Morris Mini-Traveller | 1961 | 1970 | Cream, green |
| 199 | Austin 7 Countryman | 1961 | 1970 | Red, blue |

See 1979 Catalogue for illustration of number 178. Chapter 9.

with and then without passengers. It boasted opening bonnet, boot and all four doors. After a short hiatus, it reappeared on a new number 124, this time with only the boot and front doors opening—fancy economising on a Rolls Royce! 165 FORD CAPRI is the new model but 169 FORD CORSAIR 2000E is an update of 130. 188 JENSEN FF is part of 245 SUPERFAST GIFT SET. (See: Sport Cars.)

Towards the end of the 1970s, a larger scale, 1/35, was introduced and two saloons were made, 180 ROVER 3500 which was actually manufactured in Hong Kong and 123 PRINCESS 2200HL. 170 GRANADA GHIA was planned but was not released before the factory closure.

The ubiquitous MINI turns up in four 'family' versions (provided your family was small in stature and number) and several liveried versions (see A.A.

and R.A.C. vans, Police Vehicles and other Commercials for these).

The Land Rover/Range Rover family were first represented by 27d/340 LAND ROVER which is to be found in 'Farm and Garden', and was frequently in the catalogues in Police, Ambulance and Fire versions. 202 was referred to in American Catalogues as 'Off the Road Pick-up'.

It was not normal policy to produce a vehicle that was not on the road at the time, but this rule was twice broken in the 1960s. Character Merchandise versions of both were also produced.

Four Gift Sets, some of which are a real mixture of items from various different groups were produced in the 1960s, each for only a short period of time. The colours of the models in the sets do not differ from those of the individually boxed models.

| t. No. Model | Intro. date | Deletion | Comments |
|---|---|---|---|
| 2 Range Rover | 1970 | 1980 | Gold. Later yellow. Still in production at factory closure |
| 2 Customised Land Rover | 1979 | 1980 | Yellow. Still in production at factory closure |
| 3 Customised Range Rover | 1979 | 1980 | Black. Still in production at factory closure |
| 4 Land Rover | 1970 | 1978 | Blue & red |

| t. No. Model | Intro. date | Deletion | Comments |
|---|---|---|---|
| 5 Ford Model 'T' 1908 | 1964 | 1968 | Blue, black chassis |
| 6 1913 Morris Oxford | 1965 | 1969 | Yellow and blue |

| Cat. No. Model(s) | Intro. date | Deletion | Contains |
|---|---|---|---|
| 122 Touring Gift Set | 1963 | 1964 | 188 Caravan, 193 Rambler Station Wagon, 195 Jaguar 3.4, 270 A.A. Motor Cycle Patrol, 295 Atlas Kenebrake, 796 Healey Sports Boat on trailer |
| 123 Mayfair Gift Set | 1963 | 1964 | 142 Jaguar Mark 10, 150 Rolls Royce Silver Wraith, 186 Mercedes 220 SE, 194 Bentley 'S' type, 198 Rolls Royce Phantom V, 199 Austin Countryman |
| 124 Holiday Gift Set | 1964 | 1967 | 952 Vega Major Luxury Coach, 137 Plymouth Fury Convertible, 142 Jaguar Mk 10, 796 Healey Sports Boat on Trailer |
| 126 Motor Show Gift Set | 1965 | 1969 | 133 Cortina (Later 159 Cortina) 127 Rolls Royce Silver Cloud, 151 Vauxhall Victor 101, 171 Austin 1800 |

*Fig. 158. 180 Rover 3500.*

199 Austin 7 Countryman. 2⅞" – 73 mm.

197 Morris Mini-Traveller. 2⅞" – 73 mm.

183

*Fig. 159.*

183 Morris Mini Minor (Automatic) 75 mm

*Fig. 160.*

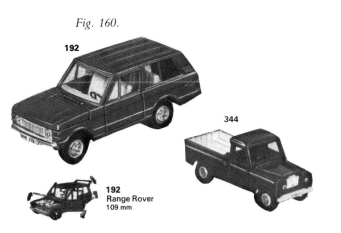

192

344

192 Range Rover 109 mm

476

475

*Fig. 161.*

145

Fig. 162. 122 Towing Gift Set.

**DINKY TOYS**

**Gift Set No.122**

**TOURING**

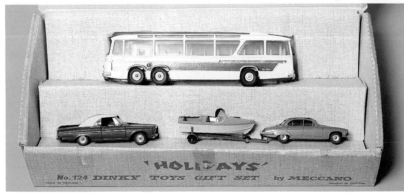

Fig. 164. 124 Holiday Gift Set

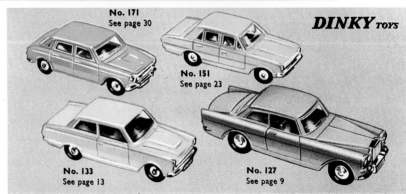

No. 171
See page 30

No. 151
See page 23

No. 133
See page 13

No. 127
See page 9

*DINKY TOYS*

Fig. 165. 126 Motor Show Gift Set.

## German Cars

The European Car Manufacturers best represented in the Dinky range are those from Germany. Their production was spread fairly evenly over the post-war period from 1956 onwards. 128 MERCEDES-BENZ 600 holds the production record as it was introduced in 1964 and was still available sixteen years later when the Binns Road Factory closed. It is closely challenged by 181 VOLKSWAGEN which was made for thirteen years and was also available in a Swiss PTT version. 186 MERCEDES-BENZ 220 SE figured in 123 MAYFAIR GIFT SET. (See: Cars—British Saloons.) The later VOLKSWAGEN 1300 SEDAN or DE-LUXE number 129 was issued in Swiss PTT and German Bundespost liveries and 154 FORD TAUNUS 17M in German Polizei colours. A few gimmicks were fitted for instance 157 BMW had flashing indicators and 176 NSU Ro 80 not only had battery operated lights but luminous seats too!

GERMAN CARS

| Cat. No. | Model | Intro. date | Deletion | Comments |
|---|---|---|---|---|
| 128 | Mercedes-Benz 600 | 1964 | 1980 | Metallic red. Still in production at factory closure |
| 129 | Volkswagen 1300 Sedan/De-luxe | 1965 | 1975 | Metallic blue |
| 144 | Volkswagen 1500 | 1963 | 1966 | White |
| 154 | Ford Taunus 17M | 1966 | 1968 | Yellow & white |
| 157 | BMW 2000 Tilux | 1968 | 1972 | Blue & white |
| 160 | Mercedes-Benz 250 SE | 1967 | 1973 | Metallic blue |
| 163 | Volkswagen 1600 TL Fastback | 1966 | 1970 | Red |
| 176 | NSU Ro 80 | 1969 | 1973 | Maroon. Later green |
| 177 | Opel Kapitan | 1961 | 1967 | Blue |
| 179 | Opel Commodore | 1971 | 1974 | Metallic blue & black |
| 181 | Volkswagen ('Beetle') | 1956 | 1969 | Grey, green, blue |
| 186 | Mercedes-Benz 220 SE | 1961 | 1966 | Blue |
| 187 | Volkswagen Karmann Ghia Coupé | 1959 | 1963 | Red & black, cream & green. |
| 516 | Mercedes-Benz 230 SL | | | See: French Dinky Products |

**157 B.M.W. 2000 Tilux** with Flashing Indicators *(Battery not included)*

6 **160 Mercedes-Benz 250 SE** with Battery Operated Stop Lights

4⅝" (117 mm.)

**144** Volkswagen 1500 3½" — 89 mm.

4½" (114 mm.)

**176 N.S.U. RO 80** with Luminous seats and Battery Operated Head and Tail Lights *(Battery not included)*

**181 Volkswagen.** 3⁹⁄₁₆" – 90 mm.

**187 Volkswagen Karmann Ghia Coupé.** 3¾" – 95 mm.

7

**177 Opel Kapitan.** 3¹¹⁄₁₆" –100 mm.

**186 Mercedes-Benz 220 SE.** 4" – 102 mm.

5

*Fig. 179.*

*Fig. 163. 123 Mayfair Gift Set.*

## American Cars

Immediately after the war, the 39 series of American cars were re-issued in a form very little different from the pre-war. (See: Pre-war—39 series.) However, in the early 1950s, two groups of the next generation of vehicles were made. The first group of three were all available in two-tone, a fad which occurred earlier in the United States than in the U.K. and was no more attractive. As a compensation, the castings are very clean and attractive. 139a FORD FORDOR was initially a single-tone, but after its renumbering to 170 it became two-tone, originally the split being at the bonnet line but later further down the side panels. 139b/171 HUDSON COMMODORE was always two-tone. To begin with only the part above the window line was painted the second colour but subsequently the whole of the centre section, i.e. roof, bonnet and boot was so treated. The 1958 catalogue shows only the lower side panels below the level of the door handles in the base colour and this version was also issued. 172 STUDEBAKER LAND CRUISER started off single-tone, changing to duo-tone and then, patterning the development of the Fordor, the colour split moved down from being along the bonnet line to part way down the side panels. The STUDEBAKER bore the number 139 with the suffix 'c' but this was restricted to internal Meccano paperwork as renumbering took place before it was issued. 139a/170 also appeared as an ARMY STAFF CAR in the U.S. on the number 675. The second group of two had single-colour bodies with luridly contrasting interiors and were fitted with drivers.

Despite the small numbers on British roads, the next group of American cars produced in the late 1950s and early 1960s proved popular with small scale purchasers because the prototypical two-toning and expanses of chrome produced a very bright and colourful appearance—'snazzy' to use the slang of the time. The casting was fine, producing clear-cut outlines, particularly important in this era of the (restrained) tail-fin. In most cases the brightness was enhanced by the use of white treaded tyres and even shiny metal hubs, for 192 DE SOTO FIREFLIGHT was the first Dinky to be fitted with these. 193 RAMBLER was included in 122 TOURING GIFT SET (See: British Saloons and Estates.)

Four of the castings in this section also appeared as Police Cars.

Overlapping with the previous group, are two, 137 PLYMOUTH FURY and 170 LINCOLN CONTINENTAL, which suffer from poor castings. 137 was part of 124 HOLIDAY GIFT SET and continued as part of the set after it had been dropped as an individual model. 115 is 137 without the hardtop and is fitted with passengers. A mere half-dozen more were produced up until 1980. 161 FORD MUSTANG was initially released with 'Mustang' and the Horse Motif as a decal but subsequently they were cast into the bonnet sides. 206 is a modified customised version of 221 CORVETTE STINGRAY. The best of the bunch is without doubt 201 PLYMOUTH STOCK CAR, which also came in a Police version. Two French Dinky models of American cars were also imported and sold in the U.K. Many of this group were fitted with breakable gimmicks—pop-up headlamps, retractable aerials, etc.

## AMERICAN CARS

| Cat. No. | Model | Intro. date | Deletion | Comments |
|---|---|---|---|---|
| 27f | Estate Car | | | See: Farm and Garden |
| 115 | Plymouth Fury Sports | 1965 | 1968 | White |
| 137 | Plymouth Fury Convertible | 1963 | 1965 | Metallic grey, green, blue |
| 161 | Ford Mustang | 1965 | 1972 | White, red interior. Later yellow, blue interior |
| 170 | Lincoln Continental | 1964 | 1969 | Metallic orange & white / Light blue & white |
| 173 | Pontiac Parisienne | 1969 | 1972 | Maroon |
| 174 | Ford Mercury Cougar | 1969 | 1972 | Blue |
| 175 | Cadillac Eldorado | 1969 | 1972 | Purple & black, later blue & black |
| 201 | Plymouth Stock Car | 1979 | 1980 | Dark blue '34'. Still in production at factory closure |
| 206 | Customised Corvette Stingray | 1979 | 1980 | Red. Still in production at factory closure |
| 221 | Corvette Stingray | 1969 | 1977 | Gold. Later white & black |
| 344 | =Estate Car= | | | Renumbering of 27f |
| 550 | Chrysler Saratoga | | | See: French Dinky Products |
| 555 | Thunderbird | | | See: French Dinky Products |

For illustration of number 206 see 1979 Catalogue. Chapter 9.

Fig. 177. 201 Plymouth Stock Car.

137 Plymouth Fury Convertible 4¹³⁄₁₆" — 122 mm.

221 Corvette Stingray

4⁷⁄₁₆" (113 mm.)

173 Pontiac Parisienne

174 Ford Mercury Cougar and retractable aerial

175 Cadillac Eldorado

with interior bonnet release catch

WITH SPEEDWHEELS

170

Fig. 178.

Fig. 166. Drawings of 132, 131, 172 and 139 B.

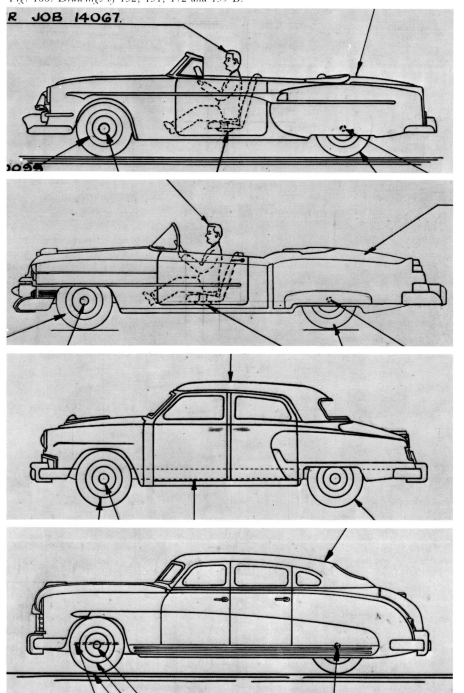

Fig. 167. 132 Packard Convertible and 131 Cadillac Eldorado.

| Cat. No. | Model | Intro. date | Deletion | Comments |
|---|---|---|---|---|
| 147 | Cadillac 62 | 1962 | 1968 | Metallic blue-green |
| 148 | Ford Fairline | 1962 | 1965 | Metallic green |
| 169 | Studebaker Golden Hawk | 1958 | 1963 | Green & fawn, fawn & red |
| 173 | Nash Rambler | 1958 | 1962 | Turquoise & red, pink & blue |
| 174 | Hudson Hornet | 1958 | 1963 | Red & cream, yellow & grey |
| 178 | Plymouth Plaza | 1959 | 1963 | Pink & green, two-tone blue |
| 179 | Studebaker President | 1958 | 1963 | Yellow & blue, two-tone blue |
| 180 | Packard Clipper | 1958 | 1963 | Fawn & pink, orange & grey |
| 191 | Dodge Royal Sedan | 1959 | 1966 | Cream & brown, green & black cream & blue |
| 192 | De Soto Fireflite | 1958 | 1964 | Grey & red, green & fawn |
| 193 | Rambler Cross-country Station Wagon | 1961 | 1968 | Yellow & white |
| 448 | Chevrolet El Camino Pick-up and Trailers | 1963 | 1967 | Car as 449. Red trailers |
| 449 | Chevrolet El Camino Pick-up | 1961 | 1968 | Green & white |

Fig. 168. 139/170 Ford Fordor showing the later type of two-toning.

**171 (139b)**
Hudson Commodore Sedan 2:8
Length 4⅞"

*Fig. 171. 139b/171 Hudson Commodore showing the first type of two-toning.*

**161  Ford Mustang**
**(Fastback 2 + 2)**

*Fig. 169. 139b/171 Hudson Commodore showing the second type of two-toning.*

| Cat. No. | Model | Intro. date | Deletion | Comments |
|---|---|---|---|---|
| 131 | Cadillac Eldorado | 1956 | 1963 | Light pink, grey seats |
| | | | | Light yellow, red seats |
| 132 | Packard Convertible | 1955 | 1961 | Fawn, red seats |
| | | | | Green, red seats |
| 139a | Ford Fordor Sedan | 1949 | 1959 | Yellow, red, green, fawn. |
| | | | | Cream & red, pink & blue |
| | | | | Renumbered 170 |
| 139b | Hudson Commodore Sedan | 1950 | 1958 | Cream & maroon, blue & fawn, blue & grey, blue & red. Renumbered 171 |
| 170 | =Ford Fordor= | | | Renumbering of 139a |
| 171 | =Hudson Commodore= | | | Renumbering of 139b |
| 172 | Studebaker Land Cruiser | 1954 | 1958 | Blue, green, red & white, fawn & cream |

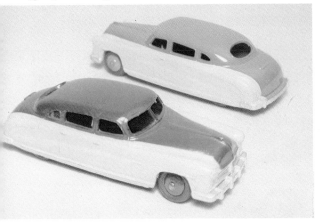

*Fig. 174. Back row 192, 180. Front row 191, 174.*

*Fig. 170. 172 Studebaker Land Cruiser showing the late and early two-toning.*

*Fig. 173. Left 178, right 173, 179 and 169.*

**147 Cadillac 62.**
4⁷⁄₁₆" – 113 mm.

**193 Rambler Cross**    *Fig. 176.*
**Country Station**
**Wagon.** 4" – 102 mm.

*Fig. 175. 448 Chevrolet El Camino Pick-up and Trailers.*

**NEW for 1971**

**179 Opel Commodore**

WITH *SPEEDWHEELS* ZIP

107 mm.

**184 Volvo 122S.**
$3\frac{13}{16}'' - 97$ mm.

**163 Volkswagen 1600 TL Fastback**

**196 Holden Special Sedan**
$4\frac{1}{4}'' - 108$ mm.

**116 Volvo 1800 S**

149

**149**
Citroen Dyane
91 mm

**172**

**154 Ford Taunus 17M**

*Fig. 180.*

**128 Mercedes-Benz 600**

**129 Volkswagen 1300 Sedan**

152

## Cars—Other Overseas Makes

Apart from American and German cars, the other overseas manufacturers are poorly represented in products from Binns Road, most of the French vehicles actually being French Dinkies imported into the U.K. Four Scandinavian cars, one of them 122 VOLVO 265DL ESTATE CAR being 1/35 scale with a very fine and detailed casting, two Italian and one Australian complete this international section. Despite the popularity of Japanese cars with the public, Dinky never made one, nor as far we know ever contemplated so doing.

## Cars—1/25 Scale

In 1973–4, three 1/25 scale FORD CAPRIS were released. This attempt to bring a larger scale to the market failed despite the fact that other toy manufacturers, e.g. Burago from Italy, habitually produced models in this size. They were nice models of the Capri and hardly seem to deserve the apathy of the purchasers which resulted in them being in shops for long after they were deleted from the catalogues. They were allocated numbers within the appropriate blocks for cars of that type with a '2' suffix added.

## CARS—OTHER OVERSEAS MAKES

| Cat. No. | Model | Intro. date | Deletion | Comments |
|---|---|---|---|---|
| 116 | Volvo 1800S | 1966 | 1971 | Red |
| 112 | Volvo 265 DL Estate Car | 1977 | 1980 | Blue & white. Still in production at factory closure |
| 149 | Citroen Dyane | 1971 | 1974 | Gold & black |
| 156 | Saab 96 | 1966 | 1970 | Metallic red |
| 166 | Renault R 16 | 1967 | 1969 | Blue |
| 172 | Fiat 2300 Station Wagon | 1965 | 1968 | Light blue & dark blue |
| 183 | Fiat 600 | 1958 | 1960 | Green, red (See Fig. 154) |
| 184 | Volvo 122S | 1961 | 1964 | Red |
| 196 | Holden Special Sedan | 1963 | 1969 | Bronze & white |
| 518 | Renault (4L) | | | See: French Dinky Products |
| 524 | Panhard 24c | | | See: French Dinky Products |
| 530 | Citroen DS 19 | | | See: French Dinky Products |
| 535 | Citroen 2cv | | | See: French Dinky Products |
| 553 | Peugeot 404 | | | See: French Dinky Products |

(Cars–1/25 scale)

| Cat. No. | Model | Intro. date | Deletion | Comments |
|---|---|---|---|---|
| 2162 | Ford Capri | 1973 | 1976 | Metallic blue and black |
| 2214 | Ford Capri Rally | 1974 | 1976 | Red & black |
| 2253 | Ford Capri Police | 1974 | 1976 | White |

Fig. 181. 166 Renault R.16.

Fig. 182. 122 Volvo 265DL Estate Car—Meccano Ltd Press release photos, dated September 30, 1977.

Fig. 183. The 1/25 Scale Ford Capris (1974 Catalogue rear cover).

153

## 25 Series—Commercials Post-war

Almost as soon as production started again after the war, the 25 series commercials were re-introduced using exactly the same body castings and diecast grilles that had been utilised before. However, a new chassis was introduced, much more solid than before with only a small circular hole in the centre instead of the three large triangular ones of the previous production. This chassis was used from 1946 probably until 1948 when a more realistic looking one was designed with a front bumper cast in, sidelights on the wings and dummy transmission cast on the underside. This new chassis changes the appearance of the vehicle quite noticeably and, despite the non-prototypical cabs, makes them look much less toy-like. At the time commercial vehicles were still restricted to 20 miles per hour, and the little white 20 in a black circle was affixed to the offside rear in most cases. The Trailer was equipped with a white T in a black square in the same position. Many and various were the colours in which the vehicles were released. In fact, there is speculation that they could have appeared in any of the colours that were in use in the factory at the time, i.e. grey, green, orange, light blue, dark blue, cream, brown, yellow, red, fawn etc., and each in several shades. Indeed a collector could spend a whole lifetime collecting post-war 25 series and still find 'new' colours when he was eighty! The chassis is usually black, but some very pretty pieces are found with one of the previously mentioned colours on the chassis. Time has taken its toll of the radiator grilles. They were all 'silver' plated and the plating has tarnished or worn off, so that most have dulled down so much that they look blackish. Some still have traces of the original silvering, particularly down the bars of the grille, giving the impression that they were originally two colour but this is not so—all had plated grilles. The attractiveness of some of the later models is enhanced by the presence of coloured wheel hubs on some of the items; for instance, there is a pretty covered wagon in cream with a red tilt and wheels. With the change from the chassis with the small circular hole to the one with dummy transmission, there occurred a change in the tyres used, from the large smooth black ones the same size as used before the war, to the small smooth black ones that were being fitted to

Fig. 185. The 25 Series trucks showing some typical colours. The Flat Truck, Tipping Wagon and Wagon are pre-war, the others are post-war.

most of the products at the time. In fact, the larger ones will fit on the latest type and some examples are found with them, but the smaller are the norm.

25a WAGON came in the previously mentioned colours, two attractive ones being cream with a red chassis, and grey also with a red chassis. 25b COVERED WAGON occurs in the same colours as 25a, as it is only the same thing with a tin tilt which itself can be green, grey, blue red, etc. 25c FLAT TRUCK utilises the above list of shades and the one with a grey body and red chassis looks rather smart. From 1948 it was only available as part of 25t FLAT TRUCK AND TRAILER which was only in the catalogue for a short time from 1948 to 1950 and consists of 25c + 25g. The truck and trailer always matched in colour and each yellow box of six ve-

Fig. 184. The various 25 series chassis, the pre-war on the left, early post-war in the centre and the later (1948) chassis on the right.

## 25 SERIES—COMMERCIALS POST-WAR

| Cat. No. | Model | Intro. date | Deletion | Comments |
|---|---|---|---|---|
| 25a | Wagon | See: Pre-war | 1950 | Re-issue |
| 25b | Covered Wagon | See: Pre-war | 1950 | Re-issue |
| 25c | Flat Truck | See: Pre-war | 1948 | Re-issue. See: 25t |
| 25d | Petrol Tank Wagon | See: Pre-war | 1950 | Re-issue |
| 25e | Tipping Wagon | See: Pre-war | 1950 | Re-issue |
| 25f | Market Gardener's Wagon | See: Pre-war | 1950 | Re-issue |
| 25g | Trailer | See: Pre-war | 1963 | Re-issue. Renumbered 429 |
| 25h | Fire Engine | | | See: Fire Engines |
| 25j | Jeep | | | See: Other Post-war Vehicles |
| 25m | Bedford End Tipper | | | See: Post-war Commercials |
| 25p | Aveling-Barford Diesel Roller | | | See: Special Purpose Vehicles |
| 25r | Forward Control Lorry | | | See: Post-war Commercials |
| 25s | Six-wheeled Wagon | | | See: Post-war Commercials |
| 25t | Flat Truck and Trailer | 1948 | 1950 | 25c — 25g |
| 25v | Bedford Refuse Wagon | | | See: Special Purpose Vehicles |
| 25w | Bedford Truck | | | See: Post-war Commercials |
| 25wm | Bedford Truck | | | See: American Military Issues |
| 25x | Breakdown Lorry | | | See: Special Purpose Vehicles |
| 25y | Jeep | | | See: Other Post-war Vehicles |
| 429 | =Trailer= | | | Renumbering of 25g |

hicles had three trucks and three trailers in it. Since there is no difference in the models it is now impossible to say whether they were originally packed in this way, unless you are lucky enough to find one of the original boxes with part or all of its contents still intact. 25e TIPPING WAGON usually had the tipping bed sprayed a different colour from the cab. 25f MARKET GARDENER'S WAGON is not found in the same rainbow of colours as the others, yellow, green and orange being the standard issues. 25g TRAILER can be distinguished from the pre-war issue by the presence of the wire towing hook which replaced the tinplate one. It came in a multitude of colours and figured as part of 25t (see above). It was in production for far longer than the rest of the series. 25d PETROL TANK WAGON as before used the same chassis with the towing hook cropped off. The colours are generally red and green but orange and fawn, etc., are found. 'Petrol' in black or white is usually stamped on either side. No Petrol Com-

| Cat. No. | Model | Intro. date | Deletion | Comments |
|---|---|---|---|---|
| 31a | Trojan Delivery Van 'Esso' | 1951 | 1957 | Renumbered 450 |
| 31b | Trojan Delivery Van 'Dunlop' | 1952 | 1957 | Renumbered 451 |
| 31c | Trojan Delivery Van 'Chivers' | 1953 | 1957 | Renumbered 452 |
| 31d | Trojan Delivery Van 'Oxo' | 1953 | 1954 | Renumbered 453 for 1 month |
| 450 | =Trojan Delivery Van 'Esso'= | | | Renumbering of 31a |
| 451 | =Trojan Delivery Van 'Dunlop'= | | | Renumbering of 31b |
| 452 | =Trojan Delivery Van 'Chivers'= | | | Renumbering of 31c |
| 453 | =Trojan Delivery Van 'Oxo'= | | | Renumbering of 31d |
| 454 | Trojan Delivery Van 'Cydrax' | 1957 | 1959 | |
| 455 | Trojan Delivery Van 'Brooke Bond Tea' | 1957 | 1960 | |

pany liveries were issued post-war on this model.

### Vans with Advertising

The decade of the 1950s was the heyday of post-war advertisement logos, and many beautifully decorated vehicles ran on the streets. Dinky, no doubt wishing to emulate their success with the 28 series of vans, made several groups of these 'vans

with advertising'. All had single piece diecast bodies and tinplate chassis.

The first to be designed was the Trojan 15cwt, which appeared with six different advertisements. The introduction of the six was spread over several years, covering both renumbering and the take-over of Oxo by Brooke Bond. This perhaps accounts for the brief appearance of the Oxo Van and its replacement by Brooke Bond. The colours were standard throughout their production run. (See photo.)

The Austin A40 10cwt van was the next subject chosen and three versions were produced. The colours, as with the Trojan vans, were standard throughout their production run. (See photo.) The 'Omnisport' van which was drawn in 1957 was a version with a special finish. It was presumably a promotional piece and it is not known whether any were produced.

Three logo schemes were also employed on the Bedford CA 10cwt. The colours were standard throughout their production run . (See photo.)

For other small vans with advertising, see under the makes of vehicle.

In December 1949, under the 'Dinky Supertoy' label, began the marketing of a range of large vans based on the Guy Vixen cab/chassis. The fineness of the castings and the detail of the transfers put these models amongst the pride of the post-war Dinkies. The cab and chassis were also used on the Guy open trucks and the casting was in production for many years. There were more than a dozen detail changes in the die over the years, but the most significant ones are as follows. Initially, the rear axles were retained by axle clips of tinplate, but after a short time axle supports were cast into the bodies. This coincided with a change to thicker axles and the more detailed 'Supertoy' wheel hubs. The drawing date for this change is 1950, but the alteration does not seem to have been put into effect until some time afterwards. In 1954, the drawing was modified to show the webs that were added either side of the numberplate, and there seems to have been a similar delay in implementation of the change. Both the diecast cab and box van have tinplate chassis. To comply with the standard Dinky practice of only issuing one model on one number, each decal run should have finished before a new one was introduced, but it is not certain that this did in fact happen. If one assumes that it did, the different quantities of each decal that seem to have survived is accounted for, but the length of time in production and the quantity produced are not necessarily related. There is a dearth of printed evidence from the late 1940s and early 1950s, so the deletion dates are tentative. The colours were standard throughout

Fig. 186. Works layouts of the transfers on the Trojan vans.

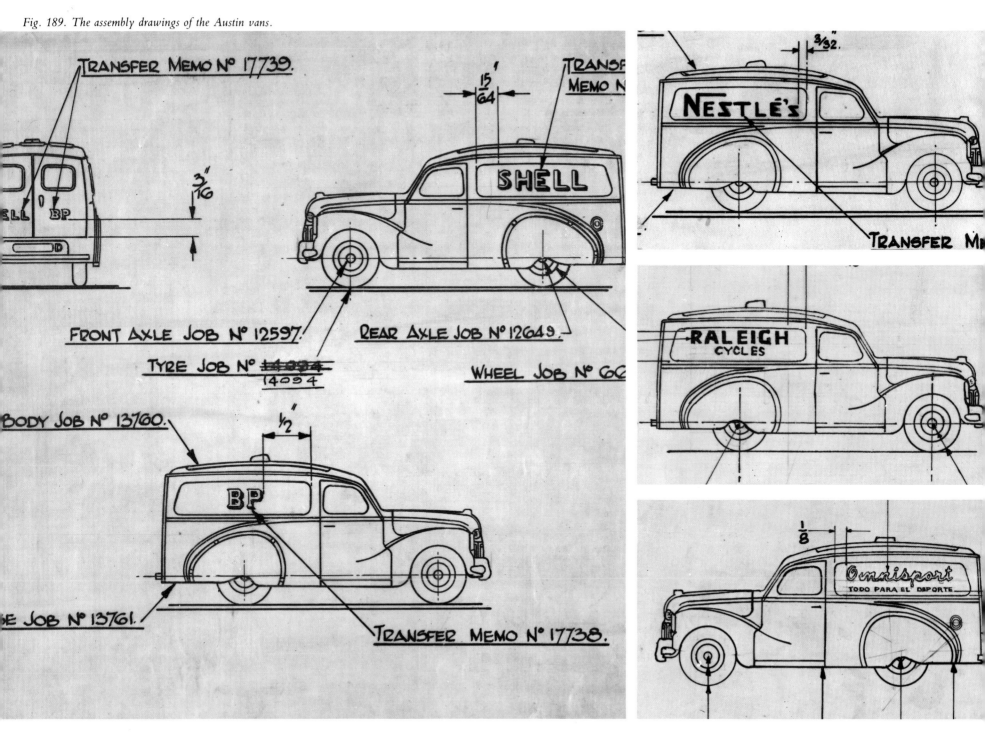

*Fig. 189. The assembly drawings of the Austin vans.*

TRANSFER MEMO Nº 17739.

SHELL

TRANS
MEMO N

15'
64

3"
16

ELL   BP

FRONT AXLE JOB Nº 12597

REAR AXLE JOB Nº 12649

TYRE JOB Nº ~~14994~~
14094

WHEEL JOB Nº 66

BODY JOB Nº 13760.

BP

1/2"

E JOB Nº 13761.

TRANSFER MEMO Nº 17738.

NESTLÉ'S

3"
32

TRANSFER M

RALEIGH
CYCLES

Omnisport
TODO PARA EL DEPORTE

1
8

157

*Fig. 190. The three Austin vans.*

*Fig. 191. The three Bedford vans.*

*Fig. 192. 465 Morris Van 'Capstan'.*

*Fig. 193. The Guy Vans.*

| Cat. No. | Model | Intro. date | Deletion | | Cat. No. | Model | Intro. date | Deletion |
|---|---|---|---|---|---|---|---|---|
| 470 | Austin Van 'Shell-BP' | 1954 | 1965 | | 514 | Guy Van 'Slumberland' | 1949 | 1951? |
| 471 | Austin Van 'Nestle's' | 1955 | 1963 | | 514 | Guy Van 'Lyons' | 1951 | 1952? |
| 472 | Austin Van 'Raleigh Cycles' | 1957 | 1960 | | 514 | Guy Van 'Weetabix' | 1952 | 1953 |
| | | | | | 514 | =Guy Van 'Spratt's'= | 1953 | 1956 |
| 480 | Bedford Van 'Kodak' | 1954 | 1956 | | 917 | =Guy Van 'Spratt's'= | Renumbering of 'Spratt's' | |
| 481 | Bedford Van 'Ovaltine' | 1955 | 1960 | | 918 | Guy Van 'Ever Ready' | 1955 | 1958 |
| 482 | Bedford Van 'Dinky Toys' | 1956 | 1960 | | 919 | Guy Van 'Golden Shred' | 1957 | 1958 |
| | | | | | 920 | Guy Warrior Van 'Heinz' | 1960 | 1960 With can till 1958 |
| 465 | Morris Van 'Capstan' | 1957 | 1959 | | 923 | Big Bedford Van 'Heinz' | 1955 | 1959 With bottle after 1958 |

The Morris 10 cwt. was only used for one.

their production run.

Two other vehicles must be dealt with in this category. The first is the Big Bedford Van which shared a cab/chassis unit with other vehicles and the second is the new Guy Warrior. Both were similarly constructed, a cab/chassis unit and a box back, the Guy using the one from the original Guy vans. And they shared transfers. The Big Bedford was initially issued with 'Heinz' and a Baked Bean can on the side, and later with a Tomato Ketchup bottle instead of the can. After the Big Bedford was deleted, the same transfer was used on the Guy Warrior. (It is possible that some Guy Warriors were issued without windows and also possible, but not probable, that it appeared initially with the Golden Shred decal, as the drawing exists, but proof of its being put into production does not.)

For other large vans with advertising see under the make of the vehicle or type of vehicle.

## Tankers with Advertising.

During almost the whole of the post-war period it was possible to buy Dinky Petrol Tankers with advertising for various petrol and oil or even chemical companies on the side. The first set were released from 1952, numbered 30p, etc. in a small scale and were models of a Studebaker cab. The motives for the choice of Studebaker is obscure as they were never seen on British roads and there were plenty of indigenous vehicles that could have been chosen— but they are pretty. There are two decal versions on the 'Mobilgas', the later having the name on a white flash (post-1957). The later Foden cab was used for 'Supertoy' sized tankers at about the same time, beautiful models these, with a plain version as well as 'Mobilgas' and 'Regent'. (See also: Fodens.) The later Leyland Octopus shares a tinplate tank with the Foden while it was carrying 'Esso' decals but when it became the 'Shell B.P.' Fuel Tanker, this was replaced by a plastic tank. There is also a 'Corn Products' promotional on this one. While the Foden was available, so also was an A.E.C. Monarch. Like the Studebakers which it dwarfs in size, it is one large diecasting with integral tank. To begin with it carried 'Shell Chemicals Ltd.' transfers but this was shortened in 1955 to 'Shell Chemicals', and in 1957

Fig. 194. The two versions of 923 Big Bedford Van 'Heinz'.

Fig. 195. 920 Guy Warrior Van 'Heinz'.

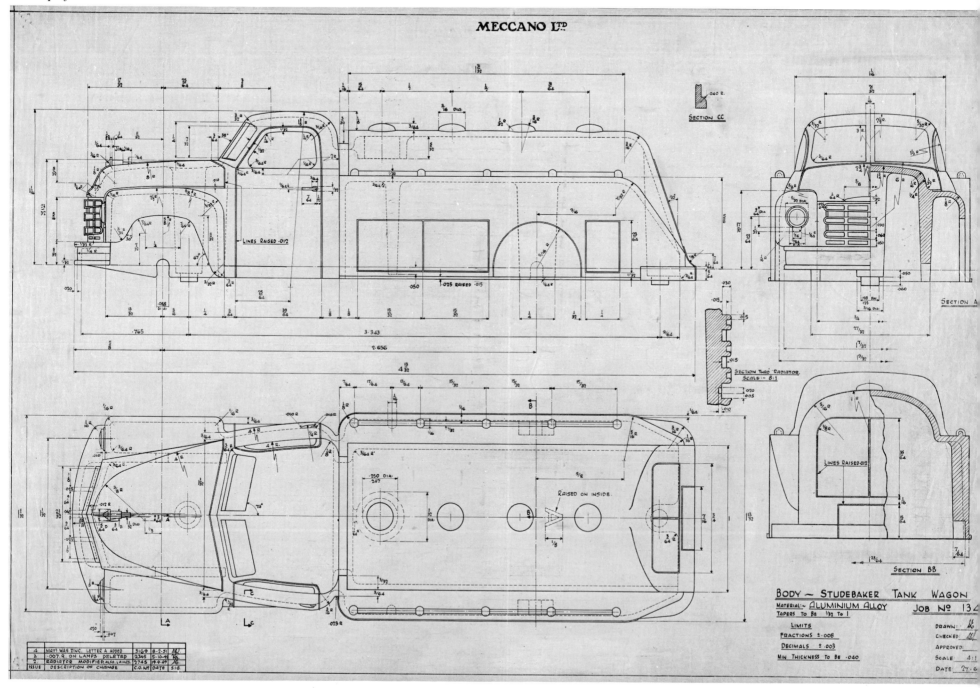

*Fig. 196. The drawing of the body casting for the Studebaker tankers. Note the reference to aluminium alloy as the material specified.*

160

*Fig. 200. The Studebaker Tankers.*

## TANKERS WITH ADVERTISING

| Cat. No. | Model | Intro. date | Deletion | Comments |
|---|---|---|---|---|
| 30p | Tanker 'Mobilgas' | 1952 | 1961 | Red. Two decal versions. Renumbered 440 |
| 30pa | Tanker 'Castrol' | 1952 | 1960 | Green. Renumbered 441 |
| 30pb | Tanker 'Esso' | 1952 | 1958 | Red. Renumbered 442 |
| 440 | =Tanker 'Mobilgas'= | | | Renumbering of 30p |
| 441 | =Tanker 'Castrol'= | | | Renumbering of 30pa |
| 442 | =Tanker 'Esso'= | | | Renumbering of 30pb |
| 443 | Tanker 'National Benzole' | 1957 | 1959 | Yellow |
| 504 | Foden 14-ton Tanker 'Mobilgas' | 1953 | 1956 | Red. Renumbered 941 |
| 591 | A.E.C. Tanker/A.E.C. Tanker 'Shell Chemicals' | 1952 | 1958 | Red & yellow. Two decal versions. Renumbered 991 |
| 941 | =Foden 14-ton Tanker 'Mobilgas'= | | | Renumbering of 504 |
| 942 | Foden 14-ton Tanker 'Regent' | 1955 | 1957 | Red, blue & white |
| 943 | Leyland Octopus Tanker 'Esso' | 1958 | 1964 | Red |
| 944 | 'Shell B.P.' Fuel Tanker | 1963 | 1970 | Yellow & white |
| 945 | A.E.C. Fuel Tanker 'Esso' | 1966 | 1976 | White |
| 950 | Foden S20 Fuel Tanker 'Burmah' | 1978 | 1980 | Red & white. Still in production at factory closure |
| 991 | =A.E.C. 'Shell Chemicals' Tanker= | | | Renumbering of 591 |
| (994) | 'Corn Products' | 1963 | 1963 | |
| (945) | 'Lucas Oil' | 1977 | 1977 | |

For illustration of 950 see 1979 Catalogue. Chapter 9.

*Fig. 201. The Foden 'Mobilgas' and 'Regent' tankers.*

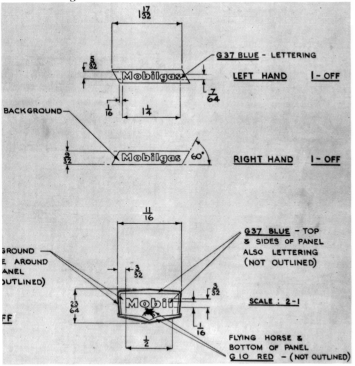

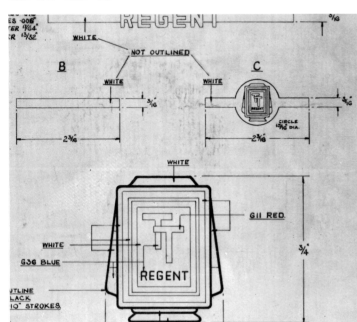

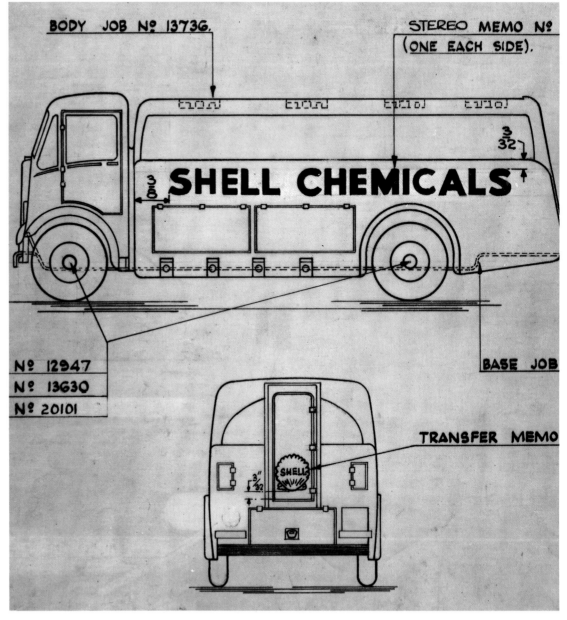

*Fig. 198. Drawings of the transfers for the Foden 'Regent' and 'Esso' tankers.*

the 20mph speed restriction roundel on the rear was deleted. For ten years from the late 1960s to the late 1970s, A.E.C. figured again on the 'Esso' tanker, utilising the cab of 915 A.E.C. WITH FLAT TRAILER, etc. This one was also used for a fairly widely available 'Lucas oil' special issue for Lucas which had a green and white base to its clear plastic package, mirroring the Lucas colours used on the vehicle. In the late 1970s this was replaced by the Foden S20 Tanker with 'Burmah' decals.

## Foden and Leyland Octopus

A big 8-wheeled group of large commercials was introduced in 1947 in the Supertoy range, based on the Foden Diesel chassis. The cab and chassis casting was one piece with a separate back, diecast for the trucks and tinplate for the tanker. The cab/chassis did not originally have slots to locate the tank, but these were added in 1948 and, since it is a common casting, the slots are found on all the vehicles from then on. Early chassis had slots for axle clips, but later, lugs to locate the axles were cast in. From about 1952–3, the more detailed 'Supertoy' wheels were fitted, but whatever the hub the tyres were large radial pattern tyres, 'Supertoy' tyres, grey rubber at first and then black. In 1952 a completely new casting for the cab/chassis was introduced, the exposed radiator being replaced by a stylised facia of chrome bars. The colours were two-tone and almost any combination can be found on any vehicle except for the tankers, which were two-tone blue or red/fawn or in petrol company colours. (For the latter see: Tankers with Advertising.) Sometimes the flash

### FODEN AND LEYLAND OCTOPUS

| Cat. No. | Model | Intro. date | Deletion | Comments |
|---|---|---|---|---|
| 501 | Foden Diesel 8-Wheel Wagon | 1947 | 1957 | Renumbered 901 |
| 502 | Foden Flat Truck | 1947 | 1960 | Renumbered 902 |
| 503 | Foden Flat Truck with Tailboard | 1947 | 1960 | Renumbered 903 |
| 504 | Foden 14-Ton Tanker | 1948 | 1953 | Note: no transfers |
| 504 | Foden 14-Ton Tanker 'Mobilgas' | | | See: Tankers with advertising |
| 505 | Foden Flat Truck with Chains | 1952 | 1964 | Renumbered 905 |
| 901 | =Foden Diesel 8-Wheel Wagon= | | | Renumbering of 501 |
| 902 | =Foden Flat Truck= | | | Renumbering of 502 |
| 903 | =Foden Flat Truck with Tailboard= | | | Renumbering of 503 |
| 905 | =Foden Flat Truck with Chains= | | | Renumbering of 505 |
| 934 | Leyland Octopus Wagon | 1956 | 1964 | |
| 935 | Leyland Octopus Flat Truck with Chains | 1964 | 1966 | |
| 936 | Leyland 8-Wheeled Chassis (with weights) | 1964 | 1969 | |
| 941 | Foden 14-Ton Tanker 'Mobilgas' | | | See: Tankers with advertising |
| 942 | Foden 14-Ton Tanker 'Regent' | | | See: Tankers with advertising |
| 943 | Leyland Octopus Tanker 'Esso' | | | See: Tankers with advertising |
| 944 | 'Shell B.P.' 4000 gallon Tanker | | | See: Tankers with advertising |

on the side of the cab was painted a contrasting colour and some late vehicles are single-tone. Colours: red/fawn, light blue/dark blue, orange/light blue, green/grey, orange/green, yellow/green, blue/orange, maroon, red, grey, green.

Another 8-wheeler overlapped for a short time with the longer-running Fodens; the Leyland Octopus. The completely different cab/chassis casting utilised three of the backs designed for the Foden. Later, another tank was designed in plastic to replace the tinplate one so that by that time, there were no parts in common with the Fodens. (For details of the Foden and Leyland tankers with transfers see: Tankers with Advertising.) A further version was the bare chassis often driven on English roads for test purposes, or for delivery to the body manufacturer.

*Fig. 205. 945 A.E.C. Fuel Tanker ESSO.*

**945  A.E.C. Fuel Tanker ESSO**

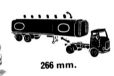

**266 mm.**

*Fig. 206. The first type Fodens.*

Fig. 202. 943 Leyland Octopus Tanker 'Esso' and 944 'Shell B.P.' Fuel Tanker.

Fig. 203. The two versions of the A.E.C. 'Shell Chemicals' tanker.

Fig. 204 (945) The 'Lucas Oil' A.E.C. Fuel Tanker.

Fig. 207. The second type Fodens.

Fig. 208. 504 Foden 14-ton Tanker, first type, showing the box lid artwork.

Fig. 209. 934 Leyland Octopus wagon, 935 flat truck with chains and 936 Leyland chassis.

Fig. 210. The early Guy lorries.

Fig. 211. The later Guy lorries, the Warrior.

Fig. 215. 522 Big Bedford Lorry.

Fig. 216. 533 Leyland Cement Wagon and 532 Leyland Comet with hinged tailboard.

**Guys**

In 1947, a new group of vehicles much larger than anything that had been made before were introduced and were designated 'Supertoys'. Most of them were accurate and magnificent models of commercial vehicles. Four were based on the Guy Vixen 4-ton truck and had a common cab/chassis unit, with different backs. Initially the rear axle was secured with tinplate tabs, but when the 'Supertoy' type wheel hubs were introduced, axle locations were cast into the body. Subsequently the lower front of the cab was modified with the addition of webs either side of the bottom of the grille. (For further details and information about the VANS see: Vans with Advertising.) All three of these open trucks had three different numbers: the one on which they were initially released as Supertoys, the number allocated at renumbering in 1954, and a new one when it was

decided to demote them from the Supertoy category in 1956. Many of the colour schemes were two-tone with the cab and chassis a different colour from the separate back, but some were single-tone: red/fawn, blue/red, blue/orange, brown/cream, red/blue, orange/blue, fawn, brown, green and grey have all been seen, though some colours are commoner than others and some colours are more usually found on one vehicle than on the others. Some had the mudguards painted black.

A new casting was introduced in 1958, based on the Warrior. Three versions were made. (For further details and information about the VAN see: Vans with Advertising.) Both the open trucks shared the same cab/chassis unit and were briefly available without window glazing. The paintwork was two-tone, green/fawn or red/green.

**Big Bedford and Leyland Comet**

The Big Bedford cab/chassis unit was the basis for two vehicles. It was designed as a Supertoy and sported 'Supertoy' dished wheels and treaded tyres. It was issued as a plain lorry and as a van with 'Heinz' transfers. (See: Vans with Advertising.) It was renumbered twice.

On the Leyland Comet cab/chassis were fitted three body styles, a Lorry which is actually fitted with a stake truck back, a Wagon with hinged tailboard, and a most attractive 'Ferrocrete' Cement Wagon. Again it was designed as a Supertoy with the appropriate wheel hubs and tyres and was renumbered twice.

*Fig. 212. Assembly drawing of 522 Big Bedford Lorry.*

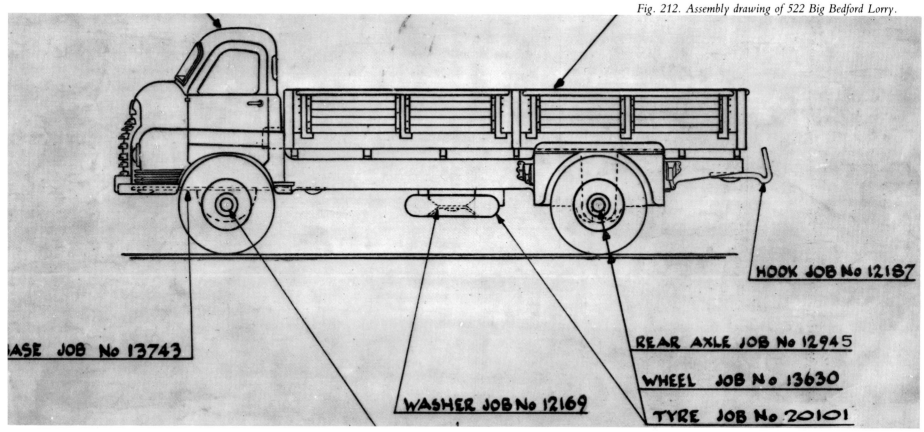

HOOK JOB No 12187

ASE JOB No 13743

REAR AXLE JOB No 12945

WASHER JOB No 12169

WHEEL JOB No 13630

TYRE JOB No 20101

## GUYS

| Cat. No. | Model | Intro. date | Deletion | Comments |
|---|---|---|---|---|
| 431 | =Guy 4-Ton Lorry= | | | Renumbering of 511/911 |
| 431 | Guy Warrier 4-Ton Lorry | 1958 | 1964 | |
| 432 | =Guy Flat Truck= | | | Renumbering of 512/912 |
| 432 | Guy Warrier Flat Truck | 1958 | 1964 | |
| 433 | Guy Flat Truck with Tailboard | | | Renumbering of 513/913 |
| 511 | Guy 4-Ton Lorry | 1947 | 1958 | Renumbered 911 & 431 |
| 512 | Guy Flat Truck | 1947 | 1958 | Renumbered 912 & 432 |
| 513 | Guy Flat Truck | 1947 | 1958 | Renumbered 913 & 433 |
| 514 | Guy Vans with Tailboard | | | See: Vans with advertising |
| 911 | =Guy 4-Ton Lorry= | | | Renumbering of 511 |
| 912 | =Guy Flat Truck= | | | Renumbering of 512 |
| 913 | =Guy Flat Truck with Tailboard= | | | Renumbering of 513 |
| 917 | Guy Van | | | See: Vans with advertising |
| 918 | Guy Van | | | See: Vans with advertising |
| 919 | Guy Van | | | See: Vans with advertising |
| 920 | Guy Warrior Van | | | See: Vans with advertising |

## BIG BEDFORD AND LEYLAND COMET

| Cat. No. | Model | Intro. date | Deletion | Comments |
|---|---|---|---|---|
| 408 | =Big Bedford Lorry= | | | Renumbering of 522/922 |
| 417 | =Leyland Comet Lorry= | | | Renumbering of 531/931 |
| 418 | =Leyland Comet with Hinged Tailboard= | | | Renumbering of 532/932 |
| 419 | =Leyland Cement Wagon= | | | Renumbering of 533/933 |
| 522 | Big Bedford Lorry | 1952 | 1963 | Renumbered 922 & 408 |
| 531 | Leyland Comet Lorry | 1949 | 1959 | Renumbered 931 & 417 |
| 532 | Leyland Comet with Hinged Tailboard | 1952 | 1959 | Renumbered 932 & 418 |
| 533 | Leyland Cement Wagon | 1953 | 1959 | Renumbered 933 & 419 |
| 922 | =Big Bedford Lorry= | | | Renumbering of 522 |
| 923 | Big Bedford Van 'Heinz' | | | See: Vans with Advertising |
| 931 | =Leyland Comet Lorry= | | | Renumbering of 531 |
| 932 | =Leyland Comet with Hinged Tailboard= | | | Renumbering of 532 |
| 933 | =Leyland Cement Wagon= | | | Renumbering of 533 |

*Fig. 213. Assembly drawing of 532 Leyland Comet with hinged tailboard.*

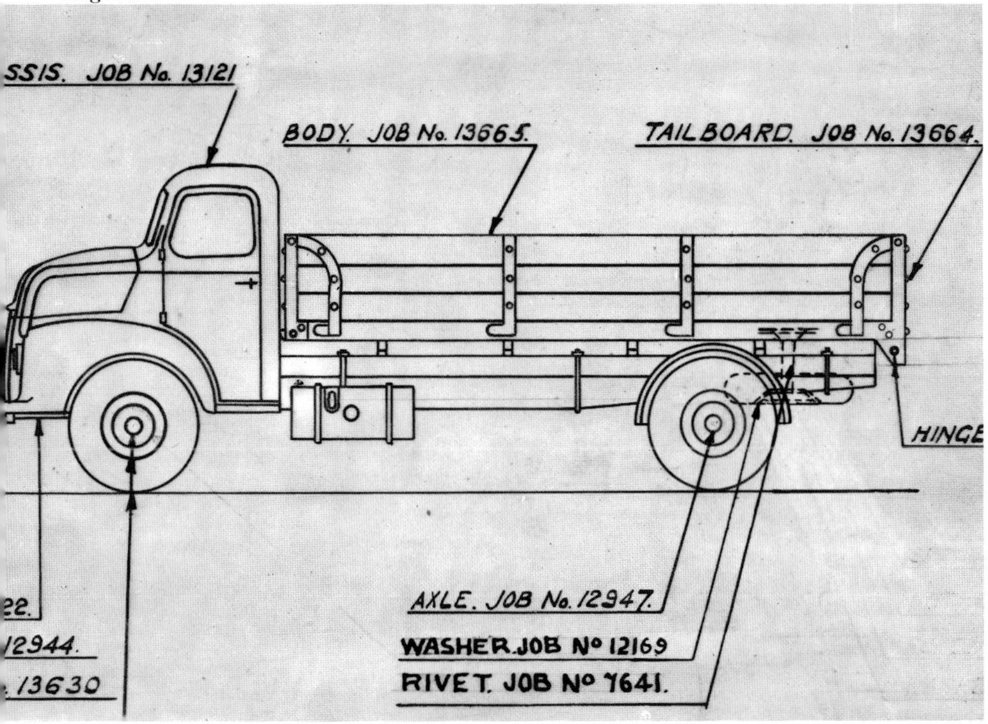

*Fig. 214. Assembly drawing of 533 Leyland Cement Wagon.*

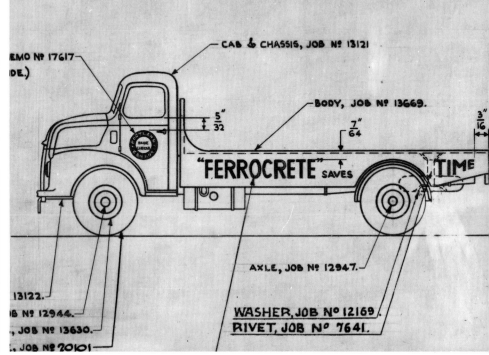

## Bedford (Dinky No. 410)

In 1972, a small Bedford Van was released in Royal Mail livery and it remained in production until the factory closure in 1979. A neat little model, it can be found with two types of 'Speed wheels', clear or blue glazing and gloss or matt black bases. Thus far is simple. Now the confusion. As the years went by it was released as 'Danish Post' in Denmark and a small number were on general sale as M.J. Hire Services (made in co-operation with this firm.) Two shops had batches made in their own livery and they were only available in their own branches: Simpson's in Canada and John Menzies (a Scottish based stationery and book chain). Two manufacturing firms had some painted their own livery: Marley Tiles sold them to customers but Belaco, manufacturers and distributors of brake and clutch parts gave them away as part of an offer to their stockists, 'Have your vans repainted free of charge if you have them painted in Belaco colours.' All of the above left the factory complete with their decals. Dinky were also prepared to produce batches of vehicles in any standard colour in use at the time without decals and the customer fitted his own. Some of these decals were fitted by the firm or a second party and were used to promote the product advertised on the side of the vehicle e.g. the 'Modellers' World' van was only available to readers of that magazine. But many had transfers affixed with no advertising or promotional intention. Most of the plethora of types that have been made fall into this category and we have not seen any documentary evidence to enable us to 'authenticate' any but the ones mentioned in this section. An A.A. van was also produced with a headboard added and a separate number allocated—412. Transfers were applied to this one with no advertising or promotional intention.

*Fig. 224. The Bedford 410 Vans with factory fitted promotional decals.*

*Fig. 226. The Bedford 'Modellers' World' van, with factory finished paint but customer applied decals.*

*Fig. 225. The Bedford Danish Post Van.*

| at. | | Date | |
|---|---|---|---|
| o. | Model | Manufactured | Comments |
| 10 | Bedford Van 'Danish Post' | | See: Foreign—Danish |
| 10 | Bedford Van 'M.J. Hire Services' | 1975/6 | White |
| 10 | Bedford Van 'John Menzies' | 1974/5 | Blue |
| 10 | Bedford Van 'Simpson's' | 1972 | Black & red |
| 10 | Bedford Van 'Marley Tiles' | 1975 | Red |
| 10 | Bedford Van 'Belaco' | 1974 | Bronze & black |
| 10 | Bedford Van 'Modeller's World' | 1976 | White |
| 10 | Bedford Van 'A.A. Service' | | See: Public Service Vehicles |
| 10 | Bedford Van 'Royal Mail' | | See: Public Service Vehicles |

*Fig. 227. The Ford Transit promotional van.*

*Fig. 229. 407 Ford Transit Van 'Hertz'.*

## Ford Transit Vans

From 1966 onwards there were always one or two versions of the current Ford Transit Vans in the catalogue. As Ford updated the vehicles, so did Dinky. There were three types altogether. Type 1 (1966–74) has a sliding driver's door and side hinging rear doors. Type 2 (1975–78) has no sliding door but a top hinging rear door. Type 3 is similar to Type 2 but with a longer bonnet. There are also wheel and headlamp variations. In the Dinky Toys Catalogue no. 6 (1970), there is illustrated a 'Colour T.V.' version. This is a photograph of one that was made up for a New Products Meeting which decided that, despite its appearance in the catalogue, it should not go into production. By 1976, the Ford Motor Com-

# FORD TRANSIT VANS

| Cat. No. | Model | Intro. date | Deletion | Comments |
|---|---|---|---|---|
| 269 | Ford Transit 'Police' | | | Type 3. See: Police Vehicles |
| 271 | Ford Transit 'Fire Service' | | | Type 2. See: Fire Appliances |
| 271 | Ford Transit 'Falck' | | | Type 2. See: Foreign—Danish |
| 272 | Ford Transit 'Police' | | | Type 2. See: Police Vehicles |
| 274 | Ford Transit 'Ambulance' | | | Type 3. See: Public Service Vehicles |
| 276 | Ford Transit 'Ambulance' | | | Type 2. See: Public Service Vehicles |
| 286 | Ford Transit 'Fire Service' | | | Type 1. See: Fire Appliances |
| 286 | Ford Transit 'Falck' | | | Type 1. See: Foreign—Danish |
| 287 | Ford Transit 'Police' | | | Type 1. See: Police Vehicles |
| 390 | Vampire Freeway Cruiser/ Customised Cruiser | 1979 | 1980 | Type 3. Metal flake blue, but no decals. Still in production at factory closure |
| 407 | Ford Transit 'Kenwood' | 1966 | 1969 | Type 1. Blue with or without white roof |
| 407 | Ford Transit 'Hertz' | 1970 | 1974 | Type 1. Yellow |
| 416 | Ford Transit 'Motorway Services' | 1975 | 1978 | Type 2. Yellow |
| 417 | Ford Transit 'Motorway Services' | 1978 | 1980 | Type 3. Yellow. Still in production at factory closure |
| | Ford Transit '1,000,000 Transits' | 1976 | 1976 | Type 2. Yellow |

For illustrations of 390 and 417 see 1979 catalogue. Chapter 9.

*Fig. 228. 407 Ford Transit Van 'Kenwood'.*

**407 Ford 'Hertz' Transit Van**

**407 Ford Transit Van**

pany had produced 1,000,000 Transit Vans and it decided to celebrate the fact with a special version of the Dinky, painted yellow with red stickers reading '1,000,000 Transits made for Ford Motor Co.' (Type 2). Fire, Police and Ambulance versions were produced. The vehicle has also been used to produce 'promotional' items but the only ones that we have been able to authenticate are the ones listed in the table.

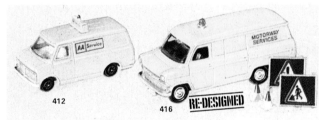

*Fig. 230. 416 Ford Transit Van Motorway Services (Type 2).*

## Small Commercials—Bedford, Commer, Austin, Dodge, Studebaker, Fordson etc.

This section deals with small commercials that were produced in the late 1940s and early 1950s They are a bit of a mixture, the linking factor being merely that Dinky decided to make them round about the same time. The sizes range from about the scale of the pre- and post-war re-issue 25 series trucks up to Supertoy size. In this latter case, numbers were given in the Supertoy 'block' and some 'Supertoy' hubs and wheels were fitted. The rest were allocated 25 and 30 series numbers and most were in production long enough to be renumbered in 1954. Only the basic vehicles are dealt with here, the specific purpose examples being referred to in the relevant section e.g. Bedford Breakdown truck and Car Transporter in Special Purpose Vehicles, Petrol Company Tankers in Tankers with Advertising, etc. In general the castings are more detailed than the earlier 25 series. Some still carry the 'early' hallmark of separate metal grilles, but now black not 'silver'.

A most attractive Bedford cab (with separate grille) was fitted to a range of vehicles and proved popular, as the cab/chassis unit was in production for sixteen years. During this time there were many detail casting changes, but the only significant difference was the fitting of windows in 1961. 25w BEDFORD TRUCK was finished in shades of green, and as 25wm, ended up in U.S. military drab for the U.S. market. (See U.S. issues) Early examples had black painted wings. 25m BEDFORD END TIPPER was commonly green or red and cream but orange, yellow and blue etc. examples are frequently found. 512 BEDFORD ARTICULATED LORRY (so numbered because of its size) usually had black wings and is commonly yellow or red.

424 COMMER CONVERTIBLE ARTICULATED TRUCK is a much later introduction, but uses the same chassis behind the cab as the Bedford. It is usually yellow or grey with windows and has two plastic pieces that slot into the trailer rear to give its 'Convertible' character—a blue plastic 'canvas' and a white plastic 'stake truck' piece. It was available as 406 without the plastic accessories. See also Special Purpose Vehicles.

25r FORWARD CONTROL LORRY later ac-

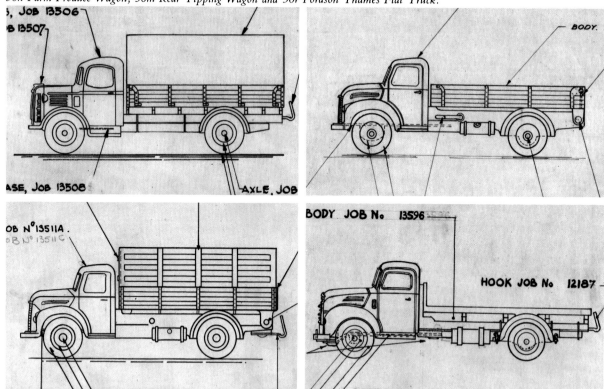

Fig. 218. Assembly drawings of 30s Austin Covered Wagon, 30n Farm Produce Wagon, 30m Rear Tipping Wagon and 30r Fordson Thames Flat Truck.

Fig. 219. 25w Bedford Truck and 25m Bedford End Tipper.

quired the nomenclature 'LEYLAND' and is the sole example of the type. Red, grey, green or cream.

The Austin also had a separate grille. 30j AUSTIN WAGON is found in blue, brown or maroon and 30s AUSTIN COVERED WAGON, which sports a tin tilt, utilises the same casting and colours with a blue or cream tilt. As 30sm, it appeared in U.S. military green (see U.S. issues).

Dodges featured as 30n FARM PRODUCE WAGON with the cab chassis in yellow or green and the back in the opposite colour, or less frequently, in red and blue, and 30m REAR TIPPING WAGON in orange and green or blue and grey.

30p PETROL TANKER had a Studebaker cab and served as the basis for several Petrol Company Tankers. (See Tankers with Advertising.) The basic type was red or green with 'Petrol' in black on the sides.

30r FORDSON THAMES FLAT TRUCK eventually had the 'Fordson' dropped from its title and came in red or green.

Some of these were included in the Gift Set No. 2 COMMERCIAL VEHICLES.

| Cat. No. | Model | Intro. date | Deletion | Comments |
|---|---|---|---|---|
| 25m | Bedford End Tipper | 1948 | 1963 | Renumbered 410 |
| 25r | Forward Control Lorry | 1948 | 1961 | Renumbered 420 |
| 25w | Bedford Truck | 1949 | 1960 | Renumbered 411 |
| 25wm | Bedford Truck | | | See also: U.S. issues |
| 30j | Austin wagon | 1950 | 1960 | Renumbered 412 |
| 30p | Petrol Tanker | 1950 | 1952 | See: Tankers with advertising |
| 30r | Fordson Thames Flat Truck | 1951 | 1960 | Renumbered 422 |
| 30m | Rear Tipping Wagon | 1950 | 1964 | Renumbered 414 |
| 30n | Farm Produce Wagon | 1950 | 1964 | Renumbered 343 |
| 30s | Austin Covered Wagon | 1950 | 1960 | Renumbered 413 |
| 30sm | Austin Covered Wagon | | | See: U.S. issues |
| 343 | =Austin Covered Wagon= | | | Renumbering of 30n |
| 406 | Commer Articulated Lorry | | | 424 without accessories |
| 409 | =Bedford Articulated Lorry= | | | Renumbering of 521/921 |
| 410 | =Bedford End Tipper= | | | Renumbering of 25m |
| 411 | =Bedford Truck= | | | Renumbering of 25w |
| 412 | =Austin Wagon= | | | Renumbering of 30j |
| 413 | =Austin Covered Wagon= | | | Renumbering of 30s |
| 414 | =Dodge Rear Tipping Wagon= | | | Renumbering of 30m |
| 420 | =Leyland Forward Control Lorry= | | | Renumbering of 25r |
| 422 | =Thames Flat Truck= | | | Renumbering of 30r |
| 424 | Commer Convertible Articulated Truck | 1963 | 1965 | |
| 521 | Bedford Articulated Lorry | 1948 | 1963 | Renumbered 921 & 409 |
| 921 | =Bedford Articulated Lorry= | | | Renumbering of 521/921 |
| Gift Set No. 2 | | | | |
| | Commercial Vehicles | 1952 | 1953 | Contains: 25m Bedford End Tipper, 27d Land Rover, 30n Farm Produce Wagon, 30p Petrol Tanker, 30s Austin Covered Wagon |

Fig. 220. The 30 series commercials.

Fig. 221. 521 Bedford Articulated Lorry and 551 Trailer.

Fig. 222. 424 Commer Convertible Articulated Truck.

Fig. 223. 25r Leyland Forward Control Lorry.

## Commercials—Special Purpose Vehicles

The vehicles covered in this section are those which were designed for a specific purpose such as road making equipment and television outside broadcast vehicles, but not Public Service Vehicles such as buses and fire engines. All of this group are post-war vehicles and cover the whole span of post-war production at Binns Road. Being on the whole large models many were marketed as Supertoys and being 'working' models are complex pieces often composed of several castings. Comments are made only about those models with major variations, basically the early ones. Colour etc. information about the others is to be found in the table at the end of the section.

Fig. 231. 1974 Catalogue

984
Atlas Digger
247 mm

963
Road Grader
238 mm

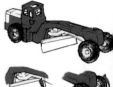

977   976   279

" SITE BUILDING "

Made in England by MECCANO LTD

Fig. 232. 900 Site Building Gift Set.

Fig. 234. 25p Aveling Barford Diesel Roller and 25v Refuse Wagon.

Fig. 233. 571 Coles Mobile Crane, 561 Blaw Knox Bulldozer and 562 Muir-Hill Dumper.

Fig. 237. 582 Pullmore Car Transporter.

Fig. 238. 983 Car Carrier and Trailer.

173

**959**
Foden Dump Truck
with Bulldozer Blade
6½" — 165 mm.

**960**
Albion Lorry
Mounted
Concrete Mixer
5⅛" — 130 mm.

*Fig. 235. 965
Terex Dump Truck.*

**DINKY TOYS**®

**436**
Atlas Copco
Compressor Lorry
3½" — 89 mm.

**975**
Ruston Bucyrus
Excavator
7½" — 190 mm.

*Fig. 236.*

924

*Fig. 231. 1974 Catalogue.*

## ROAD MAKING EQUIPMENT

| Cat. No. | Model | Intro. date | Deletion | Comments |
|---|---|---|---|---|
| 25p | Aveling-Barford Diesel Roller | 1948 | 1963 | Green, red wheels. Renumbered 251 |
| 251 | =Aveling-Barford Diesel Roller= | | | Renumbering of 25p |
| 279 | Aveling-Barford Diesel Roller | 1965 | 1980 | Orange, green wheels, windows. Still in production at factory closure |
| 430 | Johnson 2-Ton Dumper | 1977 | 1980 | Orange. Still in production at factory closure |
| 436 | Atlas Copco Compressor Lorry | 1963 | 1969 | Yellow |
| 437 | Muir-Hill 2WL Loader | 1962 | 1980 | Red, later yellow. Still in production at factory closure |
| 561 | Blaw-Knox Bulldozer | 1949 | 1964 | Red. Renumbered 961. |
| 562 | Muir-Hill Dumper | 1948 | 1965 | Yellow. Renumbered 962 |
| 563 | Heavy Tractor | 1948 | 1959 | Red. Renumbered 963 |
| 900 | Building Site Gift Set | 1964 | 1964 | Contains: 437 Muir Hill 2WL Loader. 960 Albion Concrete Mixer. 961 Blaw-Knox Bulldozer. 962 Muir-Hill Dumper. 965 Euclid Dump Truck. |
| 924 | Aveling-Barford Centaur Dump Truck | 1972 | 1976 | Red cab, yellow back |
| 959 | Foden Dump Truck with Bulldozer Blade | 1961 | 1968 | Red, silver blade |
| 960 | Albion Lorry Mounted Concrete Mixer | 1960 | 1967 | Orange, blue barrel with yellow segments |
| 961 | =Blaw-Knox Bulldozer= | | | Renumbering of 561 |
| 962 | =Muir-Hill Dumper= | | | Renumbering of 562 |
| 963 | =Blaw-Knox Heavy Tractor= | | | Renumbering of 563 |
| 963 | Road Grader | 1973 | 1976 | Orange and yellow |
| 965 | Euclid Rear Dump Truck | 1955 | 1969 | Yellow ⎫ basic same casting |
| 965 | Terex Rear Dump Truck | 1969 | 1970 | Yellow ⎬ |
| 967 | Muir-Hill Loader and Trencher | 1973 | 1978 | Orange and yellow |
| 973 | Eaton Yale Articulated Tractor Shovel | 1971 | 1976 | Yellow |
| 975 | Ruston-Bucyrus Excavator | 1963 | 1967 | Yellow, red and grey |
| 976 | Michigan 180 Tractor-Dozer | 1968 | 1976 | Yellow/red |
| 977 | Shovel Dozer | 1973 | 1978 | Yellow |
| 984 | Atlas Digger | 1974 | 1979 | Yellow |

For illustration of 430 see 1979 Catalogue. Chapter 9.

## Road Making Equipment

Diggers, bulldozers, dump trucks, etc. for building the roads on which other vehicles could then run were a constant feature of Dinky production in the post-war years. Because of the heavy road-building programme with hundreds of miles of motorway and by-passes being built in the 1960s and 1970s, this type of vehicle was a familiar sight, and many a garden was dug, graded and rolled in mimicry, leading one to believe that in years to come, it will be difficult to find these models in good condition. There are two castings to which this comment does not apply: 25p the AVELING-BARFORD DIESEL ROLLER, and 561 the BLAW-KNOX BULL-DOZER (and the same thing without the Dozer blade 563 TRACTOR), for these were extremely heavy and robust castings that were in the catalogues for many years. 561 and 563 were initially both painted red with green tracks, but later the colour was changed to yellow with a grey blade for the dozer. 961 was also issued briefly and unsuccessfully in green and orange plastic. This group were renumbered. 975 RUSTON-BUCYRUS EXCAVATOR, a type of bucket excavator, was also released in plastic. 965 EUCLID REAR DUMP TRUCK had transfer changes, the motif being green to start with and then changing to red and black. Even later, this second decal became a sticker, and the model acquired windows. Part of the way through 1979, the name was changed to 'Terex', which necessitated new decals and a casting change to the radiator and baseplate, both of which were altered to read 'Terex'. Many of this group acquired windows in 1961 or subsequently. Issues later than about 1963 were always fitted with windows. Some were available in a gift set.

**Car Transporters**

During most of the post-war era, it was possible to buy a car carrier upon which to transport your Dinky Toys. The first of these, 582 the PULL-MORE CAR TRANSPORTER, uses the Bedford Cab Unit that was used extensively in the 1950s. (See: Commercials—Small). The model will excite the variation collector, as not only were there the detail casting changes that are found on the Bedford, but over the years it was produced in several colour combinations. Commonly painted light blue all over, it is also found with a dark blue cab. Frequently, the bed of the top deck is painted fawn or even grey, and sometimes these colours are applied to the top of the cab too. The accompanying Ramp which was supplied with the transporter, or was also available separately, is always light blue. The Trailer part was always fitted with 'Supertoy' hubs, but 'Supertoy' tyres were not added until about 1959. Subsequently, the cab was fitted with windows. 'Dinky Toys Delivery Service' was applied to the side of the lower deck of the trailer by means of a rubber stamp. 'Dinky Auto Service' was applied in the same manner to the sides of the red and grey Car Carrier and Trailer. Probably based on a Thornycroft, this rather unimpressive ensemble is one of the few vehicles on which, at one time, aluminium was used for the casting. Available as Car Carrier and Trailer together or separately. Towards the end of production the casting of the front part was renumbered 989 and given a new colour scheme of yellow, grey and blue, and new decals 'Auto Transporters'. Later, the blue, yellow and red AEC HOYNER CAR TRANSPORTER using the cab on 915 AEC with flat trailer was issued with a 'Silcock and Colling' decal on the door. 528 was available in a set, having cars with it and the second set 983 consisted of the two parts of the vehicle 984 and 985. The French Dinky 894 was also imported for a short time. (See: French Dinky Products.)

**Breakdown and Crane Trucks**

There are three Breakdown Lorries (Wreck Trucks). 25x BREAKDOWN LORRY utilised the Commer Cab (See: Commercials—Small). The Bedford TK and Land Rover cabs were also utilised on other vehicles. All appeared in more than one colour and there was a Danish 'Falck' release on the Land Rover. Three Coles and a Jones Crane Trucks were issued. An oddity 'Suitable for use with gauge 'O' model railways', 752 GOODS YARD CRANE is a non-mobile model. 434 BEDFORD TK CRASH TRUCK was included in 229 MOTORWAY SERVICES GIFT SET.

Fig. 239. 989 Car Carrier.

Fig. 242. 434 Bedford TK Crash Truck.

Fig. 241. 25x Breakdown lorry.

Fig. 243. 970 Jones Fleetmaster Cantilever Crane.

Fig. 244. 972 Coles 20-ton Lorry-mounted Crane.

*Fig. 240. 950 Car Transporter Gift Set.*

**NEW**

Contents
950
**Car Transporter Gift Set**
974    Hoynor Car Transporter
136    Vauxhall Viva
138    Hillman Imp
162    Triumph 1300
168    Ford Escort
342    Austin Mini Moke

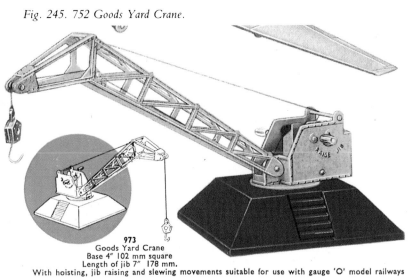

*Fig. 245. 752 Goods Yard Crane.*

973
Goods Yard Crane
Base 4" 102 mm square
Length of jib 7" 178 mm.
With hoisting, jib raising and slewing movements suitable for use with gauge 'O' model railways

## CAR TRANSPORTERS

| Cat. No. | Model | Intro. date | Deletion | Comments |
|---|---|---|---|---|
| 582 | Pullmore Car Transporter (+ Ramp) | 1953 | 1964 | Renumbered 982. Available in set 990 |
| 794 | Loading Ramp (for 582/982) | 1953 | 1964 | Renumbered 994. |
| 894 | Car Transporter | | | See: French Dinky Products |
| 950 | Car Transporter Gift Set | | | Contains: 974 Hoynor Car Transporter. 136 Vauxhall Viva. 138 Hillman Imp. 162 Triumph 1300. 168 Ford Escort. 342 Minimoke. Not issued |
| 974 | A.E.C. Hoynor Car Transporter | 1968 | 1975 | Available in Set 950 |
| 982 | =Pullmore Car Transporter (+ Ramp)= | | | Renumbering of 582 |
| 983 | Car Carrier and Trailer | 1958 | 1963 | Consists of 984 + 985 |
| 984 | Car Carrier and 'Dinky Auto Service' | 1958 | 1965 | Renumbered 989 |
| 985 | Trailer for Car Carrier | 1958 | 1963 | |
| 989 | =Car Carrier 'Auto Transporters'= | | | Renumbering of 984 |
| 990 | Car Transporter and 4 Cars Gift Set | 1956 | 1958 | Contains: 982 Pullmore Car Transporter. 154 Hillman Minx. 156 Rover 75. 161 Austin Somerset. 162 Ford Zephyr |
| 994 | =Loading Ramp= | | | |

## BREAKDOWN AND CRANE TRUCKS

| Cat. No. | Model | Intro. date | Deletion | Comments |
|---|---|---|---|---|
| 25x | Breakdown Lorry | 1950 | 1963 | Brown cab, green back<br>Grey cab, blue back. Renumbered 430 |
| 229 | Motorway Services Gift Set | 1963 | 1967 | Contains: 434 Bedford TK Crash Truck, 269 Motorway Police car, 257 Fire Chief's Car, 276 Airport Fire Tender, 263 (later 277) Criterion Ambulance |
| 430 | =Commer Breakdown Lorry= | | | Grey or fawn cab, blue back. Renumbering of 25x |
| 434 | Bedford TK Crash Truck | 1964 | 1972 | Green & white 'Top Rank'. Briefly red & white 'Auto Services' |
| 442 | Land Rover Breakdown Crane | 1973 | 1979 | Red & white 'Motorway Rescue'. See also: Danish issues |
| 571 | Coles Mobile Crane | 1949 | 1965 | Yellow and black. Renumbered 971 |
| 752 | Goods Yard Crane | 1953 | 1959 | Yellow & blue. Renumbered 973 |
| 970 | Jones Fleetmaster Cantilever Crane | 1967 | 1976 | Red & white, yellow, Metallic red & white |
| 971 | =Coles Mobile Crane= | | | Renumbering of 571 |
| 972 | Coles 20-Ton Lorry-Mounted Crane | 1955 | 1968 | Orange & yellow |
| 973 | =Goods Yard Crane= | | | Renumbering of 752 |
| 980 | Coles Hydra Truck 150T | 1972 | 1979 | Yellow |

For illustrations of 442 and 980 see 1979 Catalogue. Chapter 9.

## Cleaning and Servicing

A small selection of vehicles were available for cleaning and tidying the streets. Where applicable, windows were fitted part way through the life of the casting. 978 REFUSE WAGON using the TK chassis/cab, in the last year of production gained a new cab casting, incorporating the roof box which had, up to then, been a separate plastic part. It was supplied with two grey plastic dustbins with removable lids. 451 JOHNSTON ROAD SWEEPER was fitted with revolving brushes and renumbered 449, Johnston co-operated with Meccano in its production, and over the years received several batches in yellow and silver, initially with yellow plastic pipes and then with black. 'Johnston' on a transfer was applied by the firm itself. The last consignment were received just before the Binns Road Works closed down. Some of the early packaging, when cardboard boxes were used, have the back printed 'Johnston Road Suction Cleaners Used Worldwide' and the 'JB' logo of Johnston Brothers, but later packaging was an unmodified Dinky box. Spare buckets for the Marrel Multi-bucket Unit, which used the Albion chassis also found on the Albion Lorry Mounted Concrete Mixer, were available for some time after the model itself was deleted. 958 SNOW PLOUGH utilised the Guy Warrior cab, and is a most spectacular beast. Later, the Ford D800 appeared as a SNOW PLOUGH/TIPPER No. 439. (See: Commercials—Others). 977 SERVICING PLATFORM VEHICLE, which could be used to mend street lights, etc., is a civilian version of 677 MISSILE SERVICING PLATFORM.

## Lifting & Carrying

This group consists of three vehicles which had very long lives. 404 began with the name 'Conveyancer' and ended with 'Climax'.

*Fig. 246. 449/451 Johnston Road Sweeper. The normal production model is on the right.*

*Fig. 247. 958 Snow Plough.*

*Fig. 248. 966 Marrel Multi-bucket unit.*

*Fig. 250. 451 Johnston Road Sweeper. The early production version on the right and on the left, a prototype with the first of the yellow plastic bodies fitted to orange cab unit.*

## CLEANING AND SERVICING

| Cat. No. | Model | Intro. date | Deletion | Comments |
|---|---|---|---|---|
| 25v | Refuse Wagon, Bedford Chassis | 1948 | 1964 | Renumbered 252. Green cab, fawn back. Later: orange & silver. |
| 252 | =Refuse Wagon= | | | Renumbering of 25v |
| 449 | =Johnston Road Sweeper= | | | Renumbering of 451 (1977). All yellow. Still in production at factory closure |
| 451 | Johnston Road Sweeper | 1971 | 1980 | Renumbered 449. Orange cab, metallic green back |
| 958 | Snow Plough | 1961 | 1965 | Yellow and black |
| 966 | Marrel Multi-bucket Unit | 1960 | 1964 | Yellow, grey buckets |
| 977 | Servicing Platform Vehicle | 1960 | 1964 | Cream cab, red back |
| 978 | Refuse Wagon | 1964 | 1979 | Green, grey plastic back. 1979 casting change—Yellow, grey plastic back |
| (449/ 451) | Johnston Road Sweeper | | | Yellow. 'Johnston' decals |

For illustration of 978 see 1979 Catalogue. Chapter 9.

## LIFTING AND CARRYING

| Cat. No. | Model | Intro. date | Deletion | Comments |
|---|---|---|---|---|
| 14a | Electric Truck | 1948 | 1960 | Renumbered 400. Blue, grey |
| 14c | Coventry-Climax Fork-Lift Truck | 1949 | 1964 | Renumbered 401. Orange 9 green |
| 400 | =B.E.V. Electric Truck= | | | Renumbering of 14a |
| 401 | =Coventry-Climax Fork-Lift Truck= | | | Renumbering of 14c |
| 404 | Conveyancer/Climax Fork Lift Truck (includes plastic pallet) | 1967 | 1980 | Yellow/red. Still in production at factory closure |

For illustration of 404 see 1979 Catalogue. Chapter 9.

*Fig. 249. 977 Servicing Platform Vehicle.*

*Fig. 251. 14c Coventry Climax Fork-Lift Truck and 14a B.E.V. Electric Truck.*

179

## Horse Boxes

One Horsebox Casting appeared in three versions. 581 was issued with 'British Railways' decals in the U.K. and without in the U.S.A. though some States catalogues show the U.K. version.

*Fig. 254. 581 Horsebox (U.K. version) and 979 Racehorse Transport.*

| Cat. No. | Model | Intro. date | Deletion | Comments |
|---|---|---|---|---|
| 581 | Horsebox | 1953 | 1960 | Maroon (U.K. decals). Renumbered 981 |
| 581 | Horsebox | | | Maroon (U.S. decals). Renumbered 980 |
| 979 | Racehorse Transport (and two Horses) | 1961 | 1964 | Yellow & Grey |
| 980 | =Horsebox= | | | Renumbering of 581 (U.S.) |
| 981 | =Horsebox= | | | Renumbering of 581 (U.K.) |

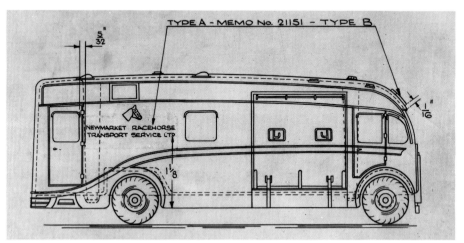

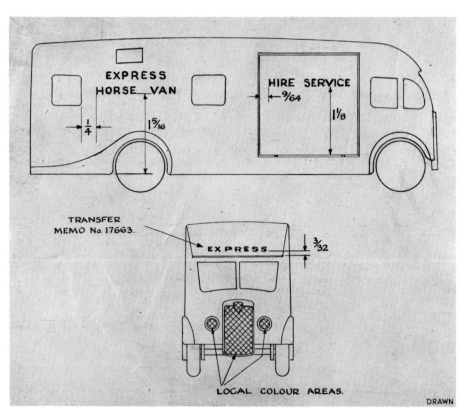

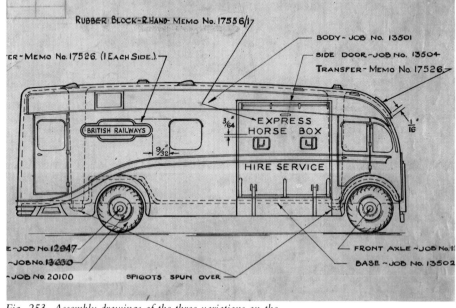

*Fig. 253. Assembly drawings of the three variations on the Horsebox.*

180

## Milk Floats

One casting initially numbered 30v was used for the N.C.B. manufactured milk float which carried the decals 'NCB' or 'Express Dairies'. The catalogue pictures cannot be relied on as a guide to when each decal was actually available, but it would appear from the captioning that 'NCB' predates 'Express Dairies', and that after renumbering, 491 'NCB' was intended for the export market, whereas 490 'Express Dairies' for the home. NCB is the scarcer of the two. As production of the model ceased, a batch of 1176 were produced in cream especially for Job's Dairies. These were decalled by the Dairy and issued to staff and business contacts.

### MILK FLOATS

| Cat. No. | Model | Intro. date | Deletion | Comments |
|---|---|---|---|---|
| 30v | Electric Dairy Van | 1949 | 1960 | NCB: Renumbered 491. Cream with red decal. Express Dairy: Renumbered 490. Cream with red decal. Grey with blue decal. |
| 490 | =Electric Dairy Van= | | | Renumbering of 30v |
| 491 | =Electric Dairy Van= | | | Renumbering of 30v |

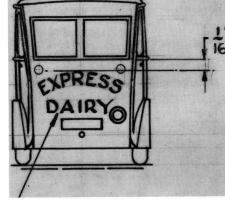

Fig. 255. The two transfers used on the Electric Dairy Van.

Fig. 257. The 'Job's Dairies' version.

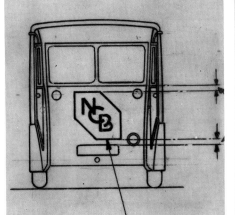

Fig. 256. 490 and 491 Electric Dairy Vans.

## T.V.

Some of the most detailed and accurate Special Purpose Vehicles that were released were Television Outside Broadcast Vehicles. 968 B.B.C. T.V. ROVING EYE VEHICLE was a landmark in production as it was the first large commercial vehicle to be fitted with windows and the catalogues burbled enthusiastically: 'These are models of the mobile camera units of the B.B.C. used for telecasting sports meetings, pageants, conferences and similar events. Finished in dark green with the B.B.C. coat of arms. Each has transparent windows in the cab, with the ones in the body glazed in green opaque material.' The production of these items was undertaken with the full knowledge of the B.B.C. Engineering & Transport Department. Later, A.B.C. T.V. (a Commercial Television Station) had its vehicles modelled and even later, there was one model of a Fiat 2300 Pathé News Camera Car.

| Cat. No. | Model | Intro. date | Deletion | Comments |
|---|---|---|---|---|
| 281 | Pathé News Camera Car | 1967 | 1969 | Black (Camera & Operator on roof) |
| 967 | B.B.C. T.V. Mobile Control Room | 1959 | 1964 | Dark Green |
| 968 | B.B.C. T.V. Roving Eye Vehicle | 1959 | 1964 | Dark Green |
| 969 | B.B.C. T.V. Extending Mast Vehicle | 1959 | 1964 | Dark Green |
| 987 | A.B.C. T.V. Control Room | 1962 | 1969 | Grey lower, blue upper (Plus camera & operator) |
| 988 | A.B.C. Transmitter Van | 1962 | 1968 | Grey lower, blue upper |

4¼" (108 mm.)

Fig. 261. 281 Pathé News Camera Car.

Fig. 259. The B.B.C. T.V. Vehicles.

Fig. 260. The A.B.C. T.V. Vehicles, 988 left, 987 right.

182

## Bank and Security

The Brinks Armoured Car was a hefty vehicle finished light grey with a dark blue base, fitted with two drivers and loaded with two crates of 'gold'. A small batch were produced with their coat of arms for Luis R. Picaso Manriques, a Mexican security firm in dark grey with a black base. The die was shipped to the United States in the late 1970s and it was issued as 'Brinks Truck' painted dark grey with a light blue base and white roof. The decals were changed slightly. Neither of these two had drivers nor gold bullion.

| Cat. No. | Model | Intro. date | Deletion | Comments |
|------|-------|-------|----------|----------|
| 275 | Brinks Armoured Car | 1964 | 1969 | Grey and blue |
| 280 | Midland Mobile Bank | 1966 | 1968 | White, blue and silver |

*Fig. 262. 275 Brinks Armoured Car and the Mexican version.*

*Fig. 263. 280 Midland Mobile Bank.*

**280** Midland Mobile Bank

$4\frac{7}{8}''$ (124 mm.)

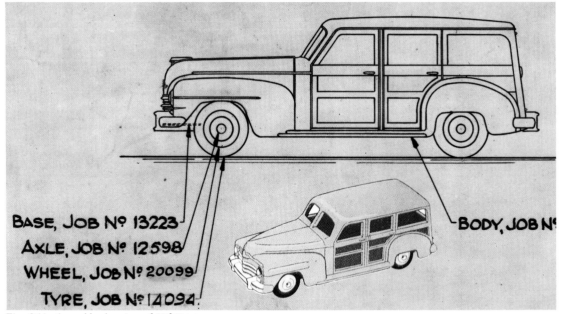

*Fig. 264. Assembly drawing of 27f Estate car.*

BASE, JOB Nº 13223
AXLE, JOB Nº 12598
WHEEL, JOB Nº 20099
TYRE, JOB Nº 14094

BODY, JOB Nº

*Fig. 265. Assembly drawing of 27n Field Marshall Tractor.*

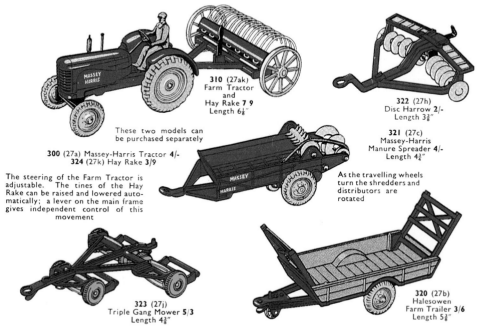

**310** (27ak)
Farm Tractor
and
Hay Rake **7 9**
Length 6⅛″

These two models can
be purchased separately

**300** (27a) Massey-Harris Tractor **4/-**
**324** (27k) Hay Rake **3/9**

The steering of the Farm Tractor is
adjustable. The tines of the Hay
Rake can be raised and lowered automatically; a lever on the main frame
gives independent control of this
movement

**322** (27h)
Disc Harrow **2/-**
Length 3⅜″

**321** (27c)
Massey-Harris
Manure Spreader **4/-**
Length 4¾″

As the travelling wheels
turn the shredders and
distributors are
rotated

**323** (27j)
Triple Gang Mower **5/3**
Length 4⅜″

**320** (27b)
Halesowen
Farm Trailer **3/6**
Length 5⅝″

**344** (27f)
Estate Car **2/11**
Length 4″

**341** (27m)
Land Rover Trailer **2/-**
Length 3⅛″
Suitable for use with
Dinky Toys
300, 301 and 340

**340** (27d)
Land Rover **4/1**
Length 3½″
This vehicle is fitted with a towing
hook and can be used with other
models of farm equipment

**301** (27n)
Field Marshall Tractor
Length 3″

**342** (27g)
Motocart **4/3**
Length 4¾″
With tipping rear platform

All models on this page can be used with Dinky Toys Nos. 300 and 301, which are fitted with towing hooks

*Fig. 266. The early Farm machinery.*

10

## Farm and Garden

Meccano certainly got their money's worth out of the dies used to produce the Farm Vehicles and Equipment as most were in the catalogues for many years, some a little less than twenty and some even more! There are very few casting changes over the years and very few colour differences also, farm equipment not being subject to fashion in the same manner as cars. 27a/300 MASSEY-HARRIS-FERGUSON TRACTOR was always red with yellow wheel hubs. The wheels were initially all metal but later rubber tyres were fitted and the front hubs became plastic. The earlier types had 'Massey-Harris' decals but later this was changed to 'Massey-Ferguson'. It appeared in a set with the Hay Rake. The accessories such as Harvest Trailer, Manure Spreader, also changed from all metal wheels to plastic hubs and rubber tyres. 27d LAND ROVER had a tinplate screen, changed its wheel hubs to plastic and had colour and minor casting changes. It also appeared in GIFT SET 2 COMMERCIAL VEHICLES. 27f ESTATE CAR is a model of the Plymouth Station Wagon. It had a colour change and eventually was fitted with shiny metal hubs. It also appeared in GIFT SET 3 PASSENGER CARS. Though a car it was almost always regarded by Dinky as a farm vehicle and appears on the 'farm' catalogue pages. 27n FIELD MARSHALL TRACTOR also had its wheels changed from all metal to plastic and rubber. All the above were renumbered. Five figured in GIFT SET 1, FARMYARD EQUIPMENT. Two other tractors were made, one in the 1960s and one in the 1970s. 564/964 ELEVATOR LOADER doesn't really fit in this section for it was designed as an accessory to 'O' Gauge trains. However children tend to regard it as part of Farm Equipment and therefore it has been included here. A model of a Barber-Greene Olding Machine it was classed as a Supertoy.

*Fig. 267. 398 Farm Vehicles Gift Set.*

## COMMERCIALS—FARM AND GARDEN

*Fig. 269. 308 Leyland 384 Tractor.*

| Cat. No. | Model | Intro. date | Deletion | Comments |
|---|---|---|---|---|
| 27a | Massey-Harris Tractor | 1948 | 1971 | Red. Renumbered 300 |
| 27ak | Farm Tractor and Hay Rake | 1953 | 1966 | 27a + 27k. Renumbered 310 |
| 27b | Halesowen Harvest Trailer | 1949 | 1970 | Brown & red. Renumbered 320 |
| 27c | Massey-Harris Manure Spreader | 1949 | 1973 | Red. Renumbered 321 |
| 27d | Land Rover | 1950 | 1970 | Orange & green. Later red. Renumbered 340 |
| 27f | Estate Car | 1950 | 1960 | Fawn with brown panels. Later grey with red. Renumbered 344 |
| 27g | Motocart | 1949 | 1961 | Green & Brown. Renumbered 342 |
| 27h | Disc Harrow | 1951 | 1971 | Red & yellow. Later white. Renumbered 322 |
| 27j | Triple Gang Mower | 1952 | 1958 | Red & yellow & green. Renumbered 323 |
| 27k | Hay Rake | 1953 | 1970 | Red & yellow. Renumbered 324 |
| 27m | Land Rover Trailer | 1954 | 1973 | Orange. Green. Renumbered 341 |
| 27n | Field Marshall Tractor | 1953 | 1965 | Orange. Renumbered 301 |
| 300 | =Massey-Ferguson Tractor= | | | Renumbering of 27a |
| 301 | =Field-Marshall Tractor= | | | Renumbering of 27n |
| 305 | David Brown Tractor | 1965 | 1975 | Yellow & red. Later white |
| 308 | Leyland 384 Tractor | 1971 | 1979 | Metallic red. Later blue. Also orange 300 + 324. |
| 310 | =Farm Tractor and Hay Rake= | | | Renumbering of 27ak |
| 319 | Week's Tipping Farm Trailer | 1961 | 1970 | Red & yellow |
| 320 | =Halesowen Harvest Trailer= | | | Renumbering of 27b |
| 321 | =Massey-Harris Manure Spreader= | | | Renumbering of 27c |
| 322 | =Disc Harrow= | | | Renumbering of 27h |
| 323 | =Triple Gang Mower= | | | Renumbering of 27j |
| 324 | =Hay Rake= | | | Renumbering of 27k |
| 325 | David Brown Tractor and Disc Harrow | 1966 | 1972 | 325 + 322. White |
| 340 | =Land Rover= | | | Renumbering of 27d |
| 341 | =Land Rover Trailer= | | | Renumbering of 27m |
| 342 | =Motocart= | | | Renumbering of 27g |
| 344 | =Estate Car= | | | Renumbering of 27f |
| 398 | =Farm Equipment Gift Set= | | | 300 + 320 + 321 + 322 + 324. Renumbering of Gift Set 1 |
| 399 | Farm and Tractor and Trailer Set | 1969 | 1971 | 300 + 428 |
| 428 | Trailer | 1967 | 1971 | Red |
| 564 | Elevator Loader | 1952 | 1968 | Yellow and blue. Renumbered 964 |
| 964 | =Elevator Loader= | | | Renumbering of 564 |
| Gift Set 1. | Farmyard Equipment | 1952 and 1964 | 1954 | 27a + b + c + h + k Renumbered 398 |

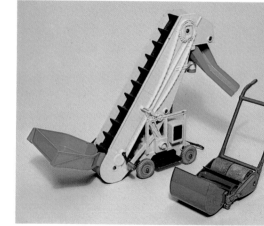

*Fig. 268. 564 Elevator Loader and 751 Lawn Mower.*

3¼" (83 mm.)

**305 David Brown Tractor**

**319 Weeks Tipping Farm Trailer**

*Fig. 270. 319, 305 and 428.*

**428 Trailer**

A very small selection of gardening tools were issued in 1948/9 and they remained in the catalogue until 1958. There are no major variations in colour or casting and Dinky did not bother to release any more at a later date. Though not normally thought of as a garden item, the Sack Truck was given a number within the 'garden' numbers and is therefore included in this section. The only remarkable model in the group is the 751/386 LAWN MOWER which at 1½in to the foot is the largest scale Dinky Toy ever produced!

| Cat. No. | Model | Intro. date | Deletion | Comments |
|---|---|---|---|---|
| 105a | Garden Roller | 1948 | 1958 | Red & green. Renumbered 381 |
| 105b | Wheelbarrow | 1949 | 1958 | Brown. Renumbered 382 |
| 105c | Four-wheeled Hand Truck | 1949 | 1958 | Green. Blue. Renumbered 383 |
| 105e | Grass Cutter | 1949 | 1958 | Red & green. Renumbered 384 |
| 107a | Sack Truck | 1949 | 1958 | Blue. Renumbered 385 |
| 381 | =Garden Roller= | | | Renumbering of 105a |
| 382 | =Wheelbarrow= | | | Renumbering of 105b |
| 383 | =Four-wheeled Hand Truck= | | | Renumbering of 105c |
| 384 | =Grass Cutter= | | | Renumbering of 105e |
| 385 | =Sack Truck= | | | Renumbering of 107a |
| 386 | =Lawn Mower= | | | Renumbering of 751 |
| 751 | Lawn Mower | 1949 | 1958 | Green & red. Renumbered 386 |

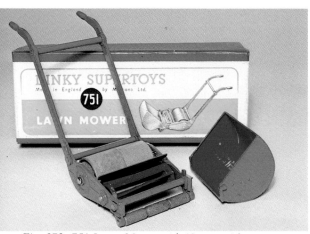

*Fig. 272. 751 Lawn Mower with 'Supertoy' box.*

**Other Commercials**

Although Meccano were very economical in the use of the main castings, there are some vehicles that are entirely individual and don't fit neatly into one section or another. There are also vehicles which, although the casting is shared with others, will not fit into any sensible descriptive scheme. In neither case does it mean that the models are any less collectable, but it does mean that this section is a disjointed hotch-potch. Only significant variations are mentioned in this text, the rest of the information being in the tables.

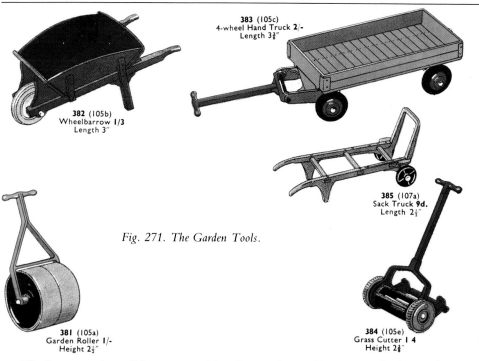

**383** (105c)
4-wheel Hand Truck 2/-
Length 3¾″

**382** (105b)
Wheelbarrow 1/3
Length 3″

**385** (107a)
Sack Truck **9d.**
Length 2½″

*Fig. 271. The Garden Tools.*

**381** (105a)
Garden Roller 1/-
Height 2½″

**384** (105e)
Grass Cutter 1 4
Height 2⅜″

The latest casting of the pre-war 28 series, Bedford type with squared grille, appears as 280 for a short time. There have been several sightings of a red one with 'Knorr' decals, but we have not ourselves seen one. With a loudspeaker on the roof, it appeared as 34c/392. In the mid to late 1960s, a nice chunky Bedford TK cab/chassis unit was made with five different backs, including a wrecker. (See: Special Purpose Vehicles). This was superceded by AEC Cab which appeared on two models in this group plus 945 TANKER, 974 CAR TRANSPORTER, 616 and 618 MILITARY TRANSPORTERS; an 'artic' with a green canopy bearing the legend 'British Road Services', and an 'artic' with flat trailer which was supplied to 'Thames Board Mills' in white. The firm applied the decals and placed simu-

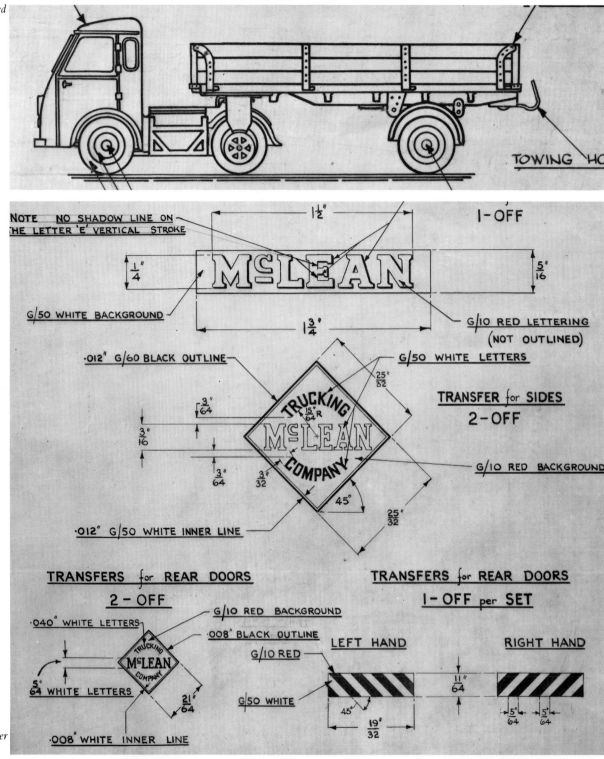

*Fig. 273. Assembly drawing of the Hindle Smart Articulated Vehicle.*

lated reels of 'Uniliner Board' in the back. 300 or so were made and given away as a trade promotion. The Ford D800 cab had opening doors in the early seventies, but as a cost saving they were deleted on the later TIPPER TRUCK No. 440. 917 MERCEDES-BENZ TRUCK and TRAILER No. 917 had a fairly long run, as the truck alone was reissued on a new number, 940, in the late 1970s. There was a promotional on 917 in green and white with 'Munster' decals, and 940 was issued in Belgium as 'Cory'. 432 FODEN TIPPING LORRY uses the same basic casting as the non-tipping military version 668. The military MIGHTY ANTAR LOW LOADER, finished in civilian colours, carried either a transformer (briefly) or a large propeller bearing a 'Scimitar' transfer. 930 BEDFORD PALLET-JEKTA from the early 1960s is a real oddity, for the truck on which it was based was produced in very small quantities. Presumably, the novel method of unloading, which works well on the model, was found wanting in reality. It acquired windows part way through its production run. The perennial Mini Van appeared as 'Vote for Somebody' (how truly impartial!) in 1964. This did not appear in the catalogues, presumably because of the transitory appeal of an election vehicle (In Britain, General Elections only being held once every five years).

The Mini Van casting was fitted with a loudspeaker on the roof and a plastic Election Candidate is shouting into a microphone. Joseph Mason, a firm that produced industrial paints including those that were used on Rolls Royces had a casting painted maroon with a small maroon plastic headboard packed in a maroon specially printed box, creating what must be the classiest promotional of all time.

*Fig. 275. 34c Loud Speaker Van.*

**492** (34c)
Loud Speaker Van 2, 3
Length 3⅛"

*Fig. 274. The transfer drawings for 948 Tractor-Trailer 'McLean'.*

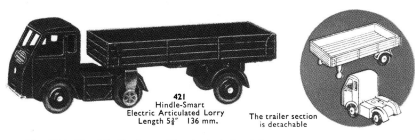

421
Hindle-Smart
Electric Articulated Lorry
Length 5⅜" 136 mm.

The trailer section is detachable

*Fig. 276. 30w Hindle Smart Electric Articulated Lorry.*

425
Bedford T.K.
Coal Wagon
4¾" — 121 mm.

*Fig. 277. 425 Bedford TK Coal Wagon.*

5⅟₁₆" (132 mm.)

438   Ford D800 Tipper Truck

*Fig. 279. 438 Ford D800 Tipper Truck.*

## OTHER COMMERCIALS

| Cat. No. | Model | Intro. date | Deletion | Comments |
|---|---|---|---|---|
| 30w | Electric Articulated Lorry | 1953 | 1959 | Maroon. Renumbered 421 |
| 33w | Mechanical Horse and Open Wagon | | | See: 33 series. Reno. 415 |
| 34c | Loudspeaker Van | 1948 | 1957 | Blue, brown, green, grey Renumbered 492 |
| 280 | Delivery Van | 1948 | 1951 | Blue, red |
| 402 | Bedford Coca Cola Truck (TK) (with crate load) | 1966 | 1968 | Red, white roof |
| 415 | =Mechanical Horse and Open Wagon= | | | Renumbering of 33w |
| 421 | =Hindle-Smart Electric Articulated Lorry= | | | Renumbering of 30w |
| 425 | Bedford TK Coal Wagon (with sacks and scales) | 1964 | 1968 | Red |
| 432 | Foden Tipping Lorry | 1976 | 1979 | White cab, yellow back, red chassis |
| 435 | Bedford TK Tipper | 1964 | 1970 | Off-white cab, light blue roof, orange back, later yellow cab, sides, silver bed |
| 438 | Ford D 800 Tipper Truck | 1970 | 1976 | Red & yellow. Later light metallic blue |
| 439 | Ford D 800 Snow Plough/Tipper | 1970 | 1976 | Blue, red and yellow. Later blue, white & yellow |
| 440 | Ford D 800 Tipper | 1977 | 1978 | Red & yellow |
| 450 | Bedford TK Box Van (Castrol) | 1965 | 1969 | Green & white |
| 492 | =Loudspeaker Van= | | | Renumbering of 34c |
| 492 | Election Mini-van (with figure with microphone | 1964 | 1965 | White, orange loudspeaker |
| 561 | Citroen Delivery Van Cibié | | | See: French Dinky |
| 579 | Simca Glazier's Lorry | | | See: French Dinky |
| 581 | Berliet Flat Truck | | | See: French Dinky |
| 893 | Unic Pipe-Line Transporter | | | See: French Dinky |
| 908 | Mighty Antar with Transformer | 1962 | 1964 | Yellow cab, grey bed |
| 914 | AEC Articulated Lorry | 1965 | 1970 | Red cab, grey back, green canopy. 'British Road Services' |
| 915 | AEC with Flat Trailer | 1973 | 1975 | Orange cab, white back |
| 917 | Mercedes-Benz Truck and Trailer | 1967 | 1976 | Blue cab, yellow back, white canopy |
| 930 | Bedford Pallet-Jekta Van (with pallets) | 1959 | 1964 | Orange cab, yellow back |
| 940 | Mercedes-Benz Truck | 1977 | 1980 | White cab, grey back. Still in production at factory closure |
| 948 | Tractor-trailer 'McLean' | 1961 | 1967 | Red cab, grey back |
| 925 | Leyland Tilt Cab and Heavy Duty Tipper/Leyland Dump Truck with Tilt Cab | 1966 | 1969 | White cab, red back |
| 986 | Mighty Antar Low Loader with Propeller | 1959 | 1964 | Red cab, grey bed |
| (274) | Mini-van 'Joseph Mason Paints' | | | Maroon |
| (915) | AEC with Flat Trailer 'Thames Board Mills' | | | White |
| (917) | Mercedes-Benz Truck and Trailer 'Munster' | | | Green & white |
| (940) | Mercedes-Benz Truck 'Cory' | | | |

For illustrations of 432 and 940 see 1979 Catalogue. Chapter 9.

*Fig. 278. 435 Bedford TK Tipper.*

*Fig. 280. 908 Mighty Antar with Transformer.*

*Fig. 281. 986 Mighty Antar Low Loader with Propeller.*

*Fig. 283. 'Joseph Mason Paints' Minivan.*

*Fig. 282. 948 Tractor-Trailer 'McLean'.*

**15 5/8" LONG**

WITH OPENING CAB DOORS

1ST AGAIN

**914 A.E.C. Articulated Lorry**

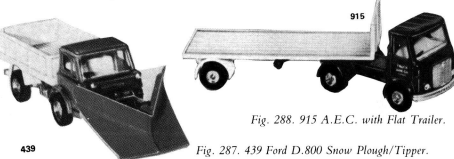

8 5/16" (210 mm.)

**917 Mercedes-Benz Truck and Trailer**

**10 SPECIAL FEATURES**

| | |
|---|---|
| 1 Opening Doors | 6 Detachable Canopies on Box Bodies |
| 2 Detailed Interior Seats | 7 Trailer couples to Truck |
| 3 Wing Mirrors | 8 Opening Tailgates |
| 4 Jewelled Headlights | 9 Suspension on Truck and Trailer |
| 5 Opening Cab Roof Ventilator | 10 Bogie wheels pivot on Trailer |

15 5/8" (397 mm.)

915

439

Fig. 288. 915 A.E.C. with Flat Trailer.

Fig. 287. 439 Ford D.800 Snow Plough/Tipper.

CASTROL

CASTROL

THE MASTERPIECE IN OILS

BEDFORD

**450 Bedford TK Box Van (Castrol)**

**925 Leyland Dump Truck with Tilt Cab**

Fig. 289. 925 Leyland Dump Truck with Tilt Cab.

DRINK Coca-Cola

**402 Bedford Coca Cola Lorry**

Fig. 286. 402 Bedford Coca Cola Lorry and 450 Bedford TK Box Van (Castrol).

**930**
Bedford Pallet-Jekta Van DINKY TOYS
(with windows)
Length 6 5/8"
14/3

MECCANO DINKY TOYS

Fig. 290. 930 Bedford Pallet-Jekta Van.

191

## Buses—Pre-war

Over the years, Meccano produced quite a few buses, and most of them stayed in the catalogues for a considerable length of time, but one cannot say that they provide much scope for the bus collector, as a very few basic castings were used with a variety of colours and decals. While, for the purist, many of the single deck buses should actually be referred to as 'coaches', the titles are used interchangeably in this chapter, as is common parlance. The first examples of this form of public transport appeared early on in mid-1934, and the two earliest numbers made a nice pair; 27 the TRAM CAR and 29a the MOTOR BUS. They are of considerably smaller scale than any other buses made, and the tram is the only example of this form of transport that Dinky ever made.

27 TRAM CAR is a mere 7.7cm in length, and is a single casting. The boom is cast into the roof and it runs on four little diecast wheels concealed within the body. Some were fitted with plastic rollers, simi-

*Fig. 298. Drawing of 'Dunlop Tyres' transfer.*

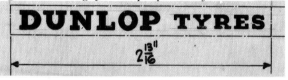

*Fig. 299. Drawing of 'Dunlop – The World's Master Tyre' transfer.*

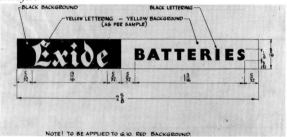

*Fig. 302. Drawing of 'Exide Batteries' transfer.*

lar to those used on the ships, etc. There are two different colour schemes, the earlier one having the lighter of the two colours covering the running gear, the lower windows and the upper windows and roof, and the later having the lighter colour only on upper windows and roof. The colours usually found are various shades of blue and cream, orange and cream, red and cream, and yellow and cream. It was issued with or without decals. The transfers were the same both sides, and read 'Drink Delicious Ovaltine Every Day'.

29 MOTOR BUS, illustrated briefly in literature with a half cab, slightly protruding bonnet and rear entrance, was not issued (illustration p. 193).

29a MOTOR BUS is a very good model of the vehicle normally known as the 'Centre Entrance Bus', having the correct number of windows both upstairs and down, and was initially numbered 29. A strange-looking vehicle to our eyes, it was actually in service in the mid-thirties. The model is only 7 cm long and came in yellow, green, and blue, with a cream or silver roof. The open door produced a requirement for some sort of interior, and this was simply produced by the addition of a baseplate which is slotted and tabbed to the body in the manner of tinplate vehicles, a method also used on the 29c DOUBLE DECKER throughout its production run. The wheels, which are on axles through the chassis, are the same as those used on the tram and have, rather incongruously, a representation of spokes on them. They were listed without decals, but most had 'Marmite Definitely Does You Good' on both sides, with 'Marmite' in silver or in red.

The next two models are a single deck coach, and the same thing as a 'Futuristic' van—well, the shape was very new and 'modern' in the Thirties, even though it looks strange to our eyes. The van is dealt with in this section, partly because of its similarity to the bus, and partly because it is such an individual item that it will not fit anywhere else.

31 HOLLAND COACHCRAFT VAN is one of the scarcest of the pre-war Dinky Toys, and was introduced in early 1935. (Holland was a firm of coachwork designers). The pre-war catalogues, which would give an accurate deletion date, have not been available to the authors, possibly because none still survive. The Holland Coachcraft Van does not

appear at all in *Meccano Magazine* advertising after the introduction of the Streamline Bus, which leads to speculation that the die for the Van was modified into that for the Bus. If one allies this with the great scarcity of the Van and the poorness of the castings around the radiator grille on many examples, one can come up with a hypothesis that the deletion date was somewhere round about May 1936, when the Streamline Bus was introduced. Its apparently short run is regretted, as it is a most delightful little item that was coloured cream, orange, blue, green or red, with coachlining in a contrasting colour and 'HOLLAND COACHCRAFT REGISTERED DESIGN' in gold or silver.

29b STREAMLINE BUS was issued in 1936 and is a single casting which mysteriously does not seem to suffer the fatigue of many other pre-war releases. The wheels are concealed within the body, and during its life it ran on white or black small tyres, both smooth and treaded. In its brief post-war existence, the tyres are usually smooth black. The pre-war castings all had an open rear window which was rather crudely filled in for post-war issue. The painting was always two-tone, with the spats and roof stripe painted a darker colour than the body. Two-tone green and blue are common, with grey allied with a variety of other colours following close behind, but the most spectacular is probably red with maroon flashes. Post-war, the colours were very similar but the roof flash was no longer applied.

29c DOUBLE DECKER MOTOR BUS is the first of the line of double deckers that featured in Dinky Catalogues from its first appearance in the Spring of 1938 until production at Binns Road ceased. It is a most attractive model of an AEC/STL and is a fairly intricate two piece casting; one for the main body and one incorporating the chassis and nearside bonnet and allied windows. More than one chassis casting was used, as can be seen from variations in the typeface of the base wording. Part of the chassis casting is the representation of stairs that lead towards the upper deck and it is this feature that most easily distinguished the pre-war issue from the post-war versions. Usually sporting 'DUNLOP TYRES' adverts along the side, the roof was nearly always grey, though this extra was dropped just before the war, and the body blue, red, maroon, green or

Fig. 291. Box of 6 no. 27 Tramcar.

Fig. 292. Box of 6 no. 29a Motor Bus.

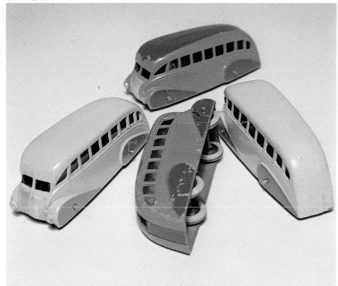

Fig. 293. 31 Holland Coachcraft Van.

Fig. 294. 29b Streamline Bus.

Fig. 295. 29c Double Decker Motor Bus (pre-war).

Fig. 296. 29c Double Deck Bus (1st post-war issue).

Fig. 297. 291 Double Deck Bus Exide.

orange with a cream upper deck.

On its post-war re-issue, it was known as DOUBLE DECK BUS and had no adverts. There were minor casting changes but the radiator remained the same being characterised by bars that produced the shape of a capital 'Y'. In 1948 and 1949, two new radiators were drawn, the first had an oblong badge centre top of the radiator cowl making it a Leyland/STL, and the second a deep 'V' in the cowl bringing it down into the pronounced vertical bars in the grille, similar to the AEC/Regent II. The Leyland grille was in use from 1948 to 1962 and the AEC from 1949 to 1959 but the two dies do not seem to have been run at the same time so that the follow-ing sequence is produced: Leyland; AEC; Leyland; AEC; LEYLAND. 29c was added to the drawing in 1951 and the drawing for the commoner post-war transfer 'Dunlop The World's Master Tyre' is dated late December 1953. From some time subsequent to this most of the castings were decorated with it. The number was changed to 290 in 1955. From about 1956 to 1960 the roof box was omitted from the body casting, but then re-introduced. In 1959, on the number 291 and utilising the Leyland chassis, a red bus with Exide decals was introduced and occasionally, the decals were applied to red and cream, or green and cream ones produced in the same era. Their two colour schemes are the standard ones, but early post-war Leylands ('Y' radiator) were also red or green lower with cream upper deck or two tone green. The odd white upper deck is also found, and there are shade variations. There are also many, many, small to important casting differences other than those mentioned, and even plastic and shiny metal hubs. It was never fitted with windows.

The double decker and subsequent models issued on No. 29 were all Dublo scale. These five were all single deck buses and coaches of various body styles. As their issue and deletion dates span from 1952 to 1960, some were renumbered, but none acquired windows.

After the deletion of 290 and 291, a completely

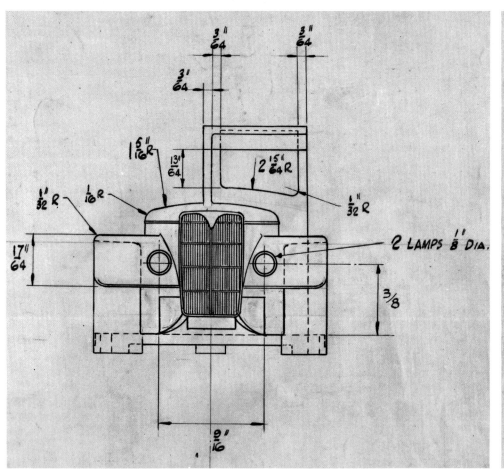

*Fig. 300. The second type A.E.C. radiator.*

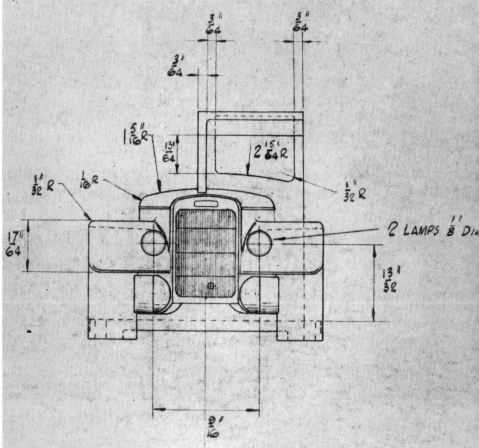

*Fig. 301. The Leyland type radiator.*

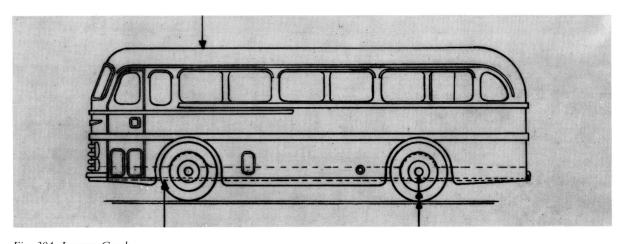

Fig. 303. Duple Roadmaster Touring Coach.

Fig. 304. Luxury Coach.

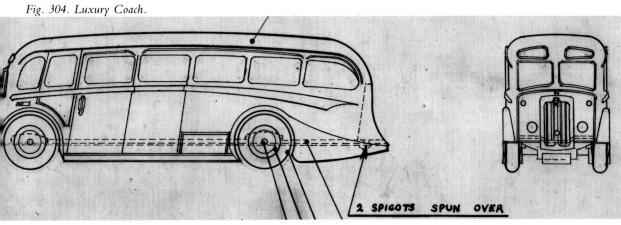

2 SPIGOTS SPUN OVER

Fig. 305. Observation Coach.

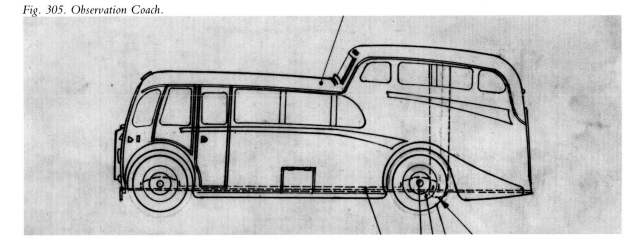

Fig. 306. Transfer drawings for 'B.O.A.C.' coach.

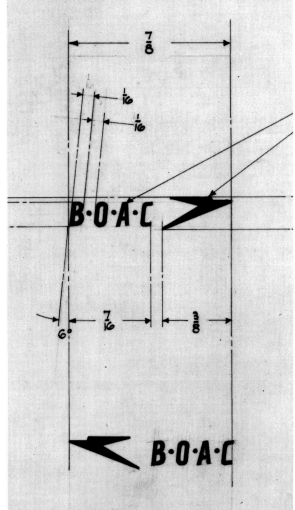

B·O·A·C

B·O·A·C

new casting, which was subject to some changes—the Atlantean—was issued on 292 and 293. 292 had a red colour scheme with 'Regent' adverts and 'Corporation Transport' fleet designation, but it was also available briefly with or without the ads, and with the fleet name, 'Ribble'—a North Country bus operator—and 293 was green with 'BP' adverts. This style was updated with 291 ATLANTEAN CITY BUS in orange, and 295 ATLANTEAN BUS in yellow with 'Yellow Pages' adverts. We are reliably informed that there are least 12 variations on this vehicle, but the most important ones are that the initial issue had the wording reversed out on the headboard, and that interior and glazing colours changed. This casting was used for the 297 JUBILEE BUS which was also specially decalled for Wool-worths.

289, the other double decker, is the London Routemaster design. In the catalogue for many years, it had a major casting change in 1977 when the nearside front wing outline was changed from a rounded to a squared-off shape to imitate the real vehicle. A new glazing piece was also fitted. It was initially issued with 'Tern Shirts' transfers, but these were quickly replaced by 'Schweppes' which in turn gave way to 'Esso Safetygrip Tyres'; this latter also in GIFT SET 300. A promotional issue was produced in 1968 for the 'Festival of London Stores'. This was on the Schweppes version, running on small hubs with the decal on the offside only, and packed in Schweppes type boxes. Even more in 1977 were made for 'Madame Tussaud's'. It's a pity they never produced one looking like the advertising bus that ran on London routes in 1974, but the decalling would have been prohibitively expensive. A very small batch were sprayed gold with Meccano/Dinky Toy decals, extracted from existing artwork for presentation to the press at the unveiling of the blue advertising vehicle.

295 ATLAS KENEBRAKE is a funny little vehicle whose main fame is that it is the first bus with windows, seats and steering wheel and was, moreover, the first vehicle fitted with a plastic interior. It also figures in internal Meccano paperwork on 628, a military number! It is part of 122 TOURING GIFT SET. (See: Cars—British Saloons). 949 is a Supertoy sized vehicle, and must have been made with the U.S. market in mind, as the U.K. did not

**Look! a real Dinky Bus!** Visitors from all over the world are amazed to see a *real* Dinky bus driving through London's heavy traffic. Painted on the body of the bus are pictures of Dinky Toys, Dinky Kits and Meccano models. And aren't people thrilled to discover they can buy Dinky Toys in their own countries! Although you can't buy one like this, you can buy your own Red Routemaster London Bus—see page 12

Fig. 309. 29f Observation Coach, 29g Luxury Coach and 29e Single Deck Bus.

Fig. 307. The Airfix real bus.

run yellow school buses to any extent. 953 CON-TINENTAL TOURING COACH utilised the same casting. 952 VEGA MAJOR LUXURY COACH, which was also part of 124 HOLIDAY GIFT SET (See: Cars—British Saloons), had flashing indicators, but later was issued as 954 without. 961 was the Swiss market P.T.T. version of the latter. 283 SINGLE DECK BUS had a working bell. The casting of 296 LUXURY COACH was used for 293 SWISS POSTAL BUS which was available in Switzerland only for two years before being released on the U.K. market. Unfortunately, 248 CONTINENTAL TOURER COACH with Liverpool Football Club livery which was shown at the 1979 Earls Court Toy Fair and which was scheduled to be released in the colours of other Clubs also, never reached the market.

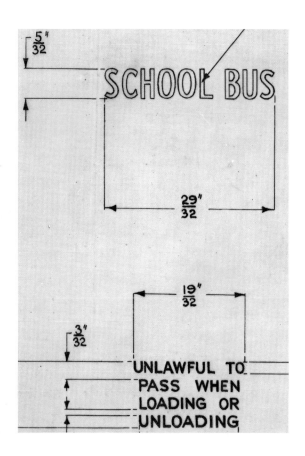

Fig. 308. Drawing for Wayne Bus transfer.

Fig. 310. 29h Duplé Roadmaster Coach.

Fig. 311. 283 B.O.A.C. Coach.

Fig. 313. Some of the variations on 292 and 293. Note the ribbed roof on the later 293.

Fig. 317. 949 Wayne School Bus and 953 Continental Touring Coach.

197

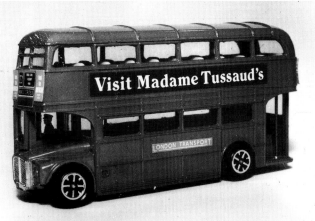

Fig. 312. 289 Routemaster London Bus.

Fig. 314. Madame Tussaud's Bus.

Fig. 315. 295 Atlantean Bus.

Fig. 323.

289 Routemaster London Bus 121 mm

295 Atlantean Bus 123 mm

291 Atlantean City Bus 123 mm

12

954

283

296

954 Vega Major Luxury Coach 245 mm

283 Single Decker Bus 167 mm

296 Viceroy Luxury Coach 119 mm

1

*Fig. 316. 297 Atlantean 'Silver Jubilee' Bus and the Woolworth variation.*

*Fig. 318 961 Vega Major Coach PTT.*

*Fig. 320. 293 Swiss Postal Bus.*

# BUSES

| Cat. No. | Model | Intro. date | Deletion | Comments |
|---|---|---|---|---|
| 27 | Tram Car | 1934 | 1939 | Colours: see text |
| 29 | Motor Bus | 1934 | 1939 | Colours: see text. Renumbered 29a |
| 29a | =Motor Bus= | | | Renumbering of 29 |
| 29b | Streamline Bus | 1936 | 1950 | Colours: see text |
| 29c | Double Decker Bus | 1938 | 1963 | Colours etc.: see text. Renumbered 290 |
| 29e | Single Deck Bus | 1948 | 1952 | Cream. blue flash. Green, dark green flash. Blue, dark blue flash |
| 29f | Observation Coach | 1950 | 1960 | Grey, red flash. Later cream, red flash. Renumbered 280 |
| 29g | Luxury Coach | 1951 | 1959 | Fawn, orange flash. Later maroon, cream flash. Renumbered 281 |
| 29h | Duple Roadmaster Coach | 1952 | 1960 | Blue, silver flash. Later red, silver flash. Then yellow, red flash. Also dark green lower, cream upper. Renumbered 282 |
| 31 | Holland Coachcraft Van | 1935 | 1936 | Colours: see text |
| 248 | Continental Tourer Coach | | | Not issued |
| 280 | =Observation Coach= | | | Renumbering of 29f |
| 281 | =Modern Coach= | | | Renumbering of 29g |
| 282 | =Duple Roadmaster Coach= | | | Renumbering of 29h |
| 283 | B.O.A.C. Coach | 1956 | 1963 | Blue, white roof |
| 283 | Single Decker Bus | 1971 | 1976 | Red. Later metallic red |
| 289 | Routemaster London Bus | 1964 | 1980 | Red. 1964–5 Tern Shirts. 1965–9 Schweppes. 1970–80 Esso. Still in production at factory closure |
| (289) | Meccano/Dinky Toys Bus | 1974 | 1974 | Gold |
| (289) | Festival of London Stores Bus | 1968 | 1968 | Red. Gold & black decal |
| (289) | Madame Tussaud's Bus | 1977 | 1979 | Red. Dark blue & white decal |
| 290 | =Double Deck Bus Dunlop= | | | Renumbering of 29c |
| 291 | Double Deck Bus Exide | 1959 | 1963 | Red |
| 291 | Atlantean City Bus | 1974 | 1978 | Orange & white. 'Kenning' |
| 292 | Atlantean Bus | 1962 | 1965 | Red & white. 'Regent', briefly 'Ribble' |
| 293 | Atlantean Bus | 1963 | 1968 | Green & white. 'BP' |
| 293 | Swiss Postal Bus | 1973 | 1978 | Yellow, cream roof. PTT. See text |
| 295 | Atlas Kenebrake Bus | 1960 | 1964 | Light blue & grey |
| 295 | Atlantean Bus | 1973 | 1976 | Yellow 'Yellow Pages' |
| 296 | Luxury Coach | 1972 | 1976 | Metallic blue |
| 297 | Atlantean 'Silver Jubilee' Bus | 1977 | 1977 | Silver |
| (297) | Woolworth's 'Silver Jubilee' | 1977 | 1977 | Silver |
| 300 | Gift Set 'London Scene' | 1979 | 1980 | Contains: 289 Esso, 284 London Taxi. Still in production at factory closure |
| 949 | Wayne School Bus | 1961 | 1964 | Yellow, red lining flash |
| 952 | Vega Major Luxury Coach | 1964 | 1971 | Grey, maroon. Flashing indicators |
| 953 | Continental Touring Coach | 1963 | 1965 | Pale blue, white roof |
| 954 | Vega Major Luxury Coach | 1972 | 1976 | White, maroon flash |
| 961 | Vega Major Coach PTT | 1973 | 1977 | Yellow, cream roof. Switzerland only |

*Fig. 324. 25k Streamlined Fire Engine with Firemen.*

## Fire Appliances

From the Spring of 1938, there was always a fire engine or two in the Dinky range. The *aficionados* of fire vehicles would say that they should be called 'Fire Appliances', but Meccano used 'Fire Engine' to designate their early ones, and the words have a ring of excitement about them that the more modern terminology does not, so that despite the efforts of the purists, 'Fire Engine' is still common parlance.

**25h STREAMLINED FIRE ENGINE** is a very good model of a mid-Thirties Merryweather design which combined efficiency with the then current passion for streamlined vehicles. The body is a one piece casting with slots in the roof to take the lugs of the tinplate ladder which had a small tinplate bell dangling from it. There was no chassis. The colour was all over red, including the wheel hubs, with

silver paint on the radiator and pumping gear. The bell is tinplate, gilded on earlier production, but becoming more silvery as time passed. It was issued as part of the set 25 Commercial Motor Vehicles before 1941, and was reintroduced post-war with no casting changes and lasted until 1962, being renumbered 250 in 1954.

**25k STREAMLINED FIRE ENGINE WITH FIREMEN** used exactly the same body casting and ladder, but had six tinplate firemen, attired in blue uniforms with red collars and wearing gold helmets, peering out of the windows. Only the heads are modelled, and they wear a somewhat lugubrious expression. They were pressed out in one continuous strip and tabbed into a tinplate chassis which was required to enable them to be fitted. This ver-

sion was available for a very short time, as it was introduced in late 1937 and had certainly been deleted by September 1939.

Post-war, there was always a selection of fire vehicles in the catalogue, and almost all of them had a very long life, so that the early ones were renumbered and spanned the without-to-with windows era, and later ones had wheel changes and tyre colour variations. As the years progressed, differences of all sorts crept in, from colour changes from metallic red to non-metallic, from the replacement of diecast parts with plastic, to grille and headlamp variations, etc.—a veritable variation hunter's paradise. Only the most obvious differences are mentioned below. Many of the later issues were also given 'Falck' decals for the Danish market, and several of the detail differences carry over into these as well. (See: Foreign Issues).

**555 FIRE ENGINE** with Extending Ladder was on a Commer chassis and gained windows as well as being renumbered, while the later **956 TURNTABLE FIRE ESCAPE** on a Bedford S-type was too late for renumbering, but also acquired windows. The Bedford 'Miles' vehicle was the basis for **259 FIRE ENGINE** and **276 AIRPORT FIRE TENDER**, which sported a flashing light on the roof. Accompanied by a selection of **008 FIRE STATION PERSONNEL**, this latter was part of GIFT SET 298 EMERGENCY SERVICES (See: Public Service Vehicles), and is found also in **299 MOTORWAY SERVICES GIFT SET** (see: Special Purpose Vehicles—Breakdown). The next one, **956 TURNTABLE FIRE ESCAPE**, is a model of a Berliet with the same ladder as the previous turntable on the Bedford S-type, and was in the catalogues for only four years, an uncharacteristically short length of time. However the Merryweather Marquise Fire Tender, which to the horror of parents had an operating water pump and was introduced in the same year, was still in production at the time when manufacture ceased at Binns Road—a total span of availability of 21 years. Needless to say, it is on this casting that most of the detailed variations are found. The **LAND ROVER FIRE APPLIANCE** No. **282** shared a front-end casting with, for instance, the Land Rover Breakdown Crane. The E.R.F. Fire Tender casting with an extending escape ladder with

*Fig. 326. 957 Fire Services Set (Nos. 956, 955 and 257).*

wheels, was numbered 266, and with a straight ladder it became an Airport Fire Tender painted yellow. Automatic hose rewind was featured on the two Ford Transits (1st and 2nd type. See: Ford Transits). The Fire Chief could travel in a version with roof light of the casting of 173 NASH RAMBLER, which was also part of 299 MOTORWAY SERVICES GIFT SET. To begin with it was called 'Fire Chief's Car', but later 'Canadian type' was added to the designation (257). But in the 1970s, he would use a Range Rover numbered 195. The latest issue was on the Convoy chassis. To add realism to play, a set of six plastic Firemen complete with hoses were released in the early sixties, along with a plastic Fire Station. Two Gift Sets were released, one in the early 1960s and one in the late 1970s.

*Fig. 325. 954 Fire Station with 259 Fire Engine.*

201

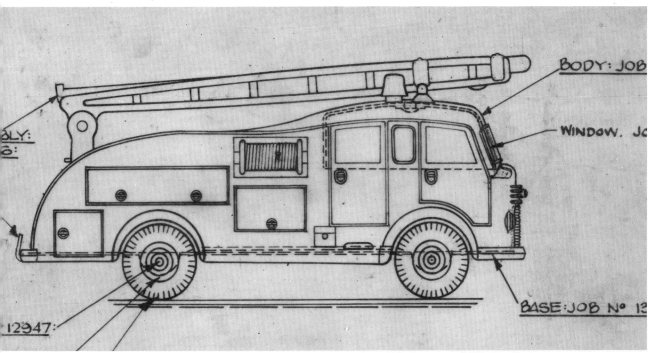

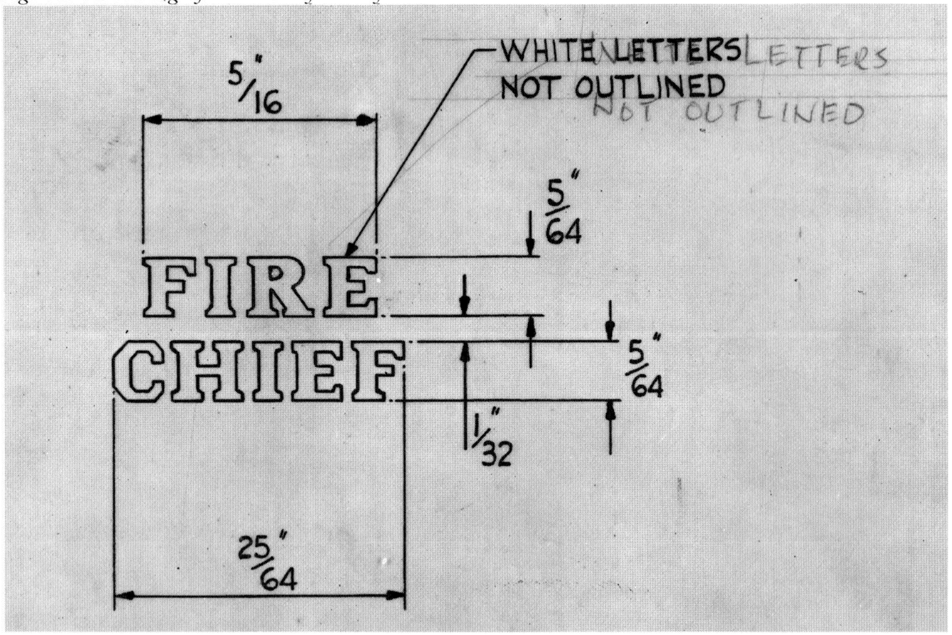

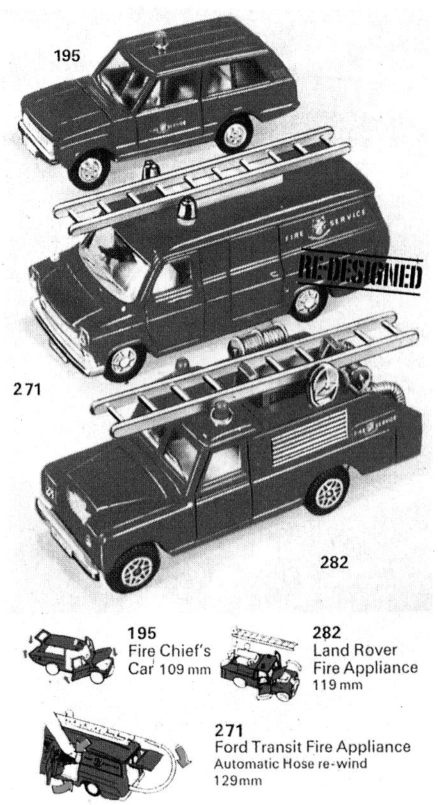

BODY: JOB
WINDOW. JO
BASE: JOB Nº 1
12947:

Fig. 328. Drawing of 955 Fire Engine.

Fig. 329. Drawing of 'Fire Chief' transfer.

WHITE LETTERS
NOT OUTLINED
5/16"
5/64"
FIRE
CHIEF
5/64"
1/32"
25/64"

195
RE-DESIGNED
271
282
195
Fire Chief's
Car 109 mm
282
Land Rover
Fire Appliance
119 mm
271
Ford Transit Fire Appliance
Automatic Hose re-wind
129mm

Fig. 330. 195, 271 and 282.

Fig. 331. 286 Ford Transit Fire Appliance.

AUTOMATIC
HOSE
RE-WIND
4 13/16" (122 mm.)
286 Ford Transit Fire Appliance

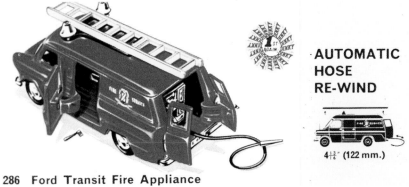

*Fig. 332.*

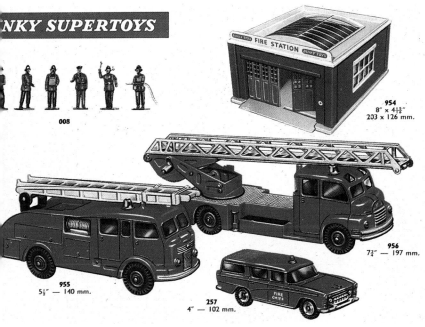

**NKY SUPERTOYS**

008

954
8″ × 4½″
203 × 126 mm.

956
7¼″ — 197 mm.

955
5½″ — 140 mm.

257
4″ — 102 mm.

FIRE
CHIEF

*Fig. 333. 956 Turntable Fire Escape—Berliet cab.*

956

## FIRE APPLIANCES

| Cat. No. | Model | Intro. date | Deletion | Comments |
|---|---|---|---|---|
| 008 | Fire Station Personnel | 1960 | 1967 | Blue uniforms |
| 25h | Streamlined Fire Engine | 1936 | 1962 | Red. Renumbered 250 |
| 25k | Streamlined Fire Engine with Firemen | 1937 | 1939 | Red, firemen blue |
| 195 | Fire Chief's Car | 1971 | 1978 | Red |
| 250 | =Streamlined Fire Engine= | | | Renumbering of 25h |
| 257 | Fire Chief's Car/Canadian Type | 1961 | 1968 | Red |
| 259 | Fire Engine | 1961 | 1969 | Red |
| 263 | E.R.F./Airport Fire Rescue Tender | 1978 | 1980 | Yellow. Still in production at factory closure |
| 266 | E.R.F. Fire Tender | 1976 | 1980 | Red. Later metallic red |
| 271 | Ford Transit Fire Appliance | 1975 | 1976 | Red |
| 276 | Airport Fire Tender | 1962 | 1969 | Red |
| 282 | Land Rover Fire Appliance | 1973 | 1980 | Red. Still in production at factory closure |
| 285 | Merryweather Marquis Fire Tender | 1969 | 1980 | Metallic red, Later red. Still in production at factory closure |
| 286 | Ford Transit Fire Appliance | 1969 | 1974 | Metallic red. Later red |
| 304 | Action Set 'Fire Rescue' | 1978 | 1979 | Contains: 384 Convoy Rescue Wagon. 195 Fire Chief's Car. 282 Land Rover Fire Appliance |
| 384 | Convoy Fire Rescue Wagon | | | See: Convoy |
| 555 | Fire Engine with Extending Ladder | 1952 | 1969 | Red and silver. Renumbered 955 |
| 954 | Fire Station | 1961 | 1964 | Plastic. Red, yellow, brick |
| 955 | =Fire Engine with Extending Ladder= | | | Renumbering of 555 |
| 956 | Turntable Fire Escape | 1958 | 1969 | Red |
| 956 | Turntable Fire Escape | 1969 | 1973 | Red & silver or black |
| 957 | Fire Services Set | 1959 | 1964 | Contains: 257 Fire Chief's Car. 955 Fire Engine with Extending Ladder. 956 Turntable Fire Escape |

For illustrations of 263, 266, 285 and 384 see 1979 Catalogue. Chapter 9.

## Police Vehicles

Police vehicles were a very late introduction to the Dinky Toy range. There were no cars released pre-war, the Force being represented by two motor cycles, two standing Policemen and a Police Box. (See: Motor cycles and Related Items). Even after the war, there was a long delay before the production of the first one, perhaps because the range did not have a vehicle that was in general use by the Police. However, in 1955, the Mersey Tunnel Police Van was made. This little vehicle on the short wheel-base Land Rover did not use the existing open Land Rover die, for it was modelled on the specialist vehicle employed to pull broken-down vehicles out of the Mersey Tunnel. One wonders if a Meccano executive was fired to suggest making it after he had found need of its services on his way home from the Liverpool factory! This model is the only one that had a die unique to itself—all the others are modifications of existing dies and minor modifications at that, for in many cases all that was required was a hole in the roof to take the light, or in later times, the roof box. Most of the variations are found on these small parts. Some of the later issues came complete with plastic policemen, road cones and notice boards, which were frequently secured alongside the vehicle in the box and visible through the 'window', making the packaging very attractive and buyable.

Reflecting the rest of the road vehicles in the range, Transatlantic Police Cars were produced from 1960 to 1975. The bases of the cars were modified to remove their 'civilian' sales number before the new version was released so that they could be fitted to either. 258 U.S.A. POLICE CAR used four different castings throughout its life (258 FORD FAIRLANE can be found in 298 EMERGENCY SERVICES GIFT SET—see Public Services Vehicles—Ambulance) but kept the same colour scheme and transfers, while 264 R.C.M.P. PATROL CAR only had two, which are the last two used for 258. The later 251 and 252 were similarly the civilian Pontiac Parisienne casting in U.S.A. and R.C.M.P. ver-

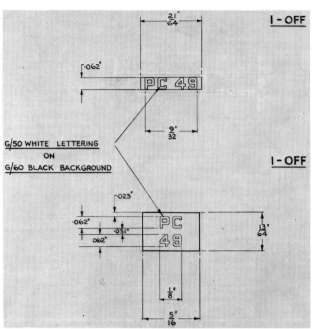

G/50 WHITE LETTERING ON G/60 BLACK BACKGROUND

Fig. 334. Drawing for 'PC 49' number plates.

Fig. 339.  270 Ford Panda Police Car.

Fig. 335. 255 Mersey Tunnel Police Van.

Fig. 337. 264 R.C.M.P. car based on 148 Ford Fairlane and 258 U.S.A. Police Car based on 192 De Soto Fireflite.

Fig. 336. 256 Police Patrol Car.

**252  R.C.M.P.  Car**

204

sions. The four British Police Cars that span the same era all had different numbers, so are easier to identify, and used Humber, Jaguar and two Ford castings. The Humber Hawk had 'PC49' number-plates—the title of a contemporary Radio show. All three Transit castings were decalled as Police Accident Units, and Minis and Land/Range Rovers figured as well. These cover the seventies and lead up to the introduction of three of the 1/35 models as Police Cars, the Rover 3500, Volvo and Plymouth. There are a few Police Gift Sets, and 269 MOTORWAY POLICE CAR is also to be found in 299 MOTORWAY SERVICES GIFT SET (See Special Purpose Vehicles—Breakdown Trucks).

*Fig. 338. 297 Police Vehicles Gift Set.*

**269** Motorway Police.
Car. 3½" – 97 mm.

*Fig. 340. 269 Motorway Police Car.*

51 **U.S.A. Police Car**

## POLICE VEHICLES

| Cat. No. | Model | Intro. date | Deletion | Based on | Colour etc. |
|---|---|---|---|---|---|
| 243 | Police Volvo | 1979 | 1980 | 122 Volvo 265 DL Estate | White. Signs, cones, policeman, dog. Still in production at factory closure |
| 244 | Plymouth Police Car | 1977 | 1980 | 201 Plymouth Stock Car | Dark blue & white. Still in production at factory closure |
| 250 | Police Mini Cooper S | 1967 | 1975 | 183 Morris Mini Minor Automatic | White |
| 251 | U.S.A. Police Car | 1970 | 1972 | 172 Pontiac Parisienne | White, black roof. Driver |
| 252 | R.C.M.P. Car | 1969 | 1974 | 172 Pontiac Parisienne | Blue, white doors. Driver |
| 254 | Police Range Rover | 1971 | 1980 | 192 Ranger Rover | White. Still in production at factory closure |
| 255 | Mersey Tunnel Police Van | 1955 | 1961 | | Red |
| 255 | Ford Zodiac Police Car | 1967 | 1971 | 164 Ford Zodiac | White. Driver |
| 255 | Police Mini Clubman | 1977 | 1979 | 178 Mini Clubman | Blue, white doors |
| 256 | Police Patrol Car | 1960 | 1964 | 165 Humber Hawk | Black. Driver and passenger |
| 258 | U.S.A. Police Car | 1960 | 1961 | 192 De Soto Fireflight | Black, white doors |
| 258 | U.S.A. Police Car | 1961 | 1962 | 191 Dodge Royal Sedan | Black, white doors |
| 258 | U.S.A. Police Car | 1962 | 1966 | 148 Ford Fairlane | Black, white doors |
| 258 | Cadillac U.S.A. Police Car | 1966 | 1968 | 147 Cadillac 62 | Black, white doors |
| 264 | R.C.M.P. Patrol Car | 1962 | 1965 | 148 Ford Fairlane | Blue, white doors |
| 264 | Cadillac R.C.M.P. Car | 1966 | 1968 | 147 Cadillac 62 | Blue, white doors |
| 264 | Rover 3500 Police Car | 1979 | 1980 | 180 Rover 3500 | White. Still in production at factory closure |
| 269 | Motorway Police Car | 1962 | 1965 | 195 Jaguar 3.4 litre | White. Driver and passenger |
| 269 | Police Accident Unit | 1978 | 1980 | 417 Ford Transit (3rd type) | White. Signs, cones, policeman |
| 270 | Ford Panda Police Car | 1969 | 1976 | 168 Ford Escort | Blue, white doors |
| 272 | Police Accident Unit | 1975 | 1978 | 416 Ford Transit (2nd type) | White. Signs, cones |
| 277 | Police Land Rover | 1979 | 1980 | 344 Land Rover | Blue, white plastic tilt. Still in production at factory closure |
| 287 | Police Accident Unit | 1967 | 1974 | 407 Ford Transit (1st type) | White and orange. Later white. Signs, cones |
| 294 | Police Vehicles Gift Set | 1973 | 1976 | | Contains: 250 Mini Cooper S, 254 Range Rover, 287 Accident Unit. Later 272 Accident Unit |
| 297 | Police Vehicles Gift Set | 1967 | 1972 | | Contains: 250 Mini Cooper S, 255 Ford Zodiac, 287 Accident Unit |
| 299 | Crash Squad Action Set | 1979 | 1979 | | Contains: 244 Plymouth Police Car, 732 Bell Police Helicopter (See: Aeroplanes) |

For illustrations of 243, 244, 254, 255, 264, 269 and 277 see 1979 Catalogue. Chapter 9.

## Ambulances

Pre-war, two ambulances were released utilising the same body, one in the 24 series and one in the 30 (see those sections for details), and 30f was re-released after the war in the same form as before. Very soon however the open side and rear windows were filled in presumably because of die wear. It was soon deleted altogether. 30h DAIMLER AMBULANCE came in in 1950 with a one-piece body, its fourteen years in the catalogue giving it the greatest longevity of all this group. It was renumbered and, in later life, acquired windows. 263 and 277

SUPERIOR CRITERION AMBULANCE based on a Cadillac shared a casting, the difference being that the higher number could be fitted with a small battery to enable the roof light to flash. The castings are fairly complex and heavy and fairly child-resistent. Both are to be found in 299 MOTOR-WAY SERVICES GIFT SET (see: Special Purpose Vehicles—Breakdown). At the same time 278 VAUXHALL AMBULANCE, used the casting of 141 VAUXHALL VICTOR ESTATE with an additional roof piece to give the illusion of increased headroom in the back. The Range Rover and the 2nd

and 3rd type Transit Van castings were also used as ambulances, but the latest releases, 267 and 288 SUPERIOR CADILLAC AMBULANCE have a body unique to themselves. The lower number this time was used for the battery-powered flashing light version. It was also produced in 'Falck' livery (see: Foreign issues–Danish). Ambulances figure in gift sets, the Ambulancemen that accompany them are 007 PETROL PUMP ATTENDANTS! A body on a stretcher covered with a red or blue blanket was supplied with many of the vehicles.

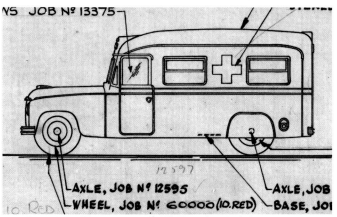

*Fig. 341. Assembly Drawing of 30h Daimler Ambulance.*

*Fig. 342. 298 Emergency Services Gift Set.*

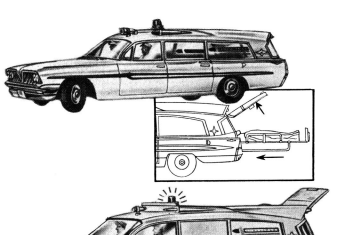

Fig. 344. 263 Superior Criterion Ambulance and 277
Superior Criterion Ambulance with flashing light.

Fig. 345. 267 Superior Cadillac Ambulance.

Fig. 346. 263 Superior Criterion Ambulance and 278
Vauxhall Ambulance.

## AMBULANCES

| Cat. No. | Model | Intro. date | Deletion | Comments |
|---|---|---|---|---|
| 24a | Ambulance | 1934 | 1941 | See: 24 series |
| 30f | Ambulance | 1935 | 1948 | Grey, cream, black chassis. See also: 30 series |
| 30h | Daimler Ambulance | 1950 | 1966 | Cream. Later white. Renumbered 253 |
| 253 | =Daimler Ambulance= | | | Renumbering of 30h |
| 263 | Superior Criterion Ambulance | 1962 | 1968 | Cream. Patient |
| 267 | Superior Cadillac Ambulance | 1967 | 1971 | White & red. Flashing light |
| 267 | Paramedic Truck | | | See: Character Toys |
| 268 | Range Rover Ambulance | 1973 | 1976 | White. Patient |
| 274 | Ford Transit Ambulance | 1978 | 1980 | White. Patient. 3rd type Transit. Still in production at factory closure |
| 276 | Ford Transit Ambulance | 1976 | 1978 | White. Patient. 2nd type Transit |
| 277 | .Superior Criterion Ambulance | 1962 | 1968 | Metallic blue & white. Flashing light |
| 278 | Vauxhall Ambulance | 1964 | 1968 | White |
| 288 | Superior Cadillac Ambulance | 1971 | 1979 | White & red |
| 298 | Emergency Services Gift Set | 1963 | 1964 | Contains: 258 U.S.A. Police Car (Ford Fairlane) 276 Airport Fire Tender. 263 & 277 Criterion Ambulances. 6 Firemen. 2 Ambulancemen. 1 Policeman |
| 302 | Action Set Emergency Squad | | | Contains: 288 Cadillac Ambulance. 267 Paramedic Truck. Not issued |

For illustrations of 267, 274 and 288 see 1979 Catalogue. Chapter 9.

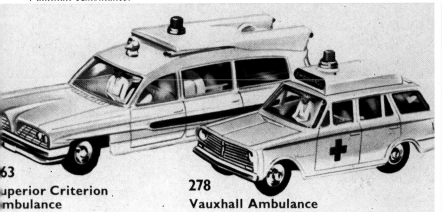

63
uperior Criterion
mbulance

**278**
**Vauxhall Ambulance**

Fig. 346. 268, 276 and 288

**268**
Range Rover
Ambulance
109 mm

**276**
Ford Transit
Ambulance
129 mm

**288**
Superior Cadillac
Ambulance
152 mm

## Taxis

The first post-war taxi was a re-issue of the pre-war 36g (see: Pre-war—36 series). It reappeared only briefly and was replaced by the long-lived 40h/254 the details of which can be found in Cars—40 series. These were both London-type taxis and the first saloon car modified for passenger carrying did not follow until 1960 when two taxis were produced using the casting of 178 PLYMOUTH. 265 PLYMOUTH U.S.A. TAXI carried the fare informa-tion on the side, and 266, which at first was only available in Canada, a transfer reading '250 Metro Cab'. The 1960 U.K. catalogue shows a picture of the Canadian version with the U.S. type's number so even before they were issued they were causing confusion! 266 was sometimes referred to a plain 'Plymouth Taxi' and sometimes as 'Plymouth Cana-dian Taxi Cab' by Meccano though amongst collec-tors, to reduce the confusion, it is often called 'Metro Cab'. From the early 1960s, the time of the 'war' between the established Licensed Hackney Carriage London Taxi drivers and the incomers who were regarded as poaching their trade, comes 268 RENAULT DAUPHINE MINI-CAB, the decall-ing of which reminds one more of a rally car than a utilitarian taxi. For some reason, perhaps its unattrac-tiveness, 282 AUSTIN 1800 TAXI had a very brief life. 284 is a 'proper' Austin London Taxi which was

*Fig. 349. 265 Plymouth U.S.A. Taxi and 266 Plymouth (Canadian) Taxi.*

*Fig. 348. 268 Renault Dauphine Mini-cab.*

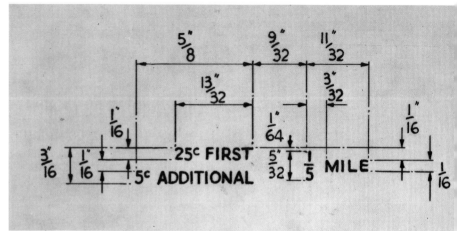

*Fig. 347. The Transfer Drawing*

in production from 1972 onwards. In 1977 it received a major casting modification to the boot having the rear light and numberplate detail removed so that it could accommodate the Union Jack decal required for 241 SILVER JUBILEE TAXI, which was heralded by the following Press Release. 'Just over 3 weeks before the first model rolled off the production line, a full-size taxi, decorated for the Queen's Silver Jubilee and driven by H.R.H. Prince Charles, appeared on a television programme. It was this item that inspired Meccano to convert their standard London Taxi into a special Jubilee Version and the job was done in record time, including the design and production of special Jubilee motifs and lettering and a special Union Jack-type display window box which required printing in huge quantities.' The job did not include altering the driver to look like the Prince of Wales and it looks as if it was done in record time as the Jubilee motif decals can appear almost anywhere on the vehicle though they are supposed to be located as on the one in the photograph. 284 appears in the Gift set 300 LONDON SCENE (see: Buses). 278 PLYMOUTH YELLOW CAB uses the casting of 201 STOCK CAR and 244 POLICE CAR. The very last offering is a nasty little toy numbered 115 U.B. TAXI and 120 HAPPY CAB. 115 was never on general release, despite its appearance in the catalogues, but was obtainable only from United Biscuits in exchange for four token wrappers from their new 'Taxi' biscuits and a small sum of money.

## TAXIS

| Cat. No. | Model | Intro. date | Deletion | Comments |
|---|---|---|---|---|
| 36g | Taxi | 1947 | 1949 | Re-issue. See: 36 series |
| 40h | Taxi | 1951 | 1962 | Renumbered 254. See: 40 series |
| 115 | U.B. Taxi | 1979 | 1979 | Blue, yellow & black |
| 120 | Happy Cab | 1979 | 1980 | White, blue & yellow. Still in production at factory closure |
| 241 | Silver Jubilee Taxi | 1977 | 1977 | Silver |
| 254 | =Taxi= | | | Renumbering of 40h |
| 265 | Plymouth U.S.A. Taxi | 1960 | 1966 | Yellow, red roof |
| 266 | Plymouth (Canadian) Taxi (Cab) | 1960 | 1966 | Yellow, red roof |
| 268 | Renault Dauphine Mini-cab | 1962 | 1967 | Red |
| 278 | Plymouth Yellow Cab | 1978 | 1980 | Yellow. Still in production at factory closure |
| 282 | Austin 1800 Taxi | 1967 | 1968 | Blue, white bonnet & boot |
| 284 | London Taxi | 1972 | 1980 | Black. Still in production at factory closure |

For illustrations of 115, 120, 278 and 284 see 1979 Catalogue. Chapter 9.

Fig. 351. 282 Austin 1800 Taxi.

**282**
**Austin 1800 Taxi**

Fig. 350. 241 Silver Jubilee Taxi.

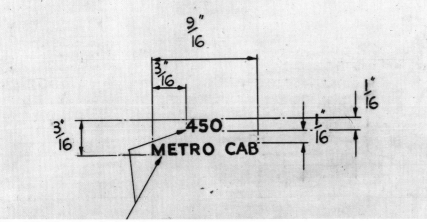

Fig. 347. The Transfer Drawing

## Mail Vans

The first Mail Van on the market after the war was 34b, a re-issue. For details of this and the telephone box and two postmen, 750, 011, 012, (see: Pre-war General). The first new vehicle was released in 1955, 260 ROYAL MAIL VAN which was a Morris J and whose red paint is subject to fading to various shades of pink. The following year it was joined by 261 TELEPHONE SERVICE VAN, a Morris Z, and one of the prettiest models of all time. As time passed, the Morris J was replaced by 410 BEDFORD ROYAL MAIL VAN which was joined by a Convoy version. This paucity of Mail vehicles partially reflects the length of time that the vehicles were in use by the G.P.O. but one wonders why Dinky missed making the commonest of all, the MORRIS MINOR VAN, in a larger scale than Dublo. The Gift Set was available for approximately one year.

MAIL VANS

| Cat. No. | Model | Intro. date | Deletion | Comments |
|---|---|---|---|---|
| 011 | =Telegraph Messenger= | | | Renumbering of 12d |
| 012 | =Postman= | | | Renumbering of 12e |
| 12c | Telephone Box | | | See: Pre-war—General |
| 12d | Telegraph Messenger | | | See: Pre-war—General |
| 12e | Postman | | | See: Pre-war—General |
| 34b | Royal Mail Van | | | See: Pre-war—General |
| 260 | Royal Mail Van | 1955 | 1961 | Red, black roof |
| 261 | Telephone Service Van | 1956 | 1961 | Green, black roof |
| 299 | Post Office Services Gift Set | 1958 | 1958 | Contains: 260 Royal Mail Van. 261 Telephone Van. 750 Telephone Box. 011 Telegraph Messenger. 012 Postman |
| 385 | Convoy Royal Mail | | | See: Convoy |
| 410 | Bedford Royal Mail Van | 1972 | 1980 | Red. Still in production at factory closure |
| 750 | =Telephone Box= | | | Renumbering of 12c |

For illustration of 410 see 1979 Catalogue. Chapter 9.

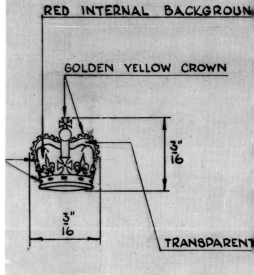

Fig. 353. Transfer Drawing for 261 Telephone Service Van.

Fig. 354. 299 Post Office Services Gift Set.

## A.A. and R.A.C.

Prewar, the A.A. and the R.A.C. were very well represented (see Motor bikes and Related Items) and some were re-issued post-war. It was however not until 1965 when the Mini Van was produced, that a new type was released. The roof sign was a peg-in plastic part and the casting was only used for A.A. and R.A.C. vehicles (and the promotional Joseph Mason's Paints. See: Vans with Advertising). Later, the 410 Bedford casting plus a roof box was used for an A.A. Van.

A.A. AND R.A.C.

| Cat. No. | Model | Intro. date | Deletion | Comments |
|---|---|---|---|---|
| 273 | R.A.C. Patrol Van | 1965 | 1969 | Blue, white roof |
| 274 | A.A. Patrol Van | 1964 | 1972 | Yellow |
| 412 | Beford Van A.A. | 1974 | 1980 | Light yellow. Later dark yellow. Still in production at factory closure |

For illustration of 412 see 1979 Catalogue. Chapter 9.

**273 RAC Patrol Van      274 AA Patrol Van**

Fig. 355. 273 R.A.C. Patrol Van and 274 A.A. Patrol Van.

Fig. 352. Transfer Drawing for 260 Royal Mail Van.

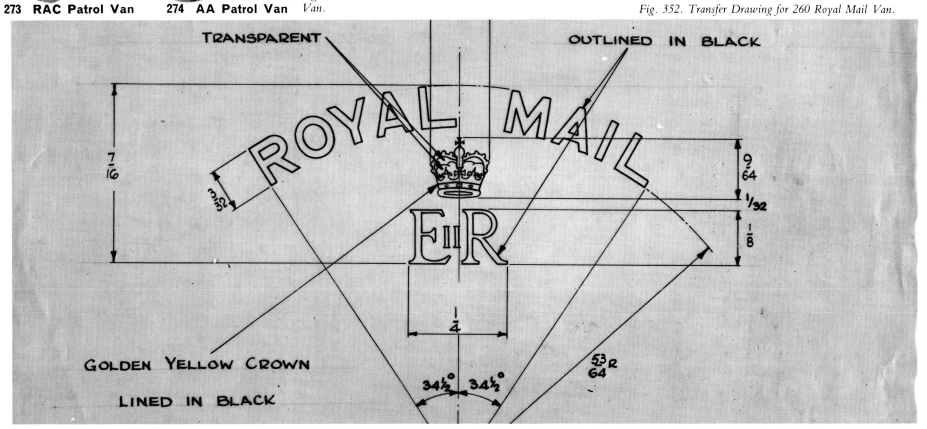

## Military Post-war

The first military items issued after the war were all pre-war items with the addition of 153a JEEP, (see: Military Pre-war and Post-war Re-issues.), and it was not until 1953 that the first of the new releases came out. This new group is to a consistent scale of 1/60 and basically spans the years from 1954 to 1970 though one of the later items 665 HONEST JOHN MISSILE LAUNCHER was last in the catalogue in 1976. The production 'record' is held jointly by 651 CENTURION TANK and 674 CHAMP both of which ran from 1954 to 1970. In the 1961 catalogue most of the vehicles to which it was feasible to fit glazing are advertised as 'with windows' but some are more commonly found so equipped than others (partly depending on the subsequent length of time they remained in the catalogue). 622 10-TON ARMY TRUCK, 623 COVERED WAGON and 689 MEDIUM ARTILLERY TRACTOR were never so fitted. Some vehicles were fitted with drivers (first diecast and later plastic), but even these did not appear 100% of the time. The driver was not issued separately but the Private (603) (diecast at first then plastic) could be bought by himself or in boxes of 12. The colour is standard—matt green with some later items in semi-gloss green. A variety of squadron markings were consistently applied to certain vehicles. 674 CHAMP has also been found in white (United Nations colours) in a shop in Germany and there have been rumours of others so coloured. The white has been oversprayed over the green and, while their authenticity because of their source is hardly open to question, no further details are known. Several of the vehicles appeared together in sets though they are not always called 'Gift Sets'. Amongst the block of numbers allocated to this selection are several which were only used for U.S. military releases. During this period some French Dinkies were also imported and sold here. The name in the right hand column of the table is the make of vehicle upon which the toy was based.

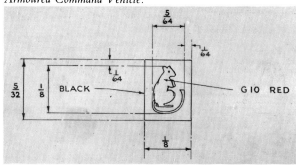

Fig. 361. Insignia drawing 'Desert Rat', used on 677 Armoured Command Vehicle.

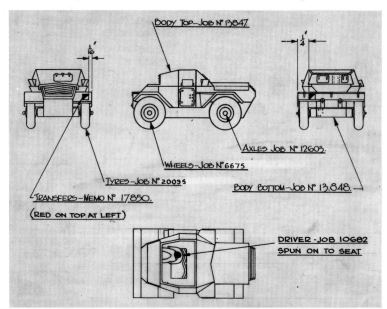

Fig. 356. 673 Scout car drawing.

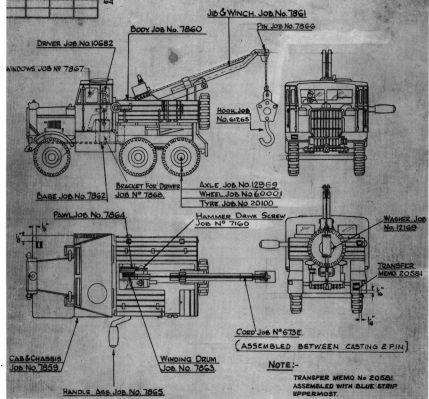

Fig. 357. 661 Recovery Tractor drawing.

212

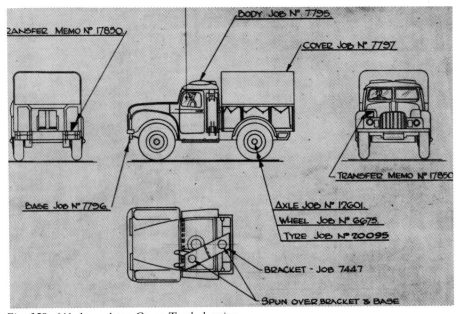

Fig. 358. 641 Army 1-ton Cargo Truck drawing.

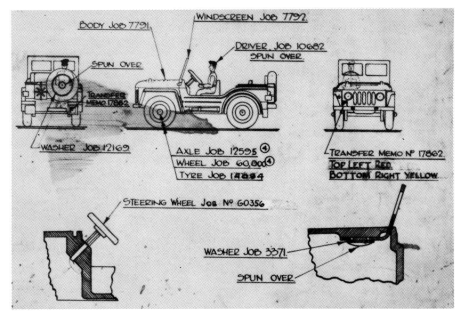

Fig. 359. 674 Austin Champ Army Vehicle drawing.

Fig. 362.

213

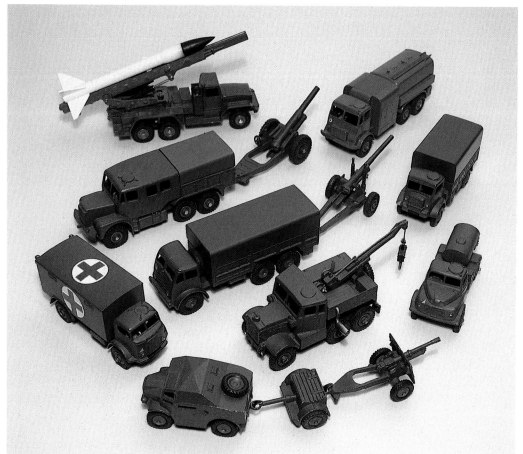

Fig. 360 Selection of military vehicles.

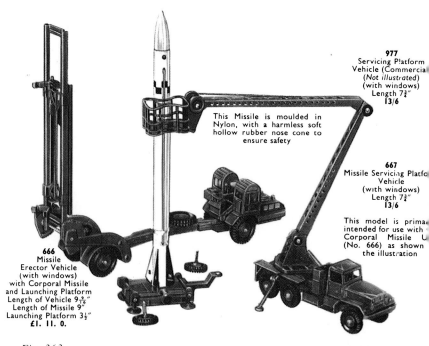

**977**
Servicing Platform
Vehicle (Commercial
(*Not illustrated*)
(with windows)
Length 7¾"
**13/6**

This Missile is moulded in
Nylon, with a harmless soft
hollow rubber nose cone to
ensure safety

**667**
Missile Servicing Platfo
Vehicle
(with windows)
Length 7¾"
**13/6**

This model is prima
intended for use with
Corporal Missile U
(No. 666) as shown
the illustration

**666**
Missile
Erector Vehicle
(with windows)
with Corporal Missile
and Launching Platform
Length of Vehicle 9 9/16"
Length of Missile 9"
Launching Platform 3½"
**£1. 11. 0.**

Fig. 363.

**622**
10-ton Army Truck
Length 5⅜"
**7/-**

**698**
Tank Transporter
(with windows)
with Tank
**£1. 3. 0.**
This fine set consists
of Tank Transporter
No. 660 and Cen-
turion Tank No. 651

**651**
Centurion Tank
Length 5¾"
**8/9**

**660**
Tank Transporter
(with windows)
Length with ramps 13¼"
**14/6**

**661**
Recovery Tractor
(with windows)
Length 5¼"
**9/6**

**689**
Medium Artillery Tractor
Length 5½"
**9/-**
This is an excellent model of a
6-wheel drive vehicle used for
towing medium artillery and
equipment over rough country

**677**
Armoured Command Vehicle
Length 5¼" 133 mm.

*Fig. 364.*

**642**
Pressure Refueller
Length 5½" 140 mm.

*Fig. 365 Military Vehicles (1).*

*Fig. 365a. 674 Champ (U.N.) and 341 Land Rover
Trailer supposedly made for the British Army (towed here by
669 U.S. Army Jeep.)*

## MILITARY POST-WAR

| Cat. No. | Model | Intro. date | Deletion | Comments |
|---|---|---|---|---|
| 1 | Military Vehicles (1) | 1955 | 1958 | Contains: 621, 641, 674, 676. Renumbered 699 |
| 603 | Army Personnel—Private Seated | 1957 | 1971 | For use with: 622, 641, 674, 689 |
| 621 | 3-ton Army Wagon | 1954 | 1963 | Bedford RL |
| 622 | 10-Ton Army Truck | 1954 | 1964 | Foden |
| 623 | Army Covered Wagon | 1954 | 1963 | Bedford QL |
| 624 | Daimler Military Ambulance | | | See: American issues |
| 626 | Military Ambulance | 1956 | 1965 | Ford |
| 641 | Army 1-Ton Cargo Truck | 1954 | 1962 | Humber |
| 642 | R.A.F. Pressure Refueller | 1957 | 1960 | Blue/grey |
| 643 | Army Water Tanker | 1958 | 1964 | Austin |
| 651 | Centurion Tank | 1954 | 1970 | |
| 660 | Tank Transporter | 1956 | 1964 | Thorneycroft Mighty Antar |
| 661 | Recovery Tractory | 1957 | 1965 | Scammell |
| 665 | 'Honest John' Missile Launcher | 1964 | 1976 | International. White-black plastic missile |
| 666 | Missile Erector Vehicle complete with 'Corporal' Missile and Launching Platform | 1959 | 1964 | White plastic missile |
| 667 | Missile Servicing Platform Vehicle | 1960 | 1964 | International |
| 669 | U.S. Army Jeep | | | See: American issues |
| 670 | Armoured Car | 1954 | 1970 | Daimler |
| 673 | Scout Car | 1953 | 1962 | Daimler |
| 674 | Austin Champ Army Vehicle | 1954 | 1970 | |
| 675 | U.S. Army Staff Car | | | See: American issues |
| 676 | Armoured Personnel Carrier | 1955 | 1962 | Alvis |
| 677 | Armoured Command Vehicle | 1957 | 1961 | AEC |
| 686 | 25-pdr. Field Gun | 1957 | 1970 | |
| 687 | Trailer for 25-pdr. Gun | 1957 | 1965 | |
| 688 | Field Artillery Tractor | 1957 | 1970 | Morris |
| 689 | Medium Artillery Tractor | 1957 | 1965 | Leyland |
| 692 | 5.5" Medium Gun | 1955 | 1962 | |
| 693 | 7.2" Howitzer | 1958 | 1967 | |
| 695 | Howitzer and Tractor | 1962 | 1965 | Contains: 689, 693 |
| 697 | 25-pdr. Field Gun Set | 1957 | 1970 | Contains: 686, 687, 688 |
| 698 | Tank Transporter and Tank Gift Set | 1957 | 1964 | Contains: 651, 660 |
| 699 | =Military Vehicles (1)= | | | Renumbering of 1 |
| 815 | Panhard Armoured Car | | | See: French Dinky Products |
| 817 | A.M.X. 13 ton Tank | | | See: French Dinky Products |
| 822 | M.3. Half-track | | | See: French Dinky Products |
| 884 | Brockway Truck with Bridge | | | See: French Dinky Products |

665 HONEST JOHN MISSILE LAUNCHER, which is more in scale with the earlier group, bridges the gap to the later production along with 601 PARA MOKE, a rehash of 342 MINIMOKE (see: Other Post-war Production), and two larger scale items, 615 U.S. JEEP and 617 VW K.D.F. These were made in the 1960s but the main group date from the 1970s, with the bulk of production being between 1973 and 1977, in which year a re-appraisal of the range resulted in the deletion of many models, some of which had only been in the catalogue for a couple of years. A few French, German and U.S. vehicles and guns were made, and these can be identified not by the name—for by this time, the armies of the Western World were buying each other's equipment—but by the colours and stickers. The colours vaguely approximate to those in actual use, and in the table the colour should be assumed to be 'British Army Green' unless another nationality's colour is specified. Over the years, the shades varied and the colours, particularly the British Green, became harsher, but the changes are impossible to express in words—one has to study the models. Most of the vehicles, etc. introduced in the 1970s were to a specified scale, and the scales in the tables are those stated in the catalogues. No doubt Meccano thought that the child interested in military models would be more aware of scales than others, becaus of the plethora of plastic kits available which always had a quoted scale. The models were 'action packed'—if a turret could rotate or a barrel elevate, it did; if there was a gun barrel, it fired garishly coloured plastic shells normally propelled by simple, inefficient pull back and release wire mechanisms. Many were supplied with military figures, camouflage nets, etc. Some castings were shared with other vehicles: 281 HOVERCRAFT used the casting of 290 SRN-6; 601 AUSTIN PARA MOKE that of the MINI MOKE; 604 LAND ROVER BOMB DISPOSAL UNIT

Fig. 366.

**Dinky TOYS**

5 MIGHTY ROCKET WEAPONS

FIRES SHELLS

**691 'Striker' Anti-Tank Vehicle** 122 mm
Fires five rockets singly

**OR ALL 5 TOGETHER**

**654 155 mm Mobile Gun** 151 mm

1/32nd. SCALE

FIRES SHELLS

**683 Chieftain Tank** 217 mm

**676 Daimler Armoured Car** 72 mm

**612 Commando Jeep** 108 mm

BOTH! GUNS FIRE

new AUTUMN '75

**699 Leopard Recovery Tank** 147mm

**696 Leopard Anti-Aircraft Tank** 152mm

**Dinky TOYS**

FIRES SHELLS

4 ROUNDS RAPID-FIRE GUN

**692 Leopard Tank** 198 mm

**690 Scorpion Tank** 120 mm

COMPLETE WITH CAMOUFLAGE NET

*Fig. 367.*

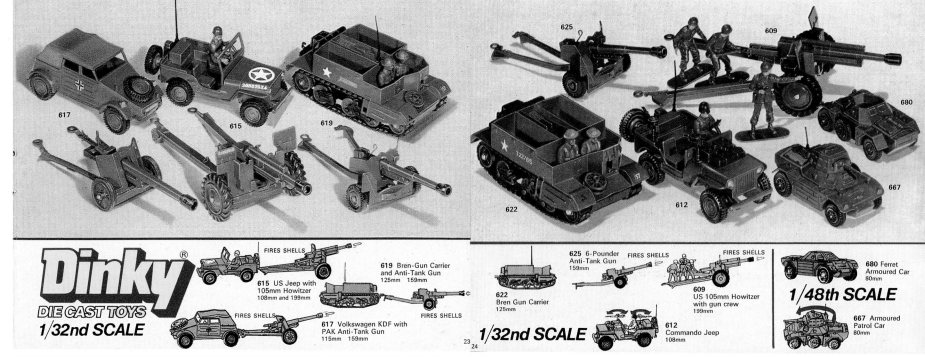

# Dinky
## DIE CAST TOYS
### 1/32nd SCALE

FIRES SHELLS

**619** Bren-Gun Carrier and Anti-Tank Gun
125mm 159mm

**615** US Jeep with 105mm Howitzer
108mm and 199mm

FIRES SHELLS

**617** Volkswagen KDF with PAK Anti-Tank Gun
115mm 159mm

FIRES SHELLS

23

---

**625** 6-Pounder Anti-Tank Gun
159mm

FIRES SHELLS

FIRES SHELLS

**622** Bren Gun Carrier
125mm

**609** US 105mm Howitzer with gun crew
199mm

**612** Commando Jeep
108mm

### 1/32nd SCALE

24

**680** Ferret Armoured Car
80mm

### 1/48th SCALE

**667** Armoured Patrol Car
80mm

---

**682** Stalwart Load Carrier
103mm  *1/65th SCALE*

**601** Austin Para-Moke with parachute
76mm

**668** Foden Army Truck
197mm

**604** Land Rover Bomb Disposal Unit  110mm

**681** DUKW Amphibian
127mm  *1/76th SCALE*

### 1/42nd SCALE

28

---

**618** A.E.C. Artic. Transporter with Helicopter
318mm

**616** A.E.C. Artic. Transporter with Chieftain Tank
318mm

# Dinky
## DIE CAST TOYS

29

had the same basic casting as 344 LAND ROVER plus a plastic tilt and engaging remote control search and destroy tracked robot; 612 and 615 JEEPS share basic castings, though the former has many plastic accessories and there are location holes for them in the casting; 616 and 618 use the cab unit of 915 AEC plus a common low loader back; 620, the BERLIET MISSILE LAUNCHER has the body of the French Dinky 816, but the casting was made in England, as can be seen from the baseplate wording; 662 is 656 STATIC 88mm GUN with added crew; 668 FODEN has the casting of 432; 676 DAIMLER ARMOURED CAR is similar to the earlier 670 but

with a new die. The two helicopters are army versions of 724 SEAKING and 732 BELL POLICE HELICOPTER. The castings were not modified, only the colours and decals. They were not available separately from the vehicles with which they were issued, and therefore did not have catalogue numbers of their own. (see: Aeroplanes). Though given military 600 numbers, 602 ARMOURED COMMAND CAR and 691 'STRIKER' ANTI-TANK VEHICLE are not models of real vehicles, and can be found in Character Merchandise. Spare shells, etc. were available and a list can be found in Accessories.

*Fig. 368.*     *pp. 27 & 29.*

680 Ferret Armoured Car 80 mm
681 D.U.K.W. 127 mm
682 Stalwart Load Carrier 103 mm
Models 680, 681 and 682 also available as 677 Task Force Set.

665 Honest John Missile Launcher 188 mm
620 Berliet Missile Launcher 150 mm
675 Motor Patrol Boat 170 mm
**FIRES MISSILES!**
281 Military Hovercraft 139 mm

27
29

| Cat. No. | Model | Scale | Intro. date | Deletion | Comments |
|---|---|---|---|---|---|
| 281 | Military Hovercraft | | 1973 | 1975 | |
| 303 | Action Set 'Commando Squad' | | 1978 | 1980 | Contains: 687 Convoy Army Truck. 667 Armoured Patrol Car, Army version 732 Bell Police Helicopter. Still in production at factory closure |
| 601 | Austin Para Moke | 1/42 | 1966 | 1977 | Parachute |
| 602 | Armoured Command Car | | | | See: Chapter 7 |
| 604 | Land Rover Bomb Disposal Unit | 1/42 | 1976 | 1977 | Orange side panels. Plastic tracked robot |
| 609 | U.S. 105mm Howitzer with Gun Crew | 1/32 | 1974 | 1977 | Three American Soldiers |
| 612 | Commando Jeep | 1/32 | 1973 | 1980 | Driver. Left hand drive. Still in production at factory closure |
| 615 | U.S. Jeep with 105mm Howitzer | 1/32 | 1968 | 1977 | 609 + 612 without standing soldiers and most Jeep accessories |
| 616 | A.E.C. Artic. Transporter with Chieftain Tank | 1/50 | 1976 | 1977 | 683 Tank. Camouflage net |
| 617 | Volkswagen KDF with PAK Anti-Tank Gun | 1/32 | 1967 | 1977 | German green |
| 618 | A.E.C. Artic. Transporter with Helicopter | | 1976 | 1980 | Army version 724 Sea King Helicopter. Camouflage net |
| 619 | Bren Gun Carrier and Anti-Tank Gun | 1/32 | 1976 | 1977 | 622 + 625 |
| 620 | Berliet Missile Launcher | | 1971 | 1973 | French green. Missile white and red plastic |
| 622 | Bren Gun Carrier | 1/32 | 1975 | 1977 | Driver and gunner |
| 625 | 6-pdr Anti-Tank Gun | 1/32 | 1975 | 1977 | |
| 654 | 155mm Mobile Gun | 1/40 | 1973 | 1980 | U.S. green. Still in production at factory closure |
| 656 | Static 88mm Gun | 1/35 | 1975 | 1980 | German green. As 662. With bogies no crew. Still in production at factory closure |
| 662 | Static 88mm Gun with Crew | 1/35 | 1975 | 1977 | German green. Three German soldiers |
| 667 | Armoured Patrol Car | 1/48 | 1976 | 1977 | As 432 but non-tipping. Green |
| 668 | Foden Army Truck | 1/42 | 1976 | 1980 | plastic tilt. Still in production at factory closure |
| 676 | Daimler Armoured Car | | 1973 | 1975 | Also seen in French Army green |
| 677 | Tank Force Set | | 1972 | 1975 | Contains: 680, 681, 682 |
| 680 | Ferret Armoured Car | 1/48 | 1972 | 1977 | Green, Khaki |
| 681 | D.U.K.W. | 1/76 | 1972 | 1977 | U.S. green |
| 682 | Stalwart Load Carrier | 1/65 | 1972 | 1977 | |
| 683 | Chieftain Tank | 1/50 | 1972 | 1980 | Still in production at factory closure |
| 687 | Convoy Army Truck | | | | See: Convoy |
| 690 | Scorpion Tank | 1/40 | 1974 | 1979 | 'Complete with camouflage net' |
| 691 | 'Striker' Anti-Tank Vehicle | | | | See: Chapter 7 |
| 692 | Leopard Tank | 1/50 | 1974 | 1980 | German green. Still in production at factory closure |
| 694 | Hanomag Tank Destroyer | 1/35 | 1975 | 1980 | German green. Still in production at factory closure |
| 696 | Leopard Anti-Aircraft Tank | 1/50 | 1975 | 1979 | German green |
| 699 | Leopard Recovery Tank | 1/50 | 1975 | 1977 | German green |

For illustrations of 612, 618, 654, 656, 668, 683, 687, 690, 691, 692 and 696 see 1979 Catalogue. Chapter 9.

# CHAPTER 6

# Foreign Issues, Production & Imports

## Models Made for Overseas Markets

Although Meccano did not boast of its exporting capabilities in its publicity, a fair proportion of the product was actually sent overseas and some items were especially made for particular markets. Immediately after the war, there was a concentration on Canada and the U.S.A., this being the market that could afford to buy toys at the time. There was considerable government pressure to export in order to improve the balance of payments situation, and some items were available on that side of the Atlantic before they were released here. (Post-war re-issues only). In the early 1950s, special paint versions were introduced for certain models, and these were given numbers slightly different from the home released items. As time passed, South Africa received a batch of raw castings, and some models were painted different colours but not allocated new numbers. Later still, special issues for European countries were released, all of them having decals relevant to that country and if necessary, special colour schemes. If a different paint colour was used, a new number was usually issued; for example, Volkswagen Swiss Post on 262 has the number 181 for the standard version, but if new decals only were fitted, the original sales number was retained, e.g. most of the Danish 'Falck' vehicles. No castings exclusive to 'abroad' were made, and details of the castings and how the models fit into the overall scheme can be found in the earlier sections, Military Post-war, Motor bikes, Buses, etc.

### U.S.A.

The post-war re-issue military models were made available to the Transatlantic market in the late 1940s and early 1950s and remained in their catalogues after they were dropped in the U.K. Indeed one, 151a MEDIUM TANK was only available overseas after the war. The number used to designate

| Set No. 5 | Military Vehicles | Contains: 153a/672 U.S. Army Jeep. 161b/690 Mobile A.A. Gun. 151a Medium Tank. 151b/620 Transport Wagon. 152b/671 Reconnaisance Car. |
| --- | --- | --- |

| Original No. | Export No. | Name |
| --- | --- | --- |
| 150 | 600 | Armoured Corps Personnel |
| 150b | 604 | Royal Tank Corps Private, sitting |
| 151b | 620 | Transport Wagon with driver |
| 152a | 650 | Light Tank |
| 152b | 671 | Reconnaisance Car |
| 153a | 672 | U.S. Army Jeep |
| 160 | 606 | Royal Artillery Personnel |
| 160b | 608 | Royal Artillery Seated Gunner |
| 161b | 690 | Mobile A.A. Gun |
| 162 | 691 | Field Gun Unit |

the items was the same as the U.K. number to begin with but because some were still available at general renumbering time, they were allocated new 600 (military) numbers. These only appear in overseas catalogues because the models themselves were only available abroad. The following numbers are those that have so far come to light. There was also a Gift Set specially created for the American market, the date of which is uncertain, but it most probably pre-dates renumbering in 1954–5.

The next group of significance were renumbered also. However, this was occasioned by the repainting of the models in American Army Olive Drab. At general renumbering they were allocated 600 numbers. They were never available in the U.K. in olive drab.

*Fig. 369. Set No. 5: Military Vehicles 'Made in England for sale in United States by H. Hudson, Dobson, 200 5th Avenue, New York'.*

221

*Fig. 374. The box of 25wm, renumbered by hand to 640
and priced at $1.25 each.*

*Fig. 373. 30hm Army Ambulance with box, 139am U.S.
Army Staff Car and 669 U.S. Army Jeep.*

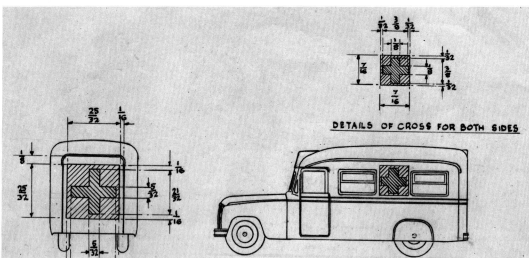

DETAILS OF CROSS FOR BOTH SIDES

*Fig. 370. Drawing of 30hm Ambulance.*

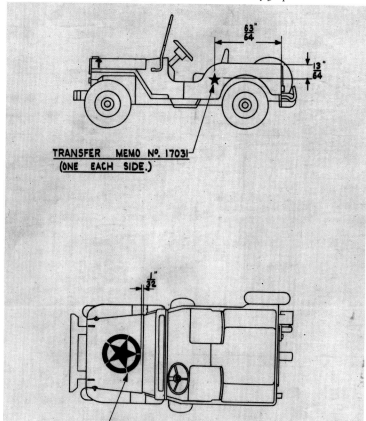

TRANSFER MEMO No. 17031
(ONE EACH SIDE.)

*Fig. 371. Drawing of 669 U.S.A. Army Jeep.*

Set No. 3 Private Automobiles, consisting of 30d Vauxhall,
36a Armstrong Siddeley, 36b Bentley, 38a Frazer-Nash, 39b Oldsmobile.
Presumably made for the American market. Late 1940s or early 1950s.

It is not surprising that Meccano should have chosen to release some of the 39 series in special colours for the American market, as these vehicles could actually have been seen on the roads over there. What is slightly puzzling is why they should only have done three in this most attractive two-toning and not all six. (Though, of course, two of the dies were shipped to France at about this time.) The American catalogue numbers were the same as the U.K. with the suffix 'u', presumably for U.S.A. They were available for two years longer in the States than in Britain, last appearing in the 1952 American Catalogues. As a matter of interest, this is the first post-war foray into two-toning. However, many of the examples found look as if the second colour has been applied by hand and not sprayed on with a spray-gun and mask as with the pre-war and the later post-war releases.

39bu OLDSMOBILE SEDAN—cream with tan wings, two-tone blue
39cu LINCOLN 'ZEPHYR' COUPE—red with maroon wings, tan and brown
39eu CHRYSLER 'ROYAL' SEDAN—yellow with red wings, two-tone green

A small group of models that were actually issued after renumbering are to be found in U.S. catalogues on the letter-suffix number which they were originally allocated. By the time they reached the market however, this earlier number was no longer in use so they were never actually sold on these numbers. 157 JAGUAR XK 120 had letter-

suffix number 139d, 172 STUDEBAKER LAND CRUISER had 139c, 470 AUSTIN VAN SHELL-BP had 32a and 673 SCOUT CAR had 153b. 129 M.G. MIDGET was an issue for the American Market only of 102/108 without driver and in red or white without racing numbers (see: 100 series). Despite the fact that the 38 series were deleted in the U.K. before renumbering, they were still available abroad, so new numbers were allocated from 100 to 105 inclusive which explains why the Austin Atlantic which appeared later was numbered 106. The renumbered ones were not necessarily the same colour as the U.K. issues. Some motor bikes and street furniture received the same treatment. The Horse Box was allocated a new number also but, in this case, there was a decal difference (see Special Purpose Vehicles—Horse Boxes).

## MODELS MADE FOR U.S.A.

| No. | Name | Notes |
|---|---|---|
| 25wm | Bedford Truck | As 25w. Renumbered 640 |
| 30hm | Army Ambulance | As 30h Daimler Ambulance. Red crosses. Renumbered 624 |
| 30sm | Austin Covered Wagon | As 30s. Renumbered 625 |
| 139am | U.S. Army Staff Car | As 170 Ford Fordor. White Star. Renumbered 170m and 675 |
| 170m | =U.S. Army Staff Car= | Renumbering of 139am |
| 624 | =Army Ambulance= | Renumbering of 30hm |
| 625 | =Austin Covered Wagon= | Renumbering of 30sm |
| 640 | =Bedford Truck= | Renumbering of 25wm |
| 669 | U.S. Army Jeep | As 405 Universal Jeep. White star |
| 675 | =U.S. Army Staff Car= | Renumbering of 139am/170m |

| Original No. | Export No. | Name |
|---|---|---|
| 37a | 041 | Civilian Motor Cycle |
| 37b | 042 | Police Motor Cycle |
| 38a | 100 | Frazer-Nash B.M.W. |
| 38b | 101 | Sunbeam Talbot |
| 38c | 102 | Lagonda |
| 38d | 103 | Alvis |
| 38e | 104 | Armstrong-Siddeley |
| 38f | 105 | Jaguar |
| 42b | 043 | Police Motor Cycle Combination |
| 44b/270 | 045 | A.A. Motor Cycle Combination |
| 47 | 770 | Road Signs |
| 47a | 773 | Robot Traffic Signal |
| 49 | 780 | Petrol Pumps |
| 581 | 980 | Horse Box |

Fig. 375. 39en Chrysler 'Royal' Sedan and 39bu Oldsmobile Sedan.

Fig. 376. 129 M.G. Midget Sports.

Fig. 377. Rambler Cross Country Station Wagon in South African colour scheme.

Around about 1966 raw castings were sent to South Africa to be assembled and painted there. This exporting technique was necessary because of importing restrictions which were biased against completed products but allowed in certain categories of unfinished items whose completion would give employment to indigenous labour. It is not known if the following list was later added to by other models, but it is unlikely as at one point stocks were cleared at reduced prices. The models were imported by the then Meccano agent for South Africa, Arthur E. Harris (Pty) Ltd., as raw castings. They were then painted (sometimes in the same colours that were used at Binns Road) but often in different ones and assembled. They were then packed in boxes patterned on the U.K. ones but printed in English and Afrikaans. Strangely, although the boxes made for the French Dinkies that received the same treatment are printed 'Assembled and finished in the Republic of South Africa', the English ones are not. The colours given are those that have been recorded as differing from the U.K. ones and the list is probably not exhaustive. The models are those that figure on the Arthur E. Harris Trade Price List dated October 17, 1966 which is headed 'DINKY Toys: Assembled and finished in the Republic of South Africa.'

Over the years, many English Dinkies were sold in France. In most cases, they were made in England and sold as English Dinkies in English boxes on the English numbers, but every so often another procedure was followed. 27ac was the English 27a MASSEY-HARRIS TRACTOR plus 27c MANURE SPREADER put together and packed in a French printed box because this combination was not marketed in the U.K. Sometimes the parts were sent to France and assembled there, and these can be identified by the baseplates which read 'Assemblé en France'. Amongst others, 562 (French No. 887) MUIR HILL DUMPER and 150 (French No. 551) ROLLS ROYCE SILVER WRAITH were so treated. However, in some cases, the die itself was shipped to Bobigny as in the case of 39a PACKARD, which was allocated the French number 24p, and can be found in gold, turquoise, cream and blue, and 39f STUDEBAKER (French No. 24o) which appeared in red, cream and metallic green. Some of these were fitted with French all-metal wheels. Later, two of the

## MODELS ASSEMBLED & FINISHED IN SOUTH AFRICA

| 112 | Austin Healey Sprite | Turquoise, deep blue, light blue |
| 113 | M.G.B. Sports Car | Red |
| 140 | Morris 1100 | |
| 141 | Vauxhall Victor Estate Car | Pinky-orange |
| 142 | Jaguar Mark X | |
| 148 | Ford Fairlane | Bright blue |
| 155 | Ford Anglia | White |
| 177 | Opel Kapitan | Dark blue |
| 181 | Volkswagen | Off-white, lime green, light blue |
| 184 | Volvo 122S Saloon | |
| 186 | Mercedes-Benz 220 SE | |
| 193 | Rambler Cross Country Station Wagon | Lime green, lavender, two-tone cream & lavender |
| 194 | Bentley Series S Coupé | Lime green, red interior. Cream, red interior |
| 195 | Jaguar Mark 10 | |
| 198 | Rolls Royce Phantom V | |
| 240 | Cooper Racing Car | |
| 241 | Lotus Racing Car | |
| 242 | Ferrari Racing Car | |
| 300 | Massey Harris Tractor | |
| 449 | Chevrolet El Camino Pick-up | Two-tone fawn & chocolate, turquoise |

Not on this list but also seen: 196 Holden — Two-tone white and turquoise
and a very much later item: 183 Mini — Red

## MODELS MADE FOR EUROPEAN MARKETS

| No. | Name | Country | Comments |
| --- | --- | --- | --- |
| 260 | Volkswagen Deutsche Bundesposte | Germany | Casting of 129 VW 1300. Yellow |
| 261 | Ford Taunus Polizei | Germany | Casting of 154 Taunus 17 M. White & green |
| 262 | Volkswagen Swiss Post | Switzerland | Casting of 181 VW. Yellow & black |
| 262 | Volkswagen Swiss Post | Switzerland | Casting 129 VW. Yellow & black |
| 266 | Plymouth Taxi | Canada | As 265 but 'Metro Cab' |
| 271 | T.S. Motor Cycle Patrol | Belgium | Casting of 44b/270. Yellow |
| 271 | Ford Transit Fire Appliance | Denmark | As 271 with 'Falck' decals |
| 272 | A.N.W.B. Motor Cycle Patrol | Holland | Casting of 44b/270. Yellow |
| 282 | Land Rover Fire Appliance | Denmark | As 282 with 'Falck' decals |
| 285 | Merryweather Marquis Fire Engine | Denmark | As 285 with 'Falck' decals. Red or metallic re |
| 286 | Ford Transit Fire Appliance | Denmark | As 286 with 'Falck' decals. Red or metallic re |
| 288 | Superior Cadillac Ambulance | Denmark | As 288 with 'Falck' decals. Red & white or black & white |
| 293 | Swiss Postal Bus PTT | Switzerland | Casting of 296. Yellow |
| 410 | Bedford Danish Post | Denmark | As 410. Yellow |
| 416 | Ford Transit Fire Appliance | Denmark | As 416 with 'Falck' decals |
| 442 | Land Rover Breakdown Crane | Denmark | As 442 with 'Falck' decals. Red or white & |
| 727 | U.S. Air Force F-4 Phantom II | America | Casting of 725. Brown & green camouflage (See: Aeroplanes) |
| 733 | F-4K Phantom Der Bundesluftwaffe | Germany & Austria | Casting of 725. Grey & green camouflage (See: Aeroplanes) |
| 956 | Berliet Turntable Fire Escape | Denmark | As 956 with 'Falck' decals |
| 961 | Vega Major Coach PTT | Switzerland | Casting of 954. Yellow |

100 series dies were shipped there: 109 AUSTIN HEALEY became French Dinky 546 and 110 ASTON MARTIN, French Dinky 506. There are also colour and wheel changes. 561 BLAW KNOX BULLDOZER became French Dinky 885. All of this type have the baseplates marked 'Fab. en France'.

Special issues were made for mainly European overseas markets using existing castings and coloured and/or decalled for that particular country.

Apart from 293 SWISS POSTAL BUS, they were all available only in the country for which they were made. 261 FORD TAUNUS 'POLIZEI' is a different casting from the French Dinky 551 which preceded it, and which was also made for Germany. Two different castings were issued as 262 VOLKS-WAGEN SWISS POST, the first using the casting of 181 VW and the second the later 129 VW 1300 SEDAN with windows and jewelled headlamps. The Danish 'Falck' or 'Rescue Service' vehicles nor-

mally have the same paint schemes as the U.K. issues except for the black and white Cadillac Ambulance with 'Falck' stickers which can vary in size. In all cases, these versions were issued during the period in which the basic castings were being used for items that appeared in the U.K. catalogues. All the items in the list were on general sale in the relevant country. Promotional models are covered in the section that deals with the appropriate basic casting.

*Fig. 378. Austin Healey Sprite, Bentley Series S Coupé and Chevrolet El Camino in South African colour schemes.*

*Fig. 379. 261 Ford Taunus 'Polizei' (Germany).*

*Fig. 380. 262 Volkswagen Swiss Post (based on 129).*

*Fig. 381. A selection of 'Falck' vehicles*

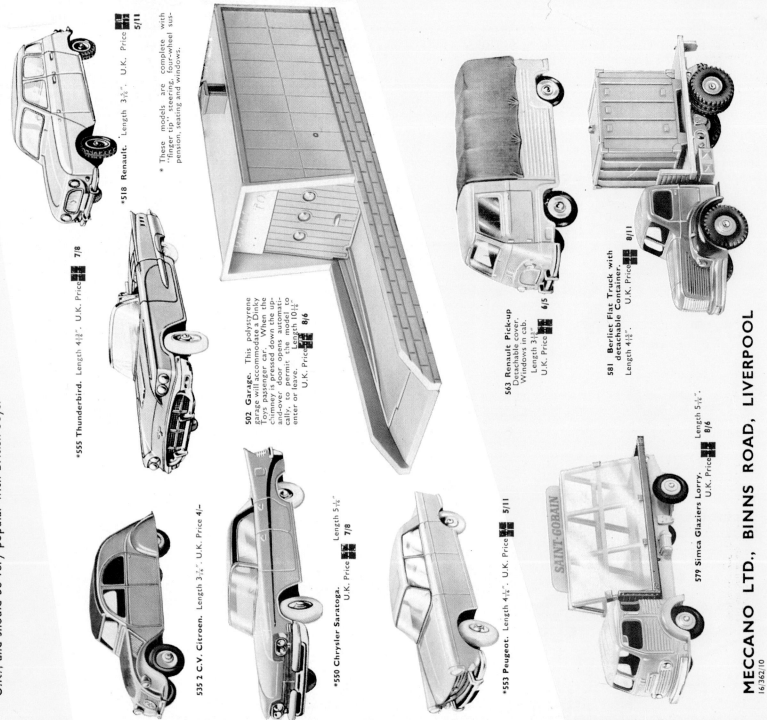

*Fig. 387. Dinky Toys and Supertoys from Paris.*

Following the withdrawal of Purchase Tax Surcharge 10th April, 1962, prices have been reduced

# DINKY TOYS from PARIS

A separate range of Dinky Toys is made by Meccano (France) in Paris. A selection of these French models has been imported into the U.K.; and should be very popular with British boys.

*518 Renault. Length 3⁵⁄₁₆″. U.K. Price 5/11

* These models are complete with "finger tip" steering, four-wheel suspension, seating and windows.

*555 Thunderbird. Length 4¹²⁄₁₆″. U.K. Price 7/8

502 Garage. This polystyrene garage will accommodate a Dinky Toys passenger car. When the chimney is pressed down the up-and-over door opens automatically, to permit the model to enter or leave. Length 10½″
U.K. Price 8/6

563 Renault Pick-up Detachable cover. Windows in cab. Length 3¹¹⁄₁₆″
U.K. Price 6/5

581 Berliet Flat Truck with detachable Container. Length 4¹³⁄₁₆″. U.K. Price 8/11

535 2 C.V. Citroen. Length 3⁷⁄₁₆″. U.K. Price 4/–

550 Chrysler Saratoga. Length 5¹⁄₁₆″. U.K. Price 7/8

*553 Peugeot. Length 4¹⁵⁄₁₆″. U.K. Price 5/11

579 Simca Glaziers Lorry. Length 5¹⁄₁₆″. U.K. Price 8/6

SAINT-GOBAIN

## MECCANO LTD., BINNS ROAD, LIVERPOOL

16/362/10

# DINKY TOYS® and SUPERTOYS

## from PARIS

**561 Citroen Delivery Van.** Length 3¾".
U.K. Price 5/5

**Dinky Supertoys No. 893. Unic Pipe-line Transporter.**
(With removable pipes. Windows in cab)
Length 8⅞". U.K. Price 12/9

**Dinky Supertoys No. 894. Car Transporter.** Length 12⁷⁄₁₆". U.K. Price 35/-
Will carry 4 Dinky Toys Cars.

DINKY TOYS SERVICE LIVRAISON

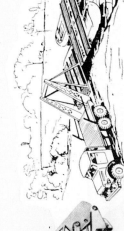

**822 Half-track M3.** Length 4⅝".
U.K. Price 9/11

**817 A.M.X. 13-ton Tank**
Rotating gun turret
Length 4¼".
U.K. Price 9/11

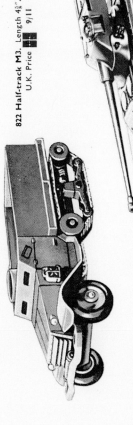

CIBIE

## CARGOES FOR DINKY TOYS

846 Oil Drums (pack of 6).     U.K. Price 1/4
847 Barrels (pack of 6).     U.K. Price 1/4
849 Packing Cases (packs of 6).     U.K. Price 1/4
850 Crates of Bottles (pack of 6). U.K. Price 1/4
851 Set of 2 each of Nos. 846, 847, 849 and 850
(pack of 8).     U.K. Price 1/9

*Suitable also for use with Hornby-Dublo Railways*

849

846

847

850

**815 Panhard Armoured Car.** Length 4⁷⁄₁₆".
Rotating gun turret     U.K. Price 8/7

**Dinky Supertoys No. 884. Brockway Military Truck with pontoon bridge.**
A lever permits the automatic unloading of the 6 lengths of bridge section and two
inflatable pontoons.     Length 6⅞".     U.K. Price 38/-

72541/02

MADE IN PARIS
BY MECCANO
(FRANCE) LTD.

*Printed in England*

227

## French Dinky Products sold in the U.K. Market

As part of the Meccano expansion during the 1930s, a factory was established in France at Bobigny outside Paris, and there Dinky Toys were manufactured. Though they made the same sort of product, there was a self-contained French Design team and French Dinkies are a completely separate range. They therefore don't fall within the scope of this book which is basically about the products of the Liverpool factory, except for a few which were not made in Britain but were marketed here. Sometime in 1937 the decision was taken to import selected French Dinky Toys and sell them alongside English Dinkies, and they first appeared in *Meccano Magazine* adverts in 1938. It must be emphasised that the dates given in this section are those during which they were sold in the U.K. and not the dates of manufacture, for they had all been in production in France for varying lengths of time before they appeared here. It is possible that all the colours that were released in France were also available here, and the colours given in the text are not exhaustive, but are the ones most commonly found.

14z THREE-WHEELED DELIVERY VAN ('Triporteur' on the French market) is rather badly named, as it is really a motor bike with two front wheels straddling a delivery box. It is basically one large and fairly complex casting, with an opening diecast lid and a tinplate insert for the bottom of the box. The catalogues show it with a front bumper but it was never issued in this form. The tyres are a type not used on British manufacture, being white with 'Dunlop' in raised letters on one side; an example of the great attention to detail exhibited by many of the French Dinkies. The bike and box were available in a variety of colours, green, grey, red, blue, yellow, etc. and the black trousered driver wore a jacket of brown, blue, green and so on, but always a different shade to that of the bike. Imported in 1938 and available while pre-war stocks lasted.

16z STREAMLINED DIESEL ARTICULATED TRAIN was imported at the same time and was also available for no more than two years. Despite the fact that the car at each end is a propulsion unit they are not the same casting, one having a concave curve and the other a convex at the end to which the coach was attached. The coach itself had curves complimentary to those on the power units to enable high speed cornering.

The internal wheels are carried on a tinplate insert

Fig. 385. 29dz Autobus.

which protrudes through the castings of the coach and trailing engine unit and acts as the coupling between the items. The painting is two-tone with the darker colour on the valance concealing the running gear and is dark blue/light blue, red/cream, green/cream etc.

24kz PEUGEOT CAR was sold for about a year in the U.K. and can be distinguished from those intended for the French market by its rubber tyres. The casting is a most attractive thinwalled single piece, with a slot to accept the tinplate front bumber and a hole in the driver's side front door which took the flag for the Taxi version, which was not released in the U.K. Available in red or blue.

*Fig. 383. 16z Streamlined Diesel Articulated Train.*

*Fig. 382. 14z Triporteur.*

*Fig. 384. 24kz Peugeot Car. This is the French Taxi version—U.K. models were single colour only (See: Display and Marketing—1939/1940 Catalogue).*

*Fig. 386. 35az Fiat Two-Seater Saloon.*

26z DIESEL RAIL CAR makes a nice companion piece to 26 G W R RAIL CAR and the construction and painting show many similarities: a one piece casting running on plastic bobbins with a bright colour, red, yellow, green, orange, etc. on the lower panel with cream or yellow windows and roof. Late production could be fitted with wheels. Available from 1938 until stocks ran out sometime in 1940 (see: Display and Marketing—1939/1940 catalogue).

29dz AUTOBUS claims to be 'A striking model of a modern French single-decker motor bus,' and indeed it is a very attractive model of the Renault Paris Bus of the time. The lower half is diecast and the roof and windows tinplate. There is a tinplate chassis and it runs on French Dinky metal wheels. It is always found in the Paris Bus colours of green (on the casting) and white (on the tinplate). It was available very briefly indeed in the U.K.

35az FIAT TWO-SEATER SALOON, though in production in France for quite some time, was only imported into Britain and advertised in the U.K. for about a year. The car of which it is a model is a Fiat 500 Topolino which was manufactured and marketed in France under licence as a Simca 5. When the toy was released in France, it was marked inside 'Simca 5', but because Fiats were imported into Britain it was advertised here as a Fiat, though no altera-

## FRENCH DINKY PRODUCTS SOLD ON THE U.K. MARKET

NOTE: The dates given below are the dates when the items were in U.K. catalogues NOT the dates during which they were manufactured in France.

| Cat. No. | Model | Intro. date | Deletion date | Comments |
|---|---|---|---|---|
| 14z | Three-wheeled Delivery Van | 1938 | 1940 | |
| 16z | Streamlined Diesel Articulated Train | 1938 | 1939 | |
| 24kz | Peugeot Car | 1939 | 1940 | |
| 26z | Diesel Rail Car | 1937 | 1940 | |
| 29dz | Autobus | 1939 | 1940 | |
| 35az | Fiat Two-seater Saloon | 1939 | 1940 | |
| 52cz | Transatlantic Liner 'La Normandie' | | | See: Ships |
| 53az | Battleship 'Dunkerque' | | | See: Ships |
| 60z | Aeroplanes | | | See: Aeroplanes |
| 60az | Arc-en-Ciel Monoplane | | | See: Aeroplanes |
| 61z | Aeroplanes | | | See: Aeroplanes |
| 64az | Amiot 370 | | | See: Aeroplanes |
| 64bz | Bloch 220 | | | See: Aeroplanes |
| 502 | Garage | 1960 | 1963 | Plastic. Light blue & grey |
| 516 | Mercedes-Benz 230 SL | 1965 | 1966 | Metallic red, cream roof |
| 518 | Renault (4L) | 1962 | 1963 | Mid-brown |
| 524 | Panhard 24c | 1965 | 1967 | Dark metallic grey |
| 530 | Citroen DS 19 | 1965 | 1966 | Light green, light grey roof |
| 535 | 2 cv Citroen | 1962 | 1963 | Maroon, grey roof |
| 550 | Chrysler Saratoga | 1962 | 1963 | Pink and white |
| 553 | Peugeot (404 saloon) | 1962 | 1963 | Off-white |
| 555 | Thunderbird | 1962 | 1963 | White, red interior |
| 561 | Citroen Delivery Van (Cibié) | 1962 | 1963 | Blue |
| 563 | Renault Pick-up | 1962 | 1963 | Orange, green plastic tilt |
| 579 | Simca Glazier's Lorry | 1960 | 1962 | Yellow and green |
| 581 | Berliet Flat Truck with detachable Container | 1960 | 1962 | Red, grey bed, grey metal container |
| 815 | Panhard Armoured Car | 1962 | 1963 | French military green |
| 817 | A.M.X. 13-ton Tank | 1962 | 1963 | French military green |
| 822 | Half-track M3 | 1962 | 1963 | French military green |
| 846 | Oil Drums | 1960 | 1962 | Plastic |
| 847 | Barrels | 1960 | 1962 | Plastic |
| 849 | Packing Cases | 1960 | 1962 | Plastic |
| 850 | Crates of Bottles | 1960 | 1962 | Plastic |
| 851 | Sets of two of each of 846, 847, 849 and 850 | 1960 | 1962 | |
| 884 | Brockway Military Truck with Pontoon Bridge | 1962 | 1963 | French military green, plastic parts |
| 893 | Unic Pipe-line Transporter | 1960 | 1962 | Fawn, grey plastic pipes |
| 894 | Car Transporter (Unic/Boilot) | 1962 | 1963 | Silver, orange trim |

*Fig. 388. 516 Mercedes-Benz 230SL, 524 Panhard 24C and 530 Citroen DS 19.*

tions were made to the name on the casting. The U.K. releases can be distinguished because the small white rubber 35 series wheels were fitted, whereas in France it had the French Dinky all-metal type or black rubber. Colours: red, blue and green with silver grilles. It fits quite nicely with the 35 series of vehicles, though the scale is fractionally larger, and is similarly a one piece casting.

The Battleship 'Dunkerque', Liner 'Normandie', and some aeroplanes in their 60 and 61 sets were also imported for about the same length of time. For details of these, see the sections on Ships and Planes.

Needless to say, after the outbreak of war, it was no longer feasible to import additional stocks, and supplies in the U.K. seem to have run out sometime during 1940.

Post-war, two batches were imported, the first and larger in about 1961 and the second in about 1966. None were in the catalogues for more than two years, and some seem to have been much more popular with purchasers than others, for it was possible to find, for instance, the Unic Pipe-line Transporter in the shops many years after importation had ceased. The numbers used in the U.K. catalogues were the same as those that were allocated in France. Some of them were renumbered just as the English Dinkies were, but this occurred before they were imported, so that it is the later all-figure number that is found.

The colours given are the commonest ones found in the U.K.

**Mini Dinky**

In 1968, Meccano made their final foray into small scale models. The cars were marked 1/65 scale and the earth moving equipment is approximately 1/130. They were not made in the Binns Road factory, (the design being undertaken at the Lines Bros. Merton factory) most of them emanating from Hong Kong and two from Holland. While some of the dies appear to be exclusive to Mini Dinky, one at least is a 'Car Lines' die (Hong Kong) and the two Dutch ones are Bestbox dies. The latter are identical to Bestbox except for the name and number on the base. The boxes, designed to be used as garages are red plastic with an opening door in one end with a clear removable roof and two sides of clear plastic. The name of the model is either impressed in yellow on the end of the box or printed in yellow on a red label. Through the clear sides can be seen the model

fixed in with plastic strips to display the 'superb detail and action features' (the legend on the bottom of the box) of the opening bonnets and boots, etc. Some of them are indeed rather pretty, accurate little models but unfortunately the casting of many leaves much to be desired and the metal of those made in Hong Kong was of such poor quality that fatigue began to show not long after manufacture. The following is the list of those that were planned. The 'X' marks those that did not go into full production. The list of colours is not exhaustive but contains those most commonly found. They were made basically in two batches, one in metallic colours probably destined for Britain and one without for the U.S.A. where they were sold either individually or in a twelve car carrying case containing the eleven cars plus one of the Bestbox Racers.

Fig. 389. A selection of standard production Mini Dinky
models and prototypes of the planned models.

Fig. 390. The two racing cars made in Holland, with the Mini Dinky box.

## MINI DINKY

| | | | |
|---|---|---|---|
| 10 | Ford Corsair | | Yellow, Metallic gold |
| 11 | Jaguar E-type | | Metallic maroon, red |
| 12 | Corvette Stingray | | Metallic blue, blue |
| 13 | Ferrari 250LM | | Metallic maroon, red |
| 14 | Chevrolet Chevy II | | Metallic maroon, yellow |
| 15 | Rolls Royce Silver Shadow | X | Blue |
| 16 | Ford Mustang | | White, off-white, metallic blue |
| 17 | Aston Martin DB6 | X | White |
| 18 | Mercedes Benz 230 SL | | White and black |
| 19 | M.G.B. | | Turquoise, blue, metallic green, red |
| 20 | Cadillac Coupe de Ville | | Silver, gold, white |
| 21 | Fiat 2300 Station Wagon | | Blue, yellow with white trim |
| 22 | Oldsmobile Toronado | X | Light metallic blue |
| 23 | Rover 2000 | X | |
| 24 | Ferrari Superfast | X | Red. Model marked 'Car Lines' |
| 25 | Ford Zephyr 6 | X | |
| 26 | Mercedes 250 SE | X | Bronze |
| 27 | Buick Riviera | X | |
| 28 | Ferrari F.1 | X | |
| 29 | Ford F.1 | X | |
| 30 | Volvo P.1800 | X | |
| 31 | Volkswagen 1600 TL Fast Back | X | Metallic green |
| 32 | Vauxhall Cresta | X | Dark green |
| 33 | Jaguar Mk X | X | |
| 60 | Cooper F.1 | X | Blue. Made in Holland |
| 61 | Lotus F.1 | X | Green. Made in Holland |
| 94 | International Bulldozer | | Yellow |
| 95 | International Skid Shovel | | Yellow |
| 96 | Payloader Shovel | | White |
| 97 | Euclid R-40 | | Yellow |
| 98 | Michigan Scraper | | Yellow |
| 99 | Caterpillar Grader | | Orange |

Fig. 391. The Mini Dinky Earth Moving Equipment.

231

Fig. 392. 001 Buick Riviera (from Hong Kong).

Fig. 393. Nicky Toys Mercedes-Benz Taxi and Jaguar 3.4 litre Police Car.

## Made in Hong Kong

In an unsuccessful attempt to reduce prices, a Hong Kong firm was contracted to produce a range of 1/42 American Cars. The quality was so low and production troubles so great that only six were produced in 1965–7 and the experiment was not repeated until 1978–9 when 180 ROVER 3500 was made and the problems re-occurred. All six U.S. cars figured in the 1965 U.S. catalogue and 001 and 003 were listed in the 1966 U.K. catalogue. In the U.K., only 001 and 003 were available and they were sold through large chain stores rather than via the normal plethora of retail outlets. They were normally two-tone with the roof in the contrasting colour. All are marked 'Made in Hong Kong' on the base.

## Dies sold abroad—Nicky Toys

In 1970, the Meccano Factory (by this time owned by Lines Bros.) wrote in the following vein after advertising to buy obsolete Dinkies. 'We are in the process of arranging for Dinky and other Lines Bros. products to be manufactured in other countries where, for various reasons, it is impossible to sell by direct export from here. Accordingly, we arrange to supply tools, either on loan or for pay-ment, and these enable local manufacturers to produce Dinky and other toys which would otherwise not be available in those countries.

'Needless to say, we can only spare tools for obsolete models which is why we wish to obtain samples, because the manufacturers in the foreign countries wished to have samples of the products they were about to manufacture, and although Meccano could provide catalogues and pictures, they did not have any stocks left of of some of the articles themselves, hence our reasons for advertising.'

How generally successful Lines Bros. were in pursuing this policy is open to question, as markets where it is difficult to sell into by direct export tend not to be wealthy enough to have produced a large toy market. However, in 1968 and 1970 some dies were shipped to India to a firm in Calcutta, S. Kumar and Co., trading as Atamco Private Ltd. The Kumar Group had very wide trading interests, including hotels, engineering, coal, cars, and mercantile and airline involvements, so the twenty-odd tools sent to them by Meccano represented a very small part of their enterprises.

Why S. Kumar & Co. chose the dies they did is a bit of a mystery, because very few of the vehicles were ever used in India, although one or two of the planes were in service with the Indian Air Force. Successful toys were usually evocative of the place and time in which they are played with, and these were strangely irrelevant to India, though with that subcontinent's known addiction to the cinema, perhaps the vehicles were familiar through that medium.

The toys are marketed as 'Nicky Toys' due to Trade Mark laws, and for this reason the words 'Dinky' and 'Meccano' have been deleted from baseplates and undersides of wings, or rather should we say, *should* have been deleted. There is a great amount of variation in the amount of effort that has been put into the removal of the names, so that on some models they do not appear at all, on others they are partially obliterated, while on yet further examples they are clearly readable. It is obvious that the indentations on the dies have been filled in with some material that is not sufficiently bonded to the block and that bits fall out during the manufacturing process. The dies are now of course very worn and the castings are therefore of inferior quality to those produced by Meccano. The boxes show similar characteristics: some are identical to the Dinky boxes

232

and have been hand altered with a ballpoint pen to transform the initial D of 'Dinky' into the N of 'Nicky' and the N to a C; some are plain; and some are a new printing based very closely on the original U.K. type with S. Kumar & Co.'s name and address substituted for Meccano's and the Nicky catalogue number for the Dinky.

Much industrial production in India is produced by outworkers in backyards, and the subsidiary parts of the models reflect this. There are many different types of wheel; the decal and sticker printing is obviously done in different places and to different artwork each time; each batch may be reproduced with a completely different colour scheme and so on. There are so many differences that it would be futile to try to list them all, so the following table gives a general description only. All the models on the list have found their way to Europe over the last few years, except 949 WAYNE SCHOOL BUS which so far hasn't been seen, and are to be found at collectors' meetings and in specialist model shops. Nicky have created new versions of some of the models; for instance, by modifying the Volkswagen 1500 with a roof light and blue and white paint into a Panda-type police car and by adding a plastic roof box to the Mercedes-Benz to create a taxi. There is a mistake in the list, probably arising from the Meccano paperwork prior to shipment of the dies. Whereas the list of dies as stated by Meccano includes 146 DAIMLER, the production is actually from 195 JAGUAR 3.4 SALOON. This is however of very minor importance as the only significant difference in the appearance of both the full size vehicles and the models is the radiator grille.

*Fig. 394. Nicky Toys Viscount Airliner and Sea Vixen.*

## MADE IN HONG KONG

| | | |
|---|---|---|
| 001 | Buick Riviera | Blue and white |
| 002 | Chevrolet Corvair Monza | Red and black |
| 003 | Chevrolet Impala | Yellow and white, all yellow |
| 004 | Dodge Polara Cabriolet | White and blue (not Dodge Charger as catalogue illustration) |
| 005 | Ford Thunderbird Coupé | Blue and white |
| 006 | Rambler Classic Wagon | Green and silver |
| 180 | Rover 3500 | White. See: Cars 1/35 scale |

## NICKY TOYS

| Dinky No. | | Date Die Shipped |
|---|---|---|
| 113 | M.G.B.   Various colours with contrasting seats | Feb 1970 |
| 115 | Plymouth Fury   Issued with the hood up and is therefore more like 137. Various colours | Feb 1968 |
| 120 | Jaguar E-type   Various colours | Feb 1970 |
| 134 | Triumph Vitesse   Nicky call this 'Standard Herald'. Various colours | Feb 1968 |
| 142 | Jaguar Mk X   Various colours | Feb 1970 |
| 144 | Volkswagen 1500   Various colours. Also produced in a 'Police' version with blue and white paintwork | Feb 1968 |
| 146 | Daimler V8 2½l.   Model produced is actually 195 Jaguar 3.4 saloon. Various colours. Also made in a red and white 'Police' version | Feb 1970 |
| 170 | Lincoln Continental   Various colours | Feb 1970 |
| 186 | Mercedes-Benz 220 SE   Various colours. Also produced in 'Taxi' form with a plastic roof-box | Feb 1968 |
| 194 | Bentley S Coupé   Various colours | Feb 1970 |
| 238 | Jaguar D-type   Various colours and number decals on the nose | Feb 1970 |
| 239 | Vanwall   Various colours and number decals | Feb 1968 |
| 295 | Standard 20 Mini Bus   Known to Dinky as Atlas Kenebrake. Various colours | Feb 1970 |
| 405 | Universal Jeep   Usually gloss brick red OR Army Jeep   Gloss khaki with U.S. star on bonnet | Feb 1970 |
| 626 | Military Ambulance   Gloss green | Feb 1970 |
| 660/908 | Mighty Antar Tank Transporter   Gloss green | Feb 1970 |
| 693 | Howitzer   Gloss brown | Feb 1968 |
| 708 | Viscount Airliner   Several civilian versions | Feb 1968 |
| 735 | Gloucester Javelin   Camouflaged and R.A.F. colours | Feb 1968 |
| 738 | Sea Vixen   At least two R.A.F. versions and in silver with Indian Roundels (white, orange and green) | Feb 1968 |
| 949 | Wayne School Bus   Not yet seen issued by Nicky | Feb 1970 |
| 962 | Dumper Truck   Various colours both civilian and military | Feb 1968 |
| 999 | Comet Airliner   Several different shades in the grey to silver band. Several different decal printings in colour and configuration | Feb 1968 |

# CHAPTER 7
# Novelty, T.V. Tie-ins & Miscellaneous

It was with some reluctance that Meccano Management was persuaded to enter the uncertain field of Character Merchandising, and to some extent their fears were justified. Although the Thunderbirds vehicles were a roaring success and others did not do too badly, terrible mistakes were made—perhaps the greatest being to introduce the toy that can be argued to be the worst Dinky Toy ever, Cinderella's Coach, which is not only unattractive to most collectors but didn't sell to children either! The first two released were invented by Meccano. In 1964, a Santa Special Model T Ford with Father Christmas, tree and sack of presents was released, and in 1965, the other 'old car', the Morris Oxford, transported three pop stars. The toy, called 'Dinky Beats', was obviously inspired by the Liverpudlian Beatles, though the plastic figures bore no resemblance to the Group. (See Figure 161). 109 GABRIEL MODEL T FORD, a magic car, suffered from the non-screening of the programme! Gerry Anderson's wonderful puppets were used to create an extremely successful T.V. futuristic adventure series, 'Thunderbirds', and two of its vehicles were modelled. 100 LADY PENELOPE'S FAB 1 was released in 1966. A sliding hood in green-tinted or clear plastic comes back to reveal Lady Penelope and her faithful Parker. It was fitted with a rocket behind the Rolls Royce grille, fired by pressing down on the front wheels, and with small rockets which emerged from the rear light clusters. There were several detail changes on that model, but 101 THUNDERBIRD II was completely reworked in 1973 and re-issued as 106, some 10mm longer and with stronger spring-down plastic legs. Inside the lowering belly capsule of both was a small yellow plastic Thunderbird IV. Captain Scarlett, also a puppet series, was represented by 103 SPECTRUM PATROL CAR which made a grinding, growling noise; by 104 SPECTRUM PURSUIT VEHICLE on which the side door slides out, and which has a rocket in the nose fired by a push-button on top, and

rear tracked wheels which flip up; and by 105 MAXIMUM SECURITY VEHICLE with a lifting side door, lowering steps and a case of gold bullion. From the Puppet Series, Joe 90, 102 JOE'S CAR had a flashing battery-powered engine exhaust amongst other working features, and 108 SAM'S CAR had a pull back and release 'keyless clockwork motor'. In addition, there was a 'World Intelligence Network Lapel Badge supplied with every Sam's Car'. The UFO series was a combination of puppets and real actors in a futuristic space/world setting. 351 UFO INTERCEPTOR could be fitted with percussion caps behind the lever and button operated rocket. 352 ED STRAKER'S CAR also had the 'keyless clockwork motor', and 353 SHADO 2 MOBILE featured a rocket mounted on a spring-loaded flip over plate on the roof. Space 1999, the most recent series to be modelled, was represented by 359 EAGLE TRANSPORTER, which had a living capsule in its belly dropped by a release catch on top (the earliest issues were without transfers), and 360 EAGLE FREIGHTER, the same casting but with four radio-active drums attached by magnets that could be lowered on 'cables' from their capsule. Not until the series was re-released in the U.K. and a film was shot were Star Trek vehicles made. Both 357 KLINGON BATTLE CRUISER and 358 USS ENTERPRISE fired round yellow 'photon' torpedoes. The latter had opening doors in the underside to allow access to a cargo hold containing a small plastic Shuttlecraft. They were also available together as a set. 372/802 and 371/801, pocket size versions of these two, were produced in VERY small quantities at Binns Road before the factory closed, but the bulk of the production appears to have been done subsequently in the U.S.A.

As well as the first two releases, existing castings were also modified into Character Merchandise. 342 MINI MOKE with a red and white striped canopy and spare wheel cover was converted into 106

'PRISONER' MINI MOKE from a 1967 fantasy film made in Portmadoc in Wales. 183 MORRIS MINI MINOR AUTOMATIC in white, yellow, red and blue became 107 STRIPEY THE MAGIC MINI with Candy, Andy and the Bearandas, from a popular children's comic 'Candy'. The Mini Moke featured again with a giraffe head poking through the yellow and white canopy as 350 TINY'S MINI MOKE from the small children's puppet show 'The Enchanted House'. For a similar age group, 'The Herbs' were represented by 477 PARSLEY'S CAR using the 1913 Morris Oxford No. 476. 211 TR 7 was featured as 112 PURDEY'S TR 7 with silver stripes across the bonnet and sides and a 'P' in the centre of the bonnet. Another member of the T.V. series 'The New Avengers', Steed, ran a Jaguar but though it was planned to be No. 113 it was not issued, and neither therefore was 307 Avengers Gift Set. 120 HAPPY CAB is a fantasy taxi with 'Smiling Flower' motifs. (See: Public Service Vehicles—Taxis).

111 CINDERELLA'S COACH was featured in the film 'The Slipper and the Rose', which was not an outstanding box-office success. The coach was diecast and finished in gold and pink with crudely modelled white plastic figures and horses. The equally garish 354 PINK PANTHER from the cartoon films had been much more successful. Bodied in pink plastic and including a removable, waving Pink Panther, the vehicle was powered by a large black plastic gyro wheel wound up by a black notched plastic strap. The other individual item was the latest to be released, 267 PARAMEDIC TRUCK from the American T.V. series 'Emergency'. It was accompanied by the figures of De Soto and Gage, and was supplied with a lapel badge. It was intended to be part of 302 ACTION SET 'EMERGENCY SQUAD'. (See: Emergency Services—Ambulances).

A selection of items were made which do not

derive from films or T.V. series. The first two made, Santa Special and Dinky Beats, were followed by a selection of Space Vehicles, the first being 355 LUNAR ROVER whose four wheel steering was controlled from a peg in the centre of the vehicle. Two white plastic astronauts rode in it. They were used

for 361 GALACTIC (or ZYGON) WAR CHARIOT which had an elevating and rotating missile launcher. 362 TRIDENT STAR FIGHTER fired stellar missiles, and featured a drop-down stairway. Numbered 363 in some catalogues, but 368 on the box, the ZYGON MARAUDER was sold as

'COSMIC CRUISER' in St. Michael boxes in Marks and Spencers before Christmas 1979. As 367, this casting was listed as 'SPACE BATTLE CRUISER'. 368 in the catalogue and 363 on the box, the ZYGON PATROLLER, was available in Marks and Spencers at the same time, but called 'COSMIC

NEW for 1971

DIRECT FROM GERRY ANDERSON'S UFO TV PROGRAMME

S.H.A.D.O.

CAP-FIRED ROCKET
Caps not included

194 mm. with Rocket

S.H.A.D.O.

351 U.F.O. Interceptor

52 Ed Straker's Car
WITH KEYLESS CLOCK-WORK MOTOR

124 mm.

Fig. 395.

107 Stripey the Magic Mini
with Candy, Andy and the Bearandas

© 1967 Century 21 Merchandising Ltd.

DINKY TOYS

2⅝" (75 mm.)

0 Tiny's Mini Moke

the TV Series

chanted use

ions Limited 1970.

with cut-out figures of Tiny's friends

73 mm.

92 mm.

With cut-out figures of Parsley's friends

477 Parsley's Car

© Filmfair, 1970, based on the BBC TV series 'The Adventures of Parsley'  15

354

354 Pink Panther *From the TV series*
175 mm Central gyroscopic road wheel with pull-through rack rod.
© Mirisch Geoffrey D.F.1964

355

355 Lunar Roving Vehicle  114 m
Front and rear wheels steered by pivoting central control column. Model Astronauts. Simulated Solar Energy Cells.

235

INTERCEPTOR'. In line with their marketing policy, the Marks and Spencers versions have no markings at all to indicate their manufacturer. The Zygon versions were not released onto the market until 1980. The confusion of numbering indicates to a certain extent the state of the firm at the time. 364 SPACE SHUTTLE was not released. In the meantime, two Army-style non-prototypical vehicles, painted green and with numbers in amongst those of the prototypical military vehicles were made. 602 ARMOURED COMMAND CAR was designed by Gerry Anderson of T.V. puppet series fame. The scanner on the top was the key with which to wind up the clockwork motor which, when the front section was opened, enabled sparks to spit out. 691 STRIKER ANTI-TANK VEHICLE was fitted with an elevating missile bed which released missiles either separately or together when pegs at the rear of the bed were depressed. 120 HAPPY CAB is also non-prototypical. (See: Taxis).

1970 Catalogue, p. 2 & 3 for 100, 101, 102, 103, 104, 105, 106 and 108.

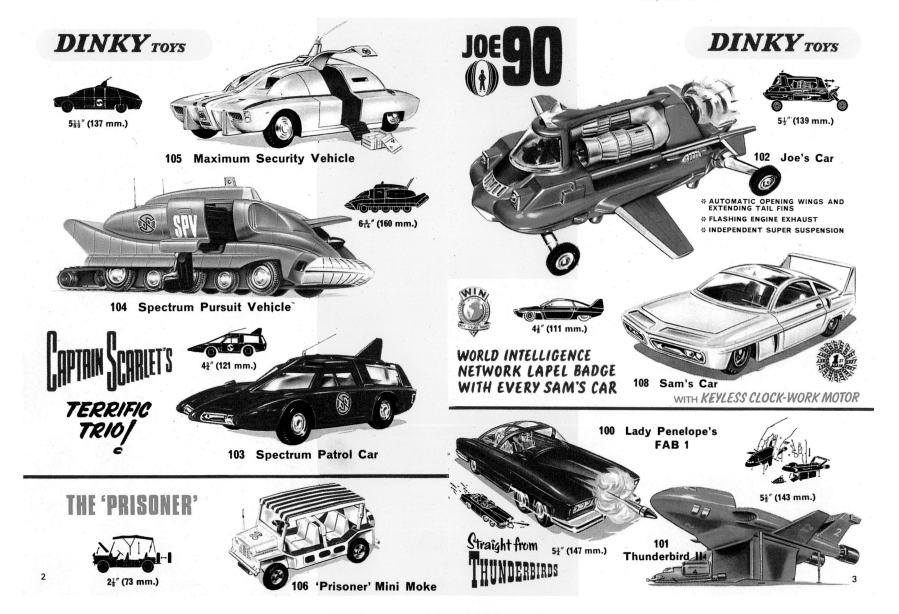

**DINKY TOYS**

5 1/3" (137 mm.)

**105 Maximum Security Vehicle**

6 5/16" (160 mm.)

SPV

**104 Spectrum Pursuit Vehicle**

4 3/4" (121 mm.)

**CAPTAIN SCARLET'S**

**TERRIFIC TRIO!**

**103 Spectrum Patrol Car**

**THE 'PRISONER'**

2 7/8" (73 mm.)

**106 'Prisoner' Mini Moke**

**JOE 90**

**102 Joe's Car**

5 1/2" (139 mm.)

※ AUTOMATIC OPENING WINGS AND EXTENDING TAIL FINS
※ FLASHING ENGINE EXHAUST
※ INDEPENDENT SUPER SUSPENSION

WIN

4 3/8" (111 mm.)

**WORLD INTELLIGENCE NETWORK LAPEL BADGE WITH EVERY SAM'S CAR**

**108 Sam's Car**

WITH *KEYLESS CLOCK-WORK MOTOR*

**100 Lady Penelope's FAB 1**

*Straight from* **THUNDERBIRDS**

5 3/4" (147 mm.)

5 5/8" (143 mm.)

**101 Thunderbird II**

**DINKY TOYS**

5 1/2" (139 mm.)

2

3

236

| Cat. No. | Model | Intro. date | Deletion | Comments |
|---|---|---|---|---|
| 100 | Lady Penelope's Fab 1 | 1966 | 1976 | Pink |
| 101 | Thunderbird II | 1967 | 1973 | Mid-green. Metallic dark green |
| 102 | Joe's Car | 1969 | 1975 | Green |
| 103 | Spectrum Patrol Car | 1968 | 1975 | Metallic red. Gold |
| 104 | Spectrum Pursuit Vehicle | 1968 | 1976 | Metallic blue |
| 105 | Maximum Security Vehicle | 1968 | 1974 | White |
| 106 | 'Prisoner' Mini Moke | 1967 | 1970 | White, red & white canopy |
| 106 | Thunderbird II | 1974 | 1979 | Metallic blue |
| 107 | Stripey The Magic Mini with Candy, Andy & the Bearandas | 1967 | 1969 | White, yellow, red & blue |
| 108 | Sam's Car | 1969 | 1971 | Silver or gold plated. Later red |
| 109 | Gabriel Model T Ford | 1969 | 1971 | Yellow |
| 111 | Cinderella's Coach | 1976 | 1977 | Pink & gold, white horses |
| 112 | Purdey's TR 7 | 1978 | 1980 | Yellow. Still in production at factory closure |
| 113 | Steed's Jaguar | | | Not issued |
| 120 | Happy Cab | | | See: Taxis |
| 267 | Paramedic Truck | 1979 | 1980 | Red. Still in production at factory closure |
| 307 | Gift Set 'Avengers' | | | Not issued |
| 309 | Gift Set 'Star Trek' | 1978 | 1980 | Contains: 357 & 358. Still in production at factory closure |
| 350 | Tiny's Mini Moke | 1970 | 1971 | Red, yellow & white canopy |
| 351 | UFO Interceptor | 1971 | 1979 | Green |
| 352 | Ed Straker's Car | 1971 | 1975 | Red. Later gold |
| 353 | Shado 2 Mobile | 1971 | 1979 | Green |
| 354 | Pink Panther | 1972 | 1980 | Pink plastic. Still in production at factory closure |
| 355 | Lunar Roving Vehicle | 1972 | 1975 | Metallic blue |
| 357 | Klingon Battle Cruiser | 1977 | 1980 | Blue & white. Still in production at factory closure |
| 358 | USS Enterprise | 1976 | 1980 | White. Still in production at factory closure |
| 359 | Eagle Transporter | 1975 | 1980 | White, metallic green legs. Still in production at factory closure |
| 360 | Eagle freighter | 1975 | 1980 | White. Still in production at factory closure |
| 361 | Galactic (Zygon) War Chariot | 1979 | 1980 | Metallic green. Still in production at factory closure |
| 362 | Trident Star Fighter | 1979 | 1980 | Black. Still in production at factory closure |
| 363 | Zygon Patroller | | | Not released until after factory closure |
| (363) | Cosmic Interceptor | Christmas 1979 | | Red & white. Made for Marks & Spencer |
| 364 | Space Shuttle | | | Not issued |
| 367 | Space Battle Cruiser | 1979 | 1979 | White |
| 368 | Zygon Marauder | | | Used casting of 367. Not released until after factory closure |
| (367/8) | Cosmic Cruiser | Christmas 1979 | | Dark blue. Made for Marks & Spencer |
| 371 | Pocket-Size USS Enterprise | | | White. Not released until after factory closure. Renumbered 801 |
| 372 | Pocket-Size Klingon Cruiser | | | Blue. Not released until after factory closure. Renumbered 802 |
| 477 | Parsley's Car | 1970 | 1972 | Green |
| 485 | Santa Special Model T Ford | 1964 | 1967 | Red & white |
| 486 | Dinky Beats Morris Oxford (Bull-Nosed) | 1965 | 1969 | White & green |
| 602 | Armoured Command Car | 1976 | 1977 | Green |
| 691 | Striker Anti-Tank Vehicle | 1974 | 1980 | Green. Still in production at factory closure |
| 801 | Mini-USS Enterprise | | | Renumbering of 371 |
| 802 | Mini-Klingon Cruiser | | | Renumbering of 372 |

For illustrations of 112, 113, 120, 267, 353, 357–62, 364, 367 and 691 see 1979 Catalogue. Chapter 9.

Fig. 396. 109 Gabriel Model T Ford.

Fig. 397. 111 Cinderella's Coach.

Fig. 398. 363 Zygon Patroller and 368 Zygon Marauder.

Fig. 399. 399 Convoy Gift Set.

## Convoy

'Complete with moulded windows and seats, the standard cab found on all the Convoy models is unusual in that it has been specially designed for Dinky by professional automotive stylists, Ogle Design of Letchworth, who also design real-life vehicles. Being specially designed, the cab is not based on a real-life subject, but Ogle see it as having the practical cab-look of the future. Dinky lead tomorrow's fashion today!' (Meccano Press Release 30 September 1977). And further from a later Press release '. . . the brand new "Convoy" range of budget-priced commercial vehicles, all equipped with similar cast metal cab/chassis units, but sporting different rear bodywork mouldings to give different identities.' What more can be said? All those with a 1980 'deletion' date were still in production at the closure of the factory.

## Dublo Dinky Toys

The December 1957 *Meccano Magazine* carries an announcement of an 'entirely new series' of road vehicles in 'OO' scale, designated 'Dinky Dublo' and intended to be used with Hornby Dublo Trains. This return to origins, for the initial concept of Modelled Miniatures was that they should be used with railways, did not prove to be the success that was hoped. It seems that railway modellers were not enthused and 'Matchbox' already had a firm grip on the market for this size of toy car. They were fitted with a solid grey plastic wheel sometimes painted black, and the Royal Mail Van, Tanker, VW Van, Bedford Truck and Land Rover had plastic windows. The castings carry no significant changes and the colours are standard throughout their production life. The 'Hornby Dublo' name on the VW Van was applied with a rubber stamp but the other decals were transfers. The Land Rover and Smiths Horse Trailer were sold together under the number 073, and the individual items were allocated the numbers 074 and 075 respectively. However, it does not appear that they were ever sold in this way. The other 'missing number' was 077 and this was intended to be an ALC Bulker Cement Transporter, but was not proceeded with. In addition to the vehicles, Dinky also made some figures to Dublo Scale (see: Trains and Modelled miniatures). For more information on the minutiae of the vehicles see: *Hornby Dublo Trains* by Michael Foster, in this series.

| Cat. No. | Model | Intro. date | Deletion | Comments |
|---|---|---|---|---|
| 380 | Convoy Skip Wagon | 1977 | 1979 | Yellow & orange |
| 381 | Convoy Farm Wagon | 1977 | 1980 | Yellow & brown |
| 382 | Convoy Dumper Truck | 1978 | 1980 | Red & grey |
| 383 | Convoy Truck 'National Carriers' | 1978 | 1980 | Yellow. Produced to coincide with the launch of 'Medallion Guaranteed Delivery Service' |
| 384 | Convoy Fire Rescue Wagon | 1977 | 1979 | Red & yellow |
| 385 | Convoy Royal Mail Truck | 1977 | 1979 | Red |
| 386 | Convoy Truck 'Avis' | | | Red. Not issued |
| 387 | Convoy Removal Truck 'Pickfords' | | | Red & blue. Not issued |
| 399 | Convoy Gift Set | 1977 | 1979 | Consists of 380, 381, 382 |
| 687 | Convoy Army Truck | 1978 | 1980 | Green |

For illustrations of individual models see 1979 catalogue. Chapter 9.

Fig. 403. 188 and 190 Caravans.

Fig. 405. 290 SRN 6 Hovercraft.

290 SRN 6 Hovercraft 139 mm

Fig. 404. 117 Caravan.

## DUBLO DINKY TOYS

| Cat. No. | Model | Intro. date | Deletion | Comments |
|---|---|---|---|---|
| 050 | Railway Staff | | | See: Trains & Modelled Miniatures |
| 051 | Station Staff | | | See: Trains & Modelled Miniatures |
| 052 | Passengers | | | See: Trains & Modelled Miniatures |
| 053 | Passengers | | | See: Trains & Modelled Miniatures |
| 054 | Station Personnel | | | See: Trains & Modelled Miniatures |
| 061 | Ford Prefect | 1958 | 1960 | Fawn |
| 062 | Singer Roadster | 1958 | 1960 | Orange |
| 063 | Commer Van | 1958 | 1960 | Blue |
| 064 | Austin Lorry | 1957 | 1962 | Green |
| 065 | Morris Pick-up | 1957 | 1960 | Red |
| 066 | Bedford Flat Truck | 1957 | 1960 | Grey |
| 067 | Austin Taxi | 1959 | 1966 | Two-tone: blue & cream |
| 068 | Royal Mail Van | 1959 | 1964 | Red |
| 069 | Massey-Harris-Ferguson Tractor | 1959 | 1964 | Blue |
| 070 | A.E.C. Mercury Tanker Shell B.P. | 1959 | 1964 | Green cab, red tank |
| 071 | Volkswagen Delivery Van Hornby-Dublo | 1960 | 1967 | Yellow |
| 072 | Bedford Articulated Flat Truck | 1959 | 1964 | Orange tractor, red trailer |
| 073 | Land Rover and Horse Trailer | 1960 | 1966 | Green vehicle, orange trailer, brown horse |
| 076 | Lansing-Bagnall Tractor and Trailer | 1960 | 1964 | Maroon, blue driver |
| 078 | Lansing-Bagnall Trailer only | 1960 | 1970 | Maroon |
| 1001 | =Station Staff= | | | Renumbering of 051 |
| 1003 | =Passengers= | | | Renumbering of 053 |

*Fig. 400. The Dublo Dinky models.*

*Fig. 401. 25j Jeep.*

*Fig. 402. 25y Jeep.*

No matter how carefully one selects categories for toy vehicles, there are some which will not fit in. The following list consists of these.

| Cat. No. | Model | Intro. date | Deletion | Comments | |
|---|---|---|---|---|---|
| 25g | Trailer | | | Renumbered 429 | See: 25 series |
| 25j | Jeep | 1947 | 1948 | Green, blue, red | See: Military Pre-war Post-war Re-issues |
| 25y | Jeep | 1952 | 1967 | Red, grey. Renumbered 405 | See: Models made for overseas—U.S.A. |
| 30g | Caravan | | | | See: 30 series |
| 117 | Four-Berth Caravan | 1963 | 1969 | Blue & cream. Later transparent roof | yellow |
| 188 | Four-Berth Caravan interior fittings | 1960 | 1963 | Blue or green & cream | See also 122 Touring Gift Set |
| 190 | Caravan | 1956 | 1963 | Yellow & cream | |
| 227 | Beach Buggy with detachable hood | 1975 | 1976 | Yellow | |

## Kits

Encouraged, no doubt, by the success of plastic kits and needing to increase sales, for at this time the firm was in financial difficulties, a range of metal kits was introduced in 1971. Though more than thirty were eventually released and though some were available from the factory for as long as seven years, they did not become very popular with the small consumer as they figured in trade price lists long after they were dropped from the retail catalogues and could be found in shops long after they were dropped from the trade lists. Initially advertised as 'Action Kits', though they didn't do anything, they were later known as 'Dinky Kits' with the military ones referred to as 'Dinky Military Kits'. The castings, plastic parts, transfers etc. required to build the toy were identical to those used to produce fully finished vehicles in the factory. Glass tubes of paint were included in the kit. Many of these kits were brought by adult collectors and painted in non-factory finish colours—many most expertly—so care must be taken in examining these models when deciding that an unusual colour or decal scheme is factory produced.

### KITS

| Cat. No. | Model | Intro. date | Deletion | Based on assembled model |
|---|---|---|---|---|
| 1001 | Rolls Royce Phantom V | 1971 | 1977 | 152 |
| 1002 | Volvo 1800S | 1971 | 1976 | 116 |
| 1003 | Volkswagen 1300 Sedan | 1971 | 1976 | 129 |
| 1004 | Ford Escort (Police Panda Car) | 1971 | 1976 | 270 |
| 1005 | Peugeot 504 Cabriolet | announced but not issued | | |
| 1006 | Ford Mexico | 1973 | 1977 | 168 |
| 1007 | Jensen FF | 1971 | 1976 | 188 |
| 1008 | Mercedes-Benz 600 | 1973 | 1978 | 128 |
| 1009 | Lotus F.1 | 1971 | 1976 | 225 |
| 1012 | Ferrari 312/B2 | 1973 | 1976 | 226 |
| 1013 | Matra Sports M530 | announced but not issued | | |
| 1014 | Beach Buggy | 1975 | 1977 | 227 |
| 1017 | Routemaster Bus | 1971 | 1977 | 289 |
| 1018 | Atlantean Bus | 1973 | 1977 | 295 |
| 1023 | Single Decker Bus | 1972 | 1978 | 283 |
| 1025 | Ford Transit Van | 1971 | 1976 | 407 |
| 1027 | Lunar Roving Vehicle | 1972 | 1976 | 355 |
| 1029 | Ford Tipper Truck | 1971 | 1978 | 438 |
| 1030 | Land Rover Breakdown Crane | 1974 | 1977 | 442 |
| 1032 | Army Land Rover | 1975 | 1978 | 344 |
| 1033 | U.S. Jeep | 1971 | 1976 | 615 Jeep only |
| 1034 | 105mm Mobile Gun | 1974 | 1978 | 654 |
| 1035 | Striker Anti-Tank Vehicle | 1975 | 1977 | 691 |
| 1036 | Leopard Tank | 1974 | 1978 | 692 |
| 1037 | Chieftain Tank | 1974 | 1978 | 683 |
| 1038 | Scorpion Tank | 1975 | 1978 | 690 |
| 1039 | Leopard Recovery Tank | announced but not issued | | |
| 1040 | Sea King Helicopter | 1973 | 1978 | 724 without capsule |
| 1041 | Hawker Hurricane Mk.IIC | 1973 | 1976 | 718 |
| 1042 | Spitfire Mk.II | 1973 | 1978 | 719 |
| 1043 | S.E.P.E.C.A.T. Jaguar | 1973 | 1976 | 731 |
| 1044 | Messerschmitt Bf109E | 1973 | 1976 | 726 |
| 1045 | Multi Role Combat Aircraft | 1975 | 1976 | 729 |
| 1050 | Motor Patrol Boat | 1975 | 1978 | 675 |

| | | | | |
|---|---|---|---|---|
| )SRN-6 Hovercraft | 1970 | 1976 | Red & black. Later blue | Same casting as 281 Military Hovercraft |
| 2 Austin Mini Moke | 1966 | 1974 | Green | See: Military Post-war & Character Merchandise |
| 5 = Universal Jeep = | | | Red, green. Later orange | Renumbering of 25y |
| 8 Trailer | | | Red | *New Model*. See: Farm & Garden |
| 8 = Trailer (large) = | | | | Renumbering of 551/951 |
| ) = Trailer = | | | | Renumbering of 25g |
| Trailer | 1948 | 1964 | Grey. Renumbered 951 & 428 | See fig. no. 221 |
| Healey Sports Boat on Trailer | 1960 | 1968 | Boat: green & white Trailer: orange | See: 122 Touring Gift Set & 124 Holiday Gift Set. See fig. no. 162 |
| 7 Healey Sports Boat | 1961 | 1963 | As 796 | |
| = Trailer = | | | Grey. Renumbering of 551 | |

*Fig. 406. 227 Beach Buggy.*

227 Beach Buggy 105mm with detachable hood.

Fig. 407. Experimental Pack for 1001 kit.

Fig. 408. The aircraft kits, showing packaging.

Fig. 409. An example of an expertly built 1029 Ford Tipper Truck in non-standard colour.

Fig. 411. 772 British Road Signs and alternative pack for 766 Countryside Set A.

### Street Furniture

Some of the street furniture accessories were re-issued post-war. These were gradually replaced with others, all in plastic except for 13a COOK'S MAN. By 1964–5 there was a wide range of little people some of which appeared in gift sets assuming a different identity, for example, the petrol pump attendant by virtue of his white coat appeared as an ambulanceman! Most were dropped from the catalogues by 1966. Odd items such as the Dinky Way Set and Galactic War Station and Blazing Inferno were released later. The designation of the latter two 'Dinky Builda' is reminiscent of 'Dinky Builder' which was used during both pre- and post-war periods for tin-plate rod-and-hinge building construction sets. The 1971 catalogue carried an advertisement for 'Zip-track', a plastic track on which to run vehicles fitted with 'Speedwheels'. This was not given a Dinky number.

Fig. 412. Dinky Builda nos. 001 and 002.

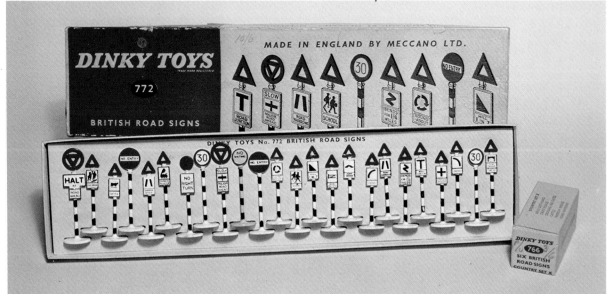

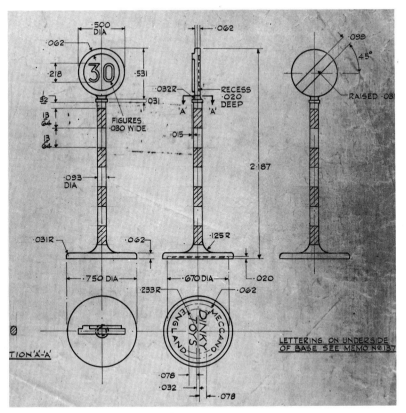

LETTERING ON UNDERSIDE
OF BASE SEE MEMO Nº 137

Fig. 413. 240 Dinky Way Set.

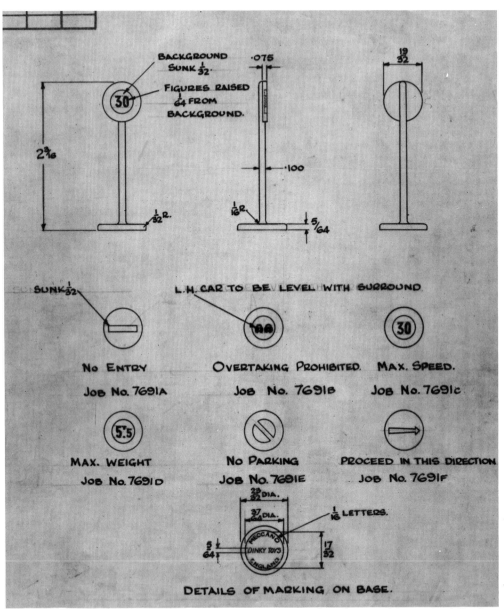

No Entry
Job No. 7691A

Overtaking Prohibited.
Job No. 7691B

Max. Speed.
Job No. 7691c

Max. Weight
Job No. 7691D

No Parking
Job No. 7691E

Proceed in this direction
Job No. 7691f

Details of marking on base.

Fig. 410. Drawings of Road Sign and International Road Signs.

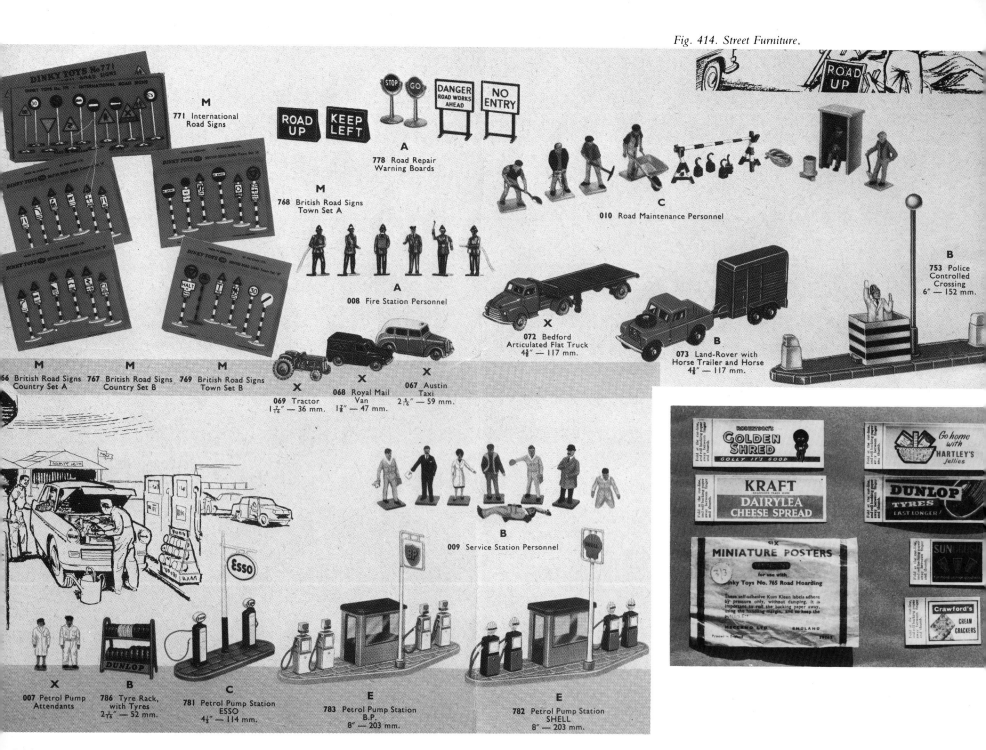

Fig. 414. Street Furniture.

**771** International Road Signs — M

ROAD UP · KEEP LEFT

STOP · GO · DANGER ROAD WORKS AHEAD · NO ENTRY

**778** Road Repair Warning Boards — A

**768** British Road Signs Town Set A — M

**010** Road Maintenance Personnel — C

**008** Fire Station Personnel — A

**072** Bedford Articulated Flat Truck 4⅝" — 117 mm. — X

**073** Land-Rover with Horse Trailer and Horse 4⅝" — 117 mm. — B

**753** Police Controlled Crossing 6" — 152 mm. — B

**766** British Road Signs Country Set A — M

**767** British Road Signs Country Set B — M

**769** British Road Signs Town Set B — M

**069** Tractor 1⅞" — 36 mm. — X

**068** Royal Mail Van 1⅞" — 47 mm. — X

**067** Austin Taxi 2⅜" — 59 mm. — X

**009** Service Station Personnel — B

**007** Petrol Pump Attendants — X

**786** Tyre Rack, with Tyres 2⅛" — 52 mm. — B

**781** Petrol Pump Station ESSO 4½" — 114 mm. — C

**783** Petrol Pump Station B.P. 8" — 203 mm. — E

**782** Petrol Pump Station SHELL 8" — 203 mm. — E

ROBERTSON'S GOLDEN SHRED · GOLLY IT'S GOOD

Go home with HARTLEY'S Jellies

KRAFT DAIRYLEA CHEESE SPREAD

DUNLOP TYRES LAST LONGER

SIX MINIATURE POSTERS for use with Dinky Toys No. 765 Road Hoarding

Crawford's CREAM CRACKERS

| Cat. No. | Model | Intro. date | Deletion | Comments |
|---|---|---|---|---|
| 001 | =Station Staff= | | | Renumbering of 1 |
| 003 | =Passengers= | | | Renumbering of 3 |
| 004 | =Engineering Staff= | | | Renumbering of 4 |
| 005 | =Train and Hotel Staff= | | | Renumbering of 5 |
| 001 | Galactic War Station | 1979 | 1979 | Dinky Builda. Card |
| 002 | Blazing Inferno | 1979 | 1979 | Dinky Builda. Card |
| 007 | Petrol Pump Attendants Set | 1960 | 1967 | Male & female in white. |
| 008 | Fire Station Personnel | | | See: Fire Appliances |
| 009 | Service Station Personnel | 1962 | 1966 | 8 various. Mainly white |
| 010 | Road Maintenance Personnel | 1962 | 1966 | 6 various |
| 011 | =Telegraph Messenger= | | | Re-issue of 12d |
| 012 | =Postman= | | | Re-issue of 12e |
| 013 | =Cook's Man= | | | Renumbering of 13a |
| 051 | =Station Staff= | | | Renumbering of 1001 |
| 052 | Passengers | | | Post-war only but see Pre-war: Trains |
| 053 | =Passengers= | | | Renumbering of 1003 |
| 054 | Station Personnel | | | Post-war only but see Pre-war: Trains |
| 1 | Station Staff | | | See: Pre-war Trains |
| 3 | Passengers | | | See: Pre-war Trains |
| 4 | Engineering Staff | | | See: Pre-war Trains |
| 5 | Train and Hotel Staff | | | See: Pre-war Trains |
| 12d | Telegraph Messenger | | | See: Pre-war Street Furniture |
| 12e | Postman | | | See: Pre-war Street Furniture |
| 12c | Telephone Box | | | See: Pre-war Street Furniture |
| 13a | Cook's Man | | | See: Pre-war Street Furniture |
| 42a | Police Box | | | Post-war issue but see Pre-war: Trains |
| 46 | Pavement Set | | | See Motor Bikes and Related Items |
| 47a | Four-face Traffic Light | | | See: Pre-war Street Furniture |
| 47d | Belisha Beacon | | | See: Pre-war Street Furniture |
| 49 | Petrol Pumps | | | See: Pre-war Street Furniture |
| 240 | Dinky Way Set | 1978 | 1979 | Contains: 255 Mini Clubman Police. 412 Bedford Van A.A. 211 TR 7. 382 Convoy Dump Truck. 20 feet of card roadway. 20 plastic road signs + decal sheet |
| 502 | Garage | | | See: Foreign Products—French |
| 750 | =Telephone Box= | 1962 | 1965 | Renumbering of 12c |
| 751 | =Police Box= | 1958 | 1962 | Renumbering of 42a |
| 753 | Police Controlled Crossing | | | Grey base. Black & white. Policeman revolves |
| 754 | Pavement Set | | | Contains: $4 \times \frac{1}{4}$ straights. $6 \times \frac{1}{2}$ straights. $2 \times \frac{1}{2}$ circles. $2 \times \frac{3}{8}$ circles. $4 \times \frac{1}{4}$ circles. $2 \times \frac{1}{8}$ circles. Card. Fawn & grey |
| 755 | Lamp Standard Single Arm | 1960 | 1964 | Grey & fawn |
| 756 | Lamp Standard Double Arm | 1960 | 1964 | Grey & fawn |
| 760 | Pillar Box | 1954 | 1960 | Red & black. EIIR |
| 763 | Posters for Road Hoardings | 1959 | 1964 | Paper. 6 various |
| 764 | Posters for Road Hoardings | 1959 | 1964 | Paper. 6 various |
| 765 | Road Hoardings | 1959 | 1964 | Plastic. Green. + 6 various paper posters |
| 766 | British Road Signs. Country Set A | 1959 | 1964 | 6 different |
| 767 | British Road Signs. Country Set B | 1959 | 1964 | 6 different |
| 768 | British Road Signs. Town Set A | 1959 | 1964 | 6 different |
| 769 | British Road Signs. Town Set B | 1959 | 1964 | 6 different |
| 770 | =Road Signs= | 1953 | 1964 | Export no. of 47. See Pre-war Street Furniture |
| 771 | International Road Signs | 1959 | 1963 | 12 |
| 772 | British Road Signs | | | 766 + 767 + 768 + 769 |
| 773 | =Four-face Traffic Light= | | | Renumbering of 47a |
| 777 | =Belisha Beacon= | | | Renumbering of 47d |
| 778 | Road Repair Warning Boards | 1962 | 1967 | 6 various |
| 781 | Petrol Pump Station 'Esso' | 1955 | 1965 | Fawn & cream |
| 782 | Petrol Pump Station 'Shell' | 1960 | 1970 | Grey, cream & green |
| 783 | Petrol Pump Station 'B.P.' | 1960 | 1965 | Grey, cream & green |
| 785 | Service Station | 1960 | 1963 | Fawn & red |
| 786 | Tyre Rack with Tyres | 1960 | 1967 | Green. 21 tyres |
| 954 | Fire Station | | | See: Fire Appliances |
| 1001 | Station Staff | | | See: Pre-war Trains |
| 1003 | Passengers | | | See: Pre-war Trains |

## Accessories—Replacement Parts

From 1954 until 1977 it was possible to buy packs of the parts most likely to get lost or damaged, many of the tyres being packed in boxes of 12. Many of the accessories remained in the catalogues or trade price lists after the models which they fitted had been deleted and many remained in the shops even longer, tucked away at the back of the shelves. For the small parts for French Dinkies sold in the U.K. (3 figure numbers beginning with '8') see that section. Generally, the packs contained only items without which the toy would not work properly, i.e. tyres and rockets and not extra pieces such as bollards.

## ACCESSORIES—REPLACEMENT PARTS TYRES

| No. | Size | Colour | Intro. Date | Deletion |
|---|---|---|---|---|
| 020 | $\frac{5}{8}$"/16mm | Black | 1969 | 1976 |
| 021 | $\frac{13}{16}$"/20mm | Black | 1970 | 1976 |
| 022 | $\frac{5}{8}$"/16mm | Black | 1971 | 1976 |
| 023 | $\frac{5}{8}$"/16mm | Black | 1971 | 1976 |
| 024 | $\frac{59}{64}$"/23mm | Black | 1971 | 1976 |
| 027 | $1\frac{1}{16}$"/27mm | Black | 1976 | 1976 |
| 030 | Tracks for 104 | Black | 1969 | 1976 |
| 031 | Tracks for 619, 622, 690, 694, 684 | Black | 1976 | 1976 |
| 032 | Tracks for 353 | Black | 1973 | 1976 |
| 033 | Tracks for 654, 683 | Black | 1973 | 1976 |
| 080 | $1\frac{1}{2}$"/38mm | Black | 1969 | 1976 |
| 081 | $\frac{9}{16}$"/14mm | White | 1964 | 1976 |
| 082 | $\frac{51}{64}$"/20mm | Black | 1964 | 1973 |
| 083 | $\frac{13}{16}$"/20mm | Grey | 1964 | 1967 |
| 084 | $\frac{11}{16}$"/18mm | Black | 1966 | 1976 |
| 085 | $\frac{19}{32}$"/15mm | White | 1964 | 1970 |
| 086 | $\frac{5}{8}$"/16mm | Black | 1966 | 1976 |
| 087 | $1\frac{25}{64}$"/35mm | Black | 1964 | 1976 |
|  |  | White | 1963 | 1963 |
| 088 | 1"/25mm | Black | 1969 | 1976 |
| 089 | $\frac{49}{64}$"/19mm | Black | 1963 | 1976 |
| 090 | $\frac{9}{16}$/14mm | Black | 1962 | 1976 |
| 091 | $\frac{1}{2}$"/13mm | Black | 1960 | 1976 |
| 092 | $\frac{19}{32}$"/15mm | Black | 1958 | 1976 |
|  |  | White | 1960 | 1963 |
| 093 | $1\frac{1}{16}$"/27mm | Black | 1956 | 1971 |
| 094 | $\frac{13}{16}$"/20mm | Black | 1954 | 1973 |
| 095 | $\frac{11}{16}$"/18mm | Black | 1956 | 1976 |
| 096 | $\frac{15}{16}$"/24mm | Black | 1954 | 1973 |
| 097 | $1\frac{1}{4}$"/32mm | Black | 1954 | 1973 |
| 098 | $\frac{21}{32}$"/17mm | Black | 1954 | 1973 |
| 099 | $\frac{13}{16}$"/20mm | Black | 1954 | 1976 |

## ACCESSORIES—OTHER REPLACEMENT PARTS

| No. | Description | Used On | Intro. Date | Deletion |
|---|---|---|---|---|
| 013 | Battery, $1\frac{1}{2}$ volt | 276, 277 | 1962 | 1962 |
| 034 | Battery, $1\frac{1}{2}$ volt | 102, 157, 160, 176, 724, 726, 1040, 1044 | 1971 | 1973 |
| 035 | Battery, $1\frac{1}{2}$ volt | 719, 1042 | 1970 | 1977 |
| 036 | Battery, $1\frac{1}{2}$ volt | 102, 724, 726, 734, 1040, 1042, 1044 | 1962 | 1977 |
| 037 | Lamp, Red | 277 | 1962 | 1971 |
| 038 | Lamp, Blue | 276 | 1962 | 1969 |
| 039 | Lamp, Clear | 952, 160 | 1966 | 1975 |
| 040 | Lamp, Clear | 157, 176 | 1969 | 1977 |
| 042 | Lamp, Clear | 102 | 1970 | 1977 |
| 645 | Shells, Six | 615, 617, 654, 683 | 1969 | 1978 |
| 751 | Missiles, Eight, and Shuttlecraft | 358 | 1971 | 1978 |
| 754 | Starter Unit | 228 | 1971 | 1971 |
| 755 | Harpoons, Six | 100 | 1967 | 1978 |
| 756 | Rocket | 100, 104, 353 | 1967 | 1978 |
| 758 | Bombs | 721 | 1970 | 1978 |
| 759 | Rocket | 351 | 1973 | 1978 |
| 760 | Rocket | 725, 730 | 1973 | 1978 |
| 787 | Lighting kit for buildings | (suitable for 785, service station, 954 fire station) | 1960 | 1964 |
| 788 | Marrel Bucket | 966 | 1960 | 1967 |
| 790 | Imitation Granite Chippings | | 1960 | 1962 |
| 791 | Imitation Coal | | 1960 | 1962 |
| 792 | Packing case & lids | | 1964 | 1964 |
| 793 | Pallets | 930 | 1960 | 1964 |
| 794/999 | Loading Ramp | See: Special Purpose Vehicles—Car Transporters | | |

# CHAPTER 8

# Planned Models that were never issued

Over the 45 years or so, many items were planned but were not proceeded with for a wide variety of reasons that are now lost in the mists of time: this one was too expensive; that one too difficult to cast; this one was felt, on reflection, not to be a good sales proposition; that one just wasn't liked by the products committee; this one had its die 'lost' during the war; that one . . . Some ideas progressed further than others: some figure in internal memos only; some reached the wooden mock-up stage before being rejected, i.e. the tram and some 39 series; some took a step further and a production drawing was made, for example, 185 RENAULT FREGATE and the BEDFORD ARTICULATED TANKER; and some even got to the production stage with a few castings being made, such as 238 FERRARI F.1, before a halt was called to further development. The above list is by no means exhaustive, for the records no longer remain to produce such a list, but serves as a reasonably objective summary based on actual evidence rather than hearsay.

With the constant requirement for new product to maintain sales, a steady stream of prototypes were made some of which reached production (see 'How Dinky Toys are Made' and 'Aeroplanes') and many that didn't. Amongst them are the wooden mock-ups of a Lincoln Zephyr Saloon, a Ford Taxi 'Luxicab' and a Hupmobile. Another example is a perfectly finished model in bronze or brass of the Aircraft Carrier 'Ark Royal' painted grey with white deck markings and complete with plastic runners. To the same scale as the rest of the ships it was no doubt shelved because the 'Ark Royal' was sunk in the war. The pre-war prototype of the Foden is also in brass in a smaller scale and has three alternative backs, a sided wagon, a flat back and the market gardener's van. The wooden tram with wheels to enable it to run on 'OO' track is a later project dating from 1975–6.

Different, i.e. cheaper, materials were constantly

sought and the feasibility of making and selling 106 THUNDERBIRD II in plastic was studied. 671 MK I CORVETTE was made in plastic also and the wheel holes were taped over to see if it would float. It didn't! Bits from one model were put on others to see what they looked like 675 MOTOR PATROL BOAT was fitted with modified ski-floats from 351 UFO INTERCEPTOR to enable a decision to be taken about the viability of a model of a hydrofoil, and 161a LORRY had its searchlight substituted by the gun from 161b. Decals from one model were fixed on another and castings painted unfamiliar colours, e.g. 410 BEDFORD in the guise of a Police Accident Unit and Army Ambulance. Other pro-

totypes in odd colours or with other variations have also been 'liberated' from the factory over the years in addition to those which the designers were allowed to remove once their use was fulfilled. Some of these are identified by tie-tags round the axle bearing thin spidery writing, such as a Weetabix Van with a hand-painted decal on one side only, a cream Oldsmobile and the Lincoln in ochre with dark brown wings, red with maroon wings and cream with green. Over the years there have been many, many more.

Lines Bros. designed a new range of 1/32 diecast toys for the States that were to be called 'Battle Lines' (Get it?), but despite the dies being produced the

39C Lincoln "Zephyr" (as a saloon)

39H(?) Ford Taxi 'Luxicab'

39G(?) Hupmobile

*Fig. 416. 4 Wooden mock-ups of proposed 39 series cars.*

project was not proceeded with and the dies lay at their Merton factory for some years until the Meccano Management, looking for new product, heard of them and since they were, at this time, the same firm, had them shipped to Binns Road where some were proceeded with and marketed as Dinky Toys, but others weren't.

Models given catalogue numbers but not put into production:

| | |
|---|---|
| 38e | Triumph Dolomite Roadster |
| 40c | Jowett Javelin Saloon |
| 52e | Queen Elizabeth |
| 62f | DH Flamingo |
| 70q | Avro Tudor |

| | |
|---|---|
| 128 | Austin-Healey (U.S.A.) |
| 138 | Commer Caravan |
| 155 | Austin Westminster Countryman |
| 177 | Standard Vanguard III |
| 185 | Renault Fregate |
| 195 | Jaguar XK 150 |
| 196 | Morris Oxford Saloon |
| 196 | Vauxhall Cresta |
| 196 | Austin Seven (Mini) Pick-up |
| 198 | Rover 105R |
| 238 | Ferrari F.1 (as French Dinky) |
| 407 | Ford Transit Van 'Colour TV' |
| 628 | Atlas Bus (Military) |
| 703 | Handley Page Herald |
| 950 | Double Deck Bus |
| 077 | ALC Bulker Cement Transporter (Dublo Dinky) |

Additional models proposed in Meccano and evidenced in written archival material, but no catalogue numbers known:

Barrage Balloon
Heinkel III
Blackburn Skua
de Havilland Dove
de Havilland Hornet
Bristol Buckmaster
Bedford Articulated Tanker
Single Deck Bus (1934)
Extension Ladder (105d?)
Taxi (Landaulette)

Models given letter-suffix numbers but not issued until after re-numbering:

| | | |
|---|---|---|
| 32a | Austin Van—Shell | (470) |
| 32c | Bedford 10cwt Van—Kodak | (480) |
| 139c | Studebaker Landcruiser | (172) |
| 139d | Jaguar XK120 | (157) |

See also export numbers in text.

See also under relevant headings for further details.

*Fig. 422. The brass prototype of the 'Ark Royal'.*

*Fig. 423. The brass prototype of the Foden Lorry, with the market gardeners' van body. The Cab of the production model shows the relative sizes.*

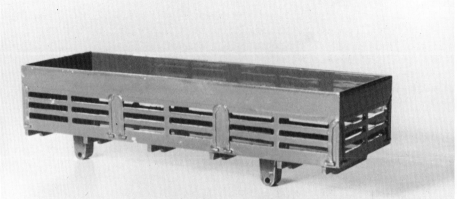

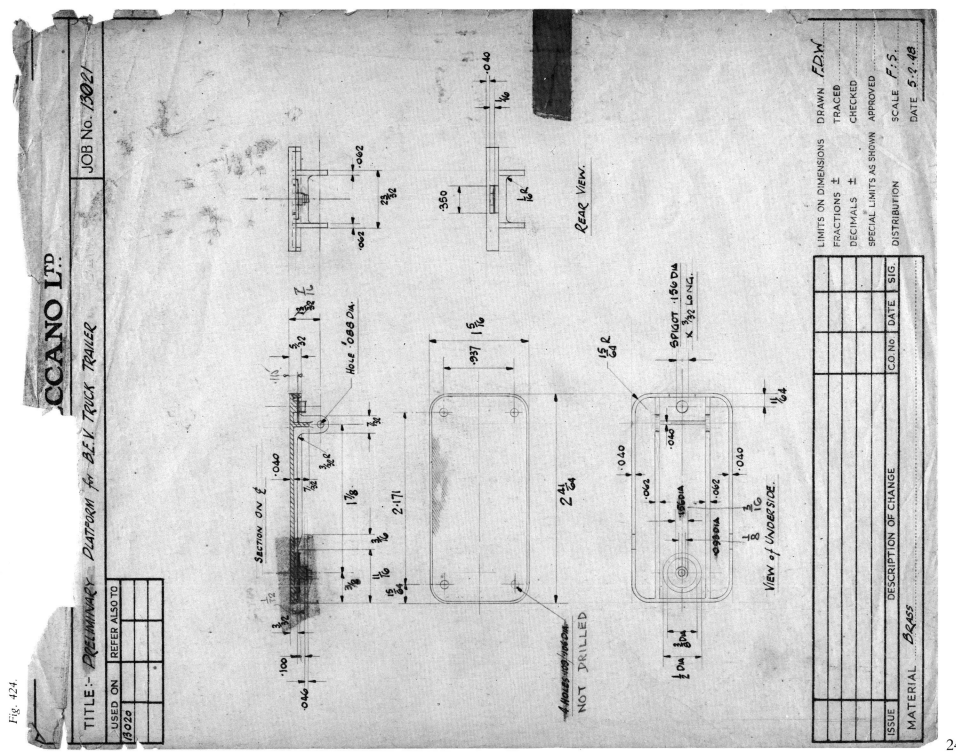

MECCANO L<sup>TD</sup>.

JOB No: 13021

TITLE:- PRELIMINARY PLATFORM for B.E.V. TRUCK TRAILER

USED ON
13020

REFER ALSO TO

REAR VIEW.

SECTION ON ₵

HOLE ·088 DIA.

4 HOLES ·103/·106 DIA.
NOT DRILLED

VIEW of UNDERSIDE.

SPIGOT ·156 DIA
X 3/32 LONG.

LIMITS ON DIMENSIONS
FRACTIONS ±
DECIMALS ±
SPECIAL LIMITS AS SHOWN
DISTRIBUTION

DRAWN    F.D.W.
TRACED
CHECKED
APPROVED
SCALE    F.S.
DATE    5·2·48.

| ISSUE | DESCRIPTION OF CHANGE | C.O. No. | DATE | SIG. |
|---|---|---|---|---|
| | | | | |
| | | | | |
| | | | | |
| | | | | |
| | | | | |

MATERIAL    BRASS

Fig. 424.

249

*Fig. 415. Wooden mock-up of proposed 'OO' gauge tram.*

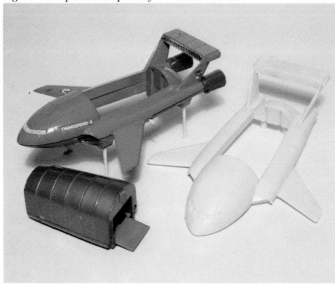

*Fig. 417. Experimental plastic for Thunderbird II.*

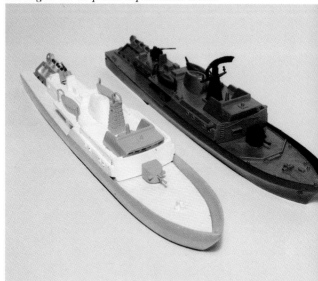

*Fig. 418. Left: the wooden mock-up of 671 MkI Corvette and Right: the all-plastic experimental model.*

*Fig. 419. Experiments with 410 Bedford vans.*

*Fig. 420. The modified 675 Motor Patrol Boat.*

*Fig. 421. Two of the Battle Lines models, the Volkswagen KDF (Dinky 617) and Jeep (Dinky 615).*

*Fig. 424. Body drawing for Bedford Articulated Tanker.*

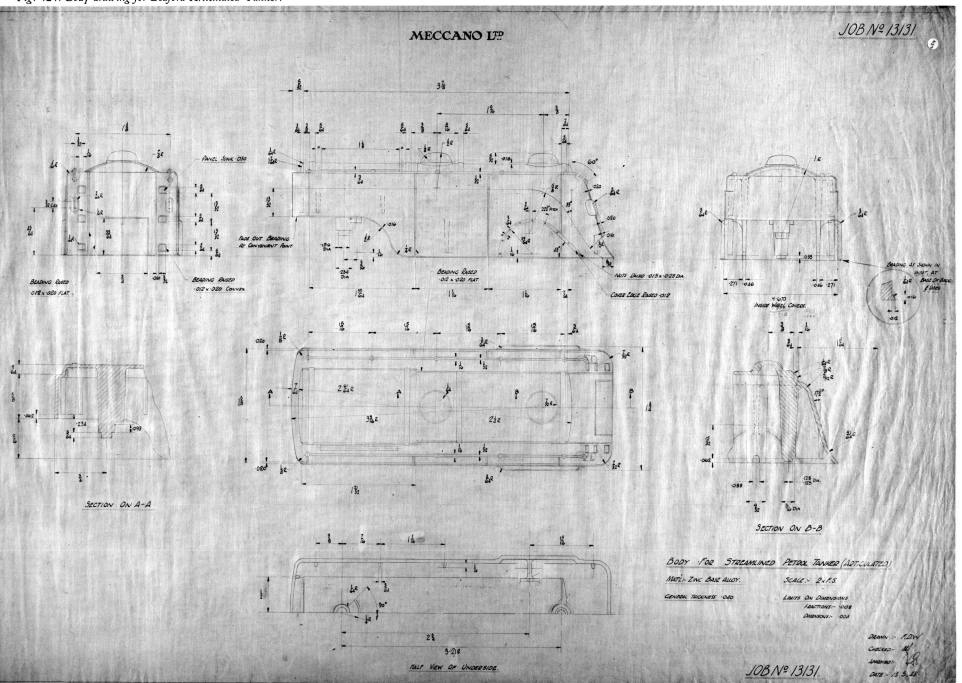

MECCANO LTD

JOB Nº 13131

SECTION ON A-A

SECTION ON B-B

HALF VIEW OF UNDERSIDE.

BODY FOR STREAMLINED PETROL TANKER (ARTICULATED)

MAT'L: ZINC BASE ALLOY.  SCALE: 2 x F.S.

GENERAL THICKNESS ·040

LIMITS ON DIMENSIONS.
FRACTIONS: ·008
DIMENSIONS: ·003

DRAWN: F.D.W
CHECKED:
APPROVED:
DATE: 13.5.48

JOB Nº 13131.

*Fig. 425. Body drawing for 185 Renault Fregate.*

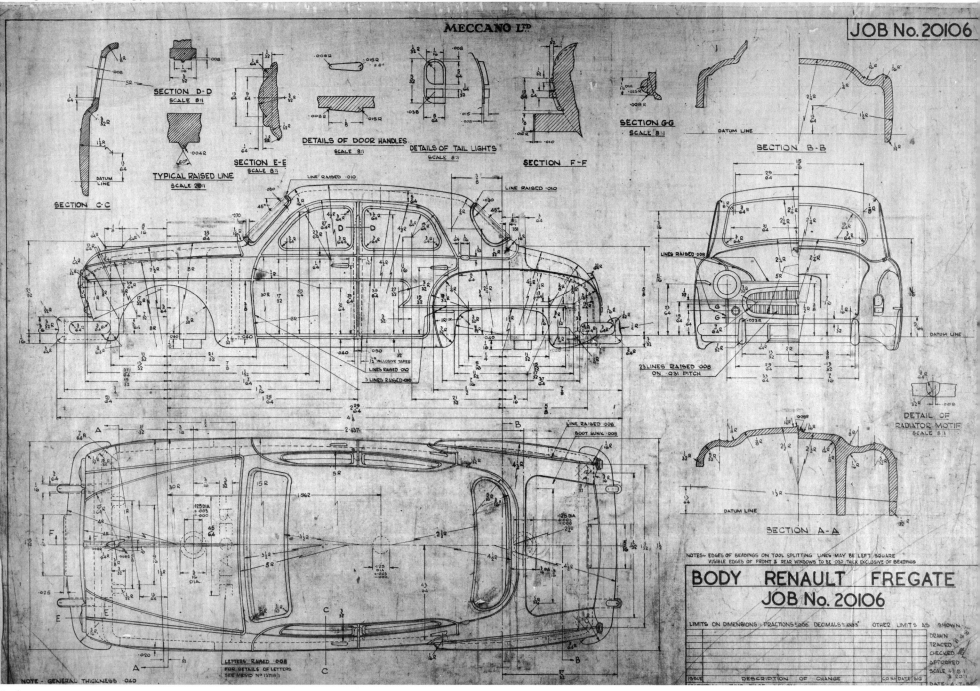

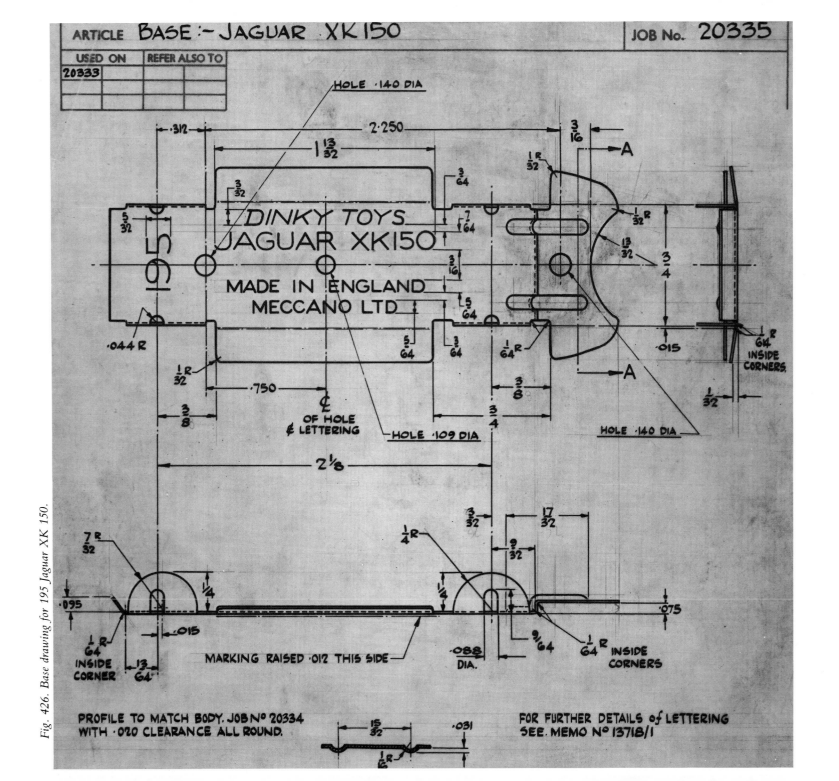

ARTICLE BASE :- JAGUAR XK150     JOB No. 20335

| USED ON | REFER ALSO TO |
|---------|---------------|
| 20333   |               |
|         |               |
|         |               |

HOLE ·140 DIA

·312

2·250

1 13/32

3/16

A

3/32

3/64

1 R 32

DINKY TOYS
JAGUAR XK150

MADE IN ENGLAND
MECCANO LTD

7/64

5/32

3/16

1/32 R

13/32

3/4

·044 R

5/64

5/64

3/64

1/64 R

·015

1 R 64 INSIDE CORNERS

1 R 32

·750

¢
OF HOLE
& LETTERING

HOLE ·109 DIA

3/8

3/4

1/32

HOLE ·140 DIA

3/8

2 1/8

3/32

17/32

7 R 32

1/4 R

9/32

·095

1/4

1/4

·075

1 R 64
INSIDE
CORNER

·015

13/64

MARKING RAISED ·012 THIS SIDE

·088
DIA.

9/64

1 R 64 INSIDE CORNERS

PROFILE TO MATCH BODY. JOB N° 20334
WITH ·020 CLEARANCE ALL ROUND.

15/32

·031

1 R 16

FOR FURTHER DETAILS OF LETTERING
SEE. MEMO N° 13718/1

*Fig. 426. Base drawing for 195 Jaguar XK 150.*

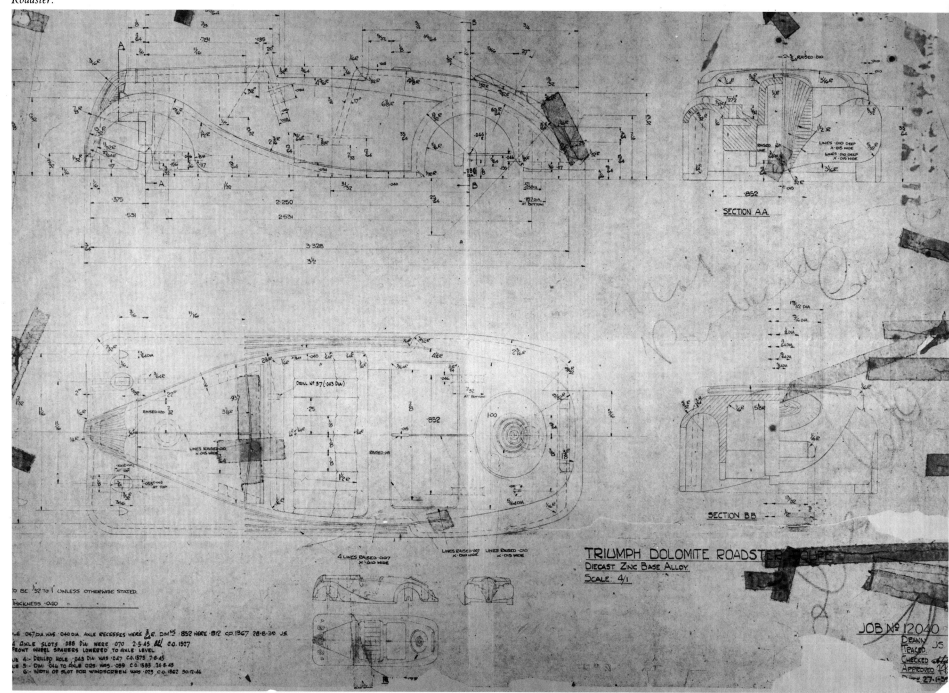

*Fig. 427. Body drawing for 38e Triumph Dolomite Roadster.*

254

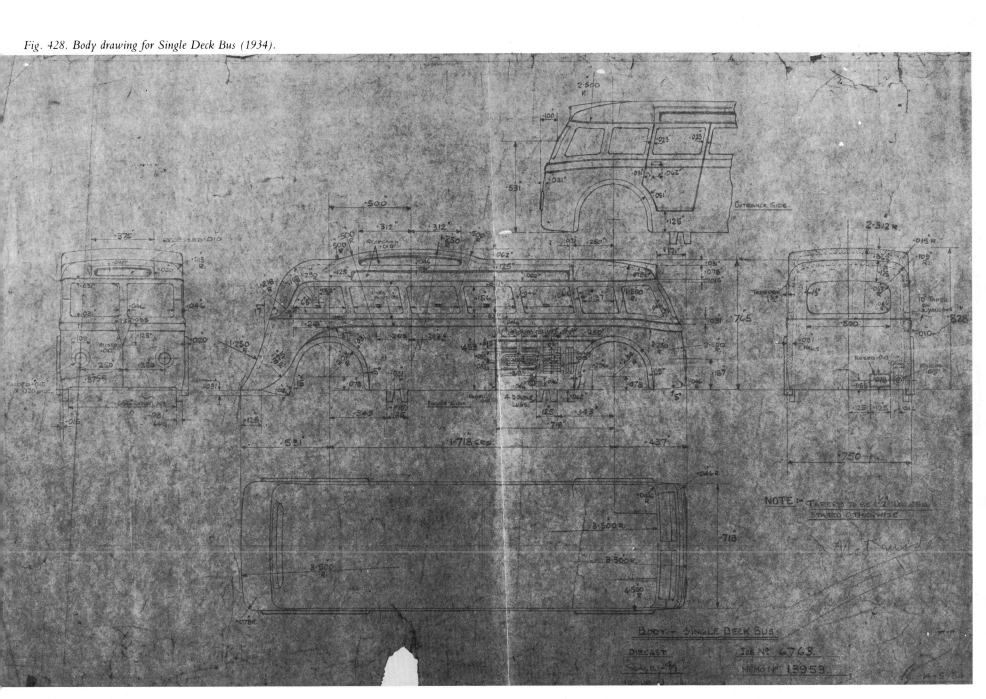

*Fig. 428. Body drawing for Single Deck Bus (1934).*

255

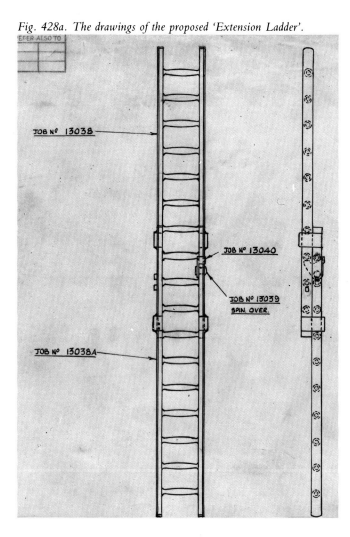

*Fig. 428a. The drawings of the proposed 'Extension Ladder'.*

JOB Nº 13038

JOB Nº 13040

JOB Nº 13039
SPIN. OVER.

JOB Nº 13038A

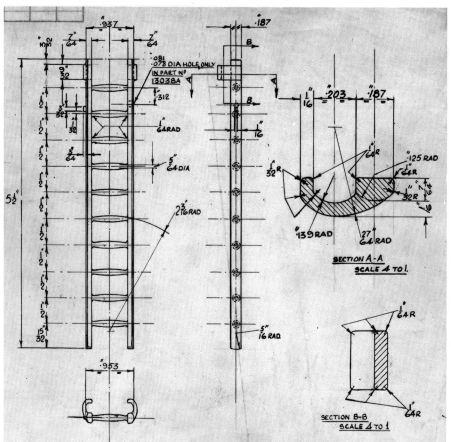

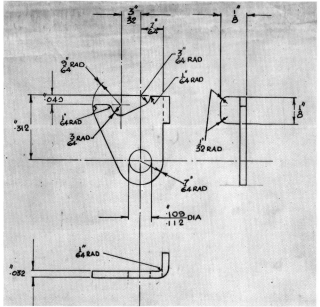

# CHAPTER 9

# Display & Marketing

## Packaging

Packaging engineers and designers did not become a fact of life with the company until the 1950s but this did not stop firms producing beautiful, effective packaging in the 1930s. Judging by the desirability of the pre-war boxes amongst collectors and the sales figures of Dinky Toys, Meccano's packaging worked without the intervention of too many specialists. Originally, the models were intended to be sold in sets following the pattern established by Meccano construction sets and Hornby Trains (see 22 series set and other Modelled Miniature boxes), but quickly, they were also available individually and were supplied to the retailer in yellow, pre-printed boxes of six, or sometimes three or twelve, of the same thing. The road vehicle set boxes were complete with a brightly coloured label on the top but the military vehicles, ships, aeroplanes and some of the smaller road vehicle sets were laid out in blue boxes with informative notes on the top. As six-of-the-same they shared the yellow boxes (see Bus section).

Post-war, sales policy changed and models were normally sold individually and only exceptionally in sets. However, they were still supplied to the shop in boxes of six, initially brown cardboard with a printed yellow label on the end and then in yellow pre-printed boxes (see 40 series). Large models were packed individually in orange boxes. In the mid-1950s, it was decided to pack the models separately each in its own yellow, thin card, box with a picture of the model on the sides showing the colours available. A colour spot was applied to the end to show which of the colours was inside. As this change roughly coincided with renumbering many of the boxes show both numbers. Supertoy boxes were originally made of rough brown (or orange) heavy card with a label on top, but soon they came in eye-catching blue and white striped boxes with the vehicle illustration, etc. printed on.

The trends in packaging led to boxes that enabled the customer to see the product without removing it from the box and, via an abortive flutter with bubble-packing (racing cars), moulded clear plastic tops, which fitted onto yellow plastic bases were introduced. This necessitated casting changes to the bases of some models to incorporate holes to enable the models to be clipped onto the plastic bases. An unsuccessful see-through box with the best part of two or three sides in clear plastic sheet was also in use for a short time but it was very flimsy and susceptible to damage. A later, longer-running type used a stiff cardboard, pre-printed fold-up plinth with a vac-formed cover designed to secure each type of model. These stacked neatly and were very firm. The latest type consisted of a modification of an earlier attempt with thin clear plastic film on front and top but with the card back projecting beyond the top of the model giving another firm structure (see 1979 catalogue in this chapter).

New ideas were constantly being formulated. The retailer must have been very thankful that the triangular design was not proceeded with! The 'Dinky Toys' logo was revised every so often to bring it more in line with up-to-date design and its development can be traced through an examination of the *Meccano Magazine* advertising and the photographs of boxes scattered throughout the book. None of the designs in the box photographs in this section were proceeded with. (Indeed neither was the idea of supplying the Eagle Transporter in kit form.)

*Fig. 429. Experimental triangular pack and mock-up of plinth type.*

*Fig. 430. Various logo designs.*

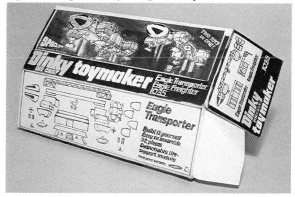
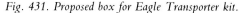

*Fig. 431. Proposed box for Eagle Transporter kit.*

For examples of the packaging including that for Gift Sets, see the text and catalogue reproduction.

Meccano were always very aware that goods do not sell themselves, and they backed up the adverts to the general public in magazines by sending dealers regular bulletins exhorting them to display the toys attractively in their windows to encourage 'the most popular of all hobbies for children . . . Collecting Dinky Toys'. To this end, in 1935 a DINKY TOY DISPLAY BOARD was produced, and it was made available both for shop display and to the retail customer. It does not seem to have been allocated a Dinky number nor does it seem to have been available for very long. The baseboard was 106×71cm (42×28in) and the overall height, including the tall tree on the right, was 20cm (8in). The catalogue tells us that 'The fun of playing with

*Fig. 432. Dinky Toy Display Board. Original Meccano photograph.*

Dinky Toys is increased enormously if these realistic miniatures are laid out in natural surroundings, such as are provided by this special display board. It represents a busy road crossing with parking ground, landing ground, garage, park and enclosed tramway track. The fencing, hedges and pavements are supplied with the board, and are permanently fixed in position, while the Dinky Toys can be purchased separately at the prices shown in this list.' A pencilled note on the back of the archive photograph reads 'One board only supplied to each dealer for display at special price of 7/6 nett. Additional boards 15/– retail subject to usual discount.' The catalogue illustration differs from the photograph only in the omission of the 'Meccano' windsock, top left in the landing ground.

A 1937 Trade Bulletin carried an advertisement

for a dealer's Royal Tank Corps Display Board.

The emphasis on point of sale display material continued with wood and glass cabinets being available for those dealers who wanted them. Many of these are still in use at collectors' meetings and to house Dinky Toy collections. Metal, plastic and card stands, stickers, notices to be incorporated in window displays and for inside the shop were readily available to aid sales. Special aluminium price tags were also supplied in the 1950s. One of the latest promotional ideas from 1979, was a set of four Kilncraft mugs from which shopkeepers and their assistants could drink the mid-morning tea or coffee and advertise Meccano and Dinky Toys at the same time. Perhaps they could also eat biscuits in the shape of a car made with what must be the most curious Meccano product of all time, a biscuit cutter which

turned up in a Liverpool junk shop with, scratched on the inside 'Meccano Ltd., Binns Road, Liverpool'!

A great deal of effort was put into displays for trade exhibitions particularly in the late 1950s and 1960s. Many consisted not just of static displays but also of working layouts with Dinky Toys moving along roadways attached to chains hidden underneath. These involved a great amount of preparation work not just in building the display and modifying the vehicles to enable them to 'move', but in calculating the distances between them and the chains and making sure all the parts of the display arrived at the same place at the same time.

The major source of publicity aimed at the consumer-child was the house magazine, *Meccano Magazine* and even before the war youngsters were ex-

Fig. 433. No. 1 Dinky Toys Display Board. Meccano Trade Bulletin, October 1937.

## DISPLAYING DINKY TOYS

Collecting Dinky Toys is now the most popular of all hobbies for children. We recommend dealers to do everything possible to encourage the collecting of these splendid miniatures by displaying groups of them attractively in their shop windows. The accompanying illustration shows an effective method of displaying the new Royal Tank Corps Dinky Toys. The various items are laid out in correct formation on a board measuring 2ft. 2in. by 1ft. 4in., finished in green to represent a field. A display of this kind at once stimulates interest, and demonstrates the possibilities of this unique collecting hobby.

It should be a simple matter to obtain a suitable board locally, but if required we can supply dealers with a very attractive board, together with a print showing the positions of the Royal Tank Corps Dinky Toys, and two descriptive cards, at the cost price of **4/-** nett. The necessary Dinky Toys for the display are taken from the dealers' own stock.

We have also available a new Dinky Toys Display Board that will accommodate a good selection of these Toys and show them to the best advantage. It is coloured in bright yellow and measures 20in. by 18in. by 1⅜in.

**No. 1 Dinky Toys Display Board** .. .. .. Price **3/6** nett

Set of pewter souvenirs.
*Dolomite, GWR Railcar, Vulcan, Bus.
Marketed by The London Toy & Model Museum
for their Golden Jubilee Dinky Toy
Exhibition*

Fig. 434. Various sales aids.

Fig. 437. The 1979 & 1983 Kilncraft Mugs.

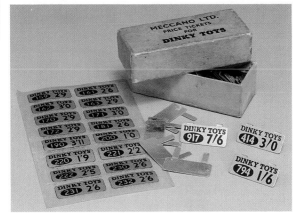

Fig. 436. The Price Tags.

Fig. 438. A Taxi mounted on a Meccano turntable from an exhibition model.

24a/30f  Ambulance in black! Ref. p. 43, 53.

413  Austin Covered Wagon. Ref. p. 171.

40e  Standard Vanguard. Ref. p. 133.

199  Austin 7 in green. Ref. p. 145.

167  AC Aceca—all white, late issue. Ref. p. 137.

25b  Covered Wagon 4th type with detailed chassis and bumper. L.H.S. olive drab painted so for the Royal Army Volunteer Reserve. R.H.S. blue and yellow, a most unusual colour combination.

430  Breakdown Lorries. Ref. p. 176.

## Dinky Toys for car park display 1958

*Sales*

| No. | Description & No. off |
|---|---|
| 061 | Ford Prefect × 1 |
| 062 | Singer Roadster × 1 |
| 063 | Commer Van × 1 |
| 064 | Austin Lorry × 1 |
| 065 | Morris Pickup × 1 |
| 066 | Bedford Flat Truck × 1 |
| 106 | Austin Atlantic Convertible × 1 |
| 108 | MG Midget × 1 |
| 152 | Austin Devon Saloon × 1 |
| 153 | Standard Vanguard Saloon × 2 |
| 154 | Hillman Minx Saloon × 1 |
| 157 | Jaguar XK120 × 2 |
| 159 | Morris Oxford Saloon × 1 |
| 160 | Austin A30 Saloon × 2 |
| 162 | Ford Zephyr Saloon × 1 |
| 164 | Vauxhall Cresta Saloon × 1 |
| 166 | Sunbeam Rapier × 1 |
| 170 | Ford Fordor Sedan × 1 |
| 171 | Hudson Commodore Sedan × 2 |
| 172 | Studebaker Land Cruiser × 2 |
| 173 | Nash Rambler × 2 |
| 174 | Hudson Hornet × 2 |
| 176 | Austin A105 × 3 |
| 181 | Volkswagen × 1 |
| 182 | Porsche × 2 |
| 183 | Fiat 600 × 1 |
| 190 | Caravan × 2 |
| 250 | Streamlined Fire Engine × 1 |
| 253 | Daimler Ambulance × 1 |
| 260 | Royal Mail Van × 1 |
| 280 | Observation Coach × 2 |
| 282 | Duple Roadmaster Coach × 2 |

| No. | Description & No. off |
|---|---|
| 283 | BOAC Coach × 1 |
| 290 | Double Deck Bus × 2 |
| 344 | Estate Car × 1 |
| 410 | Bedford End Tipper × 2 |
| 412 | Austin Wagon × 2 |
| 420 | Leyland Forward Control Wagon × 1 |
| 430 | Commer Breakdown Lorry × 1 |
| 440 | Studebaker Petrol Tanker 'Mobilgas' × 1 |
| 443 | Studebaker Tanker 'National Benzole' × 1 |
| 454 | Trojan 15cwt Van 'Cydrax' × 1 |
| 455 | Trojan 15cwt Van 'Brook Bond Tea' × 1 |
| 465 | Morris Commercial Van 'Capstan' × 1 |
| 492 | Loudspeaker Van × 1 |
| 621 | 3 Ton Army Wagon × 1 |
| 626 | Military Ambulance × 1 |
| 641 | Army 1 Ton Cargo Truck × 1 |
| 643 | Army Water Tanker × 1 |
| 670 | Armoured Car × 1 |

| No. | Description & No. off |
|---|---|
| 673 | Scout Car × 1 |
| 677 | Armoured Command Vehicle × 1 |
| 689 | Medium Artillery Tractor × 1 |
| 698 | Tank Transporter with Tank 1 set |

*Outer track*

| No. | Description & No. off |
|---|---|
| 235 | HWM Racing Car × 2 |
| 231 | Maserati Racing Car × 2 |
| 239 | Vanwall Racing Car × 2 |
| 230 | Talbot Lago Racing Car × 2 |
| 233 | Cooper Bristol Racing Car × 1 |
| 232 | Alfa Romeo × 1 |
| 234 | Ferrari Racing Car × 2 |

*Inner track*

| No. | Description & No. off |
|---|---|
| 133 | Cunningham Racing Car × 2 |
| 237 | Mercedes-Benz Racing Car × 2 |
| 238 | Jaguar Type D Racing Car × 2 |
| 236 | Connaught Racing Car × 2 |
| 163 | Bristol 450 Racing Car × 1 |

*Fig. 439. 1958 Race Track and Car Park Display.*

*Fig. 440. Other Exhibition Displays*

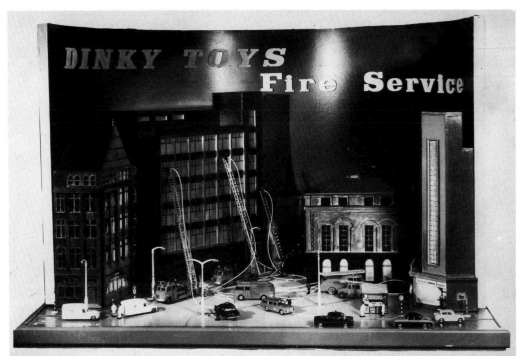

*Fig. 441. Meccano Magazine, January 1936, p. 42.*
42

THE MECCANO MAGAZINE

# Fun with Meccano Dinky Toys

## Making a Table-Top Layout

NOWADAYS everybody is talking about traffic problems, robots, Belisha beacons, and the like. These problems can be studied on the road, but it is much greater fun—and much safer!—to carry out operations on the table at home. With the wide range of vehicles of all kinds, petrol station and pumps, robots, traffic signs, etc., now available in the Meccano Dinky Toys series, street and road layouts of the most fascinating realism can be produced quickly and easily, and playing with them is fun of real interest. We know that many readers are already enthusiastic about such layouts, but for the benefit of those who have not yet tried a scheme of this kind we will describe the layout shown above.

The only materials required to make such a layout are a sheet of white or grey paper about 3 ft. square, some smooth cardboard about ⅛ in. thick, and some grey and white water colour paint. The grey paper serves as a base for the layout, and on it the exact positions of the kerbs are drawn in in pencil.

The areas of the layout that represent pavements, parks and buildings are then covered with a piece of cardboard cut to the necessary shape, a border 1⅛ in. wide being left all round the cardboard to allow room for pavements.

The pavements are made from strips of cardboard about 1½ in. wide, painted grey and lined in with black ink to represent slabs. It is a good idea to cut the large pieces of cardboard enclosed by the pavements into triangles, squares and oblongs, as when this is done it is easy to re-arrange them quickly and so make up another and quite different layout when desired. In cutting the pieces, geometrical shapes should be adhered to as far as possible. Right-angled triangles, for example, can either be used separately, or two can be placed together to form an oblong; while three such pieces will make a trapezium-shaped area. One or two of the larger rectangular pieces should be divided diagonally with a curved cut, so that if the pieces are moved away from each other curved roads are obtained.

When the pavements have been arranged and the roads planned out, the vehicles, buildings and pedestrians are placed in position. In doing this care should be taken not to overcrowd the layout, for if too many models are included a great deal of the realism will be lost.

The layout on this page includes a Dinky Toy Petrol Station and two Garages. The pavement is omitted at several points round the Petrol Station in order to provide the necessary approaches to it and the Garages. The hoardings used to finish off the edges of the layout are simply pieces of cardboard with Miniature Posters gummed to them, and any number of these may be made as required. The road island seen in the rear is a circular piece of cardboard painted grey and provided with a centre post, on the top of which is a red warning signal. A match will serve excellently for the post, and the red head makes an admirable danger lamp!

□□□□□□□□□□□□□□□□□□□□
□ **A road layout for use with Meccano Dinky** □
□ **Toys. This will provide hours of fun and un-** □
□ **limited scope for experiment, and can be assembled** □
□ **easily by any boy or girl.** □
□□□□□□□□□□□□□□□□□□□□

Two different types of crossings are shown, one being a round-about while the other is controlled by traffic lights. Pedestrian crossings are placed in judicious positions and the road studs for these are marked on the base paper with black ink.

At the robot-controlled crossing four two-face Dinky Toy Traffic Signals are used, two of these showing red and the other two green. In the illustration the signals are showing "green" to traffic proceeding along the main road past the front of the Petrol Station, and the Market Gardener's Van and the Daimler Car on the crossroad therefore are held up waiting for right of way. At the roundabout the traffic is circuiting the island, and on the right-hand road a Dinky Toy Van, and the Sportsman's Coupé, that are visible behind the Filling Station, are seen waiting to allow the Businessman to cross the road via the pedestrian crossing, which is indicated by Beacons and dotted lines.

The vicinity of the garage is a particularly realistic portion of the layout. Here good use is made of a Breakdown Car, a Petrol Tank Wagon, and one or two figures from the Hornby Engineering Staff and Passenger Sets. Two men at the rear of the garage are busy repairing and cleaning cars, and the Breakdown Car is just towing in a broken-down Van, an operation that is watched with interest by a woman standing near. Further realism is added by the Man beckoning to a Newsboy, who is shown running towards him in answer to his call.

On the other side of the layout, in the main road, a group of three Businessmen are in earnest conversation, and a Woman and a Child are walking in the foreground. Two Dogs—which look as though they are just about to start an argument—are another feature of this section of the layout.

When the layout has been completed a great deal of fun can be obtained by arranging various traffic conditions. For example an accident can be staged. This might be caused by a motorist trying to beat the "lights" at the controlled crossing, or alternatively a pedestrian could be knocked over by a negligent motorist disregarding the Belisha Crossing. In either of these cases the Dinky Toy Ambulance could be introduced with good effect.

In making a layout on these lines success depends largely on the choice of a suitable scene. An actual busy crossing with which one is familiar is the best type to tackle first of all, but when some experience of the work has been gained added interest can be obtained by making up realistic road scenes to one's own ideas. To obtain the utmost realism, however, care should be taken to see that everything is in accordance with real life. For instance motor vehicles must not be shown on road crossings while the Traffic Robots are against them, and vehicles must also be placed behind the white lines at the crossings and on the correct side of the road.

horted to have 'hours of fun with layouts such as that described in the *M.M.* for January 1936.

In 1957, a new stunt was invented and publicised through the pages of *Meccano Magazine* and also in the catalogues. A 'Dinky Toys Club' was started. Application forms were on the back page of the catalogues or were obtainable from 'your dealer'. Sending the form to Meccano with 1/– (5p) obtained a Dinky Toys Club Badge and a free 'Membership Certificate'. The following year a 'Collector's Licence' was also supplied, containing an address page, lists of car rallies, exhibitions, road signs, international car registration letters, a space for listing your collection, etc. The cover was red and mimicked the adult car driving licence. There was a monthly draw to find the lucky holder who won a 1st class rail trip to Binns Road with hotel expenses paid for the family and as a souvenir a yellow plastic badge with red lettering, 'I have visited Meccano Ltd.' The draw was to be made on the last day of the month by Stirling Moss. The scheme was so successful that it eventually collapsed under the weight of administration!

Press releases and accompanying photographs became a feature of Dinky Toys publicity as time passed with copies being sent to toy trade journals and the modelling magazines, giving ideas of how to play with the toys, featuring for instance fire engines at the scene of a fire, earthmovers in a sandpit and so on.

## Catalogues

Catalogues were regarded as part of the overall marketing strategy and the earliest containing Dinky Toys is dated 1934–5. From then until 1978 new ones were issued regularly. This earliest retail catalogue, a 60-page booklet with colour cover incorporating a space for the dealer's name, contained all the Meccano Ltd. product and a mere three pages of it was sufficient for the entire range of Dinky Toys. By 1939/40 the format of the catalogue had changed from portrait to landscape and by this time 13 of the 72 pages were of Dinkies. Blocks of parts of the catalogues were also supplied to the large mail order stores such as Hamley's and Gamages for use in their own catalogues. Wartime exigencies caused the shrinkage to the 1941 folded price list.

*Fig. 444. The Euclid Dump Truck on Location!*

*Fig. 442. Dinky Toys Club Membership Certificate and Collector's Licence.*

Follow Stirling Moss and get a free

# DINKY TOYS
### COLLECTOR'S LICENCE

Stirling Moss says: "I'm the holder of Licence No. 1"

Every Dinky Toys enthusiast can have a Dinky Toys Collector's Licence, which in the Dinky Toys world is equivalent to the driving Licences of real motorists. It has a printed registration number and a full list of Dinky Toys for keeping an up-to-date record of the models collected. Write for your Licence today to the Secretary, Dinky Toys Club, Meccano Limited, Binns Road, Liverpool 13.

**REMINDER!** Present holders are reminded that their current Licence expires on the 30th June. Application for renewal should be made to the Secretary by completing the special page in your existing Licence.

*Fig. 445. Page xii of May 1959 Meccano Magazine.*

*Fig. 443. The Dinky Toys Club badges*

Fig. 446. Catalogue

# MECCANO

**DINKY TOYS**

Meccano Dinky Toys are the most realistic and the most attractive models in miniature ever produced. They can all be purchased separately at the prices shown, or they can be obtained in complete sets. Ask your dealer to show you the complete range of Meccano Dinky Toys.

**Meccano Dinky Toys No. 5**
**TRAIN AND HOTEL STAFF**

| No. 5a | Pullman Car Conductor | ... | each 3d. |
| No. 5b | Pullman Car Waiters | ... | „ 3d. |
| No. 5c | Hotel Porters | ... | „ 3d. |
| | Price of complete set 1/3 | | |

**Meccano Dinky Toys No. 1**
**STATION STAFF**

| No. 1a | Station-master | ... | ... | each 3d. |
| No. 1b | Guard | ... | ... | „ 3d. |
| No. 1c | Ticket Collector | ... | ... | „ 3d. |
| No. 1d | Driver | ... | ... | „ 3d. |
| No. 1e | Porter with bags | ... | ... | „ 3d. |
| No. 1f | Porter | ... | ... | „ 3d. |
| | Price of complete set 1/6 | | | |

**Meccano Dinky Toys No. 4**
**ENGINEERING STAFF**

| No. 4a | Electrician | ... | each 3d. |
| No. 4b | Fitters | ... | „ 3d. |
| No. 4c | Storekeeper | ... | „ 3d. |
| No. 4d | Greaser | ... | „ 3d. |
| No. 4e | Engine Room Attendant | ... | „ 3d. |
| | Price of complete set 1/6 | | |

**Meccano Dinky Toys No. 3**
**PASSENGERS**

| No. 3a | Woman and Child | ... | ... | each 3d. |
| No. 3b | Business Man | ... | ... | „ 3d. |
| No. 3c | Male Hiker | ... | ... | „ 3d. |
| No. 3d | Female Hiker | ... | ... | „ 3d. |
| No. 3e | Newsboy | ... | ... | „ 3d. |
| No. 3f | Woman | ... | ... | „ 3d. |
| | Price of complete set 1/6 | | | |

**Meccano Dinky Toys No. 6**
**SHEPHERD SET**

| No. 6a | Shepherd | ... | each 3d. |
| No. 6b | Dog | ... | „ 3d. |
| No. 2d | Sheep | ... | „ 2d. |
| | Price of complete set 1/- | | |

**Meccano Dinky Toys No. 17**
**PASSENGER TRAIN SET**

| No. 17a | Locomotive | ... | each 9d. |
| No. 17b | Tender | ... | „ 5d. |
| No. 20a | Coach | ... | „ 7d. |
| No. 20b | Guard's Van | ... | „ 7d. |
| | Price of complete set 2/3 | | |

**Meccano Dinky Toys No. 19**
**MIXED GOODS TRAIN SET**

| No. 21a | Tank Locomotive | ... | each 9d. |
| No. 21b | Wagon | ... | „ 4d. |
| No. 21d | Petrol Tank Wagon | ... | „ 6d. |
| No. 21e | Lumber Wagon | ... | „ 5d. |
| | Price of complete set 1/11 | | |

**Meccano Dinky Toys No. 18**
**GOODS TRAIN SET**

| No. 21a | Tank Locomotive | ... | each 9d. |
| No. 21b | Wagons | ... | „ 4d. |
| | Price of complete set 1/9 | | |

**Meccano Dinky Toys No. 20**
**PASSENGER TRAIN SET**

| No. 21a | Tank Locomotive | ... | each 9d. |
| No. 20a | Coaches | ... | „ 7d. |
| No. 20b | Guard's Van | ... | „ 7d. |
| | Price of complete set 2/6 | | |

**REALISTIC MODELLED MINIATURES**

Page 54

266

**Meccano Dinky Toys No. 13**
**HALL'S DISTEMPER**
**ADVERTISEMENT**
This miniature of a well-known lineside advertisement is intended to be placed in the fields adjoining the railway track.    Price 9d.

**Meccano Dinky Toys No. 29**
**MOTOR BUS**
Assorted colours.
Price 6d. each.

25F    25B    25D    25C    25E    25A

**Meccano Dinky Toys No. 25**
**COMMERCIAL MOTOR**
**VEHICLES**
Fitted with rubber tyres and silver plated radiators.

| No. 25a | Wagon | ... | each 9d. |
|---|---|---|---|
| No. 25b | Covered Van | ... | " 9d. |
| No. 25c | Flat Truck | ... | " 9d. |
| No. 25d | Petrol Tank Wagon | ... | " 9d. |
| No. 25e | Tipping Wagon | ... | " 9d. |
| No. 25f | Market Gardener's Van | ... | " 9d. |

Price of complete set 4/6

**Meccano Dinky Toys No. 2**
**FARMYARD ANIMALS**

| No. 2a | Horses | ... | each | 3½d. |
|---|---|---|---|---|
| No. 2b | Cows | ... | " | 3½d. |
| No. 2c | Pig | ... | " | 2d. |
| No. 2d | Sheep | ... | " | 2d. |

Price of complete set 1/6

**Meccano Dinky Toys No. 27**
**TRAMCAR**
Assorted colours.
Price 6d. each.

24E    24G    24D    24F    24C    24H    24A    24B

**Meccano Dinky Toys No. 24**
**MOTOR CARS**
Fitted with rubber tyres and silver-plated radiators.

| No. 24a | Ambulance | ... | ... | each 9d. |
|---|---|---|---|---|
| No. 24b | Limousine | ... | ... | " 9d. |
| No. 24c | Town Sedan | ... | ... | " 1/- |
| No. 24d | Vogue Saloon | ... | ... | " 9d. |
| No. 24e | Super Streamline Saloon | ... | " 9d. |
| No. 24f | Sportsman's Coupé | ... | ... | " 9d. |
| No. 24g | Sports Tourer (4 seater) | ... | " 1/- |
| No. 24h | Sports Tourer (2 seater) | ... | " 1/- |

Price of complete set 6/6

22F    22B    22E    22C    22A    22D

**Meccano Dinky Toys No. 22**
**MOTOR VEHICLES**

| No. 22a | Sports Car | ... | ... | each 6d. |
|---|---|---|---|---|
| No. 22b | Sports Coupé | ... | ... | " 6d. |
| No. 22c | Motor Truck | ... | ... | " 6d. |
| No. 22d | Delivery Van | ... | ... | " 6d. |
| No. 22e | Tractor | ... | ... | " 9d. |
| No. 22f | Tank | ... | ... | " 1/- |

Price of complete set 3/9

**Meccano Dinky Toys No. 28/1**
**DELIVERY VANS**

| No. 28a | Hornby Train Van | ... | each 6d. |
|---|---|---|---|
| No. 28b | Pickford's Removals Van | ... | " 6d. |
| No. 28c | Manchester Guardian Van | ... | " 6d. |
| No. 28d | Oxo Van | ... | " 6d. |
| No. 28e | Firestone Tyres Van | ... | " 6d. |
| No. 28f | Palethorpe's Sausage Van | ... | " 6d. |

Price of complete set 3/-

**Meccano Dinky Toys No. 28/2**
**DELIVERY VANS**

| No. 28g | Kodak Cameras' Van | ... | each 6d. |
|---|---|---|---|
| No. 28h | Sharp's Toffee Van | ... | " 6d. |
| No. 28k | Marsh and Baxter's Sausage Van | " 6d. |
| No. 28l | Crawford's Biscuit Van | ... | " 6d. |
| No. 28m | Wakefield's Oil Van | ... | " 6d. |
| No. 22d | Meccano Van | ... | ... | " 6d. |

Price of complete set 3/-

---

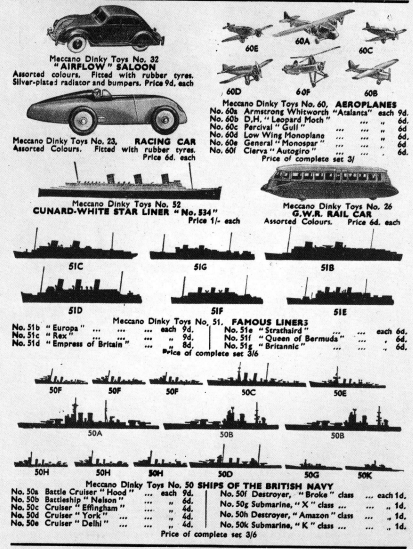

**Meccano Dinky Toys No. 32**
**"AIRFLOW" SALOON**
Assorted colours.    Fitted with rubber tyres.
Silver-plated radiator and bumpers. Price 9d. each.

**Meccano Dinky Toys No. 23,    RACING CAR**
Assorted Colours.    Fitted with rubber tyres.
Price 6d. each.

60E    60A    60C    60D    60F    60B

**Meccano Dinky Toys No. 60,    AEROPLANES**

| No. 60a | Armstrong Whitworth "Atalanta" | each 9d. |
|---|---|---|
| No. 60b | D.H. "Leopard Moth" | ... | 6d. |
| No. 60c | Percival "Gull" | ... | 6d. |
| No. 60d | Low Wing Monoplane | ... | 6d. |
| No. 60e | General "Monospar" | ... | 6d. |
| No. 60f | Cierva "Autogiro" | ... | 6d. |

Price of complete set 3/

**Meccano Dinky Toys No. 52**
**CUNARD-WHITE STAR LINER "No. 534"**
Price 1/- each

**Meccano Dinky Toys No. 26**
**G.W.R. RAIL CAR**
Assorted Colours.    Price 6d. each.

51C    51G    51B    51D    51F    51E

**Meccano Dinky Toys No. 51,    FAMOUS LINERS**

| No. 51b | "Europa" | ... | each 6d. | No. 51e | "Strathaird" | ... | each 6d. |
|---|---|---|---|---|---|---|---|
| No. 51c | "Rex" | ... | " 9d. | No. 51f | "Queen of Bermuda" | ... | " 6d. |
| No. 51d | "Empress of Britain" | ... | " 8d. | No. 51g | "Britannic" | ... | " 6d. |

Price of complete set 3/6

50F    50F    50F    50C    50E    50A    50B    50B    50H    50H    50H    50D    50G    50K

**Meccano Dinky Toys No. 50    SHIPS OF THE BRITISH NAVY**

| No. 50a | Battle Cruiser "Hood" | ... | each 9d. | No. 50f | Destroyer, "Broke" class | ... | each 1d. |
|---|---|---|---|---|---|---|---|
| No. 50b | Battleship "Nelson" | ... | " 6d. | No. 50g | Submarine, "X" class | ... | " 1d. |
| No. 50c | Cruiser "Effingham" | ... | " 4d. | No. 50h | Destroyer, "Amazon" class | ... | " 1d. |
| No. 50d | Cruiser "York" | ... | " 4d. | No. 50k | Submarine, "K" class | ... | " 1d. |
| No. 50e | Cruiser "Delhi" | ... | " 4d. | | | | |

Price of complete set 3/6

# No. 1 — No. 14

# DINKY TOYS

## STATION STAFF

**Dinky Toys No. 1**

| | | |
|---|---|---|
| No. 1a | Station-master ... | each 3d. |
| No. 1b | Guard ... | 3d. |
| No. 1c | Ticket Collector ... | 3d. |
| No. 1d | Driver ... | 3d. |
| No. 1e | Porter with bags ... | 3d. |
| No. 1f | Porter ... | 3d. |

Price of complete set **1/6**

## FARMYARD ANIMALS

**Dinky Toys No. 2**

| | | |
|---|---|---|
| No. 2a | Horses (2) ... | each 3½d. |
| No. 2b | Cows (2) ... | 3½d. |
| No. 2c | Pig ... | 2d. |
| No. 2d | Sheep ... | 2d. |

Price of complete set **1/6**

## PASSENGERS

**Dinky Toys No. 3**

| | | |
|---|---|---|
| No. 3a | Woman and Child ... | each 3d. |
| No. 3b | Business Man ... | 3d. |
| No. 3c | Male Hiker ... | 3d. |
| No. 3d | Female Hiker ... | 3d. |
| No. 3e | Newsboy ... | 3d. |
| No. 3f | Woman ... | 3d. |

Price of complete set **1/6**

## A FASCINATING COLLECTING HOBBY

Dinky Toys provide one of the most fascinating of collecting hobbies. These wonderful miniatures are unique in their realistic accuracy, rich colouring and perfection of finish. The splendid range now includes more than 300 models, among which are items that cannot fail to appeal to every boy and girl.

Splendid fun can be had in playing with Dinky Toys on the table or the floor. Exciting race games can be devised for the Sports Cars, and thrilling gliding races can be held with the Aeroplanes.

All Dinky Toys can be purchased separately, and many of them also in complete sets.

## ENGINEERING STAFF

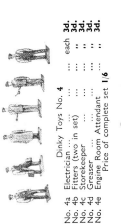

**Dinky Toys No. 4**

| | | |
|---|---|---|
| No. 4a | Electrician ... | each 3d. |
| No. 4b | Fitters (two in set) ... | 3d. |
| No. 4c | Storekeeper ... | 3d. |
| No. 4d | Greaser ... | 3d. |
| No. 4e | Engine Room Attendant ... | 3d. |

Price of complete set **1/6**

**Dinky Toys No. 5**

| | | |
|---|---|---|
| No. 5a | Pullman Car Conductor ... | each 3d. |
| No. 5b | Pullman Car Waiters (two in set) ... | 3d. |
| No. 5c | Hotel Porters (two in set) ... | 3d. |

Price of complete set **1/3**

## SHEPHERD SET

| | | |
|---|---|---|
| No. 6a | Shepherd ... | each 3d. |
| No. 6b | Dog ... | 2d. |
| | S h e e p (four in set) each | 2d. |

Price of complete set **1/-**

## POSTAL SET

| No. | | |
|---|---|---|
| 12a | Pillar Box, G.P.O. ... | each 3d. |
| 12b | Pillar Box, Air Mail ... | 3d. |
| 12c | Telephone Call Box ... | 4d. |
| 12d | Telegraph Messenger ... | each 3d. |
| 12e | Postman ... | 3d. |
| 34b | Royal Mail Van ... | 10d. |

**Dinky Toys No. 12**

Price of complete set **2/3**

## THREE-WHEELED DELIVERY VAN

**Dinky Toys No. 14z**
Fitted with opening lid. Price **10d.** each
(Made in the Meccano Factory in Paris)

## HALL'S DISTEMPER ADVERTISEMENT

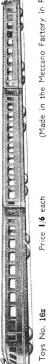

**Dinky Toys No. 13**

This miniature of a well-known lineside advertisement is intended to be placed in the fields adjoining the railway track. Price **9d.** each

268

54

---

# DINKY TOYS

# No. 15—No. 20

## STREAMLINED TRAIN SET

Richly enamelled in attractive colour combinations.

**Dinky Toys No. 16**
Price **1/6** each

## STREAMLINED DIESEL ARTICULATED TRAIN

A realistic model of the latest type of streamlined train.

**Dinky Toys No. 16z**
Price **1/6** each

(Made in the Meccano Factory in Paris)

## MIXED TANK GOODS TRAIN SET

**Dinky Toys No. 19**

| | | |
|---|---|---|
| No. 21a | Tank Locomotive ... | each 9d. |
| No. 21b | Wagon ... | 4d. |
| No. 21d | Petrol Tank Wagon ... | 6d. |
| No. 21e | Lumber Wagon ... | 5d. |

Price of complete set **1/11**

## TANK PASSENGER TRAIN SET

**Dinky Toys No. 20**

| | | |
|---|---|---|
| No. 21a | Tank Locomotive ... | each 9d. |
| No. 20a | Coaches (two in set) ... | 7d. |
| No. 20b | Guard's Van ... | 7d. |

Price of complete set **2/6**

## RAILWAY SIGNALS

**15A  15B  15C  15C  15B  15A**

**Dinky Toys No. 15**

| | | |
|---|---|---|
| No. 15a | Single Arm Signal. One "Home" and one "Distant" ... | each 2d. |
| No. 15b | Double Arm Signal. Two combined "Home" and "Distant" ... | 3d. |
| No. 15c | Junction Signal. One "Home" and one "Distant" ... | 4d. |

Price of complete set **1/6**

## PASSENGER TRAIN SET

**Dinky Toys No. 17**

| | | |
|---|---|---|
| No. 17a | Locomotive ... | each 9d. |
| No. 17b | Tender ... | 5d. |
| No. 20a | Coach ... | 7d. |
| No. 20b | Guard's Van ... | 7d. |

Price of complete set **2/3**

## TANK GOODS TRAIN SET

**Dinky Toys No. 18**

| | | |
|---|---|---|
| No. 21a | Tank Locomotive ... | each 9d. |
| No. 21b | Wagons (three in set) ... | 4d. |

Price of complete set **1/9**

55

# DINKY TOYS

## GARDNER'S M.G. RECORD CAR

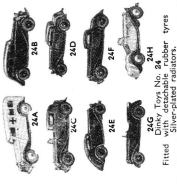

Dinky Toys No. 23p

A scale model of the car in which Major A. T. G. Gardner set up new world speed records for cars up to 1,100 c.c. on the Bitterfeld-Dessau Autobahn, Germany, in May, 1939. His speed for the flying kilometre was 203·7 m.p.h., and for the flying mile, 203·2 m.p.h.

After having the engine rebored, Major Gardner set up new records for cars up to 1,500 c.c. over the flying kilometre, mile and five kilometres, with speeds of 204·2 m.p.h., 203·8 m.p.h. and 200·6 m.p.h. respectively.    Price 10d. each

## MOTOR CARS

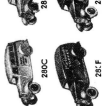

Dinky Toys No. 24
with detachable rubber tyres.
Fitted with detachable radiators.
Silver-plated radiators.

| | | | each |
|---|---|---|---|
| No. 24a | Ambulance | ... | 6d. |
| No. 24b | Limousine | ... | 6d. |
| No. 24c | Town Sedan. | ... | 6d. |
| No. 24d | Super Streamlined Saloon | | 6d. |
| No. 24e | Vogue Saloon | ... | 6d. |
| No. 24f | Sports Tourer (4-seater) | | 6d. |
| No. 24g | Sports Tourer (2-seater) | | 6d. |
| No. 24h | Sports Tourer (2-seater) | | 6d. |
| | Price of complete set 3/11 | | |

## RACING CARS

### RACING CAR

Dinky Toys No. 23
Assorted colours. Fitted with drivers and detachable rubber racing tyres.

| | | each |
|---|---|---|
| No. 23c | Mercedes-Benz Racing Car | 8d. |
| No. 23d | Auto-Union Racing Car | 8d. |
| No. 23e | "Speed of the Wind" Racing Car | 8d. |
| | Price of complete set 1/11 | |

### RACING CAR

Dinky Toys No. 23a
Assorted colours. Fitted with detachable rubber tyres.
Price 4d. each

### HOTCHKISS RACING CAR

Dinky Toys No. 23b
Assorted colours. Fitted with detachable rubber tyres.
Price 4d. each

### "THUNDERBOLT" SPEED CAR

Dinky Toys No. 23m
A fine scale model of the car in which Capt. G. E. T. Eyston set up a world land speed record of 357·50 m.p.h. at Bonneville, Utah, U.S.A.
Price 10d. each

### STREAMLINED RACING CAR

Dinky Toys No. 23s
Similar in type to the "Thunderbolt" speed car. Assorted colours.
Price 9d. each

## No. 22—No. 24

### MOTOR TRUCK

Dinky Toys No. 22c
Assorted colours. Fitted with detachable rubber tyres.
Price 6d. each

### TRACTOR

Dinky Toys No. 22e
Price 9d. each

### TANK

Dinky Toys No. 22f
Price 9d. each

### STREAMLINED SALOON

Dinky Toys No. 22h
Assorted colours. Fitted with detachable rubber tyres.
Price 4d. each

### STREAMLINED TOURER

Dinky Toys No. 22g
Assorted colours. Fitted with detachable rubber tyres.
Price 4d. each

---

## DELIVERY VANS

Dinky Toys No. 28/1
Fitted with detachable rubber tyres.

| | | | each | |
|---|---|---|---|---|
| No. 28a | Golden Shred Van | ... | | 6d. |
| No. 28b | Seccotine Van | ... | | 6d. |
| No. 28c | Manchester Guardian Van | | | 6d. |
| No. 28e | Firestone's Tyres Van | ... | | 6d. |
| No. 28f | Virol Van | ... | | 6d. |
| No. 28n | Atco Lawn Mowers Van | | | 6d. |
| | Price of complete set 3/- | | | |

Dinky Toys No. 28/2

| | | | each | |
|---|---|---|---|---|
| No. 28d | Oxo Van | ... | | 6d. |
| No. 28g | Kodak Cameras Van | | | 6d. |
| No. 28h | Dunlop Tyres Van | ... | | 6d. |
| No. 28k | Marsh & Baxter's Sausage Van. | | | 6d. |
| No. 28m | Wakefield's Castrol Oil Van | | | 6d. |
| No. 28p | Crawford's Biscuit Van | ... | | 6d. |
| | Price of complete set 3/- | | | |

Dinky Toys No. 28/3

| | | | each | |
|---|---|---|---|---|
| No. 28r | Swan Van | ... | | 6d. |
| No. 28s | Fry's Van | ... | | 6d. |
| No. 28t | Ovaltine Van | ... | | 6d. |
| No. 28w | Osram Van | ... | | 6d. |
| No. 28x | Hovis Van | ... | | 6d. |
| No. 28y | Exide and Drydex Van | | | 6d. |
| | Price of complete set 3/- | | | |

Dinky Toys No. 280

| | | | each | |
|---|---|---|---|---|
| No. 280a | Viyella Van | ... | | 6d. |
| No. 280b | Hartley's Van | ... | | 6d. |
| No. 280c | Shredded Wheat Van | | | 6d. |
| No. 280d | Bisto Van | ... | | 6d. |
| No. 280e | Yorkshire Evening Post Van | | | 6d. |
| No. 280f | Mackintosh's Van | ... | | 6d. |
| | Price of complete set 3/- | | | |

# DINKY TOYS

## FLAT TRUCK

Dinky Toys No. 25c
Fitted with detachable rubber tyres. Silver-plated radiator.
Price 9d. each

## G.W.R. RAIL CAR

Dinky Toys No. 26
Assorted colours ... Price 4d. each

## DIESEL RAIL CAR

Dinky Toys No. 26z
A realistic model of a modern Diesel-engined rail car ... Price 5d. each
(Made in the Meccano Factory in Paris).

## TRAM CAR

Dinky Toys No. 27
Assorted colours ... Price 3d. each

## WAGON

Dinky Toys No. 25a
Fitted with detachable rubber tyres. Silver-plated radiator.
Price 9d. each

## PEUGEOT CAR

Dinky Toys No. 24kz
Scale model of the new Peugeot saloon. (Made in the Meccano Factory in Paris).
Fitted with detachable rubber tyres.
Price 6d. each

## COMMERCIAL MOTOR VEHICLES

Dinky Toys No. 25
Fitted with detachable rubber tyres.
Silver-plated radiators.

| | | | each |
|---|---|---|---|
| No. 25b | Covered Van | ... | 9d. |
| No. 25d | Petrol Tank W-gon | | 9d. |
| No. 25e | Tipping Wagon | ... | 9d. |
| No. 25f | Market Gardener's Van | | 6d. |
| No. 25g | Trailer | ... | 6d. |
| No. 25h | Fire-Engine | ... | 9d. |
| | Price of complete set 4/3 | | |

## SIX-WHEELED WAGON

Dinky Toys No. 25s
An interesting model of a modern three-ton wagon. In assorted colours. Fitted with detachable rubber tyres.
Price 10d. each

# DINKY TOYS

## No. 29—No. 35

### MOTOR BUS
Dinky Toys No. 29a
Assorted colours.
Price **4d.** each

### STREAMLINED BUS
Dinky Toys No. 29b
Fitted with rubber tyres.
Price **6d.** each

Dinky Toys No. 29c
Assorted colours. Fitted with detachable rubber tyres.
Price **1/-** each

### AUTOBUS
Dinky Toys No. 29dz
A striking model of a modern French single-decker motor bus. (Made in the Meccano Factory in Paris).
Price **10d.** each

### MOTOR VEHICLES

30C   30G

30B   30E

30A   30D

Dinky Toys No. 30
Fitted with detachable rubber tyres. Silver-plated radiators.

| | | |
|---|---|---|
| No. 30a Chrysler "Airflow" Saloon | each | **6d.** |
| No. 30b Rolls-Royce | ... | **9d.** |
| No. 30c Daimler | ... | **9d.** |
| No. 30d Vauxhall | ... | **9d.** |
| No. 30e Breakdown Car | ... | **9d.** |
| No. 30f Caravan Trailer | ... | **6d.** |

Price of complete set **3/11**

## MECHANICAL HORSE AND FOUR ASSORTED TRAILERS

35F

35C   33B

33E

33A

Dinky Toys No. 33
Fitted with detachable rubber tyres.

| | | |
|---|---|---|
| No. 33a Mechanical Horse | each | **5d.** |
| No. 33b Flat Truck | ... | **6d.** |
| No. 33c Open Wagon | ... | **6d.** |
| No. 33e Dust Wagon | ... | **7d.** |
| No. 33f Petrol Tank (Esso or Wakefield Castrol) | ... | **7d.** |

Price of complete set **2/6**

### BOX VAN
Dinky Toys No. 33d
Fitted with detachable rubber tyres.
Price **7d.** each

35D

### RAILWAY MECHANICAL HORSE AND TRAILER VAN

Dinky Toys No. 33r
Fitted with detachable rubber tyres.
No. 33Ra Railway Mechanical Horse ... each **7d.**
No. 33Rd Trailer Van ... **9d.**
Price complete, L.M.S., L.N.E.R., G.W.R. or S.R." ... **1/4**

## ROYAL AIR MAIL SERVICE CAR
Dinky Toys No. 34a
In correct colours. Fitted with detachable rubber tyres.
Price **6d.** each

### SMALL CARS

35B

35C

35A

Dinky Toys No. 35   Fitted with solid rubber wheels.
No. 35a Saloon Car, each **3d.** No. 35o Racer, each **3d.**
No. 35c "M.G." Sports Car ... **3d.**
Price of complete set **9d.**

### AUSTIN SEVEN CAR
Dinky Toys No. 35d
This model is the same as No. 152c (included in the Royal Tank Corps Light Tank Set), except that it is finished in a range of different colours.
Price **4d.** each

### FIAT TWO-SEATER SALOON
Dinky Toys No. 35az
Scale model of a popular baby car. (Made in the Meccano Factory in Paris). Fitted with detachable rubber tyres.
Price **4d.** each

---

# DINKY TOYS

### MOTOR CARS
(WITH DRIVERS, PASSENGERS, FOOTMEN)

36C   36F

35B   36E

35A   36D

Dinky Toys No. 36. Fitted with detachable rubber tyres. Silver-plated true-to-type radiators.

| | | |
|---|---|---|
| No. 36a Armstrong Siddeley (Limousine) with driver and footman | each | **10d.** |
| No. 36b Bentley (Two-seater Sports Coupé) with driver and passenger | ... | **10d.** |
| No. 36c Humber (Vogue Saloon) with driver and footman | ... | **10d.** |
| No. 36d Rover (Streamlined Saloon) with driver and passenger | ... | **10d.** |
| No. 36e British Salmson (Two-seater Sports) with driver | ... | **10d.** |
| No. 36f British Salmson (Four-seater Sports) with driver | ... | **10d.** |

Price of complete set **5/-**

### TAXI WITH DRIVER

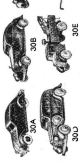

Dinky Toys No. 36g
Fitted with detachable rubber tyres.
Price **10d.** each

### MOTOR CYCLISTS

#### CIVILIAN
Dinky Toys No. 37a
Finished in attractive colours. Fitted with solid rubber wheels.
Price **6d.** each

#### POLICE
Dinky Toys No. 37b
Finished in correct colours. Fitted with solid rubber wheels.
Price **6d.** each

#### ROYAL CORPS OF SIGNALS DESPATCH RIDER
Dinky Toys No. 37c
Similar to Dinky Toys No. 37b. Finished in correct colours. Fitted with solid rubber wheels.
Price **6d.** each

### POLICE BOX, MOTOR CYCLE PATROL AND POLICEMEN

Dinky Toys No. 42
Each item is finished in correct colours.

| | | |
|---|---|---|
| No. 42a Police Box | each | **6d.** |
| No. 42b Motor Cycle Patrol | ... | **10d.** |
| No. 42c Point Duty Policeman (in White Coat) | ... | **3d.** |
| No. 42d Point Duty Policeman | ... | **4d.** |

Price of complete set **1/11**

---

## No. 36—No. 43

### SALOON CARS

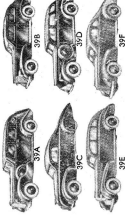

39B   39D   39F

39A   39C   39E

Dinky Toys No. 39
Fitted with detachable rubber tyres.

| | | |
|---|---|---|
| No. 39a Packard "Super 8" Touring Sedan Car | each | **10d.** |
| No. 39b Oldsmobile "Six" Sedan Car | ,, | **10d.** |
| No. 39c Lincoln "Zephyr" Coupé | ,, | **10d.** |
| No. 39d Buick "Viceroy" Saloon Car | ,, | **10d.** |
| No. 39e Chrysler "Royal" Sedan | ,, | **10d.** |
| No. 39f Studebaker "State Commander" Coupé | ,, | **10d.** |

Price of complete set **5/-**

### R.A.C. BOX, MOTOR CYCLE PATROL AND GUIDES

Dinky Toys No. 43

This set is representative of the familiar personnel and road box of the R.A.C. Each item is finished in correct colours.

| | | |
|---|---|---|
| No. 43a R.A.C. Box | each | **6d.** |
| No. 43b R.A.C. Motor Cycle Patrol | ,, | **9d.** |
| No. 43c R.A.C. Guide directing traffic | ,, | **3d.** |
| No. 43d R.A.C. Guide at the salute | ,, | **3d.** |

Price of complete set **1/9**

# DINKY TOYS

## No. 44—No. 49

### PAVEMENT SET

### ROBOT TRAFFIC SIGNAL

Dinky Toys No. 47a (Four face)
Price **2d.** each
No. **47b** (Three face) Price **2d.** each
No. **47c** (Two face) Price **2d.** each

### BEACON

Dinky Toys No. **47d**
Realistic model of the Belisha Safety Beacon. Right-angle or back-to-back. Price **1d.** each

### PETROL STATION

FILLING AND SERVICE STATION

Dinky Toys No. 48
Accurate reproduction of a filling station.
Price **1/3** each

### PETROL PUMPS

Dinky Toys No. 49
Scale models fitted with rubber feed pipes. Finished in correct colours.

No. 49a Bowser Pump each **3d.**   No. 49c Theo Pump each **3d.**
No. 49b Wayne Pump each **3d.**   No. 49d Shell Pump each **3d.**
No. 49e Oil Bin (Pratts)   each **3d.**
**Price of complete set 1/3**

Dinky Toys No. 46
The contents of this set are four 3in., six 6in., and four 12in. strips of pavement and four quarter discs for corners
Price of complete set **6d.**

### ROAD SIGNS

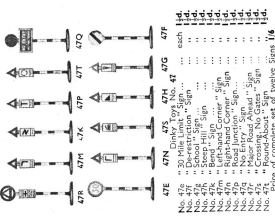

Dinky Toys No. 47

| | | |
|---|---|---|
| No. 47e | "30 Mile Limit" Sign | each **1d.** |
| No. 47f | "De-restriction" Sign | **2d.** |
| No. 47g | "School" Sign | **2d.** |
| No. 47h | "Steep Hill" Sign | **2d.** |
| No. 47k | "Bend" Sign | **2d.** |
| No. 47m | "Left-hand Corner" Sign | **2d.** |
| No. 47n | "Right-hand Corner" Sign | **2d.** |
| No. 47p | "Road Junction" Sign | **2d.** |
| No. 47q | "No Entry" Sign | **2d.** |
| No. 47r | "Major Road Ahead" Sign | **2d.** |
| No. 47s | "Crossing, No Gates" Sign | **2d.** |
| No. 47t | "Round-About" Sign | **2d.** |

Price of complete set of twelve Signs **1/6**

## No. 44—No. 49

### A.A. BOX, MOTOR CYCLE PATROL AND GUIDES

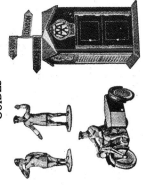

Dinky Toys No. 44
This set is representative of the familiar personnel and road box of the A.A. Each item is finished in correct colours.

| | | |
|---|---|---|
| No. 44a | A.A. Box | each **8d.** |
| No. 44b | A.A. Motor Cycle Patrol | **9d.** |
| No. 44c | A.A. Guide directing traffic | **3d.** |
| No. 44d | A.A. Guide at the salute | **3d.** |

Price of complete set **1/11**

### GARAGE

Dinky Toys No. 45
Fitted with opening double doors. Will accommodate **any** two Dinky Toys Motor Cars.

Price **1/3** each

---

# DINKY TOYS

## No. 50—No. 53

### CUNARD WHITE STAR LINER "QUEEN MARY"

Dinky Toys No. **52a** ... Price **1/-** each
Fitted with rollers and in presentation box
Dinky Toys No. **52m** ... Price **9d.** each
Without rollers and not packed in presentation box

### "NORMANDIE"

Dinky Toys No. **52c** ...
A scale model of the French Line's giant steamship. (Made in the Meccano Factory in Paris) Price **1/6** each

### CUNARD WHITE STAR LINER "QUEEN ELIZABETH"

Dinky Toys No. **52e**
The Cunard White Star Liner "Queen Elizabeth," at present building at the Clydebank yard of John Brown and Co., Ltd., was launched on 27th September, 1938, by H.M. the Queen. The vessel will be completed and ready for service sometime in 1940, and her length of 1,031 ft. and 85,000 tons gross weight will make her easily the world's largest liner. Price **1/-** each

### BATTLESHIP "DUNKERQUE"

Dinky Toys No. **53az**
Scale model of the French 26,500 ton Battleship "Dunkerque," which has an overall length of 702 ft. 9 in., and a main armament of eight 13 in. guns. (Made in the Meccano Factory in Paris) ... Price **9d.** each

# DINKY TOYS

### SHIPS OF THE BRITISH NAVY

Dinky Toys No. 50

| | | |
|---|---|---|
| No. 50a | Battle Cruiser "Hood" | each **6d.** |
| No. 50b | Battleships, "Nelson" Class (2) | **5d.** |
| No. 50c | Cruiser "Effingham" | **4d.** |
| No. 50d | Cruiser "York" | **4d.** |
| No. 50e | Cruiser "Delhi" | **3d.** |
| No. 50f | Destroyers, "Broke" Class (3) | each **1d.** |
| No. 50g | Submarine, "K" Class | **1d.** |
| No. 50g | Destroyers, "Amazon" Class (3) | **1d.** |
| No. 50k | Submarine, "X" Class | **1d.** |

Price of complete set **2/9**

### FAMOUS LINERS

Dinky Toys No. 51

| | | |
|---|---|---|
| No. 51b | "Europa" | each **6d.** |
| No. 51c | "Rex" | **6d.** |
| No. 51d | "Empress of Britain" | **6d.** |
| No. 51e | "Strathaird" | each **6d.** |
| No. 51f | "Queen of Bermuda" | **6d.** |
| No. 51g | "Britannic" | **6d.** |

Price of complete set **2/11**

# DINKY TOYS

## No. 60a—No. 60z

### BRITISH AEROPLANES

| | | each | 6d. |
| No. 60a | Imperial Airways Liner | ... | 6d. |
| No. 60b | D.H. "Leopard Moth" | ... | 5d. |
| No. 60c | Percival "Gull" | ... | 5d. |
| No. 60d | Low Wing Monoplane | ... | 5d. |
| No. 60e | General "Monospar" | ... | 5d. |
| No. 60 | Cierva "Autogiro" | ... | 5d. |
| | Price of complete set 2/6 | | |

60A 60C 60F 60D 60B 60E

### D.H. "COMET" AEROPLANE

Dinky Toys No. 60g
Price **5d.** each

### PERCIVAL "GULL" MONOPLANE

Dinky Toys No. 60k
Similar to No. 60c, but finished in aluminium and blue and lettered G-ADZO. Scale model of aeroplane used by Mr. H. L. Brook in his record-breaking South African flight.
Price **5d.** each

### FOUR-ENGINED FLYING BOAT

Dinky Toys No. 60m
Similar in type to the "Singapore" Flying Boat (No. 60h, page 63). Assorted colours.
Price **10d.** each

### EMPIRE FLYING BOAT

Dinky Toys No. 60r
Scale models of the famous Imperial Airways Liners. Twelve models available, named Caledonia, Cambria, Canopus, Corsair, Cordelia, Centurion, Calpurnia, Ceres, Clio, Calypso, Corinna and Cheviot.
Price **1/-** each

### DOUGLAS DC-3 AIR LINER

Dinky Toys No. 60t
Scale model of the Douglas DC-3 air liner, which is in regular service on American and European routes.
Price **9d.** each

### ARMSTRONG WHITWORTH "WHITLEY" BOMBER

Dinky Toys No. 60v
Scale model of the "Whitley" long-range heavy bomber adopted by the R.A.F.
Price **9d.** each

### MEDIUM BOMBER (Camouflaged)

Dinky Toys No. 60s
Similar to Fairey "Battle" Bomber (No. 60n, page 63), but with Air Ministry camouflage.
Price **4½d.** each

### FLYING BOAT "CLIPPER III"

Dinky Toys No. 60w
Scale model of the Pan American Airways flying boat that took part in the trans-atlantic experimental flights in 1937.
Price **1/-** each

### FRENCH AEROPLANES

The set consists of six models of famous French aeroplanes—"Arc-en-Ciel," Potez 58, Hanriot H180T, Breguet-Corsaire low wing monoplane, Dewoitine 500 and Cierva "Autogiro." (Made in the Meccano Factory in Paris).
Price of complete set **3/-**

### MONOPLANE "ARC-EN-CIEL"

Dinky Toys No. 60az
A scale model of the famous French triple-engined monoplane "Arc-en-Ciel." (Made in the Meccano Factory in Paris).
Price **9d.** each

### ATLANTIC FLYING BOAT

Dinky Toys No. 60x
Similar in type to Empire Flying Boat (No. 60r). Assorted colours, names and registrations.
Price **1/-** each

### REFUELLING TENDER

Dinky Toys No. 60y
Realistic model of Thompson Bros. Tender used for refuelling aeroplanes at aerodromes.
Price **8d.** each

62

---

# DINKY TOYS

## No. 61—No. 62

### R.A.F. AEROPLANES

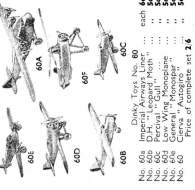

60N 60H 60P

Dinky Toys No. 61
"Singapore" Flying Boat ... ... each **10d.**
Fairey "Battle" Bomber (2) ... ... " **4d.**
Gloster "Gladiator" Biplane (2) ... " **6d.**
Price of complete set **2/6**

### FRENCH AEROPLANES

Dinky Toys No. 61z
This set consists of six models of French aeroplanes—Dewoitine 338, Dewoitine 500d, Potez 58, Potez 56, Hanriot H180M and Farman F360. (Made in the Meccano Factory in Paris).
Price **3/-**

### DEWOITINE 338

Dinky Toys No. 61az
This type of French triple-engined air liner is used by Air France, the well-known air transport company. (Made in the Meccano Factory in Paris).
Price **9d.** each

### D.H. "FLAMINGO" LINER

Dinky Toys No. 62f
Scale model of the latest British transport monoplane. It has a top speed of 245 m.p.h. and can carry 12 to 20 passengers. Price **6d.** each

### JUNKERS Ju 90 AIR LINER

Dinky Toys No. 62n
Scale model of the latest type of German air liner, having a top speed of 256 m.p.h.
Price **11d.** each

### BOEING "FLYING FORTRESS" MONOPLANE

Dinky Toys No. 62g
Scale model of a famous American long-range bomber.
Price **1/-** each

### AIRSPEED "ENVOY" MONOPLANE

Dinky Toys No. 62m
Scale model of the Airspeed "Envoy" twin-engined commercial monoplane. Assorted colours. Price **6d.** each

### THE KING'S AEROPLANE

Dinky Toys No. 62k
Scale model of the Airspeed "Envoy" supplied to the Air Council for the King's Flight.
Price **8d.** each

### HAWKER "HURRICANE" SINGLE-SEATER FIGHTER (Camouflaged)

Dinky Toys No. 62h
Scale model of the Hawker "Hurricane" single-seater Fighter extensively used by the R.A.F. Camouflaged Price **6d.** each

### ARMSTRONG WHITWORTH "ENSIGN" AIR LINER

Dinky Toys No. 62p
Scale model of the largest British air liner. Six models available named : "Ensign," "Elsinore," "Explorer," "Echo," "Ettrick," and "Elysian."
Price **1/-** each

### DE HAVILLAND "ALBATROSS" MAIL LINER

Dinky Toys No. 62r
Scale model of one of the "Albatross" mail liners built for the Air Ministry for experimental flights.
Price **10d.** each

63

---

272

**No. 62—No. 65**

### HAWKER "HURRICANE" SINGLE-SEATER FIGHTER (Aluminium Finish)

Dinky Toys No. **62s**
Similar to Dinky Toys No. 62h (page 63), but with Aluminium finish ... ... ... Price **6d.** each

### ARMSTRONG WHITWORTH "WHITLEY" BOMBER (Camouflaged)

Dinky Toys No. **62t**
Similar to Dinky Toys No. 60v (page 62), but with Air Ministry camouflage ... ... ... Price **11d.** each

### IMPERIAL AIRWAYS "FROBISHER" CLASS LINER

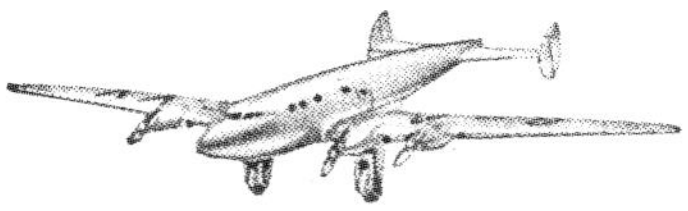

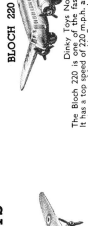

Dinky Toys No. **62w**
Scale model of the Imperial Airways "Frobisher" class liner. Three models available named: "Frobisher," "Falcon" and "Fortuna" ... ... Price **10d.** each

### BRITISH 40-SEATER AIR LINER

Dinky Toys No. **62x**
Similar in type to the Armstrong Whitworth "Ensign" Air Liner No. 62p (page 63). Assorted colours. Price **1/-** each

### GIANT HIGH-SPEED MONOPLANE

Dinky Toys No. **62y**
Similar in type to Junkers Ju 90 air liner No. 62n (page 63). Assorted colours. Price **11d.** each

### MAYO COMPOSITE AIRCRAFT

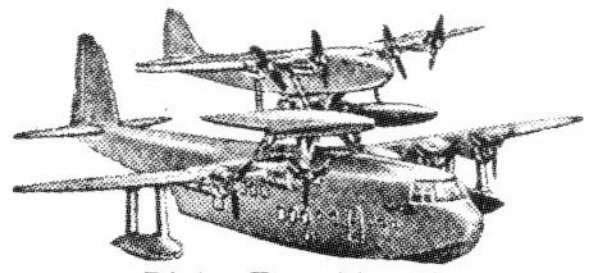

Dinky Toys No. **63**
Scale model of the Mayo Composite Aircraft. Price **2/-** each
The components of the above can be purchased separately.
No. 63a Flying Boat "Maia" ... Price **1/3** each
No. 63b Seaplane "Mercury" ... Price **9d.** each

# DINKY TOYS

### AMIOT 370

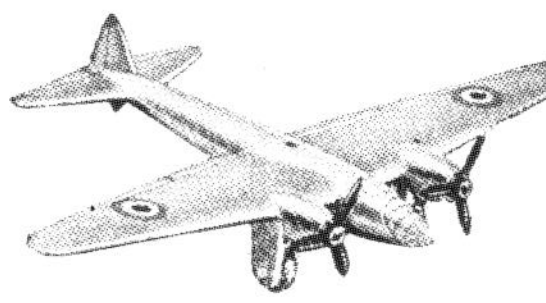

Dinky Toys No. **64az**
This high wing monoplane has been developed from the Amiot 340 long-range bomber. It is fitted with two 860 h.p. Hispano-Suiza liquid-cooled engines and is capable of the high speed of 310.5 m.p.h. When flying at 248.4 m.p.h., it has a maximum range of 4,350 miles. (Made in the Meccano Factory in Paris). Price **7d.** each

### PRESENTATION AEROPLANE SET

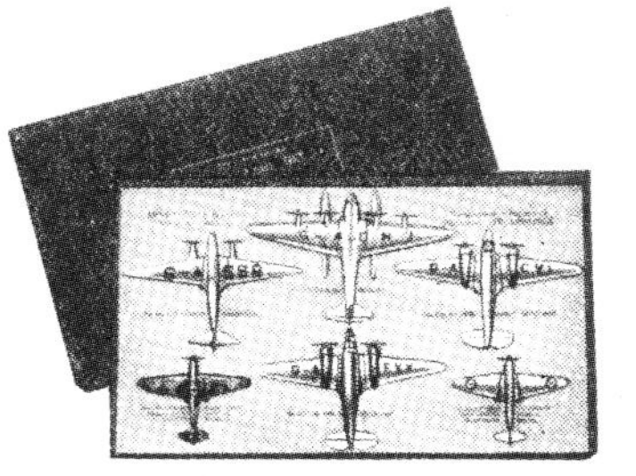

Dinky Toys No. **64**
This Aeroplane Set, in presentation box, consists of one each of the following Dinky Toys:—

No. 60g D.H. "Comet" Aeroplane,
No. 62h Hawker "Hurricane" Single-Seater Fighter (Camouflaged),
No. 62k The King's Aeroplane—Airspeed "Envoy,"
No. 62m Airspeed "Envoy" Monoplane,
No. 62s Hawker "Hurricane" Single-Seater Fighter (Aluminium Finish),
No. 63b Seaplane "Mercury."

Price **3/3**

### BLOCH 220

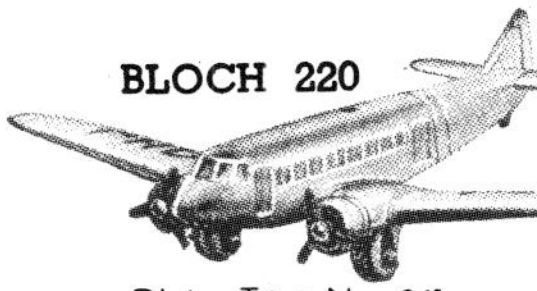

Dinky Toys No. **64bz**
The Bloch 220 is one of the fastest modern air liners. It has a top speed of 220 m.p.h. and carries 16 passengers and a crew of four. Air France have many of these twin-engined low wing monoplanes in regular service. (Made in the Meccano Factory in Paris). Price **8d.** each

### PRESENTATION AEROPLANE SET

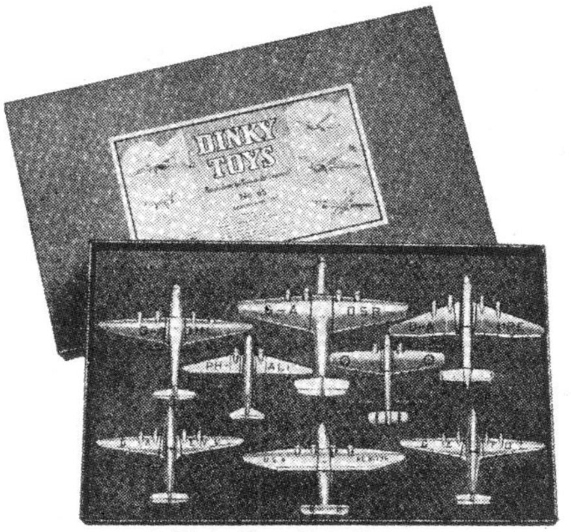

Dinky Toys No. **65**
This Aeroplane Set, in presentation box, consists of the following Dinky Toys:—

No. 60r Empire Flying Boat,
No. 60t Douglas DC-3 Air Liner,
No. 60v Armstrong Whitworth "Whitley" Bomber,
No. 60w "Clipper III" Flying Boat,
No. 62n Junkers Ju 90 Air Liner,
No. 62p Armstrong Whitworth "Ensign" Air Liner,
No. 62r De Havilland "Albatross" Air Liner,
No. 62w Imperial Airways "Frobisher" Class Air Liner,

Price **7/-**



# DINKY TOYS

**No. 101—No. 104**

### DINING ROOM FURNITURE

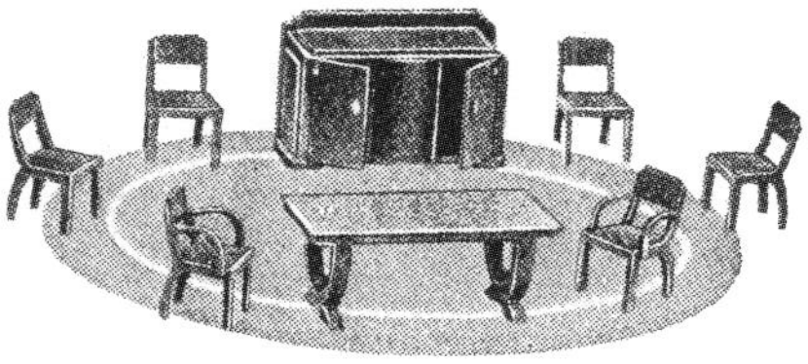

Dinky Toys No. **101** Price of complete set **1/9**

No. 101a Table ... ... ... ... each **4d.**
No. 101b Sideboard (Opening doors) ... ,, **7d.**
No. 101c Carver Chairs (two in set) ... ,, **2½d.**
No. 101d Chairs (four in set) ... ... ,, **1½d.**

Supplied in walnut brown finish only.

### BEDROOM FURNITURE

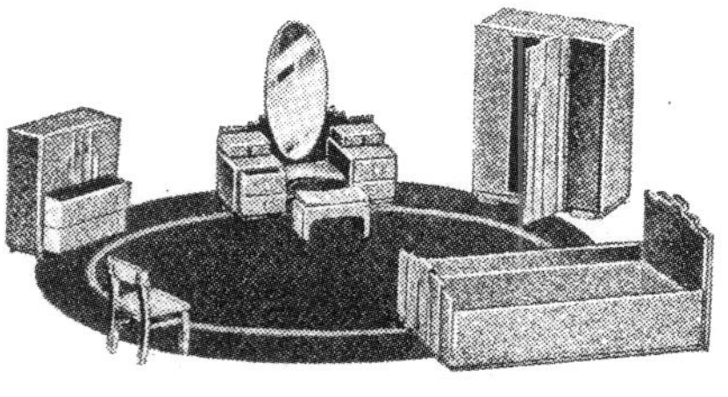

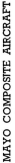

Dinky Toys No. **102** Price of complete set **2/3**

No. 102a Bed ... ... ... ... ... each **5d.**
No. 102b Wardrobe (Opening door) ... ,, **7d.**
No. 102c Dressing Table (Opening drawers) ,, **8d.**
No. 102d Dressing Chest (Opening drawer) ,, **5d.**
No. 102e Dressing Table Stool ... ... ,, **1½d.**
No. 102f Chair ... ... ... ... ,, **1½d.**

Supplied in colour or in walnut brown finish.

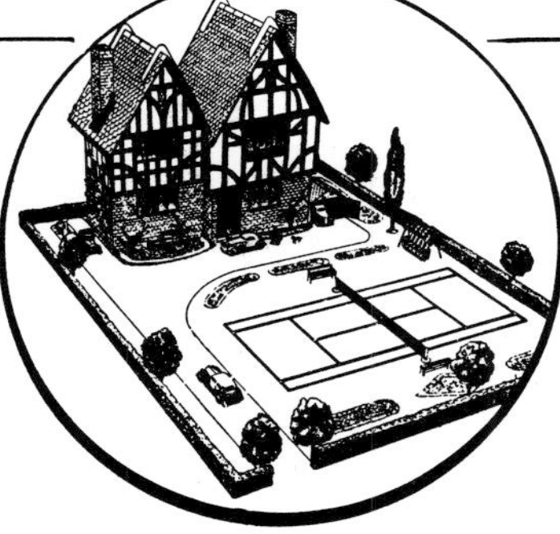

## "DOLLY VARDEN" DOLL'S HOUSE

### FOR DINKY TOYS FURNITURE

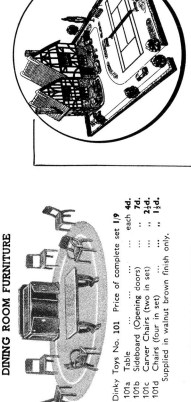

This beautifully-designed Doll's House provides a perfect setting for the Dinky Toys Doll's House Furniture illustrated and described on this page.

The exterior of the house is designed to represent a half-timbered dwelling, while the interior decorations, which are printed in nine colours, are in an attractive modern style.

Reinforced leather board is the material of which the house is constructed, and although it is collapsible it is as strong as a wood structure when set up. The container opens out to show a lovely garden, with tennis lawn, carriage drive and rockery.

Price of "Dolly Varden" Doll's House **4/11**

***The Couch Hammock, Tennis Net, Garden Seats, Dinky Toys Garage, Motor Cars and Figures, and the Hornby Trees and Hedging featured in the illustration are not included with the Doll's House and Garden.***

### KITCHEN FURNITURE

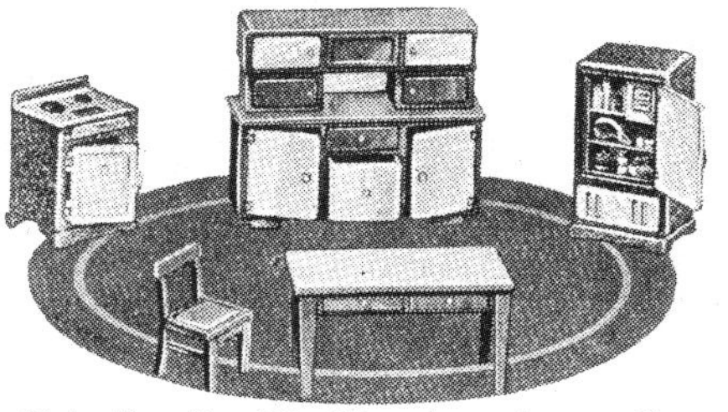

Dinky Toys No. **103** Price of complete set **2/-**

No. 103a Refrigerator (Opening door) ... each **6½d.**
No. 103b Kitchen Cabinet (Opening doors and drawer) ... ... ... ,, **8d.**
No. 103c Electric Cooker (Opening door) ,, **5d.**
No. 103d Table ... ... ... ... ,, **3½d.**
No. 103e Chair ... ... ... ... ,, **1½d.**

Supplied in two colour schemes—light blue and white, and light green and cream.

### BATHROOM FURNITURE

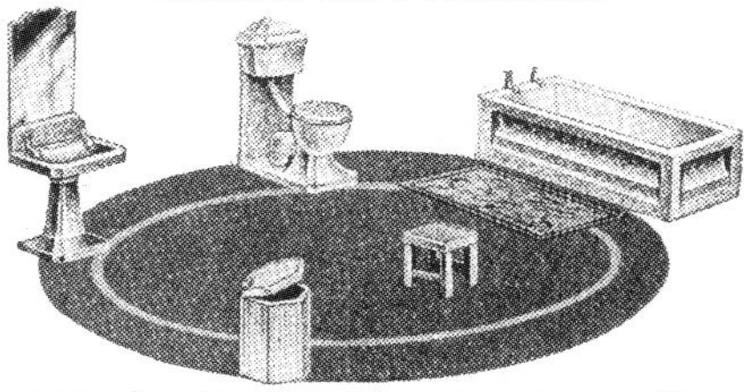

Dinky Toys No. **104** Price of complete set **1/6**

No. 104a Bath ... ... ... ... ... each **4½d.**
No. 104b Bath Mat ... ... ... ... ,, **½d.**
No. 104c Pedestal Hand Basin ... ... ,, **4½d.**
No. 104d Stool ... ... ... ... ,, **1½d.**
No. 104e Linen Basket (Hinged lid) ... ,, **3d.**
No. 104f Toilet (Hinged lid) ... ... ,, **4½d.**

Supplied in two colour schemes—pink and white, and light green and white.

# DINKY TOYS

Bring your collection up to date by including these fine models of Britain's Mechanised Army. All are made to a scale of .203in. to 1ft., and are finished in correct Service colours. Further interesting models in this Mechanised Army series will be introduced from time to time.

## ROYAL TANK CORPS PERSONNEL

Dinky Toys No. 150

| | | |
|---|---|---|
| No. 150a | Officer | each **2d.** |
| No. 150b | Private, in sitting position (two in set) | .. **1½d.** |
| No. 150c | Private, in standing position (two in set) | .. **1½d.** |
| No. 150e | N.C.O. | .. **1½d.** |
| | Price of complete set **10d.** | |

## ROYAL TANK CORPS LIGHT TANK SET

Dinky Toys No. 152

| | | |
|---|---|---|
| No. 152a | Light Tank | each **1/-** |
| No. 152b | Reconnaissance Car | .. **1/-** |
| No. 152c | Austin Seven Car | .. **4d.** |
| No. 150d | Driver | .. **1½d.** |
| | Price of complete set **2/6** | |

## ROYAL ARTILLERY PERSONNEL

Dinky Toys No. 151

| | | |
|---|---|---|
| No. 151a | Medium Tank (12 tons, 90 h.p.) | each **1/6** |
| No. 151b | Transport Wagon | .. **1/-** |
| No. 151c | Cooker Trailer, with jack stand | .. **6d.** |
| No. 151d | Water Tank Trailer | .. **4d.** |
| No. 150d | Driver | .. **1½d.** |
| | Price of complete set **3/6** | |

## ROYAL TANK CORPS MEDIUM TANK SET

## MOBILE ANTI-AIRCRAFT UNIT

Dinky Toys No. 160

For use with Dinky Toys No.161, Mobile Anti-Aircraft Unit and No. 162, 18-Pounder Quick-Firing Field Gun Unit.

| | | |
|---|---|---|
| No. 160a | N.C.O. | each **2d.** |
| No. 160b | Gunner, sitting (two in set) | .. **1½d.** |
| No. 160c | Gunlayer | .. **1½d.** |
| No. 160d | Gunner, standing (two in set) | .. **1½d.** |
| | Price of complete set **10d.** | |

Dinky Toys No. 161

Comprises scale model of a quick-firing Anti-Aircraft Gun mounted on a mobile platform, and a Searchlight mounted on a lorry. Both Gun and Searchlight have elevating and swivelling movements.

| | | |
|---|---|---|
| No. 161a | Searchlight on Lorry | each **1/6** |
| No. 161b | Anti-Aircraft Gun on Carriage | .. **1/6** |
| | Price of complete set **3/-** | |

## 18-POUNDER QUICK-FIRING FIELD GUN UNIT

Dinky Toys No. 162

Comprises scale model 18-pounder quick-firing Field Gun, Trailer, and "Light Dragon" Motor Tractor.

| | | |
|---|---|---|
| 162a | "Light Dragon" Tractor | each **1/3** |
| 162b | Trailer | .. **5d.** |
| 162c | Gun | .. **5d.** |
| | Price of complete set **2/-** | |

---

The first known post-war catalogue is a Canadian one dated 1945, a single sheet which promised more to come. From 1952, when sufficient of the product was available on the home market they were issued usually yearly, sometimes with a second or even a third edition. A variety of numbering systems were used over the years. The pre-war referencing system of two numbers followed by a separate group of three or four numbers and a final group of two was continued for a time. This code can be unravelled by looking at the centre 3 or 4 digits, e.g. the Canadian catalogue has the code 16/1145/20 and is therefore dated November 1945. The group issued between 1952 and 1964 were numbered '1st Edition' to '12th Edition' but unfortunately the early ones do not have this printed on them but are merely dated, though even this is missing on some. 1965 saw the introduction of a new system starting again at 1 though again the early ones do not have the number printed on them. The run ended in 1979 with no. 14.

As well as these, which were for the U.K. market and include French Dinkies sold in the U.K., there were also catalogues for overseas, the United States, Canada, Australia, Europe, Eire and even the Channel Islands. In addition, at certain periods export catalogues containing English and French Dinkies mixed up together were produced printed in the relevant language and currency.

Post-war, size, design and layout varied greatly. Mostly, they were in colour and the illustrations are frequently not to be trusted because they are usually line drawings washed with colour or very heavily retouched photographs. The colour though often that of the model does not reproduce the actual shade and the registration of colours leaves much to be desired. Most were entirely devoted to Dinky Toys but in later ones, 'Meccano' and 'Mogul' were included. From time to time, a general Meccano Product catalogue was produced in which Dinky Toys were featured and small flysheets were also published periodically.

## Dinky Toys—January 1941

The following list of Dinky Toys is taken from a non-illustrated fold-out leaflet printed in brown and entitled 'MECCANO PRODUCTS January 1941 and until further notice', ref. no. 16/141/25 (U.K.). All items listed were available in reasonable quantities.

# DINKY TOYS—JANUARY 1941

| Series No. | Cat. No. | Model |
|---|---|---|
| 1 | | Station Staff |
| 2 | | Farmyard Animals |
| 3 | | Passengers |
| 4 | | Engineering Staff |
| 5 | | Train and Hotel Staff |
| 6 | | Shepherd Set |
| 12 | | Postal Set |
| | 12a | Pillar Box, G.P.O. |
| | 12b | Pillar Box, Air Mail |
| | 12c | Telephone Call Box |
| | 12d | Telegraph Messenger |
| | 12e | Postman |
| 13 | | Hall's Distemper Advertisement |
| 15 | | Signals |
| | 15a | Signal, Single Arm |
| | 15b | Signal, Double Arm |
| | 15c | Signal, Junction |
| 18 | | Goods Train Set |
| 19 | | Mixed Tank Goods Train Set |
| | 22c | Motor Truck |
| | 22e | Tractor |
| | 22g | Streamlined Tourer |
| | 22h | Streamlined Saloon |
| | 22s | Searchlight Lorry (Small) |
| 23 | | Racing Cars |
| | 23a | Racing Car |
| | 23b | Hotchkiss Racing Car |
| | 23c | Mercedes-Benz Racing Car |
| | 23d | Auto-Union Racing Car |
| | 23e | 'Speed of the Wind' Racing Car |
| | 23m | 'Thunderbolt' Speed Car |
| | 23p | Gardner's M.G. Record Car |
| | 23s | Streamlined Racing Car |
| | 24a | Ambulance |
| | 24c | Town Sedan |
| | 24g | Sports Tourer (4-seater) |
| | 24h | Sports Tourer (2-seater) |
| 25 | | Commercial Motor Vehicles |
| | 25a | Wagon |
| | 25b | Covered Van |
| | 25c | Flat Truck |
| | 25d | Petrol Tank Wagon |
| | 25e | Tipping Wagon |
| | 25f | Market Gardener's Van |
| | 25g | Trailer |
| | 25h | Streamlined Fire Engine |
| | 25s | Six-Wheeled Wagon |
| | 28/1 | Delivery Vans |
| | 28/2 | Delivery Vans |
| | 28/3 | Delivery Vans |
| | 29b | Streamlined Motor Bus |
| | 29c | Double Decker Motor Bus |
| 30 | | Motor Vehicles |
| | 30a | Chrysler 'Airflow' Saloon |
| | 30b | Rolls-Royce |
| | 30c | Daimler |
| | 30d | Vauxhall |
| | 30e | Breakdown Car |
| | 30f | Ambulance |
| | 30g | Caravan Trailer |
| 33 | | Mechanical Horse and four Assorted Trailers |
| | 33a | Mechanical Horse |
| | 33b | Flat Truck |
| | 33c | Open Wagon |
| | 33d | Box Van |
| | 33e | Dust Wagon |
| | 33f | Petrol Tank |
| 33R | | Railway Mechanical Horse and Trailer Van |
| | 33Ra | Railway Mechanical Horse |
| | 33Rd | Trailer Van |
| | 34a | Royal Air Mail Service Car |
| | 34b | Royal Mail Van |
| 35 | | Small Cars |
| | 35a | Saloon Car |
| | 35b | Racer |
| | 35c | M.G. Sports Car |
| | 35d | Austin Seven Car |
| 36 | | Motor Cars |
| | 36a | Armstrong Siddeley |
| | 36b | Bentley |
| | 36c | Humber |
| | 36d | Rover |
| | 36e | British Salmson (2-seater) |
| | 36f | British Salmson (4-seater) |
| | 36g | Taxi, with Driver |
| | 37a | Motor Cyclist (civilian) |
| | 37b | Motor Cyclist (police) |
| | 37c | Royal Corps of Signals Dispatch Rider |
| | 38a | Frazer-Nash B.M.W. Sports Car |
| | 38b | Sunbeam-Talbot Sports Car |
| | 38d | Alvis Sports Tourer |
| 39 | | U.S.A. Saloon Cars |
| | 39a | Packard 'Super 8' Tourer |
| | 39b | Oldsmobile Sedan |
| | 39c | Lincoln 'Zephyr' Coupé |
| | 39d | Buick 'Viceroy' Saloon |
| | 39e | Chrysler 'Royal' Sedan |
| | 39f | Studebaker 'State Commander' Coupé |
| 42 | | Police Box, Motor Cycle Patrol and Policeman |
| | 42a | Police Box |
| | 42b | Motor Cycle Patrol |
| | 42c | Point Duty Policeman (in white coat) |
| | 42d | Point Duty Policeman |
| 43 | | R.A.C. Box, Motor Cycle Patrol and Guides |
| | 43a | R.A.C. Box |
| | 43b | R.A.C. Motor Cycle Patrol |
| | 43c | R.A.C. Guide directing traffic |
| | 43d | R.A.C. Guide at the Salute |
| 44 | | A.A. Box, Motor Cycle Patrol and Guides |
| | 44a | A.A. Box |
| | 44b | A.A. Motor Cycle Patrol |
| | 44c | A.A. Guide directing traffic |
| | 44d | A.A. Guide at the Salute |
| 45 | | Garage |
| 46 | | Pavement Set |
| 47 | | Road Signs |
| | 47a | Robot Traffic Signal (4 face) |
| | 47b | Robot Traffic Signal (3 face) |
| | 47c | Robot Traffic Signal (2 face) right angle or back to back |
| | 47d | Beacon |
| | 47e | '30 Mile Limit' Sign |
| | 47f | 'De-restriction' Sign |
| | 47g | 'School' Sign |

*Fig. 446. 1953 Catalogue*

1953

# DINKY TOYS

TRADE
MARK
REGD

## DINKY TOYS

14c Coventry Climax
Fork Lift Truck

25p Aveling-Barford
Diesel Roller

14a
B.E.V. Electric Truck

3

## DINKY TOYS

30n
Farm Produce Wagon

30s
Austin Covered Wagon

30i
Austin Wagon

30m
Rear Tipping Wagon

4

## DINKY TOYS

25h
Streamlined Fire Engine

30r
Fordson 'Thames' Flat Truck

30p Tanker

25r
Forward Control Lorry

5

277

**25x**
Breakdown Lorry

**25m**
Bedford End Tipper

**25v**
Refuse Wagon

**25w**
Bedford Truck

6

30v Electric Dairy Van

**30h**
Daimler Ambulance

**31b**
Trojan 15 cwt. Van 'Dunlop'

**40h**
Austin Taxi

27a Massey-Harris Tractor
and 27b Harvest Trailer

**27c**
Massey-Harris Manure Spreader

**27h**
Disc Harrow

8

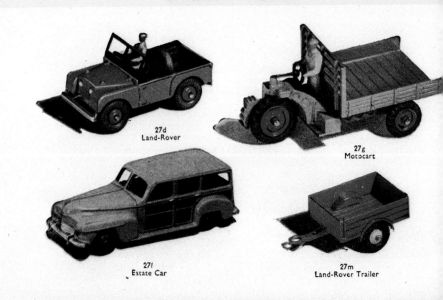

**27d**
Land-Rover

**27g**
Motocart

**27f**
Estate Car

**27m**
Land-Rover Trailer

278

40a
Riley Saloon

40d
Austin 'Devon' Saloon

40f
Hillman Minx Saloon

140a
Austin 'Atlantic' Convertible

40e
Standard 'Vanguard' Saloon

40b
Triumph 1800 Saloon

140b
Rover 75 Saloon

40g
Morris Oxford Saloon

11

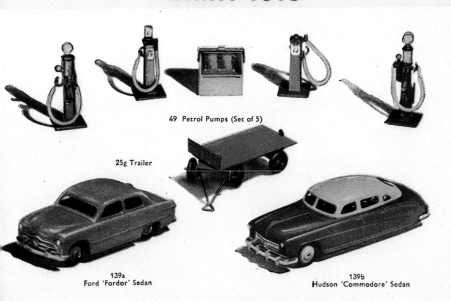

49  Petrol Pumps (Set of 5)

25g Trailer

29g
Luxury Coach

29c
Double Deck Bus

139a
Ford 'Fordor' Sedan

139b
Hudson 'Commodore' Sedan

29e
Single Deck Bus

29f
Observation Coach

13

279

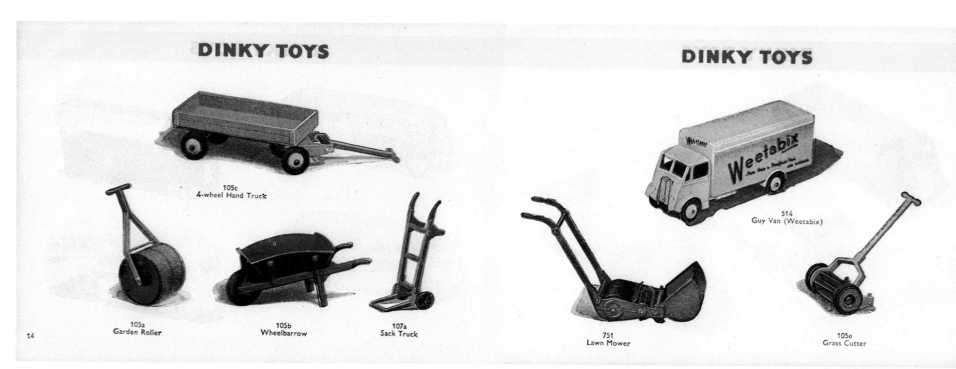

**105c**
4-wheel Hand Truck

**105a**
Garden Roller

**105b**
Wheelbarrow

**107a**
Sack Truck

14

**514**
Guy Van (Weetabix)

**751**
Lawn Mower

**105e**
Grass Cutter

**511**
Guy 4-ton Lorry

**505**
Foden Flat Truck
with Chains

**521**
Articulated Lorry

16

**513**
Guy Flat Truck
with Tailboard

**512**
Guy Flat Truck

**501**
Foden D
8-wheel V

**504**
Foden 14-ton Tanker

**502**
Foden Flat Truck
*Illustrated*

**503**
Foden Flat Truck with Tailboard

**551**
Trailer
Can be used with Dinky Toys 25p, 25x, 27a, 27d, 501–503, 505, 511–513, 521, 531 and 561–563, all of which are fitted with towing hooks.

**531**
Leyland 'Comet' Lorry

**532**
Comet Wagon
with hinged Tailboard

19

**561**
Blaw Knox Bulldozer
Runs on crawler track. The blade is raised and lowered by means of a lever.

**562**
Dumper Truck
The Front Wheels of this model are adjustable. The Bucket tips, and the Driving Seat with Driver is reversible.

**571**
Coles Mobile Crane
With hoisting, jib raising and slewing movements

563 Heavy Tractor

21

## RECENT ADDITIONS TO THE RANGE OF DINKY TOYS

555
Fire Engine with
Extending Ladder

25y
Universal Jeep

564
Elevator Loader

522
Big Bedford Lorry

23f
Alfa Romeo Racing Car

29h Duple Roadmaster Coach

22

## NEW MODELS IN PREPARATION

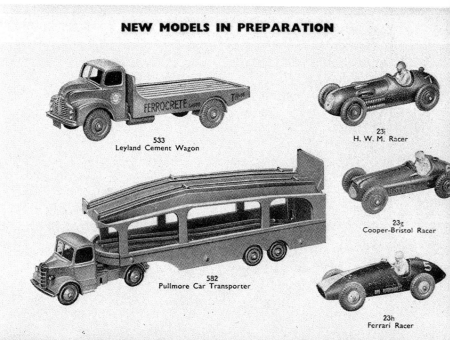

533
Leyland Cement Wagon

23j
H. W. M. Racer

23g
Cooper-Bristol Racer

582
Pullmore Car Transporter

23h
Ferrari Racer

DINKY TOYS

1st SEPTEMBER 1954

Kodak
CAMERAS & FILMS

Marked "X" for OO Gauge

2D
U.K.

U.K. JUNE 1956

DINKY SUPERTOYS
DINKY TOYS

POLICE

REGENT

J. R. INWARDS
50 HIGH STREET, RUISLIP
Tel. 3033

2d

282

# THE 1979 CATALOGUE

The last from Binns Road

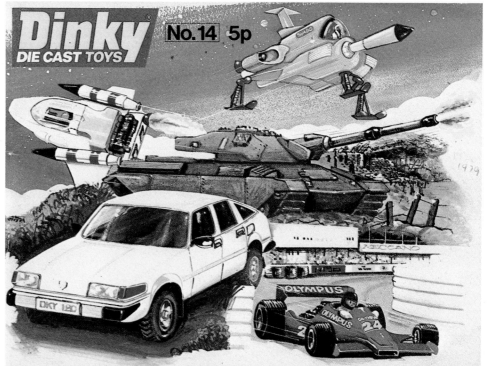

**359** Eagle Transporter
222mm

**360** Eagle Freighter
222mm

from the
successful TV series

**SPACE:1999** © 1976 ATV Licensing Ltd.

4

**351** UFO Interceptor
with rocket
194mm cap-fired rocket
*(caps not included)*

**353** Shado 2 Mobile
145mm
Rocket stows away

© 1976 ATV Licensing Ltd.

5

New

**361**
Galactic
War Chariot
126mm

**106**
Thunderbird 2
153 mm

6

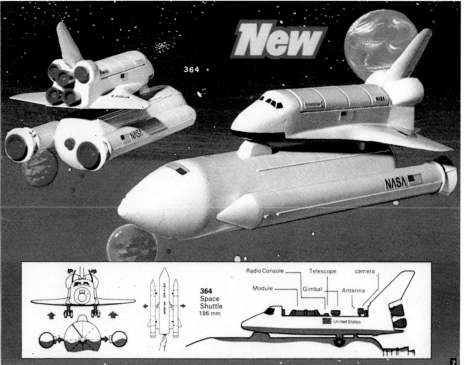

New

Radio Console — Telescope — camera

Module — Gimbal — Antenna

**364**
Space
Shuttle
186 mm

United States

7

285

**8**

211
Triumph
TR7
98 mm

123
Princess
2200 HL
Saloon
128 mm

192
Range
Rover
109 mm

**9**

178
Mini
Clubman
82 mm

180
Rover
3500   131 mm

*New*

**10**

*New*

*New*

222
Hesketh
Racing
Car 308 E
132 mm

206
Customised
Corvette
Stingray
113 mm

226
Ferrari
312/B2
121 mm

**11**

*New*

*New*

207
Triumph
TR7 Rally   98 mm

208
VW Porsche
914
89 mm

219
"Big Cat"
Jaguar
137 mm

New

**122** Volvo 265 DL Estate 128 mm

**124** Rolls Royce Phantom V 141 mm

**128** Mercedes Benz 600

**170** Granada Ghia 127·5 mm

12

**THE NEW AVENGERS**

**113** Steed's Jaguar 137 mm

**112** Purdey's TR7 98 mm

13

New    New    New

**115** U.B. Taxi 86 mm

**390** Customised Transit Van 133 mm

**120** Happy Cab 86 mm

14

New

**263** Airport Fire Rescue Tender 177mm

**384** 'Convoy' Fire Rescue Truck 126mm

**285** Merryweather Marquis Fire Tender With operating water pump 177 mm

**266** ERF Fire Tender 223mm Removable extending escape ladder with wheels

15

287

**269** Police Van

**264** New POLICE / POLICE SLOW

**255** POLICE

**277**

**255** Police Mini Clubman 82mm

**277** Police Land Rover 110 mm

**264** Rover 3500 Police Car 131 mm

**269** Police Accident Unit 129mm

16

New

**243** POLICE

**732**

**244**

**254** POLICE ACCIDENT / POLICE SLOW

**244** Plymouth Police Car 134·5 mm

**243** Police Volvo 141 mm

**732** Bell Police Helicopter 211mm

**254** Police Range Rover 109mm

17

New

**289**

Esso SafetyGrip tyres

**248** LIVERPOOL F.C.

**278** YELLOW

**284** London Taxi 112mm

**278** Plymouth Yellow Cab 134·5 mm

**248** Continental Tourer Coach 164·5 mm

Available in alternative Football club Liveries.

**289** Routemaster London Bus 121mm

288

18

**274** AMBULANCE

New

**288** AMBULANCE

**267**

**FROM THE TV SERIES "EMERGENCY"**

**267** Paramedic Truck 119mm

Free lapel Badge and Figures of De Soto and Gage.

**274** Ford Transit Ambulance 129 mm

**288** Superior Cadillac Ambulance 152 mm

19

**417 Ford Transit Van Motorway Services** 129mm

**412 Bedford Van AA** 90mm

**442 Landrover Breakdown Crane** 121 mm

**410 Bedford Royal Mail Van** 90 mm

**430 Johnson 2-Ton Dumper** 166mm

**279 Aveling Barford Diesel Roller** 116mm

**984 Atlas Digger** Powerful working shovel action 247mm

**980 Coles Hydra Truck 150T** 210mm

**432 Foden Tipping Lorry** 175mm

**449 Johnston Road Sweeper** 142mm

**978 Refuse Wagon** 162mm

**940 Mercedes-Benz Truck** 200mm

**950 Foden S20 Fuel Tanker** 266mm

# CONVOY New

386

387

383

382

380

385

| | | | | |
|---|---|---|---|---|
| **383** 'Convoy' N.C.L. Truck 110 mm | **386** 'Convoy' Avis Truck 110 mm | **382** 'Convoy' Dumper Truck 118mm | **385** 'Convoy' Royal Mail Truck 110 mm | **380** 'Convoy' Skip Truck 112mm |
| | | | **387** 'Convoy' Pickfords Truck 113 mm | |

24

308

381

404

| | | |
|---|---|---|
| **381** 'Convoy' Farm Truck 110mm | **308** Leyland 384 Tractor 86mm | **404** "Climax" Forklift Truck 97 mm |

25

FIGURES NOT INCLUDED

654

656

612

691

696

690

| | | |
|---|---|---|
| **654** 155mm Mobile Gun 151mm FIRES SHELLS | **612** Commando Jeep 108mm | **656** 88mm Gun 218mm |

26

BOTH GUNS FIRE SHELLS

**696** Leopard Anti-Aircraft Tank 152mm

**691** 'Striker' Anti-Tank Vehicle 122mm

FIRES FIVE ROCKETS SINGLY OR ALL 5 TOGETHER

**690** Scorpion Tank 120mm

FIRES SHELLS

4 ROUND RAPID-FIRE GUN COMPLETE WITH CAMOUFLAGE NET

27

290

**FIRES SHELLS**

**692** Leopard Tank
198mm

**683** Chieftain Tank
217mm

**FIRES SHELLS**

683

692

28

668

687

ARMY

618

**668** Foden Army Truck
197mm

**618** A.E.C. Artic. Transporter with Helicopter 318mm

**68** 'Convoy' Army Truck
110mm

29

741

721

**741** Spitfire MKII
Wing span 173mm

**721** Junkers Ju 87b Stuka
with dropping cap-firing bomb
Wing span 191mm

30

NAVY
66

724

722

**724** Sea King
Helicopter
179mm

**722** Hawker Harrier Jump Jet
Wing span 125mm

**724** Motor-driven main
rotor blades and
finger driven winch

(Battery not included)

31

# APPENDIX 1. Copies of Dinky Toys

During the 1930s many toy manufacturers took the easy option of 'copying' their rival's products. Sometimes there was blatant stealing with the toy from one maker being used to make the mould for another but in other cases, two manufacturers would decide to do the same thing. As the production processes were similar, only allowing certain types of construction, the toys turned out looking very similar, such as Dyson and Dinky 22b, and Johillco and Dinky 23a from Great Britain, and Ducky Toy from New Zealand with a 28 Bedford-type van and an ambulance from the Holland Coachcraft Van, all using high lead content alloys. The last two may be copies, not just 'look-alikes'. After the war, using mazak, Lemeco of Sweden made a Ford Fordor (Dinky 139a), and Austin Devon (40d), Jeep (153a), Frazer-Nash BMW (38a) and Marusan from Japan an Observation Coach (29f) and Royal Mail Van (260). Other items were also made but all of this group are easy to distinguish from the Dinky Toy, partly because many are not quite the same but also because none of them have 'Dinky Toys' or any other such wording on the base that distinguishes the Meccano product.

In the 1970s, the white metal kit industry sprang up and found that they could use a toy for a master from which to make a cheap rubber mould. Many used Dinky Toys for this purpose mostly with the permission of Meccano who merely insisted that their trade names be removed from the soft alloy before being sold. The purpose behind their manufacture was two-fold: either to produce copies of very scarce models so that collectors who could not hope to own an original could have the pleasure of looking at a copy; or because the model was a very good one in the first place and with a few chrome parts or whatever would make an acceptable model for the collector of model cars rather than toys. Despite the honorable intention of the manufacturers, some of these have been passed off as original Dinky Toys so that all unusual models should be scrutinised carefully.

One of the transfer manufacturers used by Meccano released old Meccano decals to the public and being original material it is impossible to detect if they have been affixed ex factory. Other people have had transfers and stickers made using originals, modified or not, as artwork. Some of these are easy to identify because the colours are (deliberately) slightly inaccurate or the size is wrong, but others are so perfect that only the expert eye can distinguish them. Sometimes Dinky Toys are decorated with decals that were never used at all by Dinky but were fitted to another manufacturer's toys, perhaps because they are needed for a model railway layout but frequently just because they look nice.

Many replacement parts, tyres and radiator grilles, etc. especially for pre- and immediate post-war models have been available for the last ten years or so in a variety of materials and finishes and every few months a new one is released onto the collector's market.

The message of these paragraphs can be summed up as 'caveat emptor', an ancient principle of English law, 'let the buyer beware'.

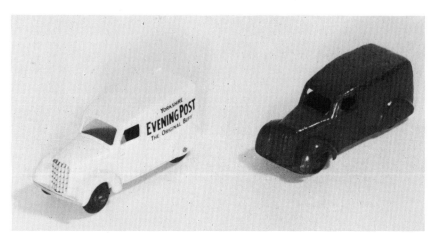

# APPENDIX 2. Scales of Dinky Toys

## MECCANO LTD.

**ARTICLE** DINKY, DUBLO & HORNBY SCALES     **MEMO No. 17157 SHT 1**

| SCALE INCHES TO 1 FT | DESCRIPTION |
|---|---|
| 5"/32 | DUBLO |
| | DOUBLE DECK BUS |
| | LUXURY COACH |
| | OBSERVATION COACH |
| | SINGLE DECK BUS |
| | TOURING COACH-DUPLE ROADMASTER |
| | B.O.A.C. COACH |
| | DUBLO DINKY TOYS |
| | ATLANTEAN O.D. BUS |
| 1"/6 | FORWARD CONTROL LORRY |
| 13"/64 | AMBULANCE (DAIMLER) |
| | END TIPPING WAGON (DODGE) |
| | FARM PRODUCE WAGON (DODGE) |
| | FLAT TRUCK (FORDSON) |
| | MECHANICAL HORSE |
| | PETROL TANKER (STUDEBAKER) |
| | TRAILER (SMALL) |
| | WAGON AUSTIN |
| | WAGON-COVERED (AUSTIN) |
| | ARMY VEHICLES & TANK |
| | MIGHTY ANTAR |
| | PRESSURE REFUELLER |
| | DOUGLAS TUGMASTER |
| | 25 Pr. GUN & HOWITZER |
| | MIGHTY ANTAR LOW LOADER |
| | 5.5 MEDIUM GUN |
| | STREAMLINED FIRE ENGINE |

| SCALE INCHES TO 1 FT | DESCRIPTION |
|---|---|
| 7"/32 | AUSTIN CHAMP |
| 15"/64 | DIESEL ROLLER |
| 1/4" | A.E.C. SHELL TANKER |
| | AUSTIN ATLANTIC A90 |
| | AUSTIN TAXI |
| | BEDFORD VEHICLES |
| | BREAKDOWN LORRY |
| | CALL BOX |
| | COMMER VEHICLES |
| | ESTATE CAR |
| | FIRE ENGINE |
| | FODEN VEHICLES |
| | FORD 'FORDOR' SEDAN |
| | GUY VEHICLES |
| | HINDLE SMART ARTICULATED |
| | HORSE BOX |
| | HUDSON COMMODORE SEDAN |
| | LEYLAND COMET & OCTOPUS |
| | LOUD SPEAKER VAN |
| | MOTOR CYCLISTS |
| | N.C.B. ELECTRIC VAN |
| | PETROL PUMPS & STATION |
| | POLICE BOX |
| | RILEY SALOON |
| | ROAD SIGNS |
| | ROYAL MAIL VAN |
| | TRAFFIC SIGNS |
| | TRAILER (LARGE) |
| | TRIUMPH SALOON |
| | TROJAN DELIVERY VAN |
| | PULLMORE CAR TRANSPORTER |
| | EUCLID REAR DUMP TRUCK |
| | STUDEBAKER LAND CRUISER |
| | SCOUT CAR |
| | 2 TON LORRY-MOUNTED CRANE |
| | TELEPHONE SERVICE VAN |
| | PACKARD |
| | CADILLAC |
| | CAR CARRIER & TRAILER |
| | TURNTABLE FIRE ESCAPE |
| | TELEPHONE KIOSK |
| | POSTMAN & MESSENGER |
| | AMERICAN RAMBLER |
| | STUDEBAKER GOLDEN HAWK |

| SCALE INCHES TO 1 FT | DESCRIPTION |
|---|---|
| 1/4" | STUDEBAKER PRESIDENT |
| | PACKARD CLIPPER |
| | HUDSON HORNET |
| | PLYMOUTH PLAZA |
| | B.B.C. T.V. MOBILE CONTROL ROOM |
| | " ROVING EYE VEHICLE |
| | " EXTENDING MAST |
| | DESOTO FIREFLITE |
| | ROLLS ROYCE SILVER WRAITH |
| | FORD ANGLIA |
| | ATLAS BUS |
| | BEDFORD PALLET 'JEKTA' VAN |
| | BENTLEY SERIES 'S' COUPE |
| | CHEVROLET EL CAMINO |
| | FOUR BERTH CARAVAN |
| | HEALEY SPORTS BOAT & TRAILER |
| | JAGUAR 3.4 LITRE |
| | LORRY MOUNTED CEMENT MIXER |
| | McLEANS TRACTOR 2 & VAN |
| | MARREL MULTI-BUCKET UNIT |
| | MERCEDES-BENZ 220 SE |
| | OPEL KAPITAN |
| | POLICE (PATROL (HUMBER HAWK)) |
| | POLICE " (USA) |
| | PLYMOUTH TAXI |
| | RAMBLER CROSS COUNTRY |
| | SNOW PLOUGH |
| | VOLVO AMAZON |
| | LAMP STANDARDS |
| | SHELL PETROL STATION |
| | BR " |
| | SERVICE STATION |
| | TYRE RACK |
| | WAYNE SCHOOL BUS |
| | FIRE STATION |
| | FODEN DUMP TRUCK |
| | MECHANICAL HORSE & TRAILER |
| | FORD FAIRLANE |
| | CRITERION AMBULANCE |
| | VAUXHALL CRESTA |
| | CADILLAC '62' |
| | ROLLS ROYCE PHANTOM V |
| | COMMER CARAVAN |

NOTE:- SCALE for AEROPLANES - 1/16 to 1 FOOT

| ISSUE | DESCRIPTION OF CHANGE | CO.No. | DATE | SIG. |
|---|---|---|---|---|
| 7 | LIST EXTENDED AND BROUGHT UP TO DATE. | | 16-2-61 | A.G. |
| 6 | LIST EXTENDED AND BROUGHT UP TO DATE. | | 29-8-60 | |
| 5 | LIST EXTENDED & BROUGHT UP TO DATE | | 29-4-57 | |
| 4 | REDRAWN: 2 SHEETS WERE 1 | | 21-6-54 | |

MATERIAL

REDRAWN
TRACED
CHECKED
APPROVED
SCALE
DATE 30-10-49

# MECCANO LTD.

ARTICLE: DINKY, DUBLO & HORNBY SCALES          MEMO No 17157 SHT: 2.

| SCALE INCHES TO 1 FT | DESCRIPTION |
|---|---|
| 17"/64 | AUSTIN DEVON SALOON. A40. |
| | AUSTIN HEALEY |
| | ASTON MARTIN. |
| | COLES CRANE |
| | CUNNINGHAM. |
| | HARVEST TRAILER |
| | HILLMAN MINX SALOON |
| | JAGUAR |
| | MORRIS OXFORD SALOON |
| | M.G. MIDGET |
| | MERSEY TUNNEL POLICE VAN |
| | ROVER 75 SALOON |
| | STANDARD VANGUARD SALOON |
| | SUNBEAM ALPINE |
| | AUSTIN SOMERSET |
| | AUSTIN VAN. |
| | FORD ZEPHYR |
| | BRISTOL 450. |
| | TRIUMPH T.R.2. |
| | VOLKSWAGEN. |
| | CARAVAN |
| | VAUXHALL CRESTA |
| | CONNAUGHT |
| | MERCEDES-BENZ |
| | JAGUAR TYPE D |
| | HUMBER HAWK |
| | PORSCHE |
| | AUSTIN A105 |
| | AUSTIN A30 |
| | SUNBEAM RAPIER |
| | FIAT 600 |
| | VANWALL |
| | A.C. ACECA UTA |
| | SINGER GAZELLE. |
| | RENAULT FRÉGATE |
| | AUSTIN SEVEN PICK UP |
| | MORRIS MINI-MINOR TRAVELLER |
| | TRIUMPH HERALD |
| | AUSTIN 7 COUNTRYMAN |

| SCALE INCHES TO 1 FT | DESCRIPTION |
|---|---|
| 2"/32 | GOODS YARD CRANE |
| | 'O' GAUGE ITEMS. |
| 19"/64 | JEEP. |
| 5"/16 | ALFA-ROMEO |
| | B.E.V. TRUCK |
| | COOPER-BRISTOL |
| | DISC HARROW |
| | ELEVATOR LOADER |
| | FARM RAKE |
| | FARM TRACTOR |
| | FERRARI |
| | FIELD MARSHALL TRACTOR |
| | GANG MOWER |
| | H.W.M. |
| | LAND ROVER & TRAILER |
| | MOTO CART |
| | MASERATI |
| | TRAILER (2 WHEELED) |
| | TALBOT LAGO |
| | MANURE SPREADER |
| | PILLAR BOX |
| | WEEKS TIPPING FARM TRAILER |

| SCALE INCHES TO 1 FT | DESCRIPTION |
|---|---|
| 5"/16 | |
| 11"/32 | BULLDOZER |
| | DUMPER TRUCK |
| | HEAVY TRACTOR |
| 13"/32 | FORK-LIFT TRUCK |
| 5"/8 | 4 WHEELED HAND TRUCK |
| | SACK TRUCK |
| 3"/4 | GARDEN ROLLER |
| | WHEELBARROW |
| 1" | GRASS CUTTER |
| 1½" | LAWN MOWER. |

NOTE:- SCALE for AEROPLANES = 1/16" TO 1 FOOT.

| ISSUE | DESCRIPTION OF CHANGE | CO. No. | DATE | SIG. |
|---|---|---|---|---|
| 7 | LIST EXTENDED AND BROUGHT UP TO DATE | | 16-2-61 | A.G. |
| 6 | LIST EXTENDED AND BROUGHT UP TO DATE. | | 29-8-60 | |
| 5 | LIST EXTENDED & BROUGHT UP TO DATE. | | 29-4-57 | RB |
| 4 | REDRAWN: 2 SHEETS WERE 1. | | 21-6-54 | |

MATERIAL

REDRAWN
TRACED
CHECKED
APPROVED
SCALE
DATE 30-10-49

# APPENDIX 3. Dinky Toys Numbering System

The first Dinky Toys inherited the numbering of their predecessors, the series of Hornby Modelled Miniatures. The figure sets (and animals) intended to enhance Hornby O Gauge Railway scenes started, logically enough, at No. 1 and went on to No. 5. A gap was then left, with the next number being No. 13, and when a miniature train set was introduced, this became No. 21, with the first set of motor vehicles No. 22. The system of leaving gaps to distinguish between different types of models—and to allow for additions to the series which could then be listed with other models of the same type, without appearing out of number order—was to remain a feature of Dinky numbering right up to the end of Liverpool production.

New vehicle models carried on from No. 22 until eventually reaching No. 40 after World War 2. A set of ships had been given the series No. 50, and aeroplanes No. 60—establishing a pattern of leaving gaps and starting series on a 'tens' basis. When accessories were introduced to complement the vehicle models, they were initially given numbers at the 'top end' of the range allocated, i.e. from No. 49 downwards as far as No. 42. When the Dinky Doll's House furniture was introduced, a long gap in numbering was left, and these items were given distinctive numbers starting at No. 101, to 104. After the war, aircraft resumed at No. 70. Garden equipment followed on from the then obsolete Furniture models, with No. 105. Army models had started pre-war at No. 150, for Tank sets and figures and 160 for artillery items, reaching 152 for the former and 162 for the latter. The post-war jeep was numbered 153a, and it seems later post-war army models continued in this 153 series, but only in the planning stage—being released after the new system of numbering was introduced in 1953–4.

The original Hornby Modelled Miniatures were initially available only in sets. After the individual pieces became available separately, and after the change of name to Dinky Toys, they took the set number plus an alphabetic character to identify them, e.g. No. 1c was a Ticket Collector from the No. 1 Station Staff Set. This part-numeric, part alphabetic numbering continued, even though from 1938 onwards many models were released separately rather than as sets—although they became parts of composite sets afterwards (e.g. the aeroplane sets Nos. 64 and 65 contained models numbered in the 60 series, but which were not in the initial 60 set of six models). Most models issued after the war were never contained in sets but continued to be numbered within the set (or series) number or range most appropriate, until 1953–4. It should be noted that in most of the series numbers, certain letters were not normally used: i, j (pre-war), l, o, q, u. The letter z was reserved for imported French Dinky Toys, many of which had the same numbers as English models, although they were different—the z was tagged on to the number to distinguish the French item from the similarly-numbered British model; e.g. 60z was the French 60 Aeroplane set, 60az a French 60a Arc-en-Ciel monoplane from the set which was also available separately in the U.K. The British 60a was an Imperial Airways Liner.

In 1947 the first Dinky Supertoys appeared. There was no question then of selling them in sets, so there was no real point in having a part-numeric and part-alphabetic numbering system for them. So there was a big jump in numbers up to 501, but the 'tens' system with gaps being left for future additions to be inserted with other models of the same type, was much in evidence, e.g. 501 to 503 were Foden Lorries, 511 to 513 Guys, 521 a Bedford articulated truck.

Later additions were a Foden Tanker numbered 504 and a Guy Van No. 514. A different type of model to these Supertoys was a short-lived Shetland Flying Boat, which was given another high number, 701; later another big jump to 751 for a Lawn Mower, 752 was later allocated to a Goods Yard Crane with no apparent connection except that perhaps a 'miscellaneous' group of models not fitting elsewhere was the idea.

The highest numbers reached in the original numbering system were 1001, the OO Gauge scale Station Staff and 1003 Passengers to the same scale. It is my view that these numbers were allocated because 1 and 3 already applied to the equivalent O Gauge sets and the inclusion of 'OO' in the number helped to identify these as being OO scale versions!

In 1953 a decision was made to introduce a new numbering system for Dinky Toys, more suitable for the then current range and taking into account that models were now being issued individually rather than in complete sets, for even a series of racing cars, etc. took a year to come out. The new numbering did away with alphabet characters completely, and was based on the allocation of blocks of 50 or 100 numbers to the different types of models, and in some cases mini-blocks of 10 or 20 numbers within a main block to further sub-divide the type of model. In the original re-numbering, the figures 1–6 kept their numbers with the addition of leading zeroes, becoming 001–006, then a few individual figures became 011 to 013, some old motor cycles (then available only for export) became 041–045, the 00 figures became 051 and 053, and boxes of spare tyres were numbered at the 'top' of this first 100 numbers, starting at 099 and going down to 094. The next number blocks went like this:

|  |  |  |
|---|---|---|
| 100–199 | Cars | Initially sub-divided<br>100 Sports and Convertibles<br>150 Saloons (British)<br>170 Sedans (American) |
| 200–249 | Racing Cars | 200 Midget Racer<br>220 Re-issues of Pre-war Racing Car and Record Breakers<br>230 Post-war Formula 2 Racing Cars |
| 250–299 | Public Service Vehicles | 250 Fire Engines, Ambulance, Refuse Wagon, Taxi etc.<br>(everything except buses and coaches)<br>280 Coaches<br>290 Buses |
| 300–399 | Farm Equipment (and Gardening) | 300 Tractors<br>320 Farm Trailers and Equipment for towing by Tractors<br>340 Farm Vehicles (other than tractors or towed implements)<br>380 Garden Equipment |
| 400–499 | Commercial Vehicles | 400 Industrial Trucks<br>450 Jeep<br>410 2-axle Rigid Trucks<br>415 Mechanical Horse<br>420 Other open Trucks (with small flat trailer being numbered<br>at 'end' of mini-blocks, 429)<br>430 Breakdown Truck<br>440 Petrol Tankers (different liveries)<br>450 Trojan Vans (different liveries)<br>470 Austin Vans (different liveries)<br>480 Bedford Vans (different liveries)<br>490 Other Vans (Electric Dairy Vans and Loudspeaker Van) |
| 500–599 | | This range was not immediately re-used, since it had been the basis of the Dinky Supertoys numbering in the old system, and immediate re-allocation could have caused confusion |
| 600–699 | Military Vehicles and Equipment | 600 Figures (at this time, export only and re-numbering<br>may not have been carried through to the actual boxes)<br>620 Army Trucks<br>640 Army Utility Trucks<br>650 Tanks<br>670 Armoured Cars, Personnel Carriers, Jeeps, Staff Cars etc.<br>690 Artillery |
| 700–749 | Aircraft | 700 Civil Aircraft<br>730 Fighters<br>750 Phone Boxes |
| 750–799 | Accessories & Miscellaneous | 770 Road Signs<br>780 Petrol Pumps<br>(The Express Passenger Train Set appeared soon after the<br>re-numbering, with a near 'top of the range' number of 798) |
| 800–899 | | This range was not used for Liverpool models, but was used together with the 500–599 range for the re-numbered French Dinky Toys and Supertoys in 1958. The French Supertoys were numbered from 899 'down', thus placing them in order with the British Supertoys from 900 onwards |
| 900–999 | | Larger models previously in the Supertoy range<br>(In 1956, when the Supertoys name was re-introduced, the models in the new range kept their 900 series numbers and others were again re-numbered, mostly in the 400–499 range). Initially, the majority of the models took their old-systems 500 series number and changed the first digit to a 9, e.g. 501 became 901, etc. and the 'tens' mini-block system was continued |

As new models were introduced, further mini-blocks came into being (e.g. 260 for Post Office vehicles, 660 for heavy military vehicles, 131–3 for American sports and convertibles, etc., and later numbers of new items ran either side of a mini-group in order to keep all types of models listed together. However, it was not until around 1977 that some numbers were beginning to run 'over' from one major block into another, e.g. some public service vehicles were being allocated to the 240s, all the numbers having been used in the 250 to 299 block and the 'mini-block' sub-divisions within this range having long disappeared.

Since about 1965 another factor has been the re-allocation of a number of a model which has been obsolete for a few years to a new model, and in some instances numbers have been used three times but in the main these have still been within the appropriate 'blocks'. Exceptions are the re-use of low 100 series numbers for Character Merchandise, and when these started to run into numbers recently or currently used for car models, a new block of numbers starting at 350 was used.

Another block of numbers starting at 1001 commenced around ten years ago when Dinky Kits were announced. The numbers of these ran from 1001 to 1050, with many gaps. However, the types of models in the range are listed in roughly the same order as the equivalent assembled Dinky Toys. A reversion to the 'tens' system occurred in a minor way with aircraft kits starting at 1040 and a solitary ship kit at 1050.

A few 1/25 scale cars were made around 1973–6, numbered 2162, 2214 and 2253. If one ignores the first digit 2 in the number, the models fit neatly into the main numbering blocks according to type.

All Meccano Products had stock code numbers in addition to the catalogue or sales numbers and in the case of Dinky Toys these originally consisted of the letter A followed by a four-digit number which bore no relation to the actual Dinky number. These 'A' numbers appear on some pre-war boxes and seem to have been allocated in strict number order as a model made its appearance. Around 1950 a new code was devised and Dinky Toys had five-digit stock numbers starting at 50001. These ran consecutively and most of the models were in the same order as their sales numbers. When the new numbering system was introduced for Dinky Toys in 1953–4, the stock code number was changed as well, but keeping the five-digit basis with 50 as the first two digits, the next three digits being identical to the new catalogue/sales number. Some boxes in the early 1950s showed the '50000' code (especially the old six- and twelve-packs) in addition to the Dinky number; and again in the early 1960s some individual boxes occasionally showed it in very small print (e.g. 50997 on a 997 Supertoys Caravelle box lid).

It may be that Meccano Ltd. were going to re-use the 800 series (previously only used in France) since a 1980 list—probably prepared just before the factory closed in late 1979—includes two pocket-sized Star Trek models 801 and 802. It seems doubtful if these models were ever issued under these numbers for they were available in the U.S.A. under different numbers, 803 and 804.

# APPENDIX 4.
## Production Suspended— September 1939 to March 1940

### Production Suspended

Production was suspended on the following items in September 1939, but they were re-introduced in March 1940. This list is 'as printed' in the *Meccano Magazine* of that month.

22g Streamlined Tourer
22h Streamlined Saloon
23a Racing Cars
23b Hotchkiss Racing Car
24a Ambulance
24c Town Sedan
24g Sports Tourer (4-seater)
24h Sports Tourer (2-seater)
28  Delivery Vans
30a Chrysler 'Airflow' Saloon
35  Small Cars
35a Saloon Cars
35b Racer Car
35c M.G. Sports Car
52a 'Queen Mary' with rollers, presentation packing

# APPENDIX 5.
## Sets & Gift Sets—Post-war

### Sets and Gift Sets

Most of the Sets and Gift Sets consist of vehicles all of the same type and the description of the contents of these sets can be found in the relevant sections, e.g. No. 4 Racing Cars in: 23 series Racing Cars, Army Vehicle Sets in: Military—Post-war, etc. However, some of the sets are a mixture of items from different sections or have a title which does not fit obviously into one of the categories. These are listed below with a note of the group with which they have been placed.

| No. 3 | Passenger Cars | Cars—40 series |
|---|---|---|
| 118 | Tow-away Glider Set | Cars—135 Triumph 2000 |
| 121 | Goodwood Racing Set | Cars—Sports Cars |
| 122 | Touring Gift Set | Cars |
| 123 | Mayfair Gift Set | Cars |
| 124 | Holiday Gift Set | Cars |
| 125 | Fun A'hoy Gift Set | Cars—130 Ford Corsair |
| 126 | Motor Show Gift Set | Cars |
| 149 | Sports Cars Gift Set | Cars—100 series |
| 240 | Dinky Way Set | Post-war—Accessories—Street Furniture |
| 245 | Superfast Gift Set | Cars—Sports Cars |
| 246 | International GT Gift Set | Cars—Sports Cars |
| 298 | Emergency Services Gift Set | Public Service Vehicles—Ambulances |
| 299 | Motorway Services Gift Set | Special Purpose Vehicles—Breakdown |
| 299 | Crash Squad | Public Service Vehicles—Police |
| 300 | Gift Set 'London Scene' | Commercials—Buses |
| 302 | Emergency Squad | Public Service Vehicles—Ambulances (Not issued) |

# Dinky TOYS

| No. | | £ | | No. | | £ |
|---|---|---|---|---|---|---|
| 106 | Thunderbird 2 | 4.25 | | 359 | Eagle Transporter | 4.75 |
| 112 | Purdey's TR7 | 1.65 | | 360 | Eagle Freighter | 4.75 |
| 120 | Happy Cab | 1.85 | | 361 | Zygon War Chariot | 2.50 |
| 122 | Volvo 265DL Estate | 1.99 | | 362 | Trident Star Fighter | 2.99 |
| 123 | Princess 2200 HL Saloon | 1.99 | | 364 | Space Shuttle | 4.50 |
| 124 | Rolls Royce Phantom V | 2.99 | | 367 | Space Battle Cruiser | 3.99 |
| 128 | Mercedes-Benz 600 | 3.35 | | 380 | Convoy Skip Truck | 1.50 |
| 170 | Ford Granada Ghia | 2.25 | | 381 | Convoy Farm Truck | 1.50 |
| 178 | Mini Clubman | 1.50 | | 382 | Convoy Dumper Truck | 1.50 |
| 180 | Rover 3500 | 2.25 | | 383 | Convoy N.C.L. Truck | 1.50 |
| 192 | Range Rover | 2.50 | | 384 | Convoy Fire Rescue Truck | 1.50 |
| 201 | Plymouth Stock Car | 2.25 | | 385 | Convoy Royal Mail Truck | 2.99 |
| 202 | Custom Land Rover | 2.85 | | 386 | Convoy Hire Van | 1.50 |
| 203 | Custom Range Rover | 2.85 | | 387 | Convoy Furniture Van | 1.50 |
| 206 | Custom Stingray | 2.25 | | 390 | Custom Freeway Cruiser | 2.99 |
| 207 | Triumph TR7 Rally Car | 1.99 | | 399 | Convoy Gift Set | 4.50 |
| 208 | VW Porsche | 1.99 | | 404 | Climax fork Lift Truck | 3.35 |
| 211 | Triumph TR7 | 1.65 | | 410 | Bedford Royal Mail Van | 1.65 |
| 219 | The Big Cat | 2.25 | | 412 | Bedford A.A. Van | 1.65 |
| 221 | Corvette Stingray | 1.85 | | 417 | Ford Transit 'Motorway Services' Van | 3.35 |
| 222 | Hesketh 308E Racing Car | 2.25 | | 430 | Johnson 2-Ton Dumper | 1.99 |
| 226 | Ferrari 312/B2 | 1.99 | | 432 | Foden Tipping Lorry | 4.25 |
| 240 | Dinky Way Set | 9.95 | | 437 | Muir Hill 2WL Loader | 3.60 |
| 243 | Volvo Police Car | 2.85 | | 442 | Land Rover Breakdown Vehicle | 2.99 |
| 244 | Plymouth Fury Police Car | 1.99 | | 449 | Johnson Road Sweeper | 4.25 |
| 254 | Police Patrol Range Rover | 2.85 | | 612 | Commando Jeep | 2.50 |
| 255 | Police Mini Clubman | 1.85 | | 618 | A.E.C. Artic. with Helicopter | 5.25 |
| 263 | Airport Fire Rescue Tender | 4.25 | | 654 | 155mm Mobile Gunn | 4.25 |
| 264 | Rover 3500 Police | 2.85 | | 656 | 88mm Gun | 4.75 |
| 266 | E.R.F. Fire Tender | 4.50 | | 667 | Armoured Patrol Car | 1.65 |
| 267 | Emergency Paramedic Truck | 2.25 | | 668 | Foden Army Truck | 3.60 |
| 269 | Police Accident Unit | 3.35 | | 673 | Submarine Chaser | 3.20 |
| 274 | Ford Transit Ambulance | 3.35 | | 683 | Chieftain Tank | 4.25 |
| 277 | Police Land Rover | 2.85 | | 687 | Convoy Army Truck | 1.50 |
| 278 | Plymouth Yellow Cab | 1.99 | | 690 | Scorpion Tank | 3.99 |
| 279 | Aveling Barford Diesel Roller | 3.15 | | 691 | Striker Anti-Tank Vehicle | 3.99 |
| 282 | Land Rover Fire Appliance | 3.20 | | 692 | Leopard Tank | 4.25 |
| 284 | London Taxi | 2.25 | | 694 | Hanomag Tank Destroyer | 4.50 |
| 285 | Merryweather Marquis Fire Tender | 5.95 | | 696 | Leopard Anti-Aircraft Tank | 3.85 |
| 288 | Superior Cadillac Ambulance | 2.99 | | 700 | RAF Diamond Jubilee Spitfire | 9.50 |
| 289 | Routemaster London Bus | 2.25 | | 721 | Junkers JU87B Stuka | 3.50 |
| 299 | Crash Squad Gift Set | 3.60 | | 722 | Hawker Harrier GR Mk 1 | 3.50 |
| 300 | London Scene Gift Set | 4.50 | | 724 | Sea King Helicopter, with Capsule | 3.75 |
| 303 | Commando Squad Gift Set | 4.75 | | 732 | Bell Police Helicopter | 1.99 |
| 304 | Fire Rescue Gift Set | 5.25 | | 741 | Spitfire Mk 2 | 3.35 |
| 308 | Leyland 384 Tractor | 1.85 | | 801 | Mini-U.S.S. Enterprise | 1.10 |
| 309 | Star Trek Gift Set | 8.99 | | 802 | Mini-Klingon Cruiser | 1.10 |
| 344 | Land Rover | 1.99 | | 940 | Mercedes-Benz Truck | 4.25 |
| 351 | U.F.O. Interceptor | 4.25 | | 950 | Foden S20 Tanker 'Burmah' | 5.50 |
| 353 | Shado 2 Mobile | 4.50 | | 978 | Refuse Wagon | 3.50 |
| 354 | Pink Panther Car | 1.10 | | 980 | Coles Hydra Truck 150T | 5.99 |
| 357 | Klingon Battle Cruiser | 3.99 | | 984 | Atlas Digger | 4.50 |
| 358 | U.S.S. Enterprise | 4.99 | | | Dinky toys Booklet | 0.05 |

**DINKY BUILDA**

| | | £ | | | | £ |
|---|---|---|---|---|---|---|
| 54001 | Galactic War Station | 0.99 | | 54002 | Blazing Inferno | 0.99 |

299

## APPENDIX 7. Dinky Toy Dimensions

**MECCANO LTD.**

**TITLE: DINKY TOYS DIMENSIONS** — MEMO No 20166 SHT. I.

| SALES No | DESCRIPTION | O'ALL LENGTH (INCHES) | O'ALL LENGTH (M/M) |
|---|---|---|---|
| 060 | | | |
| 061 | FORD PREFECT DUBLO | $2\frac{5}{16}$ | 59 |
| 062 | SINGER ROADSTER DUBLO | 2 | 51 |
| 063 | COMMER VAN. DUBLO | $2\frac{1}{8}$ | 54 |
| 064 | AUSTIN LORRY DUBLO | $2\frac{1}{2}$ | 64 |
| 065 | MORRIS PICKUP DUBLO | $2\frac{1}{8}$ | 54 |
| 066 | BEDFORD FLAT TRUCK DUBLO | $4\frac{1}{4}$ | 108 |
| 067 | AUSTIN TAXI DUBLO | $2\frac{5}{16}$ | 59 |
| 068 | ROYAL MAIL VAN DUBLO | $1\frac{7}{8}$ | 47 |
| 069 | MASSEY HARRIS FERGUSON TRACTOR DUBLO | $1\frac{7}{16}$ | 36 |
| 070 | A.E.C. MERCURY TANKER SHELL BP DUBLO | $3\frac{1}{2}$ | 90 |
| 071 | VOLKSWAGEN DELIVERY VAN DUBLO | $2\frac{5}{32}$ | 54 |
| 072 | BEDFORD ARTICULATED FLAT TRUCK DUBLO | $4\frac{5}{8}$ | 117 |
| 073 | LAND ROVER WITH HORSE TRAILER. DUBLO | $4\frac{1}{8}$ | 105 |
| 074 ▲ | LAND ROVER DUBLO | 2 | 51 |
| 075 ▲ | HORSE TRAILER DUBLO | $2\frac{3}{16}$ | 56 |
| 076 ▲ | LANSING BAGNALL TRACTOR & TRAILER DUBLO | $2\frac{15}{16}$ | 75 |
| 077 ▲ | A.C. BULKER CEMENT TRANSPORTER DUBLO | $2\frac{1}{4}$ | 57 |
| 078 | LANSING BAGNALL TRAILER DUBLO | $1\frac{15}{16}$ | 49 |
| 079 | | | |
| 080 | | | |
| 081 | | | |
| 082 | | | |
| 083 | | | |
| 084 | | | |
| 085 | | | |
| 086 | | | |
| 087 | | | |
| 088 | | | |
| 089 | | | |
| 090 | | | |
| 091 | | | |
| 100 | | | |
| 101 | SUNBEAM ALPINE TOURING FINISH. | $3\frac{11}{16}$ | 94 |
| 102 | M.G. MIDGET | $3\frac{1}{4}$ | 83 |
| 103 | AUSTIN HEALEY 100 | $3\frac{3}{8}$ | 86 |
| 104 | ASTIN MARTIN " | $3\frac{7}{16}$ | 87 |
| 105 | TRIUMPH T.R.2 " | $3\frac{3}{8}$ | 86 |
| 106 | AUSTIN ATLANTIC | $3\frac{3}{4}$ | 95 |
| 107 | SUNBEAM ALPINE RACING FINISH | $3\frac{11}{16}$ | 94 |
| 108 | M.G. MIDGET " | $3\frac{1}{4}$ | 83 |
| 109 | AUSTIN HEALEY " | $3\frac{3}{8}$ | 86 |
| 110 | ASTON MARTIN " | $3\frac{7}{16}$ | 87 |
| 111 | TRIUMPH TR2 " | $3\frac{3}{8}$ | 86 |
| 112 | | | |
| 113 | | | |
| 114 | | | |
| 115 | | | |
| 116 | | | |
| 117 | | | |
| 118 | | | |
| 119 | | | |
| 120 | | | |
| 121 | | | |
| 122 | | | |
| 123 | | | |
| 124 | | | |
| 125 | | | |
| 126 | | | |
| 127 | | | |
| 128 ▲ | AUSTIN HEALEY (U.S.A.) | $3\frac{3}{8}$ | 86 |
| 129 | M.G. MIDGET U.S.A. | $3\frac{1}{4}$ | 83 |
| 130 | | | |
| 131 | CADILLAC ELDORADO | $4\frac{11}{16}$ | 119 |
| 132 | PACKARD | $4\frac{1}{2}$ | 114 |
| 133 | CUNNINGHAM | 4 | 102 |
| 134 | | | |
| 135 | | | |
| 136 | | | |
| 137 | | | |
| 138 | | | |
| 139 | | | |
| 140 | | | |
| 141 | | | |
| 142 | | | |
| 143 | | | |
| 144 | | | |
| 145 | | | |
| 146 | | | |
| 147 | | | |
| 148 | | | |
| 149 | | | |
| 150 | ROLLS ROYCE SILVER WRAITH | $4\frac{3}{4}$ | 121 |
| 151 | TRIUMPH 1800 SALOON | $3\frac{5}{8}$ | 92 |
| 152 | AUSTIN DEVON | $3\frac{3}{8}$ | 86 |
| 153 | VANGUARD | $3\frac{5}{8}$ | 92 |
| 154 | HILLMAN MINX | $3\frac{1}{2}$ | 89 |
| 155 | FORD ANGLIA | $3\frac{3}{16}$ | 81 |
| 156 | ROVER 75 | 4 | 102 |
| 157 | JAGUAR XK 120 | $3\frac{7}{8}$ | 98 |
| 158 | RILEY SALOON | $3\frac{5}{8}$ | 92 |
| 159 | MORRIS OXFORD | $3\frac{5}{8}$ | 92 |
| 160 | AUSTIN A30 | $3\frac{1}{16}$ | 78 |
| 161 | AUSTIN SOMERSET | $3\frac{9}{16}$ | 90 |
| 162 | FORD ZEPHYR | $3\frac{13}{16}$ | 97 |
| 163 | BRISTOL 450 | $3\frac{15}{16}$ | 100 |
| 164 | VAUXHALL CRESTA | $3\frac{13}{16}$ | 97 |
| 165 | HUMBER HAWK | 4 | 102 |
| 166 | SUNBEAM RAPIER | $3\frac{9}{16}$ | 90 |
| 167 | A.C. ACECA | $3\frac{1}{2}$ | 89 |
| 168 | SINGER GAZELLE | $3\frac{5}{16}$ | 84 |
| 169 | STUDEBAKER GOLDEN HAWK | $4\frac{1}{4}$ | 108 |
| 170 | FORD SEDAN | 4 | 102 |
| 171 | HUDSON COMMODORE SEDAN | $4\frac{3}{8}$ | 111 |
| 172 | STUDEBAKER LAND CRUISER | $4\frac{1}{4}$ | 108 |
| 173 | AMERICAN RAMBLER | 4 | 102 |
| 174 | HUDSON HORNET | $4\frac{3}{8}$ | 111 |
| 175 | HILLMAN MINX | $3\frac{9}{16}$ | 90 |
| 176 | AUSTIN A105 | 4 | 102 |
| 177 ▲ | STANDARD VANGUARD III | $3\frac{7}{8}$ | 98 |
| 178 | PLYMOUTH PLAZA | $4\frac{5}{16}$ | 110 |
| 179 | STUDEBAKER PRESIDENT | $4\frac{5}{16}$ | 110 |
| 180 | PACKARD CLIPPER | $4\frac{7}{16}$ | 113 |
| 181 | VOLKSWAGEN | $3\frac{9}{16}$ | 90 |
| 182 | PORSCHE | $3\frac{1}{2}$ | 89 |
| 183 | FIAT 600 | $2\frac{13}{16}$ | 71 |
| 184 | VOLVO AMAZON | $3\frac{13}{16}$ | 97 |
| 185 ▲ | RENAULT FREGATE. | $4\frac{1}{8}$ | 105 |
| 186 | MERCEDES BENZ 220 SE | 4 | 102 |
| 187 | VOLKSWAGEN KARMAN GHIA | $3\frac{13}{16}$ | 97 |

REDRAWN BY ER 10-1-58 | TRACED BY | CHECKED BY | DATE 27-4-55 | MEMO No 20166 SHT. I.
ISSUE 4. ISSUE.G. 29-8-60.

| SALES No | DESCRIPTION | INCHES | M/M |
|---|---|---|---|
| 188 | FOUERBERTH CARAVAN | 5 5/16 | 135 |
| 189 | TRIUMPH HERALD SALOON | 3 3/32 | 86 |
| 190 | CARAVAN | 4 3/4 | 121 |
| 191 | DODGE ROYAL SEDAN | 4 7/16 | 113 |
| 192 | DESOTO FIREFLITE | 4 9/16 | 116 |
| 193 | RAMBLER CROSS COUNTRY | 4 | 102 |
| 194 | BENTLEY SERIES 'S' COUPE | 4 7/16 | 113 |
| 195 | JAGUAR 3.4 LITRE. | 3 13/16 | 97 |
| 196 | | | |
| 197 | MORRIS MINI-TRAVELLER | 2 7/8 | 73 |
| 198 | ROVER 105 R. | 4 | 102 |
| 199 | | | |
| 200 | MIDGET RACER | 2 1/4 | 57 |
| 201 | | | |
| 202 | | | |
| 203 | | | |
| 204 | | | |
| 205 | | | |
| 206 | | | |
| 207 | | | |
| 208 | | | |
| 209 | | | |
| 210 | | | |
| 211 | | | |
| 212 | | | |
| 213 | | | |
| 214 | | | |
| 215 | | | |
| 216 | | | |
| 217 | | | |
| 218 | | | |
| 219 | | | |
| 220 | SMALL OPEN RACING CAR | 3 3/4 | 95 |
| 221 | "SPEED OF THE WIND" RACING CAR | 4 1/8 | 105 |
| 222 | STREAMLINED RACING CAR | 5 | 127 |
| 223 | | | |
| 224 | | | |
| 225 | | | |
| 226 | | | |
| 227 | | | |
| 228 | | | |
| 229 | | | |
| 230 | TALBOT - LAGO RACING CAR | 4 | 102 |
| 231 | MASERATI " | 3 5/8 | 92 |
| 232 | ALFA - ROMEO " | 4 | 102 |
| 233 | COOPER BRISTOL " | 3 1/2 | 89 |
| 234 | FERRARI " | 4 | 102 |
| 235 | H.W.M. " | 3 7/8 | 98 |
| 236 | CONNAUGHT " | 3 13/16 | 97 |
| 237 | MERCEDES BENZ " | 3 7/8 | 98 |
| 238 | JAGUAR "TYPE D" " | 3 7/16 | 87 |
| 239 | VANWALL " | 3 3/4 | 95 |
| 240 | | | |
| 241 | | | |
| 242 | | | |
| 243 | | | |
| 244 | | | |
| 245 | | | |
| 246 | | | |
| 247 | | | |
| 248 | | | |

| SALES No | DESCRIPTION | INCHES | M/M |
|---|---|---|---|
| 249 | STREAMLINED FIRE ENGINE | 4 | 102 |
| 250 | AVELING BARFORD | 4 3/8 | 111 |
| 251 | REFUSE WAGON - BEDFORD | 4 1/4 | 108 |
| 252 | DAIMLER AMBULANCE | 3 3/4 | 95 |
| 253 | AUSTIN TAXI | 3 1/16 | 94 |
| 254 | MERSEY TUNNEL POLICE VAN | 2 7/8 | 73 |
| 255 | POLICE PATROL CAR (HUMBER HAWK) | 4 | 101 |
| 256 | FIRE CHIEFS CAR. | 4 1/2 | 102 |
| 257 | POLICE PATROL CAR (USA). | 4 9/16 | 116 |
| 258 | | | |
| 259 | | | |
| 260 | ROYAL MAIL VAN | 3 1/8 | 79 |
| 261 | TELEPHONE SERVICE VAN | 2 7/8 | 73 |
| 262 | SWISS POSTAL VOLKSWAGEN | 3 9/16 | 90 |
| 263 | | | |
| 264 | | | |
| 265 | PLYMOUTH TAXI (USA) | 4 5/16 | 110 |
| 266 | PLYMOUTH TAXI (CANADIAN) | 4 5/16 | 110 |
| 267 | PLYMOUTH TAXI | 4 5/16 | 110 |
| 268 | | | |
| 269 | | | |
| 270 | A.A. MOTOR CYCLE PATROL | 1 7/8 | 47 |
| 271 | | | |
| 272 | | | |
| 273 | | | |
| 274 | | | |
| 275 | | | |
| 276 | | | |
| 277 | | | |
| 278 | | | |
| 279 | | | |
| 280 | OBSERVATION COACH | 4 1/2 | 114 |
| 281 | LUXURY COACH | 4 1/2 | 114 |
| 282 | DUPLE ROADMASTER COACH | 4 3/4 | 121 |
| 283 | B.O.A.C. COACH | 4 3/4 | 121 |
| 284 | | | |
| 285 | | | |
| 286 | | | |
| 287 | | | |
| 288 | | | |
| 289 | | | |
| 290 | DOUBLE DECK BUS | 4 | 102 |
| 291 | DOUBLE DECK BUS | 4 | 102 |
| 292 | | | |
| 293 | | | |
| 294 | | | |
| 295 | ATLAS BUS | 3 3/8 | 86 |
| 296 | | | |
| 297 | | | |
| 298 | | | |
| 299 | | | |
| 300 | MASSEY HARRIS TRACTOR | 3 1/2 | 89 |
| 301 | FIELD MARSHALL " | 3 | 76 |
| 302 | | | |
| 303 | | | |
| 304 | | | |
| 305 | | | |
| 306 | | | |
| 307 | | | |
| 308 | | | |
| 309 | | | |

REDRAWN BY ER | TRACED BY | CHECKED BY | WP/: | DATE 27-4-55 | MEMO No 20166 SHT. 2.

# MECCANO LTD

## DINKY TOYS DIMENSIONS

### MEMO N° 20166 SHT. 3

| SALES N° | DESCRIPTION | O'ALL LENGTH INCHES | M/M |
|---|---|---|---|
| 310 | | | |
| 311 | | | |
| 312 | | | |
| 313 | | | |
| 314 | | | |
| 315 | | | |
| 316 | | | |
| 317 | | | |
| 318 | | | |
| 319 | "WEEKS' TIPPING FARM TRAILER" E12 | 4⅛ | 105 |
| 320 | HALESOWEN HARVEST TRAILER | 5¼ | 133 |
| 321 | MASSEY HARRIS MANURE SPREADER | 4¾ | 121 |
| 322 | DISC HARROW | 3⅜ | 86 |
| 323 | TRIPLE GANG MOWER | 4⅜ | 111 |
| 324 | HAYRAKE | 3 | 76 |
| 325 | | | |
| 326 | | | |
| 327 | | | |
| 328 | | | |
| 329 | | | |
| 330 | | | |
| 331 | | | |
| 332 | | | |
| 333 | | | |
| 334 | | | |
| 335 | | | |
| 336 | | | |
| 337 | | | |
| 338 | | 3⅝ | 92 |
| 339 | | 3⅛ | 79 |
| 340 | LAND ROVER | 4⅜ | 111 |
| 341 | "  TRAILER | 4¼ | 108 |
| 342 | MOTOCART | 4⅛ | 105 |
| 343 | FARM PRODUCE WAGON | | |
| 344 | ESTATE CAR | | |
| 345 | | | |
| 346 | | | |
| 347 | | | |
| 348 | | | |
| 349 | | | |
| 350 | | | |
| 351 | | | |
| 352 | | | |
| 353 | | | |
| 354 | | | |
| 355 | | | |
| 356 | | | |
| 357 | | | |
| 358 | | | |
| 359 | | | |
| 360 | | | |
| 361 | | | |
| 362 | | | |
| 363 | | | |
| 364 | | | |
| 365 | | | |
| 366 | | | |
| 367 | | | |
| 368 | | | |
| 369 | | | |
| 370 | | | |
| 371 | | | |

| SALES N° | DESCRIPTION | O'ALL LENGTH INCHES | M/M |
|---|---|---|---|
| 372 | | | |
| 373 | | | |
| 374 | | | |
| 375 | | | |
| 376 | | | |
| 377 | | | |
| 378 | | | |
| 379 | | | |
| 380 | | | |
| 381 | GARDEN ROLLER | HT = 2⅝ | 67 |
| 382 | WHEELBARROW | 3¼ | 83 |
| 383 | 4-WHEEL HAND TRUCK (WITH HANDLE UP 3½) | 5 | 127 |
| 384 | GRASS-CUTTER | HT= 2⅜ | 60 |
| 385 | SACK TRUCK | 2½ | 64 |
| 386 | LAWN MOWER | HT= 3½ | 89 |
| 387 | | | |
| 388 | | | |
| 389 | | | |
| 390 | | | |
| 391 | | | |
| 392 | | | |
| 393 | | | |
| 394 | | | |
| 395 | | | |
| 396 | | | |
| 397 | | | |
| 398 | | | |
| 399 | | | |
| 400 | B.E.V ELECTRIC TRUCK | 3⅜ | 86 |
| 401 | COVENTRY CLIMAX FORK LIFT TRUCK | 4½ | 108 |
| 402 | | | |
| 403 | | | |
| 404 | | | |
| 405 | UNIVERSAL JEEP | 3¼ | 83 |
| 406 | | | |
| 407 | | | |
| 408 | BIG BEDFORD LORRY | 5¾ | 146 |
| 409 | BEDFORD ARTICULATED LORRY | 6½ | 165 |
| 410 | "  TIPPING WAGON | 3⅞ | 98 |
| 411 | "  TRUCK | 4 | 102 |
| 412 | AUSTIN WAGON | 4⅛ | 105 |
| 413 | "  COVERED WAGON | 4⅛ | 105 |
| 414 | REAR TIPPING WAGON | 4 | 102 |
| 415 | MECHANICAL HORSE & TRAILER | 4 | 102 |
| 416 | | | |
| 417 | LEYLAND COMET LORRY | 5½ | 140 |
| 418 | "  WITH HINGED TAILBOARD | 5⅝ | 143 |
| 419 | "  CEMENT WAGON | 5⅝ | 143 |
| 420 | FORWARD CONTROL LORRY | 4¼ | 108 |
| 421 | HINDLE-SMART ARTIC. VEHICLE | 5⅜ | 136 |
| 422 | FORDSON FLAT TRUCK | 4⅜ | 111 |
| 423 | | | |
| 424 | | | |
| 425 | | | |
| 426 | | | |
| 427 | | | |
| 428 | LARGE TRAILER | 4¾ | 121 |
| 429 | SMALL TRAILER | 2¾ | 70 |
| 430 | BREAKDOWN LORRY (BODY 4¼) | 4⅞ | 124 |
| 431 | GUY 4 TON LORRY | 5¼ | 133 |
| 432 | "  FLAT PLATFORM | = | = |
| 433 | "  "  WITH TAILBOARD | = | = |

REDRAWN BY E.R. | TRACED BY | CHECKED BY up/. | DATE 27-4-55 | MEMO N° 20166 SHT. 3

302

# MECCANO LTD.

| TITLE | DINKY TOYS DIMENSIONS | MEMO Nº 20166 SHT. 4 |
|---|---|---|

| SALES Nº | DESCRIPTION | O'ALL LENGTH INCHES | M/M |
|---|---|---|---|
| 434 | | | |
| 435 | | | |
| 436 | | | |
| 437 | | | |
| 438 | | | |
| 439 | | | |
| 440 | STUDEBAKER TANKER – MOBILGAS | 4⅜ | 111 |
| 441 | " " " CASTROL | " | " |
| 442 | " " " ESSO | " | " |
| 443 | " " " NATIONAL | " | " |
| 444 | | | |
| 445 | | | |
| 446 | | | |
| 447 | | | |
| 448 | | | |
| 449 | CHEVROLET EL CAMINO | 4⅜ | 111 |
| 450 | TROJAN DELIVERY VAN – ESSO | 3⅜ | 86 |
| 451 | " " " – DUNLOP | " | " |
| 452 | " " " – CHIVERS | " | " |
| 453 | " " " – OXO | " | " |
| 454 | TROJAN DELIVERY VAN – CYDRAX | 3⅜ | 86 |
| 455 | " " " – BROOKE BOND | " | " |
| 456 | | | |
| 457 | | | |
| 458 | | | |
| 459 | | | |
| 460 | | | |
| 461 | | | |
| 462 | | | |
| 463 | | | |
| 464 | | | |
| 465 | MORRIS COMMERCIAL VAN – CAPSTAN | 3⅛ | 79 |
| 466 | | | |
| 467 | | | |
| 468 | | | |
| 469 | | | |
| 470 | AUSTIN VAN – SHELL | 3½ | 89 |
| 471 | " " – NESTLE'S | " | " |
| 472 | " " – RALEIGH | " | " |
| 473 | | | |
| 474 | | | |
| 475 | | | |
| 476 | | | |
| 477 | | | |
| 478 | | | |
| 479 | | | |
| 480 | BEDFORD VAN – KODAK | 3¼ | 83 |
| 481 | " " – OVALTINE | " | " |
| 482 | " " – DINKY TOYS | " | " |
| 483 | | | |
| 484 | | | |
| 485 | | | |
| 486 | | | |
| 487 | | | |
| 488 | | | |
| 489 | | | |
| 490 | ELECTRIC DAIRY VAN | 3⅜ | 86 |
| 491 | N.C.B. ELECTRIC VAN | 3⅜ | 86 |
| 492 | LOUDSPEAKER VAN | 3¼ | 83 |
| 493 | | | |
| 494 | | | |
| 495 | | | |

| SALES Nº | DESCRIPTION | O'ALL LENGTH INCHES | M/M |
|---|---|---|---|
| 496 | | | |
| 497 | | | |
| 498 | | | |
| 499 | | | |
| 600 | | | |
| 601 | | | |
| 602 | | | |
| 603 | | | |
| 604 | | | |
| 605 | | | |
| 606 | | | |
| 607 | | | |
| 608 | | | |
| 609 | | | |
| 610 | | | |
| 611 | | | |
| 612 | | | |
| 613 | | | |
| 614 | | | |
| 615 | | | |
| 616 | | | |
| 617 | | | |
| 618 | | | |
| 619 | | | |
| 620 | | | |
| 621 | 3 TON ARMY WAGON | 4½ | 114 |
| 622 | 10 TON " TRUCK | 5⅜ | 136 |
| 623 | ARMY COVERED WAGON | 4⅛ | 105 |
| 624 | AMBULANCE (DAIMLER) | 3¾ | 95 |
| 625 | AUSTIN COVERED WAGON | 4⅛ | 105 |
| 626 | MILITARY AMBULANCE | 4⅜ | 111 |
| 627 | | | |
| 628 | | | |
| 629 | | | |
| 630 | | | |
| 631 | | | |
| 632 | | | |
| 633 | | | |
| 634 | | | |
| 635 | | | |
| 636 | | | |
| 637 | | | |
| 638 | | | |
| 639 | | | |
| 640 | BEDFORD TRUCK | 3¹¹⁄₁₆ | 93 |
| 641 | ARMY 1 TON CARGO TRUCK | 3⅛ | 79 |
| 642 | PRESSURE REFUELLER | 5½ | 140 |
| 643 | ARMY WATER TANKER | 3½ | 89 |
| 644 | | | |
| 645 | | | |
| 646 | | | |
| 647 | | | |
| 648 | | | |
| 649 | | | |
| 650 | | | |
| 651 | CENTURION TANK (LENGTH WITHOUT GUN 5) | 5¾ | 146 |
| 652 | | | |
| 653 | | | |
| 654 | | | |
| 655 | | | |
| 656 | | | |

REDRAWN BY    TRACED BY    CHECKED BY    DATE 27-4-55    MEMO Nº 20166 SHT. 4.

ER    Wh WPI

ISSUE 2: 24-3-59

# MECCANO LTD.

TITLE **DINKY TOYS DIMENSIONS.** MEMO No 20166 SHT: 5.

| SALES No | DESCRIPTION | O/A LENGTH INCHES | O/A LENGTH M/M | SALES No | DESCRIPTION | O/A LENGTH INCHES | O/A LENGTH M/M |
|---|---|---|---|---|---|---|---|
| 657 | | | | 718 | | | |
| 658 | | | | 719 | | | |
| 659 | | | | 720 | | | |
| 660 | TANK TRANSPORTER | 13¾ | 337 | 721 | | | |
| 661 | RECOVERY TRACTOR | 5¼ | 133 | 722 | | | |
| 662 | | | | 723 | | | |
| 663 | | | | 724 | | | |
| 664 | | | | 725 | | | |
| 665 | | | | 726 | | | |
| 666 | CORPORAL MISSILE 9"-228 mm. MISSILE ERECTOR VEHICLE 9 9/16 242 mm LAUNCHING PLATFORM | 3½ | 89 | 727 | | | |
| 667 | MISSILE SERVICING PLATFORM | 7¾ | 197 | 728 | | | |
| 668 | | | | 729 | | | |
| 669 | JEEP UNIVERSAL (MILITARY SERVICE) | 3¼ | 82 | 730 | TEMPEST II FIGHTER WING SPAN = 2½ | 3 3/16 | 81 |
| 670 | ARMOURED CAR | 2⅞ | 73 | 731 | TWIN ENGINED FIGHTER " " = 3 | 2 | 51 |
| 671 | | | | 732 | METEOR TWIN " " = 2⅝ | 2⅝ | 67 |
| 672 | | | | 733 | SHOOTING STAR " " = 2⅜ | 2¼ | 57 |
| 673 | SCOUT CAR | 2⅝ | 67 | 734 | SUPERMARINE SWIFT " " = 2 | 2 9/16 | 65 |
| 674 | AUSTIN CHAMP | 2¾ | 70 | 735 | GLOSTER JAVELIN " " = 3¼ | 3⅝ | 92 |
| 675 | FORD "FORDOR" SEDAN (MILITARY) | 4 | 102 | 736 | HAWKER HUNTER " " = 2⅛ | 2 13/16 | 71 |
| 676 | ARMOURED PERSONNEL CARRIER | 3¼ | 83 | 737 | P1B LIGHTNING FIGHTER " " = 2 3/16. 55 | 3⅝ | 92 |
| 677 | " COMMAND VEHICLE | 5¼ | 133 | 738 | DH 110 SEA VIXEN " " = 3 5/32 | 3⅜ | 86 |
| 678 | | | | 739 | | | |
| 679 | | | | 740 | | | |
| 680 | | | | 741 | | | |
| 681 | | | | 742 | | | |
| 682 | | | | 743 | | | |
| 683 | | | | 744 | | | |
| 684 | | | | 745 | | | |
| 685 | | | | 746 | | | |
| 686 | 25 POUNDER FIELD GUN | 3½ | 89 | 747 | | | |
| 687 | TRAILER – 25 POUNDER | 2 3/16 | 56 | 748 | | | |
| 688 | FIELD ARTILLERY TRACTOR | 3⅛ | 79 | 749 | | | |
| 689 | MEDIUM " " | 5½ | 140 | 750 | TELEPHONE CALL BOX HT: = | 2 5/16 | 59 |
| 690 | | | | 751 | POLICE HUT HT: = | 2⅝ | 67 |
| 691 | | | | 752 | | | |
| 692 | 5·5 MEDIUM GUN | 5⅛ | 131 | 753 | | | |
| 693 | HOWITZER 7·2. GUN. | 5⅛ | 131 | 754 | | | |
| 694 | | | | 755 | LAMP POST HT. = 5 3/4 | | 146 |
| 695 | | | | 756 | LAMP POST HT. = 5¾ | | 146 |
| 696 | | | | 757 | | | |
| 697 | 25 Pr. FIELD GUN SET. TRACTOR 3⅛~79mm. TRAILER 2 3/16~53mm. GUN 3½~89 | 8⅜ | 212 | 758 | | | |
| 698 | | | | 759 | | | |
| 699 | | | | 760 | PILLAR BOX HT: = | 1⅝ | 41 |
| 700 | SEAPLANE. WING SPAN = 4 | 2¾ | 70 | 761 | | | |
| 701 | | | | 762 | | | |
| 702 | | | | 763 | | | |
| 703 | | | | 764. | | | |
| 704 | AVRO YORK WING SPAN = 6¼ | 4⅞ | 124 | 765 | ROAD HOARDING | 8⅛ | 206 |
| 705 | VICKERS VIKING " " = 5½ | 3⅞ | 98 | 766 | | | |
| 706 | VICKERS VISCOUNT " " = 5⅞. 149 | 5⅛ | 130 | 767 | | | |
| 707 | | | | 768 | | | |
| 708 | VICKERS VISCOUNT WING SPAN = 5⅞. | 5⅛ | 130 | 769 | | | |
| 709 | | | | 770 | | | |
| 710 | | | | 771 | | | |
| 711 | | | | 772 | | | |
| 712 | | | | 773 | TRAFFIC SIGNAL HT: = | 2½ | 64 |
| 713 | | | | 774 | | | |
| 714 | | | | 775 | | | |
| 715 | BRISTOL 173 HELICOPTER | 5 | 127 | 776 | | | |
| 716 | WESTLAND SIKORSKY | 3½ | 89 | 777 | BELISHA BEACON. HT: = | 2 | 51 |
| 717 | | | | 778. | | | |

TRACED BY .......... CHECKED BY ........ DATE 27-4-55 MEMO No 20,166 SHT: 5.

ISSUE 2. 24-3-59 ISSUE.4.29-8-60.

MECCANO LTD.

| TITLE | DINKY TOYS DIMENSIONS | MEMO Nº 20166 SHT. 6 |
|---|---|---|

| SALES Nº | DESCRIPTION | O/A LENGTH INCHES | O/A LENGTH M/M | SALES Nº | DESCRIPTION | O/A LENGTH INCHES | O/A LENGTH M/M |
|---|---|---|---|---|---|---|---|
| 779 | | | | 939 | | | |
| 780 | | | | 940 | | | |
| 781 | PETROL PUMP STATION 'ESSO' HT 4 1/2 | 4 1/2 | 114 | 941 | FODEN 14 TON TANKER "MOBILGAS" | 7 3/8 | 188 |
| 782 | PETROL PUMP STATION 'SHELL' | 8 | 203 | 942 | FODEN TANKER REGENT | 7 3/8 | 188 |
| 783 | PETROL PUMP STATION 'B.P.' | 8 | 203 | 943 | LEYLAND OCTOPUS TANKER | 7 5/8 | 194 |
| 784 | | | | 944 | | | |
| 785 | SERVICE STATION | 13 1/4 | 337 | 945 | | | |
| 786 | TYRE RACK HT=2" (51mm) | 2 1/16 | 52 | 946 | | | |
| 787 | | | | 947 | | | |
| 788 | | | | 948 | McCLEAN AMERICAN TRUCK | 11 5/8 | 295 |
| 789 | | | | 949 | WAYNE SCHOOL BUS | 8 3/4 | 222 |
| 790 | | | | 950 | | | |
| 791 | | | | 951 | | | |
| 792 | PACKING CASE | 1 3/16 SQ | 30 SQ | 952 | | | |
| 793 | | | | 953 | | | |
| 794 | LOADING RAMP – PULLMORE | 9 3/16 | 234 | 954 | FIRE STATION HT=4 15/16 (126) | 8 | 203 |
| 795 | | | | 955 | FIRE ENGINE (LADDER EXT=9") | 5 1/2 | 140 |
| 796 | HEALEY SPORTS BOAT & TRAILER | 4 1/4 | 108 | 956 | TURNTABLE FIRE ESCAPE (LADDER EXT=14 3/8) | 7 3/4 | 197 |
| 797 | HEALEY SPORTS BOAT | 3 11/16 | 94 | 957 | | | |
| 798 | EXPRESS PASSENGER TRAIN | 11 7/8 | 301 | 958 | SNOW PLOUGH | 7 3/4 | 197 |
| 799 | | | | 959 | FODEN DUMP TRUCK. | 6 17/32 | 166 |
| | | | | 960 | LORRY MOUNTED CEMENT MIXER. | 5 1/16 | 129 |
| 900 | | | | 961 | BLAW-KNOX BULLDOZER . | 5 5/8 | 143 |
| 901 | FODEN DIESEL 8 WHEELED WAGON | 7 3/8 | 188 | 962 | MUIR-HILL DUMPER | 4 3/16 | 106 |
| 902 | " FLAT TRUCK | 7 3/8 | 188 | 963 | BLAW-KNOX HEAVY TRACTOR | 4 5/8 | 118 |
| 903 | " " " WITH TAILBOARD | 7 3/8 | 188 | 964 | ELEVATOR LOADER HT: = 6 1/2. | 6 1/8 | 156 |
| 904 | | | | 965 | EUCLID REAR DUMP TRUCK | 5 5/8 | 143 |
| 905 | FODEN FLAT TRUCK WITH CHAINS | 7 3/8 | 188 | 966 | MARREL MULTI-BUCKET UNIT. | 4 5/8 | 118 |
| 906 | | | | 967 | B.B.C. T.V. MOBILE CONTROL ROOM | 5 15/16 | 151 |
| 907 | | | | 968 | " " ROVING EYE VEHICLE | 4 7/16 | 113 |
| 908 | | | | 969 | " " EXTENDING MAST " (MAST EXT=12 1/2) | 6 1/2 | 165 |
| 909 | | | | 970 | | | |
| 910 | | | | 971 | COLES-MOBILE CRANE JIB = 5 3/8 | 6 3/8 | 162 |
| 911 | | | | 972 | " -20 TON LORRY MOUNTED CRANE JIB 6 3/8 | 9 5/8 | 245 |
| 912 | | | | 973 | GOODS YARD CRANE BASE = 4" SQ JIB = 7 | | 178 |
| 913 | | | | 974 | | | |
| 914 | | | | 975 | | | |
| 915 | | | | 976 | | | |
| 916 | | | | 977 | | | |
| 917 | GUY VAN – SPRATTS. | 5 1/4 | 133 | 978 | | | |
| 918 | " " – EVER READY | " | " | 979 | | | |
| 919 | " " GOLDEN SHRED | " | " | 980 | | | |
| 920 | | | | 981 | HORSEBOX | 6 7/8 | 175 |
| 921 | | | | 982 | PULLMORE CAR TRANSPORTER | 9 3/4 | 248 |
| 922 | | | | 983 | | | |
| 923 | BIG BEDFORD VAN HEINZ | 5 3/4 | 146 | 984 | CAR CARRIER | 9 9/16 | 243 |
| 924 | | | | 985 | " " TRAILER | 9 | 229 |
| 925 | | | | 986 | MIGHTY ANTAR LOW LOADER | 12 | 305 |
| 926 | | | | 987 | | | |
| 927 | | | | 988 | | | |
| 928 | | | | 989 | | | |
| 929 | | | | 990 | | | |
| 930 | BEDFORD PALLET JEKTA VAN. | 6 5/8 | 168 | 991 | A.E.C. TANKER | 6" | 153 |
| 931 | | | | 992 | | | |
| 932 | | | | 993 | | | |
| 933 | | | | 994 | | | |
| 934 | LEYLAND OCTOPUS | 7 5/8 | 194 | 995 | | | |
| 935 | | | | 996 | | | |
| 936 | | | | 997 | | | |
| 937 | | | | 998 | BRISTOL BRITANNIA WING SPAN = 8 7/8 | 7 1/8 | 181 |
| 938 | | | | 999. | D.H. COMET " " = 7 1/4 | 5 13/16 | 148 |

TRACED BY ........ CHECKED BY ........ WP. DATE 27-4-55 MEMO Nº 20,166 SHT: 6.

ISSUE 2. 24-3-59

# MECCANO LTD.

## TITLE:- MARKING ON DINKY TOYS.

### MEMO No. 20074. SH.I.

| JOB. | DESCRIPTION. | PRESENT SALES No. | SALES No REQ. | DT OR DST | DT OR DST REQ. | CAST OR STEEL. | LOCATION OF DT MARKING | LOCATION OF SALES No. | REMARKS. |
|---|---|---|---|---|---|---|---|---|---|
| 13737 | A.E.C. TANKER. | / | 991 | DT | DST | MS | BASE. | BASE. | ADD SALES No. ALTER DT. |
| 13383 | AUSTIN ATLANTIC. | 140A | 106 | DT | DT | MS | BASE. | BASE. | ALTER SALES No. |
| 13618 | AUSTIN TAXI. | 40H | 254 | DT | DT | CAST | BASE (CAST) | BASE (CAST) | ALTER SALES No |
| 13843 | AVRO VULCAN. | 749 | 992 | DT | DST | CAST. ALUMINIUM | CASTING. | CASTING. | ALTER SALES No ALTER DT. |
| 12147 | AVRO YORK. | 704 | 704 | DT | DT | CAST | WINGS. | WINGS. | ALTERED BUT NOT ISSUED. |
| 12861 | AVELING BARFORD ROLLER. | / | 251 | DT | DT | MS | BASE. (MS) | BASE (MS) | ADD SALES No. |
| 12842 | BEDFORD END TIPPER. | / | 410 | DT | DT | CAST. | BASE 12845 | BODY 12842 | ADD SALES No. |
| FLOOR 12972 | BEDFORD REFUSE COLLECTOR. | / | 252 | DT | DT | MS | BASE 12845 | BASE No | ADD SALES No |
| 12836 | BEDFORD TRUCK. | / | 411 | DT | DT | CAST. | BASE 12845 | BODY 12816 | ADD SALES No |
| 13742 | BIG BEDFORD LORRY. | 522 | 408 | DT | DT | CAST. | CHASSIS 13741 | BODY 13742 | ALTER SALES No. |
| FLOOR 13966 | BIG BEDFORD VAN. | 923 | / | DT | DST | MS | CHASSIS 13741 | FLOOR 13966 | DST & DELETE SALES No. |
| 12919 | B.E.V. TRUCK. | / | 400 | DT | DT | MS | BASE. | BASE. | ADD SALES No. |
| 12901A | BLAW KNOX BULLDOZER. | 561 | 961 | DST | DST | MS | BASE. | BASE. | ALTER SALES No. |
| 13436 | COMMER BREAKDOWN TRUCK. | / | 430 | DT | DT | CAST. | BASE 13438 | BODY 13436 | ADD SALES No |
| 13174 | COVENTRY CLIMAX TRUCK. | / | 401 | DT | DT | MS | BASE. | BASE. | ADD SALES No |
| 13829 | COMET. | 702 | 999 | DT | DST | CAST. | CASTING. | CASTING. | ALTER SALES No. ALTER DT. |
| 13386 | DAIMLER AMBULANCE. | 30H | 253 | DT | DT | MS | BASE. | BASE. | ALTER SALES No |
| 6682 | DODGE REAR TIPPING WAGON. | 30M | 414 | DT | DT | CAST. | CHASSIS 13511 | PLATFORM 6682 | ALTER SALES No |
| 13513 | DODGE FARM PRODUCE WAGON. | 30N | 343 | DT | DT | CAST | CHASSIS 13511A | BODY 13513 | ALTER SALES No |
| 13752 | DUPLE ROADMASTER COACH. | 29H | 282 | DT | DT | MS | BASE. | BASE. | ALTER SALES No. |
| 10898 | DOUBLE DECK BUS. | 29C | 290 | DT | DT | CAST. | CASTING. | CASTING. | ALTER SALES No |
| 13696 | DRAWBAR-GANG MOWER. | / | 323 | DT | DT | CAST. | CASTING. | CASTING. | ADD SALES No SEE 12697 |
| 13651 | DISC HARROW. | / | 322 | DT | DT | CAST. | CASTING. | CASTING. | ADD SALES No. |
| 13704 | ELEVATOR LOADER. | 564 | 964 | DST | DST | CAST. | CASTING. | CASTING. | ALTER SALES No. |
| 13777 | FIRE ENGINE. (EXT. LADDER) | 555 | 955 | DT | DST | MS | BASE. | BASE. | ALTER SALES No. ALTER DT. |
| 13151 | FARM TRAILER. | 27B | 320 | DT | DT | CAST. | CASTING. | CASTING. | ALTER SALES No ALTER DT. |
| 13766 | FARM RAKE - TOWBAR. | / | 324 | DT | DT | CAST. | CASTING. | CASTING. | ADD SALES No |
| 12868 | FORWARD CONTROL LORRY. | 25R | 420 | DT | DT | CAST | BODY. | BODY. | ALTERED BUT NOT ISSUED. |
| 13596 | FORDSON THAMES FLAT TRUCK. | 30R | 422 | DT | DT | CAST | CHASSIS. | CHASSIS. | ALTER SALES No. |
| FLOOR 13014 | GUY VAN. | 514 | / | DST | DST | MS | CHASSIS 12181 | FLOOR | DST FOR VAN ONLY DELETE SALES No. |
| 12182 | GUY 4 TON LORRY. | 511 | 431 | DST | DT | CAST. | CHASSIS 12181 | BODY 12182 | ALTER SALES No ALTER DT |
| 12185 | GUY FLAT PLATFORM. | 512 | 432 | DST | DT | CAST. | CHASSIS 12181 | BODY 12185 | ALTER SALES No ALTER DST |
| 12186 | GUY FLAT PLATFORM WITH TAILBOARD. | 513 | 433 | DST | DT | CAST. | CHASSIS 12181 | BODY 12186 | ALTERED BUT NOT ISSUED. |
| 13026 | GARDEN ROLLER. | / | 381 | DT | DT | CAST. | CASTING. | CASTING. | NO MARKING. |
| 13601 | GRASS CUTTER. | 105E | 384 | DT | DT | CAST | CASTING. | CASTING. | ALTER SALES No |
| 13623 | GOODS YARD CRANE. | 752 | 973 | DST. | DT | CAST | CASTING. | CASTING. | ALTER SALES No ALTER DT. |
| 13034 | GARDEN TROLLEY. | 105C | 383 | DT | DT | CAST. | CASTING. | CASTING. | ALTER SALES No. |
| 12901 | HEAVY TRACTOR. | 563 | 963 | DST | DST | MS | BASE. | BASE. | ALTER SALES No. |

| ISSUE No. | | DRAWN. V.R. |
|---|---|---|
| DATE. | | CHECKED. 10-1-55 |
| SIGNATURE. | | APPROVED. |

# MECCANO LTD.

**TITLE:- MARKING ON DINKY TOYS.**

**MEMO No. 20074 SH.2**

| JOB. | DESCRIPTION. | PRESENT SALES No. | SALES No. REQD. | DT. OR DST. | DT. OR DST. | DT. OR DST RED. | CAST OR STEEL. | LOCATION OF DT MARKING | LOCATION OF SALES No. | REMARKS. |
|---|---|---|---|---|---|---|---|---|---|---|
| 13723 | HINDLE SMART ARTICULATED VEHICLE. | 30W | 421 | DT | DT | DT | CAST. | BODY. | BASE 13722 | ALTER SALES No. |
| 13502 | HORSEBOX. | 980 | | DST | DST | | CAST. ALUMINIUM | CASTING. | CASTING. | DELETE SALES No. |
| 13746 | JEEP - UNIVERSAL. | 25Y | 405 | DT | DT | DT | CAST. | BODY. | BODY. | ALTER SALES No. |
| 13234 | LAND ROVER. | 27D | 340 | DT | DT | DT | CAST | BODY. | BODY. | ALTER SALES No. |
| 13669 | LEYLAND COMET CEMENT WAGON. | 533 | 419 | DST | DST | DT | CAST | CHASSIS 13121 | BODY 13669 | ALTER SALES No. ALTER DST. |
| 13123 | LEYLAND COMET. | 531 | 417 | DST | DST | DT | MS | CHASSIS 13121 | BODY 13123 | ALTER SALES No. ALTER DST. |
| 13665 | LEYLAND COMET WITH HINGED TAILBOARD. | 532 | 418 | DST | DST | DT | CAST | CHASSIS 13121 | BODY 13665 | ALTER SALES No. ALTER DST. |
| 13482 | LUXURY COACH. | 29G | 281 | DT | DT | DT | MS | BASE. | BASE. | ALTER SALES No. |
| 13042 | LAWN MOWER - SIDE PLATE. | 751 | 386 | DST | DST | | CAST. | CASTING. | CASTING. | NOT ON LIST OF SUPERTOYS. |
| 13047 | " " - GRASS BOX. | | | DST | DST | | CAST. | CASTING. | CASTING. | ALTER SALES No. |
| 13272 | MORRIS OXFORD. | / | 159 | DT | DT | DT | MS | BASE. | BASE. | ADD SALES No. REDESIGN. |
| 12983 | MUIR HILL DUMP TRUCK. | / | 962 | DST | DST | DST | MS | BASE | BASE | ADD SALES No. |
| 12155 | METEOR. | 27C | 732 | DT | DT | DT | CAST. | CASTING. | CASTING. | ADD SALES No. |
| 13134 | MANURE SPREADER. | / | 321 | DT | DT | DT | CAST. | CASTING. | CASTING. | ALTER SALES No. |
| 13274 | MOTOCART. | 27G | 342 | DT | DT | DT | CAST | CASTING. | CASTING. | ALTER SALES No. |
| 7281 | MECHANICAL HORSE. | / | 415 | DT | DT | DT | CAST | CASTING. | CASTING. | ADD SALES No. |
| 13642 | N.C.B. VAN. (ELECTRIC) | 30V | 490 | DT | DT | DT | CAST. | CASTING. | CASTING. | ALTER SALES No. |
| 13426 | OBSERVATION COACH. | 29F | 280 | DT | DT | DT | MS | BASE. | BASE. | ALTER SALES No. |
| 13791 | PULLMORE CAR TRANSPORTER. | 582 | 982 | DST | DST | DST | CAST. ALUMINIUM | CASTING. | CASTING. | ALTER SALES No. JOB LIST & ASSEMBLY. |
| 12707 | RILEY SALOON. | 40A | 158 | DT | DT | DT | MS | BASE. | BASE. | ALTER SALES No. |
| 12997 | STANDARD VANGUARD. | 40E | 153 | DT | DT | DT | MS | BASE. | BASE. | ADD SALES No. REDESIGN. |
| 10990 | STREAMLINED RACING CAR. | / | 222 | DT | DT | DT | MS | BASE. | BASE. | CHANGED BUT NOT ISSUED. ALTER DST. |
| 12716 | SHOOTING STAR. | 25G | 733 | DST | DST | DT | CAST | CASTING. | CASTING. | ADD SALES No. |
| 13031 | SACK TRUCK. | / | 385 | DT | DT | DT | CAST. | CASTING. | CASTING. | ADD SALES No. |
| 10902 | SEAPLANE. | / | 700 | DT | DT | DT | CAST. | WINGS. | WINGS. | ALTERED BUT NOT ISSUED. |
| 6661 | SMALL OPEN RACING CAR. | / | 220 | DT | DT | DT | CAST. | CASTING. | CASTING. | ADD SALES No. |
| 12880 | TRIUMPH 1800 | / | 151 | DT | DT | DT | MS | BASE | BASE. | ADD SALES No. REDESIGN. |
| 12871 | TRAILER. (LARGE) | 551 | 428 | DST | DST | DT | CAST. | CASTING. | CASTING. | ALTER SALES No. ALTER DST. |
| 7263 | TRAILER. (SMALL) | 25G | 429 | DT | DT | DT | CAST | CASTING. | CASTING. | ALTER SALES No. |
| 12151 | TEMPEST II | / | 730 | DT | DT | DT | CAST | CASTING. | CASTING. | ADD SALES No. |
| 12106 | TWIN ENGINED FIGHTER. | / | 731 | DT | DT | DT | CAST. | WINGS. | WINGS. | ALTERED BUT NOT ISSUED. |
| 13028 | WHEELBARROW. | 105B | 382 | DT | DT | DT | CAST. | CASTING | CASTING. | ALTER SALES No. |
| 7776 | 20 TON LORRY MOUNTED CRANE. | 972 | 972 | DT | DST | DT | CAST. | CHASSIS | CHASSIS. | ALTER DT. |

DRAWN. VR 10-1-55

CHECKED.

APPROVED.

ISSUE No.

DATE.

SIGNATURE.

# Source Material
# & Bibliography

*History of British Dinky Toys 1934–64* by Cecil Gibson—first published by MAP latterly by MIKANSUE and *Modellers' World.*
*Dinky Toys 1964–1980* by Ed Symons—Published by the Author
*Histoire des Dinky Toys Français* by Jean-Michel Roulet—Editions Adepte.

## Notes

1. The '=' signs round the names of models indicates that the model has been renumbered.
2. In 1957, transfers were issued for use with the 100 series and 'other appropriate racing cars', each packet containing three sets of transfers of three racing numbers.
3. 401 Fork Lift Truck carrying a paperbale dated 7.6.1963, commemorating an anniversary of the Royal Dutch Paper Mill has just come into a collector's hands in Holland.
4. Page 93 'of gold or silver' should read 'of gold, red or silver'
5. Page 111 cat. no. 66 – should read 'contains 66a, b, c, d, e and f'
6. Page 48 Table refers to first castings.
7. Page 51 Table refers to second and third castings.

# DINKY TOYS

Here is the first instalment of Dinky Toys, famous for their wonderful realism and beautiful finish in attractive colours. Many other models will follow, and we have in preparation some of the latest types of Cars and Aircraft.

"Speed of the Wind" Record Car

Double Deck Bus

Packard "Super 8" Touring Sedan

"Hurricane"

Armstrong-Whitworth Air Liner

Mobile Anti-Aircraft Gun

| | | Retail Price Each cents. |
|---|---|---|
| 22c | Motor Truck | 25 |
| 23a | Racing Car | 20 |
| 23c | Racing Car | 35 |
| 23d | Racing Car | 35 |
| 23e | "Speed of the Wind" Record Car | 35 |
| 23p | MG Record Car | 45 |
| 25b | Covered Van | 40 |
| 25d | Petrol Tank Wagon | 40 |
| 25e | Tipping Wagon | 40 |
| 25f | Market Gardener's Van | 40 |
| 25h | Streamlined Fire Engine | 40 |
| 25s | Six-Wheeled Wagon | 55 |
| 28 | Delivery Van | 30 |
| 29b | Streamlined Bus | 25 |
| 29c | Double Deck Bus | 70 |
| 30e | Breakdown Car | 40 |
| 33w | Mechanical Horse and Open Wagon | 45 |
| 34b | Royal Mail Van | 90 |
| 35a | Saloon Car | 20 |
| 35b | Racer | 20 |
| 35c | MG Sports Car | 20 |
| 35d | Austin Seven Car | 20 |
| 36a | Armstrong-Siddeley Limousine | 45 |
| 36b | Bentley 2-Seater Sports Coupé | 45 |
| 36c | Humber "Vogue" Saloon | 45 |
| 36d | Rover Streamlined Saloon | 45 |
| 36e | British Salmson 2-Seater Sports | 45 |
| 36f | British Salmson 4-Seater Sports | 45 |
| 38a | Frazer Nash—BMW Sports | 60 |
| 38b | Sunbeam-Talbot Sports | 60 |
| 38d | Alvis Sports Tourer | 60 |
| 39a | Packard "Super 8" Touring Sedan | 60 |
| 39b | Oldsmobile "6" Sedan | 60 |
| 39c | Lincoln "Zephyr" Coupé | 60 |
| 39d | Buick "Viceroy" Saloon | 60 |
| 39e | Chrysler "Royal" Sedan | 60 |
| 39f | Studebaker "State Commander" Coupé | 60 |
| 60g | Light Racer | 25 |
| 60k | Light Tourer | 20 |
| 60r | Empire Flying Boat | 70 |
| 60w | Flying Boat | 65 |
| 62a | "Spitfire" | 20 |
| 62b | Medium Bomber | 35 |
| 62g | Long Range Bomber | 60 |
| 62m | Light Transport | 25 |
| 62p | Armstrong-Whitworth Air Liner | 75 |
| 62r | Four-Engined Air Liner | 55 |
| 62s | "Hurricane" | 25 |
| 63b | Seaplane | 55 |
| 151a | Medium Tank | 95 |
| 151b | Transport Wagon | 60 |
| 152a | Light Tank | 65 |
| 152b | Reconnaissance Car | 65 |
| 161b | Mobile Anti-Aircraft Gun | 95 |

## Made by Meccano Ltd., Liverpool, England

Canadian Branch :
MECCANO LTD., 187-189, CHURCH STREET, TORONTO

16/1145/20                Printed in England
*The first known post-war Dinky Toy Catalogue*

# Index

*See Contents page 5 for details
of specific vehicle types.*

311

# DINKY TOY COMPENDIUM

*Patrick French*

A full listing of all British made
Dinky Toys issued 1931 to 1979
cross-referenced to Volume 4 of
The Hornby Companion Series
'Dinky Toys & Modelled Miniatures',
by Mike & Sue Richardson

FRANK HORNBY
1863–1936

## New Cavendish Books

**LONDON**

This Compendium includes all the known production and variations of Dinky Toy equipment during its years of manufacture at Binns Road.

The listing is cross-referenced to Volume 4 of The Hornby Companion Series and thus will provide an invaluable and convenient guide which will also be more portable than the main volume.

In the best tradition of the Meccano "A" Set System, this add-on booklet will enhance access to information and be a very valuable addition to the relevant volume of the classic Hornby Companion Series.

## Acknowledgements

My thanks are due to Pete McAskie and Colin Baddiel and the many collectors who have visited their stands in Gray's Mews and allowed themselves to be pumped for information, always so willingly given and gratefully received. I hope that these people will realise who they are: By giving no names I leave no-one out! Particular thanks to Arthur Close and H. N. Twells, for supplying the dimensions for the Doll's House Furniture and pre-war Military figures, and to Hugh Sutherland for copious details.

Patrick Trench, January 1985

## Bibliography

'Dinky Toys and Modelled Miniatures' by Mike and Sue Richardson, New Cavendish Books, 1981.

'History of British Dinky Toys 1934–64' by Cecil Gibson, MAP, 1966, latterly published by Mikansue and *Modellers' World*.

'Dinky Toys 1964–80' by Ed Symons, published by the author, 1982.

'Histoire des Dinky Toys Français' by Jean-Michel Roulet, Editions Adepte, 1978.

'Collecting Dinky Toy Miniature Model Aircraft' by John Marshall, Silverdale Press, 1974.

Articles published in *Modellers' World* magazine; Meccano and Dinky Toy catalogues.

'A2Z Dinky Specialised Book' by Peter Harrington and Hugh Sutherland, Collecta-Books, 1984

**First edition published in Great Britain by New Cavendish Books – 1986**

The Hornby Companion Series

Design – John B. Cooper
Editorial direction – Allen Levy

Phototypeset by Wyvern Typesetting Ltd, Bristol.
Printed and bound in Hong Kong.

New Cavendish Books, 23 Craven Hill, London W2 3EN
Distribution: ABP, North Way, Andover, Hampshire SP10 5BE

ISBN 0 904568 85 7

# Errata

to 'Dinky Toys & Modelled Miniatures'.

1. P8, February 1932 Catalogue, date should read 1934
2. P24, Col 1, para 2: the "Speed of the Wind" *does* exist in lead (see Tables)
3. P38, (See P.00) should read p.10
4. P46, Fig 41: Caption should read ". . . *2nd type, not 1st type*".
5. P46, Fig 41. The green Tanker at top right is an early post-war version
6. P49: Captions should read:
   Fig. 52 "28e Firestone Van"
   Fig. 53 "Reverse side of 28e and 28d"
   Fig. 54 "28 Vans, 2nd Type"
   Fig. 55 "28 Vans, 3rd Type"
7. P59, Col 3, para 3: ". . . of the same colour – " *e.g.* not *i.e.*.
8. P59, Fig 67. The Armstrong Siddeley of this series is not illustrated here – see fig 68. The red and maroon 24 series Rover was illustrated to contrast with the 36 series green Rover.
9. P62, Col 2, para 2: ". . . the increase of axle slots from .070 to .088 . . ." The unit is *inches* (not specified)
10. P69: The Police, AA and RAC figures and the two figures from set 12 *are* marked, on the upper surface of the base, "Meccano Dinky Toys"
11. P73, Col 1, para 2: for "*22g* Searchlight Lorry" read *22s*
12. P78, Col 1, The 151b Transport Wagon does *not* have a tinplate base
13. P78, Col 2: The "all-cast Water Trailer" *does* have a tin base
14. P84, para 3: Heading should read "50d Cruiser 'HMS *YORK*'"
15. P111, right-hand table: The last two names in the right-hand column have been wrongly placed. The table should read:
    62r Four-Engined Liner (DH ALBATROSS)
    62s Hurricane
    63b Seaplane ('Mercury' Seaplane)
16. P154, Col 2: for "coloured *chassis*" read "coloured *wheels*"
17. P159, Left-hand table: 470 Austin "Shell BP": for *1965* read *1956*
18. P162, Fig 197: Caption should read "Drawings for the *later* transfer (see P159, Col 3)
19. P169, Table 1: Bedford "AA Service": for *410* read *412*
20. P174, Fig 236: Caption should read: "1965 catalogue illustration"
21. P175, Col 3, para 1: for *1979* read *1969*
22. P176, Col 3, para 2 and P177, Table 2: for *229* read *299*
23. P194, Col 3, line 2: for "*cream* upper deck" read "*grey* . . ."
24. P200, Col 3, para 3: for "*21 years*". read "*11 years*"
25. P219, line 10: should read "VEHICLE did exist as a real vehicle, and can be . . ."
26. P225, Fig 380: for "*129*" read "*181*"
27. P246, Table 2: for "*794/999*" read "*794/994*"
28. P296: for "*450* Jeep" read "*405* Jeep"

# Introductory notes to the tables

The page numbers in these tables refer to pages in 'Dinky Toys & Modelled Miniatures'.

1: Colours and casting variations are those known to me at the time of writing: I have no doubt that more exist.

2: Only Dinky Toys entirely produced at Binn's Road have been included: This involves the conscious omission of the following:
   A: The French production, amply covered in Jean-Michel Roulet's book.
   B: The Hong Kong production (hence the omission of 180 Rover 3500 and 219 Big Cat Jaguar).
   C: Promotionals and other limited issues where the decoration was not applied by Dinky Toys, although the paint may differ from the standard issues. These include:
   (490) Electric Milk Float 'Job's Dairies' (1960). See page 181.
   (410) Bedford Van: Many liveries by John Gay and Jean-Michel Roulet, among others, on specially finished blanks (for example the *Modellers' World* issue on page 168)
   (915) AEC Articulated Flat Truck 'Thames Board Mills' (ca. 1975) see page 188–189
   There are several cases where I have not found concrete evidence either way of the origin of the transfers or stickers. These include:
   (28 series) 'Maison de Bonneterie' Van. See page 50
   (28 series) 'Bentall's Van. See page 51
   (25b) 'M.T.S.' Covered Wagon (ca. 1946, Grey)
   (289) Routemaster Bus 'Throllenbeck' (1979, Gold, for Belgian market)
   (416) Ford Transit Van '1,000,000 Transit'. See page 169
   Some of these have, however, been included in the tables.

3: No tyres or other spare parts are listed.

4: The material is to be assumed to be zamac, unless otherwise specified in the Comments and Variations column.

5: Where no casting or colour difference is noted, pre-war and post-war examples can be differentiated by axle thickness: .062"/1.58mm to 1941; .078"/1.98mm from 1945.

6: Dates of colour and casting changes, where given, are only as accurate as the Dinky Toy catalogues from which they are taken.

General Notes on the Figures; All figures issued pre-war are made of a lead alloy, and are marked "Hornby Series" (if issued before 1934) or "Dinky Toys" on the upper surface of the stand. The marking is not always visible as the paint is often too thick. There are three main variations on the figures in sets 1, 3, 4 and 5. The first issue was to a larger size (1932); the second issue appeared in 1939; the third issue used the same castings as the second, but had simplified paint schemes. These are identified as 1:, 2:, 3: in the Colours and Variation columns. The passengers are easy to identify as regards pre- and post-war and the changes are quite specific. As regards the station and hotel staff, pre-war examples may be identified by their having shirts and ties picked out, and the colour is a deeper blue. These comments apply to sets 1–6 and 001–006, and to 12d, 12e/011, 012.

(H) = Height     Dimensions in mm.     R/ = Renumbered + date

| No. | Description | Colours | Length | Introduced | Deleted | Comment/Variations | Page |
|---|---|---|---|---|---|---|---|
| 001 | Station Staff (0 Gauge) | Blue | (H)35 | R/54 | 1956 | Renumbering of 1. | 35 |
| 002 | Galactic War Station | | | 1979 | 1979 | Dinky Builda. Card. | 242 |
| 002 | Farmyard Animals | Various | Various | R/54 | 1956 | Renumbering of 2. | 29 |
| 002 | Blazing Inferno | | | 1979 | 1979 | Dinky Builda. Card. | 242 |
| 003 | Passengers (0 Gauge) | Various | (H)35 | R/54 | 1956 | Renumbering of 3. | 268 |
| 004 | Engineering Staff (0 Gauge) | Various | (H)35 | R/54 | 1956 | Renumbering of 4. | 35 |
| 005 | Train and Hotel Staff (0 Gauge) | Various | (H)35 | R/54 | 1956 | Renumbering of 5. | 268 |
| 006 | Shepherd Set | Various | Various | R/54 | 1956 | Renumbering of 6. | 29 |
| 007 | Petrol Pump Attendants Set | White | (H)35 | 1960 | 1967 | Male and Female. Plastic. | 244 |
| 008 | Fire Station Personnel | Blue | (H)35 | 1961 | 1967 | 8 figures + hose. Plastic. | 244 |
| 009 | Service Station Personnel | Mainly White | (H)35 | 1962 | 1966 | 6 in set. Plastic. | 244 |
| 010 | Road Maintenance Personnel | Various | (H)35 | 1962 | 1966 | 6 figures + signs, etc. Plastic | 244 |
| 011 | Telegraph Messenger | Blue | (H)35 | R/54 | 1957 | Renumbering of 12d. | 66 |
| 012 | Postman | Blue, Brown sack | (H)35 | R/54 | 1957 | Renumbering of 12e. | 66 |
| 013 | Cook's man | Blue | (H)40 | R/54 | 1957 | Renumbering of 13a. | 33 |
| 050 | Railway Staff (00) (Set of 12) | Blue | | 1961 | 1969 | Plastic. | |
| 051 | Station Staff (00) (Set of 6) | Blue | | R/54 | 1959 | Renumbering of 1001. | 33 |
| 052 | Railway Passengers (00) (Set of 12) | Various | | 1961 | 1969 | Plastic. | |
| 053 | Passengers (00) (Set of 6) | Various | | R/54 | 1959 | Renumbering of 1003. | 33 |
| 054 | Railway Station Personnel (00) (Set of 12) | Mostly Blue | | 1962 | 1971 | Plastic. | |
| 061 | Ford Prefect | Fawn | 58 | 1958 | 1960 | | 240 |
| 062 | Singer Roadster | Yellow with Red seats | 50 | 1958 | 1960 | | 240 |
| 063 | Commer Van | Blue | 53 | 1958 | 1960 | | 240 |
| 064 | Austin Lorry | Green | 64 | 1957 | 1962 | Smooth or ribbed Grey or Black wheels (plastic). | 240 |
| 065 | Morris Pick-Up | Red | 54 | 1957 | 1960 | | 240 |
| 066 | Bedford Flat Truck | Grey | 107 | 1957 | 1960 | | 240 |
| 067 | Austin Taxi | Blue and Cream | 60 | 1959 | 1967 | Grey or Black plastic wheels. | 240 |
| 068 | Royal Mail Van | Red | 48 | 1959 | 1964 | Grey or Black plastic wheels. | 240 |
| 069 | Massey-Harris Ferguson Tractor | Blue | 37 | 1959 | 1964 | | 240 |

| No. | Description | Colours | Length | Introduced | Deleted | Comment/Variations | Page |
|---|---|---|---|---|---|---|---|
| 070 | A.E.C. Mercury Tanker "Shell B.P." | Red and Green | 91 | 1959 | 1964 | Grey or Black plastic wheels. | 240 |
| 071 | Volkswagen Delivery Van "Hornby-Dublo" | Yellow | 54 | 1959 | 1967 | | 240 |
| 072 | Bedford Articulated Flat Truck | Red and Yellow | 116 | 1959 | 1964 | | 240 |
| 073 | Land Rover, Trailer and Horse | Green and Orange | 103 | 1960 | 1967 | Smooth or ribbed Grey, or Black plastic wheels. | 240 |
| 076 | Lansing-Bagnal Tractor and Trailer | Maroon | 75 | 1960 | 1964 | | 240 |
| 078 | Lansing-Bagnal Trailer only | Maroon | 49 | 1960 | 1971 | | 240 |
| 1 | Station Staff (Set of 6) | Mostly Dark Blue | (H)39 | 1932 | 1939 | Contains 1a–1f (1:). | 34 |
| 1 | Station Staff (Set of 6) | Mostly Dark Blue | (H)35 | 1939 | 1941 | Contains 1a–1f (2:). | 35, 268 |
| 1 | Station Staff (Set of 5) | Blue | (H)35 | 1946 | R/54 | Contains 1b–1f (3:) Renumbered 001. | 35 |
| 1a | Station Master | Dark Blue | | | | | |
| 1b | Guard | Dark Blue | | | | 1: Blowing whistle; flag in left hand. | 34 |
| | | | | | | 2: Flag in right hand. | 35 |
| 1c | Ticket Collector | 1: & 2: Dark Blue | | | | 1: Open arms. | 34 |
| | | 3: Blue | | | | 2: Right hand only extended. | 35 |
| 1d | Driver | Blue | | | | Oil can in hand. | 34, 35 |
| 1e | Porter with bags | 1: & 2: Dark Blue | | | | 1: One round, one oblong bag. | 34 |
| | | 3: Blue | | | | 2: 2 oblong bags. | 35 |
| 1f | Porter | 1: & 2: Dark Blue | | | | 1: Walking. | 34 |
| | | 3: Blue | | | | 2: Standing still. | 35 |
| 2 | Farmyard Animals (Set of 6) | Various | Various | 1932 | 1955 | Simpler paint schemes post-war. Renumbered 002. Contains 2×2a, 2×2b, 2c, 2d. | 29 |
| 2a | Horse | Brown, White | | | | One of each colour in set. | 29 |
| 2b | Cow | Brown, Black and White | | | | One of each colour in set. | 29 |
| 2c | Pig | Pink | | | | | 29 |
| 2d | Sheep | White | | | | | 29 |
| 3 | Passengers (Set of 6) | Various | (H)39 | 1932 | 1939 | Contains 3a–3f (1:). | 34 |
| 3 | Passengers (Set of 6) | Various | (H)35 | 1939 | 1941 | Contains 3a–3f (2:). | 268 |
| 3 | Passengers (Set of 6) | Various | (H)35 | 1946 | R/54 | Contains 3a–3f (3:) Renumbered 003. | 268 |
| 3a | Mother and Child | 1: Mother in Green; Child in Red | | | | 1: Child on woman's right. | 34 |
| | | 2: Green, Red hat, Grey ruff | | | | 2: Child on woman's left. | 268 |
| | | 3: Green, Brown ruff | | | | | |
| 3b | Business Man | 1: Dark Blue suit | | | | 1: Left hand on chest. | 34 |
| | | 2: Grey suit | | | | 2: Left hand holds attache case. | 268 |
| | | 3: Brown suit | | | | | |
| 3c | Male Hiker | Brown. Khaki ruck-sack on 1: and 2: | | | | 1: Walking stick. | 34 |
| | | | | | | 2: No walking stick. | 268 |
| 3d | Female Hiker | 1: and 2: Blue skirt, White blouse. | | | | | 34 |
| | | 3: Dark Blue, later Light Blue all over | | | | | 268 |
| 3e | Newsboy | 1: Brown | | | | 1: Running with paper in hand. | 34 |
| | | 2: Dark Blue, Cream tray | | | | 2: Standing with papers in tray. | 268 |
| | | 3: Dark Blue, Grey tray | | | | | |

| No. | Description | Colours | Length | Introduced | Deleted | Comment/Variations | Page |
|-----|-------------|---------|--------|------------|---------|--------------------|------|
| 3f | Woman | 1: White skirt, Red jacket<br>2: Dark Red coat, Black ruff<br>3: Light Red coat | | | | 1: Coat over left arm, oblong case.<br>2: Round case. | 34<br>268 |
| 4 | Engineering Staff (Set of 6) | Various | (H)39 | 1932 | 1939 | Contains 4a, 2×4b, 4c, 4d, 4e. (1:). | 34 |
| 4 | Engineering Staff (Set of 6) | Various | (H)35 | 1939 | 1941 | Contains 4a, 2×4b, 4c, 4d, 4e. (2:). | 35 |
| 4 | Engineering Staff (Set of 5) | Various | (H)35 | 1946 | R/54 | Contains 2×4b, 4c, 4d, 4e.<br>Renumbered 004. | 268 |
| 4a | Electrician | Blue, White sleeves | | | | Casting as for 1e. | 34 |
| 4b | Fitter | 1: Blue or Brown, White sleeves<br>2: ditto<br>3: All-over Blue or Brown | | | | Casting as for 1f. One of each colour in set. | 35 |
| 4c | Storekeeper | 1: & 2: Brown coat, Black trousers<br>3: All-over Brown | | | | Casting as for 1a. | 34<br>35 |
| 4d | Greaser | Brown | | | | Casting as for 1d. | 34, 35 |
| 4e | Engine Room Attendant | Blue | | | | Casting as for 1c. | 34, 35 |
| 5 | Train and Hotel Staff (Set of 5) | Various | (H)39 | 1932 | 1939 | Contains 5a, 2×5b, 2×5c. (1:). | 34 |
| 5 | Train and Hotel Staff (Set of 5) | Various | (H)35 | 1939 | 1941 | Contains 5a, 2×5b, 2×5c. (2:). | 268 |
| 5 | Train and Hotel Staff (Set of 5) | Various | (H)35 | 1946 | R/54 | Contains 5a, 2×5b, 2×5c. (3:).<br>Renumbered 005. | 268 |
| 5a | Pullman Car Conductor | White Jacket, Blue Trousers | | | | Casting as for 1c. | 34 |
| 5b | Pullman Car Waiter | White jacket, Blue trousers | | | | Casting as for 1f. | 268 |
| 5c | Hotel Porter | 1: Red jacket, Brown trousers or Green jacket, Blue trousers<br>2: & 3: Brown or Blue | | | | Casting as for 1e. One for each colour in set. | 34<br>268 |
| 6 | Shepherd Set | Various | Various | 1934 | R/54 | Contains 6a, 6b, 4×2b. No casting changes. Renumbered 006. | 29 |
| 6a | Shepherd | Brown with Dark Brown hat, post-war with Green hat | (H)40 | | | | 29 |
| 6b | Dog | Black and White, post-war all-over Black | | | | | 29 |
| 12a | Pillar Box G.P.O. | Red | (H)50 | 1935 | 1940 | G.R cast on front. "POST OFFICE" and arrow on top (transfer). | 66 |
| 12c | Pillar Box, Air Mail | Blue | (H)50 | 1935 | 1940 | Casting as for 12a. "AIR MAIL" on top. | 66 |
| 12c | Telephone Box | Cream or Red | (H)58 | 1936 | R/54 | Cream pre-war only. Pre-war Red version has Black window frames. Renumbered 750. | 66 |
| 12d | Telegraph Messenger | Dark Blue, post-war Blue | (H)35 | 1938 | R/54 | Renumbered 011. | 66 |
| 12e | Postman | Dark Blue, post-war Blue | (H)35 | 1938 | R/54 | Renumbered 012. | 66 |
| 13 | Hall's Distemper Advertisement | Figures mostly White, Cream board, Red letters | (H)60 | 1931 | 1941 | 2 figures (hollow-cast lead) with cardboard plank. Early issues not marked. | 29 |
| 13a | Cook's Man | Blue | (H)40 | 1952 | R/54 | Renumbered 013. | 35 |
| 14a | B.E.V. Electric Truck | Dark Blue, Blue or Grey | 85 | 1948 | R/54 | Renumbered 400. Grey issue sometimes with Red wheels. | 179 |

| No. | Description | Colours | Length | Introduced | Deleted | Comment/Variations | Page |
|---|---|---|---|---|---|---|---|
| 14c | Coventry Climax Fork-lift Truck | Orange, Brown or Dark Red, Green fork | 108 | 1949 | R/54 | Renumbered 401. | 179 |
| 15 | Railway Signals | White poles, Black bases | (H)65 | 1937 | 1941 | Contains 2×15a, 2×15b, 2×15c | 34 |
| 15a | Single Arm Signal | | | | | Red (Home) or Yellow (Distant) tin-plate signal. One of each in set. | 34 |
| 15b | Double Arm Signal | | | | | One 'Home' arm, one 'Distant' arm. | 34 |
| 15c | Junction Signal | | | | | 2 'Home' or 2 'Distant' arms. One of each in set. | 34 |
| 16 | Streamlined Train Set | Various (see Comments) | 300 | 1937 | R/54 | Consists of engine and 2 interlocking coaches. Pre-war has pierced windows. Colours are: Silver with Red, Grey or Blue, Cream and Red, or 2-tone Blue. L.N.E.R. and 2590 cast on loco. Post-war has filled-in windows. 1: Casting otherwise as pre-war. Dark Blue loco, Brown coaches. 2: No cast letters or numbers, tin-plate base added, B.R. transfer. Green loco, Red and Cream coaches, some with Grey roofs. Renumbered 798. | 32 |
| 17 | Passenger Train Set | | | 1934 | 1940 | Contains 17a, 17b, 20a and 20b. | 32 |
| 17a | Locomotive | Maroon or Green with Black | 82 | 1934 | 1940 | Zamac boiler and cab, lead chassis. (As 21a.) | 32 |
| 17b | Tender | Maroon or Green | 62 | 1934 | 1940 | Zamac. | 32 |
| 18 | Tank Goods Train Set | | | 1934 | 1941 | Contains 21a + 3×21b. | 32 |
| 19 | Mixed Goods Train Set | | | 1934 | 1941 | Contains 21a, 21b, 21d, 21e. Replaces 21. | 32 |
| 20 | Tank Passenger Train Set | | | 1934 | 1940 | Contains 21a, 2×20a, 20b. | 32 |
| 20a | Coach | Brown, Cream roof or Green, White roof | 81 | 1934 | 1940 | Zamac, lead chassis. | 32 |
| 20b | Guard's Van | As 20a | 81 | 1934 | 1940 | Zamac body, lead chassis. | 32 |
| 21 | Hornby Train Set | | | 1932 | 1934 | Contains 21a, 21b, 21c, 21d, 21e. | 32 |
| 21a | Tank Locomotive | Red and Blue (Hornby Series) Maroon or Green and Black | 82 | 1932 | 1941 | Lead. Hornby Series or Dinky Toys. | 32 |
| 21b | Wagon | Green with Blue, Red or Black chassis, Maroon with Black chassis | 58 | 1932 | 1941 | Lead. Hornby Series or Dinky Toys. | 32 |
| 21c | Crane | Green with Blue chassis | 62 | 1932 | 1934 | Lead. Hornby Series only. | 32 |
| 21d | Tank Wagon | Red with Blue or Black chassis | 58 | 1932 | 1941 | Lead. Hornby Series or Dinky Toys. | 32 |
| 21e | Lumber Wagon | Brown log, Blue chassis or Yellow log, Red or Black chassis | 58 | 1932 | 1941 | Lead. Hornby Series or Dinky Toys. | 32 |
| 22 | Motor Vehicles | | | 1933 | 1935 | Hornby Series, later Dinky Toys. Contains 22a, 22b, 22c, 22d, 22e, 22f. | 28 |

| No. | Description | Colours | Length | Introduced | Deleted | Comment/Variations | Page |
|---|---|---|---|---|---|---|---|
| 22a | Sports Car | Red with Cream, Cream with Red, Yellow with Green, Blue with Red, Blue with Yellow, Cream with Green, Cream with Blue | 82 | 1933 | 1935 | Hornby Series or Dinky Toys. Lead. | 28 |
| 22b | Sports Coupe | Yellow with Green, Red with Cream, Red with Blue | 82 | 1933 | 1935 | Marked Hornby Series or Dinky Toys. Lead. | 28 |
| 22c | Motor Truck | Blue cab, Red rear, Red with Green, Blue with Cream | 90 | 1933 | 1935 | Always Marked Hornby Series. Lead. | 28 |
| 22c | Motor Truck | Red, Green, Blue (pre-war) Red, Green, Brown (post-war) | 84 | 1935 | 1950 | Open rear window till early post-war. | 73 |
| 22d | Delivery Van | Orange cab, Blue rear, Blue cab, Yellow rear | 84 | 1933 | 1935 | Marked Hornby Series or Dinky Toys. Meccano advertising from 1934 (in set 28). Lead. | 28 |
| 22e | Farm Tractor | Yellow with Dark Blue (Hornby), Green with Yellow, Yellow with Blue, Red or Cream with Blue or Red, Red with Blue, Blue with Cream. All with Red wheels. | 70 | 1933 | 1941 | Hornby Series (no hook) or Dinky Toys. Lead, later with zamac wheels. | 28 |
| 22f | Army Tank | Green with orange turret, Khaki, later all-over Grey. | 87 | 1933 | 1940 | Hornby Series or Dinky Toys. Lead with rubber tracks. | 28 |
| 22g | Streamlined Tourer | Green, Red, Blue, Cream, Black | 85 | 1935 | 1941 | | 75 |
| 22h | Streamlined Saloon | Green, Red, Blue, Cream. | 85 | 1935 | 1941 | | 75 |
| 22s | Small Searchlight Lorry | Green | 84 | 1939 | 1941 | Castings as for 22c and 161a. | 79 |
| 23 | Racing Car | Cream with Orange, Red, Blue, or Green flash, Blue with White flash. | 94 | 1934 | 1935 | Lead. No driver. See 23a. No racing numbers. Some have coloured tyres. | 37 |
| 23 | Racing Cars | Various | | 1936 | 1941 | Contains 23c, 23d, 23e. | 39 |
| 23a | Racing Car | Orange with Green: Yellow with Dark Blue; Cream with Red or Green; Red with Cream; White with Blue; Blue with White; Brown with Cream. | 94 | 1935 | 1941 | Reissue of 23: Zamac, driver, fish-tail exhaust. Raised circle around racing number. 3 paint schemes: 1: 2nd colour in stripes along body sides. Some have coloured tyres. 2: Front flash is broad at nose to point before cockpit. Rear flash is of even thickness along tail. 3: Circle on nose; flash is broad at cockpit, pointed at both ends (as 23). | 38 |
| | | Red or Blue with Silver or Cream; Silver with Red. | 94 | 1946 | R/54 | No raised circle, but most have racing numbers. Transverse rib(s) inside body. Painting scheme 3 only. Red with Silver flash, Silver wheels and no racing numbers is LEAD. (Early 1950's) Renumbered 220. | 126 |

| No. | Description | Colours | Length | Introduced | Deleted | Comment/Variations | Page |
|---|---|---|---|---|---|---|---|
| 23b | Hotchkiss Racing Car | Blue with Dark Blue, Red, or White flash; Yellow with Blue flash; Orange with Green flash; Green with Yellow flash. | 96 | 1935 | 1941 | | 38 |
| | | Red with Silver flash or Silver with Red flash. | 96 | 1946 | 1948 | | 126 |
| 23c | Mercedes-Benz Racing Car | Yellow, Green, Blue, Red | 92 | 1936 | 1941 | Baseplate clipped in till 1938, no name on baseplate: From 1938 baseplate rivetted and name added. | 39 |
| | | Silver or Blue | 92 | 1946 | 1950 | | |
| 23d | Auto-Union Racing Car | Red, Green, Yellow, Blue (2 shades), Silver | 100 | 1936 | 1941 | No driver till late 1936. Other comments as 23c. | 39 |
| | | Red or Silver | 100 | 1946 | 1950 | Early post-war still has driver. | |
| 23e | 'Speed of the Wind' Racing Car | Red, Green, Yellow, Blue (2 shades), Silver | 104 | 1936 | 1941 | Comment as 23c. Available also in box of 6 in 6 colours numbered 1–6. | 39 |
| | | Red or Silver | 104 | 1946 | R/54 | Lead version as 23a. Renumbered 221. | |
| 23f | Alfa-Romeo Racing Car | Red | 100 | 1952 | R/54 | Renumbered 232. | 127 |
| 23g | Cooper-Bristol Racing Car | Green | 89 | 1953 | R/54 | Renumbered 233. | 127 |
| 23h | Ferrari Racing Car | Blue, Yellow nose | 101 | 1953 | R/54 | Renumbered 234. | 127 |
| 23j | HWM Racing Car | Green | 99 | 1953 | R/54 | Renumbered 235. | 127 |
| 23k | Talbot-Lago Racing Car | Blue | 103 | 1953 | R/54 | Renumbered 230. | 127 |
| 23m | 'Thunderbolt' Speed Car | Silver with Black detail | 126 | 1938 | 1941 | Individually boxed. Union Jacks on tail. | 38 |
| 23n | Maserati Racing Car | Red | 94 | 1953 | R/54 | Renumbered 231. | 127 |
| 23p | Gardner's M.G. Record Car | Green | 104 | 1939 | 1947 | Pre-war has lateral White flash (transfer) and M.G. Magnette on base. Individually boxed. Post-war has M.G. Record Car on base. | 38, 126 |
| 23s | Streamlined Racing Car | Pre-war: Light Green, Dark Green detail; Light Blue with Dark Blue; Orange Post-war: Pale Green, Green, Dark Green or Dark Blue with Silver; Silver with Red, Green or Blue | 126 | 1938 | R/54 | Casting as for 23m. Renumbered 222. Some pre-war ones in lead. | 126 |

| No. | Description | Colours | Length | Introduced | Deleted | Comment/Variations | Page |
|-----|-------------|---------|--------|------------|---------|--------------------|------|
| 24 | Motor Cars | | | 1934 | 1940 | Contains 24a–h. | 40–43 |

Introductory notes on 24 Series:
2 chassis: 1st has diagonal bars and a central bar North–South; 2nd has diagonal bars and a central bar East–West. Earliest issues have no paint on underside of chassis, hubs with a small concentric ring (also used on 23 and 1st type 25 series lorries) and one end of each axle is rounded (also seen on 23). These very early issues can be all lead, or lead body with zamac chassis.
3 Radiator Grilles: 1st has smooth bumper; 3rd has over-riders and a radiator badge, as per 36 series Bentley. In the interim period while the 1st was being altered to the 3rd, an adapted French grille was used: Fluted bumper with diamond badge in centre.
2 bodies: The original castings were altered to make the 36 series bodies. From this time, adapted French bodies were used. The Ambulance body does not change; the changes to the Town Sedan were due to mould wear, as this body was not issued in France; the Sports Tourers have French-style bodies briefly, then as 36e and f.
The only consistency is that 1st chassis always have 1st grille and 1st body.

| No. | Description | Colours | Length | Introduced | Deleted | Comment/Variations | Page |
|-----|-------------|---------|--------|------------|---------|--------------------|------|
| 24a | Ambulance | Grey/Dark Grey chassis; Cream/Grey chassis; Cream or Grey/Red chassis; Grey/Maroon chassis; All Black | 102 | 1934 | 1940 | See 30f. All-Black version possibly export only. | 42 |
| 24b | Limousine | Maroon body with Maroon, Grey or Black Chassis; Blue/Yellow chassis; Dark Blue/Black chassis; Yellow/Brown chassis | 98 | 1934 | 1940 | Horizontal bonnet louvres. See 36a. 2nd body has these louvres diagonally above each other. (Issue ca. 1937.) | 42 |
| 24c | Town Sedan | Dark Blue/Dark Blue chassis; Cream/Dark Blue or Black chassis; Green/Red chassis; Green/Yellow chassis | 97 | 1934 | 1941 | With, later without spare wheel in wing. 2nd body has narrower boot and shorter door handles. | 42 |
| 24d | Vogue Saloon | Blue body with Blue, Maroon or Black chassis; Cream/Blue chassis; Brown/Green chassis; Pink/Green chassis; Green/Black chassis | 97 | 1934 | 1940 | Always with spare wheel in wing. See 36c. 2nd body has more domed roof line (ca. 1937). | 42 |
| 24e | Super Streamlined Saloon | Maroon body/Black chassis; Red/Dark Red chassis; Green/Red chassis; Green/Blue chassis | 97 | 1934 | 1940 | Single, long side window. See 36d. 2nd body has 13 rather than 12 bonnet louvres. | 42 |
| 24f | Sportsman's Coupe | Blue/Black chassis; Beige/Brown chassis; Cream/Dark Blue chassis; Brown/Buff chassis; 2-tone Blue | 97 | 1934 | 1940 | With, later without side-mounted spare wheel. See 36b. 2nd body has more doomed roof line (ca. 1937) | 42 |

| No. | Description | Colours | Length | Introduced | Deleted | Comment/Variations | Page |
|-----|-------------|---------|--------|------------|---------|--------------------|------|
| 24g | Sports Tourer (4-Seater) | Yellow/Black chassis; Blue/ Brown chassis; Cream/Green or Brown chassis; Royal Blue/ Maroon chassis | 100 | 1934 | 1941 | Open, later filled-in windscreen. Cast-in hub for rear-mounted spare tyre, later cast impression of cover. Steering-wheel spokes set vertically and horizontally. See 36f. Some have 36f dash/steering wheel. | 43 |
| 24h | Sports Tourer (2-Seater) | Red/Red chassis; 2-tone Green; Yellow with Green, Blue or Black chassis | 98 | 1934 | 1941 | Comments as for 24g. See 36e. | 43 |
| 25 | Commercial Motor Vehicles | | | 1934 | 1937 | Contains 25a–f. | 46 |
| 25 | Commercial Motor Vehicles | | | 1937 | 1941 | Contains 25b, d, e, f, g, h. General notes for 25a–f. Type 1:(1934): Tinplate Radiator, Chassis with 3 Pear-shaped holes. 2:(1935): Cast radiator, chassis as 1: 3:(1947): Filled-in chassis, grille as 2: 4:(1948): Chassis with transmission detail and front bumper. Grille as 2: | 269 |
| 25a | Wagon | 1: Maroon, Green or Blue, Black chassis. | 105 | 1934 | 1935 | | 47 |
| | | 2: Maroon, Green or Blue, Black chassis; Blue, Orange chassis. | 105 | 1935 | 1946 | | 46 |
| | | 3: Grey, Green or Blue, Black chassis. | 105 | 1947 | 1948 | | 154 |
| | | 4: Grey, Green, Pale Blue or Cream, Black chassis. | 110 | 1948 | 1950 | | 154 |
| 25b | Covered Wagon | 1: Blue, Cream tilt. | 105 | 1934 | 1935 | 25a + tin tilt. | 47 |
| | | 2: Green with Green, Cream or Yellow tilt; Fawn with Cream tilt; Orange with Green chassis and Cream tilt. | 105 | 1934 | 1946 | May have advertising (pre-war only): Green/Green with "Carter Paterson"; Green/Cream with "Meccano"; Fawn/Cream with "Hornby Trains". | 47 47 47 47 |
| | | 3: Green, Green tilt; 2-tone Grey; Blue, Grey tilt. | 105 | 1947 | 1948 | | 154 |
| | | 4: Green, Green tilt; 2-tone Grey; Cream, Red tilt; Yellow, Blue tilt. | 110 | 1948 | 1950 | | 154 |

| No. | Description | Colours | Length | Introduced | Deleted | Comment/Variations | Page |
|---|---|---|---|---|---|---|---|
| 25c | Flat Truck | 1:Dark Blue. | 105 | 1934 | 1935 | | 47 |
| | | 2: Green or Stone. | 105 | 1935 | 1946 | | 46 |
| | | 3: Green, Blue or Grey. | 105 | 1947 | 1948 | | 154 |
| | | 4: Green, Blue, Orange or Stone. | 110 | 1948 | 1948 | 1948–1950 as part of 25t only. | 154 |
| 25d | Petrol Tank Wagon | 1: Red: Plain or "Shell–B.P." Green: "Esso", "Power" or "Pratts". | 105 | 1934 | 1935 | | 47 |
| | | 2: Red: "Petrol", "Shell–B.P.", "Mobiloil" or "Texaco" Green: "Petrol", "Esso", "Power", "Castrol" Blue: "Redline–Glico". Grey: "Pool". | 105 | 1935 | 1946 | Advertising pre-war and very early post-war. | |
| | | 3: Red, Orange or Green, "Petrol". | 105 | 1947 | 1948 | | 154 |
| | | 4: Red, Orange or Green (pale or mid-), "Petrol". | 110 | 1948 | 1950 | | 154 |
| 25e | Tipping Wagon | 1: Maroon, Yellow rear. | 105 | 1934 | 1935 | | 47 |
| | | 2: Maroon, Yellow rear; Brown, Turquoise rear; Fawn. | 105 | 1935 | 1946 | Two-colour paint schemes pre-war only. | 46 |
| | | Grey, Stone, Green or Yellow. | 105 | 1947 | 1948 | | 154 |
| | | 4: Grey, Stone or Brown: Blue and Pink. | 110 | 1948 | 1950 | | 154 |
| 25f | Market Gardener's Van | 1: Green, Black chassis. | 105 | 1934 | 1935 | | 47 |
| | | 2: Yellow with Green or Black chassis; Green with Black chassis. | 105 | 1935 | 1946 | Green chassis pre-war only. | 46 |
| | | 3: Green or Yellow. | 105 | 1947 | 1948 | | 154 |
| | | 4: Green, Yellow or Orange. | 110 | 1948 | 1950 | | 154 |
| 25g | Trailer | Dark Blue or Green (pre-war); Stone, Green, Pale Blue or Orange (to 1950); Green or Red (post-'50) | 69 | 1935 | R/54 | Pre-war and early post-war have tin-plate draw-bar and cast-in towing hook. Wire draw-bar from 1947, tin-plate towing hook from 1948. Up to 1950, colours match 25c; post-1950 colours match 30r Fordson. Renumbered 429. | |
| 25h | Streamlined Fire Engine | Red | 101 | 1936 | R/54 | Moulded tin-plate baseplate from 1937. Renumbered 250. See 25k. | 200 |
| 25j | Jeep | Red, pale, Green, pale Blue, Brown. | 68 | 1947 | 1948 | Casting as per *later* 153a. | 240 |
| 25k | Streamlined Fire Engine with Firemen | Red | 101 | 1937 | 1939 | As per 25h but with 6 tin-plate men. | 200 |

| No. | Description | Colours | Length | Introduced | Deleted | Comment/Variations | Page |
|-----|-------------|---------|--------|------------|---------|--------------------|------|
| 25m | Bedford End Tipper | Orange, Cream or Green, later Red and Cream | 100 | 1948 | R/54 | Renumbered 410. | 170 |
| 25p | Aveling-Barford Diesel Roller | Mid-, later Pale Green, Red rollers | 110 | 1948 | R/54 | Renumbered 251. | 173 |
| 25r | Forward Control Lorry | Red, Green, Grey, Cream, Light Blue or Orange | 107 | 1948 | R/54 | Renumbered 420. | 170 |
| 25s | Six-wheeled Wagon | Brick Red (pre- or post-war); Green or Dark Blue (post-war only) with Grey tilt | 101 | 1938 | 1948 | Casting as per 151b. Holes in seat for driver and passenger (not supplied) until late post-war. No tilt pre-war. | 75 |
| 25v | Bedford Refuse Wagon | Fawn, Green doors on rear. | 106 | 1948 | R/54 | Renumbered 252. | 173 |
| 25t | Flat Truck and Trailer | Stone (Type 3), Green (3 or 4), Orange (4) | 170 or 175 | 1948 | 1950 | 25c + 25g. Trailer matches truck colour. | 155 |
| 25w | Bedford Truck | Pale Green, some with Black wings | 100 | 1949 | R/54 | Renumbered 411. | 170 |
| 25wm | Bedford Military Truck | Military Green | 100 | mid-1950's | R/54 | 25w in military colours. For U.S. market only. Renumbered 640. | 223 |
| 25x | Breakdown Lorry | Brown (Light or Mid-) cab/Green (Light or Mid-) rear, or Fawn or Grey cab/Blue rear | 123 | 1950 | R/54 | Renumbered 430. | 176 |
| 25y | Jeep | Green or Red | 83 | 1952 | R/54 | Renumbered 405. See 669. | 240 |
| 26 | G.W.R. Rail Car | Green, Blue, Yellow or Brown with Cream roof; Green with Red roof | 106 | 1934 | 1940 | Red or Green plastic rollers. Sometimes in lead. | 34 |
| 27 | Tram Car | Blue with Cream lower windows, upper windows and roof; later Red, Orange, Pale Blue or Yellow with Cream upper windows and roof | 77 | 1934 | 1939 | Plastic rollers, later metal wheels, as used on rolling stock in sets 17–21. Later paint scheme usually carries "Ovaltine" advertising. | |
| 27a | Massey-Harris Tractor | Red | 89 | 1949 | R/54 | Renumbered 300. | 184 |
| 27ak | Farm Tractor and Hay Rake | Red and Yellow | 157 | 1953 | R/54 | 27a + 27k. Renumbered 310. | 184 |
| 27b | Halesowen Harvest Trailer | Brown and Red with Brown staves | 121 | 1949 | R/54 | Renumbered 320. | 184 |
| 27c | Massey-Harris Manure Spreader | Red | 113 | 1949 | R/54 | Renumbered 321. | 184 |
| 27d | Land Rover | Orange or Green | 90 | 1950 | R/54 | Renumbered 340. | 184 |
| 27f | Estate Car | Pale Brown with Dark Brown panels | 105 | 1950 | R/54 | Renumbered 344. | 184 |
| 27g | Moto-Cart | Light or Dark Green with Brown rear | 110 | 1949 | R/54 | Renumbered 342. | 184 |
| 27h | Disc Harrow | Red and Yellow | 86 | 1951 | R/54 | Renumbered 322. | 184 |
| 27j | Triple Gang Mower | Red and Yellow and Green | 114 | 1952 | R/54 | Renumbered 323. | 184 |
| 27k | Hay Rake | Red and Yellow | 77 | 1953 | R/54 | Renumbered 324. | 184 |
| 27m | Land Rover Trailer | Orange or Green | 79 | 1952 | R/54 | Renumbered 341. | 184 |
| 27n | Field Marshall Farm Tractor | Orange with Green wheels | 75 | 1953 | R/54 | Renumbered 301. | 184 |

| No. | Description | Colours | Length | Introduced | Deleted | Comment/Variations | Page |
|---|---|---|---|---|---|---|---|
| 28/1 | Delivery Vans | | | 1934 | 1935 | Contains 28a–28f (Type 1). | |
| 28/1 | Delivery Vans | | | 1935 | 1941 | Contains 28a, b, c, e, f, n (Type 2 or 3). | |
| 28/2 | Delivery Vans | | | 1934 | 1935 | Contains 28g, h, k, l, m, n (Type 1). | |
| 28/2 | Delivery Vans | | | 1935 | 1941 | Contains 28d, g, h, k, m, p (Type 2 or 3). | |
| 28/3 | Delivery Vans | | | 1936 | 1941 | Contains 28r, s, t, w, x, y (Type 2 or 3). | |
| 280 | Delivery Vans | | | 1937 | 1940 | Contains 280a–f. | |

General Note on 28 and 280 Vans: Type 1, issued in 1934, is the same casting as 22d Delivery Van, i.e. a square-looking design, cast in lead. Type 2, issued in June 1935, is cast in zamac. The grille resembles a Ford 8/10hp. Type 3, issued in late 1939/early 1940, is also cast in zamac and resembles a Bradford. Only type 3 has open rear windows.

48–51

| No. | Description | Colours | Length | Introduced | Deleted | Comment/Variations | Page |
|---|---|---|---|---|---|---|---|
| 28a | Hornby Trains Van | Yellow | Type 1 – 84 | 1934 | 1936 | "Hornby Trains. British and Guaranteed". Type 1 or Type 2. | |
| | | | Type 2 – 81 | | | | |
| 28a | Golden Shred Van | Cream | Type 3 – 83 | 1936 | 1941 | "Golden Shred Marmalade" on right side. "Silver Shred Marmalade" on left. Type 2 or 3. | |
| 28b | Pickford's Removals Van | Dark Blue | „ | 1934 | 1935 | "Pickford's Removal and Storage. Over 100 Branches". Type 1 or 2. | |
| 28b | Seccotine Van | Blue | „ | 1935 | 1941 | "Seccotine Sticks Everything". Type 2 or 3. | |
| 28c | Manchester Guardian Van | Black and Red (Type 1) Red (Type 2 and 3) | „ | 1934 | 1941 | "The Manchester Guardian", Type 1, 2 or 3. | |
| 28d | Oxo Van | Blue | „ | 1934 | 1941 | "Oxo, Beef in Brief" on left side, "Oxo, Beef at its Best" on right. Type 1, 2 or 3. | |
| 28e | Ensign Cameras Van | Red | „ | 1934 | 1935 | "Ensign Cameras" on left side, "Ensign Lukos Films" on right. Type 1. | |
| 28e | Firestone Tyres Van | White (Type 1); Blue or White (Type 2 or 3) | „ | 1934 | 1941 | "Firestone Tyres". Type 1, 2, 3. | |
| 28f | Palethorpe's Sausages Van | Grey | Type 1 – 84 Type 2 – 81 | 1934 | 1938 | "Palethorpe's Royal Cambridge" on sides, "Palethorpe's Model Factory Tipton" on rear. Type 1 or 2. | |
| 28f | Virol Van | Yellow | Type 3 – 83 | 1938 | 1941 | "Give your child a Virol Constitution". Type 2 or 3. | |
| 28g | Kodak Cameras Van | Yellow | „ | 1934 | 1941 | "Use Kodak Film To Be Sure". Type 1, 2 or 3 | |
| 28h | Sharp's Van | Black and Red (Type 1) Red (Type 2) | „ | 1934 | 1935 | "Sharp's Toffee Maidstone". Type 1 or 2. | |
| 28h | Dunlop Van | Red | „ | 1935 | 1941 | "Dunlop Tyres". Type 2 or 3. | |
| 28k | Marsh and Baxter's Van | Green | „ | 1934 | 1941 | "Marsh's Sausages". Type 1, 2 or 3. | |

(14)

| No. | Description | Colours | Length | Introduced | Deleted | Comment/Variations | Page |
|-----|-------------|---------|--------|------------|---------|--------------------|------|
| 28l | Crawford's Biscuits Van | Red | „ | 1934 | 1935 | "Crawford's Biscuits". Type 1. See 28p. | |
| 28m | Wakefield's Oil Van | Green | „ | 1934 | 1941 | "Wakefield's Castrol Motor Oil". Type 1, 2 or 3. | |
| 28n | Meccano Van | Yellow | „ | 1934 | 1935 | "Meccano Engineering For Boys". Type 1 or 2. See 22d. (Numbered 22d till April 1935). | |
| 28n | Atco Van | Green | „ | 1935 | 1941 | "Atco Lawn Mowers Sales And Service". Type 2 or 3. | |
| 28p | Crawford's Biscuits Van | Red | „ | 1935 | 1941 | "Crawford's Biscuits". Type 2 or 3. See 28l. | |
| 28r | Swan's Van | Black | „ | 1936 | 1941 | "Swan Pens". Type 2 or 3. | |
| 28s | Fry's Van | Brown or Cream | „ | 1936 | 1941 | "Fry's Chocolate". Type 2 or 3. | |
| 28t | Ovaltine Van | Red | „ | 1936 | 1941 | "Drink Ovaltine For Health". Type 2 or 3. | |
| 28w | Osram Van | Yellow | „ | 1936 | 1941 | "Osram Lamps. A G.E.C. Product". Type 2 or 3. | |
| 28x | Hovis Van | White | „ | 1936 | 1941 | "Hovis For Tea". Type 2 or 3. | |
| 28y | Exide and Drydex Van | Red | „ | 1936 | 1941 | "Drydex Batteries" on left side: "Exide Batteries" on right. Type 2 or 3. | |
| 280 | Delivery Van | Red or Blue | 83 | 1949 | 1951 | Casting as for 28 Type 3. Filled-in rear windows. | 189 |
| 280a | Vyella Van | Blue | Type 2 – 81 | 1937 | 1940 | "Vyella For The Nursery". Type 2 or 3. | |
| 280b | Lyons Van | Blue | | 1937 | 1939 | "Lyons Tea. Always The Best". Type 2. | |
| 280b | Hartley's Van | Cream | Type 3 – 83 | 1939 | 1940 | "Hartley's Is Real Jam". Type 2 or 3. | |
| 280c | Shredded Wheat Van | Cream | „ | 1937 | 1940 | "Shredded Wheat Welwyn Garden City, Herts". Type 2 or 3. | |
| 280d | Bisto Van | Yellow | „ | 1937 | 1940 | 2 transfers: "Ah! Bisto" + design (Type 2) "Bisto" + design (Type 2 or 3). | |
| 280e | Ekco Van | Green | „ | 1937 | 1939 | "Ekco Radio", Type 2. | |
| 280e | Yorkshire Evening News | Cream | „ | 1939 | 1940 | "Yorkshire Evening News. The Original Buff" Type 2 or 3. | |
| 280f | Mackintosh's Van | Red | „ | 1937 | 1940 | "Mackintosh's Toffee". Type 2 or 3. | |
| ? | Bentall's Van | Green and Yellow | „ | ? | ? | "Bentall's Kingston-on-Thames Phone KIN 1001" Type 2. Promotional. | |
| ? | Maison de Bonneterie Van | Red | „ | ? | ? | "Maison de Bonneterie. Leverancier. Van H.M. de Koningin. Amsterdam Den Haag". Type 2. Promotional. | |
| ? | Liverpool Echo Van | ? | „ | ? | ? | Promotional. No details available. | |

| No. | Description | Colours | Length | Introduced | Deleted | Comment/Variations | Page |
|---|---|---|---|---|---|---|---|
| 29 | Motor Bus | Red, Maroon, Blue, Green or Yellow with Cream or Silver roof | 70 | 1934 | R/36 | Plastic wheels or metal wheels as used on rolling stock in sets 17–21. Renumbered 29a. Metal-wheeled variant usually has 'Marmite' advertising. | 193 |
| 29a | Motor Bus | „ | 70 | R/36 | 1939 | Renumbering of 29. Comments as above. | |
| 29b | Streamline Bus | 1: Green and Cream; Orange and Cream; Red and Cream. 2: Blue with Dark Blue; Green with Dark Green; Yellow with Orange; Red with Maroon. | 88 | 1936 | 1946 | 2 paint schemes: 1: Second colour applied to roof, pillars and tail. 2: Contrasting colour on spats and roof. Open rear window. Post-war issue only in 2-tone Blue or Green. On pre-war examples, stripe tapers to point on rear of vehicle. See below. | 270 193 |
| | | 2-tone Green; Grey with Blue. | 88 | 1947 | 1950 | Contrasting colour on spats only. Rear window filled in. | |
| 29c | Double Decker Motor Bus | Red, Blue, Dark Blue, Maroon, Green, or Orange lower part; Cream upper. | 100 | 1938 | 1941 | Early issue has Grey roof. Stairs cast in chassis. Usually has "Dunlop Tyres" on sides. A.E.C. radiator with cut-away wings. | 193 |
| | | Red or Green with Grey or Cream upper part; 2-tone Green. | 100 | 1946 | 1948 | Radiator as above. No stairs. No adverts. | 193 |
| | | Red or Green lower, Cream upper | 100 | 1948 | 1949 | Leyland radiator. No advertising. | 194 |
| | | Red or Green lower, Cream upper. | 101 | 1949 | R/54 | 2nd A.E.C. radiator with straight wings. "Dunlop, The World's Master Tyre" from 1954. Renumbered 290. *Note*: Rear wings cast with body on this version (cast with chassis on other types). | 194 |
| 29e | Single Deck Bus | Green with Dark Green flash; Blue/Dark Blue; Cream/Blue | 113 | 1948 | 1952 | | 196 |
| 29f | Observation Coach | Grey or Cream with Red flashes | 112 | 1950 | R/54 | Renumbered 280. | 196 |
| 29h | Luxury Coach | Blue/Cream flash; Fawn or Cream/ Orange flash; Maroon/ Cream flash | 113 | 1951 | R/54 | Renumbered 281. | 196 |
| 29h | Duple Roadmaster Coach | Red or Blue with Silver flashes | 119 | 1952 | R/54 | Renumbered 282. | 197 |
| 30 | Motor Vehicles | | | 1935 | 1941 | Contains 30a–f; from 1937 contains 30a, b, c, d, e, g. | 52, 270 |
| 30a | Chrysler "Airflow" Saloon | Maroon, Green, Blue, Turquoise, Cream or Red. Post-war: Green, Blue or Cream. | 103 | R/35 | 1948 | Renumbering of 32. | 52 |
| 30b | Rolls-Royce Car | Yellow with Brown chassis; Cream, Blue or Light Fawn with | 101 | 1935 | 1950 | 2 pear-shaped holes in chassis till 1946, thereafter filled in. | 52 |

| No. | Description | Colours | Length | Introduced | Deleted | Comment/Variations | Page |
|---|---|---|---|---|---|---|---|
| | | Black chassis; 2-tone Red, Grey or Green.<br>Post-war: Fawn or Dark Blue with Black chassis. | | | | | |
| 30c | Daimler | Cream, Blue, Yellow or Turquoise with Black chassis; Pink with Maroon; 2-tone Red.<br>Post-war: Fawn or Dark Green with Black chassis. | 98 | 1935 | 1950 | Comments as for 30b. | 52 |
| 30d | Vauxhall Car | 2-tone Green or Grey; Cream or Yellow/Brown chassis; Green/Black chassis.<br>Post-war: Dark Green or Brown with Black chassis. | 98 | 1935 | 1950 | Comments as for 30b. Pre-war has a spare wheel mounted on the left wing. (This feature may have appeared briefly post-war). Issued originally with an "egg-box" grille, this was replaced late pre-war by a "shield" grille. | 52 |
| 30e | Breakdown Car | Red, Yellow, Green, Brown or Grey with Black wings; Blue with Dark Blue wings.<br>Post-war: Grey or Red with Black wings (open window); Grey, Green or Red. | 92 | 1935 | 1948 | Main casting as for 22c (2nd type). | 52, 53 |
| 30f | Ambulance | Grey with Red chassis.<br>Post-war: Grey or Cream with Black chassis | 101 | 1935 | 1948 | Open rear window till 1946. Initially identical to 24a (2nd chassis), but always Grey with Red chassis. Solid moulded 36-series chassis from 1938. Open windows till 1946, thereafter filled. | 52 |
| 30g | Caravan | Cream with Blue, Green, Red or Orange; Grey and Red; Beige and Chocolate; 2-tone Green | 81 + hook | 1936 | 1941 | Roof-light windows filled in late pre-war. | 52 |
| 30h | Daimler Ambulance | Cream | 96 | 1950 | R/54 | | 206 |
| 30hm | Daimler Military Ambulance | Military Green, Red crosses on White backgrounds | 96 | Mid-50's | R/54 | Casting as for 30h. Made for U.S. market only. Renumbered 624. | 222 |
| 30j | Austin Wagon | Blue, Brown or Maroon | 104 | 1950 | R/54 | Renumbered 412. | 171 |
| 30m | Rear Tipping Wagon | Maroon or Orange cab and chassis/Pale Green rear; Blue or Dark Blue/Grey rear | 100 | 1950 | R/54 | Renumbered 414. | 171 |
| 30n | Farm Produce Wagon | Green cab and chassis with Yellow rear or these colours reversed; Red with Blue rear | 104 | 1950 | R/54 | Renumbered 343. | 171 |
| 30p | Petrol Tanker | Green or Red "Petrol". | 112 | 1950 | 1952 | Very briefly in aluminium, including some with advertising, zamac by '51. | 171 |
| 30p | Petrol Tanker "Mobilgas" | Red | 112 | 1952 | R/54 | Renumbered 440. | 161 |

| No. | Description | Colours | Length | Introduced | Deleted | Comment/Variations | Page |
|---|---|---|---|---|---|---|---|
| 30pa | Petrol Tanker "Castrol" | Green | 112 (?) | 1952 | R/54 | Renumbered 441. Some in aluminium. | 161 |
| 30pb | Petrol Tanker "Esso" | Red | 112 | 1952 | R/54 | Renumbered 442. | 161 |
| 30r | Fordson Thames Flat Truck | Red or Green | 112 | 1951 | R/54 | Renumbered 422. | 171 |
| 30s | Austin Covered Wagon | Dark Blue with Blue or Cream tilt; Maroon or Brown/Cream tilt. Maroon/Red tilt. | 104 | 1950 | R/54 | 30j + tin tilt. Tilt as per 25b. Renumbered 413. | 171 |
| 30sm | Austin Covered Wagon (Military) | Green | 112 | Mid 50's | R/54 | 30s in military colours. U.S. market only. Renumbered 625. | 223 |
| 30v | Electric Dairy Van | Cream/Red chassis or Grey/Dark Red or Blue chassis | 85 | 1949 | R/54 | Red decal on Cream van; Blue decal on Grey van: "N.C.B." (Renumbered 491) or "Express Dairy" (Renumbered 490). | 181 |
| 30w | Electric Articulated Lorry | Maroon | 135 | 1953 | R/54 | "British Railways" on front. Renumbered 421. | 189 |
| 31 | Holland Coachcraft Van | Red, Green, Dark Blue, Cream or Orange | 88 | 1935 | 1936 | Sometimes in lead. Die may have been adapted to 29b Streamline Bus. "Holland Coachcraft Registered Design" on sides. | 193 |
| 31a | Trojan 15 cwt. Van "Esso" | Red | 85 | 1951 | R/54 | Renumbered 450. | 155 |
| 31b | Trojan 15 cwt. Van "Dunlop" | Red | 85 | 1952 | R/54 | Renumbered 451. | 155 |
| 31c | Trojan 15 cwt. Van "Chivers" | Green | 85 | 1953 | R/54 | Renumbered 452. | 155 |
| 31d | Trojan 15 cwt. Van "Oxo" | Dark Blue or Blue | 85 | 1953 | R/54 | Renumbered 453. | 155 |
| 32 | "Airflow" Saloon | Maroon | 103 | 1934 | R/35 | Renumbered 30a. Sometimes in lead. | 52 |
| 33 | Mechanical Horse and 5 assorted Trailers | | | 1935 | 1937 | Contains 33a, b, c, d, e and f. | 56 |
| 33 | Mechanical Horse and 4 assorted Trailers | | | 1937 | 1940 | Contains 3a, b, c, e, f. | 57, 270 |
| 33a | Mechanical Horse | Red, Green, Blue, Yellow | 65 | 1935 | 1940 | Early issue has a shorter step beyond trailer slot on cab. (2.5mm vs. 9.5mm). See 33w. | 56 |
| 33b | Flat Truck | Red, Green, Blue, Yellow | 61 | 1935 | 1940 | | 56 |
| 33c | Open Wagon | Red, Green, Yellow, Blue | 61 | 1935 | 1940 | See 33w. | 56 |
| 33d | Box Van Trailer | Green (plain); Green "Meccano" or "Hornby Trains"; Blue "Hornby Trains" | 70 | 1935 | 1940 | Cast chassis, tinplate van body. | 56 |
| 33e | Dust Wagon | Blue or Yellow with Blue top; Grey with Green | 61 | 1935 | 1940 | 33c + tinplate cover. *May* have been issued post-war. | 56 |
| 33f | Petrol Tank | Green chassis, Red tank or vice versa; Green chassis, Red tank "Esso"; Red chassis, Green tank "Castrol" | 61 | 1935 | 1940 | 33b + tinplate tank. | 56 |

| No. | Description | Colours | Length | Introduced | Deleted | Comment/Variations | Page |
|-----|-------------|---------|--------|------------|---------|--------------------|------|
| 33r | Railway Mechanical Horse and Trailer Van | See comments | 112 | 1935 | 1940 | Maroon and Black: L.M.S. Green and Black: S.R. Blue and Black: L.N.E.R. (2 shades, earlier has red wheels.) Brown and Cream: G.W.R. | 56 |
| 33Ra | Railway Mechanical Horse | See comments | 65 | 1935 | 1940 | Liveries as 33r. | 56 |
| 33Rd | Railway Trailer Van | See comments | 70 | 1935 | 1940 | Liveries as 33r. | 56 |
| 33w | Mechanical Horse and Open Wagon. | Grey, Fawn, Dark Green, Yellow, Dark Green cab/Maroon rear; Red cab/Brown rear; Blue cab/Cream rear. | 102 | 1947 | R/54 | Re-issue of 33a and 33c. Renumbered 415. | 57 |
| 34a | Royal Mail Air Service Car | Blue | 83 | 1935 | 1941 | | 75 |
| 34b | Royal Mail Van | Red and Black | 83 | 1938 | 1952 | Open windows till 1947. Last issue has Red roof, running boards and wheels. | 66 |
| 34c | Loud-speaker Van | Green or Blue with Silver speakers; Fawn or Brown with Black speakers | 81 | 1948 | R/54 | Casting as 280 (filled-in windows) + speakers on roof. Renumbered 492. | 188 |
| 35 | Small Cars | | | 1936 | 1941 | Contains 35a, 35b and 35c. | 58 |
| 35a | Saloon Car | Grey, Dark Blue, Blue, Red, Turquoise. Post-war: Grey or Blue. | 51 | 1936 | 1948 | Some pre-war examples have spare-wheel cover in contrasting colour, e.g. Dark Blue on Blue car; Dark Grey on Grey car. White wheels (solid rubber) pre-war only; Black late pre-war and post-war. | 58 |
| 35b | Racer | Red, Silver, Yellow or Blue. Post-war: Red or Silver. | 57 | 1936 | R/54 | Original issue has no driver, driver added 1939. Comments re wheels as 35a. | 58 |
| 35c | M.G. Sports Car | Red, Pale or Dark Green, Dark Blue, Maroon. Post-war: Red, Green. | 52 | 1936 | 1948 | Some pre-war examples have windscreen, steering-wheel and spare-wheel brace in Silver. Comments re wheels as 35a. | 58 |
| 35d | Austin 7 Car | Blue, Yellow, Green, Grey, Maroon. Post-war: Blue, Fawn, Yellow. | 50 | 1938 | 1948 | Pre-war has wire screen and steering-wheel in Silver, some have hole in seat for driver (as for 152c). Some pre-war Yellow cars have Orange spare-wheel cover. Comments re wheels as 35a. | 58 |
| 36 | Motor Cars (with Drivers, Passengers, Footmen) | | | 1937 | 1941 | General notes on 36 Series: Pre-war baseplates had 2 pairs of slots to hold the tinplate figures used in the closed cars, and these slots appear briefly post-war, although the figures had | 59–60 |

| No. | Description | Colours | Length | Introduced | Deleted | Comment/Variations | Page |
|-----|-------------|---------|--------|-----------|---------|--------------------|------|
| | | | | | | been deleted. As regards the open bodies, only pre-war examples have a hole in the driver's seat. Comments re chassis also apply to 30f. Post-war chassis always Black. | |
| 36a | Armstrong Siddeley (Limousine) with driver and footman | Red, Grey | 97 | 1937 | 1941 | Vertical bonnet louvres. See 24b. | 60 |
| 36a | Armstrong Siddeley | Blue, Dark Blue, Grey, Maroon, Dark Green | 97 | 1946 | 1950 | | 61 |
| 36b | Bentley (Two-seater Sports Coupe) with Driver and Passenger | Cream/Black chassis; Yellow/Maroon chassis; 2-tone Grey | 94 | 1937 | 1941 | Tinplate figures. See 24f. | 60 |
| 36b | Bentley | Green, Blue, Dark Green, Dark Blue, Grey, Fawn | 94 | 1946 | 1950 | | 61 |
| 36c | Humber (Vogue Saloon) with Driver and Footman | 2-tone Green; 2-tone Blue; Royal Blue | 91 | 1937 | 1941 | Bonnet extended to surround radiator grille. Tinplate figures. See 24d. | 60 |
| 36c | Humber Vogue | Brown, Grey, Light Blue, Maroon | 91 | 1946 | 1950 | | 61 |
| 36d | Rover (Streamlined Saloon) with Driver and Passenger | 2-tone Green; 2-tone Red | 94 | 1937 | 1941 | 2 side windows. Tinplate figures. See 24e. | 60 |
| 36d | Rover | Light Green, Green, Blue or Dark Blue | 94 | 1946 | 1950 | | 61 |
| 36e | British Salmson (Two-seater Sports) with Driver | Royal Blue, Black chassis; Black, Red chassis; 2-tone Grey | 96 or 93 | 1937 | 1941 | Cast figure. Hole in seat for driver. Spare wheel on rear (as 24h) or smooth boot. See 24h. | 60 |
| 36e | British Salmson Two-seater Sports | Red, Pale or mid-Blue, Brown, Green | 93 | 1946 | 1950 | No hole in seat. | 61 |
| 36f | British Salmson (Four-seater Sports) with Driver | 2-tone Red or 2-tone Green. | 96 | 1937 | 1941 | Cast figure, hole in seat. Spare wheel cover in light relief on boot. See 24g. | 60 |
| 36f | British Salmson Four-seater Sports | Light Green, Green, Grey, Fawn, Brown | 96 | 1946 | 1950 | No hole in seat. | 61 |
| 36g | Taxi with Driver | (All with Black roof, wings and interior). Cream, Yellow, Grey, Dark Blue, Light Green. Post-war: Green, Light Green, Red, Maroon, Brown. | 72 | 1937 | 1950 | Open rear window till early post-war. | 60 |
| 37a | Motor Cyclist – Civilian | Blue, Green or Black rider, Black cycle. Post-war: Green or Grey rider, Black cycle. | 45 | 1937 | 1950 | Pre-war has engine and exhaust in silver. White rubber wheels till early Post-war. Produced *for export only* till 1954–5. (Renumbered 041). | 70 |
| 37b | Motor Cyclist – Police | Blue rider, Black cycle | 45 | 1937 | 1950 | Pre-war has engine and exhaust in silver, and rider has chin-strap. Produced *for export only* till 1954–5. (Renumbered 042). | 70 |

(20)

| No. | Description | Colours | Length | Introduced | Deleted | Comment/Variations | Page |
|-----|-------------|---------|--------|------------|---------|---------------------|------|
| 37c | Royal Corps of Signals Despatch Rider | Khaki rider, Green cycle | 45 | 1937 | 1941 | White rubber wheels till 1939. | 70 |
| 38a | Frazer-Nash B.M.W. Sports Car | Red with Maroon seats; Dark Blue/Putty seats; Post-war: Dark Blue, Blue, Dark Grey or Grey with Putty seats; Grey with Red seats and wheels. | 82 | 1940 | 1950 | Lacquered bare tinplate base pre-war, post-war in dirty Yellow, later Black. Filled-in steering-wheel spokes 1940 and 1946, open spokes 1941 and from 1947. Produced for export only till 1954/5 (renumbered 100 in 1954). Late issue has coloured wheels. | 62 |
| 38b | Sunbeam-Talbot Sports Car | Red/Maroon seats. Post-war: As above + Light Blue or Blue/Grey tonneau covers; Yellow/Beige or Green tonneau covers; Maroon/Grey tonneau covers; Light Green/Green tonneau covers; Brown/Blue tonneau covers. | 92 | 1940 | 1950 | Comments as above. Export No. 101. | 62 |
| 38c | Lagonda Tourer | Maroon/Dark Blue seats; Green/Black seats; Grey with Putty or Maroon seats; Green/Dark Green seats. | 102 | 1946 | 1950 | Filled-in, later open steering-wheel spokes. Produced for export only till 1954/5. Export No. 102. Late issue has coloured wheels. | 62 |
| 38d | Alvis Sports Tourer | Green/Black seats. Post-war: As above + Green with Dark Green or Brown seats; Maroon with Grey or Red seats; Light Blue with Dark Blue seats. | 95 | 1940 | 1950 | Comments as for 38a. Export No. 103. | 62 |
| 38e | Armstrong Siddeley Coupe | Grey or Light Grey with Blue seats; Light Grey with Green seats; Light Green with Grey seats; Red with Maroon seats. | 96 | 1946 | 1950 | Comments as for 38c. Export No. 104. | 62 |
| 38f | Jaguar Sports Car | Light Brown with Blue seats; Blue or Light Blue with Grey seats; Grey with Blue or Black seats; Red with Maroon seats; Putty with Black seats. | 80 | 1946 | 1950 | Comments as for 38c. Export No. 105. | 62 |
| 39 | Saloon Cars (U.S.A. Saloon Cars) | | | 1939 | 1941 | Contains 39a–f. | 61 |
| 39a | Packard Super 8 Touring Sedan Car | Light Green, Grey, Black, Yellow, Royal Blue. Post-war: Brown, Green, Olive Black, Maroon, Green. | 107 | 1939 | 1950 | Comments re base-plate and wheel colours as for 38 series apply equally to 39 Series. | 61 |
| 39b | Oldsmobile 6 Sedan | Post-war: Grey, Dark Brown, Cream, Dark Blue, Light Blue, Fawn. | 100 | 1939 | 1950 | Produced for export only till 1952. | |
| 39bu | | Cream with Dark Blue wings; 2-tone Blue. | | 1950 | 1952 | 2-colour finish only for U.S. market. | 223 |

| No. | Description | Colours | Length | Introduced | Deleted | Comment/Variations | Page |
|---|---|---|---|---|---|---|---|
| 39c | Lincoln Zephyr Coupe | Grey, Yellow, Green. Post-war: Brown, Grey, Red. | 106 | 1939 | 1950 | Comment as for 39b. | 61 |
| 39cu | | Red with Maroon wings; Tan with Brown wings. | | 1950 | 1952 | Comment as for 39bu. | 223 |
| 39d | Buick Viceroy Saloon Car | Green, Maroon, Blue, Cream. Post-war: Maroon, Fawn, Grey, Dark Blue, Green, Beige. | 103 | 1939 | 1950 | | 61 |
| 39e | Chrysler Royal Sedan | Royal Blue, Green, Grey. Post-war: Royal Blue, Light Blue, Green, Dark Green. | 106 | 1939 | 1950 | Comment as for 39b. | 61 |
| 39eu | | Yellow/Red wings; 2-tone Green. | | 1950 | 1952 | Comment as for 39bu. | 223 |
| 39f | Studebaker State Commander Coupe | Yellow, Green, Grey. Post-war: Dark Blue, Grey, Green, Olive, Yellow. | 103 | 1939 | 1950 | | |
| 40a | Riley Saloon | Light, Medium or Dull Green, Light or Dark Grey, Dark Blue or Mid-Blue. | 93 | 1947 | R/54 | Renumbered 158. Small or large lettering on base-plate. | 133 |
| 40b | Triumph 1800 Saloon | 1st casting: Grey, Black, Light Blue, Fawn. 2nd casting: Mid- or Dark Blue, Beige. | 91 | 1948 | R/54 | 1st casting has axles held by pillars from rear windows; from 1949 axles held by base-plate. Renumbered 151. | 133 |
| 40d | Austin Devon Saloon | Red, Maroon, Dark Blue, Green, Blue, Light Blue, Tan | 86 | 1949 | R/54 | Small or large lettering on base-plate. Renumbered 152. | 133 |
| 40e | Standard Vanguard Saloon | 1st casting: Tan, Maroon. 2nd: Tan, Light Blue. 3rd: Tan, Light Blue, Cream, Dark Blue. | 91 | 1948 | R/54 | 1st casting (to 1950) has open wheel arches. 1st issue has rear axle held by separate tinplate clip. 2nd casting has closed wheel arches. 3rd casting has an extra ridge across the boot, small or large lettering on base-plate. Renumbered 153. | 133 |
| 40f | Hillman Minx Saloon | Light or Dark Tan, Pale or Dark Green | 88 | 1951 | R/54 | Small or large lettering on base-plate. Renumbered 154. | 133 |
| 40g | Morris Oxford Saloon | Dark or very Dark Green, Fawn, Grey, Light Tan | 93 | 1950 | R/54 | Small or large lettering on base-plate. Renumbered 159. | 133 |
| 40h | Austin Taxi | Yellow or Dark Blue. | 94 | 1951 | R/54 | Renumbered 254. Brown chassis on Yellow taxi. | 133 |
| 40j | Austin Somerset Saloon | Red, Mid-blue, Light Blue | 89 | 1954 | R/54 | Renumbered 161. | 133 |
| 42 | Police Hut, Motor Cycle Patrol and Policemen Set | | | 1936 | 1941 | Contains 42a, b, c, and d. | 71 |
| 42a | Police Box | Dark Blue | (H)66 | 1936 | R/54 | Renumbered 751. | 71 |
| 42b | Motor Cycle Patrol | Dark Blue and Green | 47 | 1936 | 1950 | Exported till 1954/5. Export No. 043. Pre-war has engine and exhaust in silver, more careful painting on face. | 71 |

| No. | Description | Colours | Length | Introduced | Deleted | Comment/Variations | Page |
|---|---|---|---|---|---|---|---|
| | | | | | | White solid rubber wheels till 1939/40 and in 1946; Black 1940/41 and post-1946. | |
| 42c | Point Duty Policeman (in white coat) | White, Black helmet | (H)42 | 1936 | 1941 | Lead alloy. | 71 |
| 42d | Point Duty Policeman | Dark Blue, White gauntlets | (H)40 | 1936 | 1941 | Lead alloy. | 71 |
| 43 | R.A.C. Box, Motor Cycle Patrol and Guides | | | 1935 | 1941 | Contains 43a, b, c and d. | 71 |
| 43a | R.A.C. Box | Blue and White | (H)51 | 1935 | 1941 | Tinplate. | 71 |
| 43b | R.A.C. Motor Cycle Patrol | Black cycle, Blue sidecar and rider | 45 | 1935 | 1948/9 | Pre-war has engine and exhaust in Silver, rider has White shirt, Black tie and red sash. Two shades of Blue post-war. Comments re wheels as for 42b. | 71 |
| 43c | R.A.C. Guide directing traffic | Blue uniform, Red sash | (H)37 | 1935 | 1941 | Lead alloy. | 71 |
| 43d | R.A.C. Guide saluting | Blue uniform, Red sash | (H)36 | 1935 | 1941 | Lead alloy. | 71 |
| 44 | A.A. Box, Motor Cycle Patrol and Guides | | | 1935 | 1941 | Contains 44a, b, c, and d. | 71 |
| 44a | A.A. Box | Black and Yellow, White roof | (H)81 | 1935 | 1941 | Tinplate. 3 signposts on top: London, Liverpool and Glasgow. | 71 |
| 44b | A.A. Motor Cycle Patrol | Black cycle, Yellow sidecar, Tan rider | 45 | 1935 | 1950 | Exported till 1954/5. Export No. 045. Re-issued as No. 270. Pre-war has engine and exhaust in Silver, rider has Blue sash and peak, tank is Yellow. Comments re wheels as for 42b. Two badge sizes – larger is post-war only. | 71 |
| 44c | A.A. Guide directing traffic | Tan uniform, Blue sash | (H)37 | 1935 | 1941 | Lead alloy. | 71 |
| 44d | A.A. Guide saluting | Tan uniform, Blue Sash | (H)36 | 1935 | 1941 | Lead alloy. | 71 |
| 45 | Garage | Cream with Green doors, Orange roof | (Base) 127 × 90 | 1935 | 1941 | Tinplate. Doors open. | 70 |
| 46 | Pavement Set | Dark Grey | | 1937 | 1940 | @ 4 × 300mm sections; 6 × 150mm sections; 4 × 75mm sections; 4 corner pieces. Cardboard. | 67, 271 |
| | | Stone | | 1948 | 1950 | | |
| 47 | Road Signs (12) | Black on White, Red tops | | 1935 | 1950 | Contains 47e–t. Exported till 1954/5. Export No. 770. Pre-war base underside is White, post-war Black. Triangles at top filled-in pre-war, open post-war. | 67 |
| 47a | Traffic Signal 4-face | Black on White, Yellow beacon | (H)62 | 1935 | 1948 | Reissued without beacon as 773. Post-war has black under base. | 67 |
| 47b | Traffic Signal 3-face | Black on White, Yellow beacon | (H)62 | 1935 | 1941 | | 67 |
| 47c | Traffic Signal 2-face | Black on White, Yellow beacon | (H)62 | 1935 | 1941 | Right angle or back-to-back. | 67 |
| 47d | Belisha Safety Beacon | Black and White, Yellow beacon | (H)51 | 1935 | 1948 | Re-issued as 777. Post-war has black under base. | 67 |
| 47e | '30 Mile Limit' Sign | See 47 | (H)52 | 1935 | 1950 | Available post-war only in set 47. | |
| 47f | 'Derestriction' Sign | See 47 but no Red | (H)48 | 1935 | 1950 | see 47e. | |

| No. | Description | Colours | Length | Introduced | Deleted | Comment/Variations | Page |
|-----|-------------|---------|--------|-----------|---------|--------------------|------|
| 47g | 'School' Sign | See 47 | (H)51 | 1935 | 1950 | see 47e. | |
| 47h | 'Steep Hill' Sign | See 47 | (H)51 | 1935 | 1950 | see 47e. | |
| 47k | 'Bend' Sign | See 47 | (H)51 | 1935 | 1950 | see 47e. | |
| 47m | Left-hand 'Corner' Sign | See 47 | (H)51 | 1935 | 1950 | see 47e. | |
| 47n | Right-hand 'Corner' Sign | See 47 | (H)51 | 1935 | 1950 | see 47e. | |
| 47p | 'Road Junction' Sign | See 47 | (H)51 | 1935 | 1950 | see 47e. | |
| 47q | 'No Entry' Sign | See 47 | (H)48 | 1935 | 1950 | see 47e. | |
| 47r | 'Major Road Ahead' Sign | See 47 | (H)54 | 1935 | 1950 | see 47e. | |
| 47s | 'Crossing. No Gates' Sign | See 47 | (H)51 | 1935 | 1950 | see 47e. | |
| 47t | 'Round-About' Sign | See 47 | (H)51 | 1935 | 1950 | see 47e. | |
| 48 | Filling and Service Station | Mostly Yellow walls with Green or Blue base, Green, Brown or Yellow roof. | (Base) 195 × 135, (Garage) 145 × 45 × 97 | 1935 | 1941 | Tinplate. Lithographed walls with adverts etc. | 70 |
| 49 | Petrol Pumps Set | | | 1935 | 1953 | Contains 49a–e. Exported till 1954/5. Export No. 780. | 70 |
| 49a | Bowser Petrol | Green | (H)46 | 1935 | 1953 | Post-war only in set 49. White rubber hoses till early post-war, thereafter yellow plastic. | 279 |
| 49b | Wayne Petrol Pump | Pale Blue | (H)39 | 1935 | 1953 | See 49a. | |
| 49c | Theo Petrol Pump | Royal Blue (pre-war) Brown (post-war) | (H)58 | 1935 | 1953 | See 49a. | |
| 49d | Shell Petrol Pump | Red | (H)53 | 1935 | 1953 | See 49a. | |
| 49e | Oil Bin (Pratts) | Yellow | (H)32 | 1935 | 1953 | Lifting tinplate cover. "Pratt's" transfer pre-war only. | |
| 50 | Ships of the British Navy | | | 1934 | 1942 | Contains 50a, 50b × 2, 50c, 50d, 50e, 50f × 3, 50g, 50h × 3, 50k. | 82–85 |
| 50a | Battle Cruiser "Hood" | Grey | 146 | 1934 | 1942 | Name omitted from underside casting 1939/40. | |
| 50b | Battleship "Nelson" Class | Grey | 117 | 1934 | 1942 | "Nelson" or "Rodney" (one of each in set). Names omitted 1939/1940. | |
| 50c | Cruiser "Effingham" | Grey | 100 | 1934 | 1942 | See 50a. | |
| 50d | Cruiser "York" | Grey | 98 | 1934 | 1942 | See 50a. | |
| 50e | Cruiser "Delhi" | Grey | 81 | 1934 | 1942 | See 50a. | |
| 50f | Destroyer "Broke" Class | Grey | 57 | 1934 | 1942 | | |
| 50g | Submarine "K" Class | Grey | 57 | 1934 | 1942 | | |
| 50h | Destroyer "Amazon" Class | Grey | 52 | 1934 | 1942 | | |
| 50k | Submarine "X" Class | Grey | 61 | 1934 | 1942 | | |
| 51 | Famous Liners | | | 1934 | 1940 | Contains 51b–g. | 86–88 |
| 51b | (Norddeutscher Lloyd) "Europa" | Black hull, White deck, Tan funnels | 165 | 1934 | 1940 | | |
| 51c | (Italia Line) "Rex" | Black hull, White deck, Red-White-and-Green funnels | 152 | 1934 | 1940 | | |

| No. | Description | Colours | Length/Wingspan | Introduced | Deleted | Comment/Variations | Page |
|---|---|---|---|---|---|---|---|
| 51d | (CPR) "Empress of Britain" | White with Light Stone funnels | 130 | 1934 | 1940 | | |
| 51e | (Peninsular and Oriental Steam Navigation Company) "Straithard" | White with Light Stone funnels | 114 | 1934 | 1940 | | |
| 51f | (Furness Withy) "Queen of Bermuda" | Light Grey hull, White deck, Red and Black funnels | 99 | 1934 | 1940 | | |
| 51g | (Cunard White Star) "Brittanic" | Black hull, White superstructure, Tan top deck, Black and Tan funnels | 121 | 1934 | 1940 | | |
| 52 | Cunard White Star "No. 534" Cunard White Star "Queen Mary" "Queen Mary" | Black and White with Red and Black funnels | 175 | 1934 | 1935 | Name cast underneath: 1: Cunard White Star "534". 1934. 2:Cunard White Star "534" Queen Mary. 1934. 3: Cunard White Star Queen Mary. From 1935. | 89 |
| 52a | Cunard White Star "Queen Mary" with rollers | As 52 | 175 | 1935 | 1949 | Casting 3: above with tinplate insert holding 2 rollers – Red plastic pre-war, Brass post-war. Presentation Box from 1936. | 89 |
| 52b | "Queen Mary" (without rollers) | As 52 | 175 | 1935 | 1936 | Renumbering of 52. | 89 |
| 52m | "Queen Mary" (without rollers) | As 52 | 175 | 1936 | 1940 | 52b without box. | 89 |
| 60 | Aeroplanes/British Aeroplanes | | | 1934 | 1941 | Contains 60a–f. | 94 |
| 60a | Imperial Airways Liner | 1: Yellow with Blue wingtips and tail; Gold and Blue, White and Blue or Red and Cream with "Sunburst" pattern on wing. 2: Gold or Silver. | 127 | 1934 | 1941 | 1: No registration. (1934–1936) 2: G-ABTI (1936–1941) 'Imperial Airways Liner' added under wing from 1939. Tinplate Wing. Small 2-blade props. See 66a. | 94 |
| 60b | DH Leopard Moth | 1: Green and Yellow, or Dark Blue and Orange. 2: Green, Gold or Silver. | 76 | 1934 | 1941 | 1: No registration. (1934–1936). 2: G-ACPT. (1936–1941) 'DH Leopard Moth' added under wing from 1939. Side windows filled in 1939/1940. See 66b. Tinplate wing. 2-blade prop. | 94 |
| 60c | Percival Gull | 1: White with Blue wingtips and tail; Buff with Red. 2: White, Red, Yellow, Light Blue. | 76 | 1934 | 1941 | 1: No registration. (1934–1936). 2: G-ADZO in black (1936–1941). 'Percival Gull' added under wing in 1939. Side windows filled in from 1939/1940. Tinplate wing. Large 2-blade prop. See 60k and 66c. | 94 |
| 60d | Low Wing Monoplane (Vickers Jockey) | 1: Red with Cream wingtips and tail; Orange with Cream; Gold with Blue. 2: Red, Orange or Silver. | 76 | 1934 | 1941 | 1: No registration. (1934–1936). 2: G-AVYP. Pilot's head added. (1936–1941). Tinplate wing. Large 2-blade prop. See 66d. | 94 |

| No. | Description | Colours | Wingspan | Introduced | Deleted | Comment/Variations | Page |
|-----|-------------|---------|----------|------------|---------|--------------------|------|
| 60e | General 'Monospar' | 1: Gold with Red wingtips and tail; Silver with Blue. 2: Silver or Gold. | 80 | 1934 | 1941 | 1: No registration. (1934–1936). 2: G-ABVP. (1936–1941). 'General Monospar' cast under wing from 1939. Small 2-blade props (2). See 66e. | 94 |
| 60f | Cierva 'Autogiro' | Gold with Blue rotor and tail-plane tips. | Rotor Ø 72 L 49 | 1934 | 1941 | Pilot's head added in 1936. 3-blade rotor, small 2-blade prop. See 66f. | 94 |
| 60g | DH 'Comet' Aeroplane | 1: Red with Gold ailerons, elevators and fin; Gold with Red; Silver with Blue. 2: Red, Silver or Gold. | 86 | 1935 | 1941 | 1: No registration (1934–1936). 2: G-ACSR. 'DH Comet' under wing. (1936–1941). Small 2-blade props (2). | 97 |
| 60g | Light Racer | 3: Yellow, Red or Silver. | | 1945 | 1949 | 3: (Post-war). G-RACE. 'Light Racer' under wing. 3-blade props. | 97 |
| 60h | 'Singapore' Flying Boat | Silver. Some in Grey in 1940 | 126 | 1936 | 1941 | 1: No Roller or gliding-game hole. Stencilled R.A.F. roundels (red and blue circles only) (1936). 2: Red plastic, later wooden roller added. Gliding game hole in upper wing. (1936–1940). Red-White-and-Blue transfer roundels from 1939. 3: Bow cut away underneath, seat added to bow gun position, no gliding hole. (1940–1941). Tinplate wings. Large 2-blade props (4). 'Singapore Flying Boat' stamped under wing in all versions. See 60m. | 97 |
| 60k | Percival 'Gull' Monoplane | Blue with Silver wings and tailplanes | 76 | 1936 | 1941 | 60c in commemorative issue (Type 2). 1: G-ADZO in Blue. (Amy Mollison.) 2: G-ADZO in Black. (H.L. Brook) Individual boxes. | 95 |
| 60k | Light Tourer | Dark Green, Light Green, Red or Silver | 76 | 1945 | 1949 | No registration. 'Percival Tourer' or 'Light Tourer' under wing. Large or small 2-blade prop. | |
| 60m | Four-Engined Flying Boat | Red, Light Blue, Dark Blue, Light Green, Silver, Yellow | 126 | 1936 | 1941 | 60h in "civilian" colours. (Type 2 or 3). G-EUTG, G-EVCU, G-EXGF or G-EYCE in Black across top wing. 'Four Engined Flying Boat' under lower wing. | 97 |

| No. | Description | Colours | Wingspan | Introduced | Deleted | Comment/Variations | Page |
|---|---|---|---|---|---|---|---|
| 60n | Fairey 'Battle' Bomber | Silver. Some in Grey in 1940 | 75 | 1937 | 1941 | Undercarriage legs and wheels till till 1940. 'Fairey Battle Bomber' cast under wing from 1938. Red and Blue stencilled roundels till 1939, thereafter Red-White-and-Blue transfers. 3-blade prop. See 60s. | 97 |
| 60p | Gloster 'Gladiator' Biplane | Silver. Some in Grey in 1940 | 44 | 1937 | 1941 | 1: No name. Stencilled roundels. 2: 'Gloster Gladiator' cast under lower wing. Transfer roundels. (from 1939). | 100 |
| 60r | Empire Flying Boat | Silver | 156 | 1937 | 1949 | 1: Red Plastic roller, gliding hole in wing. (1937–1940). 2; Hollowed-out bow casting, no gliding hole, some have wooden roller (1940–1941). Post-war is casting 2: with Brass roller. (1945–1949). See 60x. | 100 |

Pre-war liveries:

| | | |
|---|---|---|
| Caledonia | G-ADHM | |
| Canopus | G-ADHL | |
| Corsair | G-ADVB | |
| Challenger | G-ADVD | |
| Centurion | G-ADVE | |
| Calpurnia | G-AETW | |
| Cambria | G-ADUV | |
| Capella | G-ADUY | |
| Ceres | G-AETX | |

| Clio | G-AETY |
|---|---|
| Calypso | G-AEUA |
| Camilla | G-AEUB |
| Corinna | G-AEUC |
| Cheviot | G-AEUG |
| Cordelia | G-AEUD |

Individual boxes
Post-war:

| Cambria | G-ADUV |
|---|---|
| Caledonia | G-ADHM |

| No. | Description | Colours | Wingspan | Introduced | Deleted | Comment/Variations | Page |
|---|---|---|---|---|---|---|---|
| 60s | 'Medium Bomber' | Green and Brown upper surface, Black undersurfaces. | 75 | 1938 | 1940 | 60n in Camouflage. Red-White-and-Blue roundel, with Yellow outer ring, applied to one wing only. With undercarriage. Available also in boxed mirror-image pairs. | 97 |
| 60s | Fairey 'Battle' Bomber (Camouflaged) | As above but darker shades. | 75 | 1940 | 1941 | Blue and Red roundels on both wings. No undercarriage. | 97 |
| 60t | 'Douglas DC3' Air Liner | Silver | 132 | 1938 | 1941 | PH-ALI in Black across wing. With, later without, small tail-wheel. 3-blade props (2). Individual box. | 100 |
| 60v | Armstrong Whitworth 'Whitley' Bomber | Silver | 116 | 1937 | 1941 | With, later without gliding hole. See 62t. Individual box. | 100 |
| 60w | Flying Boat 'Clipper III' | Silver | 164 | 1938 | 1941 | USA NC 16736. 'Pan American Airways Clipper III' under wing. Gliding Game hole. Red plastic roller. Individual box. | 101 |
| 60w | Flying Boat | Silver, Blue or Green | 164 | 1945 | 1949 | No registration or gliding hole. 'Flying Boat' under wing. Brass roller. | 101 |

| No. | Description | Colours | Wingspan | Introduced | Deleted | Comment/Variations | Page |
|-----|-------------|---------|----------|------------|---------|--------------------|------|
| 60x | Atlantic Flying Boat | See comments | 156 | 1937 | 1941? or 1940? | 60r in bright colours, e.g. Blue with Cream wings, 'Dauntless' on one side of nose, reg. G-AZBP; Green with Cream, 'Whirlwind' on nose, G-AZBT; Black and White 'Dreadnought', 'Atlantic Flying Boat' under wing. | 100 |
| 60y | Thompson Aircraft Refuelling Tender | Red, Black wings, Maroon driver | (L)84 | 1938 | 1940 | 3 White or Black rubber wheels. 'Shell Aviation Services' transfer. | 75 |
| 61 | R.A.F. Aeroplanes | | | 1937 | 1941 | Contains 60h (Type 2 or 3), 2 × 60n, 2 × 60p. | 108 |
| 62a | Vickers-Supermarine 'Spitfire' Fighter | Silver | 52 | 1940 | 1941 | Short nose, cockpit flush with rear of fuselage. See 62e. | 103 |
| | | | | | | Also issued as a pendant in 1940/41: marked 'Meccano Spitfire Fund'. Individual box. | 14 |
| 62a | Spitfire | Silver | 51 | 1945 | 1949 | Long nose, bubble cockpit. | 103 |
| 62b | Bristol 'Blenheim' Bomber | Silver | 78 | 1940 | 1941 | 'Blenheim Bomber' under wing. See 62d. | 105 |
| 62b | Medium Bomber | Silver | 78 | 1945 | 1949 | 'Medium Bomber' under wing. | 105 |
| 62d | Bristol 'Blenheim' Bomber Camouflaged | Green and Brown, ½ Black, ½ White undersurface | 78 | 1940 | 1941 | Casting as 62b. Red-White-and-Blue roundels, later Red and Blue with darker camouflage. | 105 |
| 62e | Vickers-Supermarine 'Spitfire' Fighter Camouflaged | Green and Brown, ½ Black, ½ White undersurface | 52 | 1940 | 1941 | Casting as 62a. Variation as 62d. | 105 |
| 62g | Boeing 'Flying Fortress' | Silver | 144 | 1939 | 1941 | 'Boeing Flying Fortress' under wing. Gliding hole. Individual box. | 105 |
| 62g | Long Range Bomber | Silver | 144 | 1945 | 1949 | 'Long Range Bomber' under wing. No gliding hole. No box. | 105 |
| 62h | Hawker 'Hurricane' Single Seater Fighter Camouflaged | Green and Brown, Black, later ½ Black, ½ White undersurface | 55 | 1939 | 1941 | Finish variation as 62d. With this change, the undercarriage and wheels were omitted. See 62s | 105 |
| 62k | Airspeed 'Envoy' King's Aeroplane | Silver wings and tailplanes, Red and Blue fuselage and engines | 91 | 1938 | 1941 | 'King's Aeroplane' under wing. Individual box. See 62m. G-AEXX. | 101 |
| 62m | Airspeed 'Envoy' | Red, Silver, Blue, Green | 91 | 1938 | 1941 | 'Airspeed Envoy' under wing. G-ACVJ, G-ADCB, G-ADAZ, G-AENA. | 101 |
| 62m | Light Transport | Red, Silver, Blue | 91 | 1945 | 1949 | 'Light Transport' under wing. G-ATMH. | 101 |

| No. | Description | Colours | Wingspan | Introduced | Deleted | Comment/Variations | Page |
|-----|-------------|---------|----------|------------|---------|--------------------|------|
| 62n | Junkers Ju 90 Air Liner | Silver | 160 | 1938 | 1941 | 'Junkers Ju 90 Air Liner' under wing. Window transfers. Gliding hole. D-AALU, D-AIVI, D-AURE, D-ADLH. See 62y and 67a. Individual box. | 101 |
| 62p | 'Ensign' Air Liner | Silver | 173 | 1938 | 1941 | 'Ensign Air Liner' under wing. Gliding Game hole. Individual box. Registrations: Ensign G-ADSR from 12/38 From 1/39: Elsinore G-ADST Explorer G-ADSV ECHO G-ADTB Ettrick G-ADSX Elysian G-ADSZ See 62x and 68a. | 104 |
| 62p | Armstrong Whitworth Air Liner | Silver, Blue or Green with Silver trim, Grey with Green trim | 173 | 1945 | 1949 | 'Armstrong Whitworth Air Liner' under wing. Explorer or Echo markings as above. No gliding hole or box. | 104 |
| 62r | De Haviland 'Albatross' Mail Liner | Silver | 145 | 1939 | 1941 | 'DH Albatross' under wing. Gliding hole. G-AEVV. Individual box. See 62w and 68b. | 104 |
| 62r | Four-Engined Liner | Grey, Light Blue or Silver, all with Red trim (with markings) Grey, Fawn, Light Blue or Silver | 145 | 1945 | 1949 | 'Four Engined Liner' under wing. No gliding hole or box. Without markings, later with G-ATPV. | 104 |
| 62s | Hawker 'Hurricane' Single Seater Fighter | Silver | 55 | 1939 | 1949 | Undercarriage and wheels till 1940 2-blade, later 3-blade prop. | 105 |
| 62t | Armstrong Whitworth 'Whitley' Bomber Camouflaged | Green and Brown | 116 | 1939 | 1941 | Camouflaged 60v. Finish variation as 62d. Individual box. | 100 |
| 62w | Imperial Airways 'Frobisher' Class Liner | Silver | 145 | 1939 | 1941 | Casting as 62r, with 'Frobisher Class Air Liner' under wing. Markings are: Frobisher G-AFDI Falcon G-AFDJ Fortuna G-AFDK Gliding hole. Individual boxes. | 104 |
| 62x | British 40-Seater Air Liner | Red with Maroon trim; Light Green with Dark Green; Yellow with Maroon; Light Blue with Dark Blue. | 173 | 1939 | 1941 | 62p in assorted colours. No box. 'British 40-Seater Air Liner' under wing. G-AZCA. Gliding hole. | 104 |

| No. | Description | Colours | Wingspan | Introduced | Deleted | Comment/Variations | Page |
|-----|-------------|---------|----------|------------|---------|--------------------|------|
| 62y | Giant High Speed Monoplane | Blue with Brown trim; Light Blue with Dark Blue; Light Green with Dark Green. Post-war: Light or Mid-Green with Dark Green; Grey with Green; Silver | 160 | 1939 | 1949 | 62n in assorted colours. 'Giant High Speed Monoplane' under wing. Pre-war: D-AZBK; post-war G-ATBK. Pre-war has gliding hole. No box. | 101 |
| 63 | Mayo Composite Aircraft | | | 1939 | 1941 | Contains 63a and 63b. | 104 |
| 63a | Flying Boat 'Maia' | Silver | 156 | 1939 | 1941 | Casting as 60r but with tinplate frame on middle of wing, and 'Mayo Composite' under wing. G-ADHK. Full bows and gliding hole, hollowed bows and no hole from 1940. Plastic roller, wooden from late 1940. Individual box. | 104 |
| 63b | Seaplane 'Mercury' | Silver | 101 | 1939 | 1941 | Tinplate clip under fuselage, 'Mercury Seaplane' under wing. G-ADHJ. With, later without gliding hole. | 104 |
| 63b | Seaplane | Silver | 101 | 1945 and 1952 | 1949 R/54 | Casting as above, but 'Seaplane' under wing and no clip. G-AVKW. Renumbered 700. | 104 |
| 64 | Presentation Aeroplane Set | | | 1939 | 1941 | Contains 60g, 62h, 62k, 62m, 62s, 63b. 62h or 62s replaced by 62a or 62s in 1940. | 106, 273 |
| 65 | Presentation Aeroplane Set | | | 1939 | 1941 | Contains 60r, 60t, 60v, 60w, 62n, 62p, 62r, 62w | 108 |
| 66 | Camouflaged Aeroplane Set | | | 1940 | 1941 | Contains 66a–f | 108 |
| 66a | Heavy Bomber | Green and Brown, Black underside | 127 | 1940 | 1941 | Casting as 60a. Dark camouflage, Red and Blue roundels. No name inscription under wing. | 108 |
| 66b | Dive Bomber Fighter | Green and Brown, Black underside | 76 | 1940 | 1941 | Casting as 60b, finish as 66a. | 108 |
| 66c | Two-Seater Fighter | Green and Brown, Black underside | 76 | 1940 | 1941 | Casting as 60c, finish as 66a. | 108 |
| 66d | Torpedo Dive Bomber | Green and Brown, Black underside | 76 | 1940 | 1941 | Casting as 60d, finish as 66a. | 108 |
| 66e | Medium Bomber | Green and Brown, Black underside | 80 | 1940 | 1941 | Casting as 60e, including 'General Monospar' under wing. Finish as 66a. | 108 |
| 66f | Army Co-operation Autogiro | Silver with Silver rotor | Rotor ∅ 72 L 49 | 1940 | 1941 | Casting as 60f. Red, White and Blue roundels. | 108 |

| No. | Description | Colours | Wingspan | Introduced | Deleted | Comment/Variations | Page |
|-----|-------------|---------|----------|------------|---------|--------------------|------|
| 67a | Junkers Ju 89 Heavy Bomber | Black with Pale Blue underside | 160 | 1940 | 1941 | Casting as 62n without gliding hole, but 'Junkers Ju 89 Heavy Bomber' under wing. Crosses on wings, swastikas on tailfins. Individual box. | 101 |
| 68 | Aircraft in Service Camouflage | | | 1940 | 1941 | Contains 2 × 60s, 2 × 62d, 3 × 62s, 3 × 62h, 62t, 68a, 68b. | 107 |
| 68a | Armstrong Whitworth 'Ensign' Liner in Service Camouflage | Green and Brown, Black underside | 173 | 1940 | 1941 | 62p in camouflage (dark) with Red and Blue roundels. No gliding hole. | 108 |
| 68b | 'Frobisher' Class Liner in Service Camouflage | Green and Brown, Black underside | 145 | 1940 | 1941 | 62r in camouflage (light or dark) with Red and Blue roundels. With or without gliding hole. | 108 |
| 70a | Avro York Air Liner | Silver | 160 | 1946 and 1952 | 1949 R/54 | G-AGJC. Individual box. Renumbered 704. 3-blade prop. | 112 |
| 70b | Tempest II Fighter | Silver | 63 | 1946 and 1952 | 1949 R/54 | RAF roundels. 4-blade prop. Large pointed spinner to 1949, flat spinner from 1952. Renumbered 730. | 112 |
| 70c | Viking Air Liner | Silver or Grey | 140 | 1947 and 1952 | 1949 R/54 | G-AGOL. Windows stencilled on fuselage. 4-blade props (2). Large pointed spinner to 1949, small spinner from 1952. | 112 |
| 70d | Twin-Engined Fighter | Silver | 76 | 1946 and 1952 | 1949 R/54 | 3-blade props. Renumbered 731. | 112 |
| 70e | Gloster Meteor Twin-Jet Fighter | Silver | 67 | 1946 and 1952 | 1949 R/54 | RAF roundels. Renumbered 732. | 112 |
| 70f | Shooting Star Jet Fighter | Silver | 61 | 1947 and 1952 | 1949 R/54 | USAF markings. Star on port wing only. Renumbered 733. | 112 |

| No. | Description | Colours | Length | Introduced | Deleted | Comment/Variations | Page |
|---|---|---|---|---|---|---|---|
| 100 | Lady Penelope's FAB 1 | Pink | 147 | 1966 | 1977 | Roof struts picked out on earlier models. | 236 |
| 101 | Dining Room Furniture | Walnut Brown | | 1936 | 1940 | Contains 101a, 101b, 2 × 101c, 4 × 101d. | 74, 273 |
| 101a | Table | See 101 | 64 | 1936 | 1940 | | |
| 101b | Sideboard | See 101 | 63 | 1936 | 1940 | Opening doors. Tin-plate back. | |
| 101c | Carver Chairs | See 101 | (H)33 | 1936 | 1940 | Armrests. | |
| 101d | Chair | See 101 | (H)34 | 1936 | 1940 | Raised 'Leather' cushion, oblong gap between seat and back. (Compare 102f.) | |
| 101 | Sunbeam Alpine (Touring Finish) | Blue or Pink-Maroon, Grey driver | 94 | 1957 | 1960 | See 107. | 132 |
| 101 | Thunderbirds II and IV | Green; Metallic Dark Green from 1973 | 143 | 1967 | 1973 | Yellow plastic legs and Thunderbird IV. See 106. | 236 |
| 102 | Bedroom Furniture | Walnut Brown; Pink | | 1936 | 1940 | Contains 102a, 102b, 102c, 102d, 102e, 102f. | 74, 273 |
| 102a | Bed | See 102 | 74 | 1936 | 1940 | | |
| 102b | Wardrobe | See 102 | (H)63 | 1936 | 1940 | Opening door. Tin-plate back. | |
| 102c | Dressing Table | See 102 | 51 | 1936 | 1940 | Tinplate mirror. Opening drawers. | |
| 102d | Dressing Chest | See 102 | (H)40 | 1936 | 1940 | Opening Drawer. Tin-plate back. | |
| 102e | Dressing Table Stool | See 102 | (H)13 | 1936 | 1940 | | |
| 102f | Chair | See 102 | (H)34 | 1936 | 1940 | See 103e. | |
| 102 | M.G. Midget (Touring Finish) | Pale Green with Cream seats; Yellow with Red seats. Grey driver | 83 | 1957 | 1960 | See 108 and 129. | 132 |
| 102 | Joe's Car | Green | 139 | 1969 | 1976 | From TV series 'Joe 90'. | 236 |
| 103 | Kitchen Furniture | Light Blue and White; Light Green and Cream | | 1936 | 1940 | Contains 103a, 103b, 103c, 103d, 103e. | 74, 273 |
| 103a | Refrigerator | See 103 | (H)50 | 1936 | 1940 | Opening door. Tinplate insert with food, tinplate back. | |
| 103b | Kitchen Cabinet | See 103 | (H)56 | 1936 | 1940 | Opening doors and drawer, tinplate back. | |
| 103c | Electric Cooker | See 103 | (H)38 | 1936 | 1940 | Opening door. Tinplate back. | |
| 103d | Table | See 103 | 52 | 1936 | 1940 | | |
| 103e | Chair | See 103 | (H)34 | 1936 | 1940 | Casting as 102f. | |
| 103 | Austin Healey 100 (Touring Finish) | Cream with Red seats; Red with Grey seats. Grey driver | 85 | 1957 | 1960 | See 109. | 132 |
| 103 | Spectrum Patrol Car | Metallic Red | 121 | 1968 | 1976 | Screaming motor. From TV series 'Captain Scarlet'. | 236 |
| 104 | Bathroom Furniture | Pink and White or Light Green and White | | 1936 | 1940 | Contains 104a–f. | 74, 273 |
| 104a | Bath | See 104. Gold taps | 69 | 1936 | 1940 | | |
| 104b | Bath Mat | Mottled Green | 50×37 | 1936 | 1940 | Rubber. | |

(Numbers 100–105 also used for 38 Series Export only, 1954–55. See 38a–f)

| No. | Description | Colours | Length | Introduced | Deleted | Comment/Variations | Page |
|---|---|---|---|---|---|---|---|
| 104c | Pedestal Hand Basin | See 104. Gold taps | (H)63 | 1936 | 1940 | Tinplate mirror. | |
| 104d | Stool | See 104 | (H)15 | 1936 | 1940 | | |
| 104e | Linen Basket | See 104 | (H)22 | 1936 | 1940 | Hinged lid. | |
| 104f | Toilet | See 104 | (H)34 | 1936 | 1940 | Hinged lid. | |
| | Although it was not given a number, the 'Dolly Varden' Doll's House should be included here with the Furniture: | | | | | | |
| | 'Dolly Varden' Doll's House | 1st storey Cream with Brown beams, Ground floor Red brick, Red roof | L 476 D 260 H 476 | 1936 | 1940 | Leather Board. | 74 |
| 104 | Aston Martin DB3S (Touring Finish) | Blue or Pink, Grey driver | 87 | 1957 | 1960 | See 110. | 132 |
| 104 | Spectrum Patrol Car | Metallic Blue | 160 | 1968 | 1976 | White rubber nose. Seat drops out till 1973, thereafter figure is attached to door. | 236 |
| 105a | Garden Roller | Green and Red | 67 | 1948 | R/54 | Renumbered 381. No marking. | 187 |
| 105b | Wheelbarrow | Brown and Red | 82 | 1949 | R/54 | Renumbered 382. | 187 |
| 105c | 4-Wheel Hand Truck | Blue or Green | O/L126 | 1949 | R/54 | Renumbered 383. | 187 |
| 105e | Grass Cutter | Yellow, Green and Red | 73 | 1949 | R/54 | Renumbered 384. | 187 |
| 105 | Triumph TR2 (Touring Finish) | Yellow or Grey, Grey driver | 84 | 1957 | 1960 | See 111. | 132 |
| 105 | Maximum Security Vehicle | White | 137 | 1968 | 1975 | Plastic crate with radioactive sticker. From TV series 'Captain Scarlet'. | 236 |
| 106 | Austin Atlantic | Black or Blue with Red seats and wheels; Pink with Cream seats and wheels | 95 | R/54 | 1958 | Renumbering of 140a. White tyres on Black car. | 140 |
| 106 | 'Prisoner' Mini Moke | White with Red-and-White striped canopy | 73 | 1967 | 1971 | See 342. | 236 |
| 106 | Thunderbirds II and IV | Metallic Blue, with White underside to 1977, thereafter Black underside | 153 | 1974 | 1979 | Redesigned 101. Yellow plastic legs and Thunderbird IV, Red plastic legs from 1977. | 237, 285 |
| 107a | Sack Truck | Blue | 65 | 1949 | R/54 | Renumbered 385. | 187 |
| 107 | Sunbeam Alpine (Competition Finish) | Pale Blue (No. 26); Pink-Maroon (No. 34). White driver | 94 | 1955 | 1959 | See 101. | 132 |
| 107 | Stripey the Magic Mini | White with Blue, Red and Yellow stripes | 75 | 1967 | 1970 | See 183. With plastic figures (4). | 235 |
| 108 | M.G. Midget (Competition Finish) | Red with Tan seats (No. 24); White with Maroon seats (No. 28). White driver | 83 | 1955 | 1959 | See 102. | 132 |
| 108 | Sam's Car | Silver or Gold; Red or Pale Blue from 1971 | 111 | 1969 | 1975 | Key-less clockwork motor. From TV series 'Joe 90'. | 236 |
| 109 | Austin-Healey 100 (Competition finish) | Cream with Red seats (No. 23); Yellow, Blue seats (No. 21). White driver | 85 | 1955 | 1959 | See 103. | 132 |

| No. | Description | Colours | Length | Introduced | Deleted | Comment/Variations | Page |
|-----|-------------|---------|--------|-----------|---------|--------------------|------|
| 109 | Gabriel Model T Ford | Yellow and Black | 83 | 1969 | 1971 | Casting as 475. From Gerry Anderson TV series 'The Secret Service'. | 238 |
| 110 | Aston Martin DB3S (Competition finish) | Grey with Blue seats (No. 20); Green, Red seats (No. 22). White driver | 87 | 1956 | 1959 | See 104. | 132 |
| 110 | Aston Martin DB5 | Metallic Red | 111 | 1965 | 1971 | 'Aston Martin DB5' and '110' on baseplate till 1967, thereafter no numbers – see 153. | 139 |
| 111 | Triumph TR2 (Competition finish) | Turquoise with Red seats (No. 25); Pink, Blue seats (No. 29). White driver | 84 | 1956 | 1959 | See 105. | 132 |
| 111 | Cinderella's Coach | Pink and Gold with White horses. | 242 | 1976 | 1978 | Plastic horses and figures. | 238 |
| 112 | Austin-Healey Sprite Mark II | Red | 78 | 1961 | 1966 | Turquoise, Dark or Light Blue assembled in South Africa | 136, 224 |
| 112 | Purdey's Triumph TR7 | Yellow | 98 | 1978 | 1980 | Casting as 211, From TV series 'The New Avengers'. | 237, 287 |
| 113 | MGB | Cream. Grey (plastic) driver | 85 | 1962 | 1969 | | 36, 224 |
| 114 | Triumph Spitfire | Metallic Grey or Red; Gold from 1966; Metallic Purple from 1970. Pale Blue (Plastic) driver | 89 | 1963 | 1971 | 'I've Got A Tiger In My Tank' transfer on boot from 1966. | 136 |
| 115 | Plymouth Fury Sports | White | 122 | 1965 | 1969 | With 2 figures and 2 aerials. Casting as 137. | 149 |
| 115 | U.B. Taxi | Yellow, Blue and Black | 86 | 1979 | 1979 | Special issue only available through United Biscuits in exchange for tokens. Casting as 120. | 209, 287 |
| 116 | Volvo 1800 S | Red or Dark Metallic Red | 105 | 1966 | 1971 | See 1002. | 152 |
| 117 | 4-Berth Caravan with Transparent Roof | Blue and Cream or Yellow and Cream | 117 | 1963 | 1970 | 188 (enlarged windows) with transparent roof. | 239 |
| 118 | Tow-Away Glider Set | Car: Cream with Blue roof; Trailer: Cream with Red and Yellow glider | 289 | 1965 | 1970 | 135 Triumph 2000 + plastic trailer and glider. 'Southdown Gliding Club' sticker on trailer. | 143 |
| 120 | Jaguar 'E' Type | Red with Black roof/Cream folded roof | 92 | 1962 | 1967 | Interchangeable plastic hardtop or folded hood. | 136 |
| 120 | Happy Taxi | White, Yellow and Blue | 86 | 1979 | 1980 | See 115. Chassis casting modified from 475 Model T Ford. | 209, 287 |
| 121 | Goodwood Racing Gift Set | | | 1963 | 1966 | Contains 112, 113, 120, 183 and 9 plastic figures. (From 009.) | 135 |
| 122 | Touring Gift Set | | | 1963 | 1965 | Contains 188, 193, 195, 270, 295, and 796. | 146 |
| 122 | Volvo 265 DL Estate Car | Metallic Blue and White | 141 | 1977 | 1980 | See 243. | 153 |
| 123 | Mayfair Gift Set | | | 1963 | 1965 | Contains 142, 150, 186, 194, 198, 199 and 4 plastic figures. (From 009.) | 148 |

| No. | Description | Colours | Length | Introduced | Deleted | Comment/Variations | Page |
|-----|-------------|---------|--------|------------|---------|--------------------|------|
| 123 | Princess 2200 HL Saloon | Bronze or White with Blue, Roof; All-over White | 128 | 1977 | 1980 | | |
| 124 | Holiday Gift Set | | | 1964 | 1967 | Contains 137, 142, 796, 952. | 146 |
| 124 | Rolls Royce Phantom V Limousine | Metallic Blue | 141 | 1977 | 1979 | 152 without opening bonnet. | 144, 287 |
| 125 | Fun A'Hoy Set | Car: Pale Blue. Trailer: as 796. | 210 | 1964 | 1969 | 130 with driver + 796 with driver from 113 and 114. | 142 |
| 126 | Motor Show Set | | | 1965 | 1969 | Contains 127, 133, 151 and 171; 127, 151, 159 and 171 from 1968. | 145 |
| 127 | Rolls Royce Silver Cloud III | Metallic Green, Gold from 1966 | 124 | 1964 | 1972 | | 142 |
| 128 | Mercedes–Benz 600 | Metallic Red; Metallic Blue from 1975 | 147 | 1964 | 1979 | 3 plastic figures till 1967; thereafter driver only. See 1008. | 152 |
| 129 | M.G. Midget | White with Maroon seats; Red with Tan seats | 83 | ? | ? | 108 without driver or numbers. For U.S. market only. | 223 |
| 129 | Volkswagen 1200 Sedan | Metallic Blue | 100 | 1965 | 1976 | Plastic Speedwheels from 1972. See 1003, 260, 262. | 152 |
| 130 | Ford Consul Corsair | Metallic Red; Pale Blue | 106 | 1964 | 1969 | See 125 and 169. | 143 |
| 131 | Cadillac Eldorado | Pink with Grey seats; Yellow with Red seats. Grey driver | 118 | 1956 | 1963 | | 150 |
| 131 | Jaguar 'E' Type 2+2 | White or Red; Bronze or Metallic Purple from 1973 | 112 | 1968 | 1975 | Plastic Speedwheels from 1972. | 138 |
| 132 | Packard Convertible | Green or Tan, Grey driver | 112 | 1955 | 1961 | | 150 |
| 132 | Ford 40-RV | Silver; Metallic Blue; Orange-Red with Yellow panels | 96 | 1967 | 1974 | Casting as for 215 except for bonnet. | 138 |
| 133 | Cunningham C-5R | White with Blue stripes. Blue driver | 99 | 1955 | 1960 | | 136 |
| 133 | Ford Cortina 1965 | Gold with White roof; Yellow | 101 | 1964 | 1969 | Facelift on 139. See 212 | 142 |
| 134 | Triumph Vitesse | Metallic Green with White flashes | 85 | 1964 | 1968 | Facelift on 189. | 143 |
| 135 | Triumph 2000 | Metallic Green, White roof; White, Blue roof | 105 | 1963 | 1969 | See 118. Some special finishes (prepared for Triumph?) including: White, Lilac or Green with Black roof; Black or Cherry with White roof; Brown, Black or Dark Green with Lilac roof. | 141 |
| 136 | Vauxhall Viva | White, Pale Metallic Blue, Blue | 93 | 1964 | 1973 | | 143 |
| 137 | Plymouth Fury Convertible | Metallic Grey, Green, Blue or Pink | 122 | 1963 | 1966 | See 115. | 149 |
| 138 | Hillman Imp | Metallic Green or Red | 85 | 1963 | 1973 | See 214. | 143 |
| 139a | Ford Fordor Sedan | Yellow, Red, Green or Tan | 102 | 1949 | R/54 | Renumbered 170. | 150 |
| 139am | US Army Staff Car (Ford Fordor) | Green | 102 | ? | R/54 | Renumbered 170m. White stars on roof and doors. | 222 |
| 139b | Hudson Commodore Sedan | Dark Blue with Tan roof; Cream with Maroon roof | 111 | 1950 | R/54 | Renumbered 171. | 150 |

| No. | Description | Colours | Length | Introduced | Deleted | Comment/Variations | Page |
|-----|-------------|---------|--------|------------|---------|--------------------|------|
| 139 | Ford Cortina | Pale Blue or Metallic Blue | 101 | 1963 | 1964 | Replaced by 133. Emerald Green issue assembled in South Africa. | 150 |
| 140a | Austin Atlantic Convertible | Blue with Dark Blue seats; Pink with Cream seats; Dark Blue with Red seats | 95 | 1951 | R/54 | Renumbered 106. | 140 |
| 140b | Rover 75 Saloon | Maroon or Cream | 101 | 1951 | R/54 | Renumbered 156. | 140 |
| 140 | Morris 1100 | Pale Blue | 87 | 1963 | 1969 | | 143 |
| 141 | Vauxhall Victor Estate Car | Yellow | 92 | 1963 | 1967 | See 278. Pink-Orange issue assembled in South Africa. | 141, 224 |
| 142 | Jaguar Mark 10 | Metallic Blue (2 shades) | 107 | 1962 | 1968 | | 143 |
| 143 | Ford Capri | Green with White roof | 90 | 1962 | 1967 | | 143 |
| 144 | Volkswagen 1500 | Cream, later Bronze | 93 | 1963 | 1967 | | 147 |
| 145 | Singer Vogue | Metallic Green or Cream | 93 | 1962 | 1967 | | 141 |
| 146 | Daimler V8 2½ Litre | Metallic Green | 95 | 1963 | 1967 | | 143 |
| 147 | Cadillac 62 | Metallic Green | 113 | 1962 | 1969 | See 258 and 264. | 151 |
| 148 | Ford Fairlane | Pale Green or Metallic Green | 111 | 1962 | 1966 | See 258 and 264. Blue-Grey, assembled in South Africa. | 150, 224 |
| 149 | Sports Cars Gift Set | | | 1957 | 1959 | Contains 107, 108, 109, 110, 111. | 132 |
| 149 | Citroen Dyane | Bronze with Black roof | 91 | 1971 | 1975 | Adapted from French Dinky 1413. | 152 |
| 150 | Royal Tank Corps Personnel | | | 1937 | R/54 | Contains 150a, 2 × 150b, 2 × 150c, 150e. Berets. Export only post-war. Renumbered for export 600. | 78 |
| 150a | Royal Tank Corps Officer | Khaki, Black beret | (H)30 | 1937 | 1941 | | |
| 150b | Royal Tank Corps Private | Black | 22 | 1937 | R/54 | Seated, folded arms. Also available in boxes of 12. Export renumbered 604 from 1954. | |
| 150c | Royal Tank Corp Private | | 30 | 1937 | 1941 | Standing. Also available in boxes of 12. | |
| 150d | Royal Tank Corps Driver | Black | 25 | 1937 | 1941 | Also available in boxes of 12. | |
| 150e | Royal Tank Corps N.C.O. | Black | 30 | 1937 | 1941 | Arms akimbo. Also available in boxes of 12. | |
| 150 | Rolls Royce Silver Wraith | 2-tone Grey | 117 | 1959 | 1964 | | |
| 151 | Royal Tank Corps Medium Tank Set | | | 1937 | 1941 | Contains 151a, b, c and d, 150d. | 78 |
| 151a | Medium Tank | Gloss Green pre-war; Matt Green post-war | 92 | 1937 | 1953/4 | Post-war for U.S. export only. Pre-war has baseplate in body colour; post-war Black. White markings pre-war only. | 78 |
| 151b | 6-Wheeled Covered Transport Wagon | Gloss Green pre-war; Matt Green or Green-Brown post-war (several shades) | 99 | 1937 | R/54 | Export only from ca. 1950. Export No. 620 in 1954. Tinplate canopy and insert for seats in rear (along sides). Hole in truck bed, under seat insert, from 1939; raised ring under rear post-war. See 25s and 161s. | 78 |

| No. | Description | Colours | Length | Introduced | Deleted | Comment/Variations | Page |
|-----|-------------|---------|--------|------------|---------|--------------------|------|
| 151c | Cooker Trailer | Gloss Green | 60 | 1937 | 1941 | Wire stand. | 78 |
| 151d | Water Tank Trailer | Gloss Green | 52 | 1937 | 1941 | | 78 |
| 151 | Triumph 1800 Saloon | Tan or Light Blue | 91 | R/54 | 1959 | Renumbering of 40b. | 133 |
| 151 | Vauxhall Victor 101 | Yellow or Metallic Red | 105 | 1965 | 1969 | | 142 |
| 152 | Royal Tank Corps Light Tank Set | | | 1937 | 1941 | Contains 152a, b, c, and 150d. | 79 |
| 152a | Light Tank | See 151b | 68 | 1937 | R/54 | Export only from ca. 1950. Export No. 650 from 1954. Other comments as 151a. | 79 |
| 152b | Reconnaissance Car | See 151b | 89 | 1937 | R/54 | Export only from ca. 1950. Export number 671 from 1954. Other comments as 151a. | 79 |
| 152c | Austin 7 Car | Gloss Green | 50 | 1937 | 1941 | Casting as 35d; wire screen and hole for driver. | 79 |
| 152 | Austin Devon Saloon | Maroon, Medium Blue, Grey-Green (2 shades); Green and Pink or Blue and Yellow. | 86 | R/54 | 1959 | Renumbering of 40d. 2-colour finish from 1956. | 133 |
| 152 | Rolls-Royce Phantom V Limousine | Dark Blue | 141 | 1965 | 1977 | Wing mirrors, driver and 2 passengers till 1967, thereafter driver only. Replaced by 124. See 1001. | 144, 287 |
| 153a | Jeep | Matt Green or Green-Brown | 69 | 1946 | R/54 | Export only from ca. 1950. ★ 1st casting has flat bonnet and may have smooth hubs and solid steering-wheel. Domed bonnet from 1947. See 25j. ★ Export No. 672 from 1954. | 81 |
| 153 | Standard Vanguard Saloon | Blue, Tan or Cream | 91 | R/54 | 1959 | Renumbering of 40e. Last issue has enlarged number-plate light on boot. | 133 |
| 153 | Aston Martin DB 6 | Metallic Blue or Metallic Green | 111 | 1967 | 1971 | | 139 |
| 154 | Hillman Minx | Tan, Pale or Dark Green; Green and Cream or Pink-Cream, Pale Blue and Pink | 87 | R/54 | 1959 | Renumbering of 40f. 2-colour finish from 1956. | 133 |
| 154 | Ford Taunus 17M | Yellow with White roof | 110 | 1966 | 1969 | See 261. | 152 |
| 155 | Ford Anglia | Pale Green | 81 | 1961 | 1966 | White issue assembled in South Africa. | 143, 224 |
| 156 | Mechanised Army Set | | | 1939 | 1941 | Contains sets 151, 152, 161, 162. | 78 |
| 156 | Rover 75 | Cream, Red or Maroon; 2-tone Green; Blue or Dark Blue and Cream | 101 | R/54 | 1959 | Renumbering of 140b. 2-colour finish from 1956. | 140 |
| 156 | Saab 96 | Metallic Red | 98 | 1966 | 1971 | | 152 |
| 157 | Jaguar XK 120 | Cream, Red, Yellow or Grey-Green; Turquoise and Pink or Yellow and Grey; White, Red, Yellow or Grey-Green | 97 | 1954 | 1962 | 2-colour finishes 1956–1959. Shiny hubs from 1959. | 136 |

| No. | Description | Colours | Length | Introduced | Deleted | Comment/Variations | Page |
|-----|-------------|---------|--------|------------|---------|--------------------|------|
| 157 | BMW 2000 Tilux | Blue and White | 121 | 1968 | 1973 | | 147 |
| 158 | Riley | Cream or Pale Green | 93 | R/54 | 1960 | Re-issue of 40a. | 133 |
| 158 | Rolls-Royce Silver Shadow | Metallic Red, later Metallic Blue | 125 | 1967 | 1973 | | 144 |
| 159 | Morris Oxford Saloon | Fawn or Green; Green and Cream or Maroon and Cream | 93 | R/54 | 1959 | Renumbering of 40g. 2-colour finish from 1956. | 133 |
| 159 | Ford Cortina Mk. II | White | 105 | 1967 | 1970 | See 205. | |
| 160 | Royal Artillery Personnel | | | 1939 | R/54 | Contains 160a, 2 × 160b, 160c and 2 × 160d. Export only post-war. Export No. 606 from 1954. | 79 |
| 160a | Royal Artillery N.C.O. | Khaki | (H)28 | 1939 | 1941 | | 79 |
| 160b | Royal Artillery Gunner | Khaki | 28 | 1939 | R/54 | Seated. Hands on knees. Export No. 608 from 1954. | 79 |
| 160c | Royal Artillery Gunlayer | Khaki | 24 | 1939 | 1941 | Seated. Hands held out. | 79 |
| 160d | Royal Artillery Gunner | Khaki | 28 | 1939 | 1941 | Standing. | 79 |
| 160 | Austin A30 | Turquoise or Tan | 77 | 1958 | 1962 | Smooth or ribbed plastic wheels. | 141 |
| 160 | Mercedes-Benz 250SE | Metallic Blue | 117 | 1967 | 1974 | | 147 |
| 161 | Mobile Anti-Aircraft Unit | | | 1939 | 1941 | Contains 161a and 161b. | 79 |
| 161a | Lorry with Searchlight | Gloss Green | 99 | 1939 | 1941 | Lorry casting as 151b. Tin insert in rear has a single bench seat behind cab. Searchlight sometimes in lead. See 22s. | 79 |
| 161b | A.A. Gun on Trailer | See 151b | 115 | 1939 | R/54 | Export only after ca. 1950. Export No. 690 from 1954. | 79 |
| 161 | Austin Somerset Saloon | Red or Pale Blue; Black and Cream or Red and Yellow | 89 | R/54 | 1959 | Renumbering of 40j. 2-colour finish from 1956. | 133 |
| 161 | Ford Mustang Fastback 2+2 | White, later Yellow | 111 | 1965 | 1973 | | 151 |
| 162 | 18-Pounder Quick-Firing Field Gun Unit | | | 1939 | R/54 | Contains 162a, b and c. Export only from ca. 1950. Export No. 691 from 1954. Box pre-war only. | 78 |
| 162a | Light Dragon Motor Tractor | See 151b | 65 | 1939 | 1955 | Some issued with 35-series Black rubber wheels. Late post-war issue has no holes in seats. | 78 |
| 162b | Trailer | See 151b | 54 | 1939 | 1955 | Pre-war baseplate in body colour; post-war Black. | 78 |
| 162c | 18-Pounder Gun | See 151b | 78 | 1939 | 1955 | Tin-plate shield. | 78 |
| 162 | Ford Zephyr Saloon | Cream and Green (2 shades) or 2-tone Blue | 96 | 1956 | 1960 | | 141 |
| 162 | Triumph 1300 | Pale Blue | 93 | 1966 | 1970 | | 144 |
| 163 | Bristol 450 Coupe | Green | 98 | 1956 | 1960 | | 141 |
| 163 | Volkswagen 1600 TL Fastback | Red or Dark Metallic Red | 102 | 1966 | 1971 | | 152 |
| 164 | Vauxhall Cresta | Grey and Green or Red and Cream | 96 | 1957 | 1960 | | 141 |
| 164 | Ford Zodiac Mk. IV | Silver, Pale Metallic Blue or Bronze | 114 | 1966 | 1971 | See 255. | 144 |

| No. | Description | Colours | Length | Introduced | Deleted | Comment/Variations | Page |
|-----|-------------|---------|--------|------------|---------|--------------------|------|
| 165 | Humber Hawk | Green with Black sides and roof *or* sides only; Maroon and Cream | 102 | 1959 | 1963 | Front number plate added to casting in 1960. See 256. | 141 |
| 165 | Ford Capri | Metallic Green or Metallic Purple | 102 | 1969 | 1976 | See 213. | 144 |
| 166 | Sunbeam Rapier | Cream and Orange or 2-tone Blue | 89 | 1958 | 1963 | | 141 |
| 166 | Renault R16 | Blue | 99 | 1967 | 1970 | French body casting (No. 537) with English baseplate and wheels. | 153 |
| 167 | A.C. Aceca | Cream, Cream with Brown roof, Cream with Maroon roof, Grey with Red roof. | 89 | 1958 | 1963 | | 137 |
| 168 | Singer Gazelle | Cream and Brown or Grey and Green | 92 | 1959 | 1963 | | 141 |
| 168 | Ford Escort | Light Blue, later Metallic Red or Metallic Blue | 97 | 1968 | 1977 | Plastic Speedwheels from 1972. See 270, 1004 and 1006. | 144 |
| 169 | Studebaker Golden Hawk | Green and Cream or Tan and Red | 106 | 1958 | 1963 | | 151 |
| 169 | Ford Corsair 2000E | Silver with Black roof | 108 | 1967 | 1969 | 130 with textured roof. | 144 |
| 170 | Ford Fordor | Yellow, Red, Green or Tan; Cream and Red or Pink and Blue. | 102 | R/54 | 1959 | Renumbering of 139, 2-colour finish from 1956: 1st scheme has entire wings and most of doors in 2nd colour; 2nd scheme has lower part of body sides only. (From 1958). | 150 |
| 170m | Ford Fordor U.S. Army Staff Car | Military Green | 102 | R/54 | R/54 | Renumbering of 139am. U.S. market only. Renumbered 675. | 222 |
| 170 | Lincoln Continental | Metallic Orange with White roof; Light Blue with White | 127 | 1964 | 1970 | | 149 |
| 171 | Hudson Commodore | Cream with Maroon roof; Dark Blue with Fawn or Grey roof. Red or Maroon with Light Blue sides; Blue with Grey sides. Red with Light Blue lower body sides; Blue with Grey | 111 | R/54 | 1959 | Renumbering of 139b. 2nd colour schemes from 1956; 3rd from 1958. | 151 |
| 171 | Austin 1800 | Metallic Blue or Pale Blue | 101 | 1965 | 1968 | See 282. | 142 |
| 172 | Studebaker Land Cruiser | Light Green or Blue; Maroon and Cream or Tan and Cream | 107 | 1954 | 1959 | 2-colour finish from 1956. | 151 |
| 172 | Fiat 2300 Station Wagon | 2-tone Blue | 108 | 1965 | 1969 | See 281. | 152 |
| 173 | Nash Rambler | Green with Red flash, Pink with Blue flash | 101 | 1958 | 1962 | Number removed from base in 1960. See 257. | 151 |
| 173 | Pontiac Parisienne | Metallic Maroon | 132 | 1969 | 1973 | See 251 and 252. | 149 |
| 174 | Hudson Hornet | Red and Cream or Yellow and Grey | 111 | 1958 | 1963 | | 151 |
| 174 | Mercury Cougar | Metallic Blue | 122 | 1969 | 1973 | | 149 |
| 175 | Hillman Minx | Blue and Grey or Green and Tan | 88 | 1958 | 1961 | | 141 |
| 175 | Cadillac Eldorado | Metallic Blue or Metallic Purple with Black roof | 133 | 1969 | 1973 | | 149 |

| No. | Description | Colours | Length | Introduced | Deleted | Comment/Variations | Page |
|-----|-------------|---------|--------|------------|---------|--------------------|------|
| 176 | Austin A105 | Cream with Blue or Grey with Red | 102 | 1958 | 1963 | 2nd colour for flash only till 1959, thereafter for roof also. | 141 |
| 176 | NSU Ro80 | Metallic Red or Metallic Blue | 114 | 1969 | 1974 | | 147 |
| 177 | Opel Kapitan | Pale Blue | 100 | 1961 | 1966 | Dark Blue issue assembled in South Africa. | 147, 224 |
| 178 | Plymouth Plaza | Pink and Green or 2-tone Blue | 108 | 1959 | 1963 | See 265 and 266. | 151 |
| 178 | Mini Clubman | Bronze or Red | 82 | 1975 | 1979 | See 255. Early issue has jewelled lights. | 144, 286 |
| 179 | Studebaker President | Yellow or light Blue with Blue flash | 108 | 1958 | 1963 | | 151 |
| 179 | Opel Commodore | Metallic Blue with Black roof | 107 | 1971 | 1975 | French body casting (No. 1420) with English baseplate and wheels. | 152 |
| 180 | Packard Clipper | Fawn and Red or Orange and Grey | 108 | 1958 | 1963 | | 151 |
| 181 | Volkswagen | Grey, Green, Dark Blue, Blue-Grey, Light Blue | 90 | 1956 | 1970 | See 262. Off-White issue assembled in South Africa. | 147, 224 |
| 182 | Porsche 356A Coupe | Cream, Red, Light Blue or Pink-Maroon | 87 | 1958 | 1966 | | 137 |
| 183 | Fiat 600 | Light Green or Red | 71 | 1958 | 1960 | Smooth or ribbed plastic wheels. | 141 |
| 183 | Morris Mini Minor (Automatic) | Red with Black roof, Metallic Blue, Metallic Red with Black roof | 75 | 1966 | 1975 | See 107, 250. Plastic Speedwheels from 1972. Cast boot detail. Some late issue uses 250 Austin casting (version with cast boot detail). | 145 |
| 184 | Volvo 122S | Red or White | 98 | 1961 | 1965 | | 152 |
| 185 | Alfa Romeo 1900 Super Sprint | Yellow or Red | 102 | 1961 | 1963 | French body casting (No. 24j) with English baseplate, seats and wheels. | 136 |
| 186 | Mercedes-Benz 220 SE | Light Blue or Grey-Blue | 102 | 1961 | 1967 | Chromed parts in plastic on later examples. | 147 |
| 187 | Volkswagen Karmann-Ghia Coupe | Red with Black roof or Green with Cream roof | 96 | 1959 | 1964 | French body casting (No. 530) with English base and wheels. | 147 |
| 187 | De Tomaso Mangusta 5000 | Red and White | 102 | 1968 | 1977 | | 138 |
| 188 | 4-Berth Caravan | Green and Cream or Blue and Cream | 132 | 1961 | 1963 | Windows enlarged in 1963, then replaced by 117. | 239 |
| 188 | Jensen FF | Yellow | 121 | 1968 | 1975 | See 1007. | 144 |
| 189 | Triumph Herald | Green and White or Blue and White | 86 | 1959 | 1964 | Some special finishes (prepared for Triumph?) including: Red; Dark Blue; Lilac; Grey-Green; Rose Taupe or Dark Blue with White roof. | 141 |
| 189 | Lambourghini Maezal | Green and White or Yellow and White; Blue and White with plastic Speedwheels (1976) | 137 | 1969 | 1978 | | 138 |
| 190 | Caravan | Orange and Cream or Blue and Cream | 118 | 1956 | 1964 | Metal, later plastic front wheel. | 239 |

| No. | Description | Colours | Length | Introduced | Deleted | Comment/Variations | Page |
|---|---|---|---|---|---|---|---|
| 190 | Monteverdi 375L | Metallic Red | 116 | 1970 | 1974 | | 138 |
| 191 | Dodge Royal Sedan | Cream with Brown flash, Green with Black flash, Cream with Blue flash | 111 | 1959 | 1964 | See 258. | 151 |
| 192 | De Soto Fireflite | Grey with Red flash and roof; Green with Fawn | 114 | 1959 | 1964 | See 258. | 151 |
| 192 | Range Rover | Bronze, later Yellow | 109 | 1970 | 1980 | See 195, 203, 254, 268. | 145 |
| 193 | Rambler Cross-Country Station Wagon | Yellow with White roof | 102 | 1961 | 1969 | Lime Green, Lavender, Cream and Lavender: assembled in South Africa. | 151, 224 |
| 194 | Bentley S Series Coupe | Grey with Red seats; Bronze with Cream seats. Grey driver | 113 | 1961 | 1967 | Plastic plated parts on late issue. Lime Green or Cream: assembled in South Africa. | 143, 244 |
| 195 | Jaguar 3.4 Litre Mark II | Maroon, Grey or Cream | 95 | 1960 | 1966 | See 269. | 141 |
| 195 | Range Rover Fire Chief | Red or Metallic Red | 109 | 1971 | 1978 | See 192. | 202 |
| 196 | Holden Special Sedan | Bronze with White roof; Turquoise with White | 106 | 1963 | 1970 | | 152 |
| 197 | Morris Mini-Traveller | White, later Green, with Brown woodwork. All-over Lime Green from ca. 1970. | 72 | 1961 | 1971 | | 145 |
| 198 | Rolls Royce Phantom V | Metallic Green and Cream; 2-tone Grey. | 125 | 1962 | 1969 | | 143 |
| 199 | Austin 7 Countryman | Blue with Brown woodwork. All-over Orange from ca. 1970. | 72 | 1961 | 1971 | | 145 |
| 200 | Midget Racer | Silver | 57 | R/54 | 1957 | Renumbering of 35b. | 58 |
| 200 | Matra 630 | Blue | 105 | 1971 | 1978 | French body casting (No. 1425) with English base and wheels. | 138 |
| 201 | Racing Car Set | | | 1965 | 1969 | Contains 240, 241, 242, 243. | 130 |
| 201 | Plymouth Stock Car | Dark Blue | 135 | 1979 | 1980 | Casting of 278 with wide wheels and stickers. | 149 |
| 202 | Fiat Abarth 2000 | Orange and White | 91 | 1971 | 1975 | French body casting (No. 1430) with English base and wheels. | 138 |
| 202 | Customised Land Rover | Yellow | 114 | 1979 | 1980 | Casting of 344 with wide wheels, plastic roll-over cage, heavy bumpers and stripes. | 145 |
| 203 | Customised Range Rover | Black | 115 | 1979 | 1980 | Casting of 192 with wide wheels, bumpers as 202 and stripes. | 145 |
| 204 | Ferrari 312P | Metallic Red, White doors | 99 | 1971 | 1975 | French body casting (No. 1432) with English base and wheels. | 138 |
| 205 | Talbot Lago (Bubble Pack) | Blue | 103 | 1962 | 1964 | 230 with plastic wheels. | 127 |
| 205 | Lotus Cortina Rally | White with Red panels | 105 | 1968 | 1973 | 159 with Rally features. Speedwheels from 1970. | 137 |

| No. | Description | Colours | Length | Introduced | Deleted | Comment/Variations | Page |
|---|---|---|---|---|---|---|---|
| 206 | Maserati (Bubble Pack) | Red with White stripe | 94 | 1962 | 1964 | 231 with plastic wheels. | 127 |
| 206 | Customised Corvette Stingray | Red | 113 | 1978 | 1980 | 221 with wide wheels and stickers. | 149, 286 |
| 207 | Alfa-Romeo (Bubble Pack) | Red | 100 | 1962 | 1964 | 232 with plastic wheels. | 127 |
| 207 | Triumph TR7 Rally Car | White with Blue and Red markings | 98 | 1977 | 1980 | 211 with rally stripes. 'Leyland' on boot. | 137 |
| 208 | Cooper-Bristol (Bubble Pack) | Green | 89 | 1962 | 1964 | 233 with plastic wheels. | 128 |
| 208 | VW Porsche 914 | Yellow. Metallic Blue with Black bonnet from 1976 | 89 | 1971 and 1976 | 1975 1980 | Plastic Speedwheels from 1976. | 138 |
| 209 | Ferrari (Bubble Pack) | Blue with Yellow triangle on nose | 101 | 1962 | 1964 | 234 with plastic wheels. | 127 |
| 210 | Vanwall (Bubble Pack) | Green | 95 | 1962 | 1964 | 239 with plastic wheels | 129 |
| 211 | Triumph TR7 Sports Car | Metallic Blue-Green, White or Red | 98 | 1976 | 1980 | Metallic Blue-Green in 1976 only. White issue was British Leyland promotional. Red issue has Pale Grey bumpers and interior till 1978, thereafter Black. | 137 |
| 212 | Ford Cortina Rally | White with Black bonnet | 102 | 1965 | 1970 | Casting as 133 with spotlights. | 137 |
| 213 | Ford Capri Rally | Metallic Red or Bronze with Black bonnet | 102 | 1970 | 1975 | Casting as 165 with spotlights and wing mirrors. Plastic Speedwheels from 1973. | 137 |
| 214 | Hillman Imp Rally | Blue | 86 | 1966 | 1969 | Casting as 138 with spotlights. | 137 |
| 215 | Ford GT Racing Car | White, Green from 1970 | 96 | 1965 | 1974 | Spoked wheels from 1966. | 139 |
| 216 | Dino Ferrari | Red, Blue with Black engine cover from 1969 | 98 | 1967 | 1975 | | 138 |
| 217 | Alfa Romeo Scarabeo OSI | Orange | 132 | 1969 | 1974 | | 138 |
| 218 | Lotus Europa | Yellow and Blue, Yellow and Black from 1973 | 96 | 1969 | 1975 | Plastic Speedwheels from 1973. | 139 |
| 220 | Small Open Racing Car | Silver with Red trim | 94 | R/54 | 1956 | Renumbering of 23a. | 126 |
| 220 | Ferrari P5 | Red | 96 | 1970 | 1975 | Plastic Speedwheels from 1973. | 139 |
| 221 | "Speed of the Wind" Racing Car | Silver with Red trim | 104 | R/54 | 1956 | Renumbering of 23e. | 129 |
| 221 | Corvette Stingray | Gold, White with Black bonnet from 1976 | 113 | 1969 and 1976 | 1975 See 206. 1978 | Plastic Speedwheels from 1976. | 149 |
| 222 | Streamlined Racing Car | Silver with Green, Red or Blue trim | 126 | R/54 | 1956 | Renumbering of 23s. | 126 |
| 222 | Hesketh Racing Car 308E | Dark Blue. | 132 | 1978 | 1980 | | 130, 286 |
| 223 | McLaren M8A Can Am | White with Metallic Blue engine cover. Metallic Green from 1976 | 94 | 1970 & 1976 | 1975 1978 | Plastic Speedwheels from 1976. | 139 |
| 224 | Mercedes Benz C111 | Metallic Red | 102 | 1970 | 1974 | | 139 |
| 225 | Lotus F.1 Racing Car | Metallic Red. Metallic Blue from 1976 | 127 | 1970 & 1976 | 1975 1978 | See 1009 | 130 |

| No. | Description | Colours | Length | Introduced | Deleted | Comment/Variations | Page |
|---|---|---|---|---|---|---|---|
| 226 | Ferrari 312/B2 | Red. Bronze from 1976, with White or Black rear wing | 121 | 1972 and 1976 | 1975 1980 | See 1012. | 130 |
| 227 | Beach Buggy | Yellow with White plastic hood. | 105 | 1975 | 1977 | See 1014. | 241 |
| 228 | Super Sprinter | Blue and Orange | 113 | 1970 | 1972 | | 130 |
| 230 | Talbot-Lago Racing Car | Blue | 103 | R/54 | 1964 | Renumbering of 23k. See 205. | 127 |
| 231 | Maserati Racing Car | Red with White stripe | 94 | R/54 | 1964 | Renumbering of 23n. See 206. | 127 |
| 232 | Alfa-Romeo Racing Car | Red | 100 | R/54 | 1964 | Renumbering of 23f. See 207. | 127 |
| 233 | Cooper-Bristol Racing Car | Green | 89 | R/54 | 1964 | Renumbering of 23g. See 208. | 127 |
| 234 | Ferrari Racing Car | Blue with Yellow nose: Triangle from 1962 | 101 | R/54 | 1964 | Renumbering of 23h. See 209. General note 230–234: Cast wheels to 1960, spun aluminium to 1962, plastic to 1964. | 127 |
| 235 | H.W.M. Racing Car | Pale Green | 99 | R/54 | 1960 | Renumbering of 23j. | 127 |
| 236 | Connaught Racing Car | Pale Green with White driver | 96 | 1956 | 1959 | | 129 |
| 237 | Mercedes-Benz Racing Car | White. Cream ca. 1960–1962. Blue driver, Yellow from 1964. | 98 | 1957 | 1969 | Spun aluminium wheels from 1960, plastic from 1962. | 129 |
| 238 | Jaguar Type D Racing Car | Turquoise. White driver, Yellow from 1964 | 86 | 1957 | 1965 | Comment as 237. | 129 |
| 239 | Vanwall Racing Car | Green. White driver, Yellow from 1962 | 95 | 1958 | 1965 | Comment as 237. See 210. | 129 |
| 240 | Cooper Racing Car | Blue with White stripes | 80 | 1963 | 1970 | Plastic engine cover. Windscreen held in by driver or tabbed into slots in body. | 130 |
| 240 | Dinky Way Gift Set | | | 1978 | | Contains 211, 255, 382, 412 + roadways and road signs. | 243 |
| 241 | Lotus Racing Car | Green | 80 | 1963 | 1970 | Plastic engine cover. See 240 Cooper. | 130 |
| 241 | Silver Jubilee Taxi | Silver. Union Jack on boot | 112 | 1977 | 1977 | Casting as 284 (no boot detail). | 209 |
| 242 | Ferrari Racing Car | Red | 89 | 1963 | 1971 | Plastic engine cover. See 240 Cooper. | 130 |
| 243 | B.R.M. Racing Car | Green or Metallic Green, Yellow engine cover | 82 | 1963 | 1971 | Plastic engine cover. See 240 Cooper. | 130 |
| 243 | Volvo Police Car | White | 141 | 1979 | 1980 | Casting as 122. | 205, 288 |
| 244 | Plymouth Police Car | Blue and White | 135 | 1977 | 1980 | Casting as 201 and 278. | 205, 288 |
| 245 | Superfast Gift Set | | | 1969 | 1973 | Contains 131, 153 and 188. | |
| 246 | International GT Gift Set | | | 1969 | 1973 | Contains 187, 215 and 216. | |
| 249 | Racing Cars Gift Set | | | R/54 | 1959 | Renumbering of Gift Set No. 4 Contains 231–235. | 128 |
| 249 | World Famous Racing Cars | | | 1962 | 1963 | Contains 230, 231, 232, 233, 234, 239. Bubble Pack. | 128 |
| 250 | Fire Engine | Red | 99 | R/54 | 1962 | Renumbering of 25h. | 200 |

| No. | Description | Colours | Length | Introduced | Deleted | Comment/Variations | Page |
|-----|-------------|---------|--------|-----------|---------|--------------------|------|
| 250 | Mini-Cooper 'S' Police Car | Off-White, later White | 75 | 1967 | 1976 | Pre-1971: Boot detail on transfer (Austin Cooper 'S') Roof sign and aerial. From 1971: Boot detail cast in (Austin Cooper 'S'). No aerial. Plastic Speedwheels from 1973. Some late issue use 183 Morris casting. | 205 |
| 251 | Aveling-Barford Diesel Roller | Green with Red rollers | 110 | R/54 | 1963 | Renumbering of 25p. | 173 |
| 251 | U.S.A. Police Car | White with Black roof | 132 | 1970 | 1973 | Casting of 173 Pontiac Parisienne with roof lights, wing mirrors and driver. | 205 |
| 252 | Bedford Refuse Wagon | Fawn with Green shutters; Green with Black shutters; Orange cab, pale Grey rear, Green shutters | 107 | R/54 | 1965 | Renumbering of 25v. Windows from 1960: 1st colour scheme with or without; 2nd and 3rd always with windows. 3rd scheme has plastic wheels and silver grille from ca 1963. Plastic side shutters on 3rd scheme. | 173 |
| 252 | RCMP Car | Blue with White front doors | 132 | 1969 | 1975 | Casting of 173 Pontiac Parisienne with roof light and driver. | 205 |
| 253 | Daimler Ambulance | Cream, later White (ca. 1958) | 96 | R/54 | 1964 | Renumbering of 30h. Windows from 1960. Plastic wheels from ca. 1962. | 206 |
| 254 | Austin Taxi | Blue or Yellow; Green and Yellow; Black | 94 | R-54 | 1962 | Renumbering of 40h. Black chassis on Yellow taxi; 2-colour scheme 1956–1959; Black from 1959. (With aluminium wheels). | 133 |
| 254 | Police Range Rover | White with Red stripes | 109 | 1971 | 1980 | Casting of 192 with roof sign. | 205, 288 |
| 255 | Mersey Tunnel Police Van | Red | 77 | 1955 | 1961 | | 205 |
| 255 | Ford Zodiac Police Car | White | 114 | 1967 | 1972 | Casting of 164 with roof sign and driver. | 205 |
| 255 | Police Mini Clubman | Blue with White doors | 82 | 1977 | 1980 | Casting of 178 with roof sign. | 205, 288 |
| 256 | Police Car | Black | 102 | 1960 | 1964 | Casting of 165 Humber Hawk with roof sign, aerial, interior and 2 figures. | 204 |
| 257 | Canadian Fire Chief's Car | Red | 102 | 1960 | 1969 | Casting of 173 Nash Rambler with light. | 201 |
| 258 | U.S.A. Police Car | Black with White front doors | see basic castings | 1960 1961 1962 1966 | 1961 1962 1966 1969 | Casting of 192 De Soto (+ interior). Casting of 191 Dodge (+ interior). Casting of 149 Ford Fairlane. Casting of 147 Cadillac 62. | 204 |
| 259 | Fire Engine | Red with Silver ladder | 115 | 1961 | 1970 | "Fire Brigade" and crest: some have transfer of 276 Airport fire tender. Ladder as 25h/250. | 201 |
| 260 | Royal Mail Van | Red with Black roof | 78 | 1955 | 1961 | | 210 |

| No. | Description | Colours | Length | Introduced | Deleted | Comment/Variations | Page |
|---|---|---|---|---|---|---|---|
| 260 | Volkswagen "Deutsche Bundespost" | Yellow | 100 | 1971 | 1972 | Casting of 129. Export issue for German market only. | 225 |
| 261 | Telephone Service Van | Green with Black roof, Silver ladder | 73 | 1956 | 1961 | Tinplate ladder. | 210 |
| 261 | Ford Taunus 17M "Polizei" | White with Dark Green panels | 110 | 1967 | ? | Casting of 154. Export issue for German market only. | 225 |
| 262 | Volkswagen Swiss PTT Car | Yellow with Black wings | 90 | 1959 | 1966 | Casting of 181. Aluminium wheels from 1960, plastic from 1962. | 225 |
| | | | 100 | 1966 | 1976 | Casting of 129. Plastic Speedwheels from 1972. Export issues for Swiss market only. | |
| 263 | Superior Criterion Ambulance | White/Cream | 127 | 1962 | 1969 | See 277. Stretcher. | 207 |
| 263 | Airport Fire Rescue Tender | Yellow | 177 | 1978 | 1980 | Casting as 266 ERF, with simple White plastic ladder. | 203, 287 |
| 264 | R.C.M.P. Patrol Car | Dark Blue with White front doors | 111 | 1962 | 1966 | Casting of 149 Ford Fairlane with roof light, aerial and 2 figures. | 205 |
| | | | 113 | 1966 | 1968 | Casting of 147 Cadillac with details as above. | |
| 265 | Plymouth Taxi | Yellow with Red roof | 108 | 1960 | 1964 | Casting for 178 Plymouth Plaza, + interior. Fare information on doors. | 208 |
| 266 | Plymouth Taxi | Yellow with Red roof | 108 | 1960 | 1966 | As 265 but 450 Metro Cab on doors: Canadian market only till 1964. | 208 |
| 266 | ERF Fire Tender | Red, White escape | 223 | 1976 | 1980 | See 263. Wheeled escape. | 203, 287 |
| 266 | ERF Fire Tender "Falck" | Red, White escape | 223 | 1976 | ? | As above. For Danish market only. | 225 |
| 267 | Superior Cadillac Ambulance | Cream and Red | 152 | 1967 | 1971 | Flashing Light. Replaced by 288. | 207 |
| 267 | Paramedic Truck | Red | 119 | 1979 | 1980 | From TV series "Emergency". 2 plastic figures and badge. | 237, 288 |
| 268 | Renault Dauphine Mini-Cab | Red | 92 | 1962 | 1967 | Advertisements. Body is French casting (24d/524) with English baseplate and wheels. | 208 |
| 268 | Range Rover Ambulance | White | 109 | 1973 | 1977 | Casting as 192 with roof sign, and interior altered to take stretcher. | 207 |
| 269 | Jaguar Motorway Police Car | White | 95 | 1962 | 1966 | Casting as 195 with roof light, aerial and 2 figures. | 205 |
| 269 | Police Accident Unit | White with Blue 'Police' sticker and Red stripe | 129 | 1978 | 1980 | Replaces 272. 3rd Transit casting: protruding grille, lights in line with grille. Roof sign only (see 272). Road signs. | 205, 288 |
| 270 | A.A. Motor Cycle Patrol | Black bike, Yellow sidecar, Tan rider | 46 | 1959 | 1962 | Re-issue of 44b. Black rubber wheels, later Grey plastic (smooth, then ribbed). | 70 |
| 270 | Ford Panda Police Car | Blue with White doors | 97 | 1969 | 1977 | Casting as 168 with roof sign. Plastic Speedwheels from 1972. See 1004. | 204 |

| No. | Description | Colours | Length | Introduced | Deleted | Comment/Variations | Page |
|-----|-------------|---------|--------|------------|---------|--------------------|------|
| 271 | T.S. Motor Cycle Patrol | See 270 | 46 | 1959 | 1962 | Casting as 270 but T.S. transfer. Belgian market only. | 70 |
| 271 | Ford Transit Fire Appliance | Red | 129 | 1975 | 1977 | Replaces 286. 2nd Transit casting: Lift-up rear door, rectangular grille, passenger's door does not open. | 202 |
| 271 | Ford Transit Fire Appliance "Falck" | Red | 129 | 1975 | 1977 | As above, Danish market only. | 225 |
| 272 | A.N.W.B. Motor Cycle Patrol | See 270 | 46 | 1959 | 1962 | Casting as 270 but A.N.W.B. transfer. Dutch market only. | 70 |
| 272 | Police Accident Unit | White. 'Police' in black on Red panel. | 129 | 1975 | 1978 | Replaces 287. 2nd Transit casting (see 271). Roof rack and radar gun. Replaced by 269. | 205 |
| 273 | R.A.C. Patrol Mini Van | Blue with White roof | 78 | 1965 | 1970 | Black, later silver baseplate. Rear doors redesigned at same time. | 211 |
| 274 | A.A. Patrol Mini Van | Yellow. White roof from 1971 | 78 | 1964 | 1973 | Comment as 273. Version with white roof has later AA logo on sticker, not transfer; oblong roof sign. | 211 |
| 274 | Mini Van 'Joseph Mason Paints' | Maroon | 78 | 1970 | 1970 | Casting as 273 and 274. Promotional | 190 |
| 274 | Ford Transit Ambulance | (Copy 276) | 129 | 1978 | 1980 | 3rd Transit casting (See 269). Replaces 276. | 280 |
| 275 | Brinks Armoured Car | Pale Grey, Dark Blue base and Blue interior. Later clear interior | 120 | 1964 | 1970 | 2 drivers to 1966, thereafter no figures. 2 plastic crates with gold bars. Brinks transfer. | 183 |
| 275 | Armoured Car "Luis R. Picaso Manriquez" | Grey with Black base | 120 | 1976 | 1976 | Promotional (Mexico). As above (no drivers) without crates. Gryphon on Red, White and Blue shield. | 183 |
| 275 | Brink's Armoured Car | Grey with White roof, Blue base, clear interior | 120 | 1979 | 1980 | Assembled in U.S.A. Metal wheels (all versions above have plastic). No driver or crates. Brink's *stickers*. | 183 |
| 276 | Airport Fire Tender | Red | 115 | 1962 | 1970 | Casting as 259 but plastic foam cannon and flashing light. "Airport Fire Control" transfers, but some have 259 transfers. | 201 |
| 276 | Ford Transit Ambulance | White with Black stick-on windows on rear | 129 | 1976 | 1978 | 2nd Transit casting (See 271). Replaced by 274. | 208 |
| 277 | Superior Criterion Ambulance | Metallic Blue and White | 127 | 1962 | 1969 | Casting as 263 but flashing light, so no stretcher. | 208 |
| 277 | Police Land Rover | Dark Blue and White | 110 | 1978 | 1980 | Casting as 344 with plastic rear. | 205, 208 |
| 278 | Vauxhall Victor Ambulance | White | 91 | 1964 | 1970 | Casting as 141 with roof box and light. Stretcher. | 208 |
| 278 | Plymouth Yellow Cab | Yellow | 135 | 1978 | 1980 | Casting as 244 and 201. | 209, 288 |

| No. | Description | Colours | Length | Introduced | Deleted | Comment/Variations | Page |
|---|---|---|---|---|---|---|---|
| 279 | Aveling Barford Diesel Roller | Orange with Grey engine covers and Green rollers. Yellow cab with Black roof, Silver rollers from 1971 | 116 | 1965 | 1980 | | 175, 289 |
| 280 | Observation Coach | Cream or Grey with Red flashes | 112 | R/54 | 1960 | Renumbering of 29f. | 196 |
| 280 | Midland Mobile Bank | White and Silver with Blue stripe | 124 | 1966 | 1969 | | 183 |
| 281 | Luxury Coach | Maroon or Blue with Cream flashes; Cream or Fawn with Orange flashes | 113 | R/54 | 1959 | Renumbering of 29g. | 196 |
| 281 | Fiat 2300 Pathé News Camera Car | Black, Yellow plastic tripod, Blue and Grey figure | 108 | 1967 | 1970 | Casting as 172 with plate on roof to take man and camera. | 183 |
| 281 | Military Hovercraft | Green | 139 | 1973 | 1976 | Casting as 290 with radar scanner moved rearward, machine gunner and aerial. | 219 |
| 282 | Duple Roadmaster Coach | Blue, Dark Blue or Red with Silver flashes; Yellow with Red flashes; Green and Cream | 119 | R/54 | 1960 | Renumbering of 29h. | 197 |
| 282 | Austin 1800 Taxi | Blue with White bonnet and boot | 101 | 1967 | 1969 | Casting as 171, without chrome window frames, with roof sign. | 209, 288 |
| 282 | Land Rover Fire Appliance | Red | 119 | 1973 | 1980 | Casting as 344 with additional casting on rear. | 202 |
| 282 | Land Rover Fire Appliance "Falck" | Red | 119 | 1974 | 1978 | As above but "Falck" stickers. Danish market only. | 225 |
| 283 | B.O.A.C. Coach | Dark Blue with White roof | 120 | 1956 | 1963 | | 197 |
| 283 | Single Decker Bus | Metallic Red or Red with White doors. | 167 | 1971 | 1977 | See 1023. | 198 |
| 284 | London Austin Taxi | Black or Very Dark Blue | 112 | 1972 | 1980 | Boot detail cast-in to 1977, then sticker. See 241. | 209, 28 |
| 285 | Merryweather Marquis Fire Engine | Metallic Red or Red | 177 | 1969 | 1980 | | 203, 287 |
| 285 | Merryweather Marquis Fire Engine "Falck" | Metallic Red or Red | 177 | 1974 | 1978 | As above but "Falck" stickers. Danish market only. | 225 |
| 286 | Ford Transit Fire Appliance | Metallic Red or Red | 122 | 1968 | 1974 | 1st Transit casting: Opening passenger door, rear doors open outwards. Replaced by 271. | 202 |
| 286 | Ford Transit Fire Appliance "Falck" | Metallic Red or Red | 122 | ? | 1974 | As above but "Falck" stickers. Danish market only. | 225 |
| 287 | Police Accident Unit | Orange and Cream, later White with Red panels | 122 | 1967 | 1975 | 1st Transit casting (See 286). Roof sign with aerial to 1971, then detail as 272, which replaced 287. | 205 |
| 288 | Superior Cadillac Ambulance | White and Red | 152 | 1971 | 1979 | Casting as 267 but stretcher replaces flashing light. See 302. | 207 |

| No. | Description | Colours | Length | Introduced | Deleted | Comment/Variations | Page |
|-----|-------------|---------|--------|------------|---------|-------------------|------|
| 288 | Superior Cadillac Ambulance "Falck" | White and Red or Black with White roof | 152 | 1974 | 1978 | As above but "Falck" stickers. Black and White version is limited issue for 1974 only. | 225 |
| 289 | Routemaster Bus | Red | 121 | 1964<br>1965<br>1969 | 1965<br>1969<br>1980 | "Tern Shirts".<br>"Schweppes". } Regular<br>"Esso Safety Grip Tyres". } issues. | 198 |
| | | Red | | 1968 | 1968 | "Festival of London Stores": Promotional. | |
| | | Gold | | 1974 | 1974 | "Meccano/Dinky Toys": Limited issue. | |
| | | Red | | 1977 | 1980 | "Madame Tussaud's": Promotional. | |
| | | Silver | | 1977 | 1977 | Silver Jubilee: Limited issue. Dividing bar on 2nd-from-rear upper rear window deleted, cast wheels fitted ca. 1973. Plastic Speedwheels fitted, dividing bars on all side windows and conductress deleted in 1977. Esso and Tussaud's available on both castings. See 1017. | |
| | | Gold | | 1979? | 1979? | "Thollenbeek's 1929–1979". Belgian Promotional. | |
| 290 | Double Decker Bus Dunlop | Green, Dark Green or Red, all with Cream upper deck and roof | 103 | R/54 | 1963 | Renumbering of 29c. A.E.C. (to 1959) or Leyland grille. Rear, later front upper deck windows enlarged ca. 1959. Small aluminium wheels from ca. 1961. | 192 |
| 290 | SRN-6 Hovercraft | Red or Metallic Red with White Yellow. Blue, later Black skirt | 139 | 1970 | 1976 | See 281. | 239 |
| 291 | Double Decker Bus Exide | Red | 103 | 1959 | 1963 | Leyland only. Comment re windows and wheels as 290. Plastic wheels from ca. 1962. | 193 |
| 291 | Atlantean City Bus | Orange and White or Pale Blue and White | 123 | 1974 | 1978 | "Kenning". See 295, 297 and 1018. Dual entrance. | 198 |
| 292 | Atlantean Bus | Red and White | 120 | 1962 | 1965 | Briefly 'Ribble' with or without 'Regent' advert., then 'Corporation Transport' with advert. See 293. | 197 |
| 293 | Atlantean Bus | Green and White | 120 | 1963 | 1968 | 'Corporation Transport' and 'BP' advert. Ribbed roof on post-'65 issue. | 197 |
| 293 | Swiss Postal Bus | Yellow with White roof | 119 | 1973 | 1978 | Casting of 296. Swiss market only till 1975. | 199 |
| 294 | Police Vehicles Gift Set | | | 1973 | 1977 | Contains 250, 254 and 287. Replaces 297. | 205 |
| 295 | Atlas Kenebrake Bus | Light Blue and Grey or all-over Light Blue. | 86 | 1963 | 1969 | | 199 |

| No. | Description | Colours | Length | Introduced | Deleted | Comment/Variations | Page |
|-----|-------------|---------|--------|------------|---------|--------------------|------|
| 295 | Atlantean Bus 'Yellow Pages' | Yellow, some with White chassis/engine cover from 291 | 123 | 1973 | 1977 | Casting as 291. Reversed 'Yellow Pages' on front later "corrected". | 198 |
| 296 | Duple Viceroy 37 Luxury Coach | Metallic Blue | 119 | 1972 | 1976 | See 293. | 198 |
| 297 | Police Vehicles Gift Set | | | 1967 | 1973 | Contains 250, 255 and 287. Replaced by 294. | 205 |
| 297 | Silver Jubilee Bus | Silver | 123 | 1977 | 1977 | 'National' stickers. Normal issue. Casting as 291. | 199 |
| 297 | Silver Jubilee Bus "Woolworth's" | Silver | 123 | 1977 | 1977 | "Woolworth's" stickers. Promotional. | 199 |
| 298 | Emergency Services Gift Set | | | 1963 | 1966 | Contains 258 (Ford Fairlane), 263, 276, 277, 007 and 008. | 206 |
| 299 | Post Office Services Gift Set | | | 1957 | 1959 | Contains 011, 012, 260, 261 and 750. | 210 |
| 299 | Motorway Services Gift Set | | | 1963 | 1967 | Contains 257, 263, 269, 276 and 434. | 177 |
| 299 | Gift Set Crash Squad | | | 1979 | 1979 | Contains 244 and 732. Renumbering of 27a. | 205 |
| 300 | Massey-Harris Tractor (Called Massey-Ferguson from 1966) | Red with Yellow wheels; Tan driver to 1964–5, thereafter Blue | 89 | R/54 | 1971 | Rubber tyres from 1962. Plastic driver and exhausts, cast-in seat from 1964–5 'Massey-Ferguson' transfer from 1966. See 310 and 399. | 184 |
| 300 | Gift Set London Scene | | | 1979 | 1980 | Contains 289 (Esso) and 284. | 199 |
| 301 | Field-Marshall Tractor | Orange with Silver, later Green wheels | 76 | R/54 | 1966 | Renumbering of 27n. Rubber tyres from 1962. | 184 |
| 303 | Gift Set Commando Squad | | | 1978 | 1980 | Contains 687, 667 and 732 in military finish. | 220 |
| 304 | Gift Set Fire Rescue | | | 1978 | 1979 | Contains 195, 282 and 384. | 203 |
| 305 | David Brown Tractor | Red cowl, Metallic Grey engine, Yellow cab and wheels | 83 | 1965 | 1967 | 'David Brown 990' stickers. | 186 |
| | | White with Metallic Grey engine. White with Red engine and wheels from 1974. | 83 | 1967 | 1975 | 'David Brown Selectamatic 990' stickers. '995 David Brown Case' stickers on Red-wheeled version. See 325. | |
| 308 | Leyland 384 Tractor | Metallic Red; Blue; Orange. Blue driver | 86 | 1971 | 1979 | | 186 |
| 309 | Gift Set Star Trek | | | 1978 | 1980 | Contains 357 and 358. | 237 |
| 310 | Farm Tractor and Hay Rake | | 157 | R/54 | 1965 | Contains 300 and 324. Renumbering of 27ak. | 184 |
| 319 | Week's Tipping Farm Trailer | Red and Yellow | 105 | 1961 | 1971 | Plastic wheels from mid 1960's | 186 |
| 320 | Halesowen Harvest Trailer | Tan and Red with Red raves, Red with Yellow raves from 1966 | 133 | R/54 | 1971 | Renumbering of 27b. Plastic wheels from 1964. Small front support wheel (plastic from early 60's) deleted in 1969. | 184 |
| 321 | Massey-Harris Manure Spreader | Red | 121 | R/54 | 1973 | Renumbering of 27c. Plastic wheels from 1962. | 184 |

| No. | Description | Colours | Length | Introduced | Deleted | Comment/Variations | Page |
|-----|-------------|---------|--------|------------|---------|--------------------|------|
| 322 | Disc Harrow | Red and Yellow. White and Red from 1967. | 86 or 79 | R/54 | 1973 | Renumbering of 27h. New colours in 1967 to match 305. No hook on this version, hence reduced length, also drawbar loses kink. See 325. | 184 |
| 323 | Triple Gang Mower | Red, Yellow and Green | 114 | R/54 | 1961 | Renumbering of 27j. | 184 |
| 324 | Hay Rake | Red and Yellow | 76 | R/54 | 1971 | Renumbering of 27k. See 310. | 184 |
| 325 | David Brown Tractor and Disc Harrow | White and Red | 152 | 1967 | 1973 | Contains 305 and 324 (See comments). | 186 |
| 340 | Land-Rover | Orange or Green, later Red. Tan driver, Blue from 1966 | 92 | R/54 | 1971 | Renumbering of 27d. Plastic driver and wheels from ca. 1966. The casting is changed at this time: Seats are shallower, spaces between front wings and bumper is filled-in. | 184 |
| 341 | Land Rover Trailer | Orange or Green, later Red. Military Green. | 79 | R/54 | 1973 | Renumbering of 27m. Military version issued in late 1950's/early 1960's – no other details known. | 184, 215 |
| 342 | Moto-Cart | Green and Tan with Tan driver | 110 | R/54 | 1961 | Renumbering of 27g. | 184 |
| 342 | Austin Mini-Moke | Metallic Green, later Metallic Green/Blue. Pale Grey canopy | 73 / 76 with Speedwheels | 1966 | 1975 | Plastic canopy, originally with 2 rear windows, later with 1. Plastic Speedwheels from ca. 1972. See 106, 350 and 601. | 241 |
| 343 | Farm Produce Wagon | Green cab, Yellow rear; Red cab, Blue rear | 107 | R/54 | 1964 | Renumbering of 30n. No bonnet louvres from ca. 1961. Late issue has plastic wheels. | 171 |
| 344 | Estate Car | Tan with Dark Brown panels | 104 | R/54 | 1961 | Renumbering of 27f. | 184 |
| 344 | Land Rover | Metallic Blue or Metallic Red. White rear interior. | 108 | 1970 | 1978 | Plastic Speedwheels ca 1973–1977. See 277, 282, 442, 604 and 1032. | 145 |
| 350 | Tiny's Mini Moke | Red, White canopy with Yellow stripes | 73 | 1970 | 1973 | 342 with giraffe driver and spare wheel cover. From TV series 'The Enchanted House'. | 235 |
| 351 | UFO Interceptor | Metallic Green with Red or Orange legs; Black, later Silver nose; White, later Yellow rocket | 194 | 1971 | 1980 | From Gerry Anderson TV Series "S.H.A.D.O.". | 235 |
| 352 | Ed Straker's Car | Red, Gold (plated) or Yellow. | 124 | 1971 | 1976 | From Gerry Anderson TV Series "S.H.A.D.O.". | 235 |
| 353 | Shado 2 Mobile | Green, late issue in Blue | 145 | 1971 | 1980 | From Gerry Anderson TV Series "S.H.A.D.O.". | 237, 285 |
| 354 | Pink Panther | Pink | 175 | 1972 | 1977 | From TV Series "The Pink Panther". Plastic, Central gyroscopic wheel with pull-through rack. Later without wheel or engine detail: this version *not* marked "DINKY TOYS". | 235 |

| No. | Description | Colours | Length | Introduced | Deleted | Comment/Variations | Page |
|---|---|---|---|---|---|---|---|
| 355 | Lunar Roving Vehicle | Metallic Blue. White plastic astronauts | 114 | 1972 | 1976 | See 1027 | 235 |
| 357 | Klingon Battle Cruiser | Blue and White | 220 | 1977 | 1980 | From TV Series "Star Trek". | 237, 284 |
| 358 | USS Enterprise | White | 234 | 1977 | 1980 | From TV Series "Star Trek". | 237, 284 |
| 359 | Eagle Transporter | White and Metallic Green | 222 | 1975 | 1980 | From TV Series "Space 1999". Life Support Module. | 237, 285 |
| 360 | Eagle Freighter | White and Red, Metallic Green legs | 222 | 1975 | 1980 | From TV Series "Space 1999". Carries 2 radioactive containers. | 237, 285 |
| 361 | Galactic War Chariot | Metallic Green and Silver, White astronauts | 126 | 1979 | 1980 | Uses figures from 355. | 237, 285 |
| 362 | Trident Star Fighter | Black | 170 | 1979 | 1980 | | 237, 284 |
| 363 | Cosmic Interceptor/ Zygon Patroller | Red and White | | 1979 | 1980 | First issued as Cosmic Interceptor in St. Michael (Marks and Spencers) packaging for Christmas 1979. Issued as Zygon Patroller in Dinky packaging in 1980. Marked only 'Made in England'. | 238 |
| 367 | Space Battle Cruiser | White | 187 | 1979 | 1980 | | |
| (367) | Cosmic Cruiser | Dark Blue | 187 | 12/1979 only | | 367 in St. Michael packaging. Marked only 'Made in England'. | 237, 284 |
| 368 | Zygon Marauder | White | 187 | 1980 | 1980 | Re-issued 367. Marked 'Dinky Toys etc'. | 238 |
| 370 | Dragster Set | Yellow and Red dragster, White, later Blue, later Red launcher | 113 | 1969 | 1976 | | 130 |
| 380 | 'Convoy' Skip Truck | Yellow and Orange | 112 | 1977 | 1979 | Shares cab and chassis with 381–385, and 687. Plastic rears. | 238 |
| 381 | Garden Roller | Green and Red | 67 | R/54 | 1958 | Renumbering of 105a. | 187 |
| 381 | 'Convoy Farm Truck | Yellow and Brown | 110 | 1977 | 1980 | See 380. | 238 |
| 382 | Wheelbarrow | Tan and Red | 82 | R/54 | 1958 | Renumbering of 105b. | 187 |
| 381 | 'Convoy' Dumper Truck | Red and Grey | 118 | 1977 | 1980 | See 380. | 238 |
| 383 | 4-Wheeled Hand Truck | Blue or Green | 128 | R/54 | 1958 | Renumbering of 105c. | 187 |
| 383 | 'Convoy' N.C.L. Truck (National Carriers Ltd.) | Yellow | 110 | 1978 | 1980 | See 380. Rear as 385. | 239, 290 |
| 384 | Grass Cutter | Red, Green and Yellow | 73 | R/54 | 1958 | Renumbering of 105e. | 187 |
| 384 | 'Convoy' Fire Rescue Truck | Red, White escape | 126 | 1977 | 1980 | See 380. | 239, 287 |
| 385 | Sack Truck | Blue | 65 | R/54 | 1958 | Renumbering of 107a. | 187 |
| 385 | 'Convoy' Royal Mail Truck | Red | 110 | 1977 | 1979 | See 380. Rear as 383. | 239, 290 |

| No. | Description | Colours | Length | Introduced | Deleted | Comment/Variations | Page |
|-----|-------------|---------|--------|------------|---------|--------------------|------|
| 386 | Lawn Mower | Green and Red | 140 | R/54 | 1958 | Renumbering of 751. Marked 'Dinky Toys'. | 187 |
| 390 | Customised Transit Van | Metallic Blue | 133 | 1980 | 1980 | 3rd Transit casting (see 369) with side wheels and 'VAMPIRE' stickers. | 287 |
| 398 | Farm Equipment Gift Set | | | R/54 | 1964 | Renumbering of Gift Set No. 1. Contains 300, 320, 321, 322 and 324. | 185 |
| 399 | Farm Tractor and Trailer Set | Red trailer | | 1969 | 1973 | Contains 300 and 428. | 186 |
| 399 | 'Convoy' Gift Set | | | 1977 | 1979 | Contains 380, 381 and 382. | 239 |
| 400 | B.E.V. Electric Truck | Grey or Blue. Tan driver | 85 | R/54 | 1960 | Renumbering of 14a. | 179 |
| 401 | Coventry-Climax Fork Lift Truck | Orange with Green Fork. Tan driver | 108 | R/54 | 1964 | Renumbering of 14c. | 179 |
| 402 | Bedford Coca Cola Lorry | Red with White roof, Brown load | 121 | 1966 | 1969 | 6 plastic trays of crates. | 191 |
| 404 | Conveyancer Fork Lift Truck | Red and Yellow, later Orange and Yellow | 97 | 1967 | 1980 | | 179, 290 |
| 405 | Universal Jeep | Green or Red, later Orange | 83 | R/54 | 1967 | Renumbering of 25y. Late issue has plastic wheels. See 669. | 240 |
| 406 | Commer Articulated Truck | Yellow cab, Grey rear | 175 | 1963 | 1966 | See 424. | 171 |
| 407 | Ford Transit | Blue with White roof: Kenwood | 122 | 1966 | 1969 | 1st Transit casting (See 286). | 169 |
| | | Yellow: Hertz Truck Rental | 122 | 1970 | 1975 | Replaced by 416. See 1025. | |
| 408 | Big Bedford Lorry | Blue with Yellow rear or Maroon with Fawn rear | 146 | R/56 | 1963 | Renumbering of 922. | 165 |
| 409 | Bedford Articulated Lorry | Yellow with Black wings | 166 | R/56 | 1963 | Renumbering of 921. Windows ca. 1961. Marked 'Dinky Toys'. | 171 |
| 410 | Bedford End Tipper | Yellow with Blue rear or Red with Cream rear | 97 | R/54 | 1963 | Renumbering of 25m. Windows from ca. 1962, in red and cream only. Marked 'Dinky Toys'. | 171 |
| 410 | Bedford Van 'Royal Mail' | Red | 90 | 1972 | 1980 | See 412. Raised rectangle on roof (base for headboard on 412) added 1974. | 168 |
| | Bedford Van 'John Menzies' | Dark Blue | 90 | 1974 | 1975 | Promotional. | |
| | Bedford Van 'Belaco' | Brown with Black roof | 90 | 1974 | 1974 | Promotional. | |
| | Bedford Van 'Marley Tiles' | Red | 90 | 1975 | 1975 | Promotional. | |
| | Bedford Van 'M.J. Hire Service' | White | 90 | 1975 | 1976 | Promotional. | |
| | Bedford Van Danish Post | Yellow | 90 | 1974 | | For Danish market only. | |
| | Bedford Van 'Simpson's' | Red with Black roof | 90 | 1972 | 1972 | Promotional (Canada). | |
| 411 | Bedford Truck | Green | 104 | R/54 | 1960 | Renumbering of 25w. | 171 |
| 412 | Austin Wagon | Blue, Maroon or Yellow | 104 | R/54 | 1960 | Renumbering of 30j. | 171 |
| 412 | Bedford Van AA | Yellow | 90 | 1974 | 1980 | 410 with headboard. | 211, 289 |
| 413 | Austin Covered Wagon | Dark Blue with Blue tilt; Maroon with Cream tilt; Red with Grey tilt | 104 | R/54 | 1960 | Renumbering of 30s. | 171 |
| 414 | Dodge Rear Tipping Wagon | Blue with Grey rear; Orange with Green; Red with Green | 99 | R/54 | 1964 | Renumbering of 30m. No bonnet. louvres from ca. 1961. | 171 |

| No. | Description | Colours | Length | Introduced | Deleted | Comment/Variations | Page |
|-----|-------------|---------|--------|------------|---------|--------------------|------|
| 415 | Mechanical Horse and Open Wagon | Blue horse, Cream trailer; Red horse, Beige trailer | 102 | R/54 | 1959 | Renumbering of 33w. | 57 |
| 416 | Ford Transit Van Motorway Services | Yellow | 129 | 1975 | 1978 | 2nd Transit casting (See 271). Replaces 407, replaced by 417. | 169 |
| —— | Ford Transit Van '1.000.000 Transits' | Yellow | 129 | 1976 | 1976 | Casting as 416. Promotional for Ford (England). | 169 |
| 417 | Leyland Comet Lorry | Blue and Yellow; Yellow and Green | 142 | R/56 | 1959 | Renumbering of 931. Tinplate rear. Marked 'Dinky Toys'. | 167, 281 |
| 417 | Ford Transit Van Motorway Services | Yellow | 129 | 1978 | 1980 | 3rd Transit casting (See 269). Replaces 416. | 169, 289 |
| 418 | Leyland Comet Lorry with hinged tailboard | Orange and Green or 2-tone Blue | 144 | R/56 | 1959 | Renumbering of 932. Marked 'Dinky Toys'. | 165 |
| 419 | Leyland Comet Wagon | Yellow | 144 | R/56 | 1959 | Renumbering of 933. Portland Portland Cement and Ferrocrete transfers. Marked 'Dinky Toys'. | 165 |
| 420 | Leyland Forward Control Lorry | Green, Red or Grey | 107 | R/54 | 1961 | Renumbering of 25r. | 171 |
| 421 | Hindle-Smart Electric Articulated Lorry | Maroon | 135 | R/54 | 1960 | Renumbering of 30w. | 189 |
| 422 | Thames Flat Truck | Red or Dark Green | 112 | R/54 | 1960 | Renumbering of 30r. | 171 |
| 424 | Commer Convertible Articulated Truck | Yellow cab, Grey rear. White stake sides. Blue tarpaulin | 175 | 1963 | 1966 | 406 with 2 interchangeable plastic inserts for rear. | 171 |
| 425 | Bedford TK Coal Wagon | Red | 121 | 1964 | 1969 | Casting of 435 without sides, with headboard on cab. Plastic scales and 6 sacks of coal. | 189 |
| 428 | Large Trailer | Grey with Red wheels. Re-issue is Red with Silver pivot and wheels | 111 | R/54 and 1967 | 1964 1971 | Renumbering of 951. Marked 'Dinky Toys'. | 171 186 |
| 429 | Trailer | Red or Dark Green. | 69 | R/54 | 1964 | Renumbering of 25g. Rivet holding swivel incorporated into main casting on late issue. | 154 |
| 430 | Commer Breakdown Lorry | Tan with Green rear; Red with Pale Grey rear; Light Tan with Blue rear | 123 | R/54 | 1964 | Renumbering of 25x. Windows from ca. 1961. Tan/Green with or without windows; other colours only with. | 176 |
| 430 | Johnson 2-ton Dumper | Orange and Red | 106 | 1977 | 1980 | | 175, 289 |
| 431 | Guy 4-ton Lorry | 2-tone Blue | 132 | R/56 | 1958 | Renumbering of 911. Marked 'Dinky Toys'. | 165 |
| 431 | Guy Warrior 4-ton Lorry | Tan and Green | 136 | 1958 | 1964 | With windows from ca. 1960. | 165 |
| 432 | Guy Flat Truck | Blue cab with Red rear or vice versa | 132 | R/56 | 1958 | Renumbering of 912. Comment as 431. | 165 |
| 432 | Guy Warrior Flat Truck | Green and Red | 136 | 1958 | 1964 | With windows from ca. 1960 | 165 |

| No. | Description | Colours | Length | Introduced | Deleted | Comment/Variations | Page |
|-----|-------------|---------|--------|------------|---------|--------------------|------|
| 432 | Foden Tipping Lorry | White cab, Yellow rear, Red chassis | 175 | 1976 | 1979 | See 668. | 189, 289 |
| 433 | Guy Flat Truck with Tailboard | 2-tone Green or Dark Blue with Orange rear | 132 | R/54 | 1958 | Renumbering of 913. Comment as 431. | 165 |
| 434 | Bedford TK Crash Truck | White with Green flash 'Top Rank'; Red or Metallic Red with Black roof and pale Grey rear from 1966 | 124 | 1964 | 1973 | | 177 |
| 435 | Bedford TK Tipper | Pale Grey cab with Blue roof and Red rear; Yellow (with or without Black cab roof) from 1966. White with Silver rear with Blue sides | 121 | 1964 | 1971 | Plastic drop-down side flaps and tailboard. | 189 |
| 436 | Atlas Copco Compressor Lorry | Yellow | 89 | 1963 | 1969 | | 174 |
| 437 | Muir Hill 2WL Loader | Red, Yellow from 1970 | 121 | 1962 | 1978 | Grille detail from 1973. See 967. | 173 |
| 438 | Ford D800 Tipper Truck | Red with Yellow rear | 132 | 1970 | 1977 | Opening cab doors – see 440. See 1029 | 189 |
| 439 | Ford D800 Snow Plough and Tipper Truck | Blue with Red, later Pale Blue, rear and Yellow snow plough | 194 | 1970 | 1978 | Casting of 438 with plough from 958 | 189 |
| 440 | Petrol Tanker "Mobilgas" | Red | 112 | R/54 | 1961 | Renumbering of 30p. Mobilgas in White letters with Blue borders to ca. 1958, thereafter in Blue letters on White background. (Unusually for the period, the change is not shown in catalogues). | 161 |
| 440 | Ford D800 Tipper Truck | Red with Yellow rear. | 132 | 1977 | 1978 | As 438 but no opening doors. | 189 |
| 441 | Petrol Tanker "Castrol" | Green | 112 | R/54 | 1960 | Renumbering of 30pa. | 161 |
| 442 | Petrol Tanker "Esso" | Red | 112 | R/54 | 1960 | Renumbering of 30pb. | 161 |
| 442 | Land Rover Breakdown Crane | White and Red | 121 | 1973 | 1979 | Motorway Rescue stickers. See 1030. | 177, 289 |
| 442 | Land Rover Breakdown Crane 'Falck' | White and Red or all Red | 121 | 1974 | ? | As above with 'Falck' stickers. Danish market only. | 225 |
| 443 | Petrol Tanker "National Benzole" | Yellow | 112 | 1957 | 1958 | | 161 |
| 448 | Chevrolet El Camino Pick-Up with Trailers | Green and White with Red trailers | 256 | 1963 | 1968 | 2 × 2-wheeled trailers: 1 open, 1 closed. | 151 |
| 449 | Chevrolet El Camino Pick-Up | Green and White | 111 | 1961 | 1969 | As above without trailers. Assembled in South Africa in Turquoise, or Cream and Brown. | 151 |
| 449 | Johnston Road Sweeper | Yellow or Lime Green | 142 | 1977 | 1980 | As 451 without opening doors. | 178 |
| 450 | Trojan Van "Esso" | | 85 | R/54 | 1957 | Renumbering of 31a. | 155 |
| 450 | Bedford TK Box Van "Castrol" | Green with White panels on rear | 143 | 1965 | 1970 | | 191 |
| 451 | Trojan Van "Dunlop" | Red | 85 | R/54 | 1957 | Renumbering of 31b. | 155 |
| 451 | Johnston Road Sweeper | Metallic Green with Orange rear | 142 | 1971 | 1977 | Opening cab doors. See 449. | 178 |
| 452 | Trojan Van "Chivers" | Green | 85 | R/54 | 1957 | Renumbering of 31c. | 155 |

| No. | Description | Colours | Length | Introduced | Deleted | Comment/Variations | Page |
|-----|-------------|---------|--------|------------|---------|--------------------|------|
| 453 | Trojan Van "Oxo" | Blue | 85 | R/54 | 1954 | Renumbering of 31d, for a few months only. | 155 |
| 454 | Trojan Van "Cydrax" | Pale Green | 85 | 1957 | 1959 | | 155 |
| 455 | Trojan Van "Brooke Bond Tea" | Red | 85 | 1957 | 1960 | | 155 |
| 465 | Morris Van "Capstan" | 2-tone Blue | 78 | 1959 | 1959 | Casting as 260. | 158 |
| 470 | Austin Van "Shell-B.P." | Green and Red | 89 | 1954 | 1956 | | 158 |
| 471 | Austin Van "Nestlés" | Red | 89 | 1955 | 1961 | | 158 |
| 472 | Austin Van "Raleigh Cycles" | Dark Green | 89 | 1956 | 1961 | | 158 |
| 475 | Ford Model 'T' 1908 | Blue body with Red, Brown or Black chassis | 83 | 1964 | 1968 | See 485, 109, 115/120. Driver and lady passenger (plastic). Plastic, later metal wheels. | 145 |
| 476 | Morris Oxford (Bull-Nosed) 1913 | Yellow body with Blue chassis and Fawn plastic hood | 92 | 1965 | 1970 | See 477 and 486. Driver from 475. Plastic wheels. | 145 |
| 477 | Parsley's Car | Green with Black chassis | 92 | 1970 | 1973 | Casting as 476 with folded hood and lion driver. From TV Series 'The Adventures of Parsley'. *Metal* wheels. | 235 |
| 480 | Bedford Van "Kodak" | Yellow | 83 | 1954 | 1956 | | 158 |
| 481 | Bedford Van "Ovaltine" | Blue | 83 | 1955 | 1960 | | 158 |
| 482 | Bedford Van "Dinky Toys" | Cream and Orange | 83 | 1956 | 1960 | | 158 |
| 485 | Ford Model 'T' with Santa Claus | Red and White | 83 | 1964 | 1968 | Casting as 475 with plastic sack on rear. | 237 |
| 486 | Dinky Beats Morris Oxford (Bull-Nosed) | Pink with Green chassis | 92 | 1965 | 1970 | Casting as 476 with folded roof and 3 beat musicians. | 237 |
| 490 | Electric Dairy Van "Express Dairy" | Grey and Blue or Cream and Red | 85 | R/54 | 1960 | Renumbering of 30v. | 181 |
| 491 | Electric Dairy Van "N.C.B." | As 490 | 85 | R/54 | 1960 | Renumbering of 30v. Export version. | 181 |
| 492 | Loud-Speaker Van | Blue with Silver speakers | 81 | R/54 | 1957 | Renumbering of 34c. | 188 |
| 492 | Election Mini-Van | White with Orange Speakers | 78 | 1964 | 1964 | Casting of 273 with plastic frame and loud-speaker on rear. Figure and microphone. | 189 |
| 501 | Foden Diesel 8-Wheel Wagon | Blue, Light Grey or Brown with Black wings and chassis; Red cab/chasis with Fawn rear; Dark Blue with Blue rear | 185 or 188 | 1947 | R/54 | Single-colour cab and rear with Black chassis has no hook and herring-bone pattern tyres. 2-colour schemes from 1948. 1st cab with exposed grille, Foden in script across grille and flash on cab sides (picked out in silver or contrasting colour) replaced in 1952. Renumbered 901. | 163 |
| 502 | Foden Flat Truck | Blue with Dark Blue trim, Green with Black trim; Orange with Green rear; Blue with Red rear. Dark Blue with Green rear (2nd grille) | 185 or 188 | 1947 | R/54 | Comments as 501. Renumbered 902. | 163 |

| No. | Description | Colours | Length | Introduced | Deleted | Comment/Variations | Page |
|-----|-------------|---------|--------|------------|---------|--------------------|------|
| 503 | Foden Flat Truck with Tailboard | Grey with Blue wings and chassis; Red with Black Trim; Blue with Orange rear; Dark Blue with Orange rear; 2-tone Green | 185 or 188 | 1947 | R/54 | Comments as 501. Renumbered 903. | 163 |
| 504 | Foden 14-Ton Tanker | Dark Blue with Blue rear; Red with Fawn rear. Red with 'Mobilgas' transfers | 188 | 1948 | R/54 | No transfers. | 163 |
| | | | 188 | 1953 | R/54 | Renumbered 941. | 161 |
| 505 | Foden Flat Truck with Chains | Green or Maroon | 188 | 1952 | R/54 | Appeared briefly with 1st cab. Renumbered 905. | 163 |
| 511 | Guy 4-Ton Lorry | Grey with Red wings and chassis; Green, Maroon or Brown; with Black wings and chassis; 2-tone Blue; Red and Fawn | 129 or 132 | 1947 | R/54 | 2-colour schemes from 1948. Renumbered 911. Marked 'Dinky Supertoys'. Tin clips holding rear axle, later cast lugs. | 165 |
| 512 | Guy Flat Truck | Yellow, Maroon, Brown or Grey with Black wings and chassis; Blue with Red rear | 129 or 132 | 1947 | R/54 | Comments as 511, Renumbered 912. | 165 |
| 513 | Guy Flat Truck with Tailboard | Yellow, Grey or Maroon with Black wings and chassis; 2-tone Green; Blue and Orange | 129 or 132 | 1947 | R/54 | Comment as 511. Renumbered 917. | 165 |
| 514 | Guy Van 'Slumberland' | Red | 134 | 1949 | 1951? | | 158 |
| 514 | Guy Van 'Lyons' | Dark Blue | 134 | 1951 | 1952? | | 158 |
| 514 | Guy Van 'Weetabix' | Yellow | 134 | 1952 | 1953 | | 158 |
| 514 | Guy Van 'Spratt's' | Red and Cream | 134 | 1953 | R/54 | Renumbered 914. | 158 |
| 521 | Bedford Articulated Lorry | Red or Yellow, Black wings | 166 | 1948 | R/54 | Renumbered 921. Marked 'Dinky Supertoys'. | 171 |
| 522 | Big Bedford Lorry | Maroon and Fawn or Blue and Yellow | 146 | 1952 | R/54 | Renumbered 922. Marked 'Dinky Supertoys'. | 165 |
| 531 | Leyland Comet Lorry | Blue or Red cab/chassis, Brown, later Yellow rear | 144 | 1949 | R/54 | Renumbered 931. Marked 'Dinky Supertoys'. | 167, 281 |
| 532 | Leyland Comet Lorry with Hinged Tailboard | Green cab/chassis, Red, later Orange rear; 2-tone Blue | 142 | 1952 | R/54 | Renumbered 932. Comment as 531. | 165 |
| 533 | Leyland Cement Wagon | Yellow | 142 | 1953 | R/54 | Renumbered 933. Comment as 531. Portland Cement and Ferrocrete advertising. | 165 |
| 551 | Trailer | Green or Grey. Black wheels | 105 (Body only) | 1948 | R/54 | Renumbered 951. Marked 'Dinky Supertoys'. | 171 |
| 555 | Fire Engine with Extending Ladder | Red with Brown, later Silver ladder | 145 | 1952 | R/54 | Renumbered 955. | 201 |
| 561 | Blaw-Knox Bulldozer | Red | 138 | 1949 | R/54 | Renumbered 961. | 173 |
| 562 | Muir-Hill Dump Truck | Yellow | 105 | 1948 | R/54 | Renumbered 962. | 173 |
| 563 | Heavy Tractor | Red, Orange or Blue | 116 | 1948 | R/54 | Casting of 561 without 'dozer blade. Renumbered 963 | 175, 281 |

| No. | Description | Colours | Length | Introduced | Deleted | Comment/Variations | Page |
|-----|-------------|---------|--------|------------|---------|--------------------|------|
| 564 | Elevator Loader | Yellow with Blue or Dark Blue chutes | 230 | 1952 | R/54 | Renumbered 964. | 186 |
| 571 | Coles Mobile Crane | Yellow and Black | 160 | 1949 | R/54 | Renumbered 971. | 173 |
| 581 | Horse Box | Maroon | 175 | 1953 | R/54 | 'British Railways' on sides and cab roof, 'Express Horse Box Hire Service' on sides: Renumbered 981. U.S. market version: 'Express Horse Van Hire Service' on sides, 'Express' on cab roof: Renumbered 980. Aluminium. | 180 |
| 582 | Pullmore Car Transporter | Pale or Mid-Blue with Fawn tracks for cars | 250 | 1953 | R/54 | Renumbered 982. Aluminium trailer. | 173 |
| 591 | A.E.C. Tanker | Red cab, Yellow rear | 151 | 1952 | R/54 | 'Shell Chemicals Limited' on sides. Renumbered 991. | 164 |
| 600 | Armoured Corps Personnel | | | R/54 | 1955? | Renumbering of 150. U.S. export only. | 221 |
| 601 | Austin Para Moke | Green with Tan hood | 73<br>76 with Speedwheels | 1966 | 1978 | 342 with plastic carrier and parachute. Comments as 342. | 218 |
| 602 | Armoured Command Car | Green, later Blue-Green | 160 | 1976 | 1978 | Gerry Anderson design for unreleased TV series. U.S. star and radar scanner | 236 |
| 603 | Army Private Seated (Army Personnel – Private Seated) | Tan with Black beret | (H)20 | 1957 | 1971 | Metal, later plastic. | 213 |
| 604 | Royal Tank Corps Private, sitting | Black | (H)22 | R/54 | 1955? | Renumbering of 150b. U.S. export only | 221 |
| 604 | Land Rover Bomb Disposal Unit | Green with Orange panels | 110 | 1976 | 1978 | Casting as 344 with plastic rear. Grey plastic tracked robot de-fuser. | 218 |
| 606 | Royal Artillery Personnel | | | R/54 | 1955? | Renumbering of 160. U.S. export only. | 221 |
| 608 | Royal Artillery Seated Gunner | Khaki with Black beret | (H)24 | R/54 | 1955? | Renumbering of 160b. U.S. export only. | 221 |
| 609 | 105mm Howitzer with gun crew | Green | 199 | 1974 | 1978 | With 3 plastic figures. See 615. | 218 |
| 612 | Commando Jeep | Green | 108 | 1973 | 1980 | Casting as 615 without screen, with 2 machine guns; gerry cans and pack on bonnet. | 218 |
| 615 | US Jeep with 105mm Howitzer | Green | 108 + 199 | 1976 | 1978 | See 609 and 1033. | 218 |
| 616 | A.E.C. Articulated Transporter with Chieftain Tank | Green | 318 | 1976 | 1978 | Militarised 974 without top deck, with 683 and camouflage net. | 218 |
| 617 | Volkswagen KDF with PAK anti-Tank Gun | Grey | 115 + 159 | 1967 | 1978 | | 216 |
| 618 | A.E.C. Articulated Transporter with Helicopter | Green | 318 | 1976 | 1980 | Militarised 974 without top deck, with militarised 724 and camouflage net. | 218 |

| No. | Description | Colours | Length | Introduced | Deleted | Comment/Variations | Page |
|-----|-------------|---------|--------|------------|---------|--------------------|------|
| 619 | Bren-Gun Carrier and Anti-Tank Gun | Green | 125 + 159 | 1976 | 1978 | 622 + 625. | 218 |
| 620 | Transport Wagon with Driver | Green | 99 | R/54 | 1955? | Renumbering of 151b. U.S. export only. | 221 |
| 620 | Berliet Missile Launcher | Green with Black plastic rear. White and Red missile. | 150 | 1971 | 1973 | French casting (No. 816) with English base and wheels. | 219 |
| 621 | 3-Ton Army Wagon | Green | 113 | 1954 | 1963 | With or without driver, with windows from 1960. Tin tilt. | 213 |
| 622 | 10-Ton Army Truck | Green | 137 | 1954 | 1963 | With or without driver. Tin tilt. | 214 |
| 622 | Bren Gun Carrier | Green | 125 | 1975 | 1978 | See 619. | 218 |
| 623 | Army Covered Wagon | Green | 105 | 1954 | 1963 | With or without driver. | 213 |
| 624 | Daimler Military Ambulance | Green | 96 | R/54 | ? | Renumbering of 30hm. U.S. export only. | 222 |
| 625 | Austin Covered Wagon | Green | 104 | R/54 | ? | Renumbering of 30sm. U.S. export only. | 222 |
| 625 | 6-Pounder Anti-Tank Gun | Green | 159 | 1975 | 1978 | See 619. | 218 |
| 626 | Military Ambulance | Green | 110 | 1956 | 1966 | With or without driver, with windows from 1961. | 213 |
| 640 | Bedford Truck | Green | 104 | R/54 | ? | Renumbering of 25wm. U.S. export only. | 222 |
| 641 | Army 1-Ton Cargo Truck | Green | 79 | 1954 | 1962 | With or without driver. Windows from 1961. Tin tilt. | 213 |
| 642 | R.A.F. Pressure Refueller | Grey | 142 | 1957 | 1961 | With or without driver. | 215 |
| 643 | Army Water Carrier | Green | 89 | 1958 | 1964 | With or without driver. Windows from 1961. | 213 |
| 650 | Light Tank | Green | 68 | R/54 | 1955? | Renumbering of 152a. U.S. export only. | 221 |
| 651 | Centurion Tank | Green | 149 | 1954 | 1971 | Metal, later plastic wheels. Rubber tracks. | 214 |
| 654 | Mobile Gun | Green | 151 | 1973 | 1980 | See 1034. | 217 |
| 656 | 88mm Gun | Grey | 218 | 1975 | 1980 | | 216 |
| 660 | Tank Transporter | Green | 335 | 1956 | 1964 | See 908. Comment as 626. | 214 |
| 661 | Recovery Tractor | Green | 134 | 1957 | 1966 | | 214 |
| 662 | Static 88mm Gun with crew | Grey | 185 | 1975 | 1978 | 656 without wheels. With three plastic figures. | 216 |
| 665 | "Honest John" Missile Erector | Green, later Green with Black. White Missile with Black nose. | 188 | 1964 | 1976 | Lorry as 667. | 214, 219 |
| 666 | Missile Erector Vehicle with Corporal Missile and Launching Platform | Green with White missile | 240 + 90 | 1959 | 1964 | | 214 |
| 667 | Missile Servicing Platform Vehicle | Green | 197 | 1960 | 1964 | See 977 and 665. | 214 |
| 667 | Armoured Patrol Car | Green | 80 | 1976 | 1978 | 680 + turret from 676. | 218 |

| No. | Description | Colours | Length | Introduced | Deleted | Comment/Variations | Page |
|-----|-------------|---------|--------|------------|---------|--------------------|------|
| 668 | Foden Army Truck | Green | 197 | 1976 | 1980 | Casting as 432. | 218 |
| 669 | U.S. Army Jeep | Green | 83 | 1956? | 1958? | Casting as 405. White Star. | 215 |
| 670 | Armoured Car | Green | 73 | 1954 | 1971 | See 676. Later issue has plastic wheels. | 213 |
| 671 | Reconnaissance Car | Green | 89 | R/54 | 1955 | Renumbering of 152b. U.S. export only. | 221 |
| 671 | Mk. 1 Corvette | White hull with Black stripes, Brown deck, Grey superstructure | 260 | 1975 | 1977 | | 91 |
| 672 | U.S. Army Jeep | Green | 69 | R/54 | 1955 | Renumbering of 153a. U.S. exports only. | 221 |
| 672 | OSA Missile Boat | Pale Grey with White and Black | 206 | 1976 | 1977 | | 91 |
| 673 | Scout Car | Green | 68 | 1953 | 1962 | | 213 |
| 673 | Submarine Chaser | Grey with White and Black. | 197 | 1977 | 1978 | | 91 |
| 674 | Austin Champ | Green or White | 69 | 1954 | 1971 | Later issue has plastic wheels, steering wheel and driver. White (U.N.) version for export only. | 213, 215 |
| 674 | Coastguard Amphibious Missile Launch | White with Blue, Red and Yellow | 155 | 1976 | 1978 | | 91 |
| 675 | U.S. Army Staff Car | Green | 102 | R/54 | 1959? | Renumbering of 170m. U.S. export only. | 222 |
| 675 | Motor Patrol Boat | Grey with Cream, Black and Red. | 170 | 1973 | 1977 | | 91 |
| 676 | Armoured Personnel Carrier | Green | 82 | 1955 | 1962 | | 213 |
| 676 | Daimler Armoured Car | Green | 73 | 1973 | 1976 | Re-issue of 670 with extra detail and Speedwheels. Also assembled in France with French wheels, paint, box and camouflage net, still marked Made in England. (1973–74). | 217 |
| 677 | Armoured Command Vehicle | Green | 134 | 1957 | 1962 | | 215 |
| 677 | Task Force Set | | | 1972 | 1975 | Contains 680, 681 and 682. | 219 |
| 678 | Air Sea Rescue Launch | Black with Grey and Yellow | 170 | 1974 | 1977 | With pilot and dinghy. | 91 |
| 680 | Ferret Armoured Car | Green or Tan | 80 | 1972 | 1978 | See 667. | 219 |
| 681 | D.U.K.W. | Green | 127 | 1972 | 1978 | | 219 |
| 682 | Stalwart Load Carrier | Green | 103 | 1972 | 1978 | | 219 |
| 683 | Chieftain Tank | Green | 217 | 1972 | 1980 | See 1037. | 217 |
| 686 | 25-pounder Field Gun | Green | 90 | 1957 | 1971 | Later issue has plastic wheels. See 697. | 213 |
| 687 | Trailer for 25-pounder Field Gun | Green | 58 | 1957 | 1966 | Comment as 686. | 213 |
| 687 | Convoy Army Truck | Green | 110 | 1978 | 1980 | | 220, 239 |
| 688 | Field Artillery Tractor | Green | 81 | 1957 | 1971 | Comments as 626 and 686. | 213 |
| 689 | Medium Artillery Tractor | Green | 140 | 1957 | 1966 | With or without driver. | 214 |
| 690 | Mobile A.A. Gun | Green | 115 | R/54 | 1955 | Renumbering of 161b. U.S. export only. | 221 |

| No. | Description | Colours | Length/Wingspan | Introduced | Deleted | Comment/Variations | Page |
|---|---|---|---|---|---|---|---|
| 690 | Scorpion Tank | Green | 120 | 1974 | 1980 | With camouflage net. See 1038. | 217 |
| 691 | Field Gun Unit | Green | | R/54 | 1955 | Renumbering of 162. U.S. export only. | 221 |
| 691 | 'Striker' Anti-Tank Vehicle | Green | 122 | 1974 | 1980 | | 217 |
| 692 | 5.5″ Medium Gun | Green | 131 | 1955 | 1962 | | 213 |
| 692 | Leopard Tank | Grey | 198 | 1974 | 1980 | | 217 |
| 693 | 7.2″ Howitzer | Green | 130 | 1958 | 1967 | | 213 |
| 694 | Hanomag Tank Destroyer | Grey | 171 | 1975 | 1978 | | 216 |
| 695 | Howitzer and Tractor | Green | | 1962 | 1966 | Contains 689 and 693. | 214 |
| 696 | Leopard Anti-Aircraft Tank | Grey | 152 | 1975 | 1979 | | 217 |
| 697 | 25-pounder Field Gun Set | Green | 220 | 1957 | 1971 | Contains 686, 687 and 688. | 213 |
| 698 | Tank Transporter and Tank | Green | 335 | 1957 | 1965 | Contains 651 and 660. | 214 |
| 699 | Military Vehicles Gift Set (1) | | | R/55 | 1958 | Contains 621, 641, 674 and 676. Renumbering of Military Gift Set No. 1. | 215 |
| 699 | Leopard Recovery Tank | Grey-Green | 147 | 1975 | 1978 | | 217 |
| 700 | Seaplane | Silver | 101 | R/54 | 1955 | Renumbering of 63b. | 104, 111 |
| 700 | Spitfire Mk. II Diamond Jubilee of the R.A.F. | Chrome plated and Black | 173 | 1979 | 1979 | Mounted on plinth. Limited issue. | 119 |
| 701 | Shetland Flying Boat | Silver | 236 | 1947 | 1949 | G-AGVD | 112 |
| 702 | D.H. Comet Jet Airliner | White and Blue with Silver wings | 183 | 1954 | R/55 | G-ALYV. Renumbered 999. B.O.A.C. livery. | 114 |
| 704 | Avro York Air Liner | Silver | 160 | R/54 | 1959 | Renumbering of 70a. | 112 |
| 705 | Viking Airliner | Silver | 140 | R/54 | 1962 | Renumbering of 70c. | 112 |
| 706 | Vickers Viscount Airliner (Air France) | Silver with Blue and White | 149 | 1956 | 1957 | Replaced by 708. | 115 |
| 708 | Vickers Viscount Airliner (B.E.A.) | Silver with White, later Metallic Grey and White | 149 | 1957 | 1965 | Metallic Grey issue has plastic wheels. | 115 |
| 710 | Beechcraft S.35 Bonanza | Red and White; Bronze and Yellow with Black cowl from ca. 1971; Red, Blue and White from ca. 1975 | 133 | 1965 | 1976 | | 119 |
| 712 | U.S. Army T-42A | Grey-Green | 153 | 1972 | 1977 | Casting of 715 with wint-tip tanks. | 119 |
| 715 | Bristol 173 Helicopter | Turquoise with Red rotors and stripes | 53 Rotor ø 72 (L)86 | 1956 | 1962 | | 118 |
| 715 | Beechcraft C-55 Baron | White with Yellow cowls, Red with Yellow from 1972 | 150 | 1968 | 1976 | See 712. | 119 |
| 716 | Westland Sikorsky S51 Helicopter | Red and Cream | (L)66 Rotor ø 72 | | | | 118 |
| 717 | Boeing 737 | White with White, later Blue engine pods | 152 | 1970 | 1975 | Lufthansa livery. | 119 |

| No. | Description | Colours | Wingspan | Introduced | Deleted | Comment/Variations | Page |
|-----|-------------|---------|----------|------------|---------|--------------------|------|
| 718 | Hawker Hurricane Mk IIc | Camouflage | 188 | 1972 | 1975 | See 1041. | 119 |
| 719 | Spitfire Mk II | Camouflage | 173 | 1969 | 1977 | Battery motor for propeller. Replaced by 741. See 1042. | 119 |
| 721 | Junkers Ju87B Stuka | Camouflage Grey-Green | 191 | 1969 | 1980 | | 119 |
| 722 | Hawker Harrier | Camouflage Light Blue and Olive Green | 125 | 1970 | 1980 | | 119 |
| 723 | Hawker Siddeley HS125 Executive Jet | Yellow and White; Metallic Blue and White from ca. 1971 | 132 | 1970 | 1975 | See 728. | 119 |
| 724 | Sea King Helicopter | White with Metallic Blue | (L)179 | 1971 | 1979 | With White plastic Apollo space capsule. See 1040, 736 and 618 | 122 |
| 725 | F-4K Phantom II | Dark Blue and Pale Blue | 132 | 1972 | 1977 | See 727, 730 and 733. | 122 |
| 726 | Messerschmitt Bf 109E | Pale Brown desert camouflage, Grey-Green from ca. 1974 | 165 | 1972 | 1976 | See 1044. | 122 |
| 727 | U.S. Air Force F-4 Phantom II | Brown and Green camouflage | 132 | 1976 | 1977 | Casting as 725. American market only. | 112 |
| 728 | R.A.F. Dominie | Metallic Blue and Green camouflage | 132 | 1972 | 1975 | Casting as 723. | 119 |
| 729 | Multi-Role Combat Aircraft | Grey and Dark Green camouflage. | 164 (open wings) | 1974 | 1976 | | 122 |
| 730 | Tempest II Fighter | Silver | 63 | R/54 | 1955 | Renumbering of 70b. | 112 |
| 730 | U.S. Navy Phantom | Grey and White | 132 | 1972 | 1976 | Casting as 725. | 123 |
| 731 | Twin-Engined Fighter | Silver | 76 | R/54 | 1955 | Renumbering of 70d. | 112 |
| 731 | S.E.P.E.C.A.T. Jaguar | Metallic Light Blue and Green camouflage | 106 | 1973 | 1976 | See 1043. | 123 |
| 732 | Gloster Meteor Twin-Jet Fighter | Silver | 67 | R/54 | 1962 | Renumbering of 70e. | 112 |
| 732 | Bell Police Helicopter | Blue, Orange and White | (L)211 | 1974 | 1980 | See 303. | 123 |
| 733 | Shooting Star Jet Fighter | Silver | 61 | R/54 | 1962 | Renumbering of 70f. | 112 |
| 733 | F-4K Phantom II Der Luftwaffe | Grey-Green camouflage | 132 | 1973 | 1976? | Casting as 725. Austrian and German market only. | 123 |
| 734 | Supermarine Swift | Grey and Dark Green camouflage | 51 | 1955 | 1962 | | 115 |
| 734 | P47 Thunderbolt | Silver-Grey | 190 | 1975 | 1978 | | 123 |
| 735 | Gloster Javelin Delta Wing Fighter | As 734 | 83 | 1956 | 1966 | | 115 |
| 736 | Hawker Hunter | As 734 | 53 | 1955 | 1963 | | 115 |
| 736 | Bundesmarine Sea King Helicopter | Grey with Orange | (L)179 | 1973 | 1978 | | 123 |
| 737 | P.1B Lightning Fighter | Silver, later Metallic Grey | 55 | 1959 | 1968 | Metal wheels with Silver finish; Black plastic with Metallic Grey. | 118 |
| 738 | D.H. 110 Sea Vixen Fighter | Grey and White | 80 | 1960 | 1965 | | 118 |
| 739 | A6M5 Zero-Sen | Metallic Green and Grey | 184 | 1975 | 1978 | | 123 |
| 741 | Spitfire Mark II | Green, Brown and Eggshell; Green camouflage | 173 | 1978 | 1980 | As 719 but without motor. | 119 |
| 749 | Avro Vulcan Delta Wing Bomber | Silver | 156 | 1955 | 1956 | (This is the number cast on the model, although catalogued and boxed as 992). Canadian market only. Aluminium. | 114 |

| No. | Description | Colours | Length | Introduced | Deleted | Comment/Variations | Page |
|---|---|---|---|---|---|---|---|
| 750 | Telephone Call Box | Red and Silver | (H)58 | R/54 | 1962 | Renumbering of 12c. | 210 |
| 751 | Lawn Mower | Green and Red | 140 | 1949 | R/54 | Renumbered 386. Marked Dinky Supertoys. | 18 |
| 751 | Police Box | Dark Blue | (H)66 | R/54 | 1960 | Renumbering of 42a. | 71 |
| 752 | Goods Yard Crane | Yellow and Blue or Dark Blue | (Base) 100 (H) 195 | 1953 | R/54 | Renumbered 973. Some with cast-iron base. | 177 |
| 753 | Police Controlled Crossing | Grey base, Black and White | 151 | 1962 | 1967 | Plastic. | 244 |
| 754 | Pavement Set | Fawn and Grey | | 1958 | 1962 | Card. Contains: 6 × ½ straights; 4 × ¼ straights; 2 × ½ circles; 4 × ¼ circles; 2 × ⅜ circles; 2 × ⅛ circles. | 245 |
| 755 | Lamp Standard Single Arm | Grey and Fawn | (H)145 | 1960 | 1964 | Plastic lamp; metal base. | 245 |
| 756 | Lamp Standard Double Arm | Grey and Fawn | (H)145 | 1960 | 1964 | Comment as 755. | 245 |
| 760 | Pillar Box | Red and Black | (H)42 | 1954 | 1960 | E II R cast in. | 245 |
| 763 | Posters for Road Hoardings | | | 1959 | 1964 | Paper. 6 different. | 244 |
| 764 | Posters for Road Hoardings | | | 1959 | 1964 | Paper. 6 different. | 244 |
| 765 | Road Hoardings | Green hoardings | 205 | 1959 | 1964 | Plastic. With 6 posters. | 245 |
| 766 | British Road Signs. Country Set A. | Black and White with Red | (H)55 average | 1959 | 1964 | White base. (see 47). All castings different to 47 set. Contains: Narrow Bridge; Bend (Left); Crossing No Gates; Cattle; Cross Roads; Road Narrows'. | 244 |
| 767 | British Road Signs. Country Set B. | As 766 | As 766 | 1959 | 1964 | See 766. Contains: Bend (Right); Level Crossing; Hill 1 in 7; Hump Bridge; Bends for 1¼ miles; Low Bridge Hdr'm 14'. | 244 |
| 768 | British Road Signs. Town Set A. | As 766 | As 766 | 1959 | 1964 | See 766. Contains: No Entry (2); No Right Turn; Children; Round-About; Slow – Major Road Ahead. | 244 |
| 769 | British Road Signs. Town Set B. | As 766 | As 766 | 1959 | 1964 | See 766. Contains: Halt at Major Road Ahead; No Waiting; Road Junction; School; 30/Derestriction (2). | 244 |
| 770 | Road Signs (12) | As 766 | As 766 | R/54 | 1955 | Renumbering of 47. U.S. export only. | 67 |
| 771 | International Road Signs (12) | Silver with White, Red and Black. | (H)35–45 | 1953 | 1965 | | 244 |
| 772 | British Road Signs (24) | As 766 | As 766 | 1959 | 1963 | Contains 766, 767, 768 and 769. | 242 |
| 773 | Traffic Signal 4-Face | Black and White | (H)62 | 1958 | 1963 | No Orange globe on top. (Compare 47a). | 67, 245 |
| 777 | Belisha Beacon | Black and White, Orange beacon | (H)51 | 1958 | 1963 | Reissue of 47d. | 67 |
| 778 | Road Repair Warning Boards | | | 1962 | 1967 | Plastic. 6 different. | 244 |

| No. | Description | Colours | Length | Introduced | Deleted | Comment/Variations | Page |
|---|---|---|---|---|---|---|---|
| 781 | Petrol Pump Station Esso | Tan base, Red and White | 114 | 1955 | 1966 | Esso and Esso Extra pumps. | 244 |
| 782 | Petrol Pump Station Shell | Grey base, Cream and Green kiosk, Red and Yellow pumps with White tops | 203 | 1960 | 1971 | Plastic except for pump bodies. | 244 |
| 783 | Petrol Pump Station B.P. | Base and kiosk as 782, Green and White pumps | 203 | 1960 | 1971 | Comment as 782. | 244 |
| 784 | Dinky Goods Train Set | Blue Loco., 1 Red truck, 1 Yellow truck | (Loco) 115 (Trucks) 92 | 1972 | 1974 | | 35 |
| 785 | Service Station | Tan and Red | 335 × 185 | 1960 | 1964 | Plastic. | 245 |
| 786 | Tyre Rack with Tyres | Green rack 'Dunlop' | 52 | 1960 | 1967 | With 21 tyres. | 244 |
| 787 | Lighting Kit for Buildings | | | 1960 | 1964 | | 246 |
| 788 | Marrel Bucket for No. 966 | Grey | 68 | 1960 | 1969 | | 246 |
| 790 | Imitation Granite Chippings | Grey | | 1960 | 1964 | Plastic. | 246 |
| 791 | Imitation Coal | Black | | 1960 | 1964 | Plastic. | 246 |
| 792 | Packing Cases (3) | Fawn | 30 × 28 × 19 | 1962 | 1969 | Plastic. | 246 |
| 793 | Pallets | Orange | 29 × 35 | 1960 | 1964 | Plastic. For use with 930, later included with 404. | 246 |
| 794 | Loading Ramp | Pale Blue | 233 | 1955 | 1964 | Tinplate. Renumbered 994 in 1954–1955 only. | 177 |
| 796 | Healey Sports Boat on Trailer | Green and White boat, Orange trailer | 112 | 1960 | 1969 | Plastic boat. See 125. | 146, 241 |
| 798 | Express Passenger Train | Green and Black loco.; Red and Cream carriages, early issue has Grey roofs. | 297 | 1954 | 1960 | Re-issue of 16. British Railways crest on tender. | 32 |
| 801 | Mini-USS Enterprise | White | 100 | 1980 | 1980 | Marked '© 1979 Paramount Pictures. Corp. Made in England'. Not released until after factory closure. | 237 |
| 802 | Mini-Klingon Cruiser | Metallic Dark Blue | 100 | 1980 | 1980 | Marked 'Dinky Toys' and as 801. Comment as 801. | 237 |
| 900 | Building Site Gift Set | | | 1964 | 1970 | Contains 437, 960, 961, 962, 965. | 173 |
| 901 | Foden Diesel 8-wheel Wagon | Red and Fawn or 2-tone Blue | 188 | R/54 | 1957 | Renumbering of 501. See 934. | 164 |
| 902 | Foden Flat Truck | Orange and Green, Red and Green, Dark Blue and Green, Yellow and Green | 188 | R/54 | 1960 | Renumbering of 502. Late issue has rear adapted from 905: No holes for posts but raised rings underneath. | 164 |
| 903 | Foden Flat Truck with Tailboard | Dark Blue and Orange; Blue and Pale Orange from ca. 1957 | 188 | R/54 | 1960 | Renumbering of 503. | 164 |
| 905 | Foden Flat Truck with Chains | Green or Maroon; Red and Pale Grey from ca. 1957 | 188 | R/54 | 1964 | Renumbering of 505. See 935. | 164 |
| 908 | Mighty Antar with Transformer | Yellow and Grey. | 295 | 1962 | 1966 | Low loader as 660. French Dinky plastic transformer (No. 833). | 190, 190 |
| 911 | Guy 4-ton Lorry | 2-tone Blue; All Blue | 132 | R/54 | R/55 | Renumbering of 511. Lugs at sides of numberplate are triangular. Marked Dinky Supertoys. Renumbered 431. | 165 |

| No. | Description | Colours | Length | Introduced | Deleted | Comment/Variations | Page |
|-----|-------------|---------|--------|------------|---------|--------------------|------|
| 912 | Guy Flat Truck | Blue and Red or Red and Blue | 132 | R/54 | R/55 | Renumbering of 512. Comment as 911. Renumbered 432. | 165 |
| 913 | Guy Flat Truck with Tailboard | Blue and Orange or 2-tone Green | 132 | R/54 | R/55 | Renumbering of 513. Comment as 911. Renumbered 433. | 165 |
| 914 | A.E.C. Articulated Lorry | Red cab, Grey rear, Green tilt | 210 | 1965 | 1970 | British Road Services markings. | 191 |
| 915 | A.E.C. with Flat Trailer | Orange Cab, White rear | 210 | 1973 | 1975 | | 191 |
| 917 | Guy Van 'Spratt's' | Red and Cream | 132 | R/54 | 1955 | Renumbering of 514. Comment as 911. | 158 |
| 917 | Mercedes-Benz Truck and Trailer | Blue, Yellow and White | 397 | 1967 | 1977 | Plastic tilts. See 940. | 191 |
| 918 | Guy Van 'Ever Ready' | Blue | 132 | 1955 | 1958 | | 158 |
| 919 | Guy Van 'Golden Shred' | Red | 132 | 1957 | 1958 | | 158 |
| 920 | Guy Warrior Van 'Heinz' | Red and Yellow | 137 | 1960 | 1960 | Rear as per 914, transfer as 923 (with bottle). | 159 |
| 921 | Bedford Articulated Lorry | Yellow with Black wings. | 166 | R/54 | R/56 | Renumbering of 521. Renumbered 409. | 171 |
| 922 | Big Bedford Lorry | Maroon and Tan or Blue and Yellow | 146 | R/54 | R/56 | Renumbering of 522. Renumbered 408. | 165 |
| 923 | Big Bedford Van 'Heinz' | Red and Yellow | 146 | 1955 | 1959 | With baked beans can to 1958; thereafter with ketchup bottle. | 159 |
| 924 | Aveling-Barford Centaur Dump Truck | Red and Yellow | 180 | 1972 | 1976 | | 174 |
| 925 | Leyland Dump Truck (with Tilt Cab) | White cab/chassis with Blue roof; Red rear with White tailgate | 192 | 1966 | 1969 | | 191 |
| 930 | Bedford Pallet-Jekta Van | Orange and Cream | 177 | 1960 | 1964 | 'Dinky Toys' transfers. With 3 plastic pallets. (No. 793). | 191 |
| 931 | Leyland Comet Lorry | Red and Yellow or Blue and Yellow | 144 | R/54 | R/56 | Renumbering of 531. Renumbered 417. | 167, 281 |
| 932 | Comet Wagon with Hinged Tailboard | Green and Orange or 2-tone Blue | 142 | R/54 | R/56 | Renumbering of 532. Renumbered 418. | 165 |
| 933 | Leyland Cement Wagon | Yellow | 142 | R/54 | R/56 | Renumbering of 533. Renumbered 419. | 165 |
| 934 | Leyland Octopus Wagon | Yellow/Green; Blue/Yellow | 194 | 1956 | 1964 | Rear as 901. | 164 |
| 935 | Leyland Octopus Flat Truck with Chains | Green or Blue cab/chassis, Pale Grey rear | 194 | 1964 | 1966 | Rear as 905. | 164 |
| 936 | Leyland 8-Wheeled Chassis | Red 'cab', Silver chassis, Yellow weights | 197 | 1964 | 1969 | With 3 weights (marked '5 Tons'). Plastic open cab and driver. | 164 |
| 940 | Mercedes-Benz Truck | White cab and rear, Red chassis, Grey tilt | 200 | 1977 | 1980 | Reissue of 917 without opening doors or roof ventilator. | 189, 289 |
| 941 | Foden Tanker 'Mobilgas' | Red | 188 | R/54 | 1956 | Renumbering of 504. | 161 |
| 942 | Foden Tanker 'Regent' | Dark Blue and Red | 188 | 1955 | 1957 | | 161 |
| 943 | Leyland Octopus Tanker 'Esso' | Red | 192 | 1958 | 1964 | Rear as 942. | 164 |
| 944 | 'Shell-B.P.' Fuel Tanker | | 192 | 1963 | 1970 | Cab/chassis as 943. Plastic tank. | 164 |

| No. | Description | Colours | Length | Introduced | Deleted | Comment/Variations | Page |
|---|---|---|---|---|---|---|---|
| (944) | 'Corn Products' Tanker | White cab, Black chassis, Cream rear | 192 | 1963? | | Castings as 944. Stickers: 'Sweeteners for Industry'; 'Corn Products (Sales) Ltd. A Member of the Brown and Polson Group'. 'Corn Products' *transfer* on cab roof. Promotional. | 159–161 |
| 945 | A.E.C. Fuel Tanker 'Esso' | White | 266 | 1966 | 1977 | Cab as 914. With 2 Esso transfers per side to 1975, thereafter with 1. | 163 |
| (945) | Lucas Oil Tanker | Green | 266 | 1977 | 1977 | Promotional. | 164 |
| 948 | Tractor-Trailer 'McLean' | Red cab, Grey trailer | 290 | 1961 | 1967 | Plastic box van on metal base. | 190 |
| 949 | Wayne School Bus | Orange with Red trim | 195 | 1961 | 1966 | See 953. | 197 |
| 950 | Foden S20 Fuel Tanker | Red and White | 266 | 1978 | 1980 | Burmah stickers. Cab as 432 tank as 945 but trailer slightly modified. | 161, 289 |
| 951 | Trailer | Grey with Red wheels | 105 | R/54 | R/56 | Renumbering of 551. Renumbered 428. | 171, 240 |
| 952 | Vega Major Luxury Coach | Pale Grey with Maroon flash (Sticker) | 242 | 1964 | 1971 | With flashing indicators. See 954. | 198 |
| 953 | Continental Touring Coach | Turquoise with White roof | 195 | 1963 | 1966 | Casting as 949. | 197 |
| 954 | Fire Station | Red, Yellow and Brick | (Base) 252 × 203 | 1961 | 1964 | Plastic. | 203 |
| 954 | Vega Major Luxury Coach | As 952 | 242 | 1972 | 1977 | Casting as 952 without flashing indicator. | |
| 955 | Fire Engine with extending Ladder | Red with Silver ladder | 145 | R/54 | 1970 | Renumbering of 555. With windows from ca. 1960, later with plastic wheels. | 203 |
| 956 | Turntable Fire Escape | Red with Silver ladder | 200 | 1958 | 1970 | Bedford cab. With windows from ca. 1960. Later with plastic wheels. Tinplate 2-part escape. Replaced by next item. | 203 |
| 956 | Turntable Fire Escape | Metallic Red with Silver or Black platform at rear | 200 | 1970 | 1974 | Berliet cab. French casting (No. 568) with English base, wheels and finish. Ladder as Bedford. Issued in Falck livery for Danish market in 1974. | 203 |
| 957 | Fire Services Gift Set | | | 1959 | 1966 | Contains 257, 955 and 956. | 203 |
| 958 | Snow Plough | Yellow and Black | 195 | 1961 | 1966 | Guy Warrior cab/chassis. See 439. | 179 |
| 959 | Foden Dump Truck with Bulldozer Blade | Red and Silver | 165 | 1961 | 1968 | | 174 |
| 960 | Albion Lorry-Mounted Concrete Mixer | Orange Truck, Yellow and Blue Mixer | 128 | 1960 | 1969 | | 174 |
| 961 | Blaw-Knox Bulldozer | Red; Yellow and Grey from ca. 1958. Tan driver, Blue from ca. 1963 | 138 | R/54 | 1964 | Renumbering of 561. | 173 |
| 961 | Blaw-Knox Bulldozer | Orange and Green, Blue driver | 138 | ca. 1964 | | Plastic. Casting as metal version but with engine detail. | 175 |

| No. | Description | Colours | Length | Introduced | Deleted | Comment/Variations | Page |
|---|---|---|---|---|---|---|---|
| 961 | Vega Major Luxury Coach PTT | Yellow with White roof | 242 | 1973 | 1977 | Casting as 954. Swiss market only. | 199 |
| 962 | Muir-Hill Dumper | Yellow | 105 | R/54 | 9166 | Renumbering of 562. Rubber tyres from ca. 1962. | 173 |
| 963 | (Blaw-Knox) Heavy Tractor | Red or Orange; Yellow from ca. 1958 | 116 | R/54 | 1959 | Renumbering of 563. | 175, 281 |
| 963 | Road Grader | Orange and Yellow | 238 | 1973 | 1976 | Cab as 973. | 172 |
| 964 | Elevator Loader | Yellow with Blue chutes, reversed colours from ca. 1966 | 156 | R/54 | 1969 | Renumbering of 564. | 186 |
| 965 | Euclid Rear Dump Truck | Yellow | 142 | 1955 | 1969 | Euclid transfer on doors. Euclid logo on Grey background to 1956, thereafter on Red. With windows from ca. 1961. | 173 |
| 965 | Terex Dump Truck | Yellow | 142 | 1969 | 1970 | Casting as above but Terex cast under cab. Terex sticker on doors. | 174 |
| 966 | Marrel Multi-Bucket Unit | Yellow with Grey skip | 115 | 1960 | 1964 | See 788. | 179 |
| 967 | B.B.C. TV Mobile Control Room | Green | 149 | 1959 | 1964 | See 987. | 182 |
| 967 | Muir Hill Loader and Trencher | Yellow and Orange | 163 | 1973 | 1978 | 437 (grille detail) with trencher on rear. | 172 |
| 968 | B.B.C. TV Roving Eye Vehicle | Green | 110 | 1959 | 1964 | With cameraman on roof and plastic aerial. See 988. | 182 |
| 969 | B.B.C. TV Extending Mast Vehicle | Green | 195 | 1959 | 1964 | Plastic collector on tinplate mast. | 187 |
| 970 | Jones Fleetmaster/Cantilever Crane | Red, Black and White; Yellow or Metallic Red and Black with White crane from ca. 1971. | 178 | 1967 | 1977 | | 176 |
| 971 | Coles Mobile Crane | Yellow and Black | 160 | R/54 | 1966 | Renumbering of 571. Last issue has Silver crane, plastic wheels and driver. | 173 |
| 972 | Coles 20-ton Lorry-Mounted Crane | Yellow and Orange | 240 | 1955 | 1970 | With black-and-white Long Vehicle markings from ca. 1962. Later with plastic wheels. | 196 |
| 973 | Goods Yard Crane | Yellow and Blue | (Base) 100 × 100 (H)195 | R/54 | 1959 | Renumbering of 752. | 176 |
| 973 | Eaton Yale Articulated Tractor Shovel | Yellow and Orange | 178 | 1971 | 1976 | See 963. | 172 |
| 974 | AEC Hoynor Car Transporter | Blue cab with Yellow and Red trailer | 322 | 1968 | 1976 | See 616 and 618. | 177 |
| 975 | Ruston-Bucyrus Excavator | Red, Yellow and Grey | 190 | 1963 | 1968 | Plastic body. | 174 |
| 976 | Michigan 180 III Tractor Dozer | Yellow and Red | 147 | 1968 | 1977 | | 173 |
| 977 | Servicing Platform Vehicle (Commercial) | Red and Cream | 197 | 1960 | 1964 | 667 in civilian guise. | 179 |
| 977 | Shovel Dozer | Yellow and Red | 151 | 1973 | 1978 | | 172 |
| 978 | Refuse Wagon | Metallic Green or Green with Grey rear; Yellow or Lime Green with Grey from 1979 | 152 | 1964 | 1979 | Plastic rear; plastic roof box to 1979, then cast in with cab. | 179, 289 |

| No. | Description | Colours | Length/Wingspan | Introduced | Deleted | Comment/Variations | Page |
|-----|-------------|---------|-----------------|------------|---------|--------------------|------|
| 979 | Racehorse Transport | Light Grey and Yellow | 173 | 1961 | 1964 | Casting as 981. Newmarket transfers. 2 plastic horses. | 180 |
| 980 | Horsebox | Maroon | 173 | R/54 | 1960 | Renumbering of 581. (U.S. decals) | 180 |
| 980 | Coles Hydra Truck 150 T | Lemon Yellow, Yellow or Orange, Black wings | 210 | 1972 | 1979 | Operating handles at side and rear (Lemon Yellow). One handle each side (Yellow or Orange). | |
| 981 | Horsebox | Maroon | 173 | R/54 | 1960 | Renumbering of 581. (U.K. decals) | 180 |
| 982 | Pullmore Car Transporter | Pale Blue with Fawn tracks, then Blue cab, Pale Blue rear | 250 | R/54 | 1964 | Renumbering of 582. With windows from ca. 1960. Supplied with ramp (794 or 994) | 173 173 |
| 983 | Car Carrier and Trailer | | | 1958 | 1963 | Contains 984 and 985 | 173 |
| 984 | Car Carrier | Red and Grey | 240 | 1958 | 1963 | Rear in aluminium. See 989. | 173 |
| 984 | Atlas Digger | Yellow, Red and Black | 247 | 1974 | 1979 | | 172 |
| 985 | Trailer for Car Carrier | Red and Grey | 196 | 1958 | 1963 | | 173 |
| 986 | Mighty Antar Low Loader and Propeller | Red and Grey, Brown propeller | 295 | 1959 | 1964 | Plastic propeller. With windows from ca. 1961. | 190 |
| 987 | A.B.C. TV Control Room | Light Blue and Light Grey | 149 | 1962 | 1970 | Casting as 967, with plastic camera and operator. | 182 |
| 988 | A.B.C. TV Transmitter Van | Light Blue and Light Grey | 110 | 1962 | 1969 | Casting as 968, but roof altered to take collecting dish from 969. | 182 |
| 989 | Car Carrier | Yellow, Light Grey and Blue | 240 | 1963 | 1965 | Casting as 984. Auto Transporters decal. | 176 |
| 990 | Pullmore Car Transporter + four cars | | | 1957 | 1958 | Contains 154, 156, 161, 162 and 982. | 177 |
| 991 | A.E.C. Tanker | Red and Yellow | 150 | R/54 | 1958 | Renumbering of 591. 'Shell Chemicals Limited' to 1955, thereafter 'Shell Chemicals'. | 164 |
| 992 | Avro Vulcan Delta Wing Bomber | Silver | 156 | 1955 | 1956 | See 749 | 114 |
| 994 | Loading Ramp for 982 | Pale Blue | 233 | R/54 | R/55 | Brief renumbering of 794 | 177 |
| 997 | Caravelle SE210 Airliner | Silver with Blue and White | 180 | 1962 | 1965 | Adapted French casting (No. 60f/891) marked Made in England. Air France markings. Black plastic wheels in 1965. | 118 |
| 998 | Bristol Britannia Airliner | Silver and White with Blue lines on fuselage and tail; Red lines from ca. 1961. Metallic Grey and White from ca. 1964 | 225 | 1959 | 1965 | Canadian Pacific livery. | 118 |
| 999 | D.H. Comet Airliner | Silver with Blue and White | 184 | R/55 | 1965 | Renumbering of 702. G-ALYX from ca. 1959. | 114 |
| 1001 | Station Staff (Set of 6) 00 Gauge | | | ? | R/54 | Originally issued pre-war as Hornby-Dublo. No. D1 Renamed Dinky Toys (still marked HD on bases) before 1952. Renumbered 051. | 36 |
| 1003 | Passengers (Set of 6) 00 gauge | | | ? | R/54 | Comments as 1001. Renumbered 053. Original No. D2 | 36 |

Action Kits: These were issued unpainted, the colour shown being that of the paint supplied with the model, which in some cases differs from that of the standard model. For dimension and casting details, refer to the number under comments.

| No. | Description | Colours | Length | Introduced | Deleted | Comment/Variations | Page |
|---|---|---|---|---|---|---|---|
| 1001 | Rolls Royce Phantom V Limousine | Blue | | 1971 | 1977 | 152. | 241– |
| 1002 | Volvo 1800S | Yellow | | 1971 | 1975 | 116. | 242 |
| 1003 | Volkswagen 1300 Sedan | Red | | 1971 | 1975 | 129. | |
| 1004 | Ford Escort Police Car | Blue | | 1971 | 1977 | 270. Police transfers. | |
| 1006 | Ford Mexico | Red | | 1973 | 1977 | 168. Mexico stripes. | |
| 1007 | Jensen FF | Blue | | 1971 | 1975 | 188. | |
| 1008 | Mercedes–Benz 600 | Red | | 1973 | 1977 | 128. | |
| 1009 | Lotus F.1 Racing Car | Green | | 1971 | 1975 | 225. Gold Leaf transfers. | |
| 1012 | Ferrari 312–B2 | Red | | 1973 | 1975 | 226. Shell decals. | |
| 1014 | Beach Buggy | Blue | | 1975 | 1977 | 227. | |
| 1017 | Routemaster Bus | Red | | 1971 | 1977 | 289. Esso Safety Grip Tyres transfers. | |
| 1018 | Atlantean Bus | White | | 1974 | 1977 | 295. National transfers. | |
| 1023 | Single Decker Bus | Green | | 1972 | 1977 | 283. Green Line transfers. | |
| 1025 | Ford Transit Van | Red | | 1971 | 1975 | 407. Avis transfers. | |
| 1027 | Lunar Roving Vehicle | Blue | | 1972 | 1975 | 355. | |
| 1029 | Ford D800 Tipper Truck | Green | | 1971 | 1977 | 438. | |
| 1030 | Land Rover Breakdown Truck | White | | 1974 | 1977 | 442. | |
| 1032 | Army Land Rover | Military Green | | 1975 | 1977 | 344. | |
| 1033 | U.S. Jeep | Military Green | | 1971 | 1977 | 615. | |
| 1034 | Mobile Gun | Military Green | | 1975 | 1977 | 654. | |
| 1035 | Striker Anti-Tank Vehicle | Military Green | | 1975 | 1977 | 691. | |
| 1036 | Leopard Tank | Military Green | | 1975 | 1977 | 692. | |
| 1037 | Chieftain Tank | Military Green | | 1974 | 1977 | 683. | |
| 1038 | Scorpion Tank | Military Green | | 1975 | 1977 | 690. | |
| 1040 | Sea King Helicopter | White (and Orange?) | | 1971 | 1977 | 724. U.S.A.F. markings. | |
| 1041 | Hawker Hurricane Mk IIC | ? | | 1973 | 1976 | 718. R.A.F. markings. | |
| 1042 | Spitfire Mk II | ? | | 1971 | 1977 | 719. R.A.F. markings. | |
| 1043 | S.E.P.C.A.T. Jaguar | ? | | 1974 | 1976 | 731. R.A.F. markings. | |
| 1044 | Messerschmitt B.F. 109E | ? | | 1972 | 1975 | 726. Luftwaffe markings. | |
| 1045 | Multi-Role Combat Aircraft | ? | | 1975 | 1976 | 729. | |
| 1050 | Motor Patrol Boat | ? | | 1975 | 1977 | 675. | |

1:25 Scale Models

| No. | Description | Colours | Length | Introduced | Deleted | Comment/Variations | Page |
|---|---|---|---|---|---|---|---|
| 2162 | Ford Capri | Metallic Blue and Black | 175 | 1973 | 1976 | | 153 |
| 2214 | Ford Capri Rally Car | Red and Black | 175 | 1974 | 1976 | | 153 |
| 2253 | Ford Capri Police Car | White | 175 | 1974 | 1976 | | 153 |

| No. | Description | Colours | Length | Introduced | Deleted | Comment/Variations | Page |
|-----|-------------|---------|--------|------------|---------|--------------------|------|
| Gift Sets: | | | | | | | |
| No. 1 | Farmyard Gear | | | 1952 | R/54 | Contains 27a, 27b, 27c, 27g, and and 27h. Renumbered 398. | 186 |
| No. 2 | Commercial Vehicles | | | 1952 | 1954 | Contains 25m, 27d, 30n, 30p (Mobilgas) and 30s. | 171 |
| No. 3 | Passenger Cars | | | 1952 | 1954 | Contains 27f, 30h, 40e, 40g, 40h and 140b | 134 |
| No. 4 | Racing Cars | | | 1953 | R/54 | Contains 23f, 23g, 23h, 23j, and 23n. Renumbered 249. | 129 |
| Military | | | | | | | |
| No. 1 | Miltary Vehicles | | | 1955 | R/55 | Contains 621, 641, 675 and 676. Renumbered 699. | 215 |

# Corrections for the 3rd edition Dinky Toys & Modelled Miniatures
## The Hornby Companion Series Vol 4.

This list of corrections and additions to our original manuscript is, of necessity, all too brief. An attempt was made in the original work to include all really important information and to omit less important variations in the interests of producing a readable reference work. Since the first publication, the interest in Dinky Toys has exploded and, almost daily, new variations turn up. Many collectors have written to us and Alan Dimmock telling us of these and we have selected from this wealth of information the following items. We have concentrated on those parts of the text in which there were errors or misleading wording and have as far as possible corrected those. We have not added many colour variations as many of the most important ones are included in the Compendium listing compiled by Patrick Trench and bound at the end of the book. We would like to emphasise that the Tables included by us in the main body of the text give the deletion date as the last date the model is to be found in a U.K. catalogue, whereas the date given by Patrick Trench in the Compendium listing is the first year that it did not appear in any catalogue. Thus these dates are usually a year later than those in the main text. We would like to thank most heartily, all those who have helped in updating this edition.

*Page No.*

| | |
|---|---|
| 8 | February 1932 Catalogue, date should read 1934. |
| 14 | Spitfire Fund. Colours of Spitfire as listed on the box lid: light grey, red, yellow, light blue, dark blue, emerald green, medium green, magenta and special finish camouflage. |
| 19/21 | Hand operated 'Kip' diecasting machines were used until the mid-sixties. They were gradually phased out, after Lines Bros. takeover in 1964, in favour of automatic machines. All the Kip machines were thrown away and since the dies designed for the hand operated machines could not be used on the automatic ones, all the earlier models were phased out and could not be re-introduced. |
| 38 | (See P. 00), should read P. 10. |
| 39 | White tyres with the herringbone pattern are also found on the 23 Series. |
| 46 | Fig 41. The green Tanker at top right is an early post-war version. |
| 51 | 28 Series Van, 2nd casting has been found painted chocolate brown with transfers 'De Bijenkorf Amsterdam, den Haag, Rotterdam' |
| 57 line 8 | factors, should read factory. |
| 57 table | 33e Dust Wagon was issued post-war. |
| 59 | Fig 67. The Armstrong Siddeley of this series is not illustrated here—see fig 68. The red and maroon 24 series Rover was illustrated to contrast with the green 36 series Rover. |
| 67 | 47k Bend—early pre-war a Z-bend was shown. 47k/770 Bend—later a gentle left hand curve was shown. |
| 68 | 48 Petrol Station also came with an orange base. |
| 68 | 49c Theo petrol pump was blue pre-war and brown post-war, should read was blue pre- and early post-war and brown later. |

| | |
|---|---|
| 69 | 43c & 43d R.A.C. Guides are similar castings to 44c & 44d A.A. Guides, but are not identical. The R.A.C. figures have a curved pouch on their backs, the A.A. a square one. |
| 69 | A.N.W.B.—Dutch motoring organisation. Algemene Nederlandse Wielrijders Bond. (General Dutch Cycle Union) |
| 78 | 151b Transport Wagon does not have a separate chassis. |
| 78 | 152a Light Tank has a tinplate base. |
| 80 | 162b Trailer has a tinplate base. |
| 81 | 153a Army jeep is always matt green, should read is usually matt green but can be chocolate brown. |
| 89 | 52a Queen Mary (1st casting) also came with brass rollers. 52a (2nd casting) also came with red plastic rollers. |
| 91 | 674 Coastguard Amphibious Missile Launcher has a plastic hull. The decking is diecast. |
| 93 | 60a Imperial Airways Liner also red with G-ABTI in standard lettering. |
| 96 | 60m Four-Engined Flying Boat also gold with letters G-EXFE. |
| 98 | 60x Atlantic Flying Boat also dark blue fuselage 'Enterprise' name in silver by nose, cream wings, G-AZBR lettering. Also green and cream, 'Whirlwind', lettered G-AZBT. |
| 103 | 62x British 40-seater Airliner, pre-war version with that name cast, in a medium shade of blue with silver trim and propellors. |
| 103 | 62g Flying Fortress was released with gliding game hole and finished in grey. |
| 106 | 68a Ensign has been found in original camouflage and with the gliding game hole. The Ensign was available in dark or light camouflage. |
| 125 | Beechcraft Baron—also bronze. |
| 134 | 40j Austin Somerset issued in 1953 (not 1954). |
| 136 | 120 Jaguar E-type—early and briefly issued in metallic blue & white. |

| No. | Description | Colours | Length | Introduced | Deleted | Comment/Variations | Page |
|---|---|---|---|---|---|---|---|
| **Gift Sets:** | | | | | | | |
| No. 1 | Farmyard Gear | | | 1952 | R/54 | Contains 27a, 27b, 27c, 27g, and and 27h. Renumbered 398. | 186 |
| No. 2 | Commercial Vehicles | | | 1952 | 1954 | Contains 25m, 27d, 30n, 30p (Mobilgas) and 30s. | 171 |
| No. 3 | Passenger Cars | | | 1952 | 1954 | Contains 27f, 30h, 40e, 40g, 40h and 140b | 134 |
| No. 4 | Racing Cars | | | 1953 | R/54 | Contains 23f, 23g, 23h, 23j, and 23n. Renumbered 249. | 129 |
| **Military** | | | | | | | |
| No. 1 | Miltary Vehicles | | | 1955 | R/55 | Contains 621, 641, 675 and 676. Renumbered 699. | 215 |

# Corrections for the 3rd edition Dinky Toys & Modelled Miniatures

## The Hornby Companion Series Vol 4.

This list of corrections and additions to our original manuscript is, of necessity, all too brief. An attempt was made in the original work to include all really important information and to omit less important variations in the interests of producing a readable reference work. Since the first publication, the interest in Dinky Toys has exploded and, almost daily, new variations turn up. Many collectors have written to us and Alan Dimmock telling us of these and we have selected from this wealth of information the following items. We have concentrated on those parts of the text in which there were errors or misleading wording and have as far as possible corrected those. We have not added many colour variations as many of the most important ones are included in the Compendium listing compiled by Patrick Trench and bound at the end of the book. We would like to emphasise that the Tables included by us in the main body of the text give the deletion date as the last date the model is to be found in a U.K. catalogue, whereas the date given by Patrick Trench in the Compendium listing is the first year that it did not appear in any catalogue. Thus these dates are usually a year later than those in the main text. We would like to thank most heartily, all those who have helped in updating this edition.

| | |
|---|---|
| 139 | 210 Alfa Romeo 33 Tipo Le Mans. Colour should read, fluorescent orange-red with black bonnet cover. |
| 153 | 112 Volvo 265DL Estate, should read 122. |
| 154 | 25b Covered Wagon. Also olive drab for the Royal Army Volunteer Reserve. |
| 155 | 25g Trailer. Early postwar issues also had the tinplate towbar. |
| 159 table | 920 and 923 should read, 920 Guy Warrior Van 1960–1960 Heinz with bottle 923 Big Bedford Van 1955–1959 Heinz with can till 1958, with bottle after 1958. |
| 161 | 950 Foden S20 Fuel Tanker also available with Shell labels circa 1979. |
| 169 table | 390 Customised Transit Van, dark blue with 'Vampire' decals or metal flake pale blue with no decals. |
| 178 | 451 Johnston Roadsweeper should read, had its opening doors deleted and was renumbered 449. |
| 178 caption | 449/451 should read 451 only. |
| 179 table | 449 Johnston Road Sweeper 1977–1980 yellow or lime green 451 Johnston Road Sweeper 1971–1977 orange cab, metallic green back |
| 179 table | 439 Ford D800 Snow Plough and Tipper Truck 1970–1978 |
| 179 | 958 Snow Plough. Blade also painted grey. |
| 189 | (274) Joseph Mason Paints. Given away by Mason's around Christmas 1969. |
| 189 | 930 Pallet Jekta should read, two-tone yellow/orange cab & back |
| 196 | 289 Routemaster Bus. Casting changes described incorrectly. See Compendium 4a Tables p(48). |
| 203 | 956 Turntable Fire Escape 1969–1973 red, should read metallic red. |
| 219 | 691 'Striker' Anti-tank Vehicle IS a model of a real vehicle, based on an Alvis. See also p 236. |
| 220 | 691 'Striker' Anti-Tank vehicle. Delete See Chapter 7. Add 1974–1980 Green. Still in production at factory closure. |

| | |
|---|---|
| 221 table | Set No. 3 Private Automobiles Contains; 30d Vauxhall, 36a Armstrong Siddeley, 36b Bentley, 38a Frazer Nash, 39b Oldsmobile. |
| 221 | Dies sent to New Zealand in 1977. A correspondent in New Zealand was supplied by Models Ltd., the New Zealand Meccano Agent, with a list of dies sent to them by Meccano in 1977. No models were produced because Models Ltd could not reach a satisfactory agreement with Underwood Engineering (Fun Ho!) to produce the models. The list is as follows: 131 Jaguar E-type   216 Ferrari Dino 163 Ford Capri   224 Mercedes C111 176 NSU Ro80   354 Pink Panther 187 de Tomaso   370 Dragster 190 Monteverdi   717 Boeing 737 210 Alfa Romeo |
| 225 | Models made for European markets. Occasionally models were sold in countries for which they were not intended e.g. the Falck Landrover Breakdown Crane was found in a Scottish shop. |
| 233 | 004 Dodge Polara Cabriolet should read Oldsmobile Dynamic 88 Sedan. |
| 233 | 735 Gloster Javelin: also Indian Air Force markings. |
| 234 | Pink Panther Car. Last issue sold in a bubble pack did not have any mechanism. |
| 236 | 364 Space Shuttle was made at the factory before closure but was distributed patchily being easily available in some areas but not in others. Possibly also made later in Hong Kong. |
| 236 | 691 Striker Anti-Tank Vehicle is a real vehicle so it should not appear in this Chapter. |
| 237 | 364 Space Shuttle. 1979–1980 Still in production at factory closure. |
| 237 | 691 Delete all this reference. |
| 248 | Models planned but not issued. Mentioned in the Planning Committee Minutes for 9 October 1963—Vickers VC 10. The drawings were sent to a Hong Kong industrial company for assessment but production was not proceeded with. |

# Collection Notes

| Description | Date purchased | Cost | Description | Date purchased | Cost |
| --- | --- | --- | --- | --- | --- |